PRESIDENTS

A BIOGRAPHICAL DICTIONARY

Second Edition

Neil A. Hamilton

Checkmark Books®
An imprint of Facts On File, Inc.

Presidents: A Biographical Dictionary, Second Edition

Copyright © 2005, 2001 by Neil A. Hamilton

All rights reserved. No part of this book may be reproduced or utilized in any form or by any means, electronic or mechanical, including photocopying, recording, or by any information storage or retrieval systems, without permission in writing from the publisher. For information contact:

Checkmark Books
An imprint of Facts On File, Inc.
132 West 31st Street
New York NY 10001

Library of Congress Cataloging-in-Publication Data
Hamilton, Neil A., 1949–
Presidents : a biographical dictionary / Neil A. Hamilton.—2nd ed.
p. cm.
Includes bibliographical references and index.
ISBN 0-8160-5733-8 (hardcover)—ISBN 0-8160-6424-5 (pbk.: acid-free paper)
1. Presidents—United States—Biography—Dictionaries. I. Title.

E176.1.H215 2001
973'.09'9—dc21
[B] 00-053547

Checkmark Books are available at special discounts when purchased in bulk quantities for businesses, associations, institutions, or sales promotions. Please call our Special Sales Department in New York at (212) 967-8800 or (800) 322-8755.

You can find Facts On File on the World Wide Web at http://www.factsonfile.com

Text design by Rachel L. Berlin

Printed in the United States of America

VB FOF 10 9 8 7 6 5 4 3 2 1

This book is printed on acid-free paper.

For my mother and my brother

Contents

Preface
and Acknowledgments vi
Introduction vii
George Washington 1
John Adams 12
Thomas Jefferson 21
James Madison 31
James Monroe 40
John Quincy Adams 49
Andrew Jackson 58
Martin Van Buren 68
William Henry Harrison 76
John Tyler 83
James K. Polk 90
Zachary Taylor 98
Millard Fillmore 105
Franklin Pierce 113
James Buchanan 120
Abraham Lincoln 128
Andrew Johnson 139
Ulysses S. Grant 148
Rutherford B. Hayes 158
James A. Garfield 167
Chester A. Arthur 175
Grover Cleveland 183
Benjamin Harrison 193
William McKinley 201
Theodore Roosevelt 210
William Howard Taft 221
Woodrow Wilson 229
Warren G. Harding 239
Calvin Coolidge 247
Herbert Hoover 255
Franklin Delano Roosevelt 263
Harry S. Truman 276
Dwight David Eisenhower 286
John Fitzgerald Kennedy 295
Lyndon Baines Johnson 304
Richard M. Nixon 314
Gerald Ford 325
James Earl Carter, Jr. 333
Ronald Reagan 344
George H. W. Bush 356
William Jefferson Clinton 365
George Walker Bush 379
Appendix 400
Bibliography 461
Index 463

Preface and Acknowledgments

I have endeavored in this book to present profiles about America's presidents in largely chronological narratives that avoid academic wordiness. My aim has been to reveal character alongside policies and social developments alongside politics. I found all of the presidents, even the most obscure, intriguing. Each had his own challenges, achievements, and failures, shaped by institutional requirements and individual personalities, and I have tried to capture them through anecdotes while maintaining the format required for an encyclopedic reference book.

I would like to thank two colleagues at Spring Hill College in Mobile, Alabama, for their help in uncovering sources and tracking down little-known facts: Bret Heim, the Government Documents and Reference Librarian, and Richard Weaver, the Instructional/Access Librarian, both at Thomas Byrne Memorial Library. In addition to their work, Phyllis Compretta helped acquire numerous books and articles through interlibrary loan in her usual prompt and courteous manner.

I owe a special debt of thanks to Nicole Bowen, executive editor for American history at Facts On File. She originated the idea for this book and provided invaluable guidance in seeing it through to publication. Her professionalism made my work more productive and enjoyable while keeping my nose to the grindstone. My thanks go also to Ellen Scordato for her expertise in line editing the manuscript and to Tracy Bradbury for helping to pull together the completed copy.

Finally, I would like to thank my mother for the time she took in reading the profiles and offering innumerable suggestions that added clarity and smoothness to my writing, ridding it of characteristics that would have detracted from its final form. Her keen insight has made this book stronger.

My hope is that the reader will find as much value and pleasure in this volume as I did in similar volumes written by others and read by me in my childhood. Those stories of presidents stirred my imagination and enticed me to delve into biographies that told more about the role of individuals in shaping America's development.

INTRODUCTION

Presidential Power

In the fall of 1948, work began on renovating the White House, gutting its interior while leaving only the original outside stone walls. Harry S. Truman, president at that time, insisted that nothing be done to change the building's outer appearance. He even refused to let the workers break open a passageway so a tractor could be brought inside. Instead, the machine was dismantled piece by piece, carted through an existing portal, and then reassembled.

Truman, who was forced to live at Blair House during the construction, personally supervised the remodeling, even roaming the catwalks and issuing directives. By the time the workers completed the project in 1951, they had used 66 tons of steel to build a skeleton that removed pressure from the walls by redistributing the weight, and although the refurbished rooms were new in most respects, they reinstalled the original mantels, wood floors, and paneling. In effect, Truman presided over an architectural rebirth that left the exterior unchanged while the inner structure worked differently.

The gutting of the White House as the cold war began symbolized a change in the American presidency. Even while the nation's highest office maintained many of its traditional trappings, a fundamental shift brought it greater powers and responsibilities shaped by America's status as a military and commercial force competing with the Soviet Union for international leadership.

The cold war and its immediate predecessors, the Great Depression and World War II, redefined and reshaped the presidency more than any event since the Civil War. A cynic might say that the office has declined since the noble days of George Washington and Thomas Jefferson, with a modern electorate more interested in entertainment than voting and presidents more interested in self-centered power than selfless governance. That view, however, ignores the political plotting and maneuvering that has been inherent in government since its inception, as well as the personal limitations of several early occupants of the White House.

A contrast of the American presidency with the parliamentary system used by most Western democratic countries illustrates the powers that the chief executive can wield. Unlike the president, a prime minister does not have to worry about trying to govern while an opposition political party controls the legislature. By the very nature of a parliamentary system, a prime minister retains power only while his or her party holds a majority of seats, either on its own or through a coalition arrangement. This means that a prime minister can exert considerably more power in the legislature than can a president. One study has found that while on average less than 50 percent of all presidential proposals pass Congress, in Great Britain the pass rate in Parliament is much higher; between 1959 and 1967, for example, it stood at 96 percent.

The prime minister's power is further enhanced by the method of choosing a cabinet. The PM usually selects a cabinet's members from those who serve in the parliament and exert the most influence over it. Seldom does an American president nominate a member of Congress for a cabinet post, and he selects his appointees less for their influence on Capitol Hill than for how his choice will affect public opinion; how it will satisfy ethnic, gender, racial, or geographic constituencies; or how much it will add to needed expertise.

Lacking a strong base in Congress and precisely defined powers in the Constitution, a president must rely heavily on his ability to persuade if he is to wield considerable influence. He must especially try to sway his fellow politicians in Washington. According to political scientist Richard E. Neustadt in *Presidential Power and the Modern Presidents,* this group exceeds all others in importance; if the leadership elite perceives that a president is weak, indecisive, or inept, he will be doomed to failure. But the president must also persuade party activists and officeholders outside the nation's capital by appealing to their principles and programs; and he must persuade the public, a diverse group that some politicians think can be read and led through opinion polls.

In trying to wield power, presidents actually have little influence over whether a congressional representative is elected or reelected. Most often, a congressional election turns on local matters and a candidate's own abilities. In any event, the president's party often loses seats in Congress during midterm elections, and incumbents stand little chance of losing. Yet congressional representatives do take some risks if they oppose a well-liked and widely supported president. Thus, popularity becomes all the more important if the chief executive wants to exert influence.

For all the limits on presidential power, there are notable ways in which it can be exercised and in which it has grown. The chief executive can veto or threaten to veto a bill. This allows him to shape legislation through negotiation. Presidents Grover Cleveland, Franklin D. Roosevelt, Harry S. Truman, Dwight D. Eisenhower, and Gerald Ford used their veto power extensively, knowing full well that any bill rejected by a president stands little chance of making it through Congress. From the beginning of the constitutional government in 1789, Congress has overridden less than 4 percent of all presidential vetoes.

Presidents have also claimed executive privilege based on the belief that the separation of powers established in the Constitution substantially prevents one branch of the federal government from interfering with another. Executive privilege underwent its greatest court test in 1973 with the case of *United States v. Nixon,* when President Richard Nixon asserted he could withhold his Watergate tapes from Congress. But the Supreme Court ruled, 8-0, that a president has no absolute claim to executive privilege, and that Nixon had to turn over the tapes to congressional investigators in what was a criminal case. The court did, however, say there could be good reasons for the claim of executive privilege, such as when sensitive military matters might be endangered.

With America's status as a global power, a president can flex considerable muscle overseas as commander in chief of the military. Presidents have been able to maneuver troops to ignite wars, and during the cold war they engaged in secret actions that overthrew governments and incited rebellions.

Since the 1930s, presidents have surrounded themselves with a large bureaucracy that has allowed them to take the lead in setting policies. For example, the Executive Office of the President includes the Office of Management and Budget (OMB), which does more than compile figures; it studies how the executive branch operates, develops plans for agencies, and reviews proposals coming from the various cabinet departments to create a coordinated executive branch. Increasingly, the OMB advocates policies that others in the federal government must react to, and as a result it sets the basis for debate.

A president can also generate massive support for his programs through "sheer command," though, according to Richard Neustadt, this involves a confluence of several elements: He must be clear about what he wants; he must express his desires lucidly; he must mobilize widespread public support; and he must convince others that what he wants done should be done and that it is within his power to get it done.

Whatever the limits or prerogatives of presidential power, Americans have looked increasingly to their chief executives for strong leadership. In a bureaucratic world, the president is an individual on whom blame or credit can be laid and toward whom a voter on election day can vent frustrations or express support.

Presidential Categories

Historically, America's presidents can be placed into six categories and two subcategories based on their relationship to the people, historical developments, and, importantly, the nature and status of their power. Any such labeling, though, is arbitrary, and the shift from one group of presidents to another is seldom clear and often filled with contradictions, along with continuities, across time. Writing in *The Personal President,* Theodore J. Lowi cautions us that "separation serves exposition but ultimately it is the combined and cumulative effect that shapes the modern presidency." Further, the unique qualities of every individual who has served as president—especially that which political scientist Fred I. Greenstein in *The Presidential Difference* calls their "emotional intelligence"—makes generalizations dangerous. Yet categorizing the presidents reveals something about the context in which they governed as well as changes in the office itself.

The first category, the formative or republican presidents, comprises George Washington through James Monroe. Like pioneers trekking into unknown territory, these presidents faced the daunting task of developing the office from scratch—with the Constitution an indistinct guide—and placing it within the emerging political system. Washington (in office 1789–97) embellished the presidency with dignity, drawing a line between the ruling elite and the masses. He met the public (only the "better sort") at weekly receptions but kept a studied distance. He stood in front of the fireplace, his face toward the entry door, and received each visitor with a bow while making it clear through his actions that he would not shake hands. About town, he rode in a yellow chariot adorned with gilded cupids and his coat of arms, and he staffed his executive mansion with 14 white servants and seven slaves.

George Washington and Congress set precedents for the relationship of the executive and the legislative branches. In 1789 he appeared before the Senate to present a proposed Indian treaty, to which the senators reacted by saying they would have to deliberate the details without his presence. Washington left in a huff, vowing never to appear before Congress again, and he kept his word. On another occasion Congress rejected attempts by Alexander Hamilton, Washington's secretary of the treasury, to treat it as a parliament and himself as a prime minister representing the president. Such disagreement characterized the federal legislature's determination to be independent.

Washington also set out to define the president's role on his own terms. In 1796, when the House of Representatives demanded that he turn over all of his papers relating to the controversial Jay Treaty (sometimes called Jay's Treaty) with England, he refused, reminding the congressmen that there was no requirement in the Constitution that a treaty be approved by them. When war erupted between Britain and France, he declared America's neutrality, even though the Constitution did not give him that power.

The founding document said nothing about a cabinet either, but Washington formed one. In time he developed the principle that appointments to the cabinet should be based on the prospective member's agreement with presidential policies. After a rift developed between Alexander Hamilton and Secretary of State Thomas Jefferson, Washington said he would no longer "bring a man into office of consequence . . . whose political tenets are adverse to the measures which the general government are pursuing. . . ."

Never desirous of establishing a dictatorship, Washington recognized Congress's predominant role in writing legislation. He believed a bill should be vetoed only if it were unconstitutional; with that in mind, he used this power only twice. He also viewed the president as the sole representative of all the people since he was the only federal official elected by a nationwide vote.

Working through Alexander Hamilton, Washington took the lead in establishing the federal government's financial structure, including taxes and a national bank. Congress reacted to these actions by allowing the presidential administration to take a significant role in proposing and formulating legislation. John Adams (1797–1801) lost most of this initiative to Congress, but Thomas Jefferson (1801–09) again set an ambitious agenda with his war on the judiciary and his efforts to lower taxes, decrease military spending, and eliminate the national debt. His purchase of Louisiana from France stands as another bold presidential stroke, since the Constitution fails to give explicit authority for such a purchase.

Jefferson enhanced the power of the presidency by building a political party, the Democratic-Republicans, that he headed. As a result, a president could exert power by means other than through a government body or agency. Indeed, all of the early presidents, beginning with Washington's second term, faced the formative task of dealing with political parties, neither provided for in the Constitution nor anticipated by many observers.

In 1812 James Madison (1809–17) tackled the task of a president at war, another first. For this he not only had to organize armies and devise strategies, but he also had to rally public support, which he did, albeit ineffectually, by portraying the conflict with Britain as a fight to protect the republican community—meaning industry, commerce, banking, and agriculture—from foreign assault. James Monroe (1817–25) built on the Washingtonian legacy of the president representing all the people when he traveled the country on behalf of national unity during the Era of Good Feelings.

Each one of these formative presidents governed in a republican political setting different from today's democratic one. Candidates were supposed to stand for office without appealing directly to the people. As with other political leaders, presidents were expected to distinguish themselves from the masses by possessing a superior character—one that political scientist Bruce Miroff, writing in *Presidential Studies Quarterly,* describes as "dignified, grave, and measured"—and by combining it with balanced judgment that controlled passions. Washington epitomized the republican character and the republican political behavior—a man of extraordinary qualities who would never stoop to campaigning.

Yet the republican presidencies changed. Although John Adams retained the remote and dignified Washingtonian qualities, he resorted to a more direct appeal to the people through public addresses late in his presidency. Thomas Jefferson resorted to such devices much more and in certain ways liked to present himself as one with the people, as when he greeted visitors to the White House in his bathrobe. Further, he considered his politics, such as the reduction of the national debt, to be much truer to republicanism than had been the politics of Washington and Adams. The election of Jefferson over Adams, in fact, provided another benchmark with the passing of presidential power from one political party, the Federalists, to another, the Democratic-Republicans. This was a testament to the greater acceptance of party competition, which would eventually weaken the republican context. After Monroe, John Quincy Adams (1825–29) became a transitional chief executive leading into the second category, the democratic presidents.

Just as George Washington represented the republican mentality, Andrew Jackson (1829–37) represented the democratic one. At the time that property qualifications for voting were relaxed, enabling nearly all adult white men to cast ballots, Jackson and his supporters, most notably Martin Van Buren, crafted a political party in the late 1820s that used modern campaign tactics—namely, hoopla, parades, and slogans that could push any serious discussion of issues into the background. Jackson rallied the masses and, more emphatically than any previous president, asserted that he was the people's voice.

When the Whig party formed to challenge the Democrats, it affirmed the shift to a democratic age by adopting the techniques of mass appeal. William Henry Harrison (1841) came into the White House as a military hero whose stand on the issues few people knew or cared about. Democrat James K. Polk (1845–49) continued the Jacksonian appeal when he pursued the acquisition of Oregon and started a war against Mexico to fulfill the widespread (but far from universal) desire to expand westward as part of the popular belief in Manifest Destiny.

The remaining presidents through the 1850s owed their elections to similar popular appeals, with their nominations produced by national conventions, another innovation from the Jackson era. Nevertheless, as chief executives they displayed little vigor, and in James Buchanan's case (1857–61) a weakness so severe that it encouraged secessionists to revolt against the Union. It could be argued that the rise of mass-based political parties that often avoided serious discussions of critical issues contributed to the outbreak of the Civil War by letting sectional problems fester rather than meeting them head-on and defusing them.

With Abraham Lincoln (1861–65), the category of Civil War presidents began, so defined because the war, or its aftermath, dominated their actions, either encouraging an expansion in presidential power, as with Lincoln, or forcing a contraction, as with his immediate successors. The war changed Lincoln's preference, as a Republican and former Whig, for limited executive action. As the South seceded, Northerners looked to Lincoln for leadership, and in dealing with an unprecedented rebellion, he assumed greater powers for the presidency. Lincoln defined the fight as primarily one to preserve national unity. In so doing he reflected Northern views and became a symbol for the Union itself. "One duty paramount to all others was before me," he said to a group gathered at the White House in 1863, "namely, to maintain and preserve at once the Constitution and the integrity of the federal republic."

Acting without prior congressional approval, President Lincoln raised an army, spent money, blockaded Southern ports, suspended the writ of habeas corpus, and changed the tenor of the war and its objectives by issuing the Emancipation Proclamation. He based his actions on his role as commander in chief and on the extraordinary circumstances of rebellion, along with the responsibility the Constitution gave him to maintain order. The suspension of the writ of habeas corpus, he insisted in a letter he wrote during the summer of 1863, was in accordance with the constitutional provision that civil liberties can be held in abeyance "in cases of Rebellion or Invasion [when] the public safety may require it." In another statement he said the Emancipation Proclamation was an "act of justice, warranted by the Constitution, upon military necessity."

Shortly before his death, Lincoln proposed a reconstruction plan for after the war, indicating that he would take the lead in that project as well. Congress, however, contested it, and had Lincoln escaped assassination and served his full second term, he may well have seen his presidential power eroded.

That is what happened under his successor, Andrew Johnson (1865–69). Though the military battlefields stood silent, the Civil War continued to rage as an issue, as it would through the 1880s. In the continuing debate over reconstruction, Congress acted to contain the president by devising and implementing its own plan; it even forbade him from firing cabinet members and other officials whose appointment to office required the Senate's consent. When Johnson defied the Congress he was impeached, and although acquitted by one vote, he and the presidency were humbled.

Ulysses S. Grant (1869–77) may have been able to use his enormous prestige as a military hero to end congressional domination of the national government, but his ineptitude as an administrator—evident when he filled his first cabinet largely with cronies—and the scandals that swept through his presidency quickly ended that possibility. Rutherford B. Hayes (1877–81) owed his election to "waving the bloody red shirt" of the Civil War, reminding Northerners that a Republican should occupy the White House, not someone like his opponent from the "disloyal" Democratic Party (which many identified with secession). He owed his election as well to voting irregularities directly related to reconstruction. Once in office, he toiled under the congressional domination that had also contained Johnson and Grant, though he did win back some power for the presidency through his crusade for civil service reform and his use of the veto.

Democrat Grover Cleveland (1885–89; 1893–97), his two presidencies interrupted by Benjamin Harrison's one term, exerted the most executive power since Abraham Lincoln. For example, through his control of patronage appointments, he convinced the Senate in 1893 to approve the repeal of the Sherman Silver Purchase Act. He wielded his veto power often, but in that sense was more of a negative force than a positive one. Republican William McKinley (1897–1901) was, like Cleveland, a transitional president, the last one elected who had actually fought in the Civil War, and a Republican most noted for presiding over the Spanish-American War, a conflict whose outbreak owed more to congressional than presidential leadership.

The ascent of Theodore Roosevelt (1901–09) to the White House after McKinley's assassination brought about the era of the Progressive presidents, the fourth category. These chief executives accepted, protected, and promoted the new economic system of corporate capitalism but sought to control its worst abuses. Toward that end, they exerted presidential power against conservatives in Congress whose "laissez-faire attitude" and opposition to change amid a tide of popular demands for reform enhanced the president's status as leader of the people. Roosevelt worked to reaffirm the prestige of the White House not only against Congress, but also against the corporate giants who believed they owned the national government.

By sheer personality alone—he was confident, strong, and zestful—Roosevelt strengthened the presidency. One observer later said: "Theodore Roosevelt could get the attention of his fellow citizens and make them think. He knew how to put the hard questions a little before they became obvious to others; . . . how to startle the country into informed debate; and how to move people into their thinking beyond short-run self-interest and toward some longer view of the general welfare."

In more concrete terms, Roosevelt showed early on he would tackle what he called "bad corporations"—those that injured the public—when he sued the Northern Securities Company for its monopolistic practices. In embracing conservation, he pushed environmental reform to the top of the national agenda and showed he would fight congressional restrictions on such practices as setting aside forestlands.

Although criticized by Roosevelt as a pusillanimous conservative, William Howard Taft (1909–13), also a Republican, continued much of the progressive reform begun by his predecessor. Woodrow Wilson (1913–21) grabbed the progressive mantle for the Democratic Party as he shifted from seeking to break up big businesses to establishing polices that regulated them. Today, most Americans remember Wilson for his leadership in World War I. To Wilson, the war was an extension of progressive reform; consequently, he attempted to apply democratic ideals and regulatory principles to the international scene and to "uplift" countries overseas.

Theodore Roosevelt had felt much the same way and insisted that as a superior country America must stand first among all nations. With these attitudes in mind, the Progressive presidents can also be labeled the first global presidents, as they promoted interventionist policies and hastened the day when the United States would become a world power.

Not even the fifth group of presidents, the Republican reactionaries Warren G. Harding, Calvin Coolidge, and Herbert Hoover, could overturn this trend. True, they represented an American revulsion toward Woodrow Wilson's League of Nations and placed domestic rather than overseas policy on the political front burner (while encountering a largely isolationist Congress), but even they sent observers to League meetings and participated in League conferences.

Nor could they completely rout progressivism. They were reactionaries, however, because they tried to undo many reform measures while striving for economic development over social reform. In an era when a best-selling book by Bruce Barton, titled *The Man Nobody Knows,* sought to praise Jesus Christ by likening him to a salesman, Warren Harding (1921–23) talked about a return to normalcy, a pre-reformist time when government stayed out of people's lives; and Calvin Coolidge (1923–29) preached traditional small town verities while promoting corporate acquisitiveness. He extolled Charles Schwab, who built Bethlehem Steel into a giant, and called the industrialist's company "a great manufacturing plant for the service of the people of America." Herbert Hoover (1929–33) was yet another transitional president, forced late in his term by America's economic collapse to exert more power and develop emergency programs.

The founder of the modern presidency, the sixth category, was Franklin D. Roosevelt (1933–45). According to Fred I. Greenstein, with FDR "the president became the most visible landmark in the political landscape, virtually standing for the federal government in the minds of many Americans."

The Great Depression and, later, World War II, combined with Roosevelt's personality and leadership qualities to enhance the powers of the president and make the office dominant over Congress. Continuity was evident when FDR referred to the record of his cousin, Theodore Roosevelt, for guidance and built on the executive powers established by the Progressive presidents. In the case of the Great Depression, Congress had failed to revive the economy, and as banks folded and businesses shuttered their doors, Americans desperately looked to their president for help.

FDR gladly accepted the burden. He loved politics, enjoyed publicity, and liked wielding power. On top of that, he exuded confidence and seldom wavered in exerting his will. He put himself directly in the political spotlight when in his first inaugural address he declared, "The only thing we have to fear is fear itself," and insisted, "I am prepared under my constitutional duty to recommend the measures that a stricken nation in the midst of a stricken world may require." He made it clear he would act boldly when he announced, "I shall ask the Congress for . . . broad executive power to wage a war against the emergency as great as the power that would be given me if we were in fact invaded by a foreign foe." Greenstein says Roosevelt's determined statement showed there would be "a quantum increase in autonomous presidential policymaking."

On its very first day in session, Congress passed FDR's banking bill without even having its text available to read. Clearly the initiative had shifted from the legislative to the executive branch. With the modern presidency, the president became the central figure in the national government; he largely compiled the legislative agenda, involving himself in it at almost every step, and exerted influence not only through his personal will but also through the support of a large staff.

Roosevelt created the Executive Office of the President and maximized his information by going beyond official channels and using private and informal sources. He made sure that lines of authority in the bureaucracy overlapped to encourage competition among staff members, and he recruited advisers with differing views and temperaments to promote an exchange of ideas.

As Arthur M. Schlesinger, Jr., writes in *The Imperial Presidency,* World War II also greatly changed the nature of executive power. Whereas for his New Deal programs Roosevelt had relied on authority contained in specific statutes passed by Congress, "the urgencies of war led him to turn increasingly to less particularized authority—in part on the powers he asserted as 'Commander in Chief in wartime' and even more on the emergency powers released by his proclamations. . . ."

With the end of World War II, the cold war presidency emerged as the United States and the Soviet Union battled for international supremacy. Since the characteristics of the modern presidency continued into the new era, this category more accurately represents a subcategory stemming from FDR's executive practices, but it should be emphasized that the cold war created a new environment and greatly intensified the role of the president as the nation's leader.

All of the cold war presidents from Harry Truman through Ronald Reagan, though at odds ideologically on many policies and quite different from one another in personal style, expanded the power and reach of the national government overseas and into the lives of the American people. A more secretive and intensive government emerged—a cloak-and-dagger enclave that often violated the Constitution and trampled individual liberties. That Congress frequently acquiesced in such activities only emboldened the executive branch. By and large, this subterranean realm was justified by those in power as necessary to fight the cold war and defeat communism.

With congressional approval, Harry Truman (1945–53) formed the National Security Council (NSC) in 1947 to help him develop policies important in protecting America from foreign enemies. Over time, the NSC went beyond advising and started *making* policy without congressional oversight; under President Ronald Reagan in the 1980s, it engaged in illegal and unconstitutional acts that involved sending money to rebels in Nicaragua.

Near the beginning of the cold war presidency, Truman waged war in Korea without obtaining a declaration from Congress. Dwight Eisenhower, John Kennedy, and Lyndon Johnson all deepened American involvement in Vietnam through secret maneuvers that violated international agreements or domestic laws. Dwight Eisenhower (1953–61) approved the overthrow of a leftist regime in Guatemala through a clandestine plan directed by the Central Intelligence Agency (CIA). John Kennedy (1961–63) backed an invasion by Cuban exiles against Fidel Castro in 1961 as part of a covert plot whose public exposure turned it into a fiasco.

Lyndon Johnson (1963–69) began Conus Intel, a top-secret program to spy on the American public, and Richard Nixon (1969–74) expanded it. Conus Intel involved using approximately 1,000 U.S. Army agents to gather background information on civilians. By the early 1970s, the military had dossiers on 25 million Americans.

Johnson engaged American troops in direct combat in Vietnam without the explicit approval of Congress, while Nixon waged an air war against Cambodia without even telling Congress. Gerald Ford (1974–77) sent $25 million to Angola to back a rebel group there and approved a plan to have the CIA hire mercenaries to help them—all through maneuvers that kept Congress and the American public in the dark.

Richard Nixon's Watergate violations revealed numerous presidential abuses of power but failed to end many of them, largely because most Americans looked at them as the fault of Nixon rather than the political system. Historian Joan Hoff, writing in *Nixon Reconsidered*, bemoans the lawlessness of presidents since 1945 and claims that their abuses resulted from the "semi-state of war the nation had waged" against communism. The failure to see beyond Nixon's personal faults, she says, led to the Iran-Contra scandal under Ronald Reagan (1981–89) and ultimately to Reagan's popularity prevailing over justice, trust, and responsibility. As a result, he went unpunished and the presidency escaped full accountability.

Ronald Reagan issued more than 300 National Security Decision Directives (NSDDS), largely secret orders under the supervision of the National Security Council. Directive 145 led to the government asking commercial databases for lists of subscribers to see if people were accessing "sensitive but unclassified" government information. At the time, Tulane University historian Anna Nelson charged that "Some of [Reagan's] NSDDS are action documents bypassing even normal agency channels, let alone the Congress.

The arrogance of this arrangement is incredible." One of Reagan's directives launched the 1983 invasion of Grenada.

Enhanced presidential power, of course, comes from more than covert plots. Truman, for example, built on Franklin Roosevelt's Executive Office of the President, and under him the Bureau of the Budget began reviewing policies to see if they conformed with the presidential agenda. According to Greenstein, "The result was a set of operating procedures that [today] make presidential leadership of Congress automatic rather than a function of the individual who happens to occupy the White House." And when Dwight Eisenhower established a committee outside the Republican Party to lead his presidential campaign, he began the era of what Theodore J. Lowi calls "the personal president," one characterized by "a virtual cult of personality revolving around the White House." This form has continued into the 21st century.

After George Bush (1989–93), the post–cold war presidency, a second subcategory, began with Bill Clinton (1993–2001). For Clinton, continuity with the cold war presidents remained strong. For despite a surge in congressional power with the Republican election victory in 1994 and the impeachment of the president four years later, and despite abysmal voter turnouts for presidential elections, most Americans still placed great demands on the presidency and expected the chief executive to handle any big problem that developed.

Bruce Miroff believes that Bill Clinton's impeachment revealed a different context for the presidency than the republican one that prevailed in the 1790s and early 1800s. He calls it the "democratic character" by which a president "need not be better than most of us; he need only be like most of us." (His essay traced this character trait back to Andrew Jackson in the 1820s.) The prevalence of democratic character, Miroff claims, accounts for why Clinton avoided removal from office—that is, most Americans thought his job performance remained unhindered by his personal flaws, with which they could identify.

Miroff may be right, though it can be argued that as much as Americans thought of their presidents as "one of the people" and were willing to ask a presidential candidate what kind of underwear he wore—as happened to Clinton on national television—many still wanted their president to exhibit superior qualities that could be found in the traditional model of republican character.

The post–cold war presidency took a sudden turn in the wake of the terrorist attacks on the United States in September 2001. Americans found themselves in a new era, one defined by President George W. Bush's war on terror and his pronounced doctrine, whereby the United States committed itself to waging preventive war against any group or country that threatened American interests and dedicated itself to maintaining military supremacy by preventing any other nation from emerging as its rival.

The executive branch amassed much greater power at the expense of Congress and the judiciary, and the federal government reached ever deeper into personal lives under the name of national security. Defense spending increased, and when Bush involved the United States in a war against Iraq under the guise of fighting terrorism, foreign entanglements became greater and messier. Moreover, the credibility of the presidency became more tenuous when the primary reasons offered by Bush for the invasion turned out to be false.

To many Americans, Bush exhibited the superior republican qualities found in tradition. He took the reins in a difficult situation and responded forcefully to protect American lives and liberties. To many other Americans, Bush exhibited the qualities quite opposite the model of republican character; he lied, deceived, and used excessive power.

With Bush in the White House, America became increasingly polarized. The country had entered an uncharted and perilous time, filled with doubts at home, animosity overseas, and a presidency certain to undergo considerable change.

Each of the profiles presented in this book, *Presidents: A Biographical Dictionary,* traces the points at which presidential character, the exercise of power, and external events intersected. It is meant to present information suitable for exploratory research or for a casual reading of the history of America's chief executives. Each profile includes suggestions for further reading and a chronology. A general bibliography follows at the end of the book, along with an appendix that presents personal facts about the presidents, election results, and information about the presidential cabinets.

No one can say what events will define the presidency of the future when changed circumstances may generate different categories from those discussed here. Whatever the challenges, the words that historian Henry Adams used to describe the president in the 1870s remain valid today. "[He] resembles the commander of a ship," Adams said. "He must have a helm to grasp, a course to steer, a port to seek." How firmly he steers and how skillfully he enters the as yet indefinable port may well determine the legacy beyond any one presidency and shape the institution for many years to come.

George Washington (1732–1799)

First President, 1789–1797

George Washington
(painting by Charles Peale Polk, West Point Museum Art Collection, United States Military Academy)

"The destiny of the republican model of government are justly considered . . . staked on the experiment entrusted to the hands of the American people."

—Inaugural words, first term, April 30, 1789

Many years ago historian Marcus Cunliffe tracked the historical traces left by George Washington and found it nearly impossible to separate myth from fact. Americans, he said, had inherited a picture of their revolutionary hero and first president as a demigod, and in many ways a cold and boring one at that. But as Cunliffe discovered, while Washington's contemporaries recognized his greatness, they also recognized his limitations; while they praised him, they also criticized him. In short, Washington turned out to be more complex than the one-dimensional "founding father" later enshrined in legend.

—⁓—

George Washington was born to Augustine Washington, a prosperous farmer, and Mary Ball on February 11, 1732, in Westmoreland County, Virginia, on a plantation later called Wakefield. His father died when George was only 11. The youngster subsequently lived on the family farm near Fredericksburg with his mother. Washington's childhood remains shrouded in the fanciful stories of Parson Weems, who in the early 1800s told how George had chopped down a cherry tree with his hatchet and then admitted having done so, saying that he could never tell a lie.

Young George obtained a limited formal education, roughly equivalent to an elementary level today. John Adams, the Massachusetts political leader and later president, said that Washington was "too illiterate, unlearned, unread for his station and reputation." But what Washington lacked in classroom schooling, he made up for in other ways, and he developed a love for reading. That he devoured many political essays, including *The Federalist,* during the public debate over the Constitution; that in retirement he subscribed to 10 newspapers; and that at his death he had a large library—900 books—shows that Adams, long jealous of the Virginian, may have exaggerated.

In his youth, Washington read the *Morals,* written by Seneca, a first-century A.D. Roman philosopher. Conscious of his own thin-skinned nature that sometimes unleashed a violent temper, he tried to adopt the author's advice that men should control their anger. (An acquaintance once told George's mother when the youngster was 16, "I wish I could say he governs his temper.") *Cato,* a drama written by Joseph Addison in 1713, attracted Washington for its insistence that everything other than great exploits, justice, and wisdom amounts to nothing more than "frenzy and distraction." When Washington read yet another work, "The Rules of Civility and Decent Behavior in Company and in Conversation," an English version of which first appeared in the mid-1600s, he copied it word for word and through its lessons learned to accept honor with reluctance and modesty.

By age 16, Washington was running survey lines in the vast expanse beyond Virginia's Blue Ridge Mountains. In 1749 he worked as an assistant surveyor. The following year, as a surveyor, he staked out and laid claim to 1,450 acres for himself. By 1753 he was living in considerable comfort; in addition to his own land claims, he had inherited 4,000 acres, owned many slaves, and leased Mount Vernon from his sister-in-law before buying it a few years later. Mount Vernon came to encompass five separate farms over 13 square miles. With his slaves and landed wealth, he affirmed his standing in the Virginia gentry, a planter class which, though never large in size, exerted enormous power and directed Virginia's political affairs.

Washington grew into a commanding figure. At 6'2", big-boned with wide shoulders, long legs and arms, and a sculpted face, the Virginian appeared strong in body and character, and he was. He once boasted that he threw a stone to the top of the 215-foot-high Natural Bridge in the Shenandoah Valley. He complemented these qualities with amazing endurance and impressive horsemanship, an important trait in a society that counted horses as essential to survival in war and peace.

During the time that Washington developed into a wealthy planter, he fell in love with Sally Fairfax, whom he first met when he was 16. In old age he wrote her that neither a single accomplishment "nor all of them together had been able to eradicate from my mind those happy moments, the happiest of my life, which I have enjoyed in your company." Yet in Washington's early years his love for her posed a problem: She was married to his close friend, George William Fairfax.

Although his quest for Sally Fairfax would end in frustration, his quest for glory soon brought him renown. In the early 1750s, Britain and France clashed over the Ohio Valley. As French settlers moved southward from Canada, prominent Virginians secured a half-million acre land grant for the Ohio Company, through which they intended to engage in speculation. In 1753 Washington offered his services to Virginia's lieutenant governor, Robert Dinwiddie, to lead a mission into Ohio to warn the French out.

After making the arduous journey and serving notice on the French, Washington told Dinwiddie that the enemy showed no signs of leaving. In 1754 the young Virginian, ordered to hold onto the Ohio Valley for Britain, led 159 men into the disputed territory. At one point he attacked and defeated a group of French soldiers. The dead included a French diplomat, M. de Jumonville, who had been on a mission to push the British out of Ohio.

Washington then blundered. He built a stockade called Fort Necessity in an indefensible location and in such a way that when it rained, the structure flooded. In July 1754 the French launched a withering attack, the rains came, and together they forced Washington to surrender and sign a document in which he agreed that France had acted only to avenge the death of Jumonville. His admission raised an international furor, as it seemed to confirm that Washington had purposely killed a diplomat. The militarily inexperienced Virginian stood chastised, but many of his fellow colonists praised him nonetheless for having confronted the French.

In 1755 Washington journeyed west again, this time as aide to General Edward Braddock, who led a British army accompanied by an army of colonists into the Ohio Valley. Their mission turned disastrous when the French killed Braddock and shot Washington's horse from under him—twice. With 900 men dead or wounded, the Virginian, thrust into command on Braddock's death, led his men to safety and retreated to Philadelphia. Despite this defeat, the colonists extolled Washington's bravery.

The territorial conflict ignited the Seven Years' War, called the French and Indian War in North America. Virginia created its own army and appointed George Washington, then a colonel, to command a regiment of infantry and defend the colony's frontier. Washington, however, never received the supplies or men he needed, and he became angry when the British refused to allow him much authority. He longed for a regular commission in the British army, but never got one due to his "inferior" status as a colonist. When the war ended in a British victory in 1763, Washington returned to his plantation having seen little action after the Braddock defeat—though he did participate in the westward march to capture Fort Duquesne, which fell peacefully—and having developed a deep dislike for the way Britain treated the colonists.

During the war Washington had won election to Virginia's legislature, the House of Burgesses, in which he would serve for 15 years. This further advanced his standing within the colony's elite. So, too, did his marriage in January 1759 to Martha Dandridge Custis, a wealthy widow with two small children. The wedding occurred shortly after he had written Sally Fairfax professing to love only her.

Within a few years, Washington's newfound domestic life was shattered by the American Revolution. By spring 1769, two years after the British Parliament tried to levy internal taxes on the colonies through the Townshend Acts, the Virginian began to think that armed rebellion was possible. When Parliament reacted to the Boston Tea Party of 1773 by closing Boston harbor and suspending town meetings in Massachusetts, Washington called the action tyranny.

In 1774 Virginia made him a delegate to the Continental Congress, called into session by the colonies to consider strategy. While there, he said little but voted for commercial sanctions, which were enacted, and supported warning Britain that should it use force, the colonists would respond in kind.

Washington served as a delegate to the Second Continental Congress in May 1775. He wore his blue and buff military uniform, probably as a way to show the willingness of Virginia to fight and his own willingness to head his colony's forces. Some historians claim he wanted to promote himself as commander of the intercolonial army. Yet when reports circulated that he would indeed be chosen commander in chief, he privately urged some of the Virginia delegates to block the appointment.

They refused, and Congress made him its unanimous choice to lead the Continental army gathered outside Boston. Even John Adams supported Washington for his bravery in the French and Indian War, his integrity and strength, and his Virginia origins, which the delegates felt would diversify an army that was heavily New England in its makeup.

Washington, who almost always blended his ambition with diffidence—a mix that produced the humble quality prized in the "Rules of Civility"—accepted his appointment and told Congress: "But lest some unlucky event should happen . . . I beg it may be remembered, by every gentleman in this room, that I, this day, declare with the utmost sincerity, I do not think myself equal to the command I am honored with."

Washington's first months as general sorely tried the revolutionary cause. When he arrived at Cambridge, Massachusetts, he found 14,000 soldiers and confusion bordering on chaos. The army had little gunpowder, and the men lacked discipline, failing to even build privies and living in disease-threatening stench. The officer corps was so unreliable that Washington prosecuted some of its members for incompetence. He resolutely believed that quality officers were essential to victory and never favored hit-and-run guerrilla tactics; rather, he admired British military skill and wanted to emulate it. He quickly achieved discipline, partly because his men respected his bearing, frugality, and hard work.

For their part, the British assembled an enormous expeditionary force: 10 ships of the line, 20 frigates, and 32,000 regular troops. Washington thought the war would last only a few weeks because Parliament would compromise. He favored an agreement himself, until he read Thomas Paine's pamphlet *Common Sense* and wrote to the Continental Congress that if Britain intended tyranny, then the colonists must intend independence.

After the British army evacuated Boston in March 1776, it set its sights on conquering New York City. Washington faced a daunting task, for Manhattan's large size alone made it difficult to defend. He decided to place his troops, 19,000 men, across the East River at Brooklyn Heights. On August 27, 1776, though, the British surprised him by attacking from another direction. Having been routed, the general brought his survivors together—500 Americans had been killed and 1,000 captured—and two nights later retreated. His army met the British again in September, when the redcoats attacked Manhattan from Kips Bay, their naval guns blasting and barges bringing troops ashore. The Americans reacted to the ferocity by running. Astride his horse, Washington tried to rally his men but was nearly captured himself. "Good God!" he cried. "Have I got such troops as these?"

The general suffered an even worse defeat when British troops captured a fort under the command of Nathanael Greene. Washington watched the loss from nearby Fort Lee, which itself soon fell to the British. The Virginian did what his critics thought he did best and again retreated.

Several contemporaries and later historians disparaged Washington's retreat as a sign of incompetence, especially when viewed in contrast to the victory a year later by Horatio Gates over the large British army commanded by John Burgoyne at Saratoga, New York. But his defenders presented a different picture. To them the general showed skill in saving his outclassed army, slipping through British lines, and keeping the enemy off guard. In time, Washington's maneuvers exhausted the British, who found themselves burdened by having to replace casualties with men from across the Atlantic.

After a battle at White Plains, New York, in October 1776, Washington retreated to Pennsylvania. He desperately needed a victory to boost morale. On Christmas Day he and his troops crossed the Delaware and attacked Hessian soldiers—Prussian mercenaries fighting for the British—at Trenton, New Jersey. By forging ahead through snow and ice, he completely surprised the enemy, and his victory convinced Britain to abandon as unworkable its plan to build military outposts throughout the Northeast.

On January 3, 1777, Washington attacked at Princeton and for the first time caused a British line to break. The redcoats, however, triumphed again in September 1777 at Brandywine Creek in Pennsylvania and the following month at Germantown. Then they captured Philadelphia, the seat of the U.S. government, and sent the Continental Congress fleeing. While the British spent that winter in comfort, supplied by American collaborators, Washington's army suffered at Valley Forge in makeshift log cabins, short on fuel, clothing, and food. The general could have raided the countryside for provisions, but he refused, believing it would only antagonize local farmers. He wanted the onus for depredations left on the British, who often resorted to taking what they needed.

During that winter a cabal led by Brigadier General Thomas Conway attempted to strip Washington of his command. The complex plot unraveled when the Virginian's supporters both within and outside Congress rallied to his side.

The Americans received a boost in 1778 when France, long Britain's archenemy and buoyed by Gates's victory at Saratoga, recognized the United States as an independent nation. That June, Washington engaged the British in battle at Monmouth, New Jersey, that, despite its indecisive outcome, caused the redcoats to garrison at New York City.

During the battle, Washington had a falling out with Major General Charles Lee, considered among the army's more talented commanders. Washington publicly upbraided Lee for allowing his men to retreat, and Lee never forgave him for the humiliation. In June, Lee wrote Washington a letter saying, "I must pronounce [you] . . . guilty of an act of cruel injustice. . . ." He tempered his accusation, however, by saying he believed Washington's criticism of him originated elsewhere, with "some of those dirty earwigs who will for ever insinuate themselves near persons in high office. . . ." Lee was eventually court-martialed and found guilty of disobeying orders.

In all, from the summer of 1776 through the summer of 1778, Washington fought seven battles in the New York to Philadelphia theater, winning just two. By 1780 French forces were heavily involved in the war, and the following year French commanders planned Britain's *coup de grace*. While ignoring George Washington's advice to attack New York City, the comte de Rochâmbeau prepared to have a combined French and American army march to Yorktown, Virginia, where Lord Cornwallis had stationed his large British force.

In August 1781, as the allied troops headed south, Washington employed a ruse: He built baking ovens in New Jersey to trick enemy spies into thinking his army would be stationed there as part of an offensive in the Northeast. By the time the British realized what was really happening, the allied armies were at the Delaware River; Cornwallis received news of the advance only after his enemy was upon him. With the French and American troops blocking Cornwallis on land and pounding him and the French navy blocking his ocean exit, he capitulated in October 1781. As the British fife and drums played "The World Turned Upside Down," Washington received the surrender. The battle broke the British military resistance in America, though fighting continued for two more years.

Washington faced one more challenge as general. In 1783 his troops at Newburgh, New York, threatened rebellion after Congress failed to pay them. He then met with his officers on March 15 and told them that although the government was acting slowly, it would act justly. The officers were unmoved until, in a dramatic gesture likely planned by him but made to appear spontaneous, he told them he wanted to read them a letter. He then took a pair of eyeglasses from his pocket, hesitated, and said: "Gentlemen, you will permit me to put on my spectacles, for I have not only grown gray but almost blind in the service of my country." With those words touching the officers' sense of sacrifice, they abandoned their rebellious thoughts, and Washington soon returned to Virginia and his beloved Mount Vernon.

Public service called Washington again when he was chosen in 1787 as a delegate to the Constitutional Convention. He arrived in Philadelphia a strong nationalist devoted to increasing the power of the central government. Based on his reputation from the Revolutionary War, the delegates unanimously chose him to serve as convention president, and he used his calm demeanor to keep the meeting from collapsing.

As a substantial slaveholder, Washington did nothing at the Constitutional Convention to attack or even question slavery, nor would he as president of the United States. On several occasions he privately expressed his dislike for the peculiar institution and hoped it would be ended; but he said, "to set [slaves] afloat at once would, I really believe, be productive of much inconvenience and mischief."

Washington refused any active role in ratifying the Constitution. About the document he stated, "What will be the general opinion on, or the reception of it, is not for me to decide, nor shall I say anything for or against it. If it be good, I suppose it will work its way good. If bad, it will recoil on the framers." Yet by signing the Constitution he put his enormous prestige behind it.

George Washington reacted to his election as president of the United States in 1789 with trepidation. He told a friend, "My movements to the chair of Government will be accompanied with feelings not unlike those of a culprit who is going to the place of his execution, so unwilling am I . . . to quit a peaceful abode for an ocean of difficulties." He traveled slowly overland to the first national capital, New York City, receiving the huzzahs of supporters along the way, and in April took the oath of office at city hall. His hand over his heart, Washington bowed several times to a huge crowd as they cheered him.

Despite hopes for national unity, political disputes erupted almost from the start. At first they seemed trivial, such as the debate over how Washington should be addressed; should it be as "His Excellency"? Such pretension occupied the portly vice president, John Adams, leading his critics to retaliate by calling him "His Rotundity." Congress finally settled on simply referring to Washington by his constitutional title, "president." As frivolous as the debate seems today, it was loaded with meaning. Political leaders knew that the trappings of office said much about power; when leaders are lavished with courtiers, impressive ceremonies, and imposing names, they assume an exalted state. Every president still realizes this and shapes his actions accordingly.

Politics quickly heated up over money and sparked a dispute between Secretary of State Thomas Jefferson of Virginia and Secretary of the Treasury Alexander Hamilton of New York. Because the government needed to arrange its finances, the highly intelligent, talented, and brash Hamilton unfolded a complex financial tapestry—so complex that few understood it besides him. First, in 1790 he proposed to Congress that the national debt be funded. Linked to this, he proposed the national government assume state debts. Jefferson and his fellow Virginian James Madison, then serving in Congress, protested that because the northern states carried the most debt, the policy, which would have to be supported with taxes, would hurt the southern states. Hamilton's proposal passed after his congressional allies agreed to place the new national capital in the South, near the Potomac River.

By having the national government take over the state debts and make interest payments, Hamilton shifted the allegiance of those wealthy capitalists who bought securities; they now looked to the national government rather than the state governments as a source for their income. Further, in eradicating state debts he hoped the states would have no need to levy taxes, that this power could be used exclusively by the national government, and that the states would become irrelevant. Although less extreme in his nationalism than Hamilton, Washington supported his treasury secretary.

Hamilton raised an even greater storm of controversy in 1791 when he proposed a national bank to serve as an engine for economic development by making loans primarily to commercial and manufacturing interests. The bank would be capitalized mostly by the wealthy, giving them a greater influence in the government. This arrangement, he believed, would create a strong pillar of support: The wealthy would want to see the government thrive so the bank could prosper.

Clearly, Hamilton's national bank would nudge America from an agrarian society to a more commercial one, as he desired. Jefferson and Madison, however, vehemently opposed the bank. They argued that the government had no power under the Constitution to create it. After Congress approved the bank and Washington heard Jefferson's objections, he asked Hamilton to respond. The treasury secretary submitted a brilliant rebuttal, arguing that the government had implied powers, which in this case came from the right to regulate currency. Should the government fail to use its implied powers, Hamilton warned, it would be shackled. Washington again agreed with him and signed the legislation.

The president drew the line, however, when he refused to support Hamilton's "Report on Manufactures" that would have committed the government to financing projects aimed at expanding industry. Washington said Hamilton's proposal would require excessive government power.

President Washington wanted to return home when his first term ended, and he convinced Madison to write a farewell address for him. But others dissuaded him. Jefferson later said he told the president "that as far as I knew . . . he was the only man in the U.S. who possessed the confidence of the whole. . . ." Had he left, the presidency may have been changed forever. Biographer Richard Norton Smith says that Washington may have "established a precedent of quitting. It might have become an almost parliamentary kind of government." In 1792, the electoral college again cast a unanimous vote for Washington.

His presidency, though, soon came under attack. Conflict between the Jeffersonians and Hamiltonians, then gathering into factions, intensified after the treasury secretary convinced Congress to pass excise taxes necessary to support the new financial programs, including a levy on whiskey. Along the frontier, whiskey served as a means of exchange, and in western Pennsylvania farmers refused to pay the taxes, which they considered loathsome and oppressive. They even tarred and feathered revenue collectors.

For his part, Hamilton purposefully antagonized the frontier settlers. Only hours before a new federal law forbade the government from forcing people in remote locations to travel long distances for trials, he ordered that writs be served on 75 distillers to appear in Philadelphia. For most of them, the city was far from their homes. Hamilton obviously wanted to foment armed rebellion and was looking for an excuse to wield the military so he could show the government's clout.

In July 1793 about 500 frontiersmen attacked and destroyed the house of excise collector John Neville and killed an armed guard. In August Hamilton and Washington—who, like his treasury secretary, considered the "Whiskey Rebellion," as it was called, to be a threat to order—decided to send an army into western Pennsylvania. Madison called it an excuse to "establish the principle that a standing army was necessary for *enforcing the laws.*"

President Washington led the army a short distance, Hamilton the rest of the way. Rather than facing armed revolutionaries, however, the secretary faced derision in newspapers and in Congress when no rebellion could be found. As it turned out, the few frontiersmen who supported armed action had scattered and disappeared. (Only two of the insurgents were convicted of treason, and they were pardoned by Washington.) Still, Hamilton rejected his critics and praised the mission as having proved the government could restore order.

Washington raised the political conflict another notch when he claimed the Whiskey Rebellion had been fomented by groups called Democratic Societies, which had formed to oppose Hamilton's policies. Given Washington's prestige, when he criticized them he effectively killed them. In siding with those who wanted to limit free expression, Washington may have been mindful of the shrill taunts of opposition newspapers that called him "a man in his political dotage" and a "supercilious tyrant."

To Washington, the Democratic Societies carried another danger: intrigue linked to the French Revolution. When the French monarchy fell in 1789 and revolutionaries sent the heads of Louis XVI and Marie Antoinette tumbling from a guillotine in 1793, many Americans embraced the uprising as an extension of their own quest for republican government. Many others, however, cringed at the bloodshed, and as the French Revolution took a radical course, they considered it dangerous. To complicate matters, at the same time the revolution was engulfing France, the nascent French Republic found itself fighting a war with Britain.

The French Revolution shaped the conflict between Jeffersonians and Hamiltonians. The Jeffersonians supported the uprising as an expression of republican ideals and insisted the United States was obligated to stand by France against Britain due to a treaty of alliance signed in 1778. The Hamiltonians condemned the revolution as anarchy and warned that if it were given any support it would spread to the United States, and they also believed that America's economic interest lay with its chief trading partner, Britain. In this way foreign affairs merged with the debt, national bank, and tax issues to shape domestic politics.

On the foreign policy front, in April 1793, soon after Britain and France went to war, President Washington declared American neutrality. "The duty and interest of the United States," he said, "require that they should with sincerity and good faith adopt and pursue a conduct friendly and impartial towards the belligerent powers."

George Washington found neutrality a difficult course. First, the French sent Edmund Genet as their minister to the United States. Genet decided to defy Washington, and after he arrived in Charleston, South Carolina, he began recruiting men for an expeditionary force to wrest Louisiana from Spain. He also outfitted privateers to attack British ships. As Genet traveled overland to see Washington at Philadelphia, he harangued huge crowds and expressed confidence that his popularity would humble the president. Jefferson initially embraced Genet, but he backed away as the Frenchman brazenly defied the government. Ultimately, Genet was removed from his post.

Second, the British intensified their raids on American ships, confiscating cargo and even forcing sailors into their navy. This mortified the Hamiltonians, who feared the United States would go to war against Britain and help France. President Washington believed any war would greatly harm America, still politically and militarily weak.

As a result, he sent John Jay to London to negotiate on behalf of the United States. Jay's Treaty, completed in 1795, stunned Washington, for it conceded much to Britain while gaining little for America. Although some money would be provided to compensate for the raids on American ships, the treaty failed to provide for any punishment; although Britain opened its West Indies islands to American trade, the treaty greatly restricted the size of the ships allowed; and although Britain agreed to remove its troops from American territory near the Great Lakes—which it should have done under the terms of an earlier agreement—the treaty refused to recognize America's rights officially as a neutral nation.

Washington believed Jay's Treaty would so outrage the American public, which still disliked Britain from the days of the American Revolution, that when he sent it to the Senate for consideration, that body held its sessions in secret. The Senate approved the treaty, minus the restrictions on ship sizes in the West Indies trade, by exactly the two-thirds vote required.

Before Washington could sign Jay's Treaty, news of its provisions leaked to the public, and demonstrations erupted across the country. Americans considered it a sellout. Amid the controversy, the president faced another crisis: Edmund Randolph, who had replaced Jefferson as secretary of state, was found to have given information about American internal affairs to the French. Randolph's betrayal angered Washington, and he feared that if he rejected the treaty, his entire administration would be perceived as being under French influence. So even though the British were still raiding American ships, in August 1795 he signed the agreement.

A fortuitous development enabled Americans to accept his decision when at about the same time Thomas Pinckney concluded a treaty with Spain, which gave the United States access to the Mississippi River for shipping goods through New Orleans, a critical route for westerners. Where Jay's Treaty had ignited protest, Pinckney's Treaty won praise.

Jay's Treaty cut deep into American society and polarized the nation, helping to shape the warring Jeffersonian and Hamiltonian factions into opposing political parties. The Jeffersonians took the name Republican, and the Hamiltonians took the name Federalist. The Republicans believed that if the Federalists stayed in power—and they considered Washington one of them even though he rejected both parties—monarchy would take hold. The Federalists believed that if the Republicans gained power, a French-style popular uprising would destroy order. Washington decried the rise of these parties as evidence of a country losing its unity and falling prey to domestic violence, foreign schemers, and manipulative demagogues.

Dispirited and still longing for Mount Vernon, President Washington decided against a third term. In his farewell address, presented September 17, 1796, he bemoaned political parties. "Let me . . . take a . . . comprehensive view," he said, "and *warn* you, *in the most solemn manner,* against the baneful effects of the Spirit of Party. . . ." Thinking of the turmoil in Europe, he advocated neutrality in foreign affairs. "The great rule of conduct for us, in regard to foreign Nations," he said, "is, in extending our commercial relations, to have with them as little *Political* connection as possible. . . . [it] is our true policy to steer clear of permanent alliances, with any portion of the foreign world. . . ."

Federalists refused to let the old soldier fade away, though. In 1798 they pressured President John Adams to appoint Washington as commander of a provisional army then being organized to protect the United States against a possible French invasion. Alexander Hamilton expected Washington to appoint him second in command, and he did.

Just a little more than two years after leaving office, on December 14, 1799, George Washington died at Mount Vernon, his wife Martha by his side. He had contracted a respiratory disease and doctors worsened his health by "bleeding" him, a treatment that killed many patients it intended to save. In his will, he freed his slaves, effective on Martha's death.

No number of words can fairly measure Washington's legacy. Without his leadership in the Revolution, America could well have faltered; without his presence at the Constitutional Convention, the delegates may have produced nothing more than wrangling; without his guidance as president, committed to moderation and republicanism, the nation may have suffered a tyrant. Marcus Cunliffe was right about the difficulty in knowing the true Washington, but the first president's principles remain engrained in the American conscience. To Washington, "the sacred fire of liberty and the destiny of the republican model of government," as he put it, relied on "the experiment intrusted to the hands of the American people."

Chronology

1732 Born February 11

1749 Appointed assistant surveyor

1750 Appointed county surveyor

1752 Receives appointment in Virginia militia

1754 Attacks French in Ohio Valley

Surrenders at Fort Necessity

1755 Fights French as an aide to General Braddock

Appointed commander in chief of militia

1758 Elected to House of Burgesses

1759 Marries Martha Dandridge Custis

1773 Condemns British for closing Boston harbor

1774 Serves in First Continental Congress

1775 Serves in Second Continental Congress

Elected commander in chief of the army

1776 Takes over defense of Boston

Loses New York in battles of Long Island and White Plains

Retreats through New Jersey

1777 Breaks through British lines at Princeton

Loses at Brandywine Creek and Germantown

Encamps at Valley Forge

Turns back Conway Cabal

1781 Receives surrender of Cornwallis at Yorktown

1783 Bids farewell to his officers

Resigns his commission

1787 Elected president of Constitutional Convention

1789 Elected president

1790 Signs assumption of states' debt bill

1791 Signs national bank charter

Approves excise tax

1792 Reelected president

1793 Issues Neutrality Proclamation

Demands recall of Edmund Genet

Sends army against Whiskey Rebellion

1795 Signs Jay's Treaty

1796 Publishes Farewell Address

1797 Retires to Mount Vernon

1798 Appointed commander of provisional army

1799 Dies December 14

Further Reading

Abbot, W. W., ed. *The Papers of George Washington.* Charlottesville: University Press of Virginia, 1983.

Brookhiser, Richard. *Founding Father: Rediscovering George Washington.* New York: Free Press, 1996.

Burns, James MacGregor. *George Washington.* New York: Times Books, 2004.

Cunliffe, Marcus. *George Washington, Man and Monument.* Boston: Little, Brown, 1958.

Ellis, Joseph. *His Excellency: George Washington.* New York: Alfred A. Knopf, 2004.

Ferling, John E. *The First of Men: A Life of George Washington.* Knoxville: University of Tennessee Press, 1988.

Fischer, David Hackett. *Washington's Crossing.* New York: Oxford University Press, 2004.

Fitzpatrick, John C., ed. *Diaries of George Washington, 1748–1799,* 4 vols. Boston: Houghton Mifflin, 1925.

———, ed. *The Writings of George Washington.* Washington, D.C.: U.S. Government Printing Office, 1931–1944.

Flexner, James Thomas. *George Washington,* 4 vols. Boston: Little, Brown, 1965–1972.

Freeman, Douglas Southall. *George Washington: A Biography,* 7 vols. New York: Scribner's, 1948–1957.

Higginbotham, Don, ed. *George Washington Reconsidered.* Charlottesville: University Press of Virginia, 2001.

According to biographer Page Smith, "Adams was stirred in his deepest being. . . . It is only given a man to be once so moved, so transported as John Adams was. . . . these are the moments in which truth seems to have descended from heaven in the inspired word."

Nearly four decades later, having lost reelection to Thomas Jefferson, Adams prepared to leave the presidency. Legend has it that as he sat amid trunks and packing crates in the sparsely furnished building later called the White House, he feverishly signed appointments of conservative judges to office in a last-minute act intended to thwart Jefferson's libertarian principles. Who, then, was the real Adams—the inspired crusader for liberty, or the vengeful reactionary seeking to contain it?

John Adams was born on October 19, 1735, to John and Susanna Boylston Adams at Braintree, Massachusetts, near Boston. He grew up on his family's farm, more attracted to agriculture and boyhood idylls than to school. "I spent my time . . . in making and sailing boats and Ships upon the Ponds and Brooks," he wrote much later in his autobiography, "in making and flying Kites, in driving hoops, playing marbles, playing Quoits, Wrestling, Swimming, Skating, and above all in shooting, to which Diversion I was addicted to a degree of Ardor which I know not that I ever felt for any other Business, Study, or Amusement."

Still, no farm could satisfy his brilliant, penetrating mind, and in 1751, at age 16, he enrolled at Harvard. Since his uncle, Joseph Adams, had graduated from there and had gone on to become a schoolmaster and clergyman, many in the Adams family expected young John would do the same. At first events appeared to be unfolding that way when, on receiving his degree in 1755, he found employment as a schoolmaster in Worcester, west of Boston.

At this time Adams began keeping a diary, and for nearly 30 years he recorded observations historians still turn to in assessing early America. He used his diary as a magnifying glass, frequently turning it on himself to closely investigate his own character and what motivated him. In this he followed the example of his Puritan ancestors, who had made introspection fundamental to their lives. His diary entries reveal all the traditional Puritan concern—some might call it preoccupation—with ambition and worldly gains and how they corrupt the human spirit.

His writings also reveal his feelings of guilt over failing to work hard enough. In one of his early entries, he lamented: "I am constantly forming, but never executing good resolutions." Yet Adams assiduously pursued self-improvement. In the early morning and again late at night he read ancient and some modern works, and during the school day he let his students teach one another while he sat at his desk and wrote.

He had no desire to spend his entire life in the classroom—he referred to his students as ignorant "little runtlings"—but lacked clear plans for the future. He considered the ministry, but after he became friends with James Putnam, a local lawyer, he began studying law. He did so with considerable dread, for many colonists distrusted all lawyers. "In this situation I remained for about two Years," Adams later wrote, "Reading Law in the night and keeping School in the day."

In 1758 he completed his training under Putnam and returned to his beloved Braintree to open his own practice. Without a reputation and dwarfed by the legal lights in Boston, Adams struggled to make a living. As he yearned to be a successful lawyer, he met with Jeremiah Gridley, the most prominent member of the Boston bar, who befriended him and gave him full use of his extensive library. At the same time he studied the political leaders in Braintree and how they worked with the townspeople in order to maintain power. From an early date, Adams believed politics was "psychology writ large, a heaving collection of irrational urges that moved across the social landscape." Ambitious, he mused, "How shall I spread an opinion of myself as a lawyer of distinguished genius, learning and virtue?"

He soon found that the events leading to the American Revolution provided him a grand stage on which to display his qualities. Eager to learn from outstanding lawyers around him and caught up in an intensifying controversy between Massachusetts and Britain, in 1761 Adams—with paper, pen, and ink pot in hand—attended the court hearing in which James Otis argued against the writs of assistance. For years the colonists had been subject to import duties and to restrictions on which ports they could trade with, but these laws had been enforced only erratically. Now the Crown wanted to hold the colonists to them and began using the writs to search ships for any violations. Jeremiah Gridley argued for the Crown with logic so tight that Adams thought it impregnable. Gridley insisted the writs rested on several centuries of statutory law.

Then Otis arose. He, too, reached back into the centuries, but in his case it was to the fight of English people against arbitrary rule. He said that a law-abiding orderly person "is as secure in his house as a prince in his castle" and that any Parliamentary act that conflicted with the British constitution or "natural equity" must be voided by the courts.

Adams marveled at Otis's argument, both the reasoning he used and the forceful way in which he presented it. Adams believed Americans would never sacrifice their English liberties, "at least without an entire devastation of the country and a general destruction of their lives."

Despite his rational exterior, John Adams harbored deep emotional feelings toward women. He fell in and out of love several times before marrying Abigail Smith in 1764. She was well-read and articulate and seldom hesitated to voice her political views. Over the years they had five children.

Much as Adams sought throughout his life to purge himself of impure motives, he sought to purge America of Britain's impurities, its trampling of liberty. In 1765, when Parliament passed the Stamp Act, a tax on printed items, Adams protested. He gained attention throughout Massachusetts—his genius, learning, and virtue at last recognized—when he wrote the instructions used to guide the Braintree delegates to the colonial assembly. In his instructions he said the Stamp Act violated the colonists' rights and liberties because it was a tax imposed without representation. "With the submission to Divine Providence . . . ," he wrote, "we never can be slaves." The General Court followed Adams's argument and declared that no taxes could be imposed on the colonists except "by their respective legislatures."

Colonial protests, including a boycott of trade with England, forced Parliament to rescind the Stamp Act. In his diary Adams told of stamp tax collectors from New England to Georgia being forced to resign their offices and of colonists "more determined to defend" their liberties than ever before. He moved closer in thought to his cousin Samuel Adams, an increasingly radical dissident who, John Adams said, exhibited "refined policy, steadfast integrity, exquisite humanity, genteel erudition . . . [and] engaging manners." The young lawyer socialized more and more with the emerging patriot leaders. "The year 1765 has been the most remarkable year of my life . . . ," he said.

Although repeal of the Stamp Act heartened Adams, he sensed more trouble brewing, and it came in 1767 when Parliament passed the Townshend Acts and levied taxes on goods imported into the colonies. The taxes angered Adams, and early in 1768 he moved to Boston to be at the center of protest and in a place more congenial to building his law practice. "Am I grasping at money or scheming for power?" he worried in words that could be just as easily applied to Britain or the colonies in the deepening political crisis.

Adams stunned his fellow Patriots in 1770 when he decided to defend Captain Thomas Preston and six British soldiers indicted for murder in the Boston Massacre. He realized this would be a historic case with great legal and political impact for years to come and that it would resound in law books—as would his name. He realized, too, the case would make him widely, if only temporarily, unpopular. According to Peter Shaw in *The Character of John Adams,* such behavior was a theme in the Patriot's life: "He courted not popularity but unpopularity as a mark of distinction."

The redcoats, so the charge went, had fired unprovoked into a crowd of Bostonians, killing and injuring several of them. In a brilliant defense, Adams proved that the colonial crowd—really a mob—had threatened the soldiers, causing them to fire in panic. In two separate trials, juries acquitted Preston and his men of murder, while finding two of the soldiers guilty of manslaughter. The Patriot press subsequently vilified Adams, and he temporarily retreated from politics.

Yet revolutionary events combined with his ambition and principles to soon make him return to the fight. In late 1773 a flyer appeared in Boston declaring: "Friends! Brethren! Countrymen! That worst of plagues, the detested TEA . . . is now arrived in this harbor." The *Dartmouth* had come into port bearing 114 chests of tea and enough political baggage to shake two continents. Parliament had recently passed the Tea Act, which allowed the financially troubled British East India Company to sell the product in the colonies without going through local middlemen. That arrangement made the company's tea cheap and attractive to consumers. If the colonists bought it, however, they would be paying the tax, a holdover from the Townshend Acts. (Unknown to most of them, importers had been paying it for years.) Many colonists saw the Tea Act as a sly way to get them to admit Parliament's right to tax them. Consequently, they determined to stop the *Dartmouth* from unloading its chests.

At a rally called by the radical Sons of Liberty and held at Faneuil Hall, Samuel Adams addressed a crowd of 7,000. When he declared, "This meeting can do nothing more to save the country," a war whoop went up from several colonists disguised as Indians, who then boarded the *Dartmouth* and for three hours dumped its cargo of tea into Boston harbor.

John Adams heard about the Boston Tea Party on his return from a trip and in his diary noted: "This destruction of the tea is so bold, so daring, so firm, intrepid and inflexible, and it must have so important consequences, and so lasting, that I can't but consider it as an epoch in history!"

Property had been destroyed, which to Englishmen was an attack on the very foundation of civilized society. Parliament therefore reacted with a vengeance. "The town of Boston ought to be knocked down about their ears . . .," said one member before Parliament passed the Coercive Acts—called the Intolerable Acts by the colonists—which closed the port of Boston and restricted the colony's town meetings.

The acts combined with another colonial protest led by John Adams over a declaration of Parliament that required judges' salaries be paid by the Crown rather than the colonial assembly. This measure was intended to lessen colonial influence over the judiciary. Adams convinced the colonial assembly to impeach Chief Justice Peter Oliver for taking such pay. When the Governor's Council refused to hear the impeachment, colonists across Massachusetts refused to serve as jurors, thereby paralyzing the Superior Court.

In 1774 Adams served as a delegate from Massachusetts to the First Continental Congress at Philadelphia, where he worked to get the Suffolk County Resolves adopted. This was a call for complete defiance of the Intolerable Acts, including taking up arms, a move favored by radicals who outvoted the conservatives. Adams frequently socialized with delegates from the other colonies with the goal, as he put it, "to get acquainted with the tempers, views, characters, and designs of persons." A few months later, he wrote his *Novanglus* essays, in which he argued that Parliament had no authority over the colonies. In *John Adams,* Page Smith states, "*Novanglus* was the most learned and laborious statement of the strictly constitutional grounds for colonial resistance."

When the colonies met as the Second Continental Congress in 1775, after the first shots had been fired between colonial militias and British troops at Lexington and Concord, Adams again cut a wide swath. He served on numerous congressional committees, sometimes working from 7:00 in the morning to 11:00 at night. He tirelessly promoted the radical drive for a complete break with Britain, and he nominated George Washington to command the emerging colonial army.

Adams was sensitive to criticism and was embarrassed when the British intercepted and made public a letter he had written in which he called Pennsylvania delegate John Dickinson a "piddling genius." Nevertheless, most in Congress respected him. In 1776 he served on the committee that put together the Declaration of Independence. Although the document was largely written by Thomas Jefferson, Adams claimed he participated extensively in committee discussions that preceded Jefferson's work and that he was the one who asked Jefferson to do the writing. Adams later drafted the Plan of Treaties, from which evolved a treaty with France. He was also the unanimous choice to head the Board of War and Ordnance and did so for over a year, equipping the army and establishing civilian control over it.

With independence declared in July 1776, Adams served as a diplomat to France, making two trips there, one in 1778 and the other in 1780. In 1782 he negotiated a much-needed loan at The Hague, and the following year, along with Benjamin Franklin and John Jay, he signed the Treaty of Paris, in which Britain recognized the United States as an independent nation. He was appointed by Congress as the first American minister to London and began serving there in 1785, but the British government rejected his efforts to establish closer relations.

Soon after John Adams returned home, the Constitution was ratified, and in 1789 the electoral college chose him to serve as the country's first vice president. The electors did so after George Washington made it clear he preferred Adams for the job. Washington believed that Adams would strongly defend the Constitution and protect it against crippling amendments as advocated by some of its critics. Nevertheless, the vice presidency proved not to Adams's liking. To his wife Abigail he wrote: "My country has in its wisdom contrived for me the most insignificant office that ever the invention of man contrived or his imagination conceived." As Senate president, however, he broke 20 tie votes, all in support of President Washington's policies, and he accepted a second term in 1792 because he expected it would lead to the presidency.

When Washington retired, his expectation came true. Yet Adams, who was aligned with the Federalist Party, won the presidency in 1796 by just three electoral votes over Thomas Jefferson, who was aligned with the Republican Party. That narrow victory rankled him, as did the enmity of a fellow Federalist, the powerful former treasury secretary Alexander Hamilton, who had plotted to have South Carolinian Thomas Pinckney elected president.

John Adams entered the presidency under difficult circumstances. As Thomas Jefferson, the new vice president, said to a friend: "[George Washington] is fortunate to get off just as the bubble is bursting, leaving others to hold the bag. Yet, as his departure will mark the moment when the difficulties begin to work, you will see that they will be ascribed to the new administration. . . ."

Many of the difficulties came from the continuing revolution in France and war between that country and Britain, which threatened to envelop the United States and incite Americans to take up arms against one another. Although Adams represented the Federalist Party, he often acted independently of it. Consequently, when he began his term he hoped to bridge the gap between himself and Jefferson by turning to the vice president for help in shaping policy. Like most Republicans, Jefferson strongly supported France, and because he feared Adams might take a strong pro-British stand and link him to it, he rejected the president's overtures.

Relations between Adams and Jefferson soon worsened. In May 1797, after France stated it considered the United States too closely aligned with Britain and would refuse to recognize American ships as neutral, Adams called for Congress to form a provisional army to prepare for war. Jefferson criticized the president's message, and in reaction Adams privately said the Virginian showed evidence of "a mind, soured, yet seeking for popularity, and eaten to a honeycomb with ambition, yet weak, confused, uninformed and ignorant." Just weeks after the president's call for preparedness, Secretary of State Timothy Pickering reported that French cruisers had attacked 316 American ships over the previous year.

Adams wanted to avoid war with France while getting that nation to respect American neutrality, a difficult chore given that the United States lacked a powerful military. At the same time, he rejected any alliance with Britain; foreign entanglements, he believed, would only involve his countrymen in distant wars, in this case one that would likely tear the nation into two armed camps, one pro-French and the other pro-British.

In the fall of 1797, President Adams sent John Marshall, Charles Pinckney, and Elbridge Gerry on a peace mission to Paris. A few months later he announced the mission had failed. The news stunned Republicans, who asserted that pro-British Federalists had undermined the delegates. They demanded that all the relevant diplomatic correspondence be made public.

Adams happily obliged, for he knew what had really happened in Paris. The French government had refused to meet with the Americans until they acquiesced to three demands: an apology from President Adams for his "disparagement" of France in his recent address to Congress, a payment to the ruling French Directory, and a loan from the U.S. government. Now the Republicans were stunned as the demands, interpreted as an insult to American sovereignty and morality, produced a frenzied reaction against France. At rallies crowds shouted "Adams and Liberty!"

In July 1798 Congress authorized the capture of French armed ships and declared previous treaties with France to be void. An undeclared naval war erupted, and the tiny U.S. Navy, aided by privateers, captured more than 80 ships flying the French flag. In responding to an address from a group in South Carolina, Adams declared: "I know of no government ancient or modern that ever betrayed so universal and decided a contempt of the people of all nations, as the present rulers of France."

At the same time Congress passed the Alien and Sedition Acts. The Alien Act, aimed at French immigrants, authorized the president to arrest and deport aliens involved in "treasonable" activities. The more controversial Sedition Act set heavy fines and even imprisonment for writing, speaking, or publishing anything "false, scandalous and malicious" against the government. The Alien Act was never used, but the Sedition Act was—in each instance to prosecute Republicans.

Adams never asked for these laws (which were allowed to expire in 1800), but he signed them, and many historians have criticized the Federalist president and Congress for essentially trampling free speech. Yet Adams acted in an explosive time when several thousand French agents were operating within the United States and newspapers were exciting the citizenry with charges about supposedly treasonous activities.

The turmoil over France produced a headache for Adams in the form of the provisional army. Although he preferred to strengthen the navy, Congress established a bigger army than he wanted. In addition, the Hamiltonian Federalists offended him when, after former President Washington was made the army's commander, they maneuvered Alexander Hamilton into the position of second-in-command. Nothing riled Adams more than to have his archenemy in that position.

The president feared that Hamilton and his faction among the Federalists would use the army against domestic enemies and begin rounding up Republicans. There was some truth in this as a few Federalists advocated such an attack, and with Republicans in Virginia gathering arms to defend themselves, the country moved perilously close to civil war.

In February 1799 Adams stunned the Hamiltonians, and the nation as a whole, when in response to French overtures he announced a new peace mission. The Hamiltonians exploded. They accused the president of giving in to France, and they accused him of ruining the Federalist Party by defusing the excitement against France that had damaged the Republicans.

Adams sent the peace mission for several reasons. First, he wanted to weaken Hamilton. Second, he realized that militarism was becoming unpopular; by 1799 the public was tiring of the political fervor, was more critical of the Sedition Act, and had become increasingly resentful at having to pay taxes levied to support the army. Third, his attachment to peace with honor remained unchanged. Finally, he realized that with a successful peace mission he could win popular support and reelection. In *The Presidency of John Adams,* Stephen Kurtz writes that the president "was a patriot, but he was also a far more astute politician than most historians have given him credit for being. When he saw an opportunity to benefit the nation and the political fortunes of John Adams he quite naturally seized on it."

While Adams absented himself at his home near Boston, Hamiltonians within his cabinet worked to keep the peace commission from departing. Although told about the underhanded maneuver, Adams at first did nothing, perhaps because continuing political turmoil in France caused him to doubt the French government would engage in any talks. But in the spring of 1799 he acted. After a tense meeting with Hamilton at Trenton, New Jersey, at which the former treasury secretary tried to persuade the president to cancel the peace mission (Adams later said Hamilton acted like a fool), he ordered the three emissaries to leave for Paris.

John Adams correctly read public opinion, and the peace mission boosted his popularity. But as he sought reelection in 1800, the Federalist Party split when Hamilton and his faction supported Charles C. Pinckney for president. Thomas Jefferson sought the presidency as a Republican. As the election neared, Hamilton wrote a pamphlet, published by some friends, that detailed Adams's character flaws and called him "unfit for the highest office of Chief Magistrate." Hamilton observed: "It is a fact that he is often liable to paroxysms of anger, which deprive him of self command, and produce very outrageous behavior to those who approach him."

In the spring of 1800, John Adams found his impending defeat unbearable. After all, he had stood up to the Jeffersonian and Hamiltonian extremists, had prepared the nation militarily while tempering the militarists, and had begun peace talks with France—all this, yet he faced little chance of an election victory. In October the Treaty of Morfontaine ended the French crisis, adding to his accomplishments. On November 1 Adams became the first chief executive to occupy the new presidential residence that by 1809 was being called the White House for its white-grey sandstone exterior, which contrasted with the brick buildings nearby.

Adams nearly won reelection; a few hundred votes in New York switched his way would have made the difference. Shortly after he was defeated, however, he appointed fellow Federalist John Marshall as Chief Justice of the United States. This appointment rankled Republicans, but the story that John Adams spent his last hours as president appointing Federalists to the courts to get back at Jefferson holds no truth. Actually, most observers at the time expressed surprise at his magnanimity toward Jefferson and his praise for the Virginian's talents. Embittered by defeat, Adams refused to attend Jefferson's inauguration, but the person he hated and never forgave was Hamilton.

Adams spent his remaining years at his home in Quincy (formerly Braintree), Massachusetts, tending to his farm and writing. On the first day of 1812 he sent a friendly letter to Thomas

Jefferson, by then also a former president, and proposed that they correspond. Thus began 14 years of exchanging ideas about politics, philosophy, and the past. Jefferson consoled Adams over Abigail's death in 1818 and shared Adams's joy when his son, John Quincy Adams, was elected president.

John Adams died on July 4, 1826, just hours after Jefferson. Not knowing that Jefferson had already passed away, Adams's last words were, "Jefferson still survives." Often thwarted by Hamilton and attacked by his own party, unable to establish an effective working relationship with Congress, principled more than charismatic, John Adams led America to independence as a revolutionary and preserved peace as an embattled president amid a trying crisis with France.

CHRONOLOGY

1735 Born October 19

1751 Enters Harvard

1758 Admitted to the bar

1764 Marries Abigail Smith

1765 Denounces Stamp Act

1770 Defends Thomas Preston

1774 Serves as delegate to First Continental Congress

1775 Serves as delegate to Second Continental Congress
Nominates George Washington to command Continental army

1776 Signs Declaration of Independence
Heads Board of War and Ordnance

1778 Serves in France as diplomat

1779 Returns to Boston

1780 Returns to France as diplomat

1782 Negotiates loan at The Hague

1783 Signs Treaty of Paris

1785 Arrives in London as minister to Britain

1788 Returns to Massachusetts

1789 Elected vice president

1792 Reelected vice president

1796 Elected president

1797 Sends peace mission to France

1798 Signs Alien and Sedition Acts
Appoints George Washington to command provisional army

1799 Sends second peace mission to France

1800 Signs Treaty of Morfontaine
Moves into presidential residence (later called the White House)
Loses reelection

1801 Retires to Quincy

1812 Resumes correspondence with Thomas Jefferson

1826 Dies July 4

FURTHER READING

Butterfield, L. H., ed. *Diary and Autobiography of John Adams.* Cambridge, Mass.: Harvard University Press, 1962.

Ellis, Joseph. *Passionate Sage: The Character and Legacy of John Adams.* New York: W. W. Norton, 1993.

McCullough, David. *John Adams.* New York: Simon & Schuster, 2001.

Shaw, Peter. *The Character of John Adams.* New York: W. W. Norton, 1976.

Shephard, Jack. *The Adams Chronicles: Four Generations of Greatness.* Boston: Little, Brown, 1975.

Smith, Page. *John Adams.* 2 vols. Garden City, N.Y.: Doubleday, 1962.

Vidal, Gore. *Inventing a Nation: Washington, Adams, Jefferson.* New Haven, Conn.: Yale University Press, 2003.

*T*HOMAS *J*EFFERSON (1743–1826)

Third President, 1801–1809

THOMAS JEFFERSON
(National Archives)

> *"We are all Republicans, we are all Federalists. If there be any among us who would wish to dissolve this Union or to change its republican form, let them stand undisturbed as monuments of the safety with which error of opinion may be tolerated where reason is left free to combat it."*
>
> —Inaugural words, first term, March 4, 1801

When in the spring of 1999 Thomas Jefferson's white descendants met at his Monticello estate in Virginia, they encountered a storm of criticism from African Americans. A recent DNA study had concluded Jefferson most likely fathered at least one of the six children born to his slave, Sally Hemings (who was also a half-sister to his wife, Martha). Despite that finding, the descendants, organized as the Monticello Association, refused to admit Hemings's black relatives as members. One dissident of the association called the decision "racist," saying, "They don't want black people buried in that [Monticello] graveyard."

Charges of racism have dogged Jefferson's legacy for many years—and understandably so, for although he wrote the Declaration of Independence, which became an engine for equality; dedicated his presidency to creating an "empire of liberty"; and, in old age, claimed he had opposed human bondage for 40 years, he owned slaves throughout his adult life. For Jefferson, as for many Americans, liberty and race shaped the contours of society.

Thomas Jefferson was born on April 13, 1743, at Shadwell, his family's farm in Albemarle County, Virginia, with the colony's Blue Ridge Mountains and western frontier near his doorstep. Of his mother, Jane Randolph Jefferson, little is known. His father, Peter Jefferson, a physically robust and strong man, had probably never attended school but prospered as a farmer, surveyor, and land speculator.

From ages two until nine Thomas lived at Tuckahoe, a plantation owned by his father's friend William Randolph. The elder Jefferson moved his family there after Randolph died and left instructions in his will for Peter to take charge of the property. In 1752 Peter moved his family back to Shadwell. By the time of his own death in 1757, Peter Jefferson had achieved a solid standing among Virginia's western planters, providing his widow, six daughters, and two sons with land, hogs, cattle, horses, and slaves.

Thomas Jefferson learned Greek and Latin from a local schoolmaster and then enrolled in 1759 at the College of William and Mary in Williamsburg. Quiet and reclusive, he devoted long hours to reading and to practicing his violin. He graduated in 1762 and then studied law under George Wythe. He prepared himself thoroughly for his cases but earned a reputation as a cautious rather than innovative lawyer. Jefferson spoke poorly in public, a trait that time and again caused him to embrace writing as the best way to convey his thoughts.

In 1768 Jefferson decided to build his own home on land inherited from his father. He later named it Monticello. Virginians expected anyone with substantial land and slaves to hold important political office, an arrangement that kept power within a wealthy elite. Jefferson fulfilled this expectation when he ran for the House of Burgesses and in 1769 took his seat as the protégé of two influential planters, Peyton Randolph and Edmund Pendleton. Three years later he enhanced his social standing when he married Martha Wales Skelton, another member of Virginia's elite. The marriage brought the added advantage to Jefferson of doubling his land holdings. The couple had six children, but their only son and two of their daughters died in infancy; daughter Lucy, born in 1782, died in 1785.

At the time Jefferson entered the House of Burgesses, relations between the colonies and Britain were deteriorating. Parliament's attempts to tax the colonies had evoked strong protests from Virginia. Jefferson opposed the tax bills as a violation of the rights of Englishmen and agreed with those who said "no taxation without representation." He supported an embargo against British goods, or what the colonists called nonimportation.

In 1774, Parliament's decision to pass the Coercive Acts (known as the Intolerable Acts in America) and close the port of Boston as punishment for the Boston Tea Party caused the colonies to send delegates to the Continental Congress in Philadelphia. Jefferson was passed over for this session, but he drafted instructions to the Virginia delegation, which friends published as "A Summary View of the Rights of British America."

Jefferson proclaimed: "His majesty . . . is no more than the chief officer of the people, appointed by the laws, and circumscribed with definite powers, to assist in working the great machine of government, erected for their use, and consequently subject to their superintendence." With those words he attacked the theory of divine right and made the king a mere servant of the people.

The Virginian presented a theory common to the revolutionary leaders and later expressed in the Declaration of Independence: "These are our grievances which we have thus laid before his majesty, with that freedom of language and sentiment which becomes a free people claiming their rights, as derived from the laws of nature, and not as the gift of their chief magistrate. . . ." In sum, he believed everyone possessed rights inherent in nature and coming from it, not from kings or any government. But the delegates considered his claim that Parliament had no right to exercise authority over the colonies as too radical and rejected his instructions.

Jefferson's pen had revealed his sharp mind, and in 1775 he was chosen as an alternate to congressional delegate Peyton Randolph. When Randolph decided to remain in Virginia, Jefferson headed for Philadelphia in a phaeton pulled by four horses and accompanied by three slaves. At age 32, he arrived as an impressive figure: 6'2" tall—an imposing height for that day—his sandy red hair full and thick and tied behind his neck, his thin face freckled and ruddy, his posture erect—a man in full stride intellectually, with wealth and status to complement his physique and mind.

Jefferson said little in Congress and even refrained from participating in the oral debates used by delegates to contend for influence and prestige. He went back to Monticello in May 1775 to care for his wife and daughter, who were both ill, and remained there until May 1776. Soon after returning to Philadelphia, his pen again became his voice. In June Congress appointed him to a committee of five with an assignment to write a "Declaration of the Causes and Necessity for Taking Up Arms." The committee chose Jefferson to write the draft.

In a room on the second floor of a brick house at the corner of Market and Seventh streets, he surrounded himself with his papers, and from June 13 to June 28 he wrote in the early mornings and evenings. Jefferson had no intention of developing new ideas. Pressed for time, he borrowed heavily from the English philosopher John Locke and from his own earlier "Summary View." His experience in Virginia influenced him as well, since he saw in the frontier an independent spirit that had to be preserved against government oppression.

"We hold these truths to be self-evident: that all men are created equal; that they are endowed by their creator with inherent and inalienable rights," Jefferson wrote, "that among these are life, liberty, and the pursuit of happiness. . . ." He submitted the draft to Congress on June 28. Then the sensitive author sat, fumed, and brooded as the other delegates changed his words. In one instance, "inherent and inalienable rights" became "certain inalienable rights." Most galling, Congress removed his entire passage condemning the king for promoting the slave trade. "He has waged cruel war against human nature itself, violating its most sacred rights of life and liberty in the persons of a distant people who never offended him, captivating and carrying them into slavery in another hemisphere," he wrote. Delegates from the South and a few from the North caused the words to be struck.

Although Jefferson's passage can be read as an antislavery statement, it stopped well short of calling for abolition. He knew that many Virginia slave owners opposed the slave trade, not because they disliked it on humanitarian grounds but because they feared the effects of a slave surplus that was lowering the value of their bound labor. And his argument in one way protected slavery, for by blaming the king for the slave trade, he absolved the colonists both of their responsibility for the practice and of finding ways to end it.

Congress deleted about 25 percent of Jefferson's text, but it remained a ringing proclamation, asserting that human rights came from nature and preceded government, that government had as its first duty to protect those rights, and that if it failed to, then the people were obligated to change it. During the spring of 1776, Jefferson wrote a new constitution for Virginia that expressed more of his principles, among them extensive suffrage, development of the West by yeoman farmers, and protection of citizens from totalitarian rule. Again some of his ideas proved too liberal, and the Virginia convention adopted only a small portion of his work.

Jefferson remained in Congress until September 1776 and then returned to Monticello. A few weeks later he entered the Virginia Houe of Delegates. Over three years he proposed 126 bills, and the House passed most of them. His legislation abolished hereditary restrictions on property (called entail and primogeniture), which he considered antirepublican, and established a state library and a new system of state courts.

In 1779 Jefferson introduced his "Bill for Establishing Religious Freedom." Although it was not adopted until 1786, this bill served as another call for liberty and a statement of natural rights that shaped political debate. "Our civil rights have no dependence on our religious opinions, any more than our opinions in physics or geometry," Jefferson said. "Therefore the proscribing any citizen as unworthy the public confidence . . . unless he profess or renounce this or that religious opinion, is depriving him injuriously of those privileges and advantages to which . . . he has a natural right." Jefferson's bill declared that "no man shall be compelled to frequent or support any religious worship, place, or ministry whatsoever . . . that all men shall be free to profess, and by argument to maintain, their opinions in matters of religion. . . ."

Amid the Revolutionary War, on June 1, 1779, Jefferson became governor of Virginia. Disaster followed, for the philosophically minded chief executive had little aptitude for military matters, and when British troops under Benedict Arnold entered Richmond, he fled. The British burned the city to the ground, and their cavalry units nearly captured Jefferson at Monticello. With Virginia's honor besmirched and its economy in shambles, the legislature investigated Jefferson for misconduct; he was cleared in 1781. In the meantime, he retired from the governorship.

That same year, Jefferson published his *Notes on the State of Virginia*. Presented as a series of queries followed by answers, it outlined the geography, economy, and history of Virginia and revealed Jefferson's continuing dilemma over the issue of race. Typical for whites of his day, he said about African Americans: "Comparing them by their faculties of memory, reason, and imagination, it appears to me, that in memory they are equal to the whites, in reason much inferior, as I think one could scarcely be found capable of tracing and comprehending the investigations of Euclid. . . ." Black males, he said, "are more ardent after their females" than whites but lack the "tender delicate mixture of sentiment and sensation" found in love.

Jefferson repeated the widespread story that in Africa orangutans preferred black women to their own species, and he described blacks as inferior to whites in appearance. He wanted blacks to be freed but sent abroad, for otherwise there would be convulsions "which will probably never end but in the extermination of the one or the other race." In any race war, he believed, God would side with blacks as retribution for slavery. "I tremble for my country when I reflect that God is just," Jefferson said, "that his justice cannot sleep for ever. . . ."

Jefferson was devastated in 1782 when his wife, Martha, died. Seeking diversion from the tragedy, he reentered politics and in June 1783, as the war with Britain ended, he won election to the national Confederation Congress. The following year he sailed for Paris to join Benjamin Franklin and John Adams as American emissaries.

In 1785 Jefferson succeeded Franklin as minister to France. He served for four years with little to do. At one point he tried to refute claims by French naturalist Georges de Buffon that North American mammals and plants were inferior to European ones. He obtained a dead moose from New England and placed it on display in Paris to show it was much larger than any European deer, but he fretted when the moose's hair kept falling out.

While in France, Jefferson fell in love with Maria Cosway, the wife of Richard Cosway, a prominent miniaturist painter. Golden-haired, Anglo-Italian, and graceful, Maria enraptured Jefferson, who in October 1786 sent a 12-page letter to her in England that he called "a dialogue between the Head and the Heart." Despite his feelings, by the summer of 1787 the relationship had cooled.

Living with Jefferson at this time was 16-year-old Sally Hemings, his daughter's servant. Nearly white in appearance, Sally Hemings was considered pretty with "long straight hair down her back;" at Monticello she was called "Dashing Sally." In Paris she soon became pregnant with a son. Another son, Madison (born in 1805), would later recount in his family's history that soon after Jefferson returned to Monticello in 1789 with Sally Hemings, "she gave birth to a child, of whom Thomas Jefferson was the father."

While in Paris, Jefferson followed the debate in America over whether to ratify the Constitution. He supported the document, but reluctantly, since he believed it created too strong a national government. He also followed the course of the French Revolution. At first he thought the French would reform their monarchy without bloodshed. In 1789 he sent the Marquis de Lafayette proposals for changing the government, which became the basis for the Declaration of Rights that Lafayette submitted to the National Assembly in June. When violence rocked Paris, Jefferson expressed shock but saw it as necessary to a just cause.

That same year, soon after Jefferson returned to Monticello, President Washington chose him to serve as the nation's first secretary of state. Taking office in 1790, he soon found himself drawn into conflicts with Alexander Hamilton, the secretary of the treasury, who vigorously pursued policies Jefferson disliked. Where Jefferson wanted a limited government, Hamilton wanted an expansive one; where Jefferson promoted farming, Hamilton promoted industry; where Jefferson supported the French Revolution, Hamilton hated it. Their differences stimulated the formation of two political parties: the Federalists, led by Hamilton, and the Republicans, organized by Jefferson's friend James Madison.

While these parties were forming, Jefferson, exhausted by his duties, quit Washington's cabinet and returned to Monticello early in 1794. Two years later he reentered national politics when he was elected vice president at the same time that John Adams was elected president. Because of rules then in effect, the election resulted in the president and vice president coming from two different parties, with Adams from the Federalist Party and Jefferson from the Republican Party.

Jefferson had no role in Adams's presidency. He opposed Adams for his pro-British policies in a war then under way between Britain and France and criticized the Alien and Sedition Acts passed by the Federalist Congress to silence the Republicans. Jefferson even convinced the Kentucky legislature to adopt resolutions declaring the acts unconstitutional. At the same time his colleague and friend, James Madison, pushed similar resolutions through the Virginia legislature.

All through the late 1790s, differences between the Federalists and Republicans intensified. On one side the Federalists supported Britain in its fight against France as a counterweight to the French Revolution that to them stood for nothing less than anarchy. They believed that if the Republicans gained the presidency, mobs would rule America. On the other side the Republicans expressed sympathy for France and considered its revolution an extension of the American fight for liberty. They believed that if the Federalists continued to hold the presidency, monarchy would take over.

It was in this atmosphere that Jefferson ran for president in 1800. "I do wish an inviolable preservation of our present federal constitution," he told his friend Elbridge Gerry. "And I am opposed to the monarchising [of] its features . . . with a view to conciliate a first transition to a President & Senate for life, & from that to a hereditary tenure of these offices, & thus to worm out the elective principle." He benefited from a schism within the Federalist party when Alexander Hamilton broke with Adams and supported Charles C. Pinckney of South Carolina for president.

Pinckney fared no better than fourth in the electoral college, but the system of balloting, in which electors made no distinction between their choice for president and vice president, placed Jefferson in a tie with New Yorker Aaron Burr. After 36 ballots the House of Representatives broke the tie early in 1801, choosing Jefferson over Burr largely because Hamilton, who disliked both men, urged his fellow Federalists to hold their noses and support the Virginian.

For all the differences between Federalists and Republicans, America experienced an unusual development for countries back then: a peaceful transfer of power from the leaders of one political party to those of another. When Thomas Jefferson arrived in Washington for his inauguration in March 1801, he found the Capitol still under construction, with the House chamber lacking a roof and columns intended for the front facade lying scattered on the ground. In his inaugural address he tried to pick up the pieces of animosity and assemble a new unity. "Every difference of opinion is not a difference of principle," he said. "We have been called by different names brethren of the same principle. We are all republicans—we are all federalists." Although in referring to republicans and federalists, he was probably talking more about philosophies than political parties, many people at the time thought he had extended an olive branch.

Jefferson entered the presidency amid an improved international and domestic scene: England and France had entered a truce; the Alien and Sedition Acts were about to end; the domestic economy was prospering; and the Republicans held majorities in both houses of Congress. The president bolstered his own cause when he appointed a first-rate cabinet that included James Madison as secretary of state and Albert Gallatin as secretary of the treasury.

Jefferson governed simply. He rejected lavish entertainment and held three dinner parties each week, thinking if he brought together members of Congress and other leaders over a meal, it would be more difficult for them to be enemies. He avoided public appearances and conducted business mainly through correspondence, sitting at his writing desk about 10 hours per day.

For President Jefferson, frugality and limited government became cardinal principles, or, as he said at his inauguration: "Economy in the public expense, that labor may be lightly burthened." Toward that end, he determined to eliminate the national debt. Where Hamilton had considered the debt beneficial, Jefferson considered it harmful, requiring taxes that hurt the common people and created power and privilege for the moneyed class. After he and Gallatin decided that the national government should rely only on tariff revenues and Congress repealed all internal taxes, Jefferson reduced the government bureaucracy and slashed military spending. These moves cut the $82 million debt in half.

Frugality even figured in Jefferson's fight with Barbary pirates. When the pasha of Tripoli declared war on the United States after it failed to pay him adequate tribute for shipping in the Mediterranean Sea, Jefferson reacted by sending a naval squadron into battle. (He hated maintaining a navy but hated the pirates even more.) But when spending for the fight topped $1 million, he decided to end his mounting financial burden and settle with the pasha by paying him $60,000 for a treaty of commerce. Due to America's impressive victories at sea, the terms turned out to be better than those obtained by any other nation.

In today's government the civil service fills most jobs, but President Jefferson faced a different patronage situation. When he took office, Federalists held nearly all the positions in the national government, and few people thought it proper to replace them with Republicans as a reward for their party loyalty. Yet Jefferson knew that if the Federalists retained so many offices they would frustrate his programs. To prevent this, as vacancies appeared he nearly always appointed Republicans to fill them. To keep the government from being disrupted, however, he decided against a wholesale purge, cleaning house only in a few hard-core Federalist regions, such as Connecticut. He believed that men from his own party should eventually hold half the government offices.

In a similar way Jefferson worried that Federalist judges would overturn Republican legislation. Although he deeply disliked the conservative judiciary for dampening the populist spirit of the American Revolution, he decided against radical structural change and instead went after Federalist judges whom he disliked for their vitriolic attacks on Republicans. In the most famous incident of his "war on the judiciary," the Republican House of Representatives impeached Supreme Court Justice Samuel Chase in January 1805. When the Senate failed to convict Chase, Jefferson ended his assault, but he had served notice that Federalist judges must temper their partisanship.

Many historians rank Jefferson's purchase of Louisiana as his greatest presidential achievement. When French ruler Napoleon Bonaparte acquired the territory from Spain, Jefferson saw it as a threat to American expansion and prosperity. Americans living west of the Appalachian Mountains relied on the Mississippi River as a means to ship their produce, and should the port at New Orleans be closed, trade would be hampered. Exactly that happened in October 1802 when the United States lost its right to deposit goods there. Jefferson had already sent James Monroe to France to help U.S. minister Robert Livingston purchase New Orleans and as much of the Mississippi Valley as possible. Now the mission became an urgent one.

Fortunately for the United States, Napoleon's plans to combine Louisiana with Hispaniola and create a great American empire failed when a slave uprising in Haiti and yellow fever decimated French troops sent to the Caribbean. Napoleon then surprised Livingston before James Monroe arrived on his mission by agreeing to sell all of Louisiana for $15 million. The deal increased the size of the United States by 140 percent and forced Jefferson to contradict his own stand against loose interpretation of the Constitution, for nothing in it specifically allowed him to buy the land.

Shortly before the purchase, Jefferson planned to send an expedition to the Pacific; Congress secretly agreed to fund the trip. The president commissioned Meriwether Lewis and William Clark to explore and map the western lands. They began their trip in May 1804 and concluded it with a report to the president in January 1807.

Jefferson considered the West a mystical place, a "secret weapon," says Joseph Ellis in *American Sphinx*, "that made the American experiment in republicanism immune to the national aging process, at least for the remainder of the century. It was America's fountain of youth." And it was part of what Jefferson called his "empire of liberty," a place where yeoman farmers could reasonably obtain land. (As for the Indians who lived there, he believed they had no choice but to adapt to white society.) Contrary to his vision, land speculators monopolized large tracts, and planters took slaves with them into the wilderness.

Slavery figured heavily in national politics, and during Jefferson's first term a scandalous story published by newspaperman James Callender shocked sensibilities. "The man, *whom it delighteth the people to honor*," Callender said in reference to the president, "keeps, and for many years has kept, as his concubine one of his own slaves." He meant Sally Hemings, whom he derisively called "Sally the sable." Callender's story was surprising, since he had once worked with Jefferson and in 1798 had issued a pamphlet titled "The Prospect Before Us" that slandered John Adams.

When the Sally Hemings story broke, Jefferson denied any close relationship with Callender, but Callender published letters from Jefferson in which the Virginian stated he had read the proof sheets for the anti-Adams pamphlet. The president was therefore caught in a lie. Yet he never publicly commented about his relationship with Sally Hemings, and until the DNA tests of 1998, most historians considered Callender's story ludicrous.

Despite the Sally Hemings story, Thomas Jefferson was enormously popular as his first term neared its end. He had acquired Louisiana, lowered the national debt, cut taxes, put the Barbary pirates in their place, and presided over a strong economy. In addition, he seemed to care about the common people and carefully cultivated that image. Britain's minister to the United States described Jefferson in 1804 as looking "much like that of a tall, large-boned farmer"—exactly the reaction Jefferson wanted.

Although he was saddened by the death of his daughter Maria in 1804, Jefferson decided to seek reelection that year and had little problem defeating his Federalist opponent, Charles C. Pinckney. But his second administration suffered numerous setbacks, one involving Aaron Burr. Burr quit the vice presidency in 1805 after having shot and killed Alexander Hamilton in a duel, and from there he plunged into a murky conspiracy. He traveled to St. Louis and along the way met with prominent Westerners. To them he revealed a plan to attack Mexico and convince the western states to secede. Apparently he wanted to join the two lands together, with himself as ruler. Toward that end he and a small band of followers reached Natchez, Mississippi, in January 1807, only to flee after an American general ordered their arrest. Captured in Pensacola, Florida, Burr was taken to Richmond, Virginia, where he stood trial for treason.

Jefferson hated Burr, partly for Burr's refusal to renounce any desires for the presidency in 1801, when the two men were tied in the electoral college. Now the Virginian threw all constitutional regulations to the wind and worked behind the scenes to get Burr convicted. Unfortunately for Jefferson, his old Federalist enemy, Chief Justice John Marshall, presided over the case and interpreted the treason clause of the Constitution narrowly. As a result, Burr won acquittal.

President Jefferson faced an even bigger problem when Britain and France, their truce over, attacked American ships. His frugality had weakened the U.S. Navy, and since he had little stomach for war, he decided to use economic sanctions. In 1807 he convinced Congress to pass the Embargo Act, which prohibited trade overseas until either Britain or France recognized America's neutrality and ended their attacks. He believed the embargo would especially hurt Britain, with whom the United States traded the most, and force concessions.

Instead, it ruined the American economy. In a giant chain reaction, merchants suffered, sailors sat idle, shipbuilders laid off their carpenters, and so on. The effects rippled beyond the port cities and into the countryside, where farmers who exported their crops suffered from declining prices. Salem, Massachusetts, among New England's most vibrant coastal towns, suffered so much damage it never recovered its prosperity. Ironically, the embargo encouraged manufacturing in the middle states and worked against Jefferson's vaunted agrarianism.

Once the Embargo Act passed Congress, Jefferson showed little leadership. Discouraged by protests, tired with politics, and frequently incapacitated by migraine headaches, he drifted. Acting without the president's guidance, Congress in March 1809 repealed the Embargo Act and replaced it with a less restrictive measure. By that time America's exports had declined 80 percent.

When Thomas Jefferson left office in March 1809, he retired to his home in Virginia. There he tended to his farming, his inventions, and his books and earned the nickname "Sage of Monticello." He lived in so much debt that friends were forced to raise money to help him.

Jefferson spent much of his retirement founding the University of Virginia at Charlottesville. He designed its buildings and supervised their construction. He helped select professors and library books and also helped devise the curriculum. Jefferson insisted that the university "be based on the illimitable freedom of the human mind," following "truth wherever it may lead." In politics he advised Presidents Madison and Monroe and continued to promote a frugal, limited government.

In 1801 Jefferson had said in his inaugural address, "I have learnt to expect that it will rarely fall to the lot of imperfect man to retire from this station with the reputation and the favor which bring him into it. . . . I shall often go wrong through defect of judgment. When right, I shall often be thought wrong by those whose positions will not command a view of the whole ground. I ask your indulgence for my own errors. . . ."

As Jefferson had predicted, he left the White House in less "favor" than when he entered. In time, though, Americans looked upon his presidency as enlightened and his commitment to liberty as sincere. He understood that slavery contradicted his humanitarian principles and kept America from fulfilling its republican promise. He compared slavery to holding a wolf by its ears, and he prayed that public opinion would one day end it.

Thomas Jefferson and John Adams died on the same day—July 4, 1826. On his death bed at Monticello, Jefferson murmured, "This is the Fourth?" In his last letter to Adams, he reflected on liberty:

> The general spread of the light of science has already laid open to every view the palpable truth, that the mass of mankind has not been born with saddles on their backs, nor a favored few booted and spurred, ready to ride them legitimately, by the grace of God.

Did Jefferson's opposition to slavery stem, at least in part, from the bondage in which he saw Sally Hemings and her—or their—children live? (He eventually freed five members of the Hemings family, but not Sally.) If his relationship with her was as it appears—the evidence is so strong that the Monticello foundation now acknowledges it on tours of the Jefferson home—it may well have contributed to his struggle with the meaning of liberty.

Chronology

1743 Born April 13

1762 Graduates from the College of William and Mary

1767 Admitted to the bar

1768 Begins building Monticello
Elected to Virginia House of Burgesses

1772 Marries Martha Skelton

1774 Drafts *A Summary View of the Rights of British America*

1775 Elected alternate delegate to Second Continental Congress

1776 Writes Declaration of Independence
Elected to Virginia House of Delegates

1779 Introduces Act for Establishing Religious Freedom
Elected governor of Virginia

1781 Retires as governor
Publishes his *Notes on the State of Virginia*

1783 Drafts Virginia constitution
Elected to Confederation Congress

1785 Named minister to France

1789 Appointed secretary of state

1794 Retires to Monticello

1796 Elected vice president

1798 Drafts Kentucky Resolutions

1801 Elected president by House of Representatives
Sends navy to Mediterranean to fight Barbary pirates

1803	Approves Louisiana Purchase Commissions Lewis and Clark Expedition
1804	Reelected president
1807	Signs Embargo Act
1809	Signs Non-Intercourse Act Retires to Monticello
1819	Becomes rector of University of Virginia
1826	Dies July 4

Further Reading

Appleby, Joyce. *Thomas Jefferson.* New York: Times Books, 2003.

Bernstein, R. B. *Thomas Jefferson.* New York: Oxford University Press, 2003.

Boorstin, Daniel. *The Lost World of Thomas Jefferson.* New York: Henry Holt, 1948.

Cunningham, Noble E., Jr. *In Pursuit of Reason: The Life of Thomas Jefferson.* Baton Rouge: Louisiana State University Press, 1987.

———. *The Process of Government under Jefferson.* Princeton, N.J.: Princeton University Press, 1978.

Ferling, John E. *Adams Vs. Jefferson: The Tumultuous Election of 1800.* New York: Oxford University Press, 2000.

———. *Setting the World Ablaze: Washington, Adams, Jefferson and the American Revolution.* New York: Oxford University Press, 2000.

Johnstone, Robert, Jr. *Jefferson and the Presidency: Leadership in the Young Republic.* Ithaca, N.Y.: Cornell University Press, 1978.

Levy, Leonard. *Jefferson and Civil Liberties: The Darker Side.* Cambridge, Mass.: Harvard University Press, 1963.

Malone, Dumas. *Jefferson and His Time,* 6 vols. Boston: Little, Brown, 1948–1981.

McDonald, Forrest. *The Presidency of Thomas Jefferson.* Lawrence: University Press of Kansas, 1976.

Miller, John Chester. *The Wolf by the Ears: Thomas Jefferson and Slavery.* New York: Free Press, 1977.

Onuf, Peter. *Jefferson's Empire: The Language of American Nationhood.* Charlottesville: University Press of Virginia, 2000.

Peterson, Merrill D. *The Jefferson Image in the American Mind.* New York: Oxford University Press, 1960.

———. *Thomas Jefferson and the New Nation: A Biography.* New York: Oxford University Press, 1970.

———, ed. *Thomas Jefferson Writings.* New York: Viking Press, 1984.

Weisberger, Bernard. *America Afire: Jefferson, Adams, and the Revolutionary Election of 1800.* New York: William Morrow, 2000.

JAMES MADISON (1751–1836)

Fourth President, 1809–1817

JAMES MADISON
(Library of Congress)

"On the issue of the war are staked our national sovereignty on the high seas. . . . Not to contend for such a stake is to surrender our equality with other powers on the element common to all and to violate the sacred title which every member of the society has to its protection."

—Inaugural words, second term, March 4, 1813

As British troops neared the White House during the War of 1812, First Lady Dolley Madison grabbed Gilbert Stuart's painting of George Washington, hurriedly removed it from its frame, rolled it up, and gave it to someone for safekeeping. Soon after, the British arrived and burned the presidential residence, leaving it scorched and the country humiliated.

President James Madison, absent from the scene, had for several years worked beside Washington's canvas presence; the general's stature as revolutionary hero and foremost founding father served as a constant reminder of wise leadership. Now Madison's conduct in allowing the British to invade gave an opposite impression; it appeared to be the epitome of incompetence, even cowardice. "A lot of people consider [Madison] very nearly a failure as a President," says historian Lance Banning, "a very mediocre President at best."

James Madison was born on March 16, 1751, at Port Conway, Virginia, to James Madison and Eleanor Conway Madison and grew up on his family's plantation in Orange County. His father owned thousands of acres and served as leader of the local militia, justice of the peace, and vestryman in the Anglican Church. Young James received a basic education from his parents and at age 11 entered a school taught by Donald Robertson on a nearby plantation. Wealth surrounded James in his youth, as did the structure and pace of a planter's life—the sheds, barns, harvests, and, most tellingly, the slave cabins.

At age 18, James debated whether to continue his education by enrolling at the College of William and Mary. Many planters' sons went to school there, but James disliked both the unhealthy climate in Williamsburg and the reputation the college had for dissolute and drunken professors. As a result, in 1769 he entered the College of New Jersey (later renamed Princeton).

He arrived a serious and bookish young man, and although as a student he participated fully in the college's social life, including pranks pulled on classmates, he remained a voracious reader who would go weeks at a time sleeping only four to five hours a night in order to pursue his studies. His friends often sought him out to discuss philosophy.

When he graduated in September 1771, Madison initially had no idea what to do with his future. Life as a planter held little appeal, and, besides, he liked his books. As a result, he stayed at the college until April 1772, during which time he pursued his intellectual activities. He then returned to Virginia sickly and still undecided; his friends described him as feeble and pale, and he probably suffered from a nervous disorder.

James decided to study law, but more as a way to understand politics better than to become a trial lawyer. He wrote a friend: "I intend myself to read Law occasionally and have procured books for that purpose so that you need not fear offending me by Allusions to that science." He often read all morning and afternoon, sometimes staying in his room until evening, when he ate dinner and socialized with his family.

Soon a momentous event gave him direction: the American Revolution. In 1774 Britain reacted to the Boston Tea Party by imposing the Coercive Acts (known as the Intolerable Acts in the colonies), which sought to isolate Massachusetts through punitive measures. Madison condemned the laws and said Parliament had no legislative authority over the colonies. In December he and his father won election to the Orange County Commission, organized to enforce legislation passed by the Continental Congress. At the same time they helped obtain arms and supplies for the militia. An ardent supporter of the Revolution, young Madison was "suspicious of anyone who showed, or seemed to show, the slightest backwardness or caution" toward the Patriot cause.

In April 1776, just weeks before America declared its independence, Madison won election to the Virginia Convention, knowing that it would formally establish a government outside British control. He served on a committee to compose a declaration of rights but exerted little influence until, in a debate over religious freedom, he convinced his colleagues to accept language that made possible the separation of church and state.

Beginning in November 1777, Madison served on the governor's council. When Thomas Jefferson succeeded Patrick Henry as governor in 1779, Madison developed a close friendship with the new executive. Although Jefferson was Madison's senior by several years, they had earlier exchanged ideas and now found themselves in unison on several topics, particularly religious freedom.

In December 1779 Madison accepted appointment to the Continental Congress and became its youngest delegate. He arrived in Philadelphia with his slave servant the following March. Here he developed more thoroughly his position on national issues, and despite an innate shyness he quickly earned respect for his sharp mind. A nationalist, he favored a vibrant central government supported by the power to tax. Otherwise, he said, the government would be feeble, the states would be divided by factions, and foreign aid would "be called in by first the weaker [and] then the stronger side, and finally both be made subservient to the wars and politics of Europe." An internationalist, he firmly supported an alliance with France and wanted America to exert its influence on European affairs.

Observers at Philadelphia reached different conclusions about Madison's character. One claimed he was impetuous, that he lacked grace and ease; another pictured him as "a gloomy, stiff creature . . . the most unsociable creature in existence." Yet another called him "well-educated, wise, temperate, gentle, [and] studious." Most considered the diminutive Madison cold and aloof in large gatherings, congenial in small ones, and a skillful politician.

When the new nation's governing document, the Articles of Confederation, proved inadequate, Madison supported change and was among the 55 delegates to the Constitutional Convention that convened at Philadelphia in May 1787. There he expressed his nationalist views and insisted the government needed effective taxing power. Madison emerged as the most important figure in writing the Constitution; he proposed most of the major ideas, including the Virginia Plan, which called for each state's representation in Congress to be based on population.

The convention agreed to that formula for the House of Representatives, but a dispute arose over whether to count slaves as people in determining the number of seats. Southerners wanted to count them; Northerners did not. Madison then suggested a compromise, eventually adopted, whereby each slave would be counted as three-fifths of a person. Despite aligning with his fellow Southerners, Madison differed from many of them in his hatred of slavery. Believing it to be economically unwise and morally unjust, he longed for the day it would be ended but submerged his views for the sake of building a united national government.

Once written, the Constitution required ratification by the states to take effect—from Madison's view an event essential to saving the nation. The tight battle between those who supported and those who opposed the Constitution resulted in Madison joining New Yorkers Alexander Hamilton and John Jay to write a series of essays that appeared in newspapers. Later called *The Federalist,* they eloquently parried complaints about the Constitution. Jay wrote only five of the 77 treatises, Hamilton over half, Madison the rest.

Madison's *Federalist No. 10,* published in the *New York Advertiser* on November 22, 1787, ranked among the most important of the essays, for in it he argued effectively against the widely held belief that a republic could never survive in a large country. He wrote that a small country would be susceptible to a few parties and factions running the government and oppressing the people. But, "extend the sphere, and you take in a greater variety of parties and interests; you make it less probable that a majority of the whole will have a common motive to invade the rights of other citizens; or if such a common motive exists, it will be more difficult for all who feel it to discover their own strength, and to act in unison with each other."

In 1789 Madison won election to the U.S. House of Representatives, where he served for eight years. They turned out to be eventful ones, for during that time a two-party system emerged in Congress in reaction to financial proposals made by the treasury secretary, Alexander Hamilton and to diplomatic relations with Britain and France. After Hamilton and his supporters organized the Federalist Party, Madison joined Thomas Jefferson in forming the Republican Party.

In 1794 Madison married Dorothea Payne Todd, called Dolley, the 26-year-old widow of a Quaker lawyer. Born in North Carolina and raised in Virginia, Dolley had lived in Philadelphia since 1783, when her father moved his family there. Three years after Madison married Dolley, he retired from Congress and returned to Montpelier, the 5,000-acre family plantation in Orange County, Virginia, where his aging father needed help. He worked to diversify the crop, to rely less on tobacco, and to speculate in western lands. He relied heavily on slave labor, though he was uncomfortable with it.

While Madison was at Montpelier, in 1798 the Federalist-dominated Congress, reacting to a crisis that threatened war with France, passed the Alien and Sedition Acts, which made it illegal to criticize the national government. In response, Madison wrote a document for his state legislature, called the Virginia Resolutions, in which he asserted the acts violated the principles of free government and of the Constitution. He said the states have the right to protect liberty from such assaults, and he called for other states to join Virginia in declaring the acts unconstitutional. He refused, however, to claim that any state could nullify a law passed by Congress.

Madison returned to national politics in 1801 when he accepted an appointment as President Thomas Jefferson's secretary of state. He accomplished little, though, largely because Jefferson handled most of the department's affairs himself. Still, his position in the government and his continuing friendship with Jefferson placed him next in line for the presidency.

Although Virginia congressman John Randolph of Roanoke, an intemperate, eccentric, but powerful leader in the House, tried to excite opposition among his fellow Republicans to Madison's candidacy for president, he failed. Madison, whom Jefferson once called "the greatest man in the world," went on in 1808 to defeat Federalist candidate Charles Cotesworth Pinkney by an electoral vote of 122 to 47.

When Madison entered the presidency, the still young United States was composed of 17 states; its territory stretched to the Rocky Mountains, but with a free population of about 7 million, vast stretches remained unpopulated or lightly populated by whites.

James Madison arrived at his inauguration in plain dress: black knee breeches, a black jacket, light vest, scarf, and stockings. Louisa Catherine Adams, wife of John Quincy Adams, described him as "a *very* small man in his *person,* with a *very* large *head*—his manners were peculiarly unassuming; and his conversation lively, often playful. . . . His language was chaste, well suited to occasion, and the simple expression of the passing thought . . . in harmony with the taste of his hearers."

Madison's plain style complemented his republican outlook. He believed America's survival and growth proved that people could govern themselves, and he wanted the nation to continue that way by emphasizing farming. In an agrarian society, he said, each person could own his own land and maintain his independence. Madison also wanted some diversity in the economy and advocated a laissez-faire policy, whereby the government would intervene little in business and finance. As a strong unionist, he sought to expand the nation in a way that would benefit all sections while keeping America out of war. To this end, he realized that something would have to be done about Jefferson's foreign policy, which had failed to protect America's neutrality in the conflict then underway between Britain and France.

From the start of his presidency, Madison encountered opposition from Federalists. Several of them believed the Virginian wielded little real power and that either Jefferson or some Republican group manipulated him. Samuel Taggart, a congressman from

Massachusetts, said in a letter: "M———n is a mere puppet or a cypher managed by some chief faction who are behind the curtain."

Troubles with fellow Republicans may have given the impression that Madison worked from a position of weakness rather than strength. When the president notified Senator William Branch Giles that he intended to nominate Albert Gallatin for secretary of state, the senator, who thought himself more worthy of the office and, in any event, disliked Gallatin's opposition to his patronage requests, rallied others to thwart the plan. To avoid what would likely be a losing fight, Madison reconsidered, though to keep Gallatin in the cabinet he appointed him secretary of the treasury. For Giles and others in Congress, the real substance to the battle was to see who would rule the roost—and Madison had his feathers plucked.

Like Thomas Jefferson, James Madison believed that a high national debt was injurious to republicanism because it unduly benefited a wealthy elite. In addition to lowering the debt, he wanted to lower taxes and establish a frugal government. His tight budgets kept the diplomatic corps small and, some said, understaffed and restricted the army to only a few frontier posts while keeping the navy's battleships in dry dock. From his home in Virginia, Jefferson agreed with these measures, telling Gallatin that debt reduction was "vital to the destinies of our government."

To Madison's critics, his handling of a scandal involving General James Wilkinson confirmed his pusillanimous nature. Ordered to take his men to New Orleans to guard against a foreign invasion, Wilkinson stationed them at Terre aux Boeufs in swampy terrain. Although malaria and scurvy exacted an enormous toll and 800 men died, Wilkinson refused to relocate. The deaths, along with letters of complaint written by soldiers to their congressmen, led to a court-martial and a report that pointed to Wilkinson as incompetent. It was left up to Madison to determine his fate. If the president removed Wilkinson, it would be a slap at Thomas Jefferson who had promoted the besmirched figure to general. After reporting the matter to Jefferson, Madison decided to place Wilkinson back in the command from which he had been suspended. His decision helped to politicize the army and assure he would be surrounded by incompetent generals. Historian Robert Allen Rutland says that with this move Madison "in effect became a buck-passer instead of a courageous leader."

Yet the president passed no buck when American settlers in Spanish-controlled West Florida declared their independence in 1810. In October he sent in troops and proclaimed the territory a part of the United States, saying it was included in the Louisiana Purchase made seven years earlier. In 1811 Madison took military action against rebellious Indians led by Tecumseh in Indiana Territory; and William Henry Harrison defeated the Native Americans at Tippecanoe.

Madison's most important challenge, however, came from Britain. Since the 1790s the British, at war with France, had been stopping and searching American merchant ships in an attempt to disrupt trade and force sailors into the Royal Navy, a policy known as impressment. Madison agreed with Jefferson that in violating America's neutrality, Britain was a great enemy, and he deplored both the presence of the Royal Navy near American ports and America's close ties to the British economy. Still, the president opposed war with any European nation as disruptive to the unsettled American experiment in republican government. His view was in keeping with his earlier role in formulating President Jefferson's disastrous embargo, which had tried to squeeze the British economy and force concessions by prohibiting American ships from engaging in overseas trade.

In 1810 Congress passed Macon's Bill No. 2, which allowed American ships to trade with both Britain and France but stated that if either nation recognized American neutrality, the United States would end its trade with the other, unless the recalcitrant nation also took the same action. As a result, French ruler Napoleon declared that his country would end its attacks on American ships. President Madison then publicly announced Napoleon's promise and said the British must do likewise or American trade with them would be halted. Madison having made his warning, Napoleon double-crossed him by seizing American ships in French ports. The president could either embarrass himself by rescinding his proclamation, or he could ignore Napoleon's seizures. He chose to ignore them. War seemed likely anyhow, and when it came he wanted it to be with Britain rather than France.

Madison would get his preference. The British refused to suspend their assaults on American ships. At the same time, War Hawks, the congressional faction that favored military action, looked voraciously at Canada, then owned by Britain. War, they believed, would allow the United States to conquer the territory quickly. For his part, President Madison was disgusted with Britain for treating the United States like a colony unworthy of inclusion in international councils. War seemed the surest way to reaffirm America's independence and protect its republican experiment.

In June 1812 Congress, meeting in closed session, declared war on Britain by a 79-49 vote in the House and a close 19-13 vote in the Senate; if only three more senators had decided against war, Madison would have been humiliated by a tie. The war declaration actually came after Britain had decided to end its attacks on American ships but before news of the decision reached Madison and Congress.

The War Hawks talked brashly about an easy victory. South Carolina senator John C. Calhoun said: "I believe that in four weeks . . . the whole of Upper Canada and a part of Lower Canada will be in our power." Madison concurred, stating that an adequate force could "be obtained in a short time, and be sufficient to reduce Canada from Montreal upward." He also believed that with the Atlantic Ocean serving as a barrier between the United States and Britain, the British would be hard pressed to either defend Canada or launch an assault on American soil.

The president, however, almost immediately encountered problems that threatened doom. First, he presided over a poorly equipped military, the responsibility for which rested largely with him and his fellow Republicans. As seen with the Wilkinson affair, Madison had allowed incompetent generals to lead the army, and his pursuit of a balanced budget had cost the military dearly in troops and ships. Second, he contrived a faulty strategy for attacking Canada, a three-pronged assault that by November was clearly a failure. Third, as the vote in the Senate had revealed, America was deeply divided over the war. New England offered the fiercest opposition, fearing a conflict would ruin its trade with Britain. The region which, because of its extensive shipping, stood to benefit most from forcing Britain to respect American neutrality, ridiculed the entire venture by calling it "Mr. Madison's War."

Americans did celebrate a few victories in the early stages of the conflict, most notably Commander Oliver Hazard Perry's defeat of a British fleet on Lake Erie. "We have met the enemy and they are ours," Perry said, adding to the country's patriotic lexicon. By and large, though, the fighting went miserably—the British, for example, captured Buffalo, New York, in 1813—with no indication that Canadians wanted to join the United States or that James Madison could serve as an effective commander in chief.

The picture grew darker when in April 1814 Napoleon abdicated as ruler of France, signaling a British victory in Europe. Britain could now turn its full military power against America. Washington buzzed with rumors: Thousands of British troops would soon attack the capital, and Britain would force the United States to return Louisiana to Spain.

As President Madison dropped his demand that impressment be covered in any agreement to end the war, the first rumor came true. On August 22, 1814, about 4,000 British troops marched along the banks of the Potomac River, headed for Washington. The following day chaos took over as thousands of residents fled in wagons loaded with personal items and clogged the roads west of the capital. On August 24 militiamen assigned to defend Washington joined the flight; one British officer who witnessed the behavior said he had never seen troops behave so poorly. Madison had thus been wrong in thinking the militia could effectively defend the capital, and he blundered in allowing an incompetent leader to command the forces.

With the British troops closing in, Dolley Madison hurriedly loaded a wagon with silver items from the White House and retrieved the Gilbert Stuart painting. She left just ahead of the invaders to join her husband outside the city. The British soldiers marched into Washington and torched the White House, the Capitol, and several offices used by the executive departments. Although the troops pillaged little, the raid and word of America's leaders retreating caused deep embarrassment for the young nation.

Several days after the attack, a British fleet bombarded Fort McHenry, near Baltimore. American gunners kept the enemy far enough away that the assault caused little damage, but the battle's exploding bombs were witnessed by Francis Scott Key, who memorialized the scene in "The Star-Spangled Banner."

In September Captain Thomas McDonough achieved an American naval victory on Lake Champlain, stopping British plans to sweep through upstate New York. Weary from its long war with France and seeing there would be little to gain in continuing its fight, Britain decided to soften its position at negotiations in Ghent, Belgium, and reach a settlement with the United States.

Before this occurred, however, delegates from Massachusetts, Connecticut, and Rhode Island met at a regional conference called the Hartford Convention. A few extremists at the meeting raised the possibility that New England might secede from the Union should the war continue. At the same time one Federalist newspaper in Boston went so far as to say Madison should resign as a peace offering to Britain.

While the extremists tried to rally more support, negotiators from the United States and Britain signed the Treaty of Ghent on December 24, 1814, officially ending the War of 1812. Despite the treaty, a bloody fight occurred at New Orleans on January 8, 1815, as slow communications delayed news of the signing. During the Battle of New Orleans, British forces launched a frontal assault against American troops commanded by Andrew Jackson. In less than two hours British casualties surpassed 2,000, while the Americans lost only 13 dead and 39 wounded. News of the American victory reached Washington on February 4, sending the city into a raucous celebration. Like a chameleon against the political landscape, Madison had suddenly changed color, from blunderer to hero.

The Treaty of Ghent, which reached the president on February 14, stipulated there would be no territorial changes or reparations; all prisoners of war would be sent home; slaves taken from American planters would be returned to them; and commissions would be established to settle boundary disputes. Though the treaty ignored the issue of impressment, the Senate ratified it on February 16.

An objective observer would say the United States won little from the war. The great prize, Canada, remained British, and the seizure of American sailors remained unresolved. But the Battle of New Orleans bathed everything in red, white, and blue; it seemed to have saved the country from defeat, and even if it had not, it lent force to the view that America had stood up for its rights against the most powerful nation on earth in what amounted to a second war of independence. Albert Gallatin commented: "The war has renewed and reinstated the national feelings . . . which the Revolution had given, and which were daily lessened."

With the war over, President Madison reversed the Republican policy that previously favored limited government. In December 1815 he called for Congress to charter a national bank, fund internal improvements, and levy a protective tariff. Madison differed from earlier Republican politics in another way: The national debt, which he and Jefferson had once considered anathema, stood at a record high of $120 million as a result of the war. Although some Republicans fought Madison's proposals, in the spring of 1816 Congress approved a national bank and voted money to build the Cumberland Road, which began in Maryland. In time this reversal in Republican policy would breed enough dissent to form a new political party.

At the end of his second term in March 1817, James Madison returned with Dolley to their home in Virginia. He retired from public life for nearly a decade and then succeeded Jefferson as rector of the University of Virginia in 1826. Three years later he served as a delegate to the Virginia Constitutional Convention, where he criticized the power wielded by eastern slaveholders in the state legislature.

Madison died on June 28, 1836, after a series of illnesses, including a painful eruption over his entire body that weakened him greatly. His valet, Paul Jennings, reported: "For six months before his death, he was unable to walk, and spent most of his time reclining on a couch."

James Madison has often been compared to his predecessors in the White House and found wanting. More than any other event, the War of 1812 defined his presidency, and the attack on Washington sullied it. Yet Madison left office with the national economy prosperous and with the country more united than ever, steeped in a fervid nationalism that came from having stood up to Britain. Moreover, his career included his invaluable, even indispensable role as "father of the Constitution." The measurement of Madison's accomplishments may have less to do with burned structures in Washington than with the mortar of nationalism he applied to the building of American liberty.

CHRONOLOGY

1751 Born March 16

1769 Enters College of New Jersey

1774 Becomes member of Orange County Committee of Safety

1776 Attends Virginia Convention

Elected to Virginia legislature

1777 Serves on governor's council

1780 Attends Continental Congress

1784 Elected to Virginia legislature

1786 Attends Annapolis Convention

1787 Attends Constitutional Convention

Proposes Virginia Plan

Writes essays for *The Federalist*

1788 Attends Virginia ratifying convention

1789 Elected to U.S. House of Representatives

1794 Marries Dolley Payne Todd

1798 Writes Virginia Resolutions

1801 Appointed secretary of state by Thomas Jefferson

1808 Elected president

1812 Proclaims war with Britain

Reelected president

1814 Evacuates White House as British troops attack

1815 Signs Treaty of Ghent

1816 Proposes nationalist program

1817 Retires to Montpelier

1826 Appointed rector of University of Virginia

1829 Serves as delegate to Virginia Constitutional Convention

1836 Dies June 28

Further Reading

Brant, Irving. *James Madison,* 6 vols. Indianapolis, Ind.: Bobbs-Merrill, 1941–1961.

Hutchinson, William T., et al., eds. *The Papers of James Madison,* 16 vols. Chicago and Charlottesville: University of Chicago Press and University Press of Virginia, 1962.

Ketcham, Ralph. *James Madison: A Biography.* New York: Macmillan, 1971.

Koch, Adrienne. *Jefferson and Madison: The Great Collaboration.* New York: Alfred A. Knopf, 1950.

Peterson, Merrill, ed. *James Madison: A Biography in His Own Words,* 2 vols. New York: Newsweek Books, 1974.

Rakove, Jack N., ed. *James Madison: Writings.* New York: Library of America, 1999.

Rutland, Robert Allen. *James Madison and the Search for Nationhood.* Washington, D.C.: Library of Congress, 1981.

———. *James Madison: The Founding Father.* New York: Macmillan, 1987.

———. *The Presidency of James Madison.* Lawrence: University Press of Kansas, 1990.

Schultz, Harold. *James Madison.* New York: Twayne, 1970.

Wills, Garry. *James Madison.* New York: Times Books, 2002.

*J*AMES MONROE (1758–1831)

Fifth President, 1817–1825

JAMES MONROE
(Library of Congress)

"Equally gratifying is it to witness the increased harmony of opinion which pervades our Union. Discord does not belong to our system. Union is recommended as well by the free and benign principles of our Government, extending its blessings to every individual. . . ."

—Inaugural words, first term, March 4, 1817

Ingrained in America's heritage, the Monroe Doctrine declares the Western Hemisphere to be in a "free and independent condition" and asserts that the countries within it "are henceforth not to be considered as subjects for future colonization by any European powers." For President James Monroe the doctrine expressed his determination to protect U.S. security and promote the spirit of revolutionary freedom then taking hold in Spanish America.

Monroe was the last president to have fought as an officer in the American Revolution, and he wanted the ideals of 1776 to remain alive as a beacon to people overseas and to citizens at home, who would live in unity attached to republican principles. Yet domestically his desires ran into problems. In his first term he overcame party divisions and brought Americans together into an "Era of Good Feelings;" but during his second term a divisive sectional conflict threatened the very survival of the United States.

—m—

Like Presidents George Washington, Thomas Jefferson, and James Madison, Monroe came from Virginia's landed class, but his family belonged to the gentry's lower ranks. Born on April 28, 1758, in Westmoreland County to Spence Monroe and Elizabeth Jones Monroe, James grew up on a 500-acre farm worked by slaves.

His formal education began at age 11 when he enrolled at Campbelltown Academy. In 1774 his father died, and James and his uncle, Joseph Jones, a judge in Fredricksburg, managed the estate. Jones encouraged young Monroe to pursue politics and thought his prospects could be enhanced if he attended the College of William and Mary. James had learned his Latin and math so thoroughly that when he enrolled there later that year, he was placed in its upper division.

Events soon took James away from William and Mary, however. In 1775 fighting erupted between colonial and British troops in Massachusetts, and the following year the colonies declared their independence from Britain. Caught up in the revolutionary fervor, James enrolled as a cadet in the Third Virginia Infantry and was quickly commissioned a lieutenant. In December 1776, when George Washington's troops crossed the Delaware to attack Hessian soldiers, Monroe led a company against two cannon. His men captured the weapons, but in the battle a Hessian severely wounded him in the shoulder with a musket shot.

For his valor, James Monroe was promoted to captain and eventually to major. With no field command, though, he returned to Virginia in 1778. Acting on Washington's recommendation, the legislature commissioned Monroe a lieutenant colonel. Unable to raise a regiment, he reentered William and Mary in 1780 and at the same time began reading law under Thomas Jefferson, who was then governor. When the state capital was moved from Williamsburg to Richmond, Monroe again left William and Mary, this time to continue his studies under Jefferson. In working together, the two men established a lasting friendship.

Monroe entered politics in the spring of 1782 when he was elected to the Virginia House of Delegates. The following year, the legislature chose him to serve in the Confederation Congress at Philadelphia, where he shared lodgings with another delegate, his friend Thomas Jefferson.

Several friends and acquaintances offered their assessment of Monroe's character in the early stage of his political career:

> "He is a man whose soul might be turned wrong side outwards without discovering a blemish to the world," Jefferson said.
>
> "My impressions of Mr. Monroe are very pleasing. He is tall and well-formed. His dress plain and in the old style, small clothes, silk hose, knee-buckles, and pumps fastened with buckles. His manner was quiet and dignified. From the frank, honest expression of his eye, which is said to be 'the window of the soul,' I think he well deserves the encomium passed upon him by the great Jefferson . . . ," another Virginian said.
>
> "There is often in his manner an inartificial and even an awkward simplicity. . . . Mr. Monroe is a man of a most sincere and artless soul," said a Briton, William Wirt.

With a plain but friendly face and a warm smile, Monroe radiated honesty and sincerity. Though many found his intellect more limited than Jefferson's, his commitment to hard work earned him praise. A traditionalist down to his knee buckles, throughout his career he firmly defended the republican principles he fought for in 1776.

After Congress began holding its sessions in New York City in 1785, James Monroe met Elizabeth Kortright, the daughter of a wealthy but financially troubled merchant. He wrote to his friend James Madison, "If you visit this place shortly I will present you to a young lady who will be adopted a citizen of Virginia in the course of this week." The couple married in 1786, and Monroe moved to Fredericksburg, where he practiced law. They had two daughters, only one of whom survived into adulthood.

Monroe seldom strayed far from politics, and as the national government foundered, he supported action to strengthen it. After the Constitution was written to replace the Articles of Confederation, he was elected in 1788 as a delegate to the Virginia Ratifying Convention. Despite his desire for a stronger national government, he disliked the Constitution, viewing it as a threat to republican principles. He thought the Senate and the president should be popularly elected; he opposed giving Congress the power to levy direct taxes; he preferred militias to a standing army; and he wanted a bill of rights. In fact, five state ratifying conventions demanded such a bill when they called for immediate amendments to the Constitution to protect freedom of speech, freedom of religion, the right to a jury trial, and other basic liberties. After the Constitution was ratified, Congressman James Madison took the lead in recommending 12 amendments suggested by the states. Of these, 10 were approved. In the meantime, Virginia ratified the Constitution on a close 89-79 vote, putting Monroe on the losing side.

The constitutional battle over, Monroe ran for Congress in 1788. James Madison, who had advocated ratification, defeated him, and the outcome reaffirmed Virginia's support for the new document.

In August 1789 Monroe moved from Fredericksburg to a farm in Charlottesville, near Jefferson's home, Monticello. He returned to public office the following year when the state legislature elected him to the U.S. Senate. Monroe joined in the political battle then building in Congress. On one side of a heated debate, Secretary of the Treasury Alexander Hamilton pushed for a stronger national government that could use implied powers found in the Constitution to make the states impotent. On the other side, Congressman James Madison, along with Secretary of State Thomas Jefferson, opposed implied powers as dangerous to state prerogatives and individual liberty.

Monroe joined his two Virginia colleagues in organizing the Republican Party to fight Hamilton's Federalist Party. He rallied supporters in the Senate and told Jefferson: "Upon political subjects we perfectly agree, and particularly in the reprobation of all measures that may be calculated to elevate the government above the people." In several essays he wrote for the *National Gazette,* a newspaper founded by fellow Republican Philip Freneau, he likened the French Revolution, which had begun in 1789, to the American Revolution and said those who condemned it condemned republicanism.

Monroe's strong sympathies for France soon caused him trouble. After President George Washington appointed him minister to that country in 1794, he made several public statements that compromised American negotiations with Britain. He called France America's "ally and friend" and praised the "heroic valor of her troops." As a result, Washington, who was under pressure from Federalists who hated the French Revolution for its assault on order, recalled Monroe. Once he returned home, the former minister vilified Washington's foreign policy in a widely circulated pamphlet, one that Federalist leader Oliver Wolcott, Jr., condemned as "a wicked misrepresentation of facts." With this attack Monroe deepened the rift between Republicans and Federalists.

When the Republican-dominated Virginia legislature sought a governor in 1799, it recognized Monroe's party loyalty and elected him. He won reelection in 1800 and again in 1801. Although the state constitution gave the governor little power, Monroe advocated several reforms, among them a system of public education, which he thought essential to a society where decisions depended on learned citizens. The legislature, however, rejected his proposal.

Monroe returned to France in 1803 when President Thomas Jefferson sent him to join New Yorker Robert R. Livingston in negotiations for the purchase of Louisiana. Napoleon agreed to sell the territory before Monroe reached Paris, but he and Livingston negotiated the final treaty, an achievement that was hailed in the United States. Monroe then served as minister to Britain and tried but failed to resolve an Anglo-American dispute over shipping.

Differences with James Madison caused Monroe to refrain from endorsing his colleague for the presidency in 1808. Instead, he allowed his own name to be offered as an alternative, though he did not promote himself. Madison's subsequent victory seemed to signal Monroe's political ruin, but he pledged to support the new president, and Jefferson stepped in to help heal the rift between them. Their relations again cooled after Madison offered Monroe the governorship of Louisiana Territory, which Monroe refused. He thought it an inferior position and considered its proffering an insult. Once more Jefferson smoothed the ruffled feathers.

Monroe won election to the Virginia legislature in 1810, and in January 1811 he was again elected governor. In March President Madison asked him to serve as secretary of state, a post considered a stepping stone to the presidency; Monroe accepted. For Madison the appointment was opportune: It helped soothe factional divisions within the Republican Party at a time when the Federalists were gaining recruits to oppose his foreign policy, which was pointing toward war with Britain.

The appointment served another purpose: It notified the British of Madison's intent to deal firmly with them as they continued to violate American neutral rights by raiding ships flying the U.S. flag. Monroe had said the time was fast approaching for the United States to end "dealing in the small way of embargoes, non-intercourse, and non-importation with menaces of war." His biographer Harry Ammon says the Virginian's entry into the cabinet "made a resolution" of the dispute between Britain and the United States "inevitable," either through treaty or force.

When war erupted in 1812, and Madison's discredited secretary of war, William Eustis, resigned that December, Monroe took over the post on an acting basis. Like many political leaders, he miscalculated when he thought the British were too preoccupied with their war in Europe to launch an effective attack against the United States, and he thought Canada an easy target for the American army. Before long, Monroe relinquished his war post and resumed his duties as secretary of state. He returned to lead the war department again in 1814, while retaining his post in the state department, after the British invaded and burned Washington, D.C. During the invasion, Monroe led a scouting party to gather information about enemy troop movements. At the War Department he enacted needed reforms and made the military more effective. As secretary of state he supervised the peace negotiations with Britain and drafted instructions for the negotiators to drop their demands that the enemy promise to end its impressment of American sailors, a decision on his part that helped speed an end to the war with the signing of the Treaty of Ghent. In March 1815, with the war over, he once more served full-time as secretary of state while preparing for the 1816 presidential contest.

Although the United States did no better in the War of 1812 than fight Britain to a draw, Andrew Jackson's defeat of the British at the Battle of New Orleans persuaded most Americans that they had won. Monroe received widespread acclaim for his work in the cabinet, and when added to his Revolutionary War background, it made him the leading candidate to succeed James Madison.

A caucus of congressional Republicans made Monroe the party nominee in March 1816, picking him by a slight margin over William H. Crawford, Madison's new secretary of war. To receive the nomination meant winning the presidency, for the Federalists had grown so weak that they had no official candidate, though they generally considered New York Senator Rufus King their standard bearer. Monroe won easily in the electoral college, with King carrying only three states. The New Yorker later said of his opponent: "[He] had the zealous support of nobody, and he was exempt from the hostility of Everybody."

When James Monroe entered the White House, he led a nation that was gradually moving away from its agrarian and rural roots. Even though the decade 1810 to 1820 was the only one in American history in which urbanization had failed to increase, the War of 1812 boosted manufacturing and made cities economically more important. At the same time, America's population, concentrated heavily in the New England and Mid-Atlantic states, continued to push westward, with the number of people living in the Mississippi Valley increasing from 1.4 million in 1810 to 2.4 million in 1820. In yet another indication of America's growth, five states entered the Union between 1817 and 1825, bringing the total to 24.

In March 1817 Monroe departed on a tour of several northern states to survey the nation's development. He hoped few people would notice him, but everywhere he went citizens poured out to greet him. In Trenton, New Jersey, bells rang and guns fired in salute, while city leaders, volunteer organizations, and large crowds hailed his arrival.

Almost everyone thought such enthusiasm would be lacking in New England, an old Federalist stronghold. Amazingly, when the president arrived there the warm reception and excitement over his visit outshone the previous celebrations. Although a few Federalists criticized Monroe, partisan differences evaporated. The *Independent Chronicle and Boston Patriot* declared: "The visit of the *President* seems wholly to have allayed the storms of party. People now meet in the same room who would before scarcely pass the same street—and move in concert, where before the most jarring discord was the consequence of an accidental encounter." William Crawford wrote to a friend: "A general absolution of political sins seems to have been mutually agreed upon."

Boston's *Columbian Centinel* went so far as to declare an "era of good feelings." Americans everywhere were basking in their self-proclaimed triumph over Britain, and the mauling of the redcoats at New Orleans was encouraging an all-embracing national unity. When Monroe traveled as far west as Detroit, he showed his oncern for the frontier as an integral part of the nation and expressed a nationalism that superseded any sectional differences. (Two years later he traveled to the South and West on an itinerary that included Augusta, Georgia, and Nashville, Tennessee.)

America's growth confronted the national government with an important issue: whether Congress should fund the development of internal improvements, such as roads and canals. On his trip Monroe learned how strongly the country wanted such projects for economic development. He favored the improvements, but with a logic that seems as tortured today as it was back then, he said Congress had no power under the Constitution to pay for them.

Monroe had long held strong reservations about centralized power and had opposed the Constitution for that reason. True to his republican principles—some said blinded by them—he proposed that Congress send a constitutional amendment to the states for ratification, specifically enabling the national government to fund internal improvements. Most congressmen, however, not only favored building roads and canals, they believed Congress already possessed the power to finance them.

Consequently, Monroe and Congress came to a stalemate. Within two years, though, the issue faded as the states paid for local improvements and an economic downturn pinched the national treasury, making money difficult to come by.

President Monroe dealt with an overwhelmingly Republican Congress. Although in certain ways the political balance worked to his benefit, in other ways it worked against him.

Bereft of strong opposition, the Republicans no longer felt compelled to maintain strict discipline, and they often opposed Monroe's plans. At the same time several congressmen, such as Kentuckian Henry Clay, showed a greater interest in jockeying for the presidency than in supporting their Republican president. Still, Monroe won congressional approval for several of his programs.

In working with his cabinet, Monroe sought to build consensus on important issues. According to Harry Ammon, "Some of the lengthiest sessions were those devoted to harmonizing conflicting opinions." Monroe particularly turned to his cabinet for advice and support in a controversy involving General Andrew Jackson. In January 1818 Jackson was ordered by the secretary of war to contain and punish any Seminole Indians raiding American settlements from Florida, a territory then owned by Spain. In April Jackson crossed into Florida and seized the Spanish fort at St. Marks, claiming it was providing refuge to the Seminole Indians. While there he hanged two British citizens for inciting the Seminole tribe to war.

In May Jackson attacked a fort in Pensacola and forced its surrender, heavy-handed tactics that inevitably caused problems with Spain. President Monroe told Congress he had given Jackson permission to enter Florida, but only in pursuit of the Indians, and then only with due respect for Spanish authority. (Secretary of War John C. Calhoun later contradicted this account when he said Jackson had been given full power to wage war as he thought best.) Monroe discussed Jackson's military actions with his cabinet, and all except Secretary of State John Quincy Adams agreed the general had exceeded his orders in capturing the fort at Pensacola. Even Adams offered no resistance when the cabinet decided to renounce Jackson's aggression and return the fort to Spain.

A heated debate erupted in Congress over whether to censure Jackson, but the motion died when many congressmen concluded that to pass it would be interpreted as a slap at Monroe. Jackson later said the president had sent him a secret letter authorizing his incursion into Florida, but no evidence ever emerged to support his claim.

Nevertheless, Monroe clearly knew the general's temperament before he sent him to quell the Indian raids, and he himself wanted the Spanish removed from Florida. Historian Robert Remini asserts: "It would have been an act of supreme folly and irresponsibility to send Jackson on this mission if the administration truly meant to preserve the territorial integrity of Spanish Florida."

In February 1819 Monroe solved his border problem when John Quincy Adams negotiated a treaty with Spain after indicating that Andrew Jackson might again raid the territory. Under the Adams-Onís Treaty, the United States agreed to buy Florida for $5 million. In addition, the treaty settled the southwestern boundary with Spanish Texas.

While the Era of Good Feelings defined Monroe's early presidency, economic and sectional crises soon soured the atmosphere. In 1819 a depression hurt trade and caused high unemployment. Since few people at that time looked toward the national government for help in stimulating the economy, Monroe suffered little political damage, but the accompanying gloom punctured America's optimism.

Then in late 1819 differences between the North and South over slavery reached a fever pitch, ignited by Missouri's request to be admitted into the Union as a slave state. Antislavery groups pushed for the emancipation of all slaves in Missouri prior to statehood, and while a bare majority of congressmen in the House supported the measure, the Senate opposed it. Virginia senator James Barbour observed: "Who would have thought that the little *speck* . . . was to be swelled into the importance that is has now assumed, and that upon its decision depended the duration of the Union."

Monroe worked behind the scenes, voicing his opinion to several congressmen and placing pressure on state leaders in Virginia, the most populous of the Southern states and thus politically powerful, to accept a compromise. He wanted to preserve the Union and settle the issue before his reelection; yet as a slaveholder from a slave state, he considered the North too aggressive with its criticism (though he also hoped the South would eventually end slavery and ship blacks to Africa). Northerners, Monroe said to a fellow Southerner, should "show some regard for our peculiar situation." In that respect he encouraged an ally to write an essay opposing any rule that would require Missouri to abandon slavery. He advised: "A paper showing that Congress [has] no right to admit into the Union any new state on a different footing from the old . . . would be eminently useful, if published immediately."

Yet he agreed that Congress could prohibit slavery in the territories if it wanted, and when the Missouri Compromise reached his desk he signed it. The legislation admitted Missouri as a slave state, prohibited slavery in the Louisiana Purchase territory north of latitude 36°30', and brought Maine into the Union as a free state.

Later in 1820, Monroe won reelection, receiving 231 out of 232 electoral votes. The lone elector who voted against him did so only to preserve for George Washington the distinction of being the one candidate elected unanimously to the presidency. The Federalist Party, in complete disarray, reached the point where only four of its members sat in the Senate and only 25 in the House.

Without an organized opposition, Republicans fell victim to more bickering, and Monroe's power in Congress waned. Henry Clay went so far as to conclude, with some exaggeration, that the president "had not the slightest influence in Congress. His career was considered as closed." Senator Rufus King claimed Monroe's plans "are without friends in Congress."

Yet the president scored a momentous achievement in foreign policy. Long sympathetic with revolutionary movements underway against Spanish rule in South America, in 1822 he informed Congress he would act to recognize the emerging nations. This revealed his continuing attachment to republican principles—the fabric of America's own revolution—along with something more prosaic: He feared European nations would use the cover of revolution and all the turmoil surrounding it to slip in, crush the independence movements, establish their own empires, and invade the United States.

In autumn 1823, Britain's foreign minister George Canning proposed that the United States join his country in declaring Latin America off limits to any European expansion. Canning believed this would contain Britain's archenemy, France. Secretary of State John Quincy Adams advised Monroe to reject Canning's proposal. He wanted the United States to stand on its own against Europe, and the president agreed. As it turned out, Canning backed away from his proposal before it was officially rejected.

As a result of Adams's advice, in December 1823 Monroe incorporated a special message into his annual address to Congress. His words, which became known as the Monroe Doctrine, declared the Americas closed to European colonization. He announced: "We should consider any attempt on their part to extend their system to any portion of this hemisphere as dangerous to our peace and safety." Such action, he asserted, would be viewed "as the manifestation of an unfriendly disposition toward the United States." He added: "In the wars of the European powers, in matters relating to themselves, we have never taken any part, nor does it comport with out policy to do so."

When Monroe proclaimed his doctrine, the United States had neither the army nor the navy to back it, and as a unilateral measure it had no standing in international law. Monroe figured that for the time being the British would want to prevent competitors from expanding into the Americas and would use their navy to help enforce the doctrine. Most Americans supported Monroe's policy. Speaking in 1826, Daniel Webster said, "I look on the message of December 1823 as forming a bright page in our history."

Although John Quincy Adams had proposed the Monroe Doctrine, the president produced its final wording and added force to it by including it in a speech rather than burying it in diplomatic communiqués, as Adams had originally suggested. In so doing he boldly exerted the chief executive's power to formulate foreign policy.

In his last year as president, Monroe showed some flexibility regarding internal improvements when he signed a bill that provided money to survey land for roads and canals. True to his republican principles, he still insisted that Congress lacked the constitutional authority to actually build the improvements.

Monroe's second term ended in March 1825, at which time he retired to Oak Hill, his home designed by Thomas Jefferson and located in Virginia's Loudoun County. He returned briefly to politics in 1829 when he served as presiding officer at the Virginia Constitutional Convention. After his wife Elizabeth died in 1830, financial difficulties forced him to sell Oak Hill, and he moved to New York City, where he lived with his daughter. He died there on July 4, 1831, drawing his last breath on the patriotic holiday dedicated to the republican principles he fought hard to establish and preserve.

CHRONOLOGY

1758 Born April 28

1775 Leaves William and Mary to join army

1776 Promoted to first lieutenant
Wounded at Trenton
Promoted to captain

1777 Fights at Brandywine and Germantown

1778 Fights at Monmouth
Returns to Virginia

1780 Studies law under Thomas Jefferson

1782 Elected to Virginia House of Delegates
Elected to Confederation Congress

1786 Marries Elizabeth Kortright

1788 Elected to Virginia State Convention
Defeated in election to U.S. House of Representatives

1790 Elected to U.S. Senate

1794 Appointed minister to France

1796 Recalled from France

1799 Elected governor of Virginia

1800 Reelected governor

1801 Reelected to third term as governor

1803 Participates in purchase of Louisiana Territory
Appointed minister to Britain

1810 Elected to Virginia Assembly

1811 Elected governor of Virginia
Appointed secretary of state

1814 Appointed secretary of war

1816 Elected president

1817 Tours northern states

1819 Signs Adams-Onís Treaty

1820 Approves Missouri Compromise
Reelected president

1823 Announces Monroe Doctrine

1829 Serves as presiding officer at Virginia Constitutional Convention

1831 Dies July 4

FURTHER READING

Ammon, Harry. *James Monroe: The Quest for National Identity.* 1971. Reprint, Charlottesville: University Press of Virginia, 1990.

Cresson, W. P. *James Monroe.* Chapel Hill: University of North Carolina Press, 1946.

Cunningham, Noble E., Jr. *The Presidency of James Monroe.* Lawrence: University Press of Kansas, 1996.

Hamilton, Stanislaus M., ed. *The Writings of James Monroe,* 7 vols. 1898–1903. Reprint, New York: AMS Press, 1969.

May, Ernest R. *The Making of the Monroe Doctrine.* Cambridge, Mass: Harvard University Press, 1975.

Sellers, Charles. *The Market Revolution: Jacksonian America, 1815–1846.* New York: Oxford University Press, 1991.

John Quincy Adams (1767–1848)

Sixth President, 1825–1829

John Quincy Adams
(Library of Congress)

"To the topic of internal improvement . . . I recur with peculiar satisfaction. . . . The magnificence and splendor of their public works are among the imperishable glories of the ancient republics. The roads and aqueducts of Rome have been the admiration of all after ages, and have survived thousands of years after all her conquests have been swallowed up in despotism or become the spoil of barbarians."

—Inaugural words, March 4, 1825

In 1777, when John Quincy Adams was only 10, his father, John Adams—then a leader in the American Revolution—made it clear he expected the youngster to commit his life to public service. Just four years later JQA—the moniker he used in his letters to distinguish himself from his father—was in St. Petersburg, Russia, as secretary to the American minister. His public service under way, it would continue to his deathbed, wrapped in his parent's expectations, a constant din in his mind to avoid idleness, reject vice, and strive without being aggressive. The pressure placed on him, mixed with a personality noted for stubbornness, sensitivity to criticism, and self-righteousness, resulted in both notable accomplishments and what most historians consider a great failure: his presidency. An Adams biographer, Paul Nagel, says of him: "The poor fellow really was impotent as a President."

John Quincy Adams was born in Braintree, Massachusetts, on July 11, 1767, the second child and first son of John and Abigail Adams. He grew up in a household imbued with revolutionary spirit as his father joined the fight to end British control of the American colonies. In 1775, with the elder Adams serving in the Continental Congress at Philadelphia, John Quincy and his mother climbed Penn Hill, near their farm, from where they watched the Battle of Bunker Hill. The distant cannon and smoke impressed JQA, and the sacrifices made for independence forever remained fixed in his mind.

Young Adams made his first trip to Europe in February 1778 when he sailed with his father to France, where the elder Adams joined Benjamin Franklin in representing the United States. After a brief return to Massachusetts, they sailed to France a second time when John Adams was appointed minister plenipotentiary to seek a peace with Britain. In July 1780 they traveled to the Low Countries (present-day Holland and Belgium), and JQA kept a diary in which he described Brussels, Rotterdam, Leyden, and The Hague. As a result of his trips, he saw more of the world than almost any American boy his age could ever expect to see, and his outlook became less provincial and more cosmopolitan. (In his lifetime, he spent a total of 21 years overseas.) In January 1781 JQA enrolled at Leyden University to pursue his higher education.

His stay was brief. That July he made his trip to St. Petersburg, Russia, accompanying Francis Dana, a former delegate to the Continental Congress, on a diplomatic mission. In addition to serving as Dana's secretary, JQA acted as an interpreter at the Russian court, which conducted its state business in French. After he returned to The Hague early in 1784, he translated Latin and French classics into English. By that time, however, the elder Adams had decided his son had been much too long in Europe and sent JQA home in 1785 to enroll at Harvard.

Accustomed to keeping company with adults, the young man despaired at the sight of a group of sophomore students who went on a drunken spree and broke windows in rooms occupied by the college's tutors. "Such are the great achievements of many of the sons of Harvard," he said sarcastically. He avoided such drunken bouts, but he joined in the social scene and complained more about the faculty, whom he thought inferior in mind, than about his fellow students.

John Quincy Adams graduated from Harvard in 1787, having earned praise from its president. He then began studying law under Theophilus Parsons. Although Parsons was renowned as a teacher, JQA hated the study of law, which meant three years of supervised reading. This bored him, but he pursued it because his parents insisted and because he could think of nothing better to do. With constant commands from his mother and father to work hard, he attributed his reluctance to study to his own laziness: "Indolence, indolence, I fear, will be my ruin." He soon plunged into depression, which forced him to suspend his studies for six months. In 1790 however, he passed the bar and set up practice in Boston, though he had no desire for a long legal career.

With America's constitutional government just beginning in 1791, JQA entered a debate over how populist it should be with the publication of his *Letters of Publicola* in the *Columbian Centinel* of Boston. The young man displayed a conservative outlook in such agreement with his father that many people thought the elder Adams was the author. JQA criticized Thomas Paine's *The Rights of Man,* a prodemocratic treatise that defended the French Revolution, and warned about passion ruling reason. His writing reflected his love for literature and his intensifying attraction to politics. Although he at times combined the two in his long career, for the most part he professed his greater liking for books while committing most of his time to public office, a predicament that tormented him.

When President George Washington appointed JQA American minister to the Netherlands in 1794, Adams expressed reservations that his father, then vice president, may have arranged the assignment. There was some truth in this, since the elder Adams had discussed the post with the secretary of state. But upon speaking with his father JQA found "that my nomination had been as unexpected to him as to myself, and that he had never uttered a word . . . which . . . could be presumed that a public office should be conferred upon me."

By going to the Netherlands, JQA could get away from his dreary law practice and reenter public service in the European society he found attractive for its brilliance and gaiety. Soon after he arrived, he renewed his diary, so remarkable in detail about contemporary events that historians still use it as an important resource.

In November 1795 Washington sent John Quincy to London to exchange with Britain the ratification documents relating to the Jay Treaty. Delayed in his journey, he arrived too late for his assignment, but while in the city he often visited with Joshua Johnson, a wealthy Briton who entertained lavishly. JQA fell in love with Johnson's daughter, Louisa, and married her in July 1797, a few months after his father was inaugurated as the second president of the United States. They eventually had three sons and a daughter.

Before long, John Quincy and his new wife were heading for Berlin, President Adams having appointed him minister to Prussia. There he concluded a treaty of commerce and friendship. In addition to his diplomatic work, he translated several books from German to English.

In 1801 John Adams lost his bid for reelection to Thomas Jefferson and recalled his son to preclude any possibility the incoming president might do so. After once again sailing across the Atlantic, JQA reopened his law practice in Boston and descended back into the profession he loathed.

For the first time, the domestic political scene beckoned, and in 1802 Adams won election to the Massachusetts senate, where he served into the following year. Until this time, he had long said he would avoid political office because it represented a clawing aggressiveness he found repulsive. He later said he changed his mind so he could get away from his tedious law routine and serve the public as an independent leader standing above party rancor and favoritism.

Over the years, Adams hid his ambition beneath his insistence that political office had caused him to sacrifice himself for the public good. He always believed he should stand for election, not run for office, and portrayed his victories as the people calling him, rather than as an Adams debasing himself by seeking their vote. His sanctimoniousness served him well at times by making him appear to be more honorable than his opponents; at other times, when his political ambitions were obvious, it made him appear hypocritical. And sometimes he could not decide how to play the political game, an indecisiveness that made him appear weak and vacillating.

In 1803, having lost a race for Congress, Adams hoped the Massachusetts legislature would elect him to a seat in the U.S. Senate. The legislature obliged, and although Adams went to Washington as a member of the Federalist Party, he immediately took an independent course. He arrived after the initial vote on Thomas Jefferson's Louisiana Purchase but supported several bills needed to complete the Republican president's deal. This put him at odds with many other New England Federalists who believed that acquiring and quickly settling the land would drain the northeastern states of people and resources. Adams thought differently; a strong nationalist, he insisted that programs to help the West would in time benefit the entire nation.

Just as many Federalists began suspecting JQA had abandoned them for the Republican Party, he took a strong stand against Jefferson's orchestrated impeachment of Samuel Chase, a Federalist Supreme Court justice. To remove Chase from office based on the flimsy charges that faced him, Adams said, would make a mockery of the constitutional separation of powers. As it turned out, the House impeached Chase, but the Senate acquitted him. Those puzzled by JQA's peculiar politics could find some answers in statements he made about political parties, which showed his dislike for them. At one point he lamented, "The country is so totally given up to the spirit of party, that not to follow blindfold the one or the other is an inexpiable offense."

In a move that tempered Adams's political ambition, Harvard chose him in 1805 for its new chair of rhetoric and oratory. Though Adams continued serving in the Senate—"I could neither bind myself to residence at Cambridge, nor to attendance more than a part of the year," he said—he accepted his professorial duties with enthusiasm and presented several lectures well-received by students.

His academic experience may have provided some compensation for his much rockier ordeal in politics. After the British frigate *Leopard* fired on the American ship *Chesapeake* in 1807, killing several on board, Adams joined the general outrage against the attack. Once again he broke with numerous New England Federalists, who in this instance feared that any retaliation directed at Britain would lead to war and damage overseas trade. Adams fumed that these New Englanders would rather submit to British indignities for the sake of the dollar than defend American rights. On several occasions he engaged in angry shouting matches with his Federalist colleagues. His position in the Senate had clearly become untenable, and it was made all the more so when he joined Republicans in supporting an embargo of all overseas trade to keep Britain and France from raiding American ships.

In June 1808 Federalists in the Massachusetts House voted to name a successor to Adams's Senate seat well ahead of schedule—making it clear that he would not be returned to office. He could have stayed in the Senate until 1809, but when the legislature instructed him to vote for a measure to repeal the embargo, he refused and quit. He then resumed his law practice.

Before long Adams was again packing his bags for Europe. He had let it be known to President James Madison, a Republican, that he desired a government appointment, and in July 1809 he gave his final lecture at Harvard before assuming his duties as minister to Russia. There Adams developed a close friendship with Czar Alexander I. They often took lengthy walks together and talked about everything from international developments to personal matters.

President Madison nominated John Quincy Adams for justice of the Supreme Court in 1810, and the Senate confirmed his appointment, but he declined the post. In a letter to his brother he revealed an important reason for his decision: He preferred his role as a political partisan. It was one of the few times when he admitted ambition as a ruling passion over selfless service.

In the spring of 1814 Adams joined the American diplomatic team at Ghent to negotiate a peace with Britain to end the War of 1812. His colleagues considered him ill-tempered and rude, but he was instrumental in getting an acceptable treaty when he advised them against trying to obtain British concessions on issues such as neutral rights. Instead, he insisted, they should settle for conditions as they existed before the war. He accurately understood that by this time Americans and Britons alike were anxious for peace.

Soon after the treaty talks, President Madison appointed Adams minister to Britain. He accomplished little, but in 1817 another

Republican president, James Monroe, appointed him secretary of state. Monroe chose Adams partly because of his diplomatic background and partly because he wanted to balance his cabinet geographically and needed a New Englander. The time had come for John Quincy Adams to make his last transatlantic voyage.

Once in Washington, Adams found himself attacked early and hard by his political opponents, in part because of his personality. Many fellow politicians considered him cold, snobbish, and aloof. The last characteristic he readily admitted, saying it came from an aversion to idle conversation. But the opposition was more intensely stirred by politics. Adams had assumed an office many saw as a stepping stone to the presidency—a route previously followed by Jefferson, Madison, and Monroe. As a result, others who desired the executive office battled him from the start. Among them was Henry Clay, the Speaker of the House, who had hoped to be secretary of state himself and was now determined to run foreign affairs.

Despite all the in-fighting, Adams possessed Monroe's confidence and was given wide latitude in pursuing policy. The president, however, always made the final decisions, closely reviewed his secretary's official papers, and made numerous changes to them. JQA's accomplishments set a high standard that future secretaries of state would find difficult to match. In 1818 he arranged a treaty with Britain that set the northwest boundary between Canada and the United States at the 49th parallel out to the Rocky Mountains and reaffirmed the right of Americans to fish off the coasts of Newfoundland and Labrador. The following year he settled the boundary between the Louisiana Purchase territory and Spanish Texas, and he signed the Adams-Onís Treaty with Spain, by which the United States acquired Florida for $5 million.

In 1821, with Spain's colonies in the Americas seeking independence and other European countries threatening to intervene, JQA stated publicly that the Western Hemisphere should never again "be encroached upon by foreign powers." That view was refined and formalized as the Monroe Doctrine in 1823, after Adams advised the president that the United States should defend North and South America on its own, without British help. He wrote in his diary: "It would be more candid, as well as more dignified, to avow our principles explicitly to Russia and France, than to come in as a cock-boat in the wake of the British man-of-war." Monroe declared the Western Hemisphere closed to further colonization by European powers. He said the United States would keep out of European affairs and that any attempt by European nations to expand into the Americas would be considered a threat to U.S. security.

The fears of JQA's opponents that he would move from the state department to the White House proved well-founded. In 1824 Adams worked as hard as anyone else in seeking the presidency, even holding a grand ball to honor General Andrew Jackson in an unsuccessful attempt to rally him behind the Adams campaign. A bitter and divisive four-way race—what one historian has called "America's most fractured Presidential election ever"—involved Adams, Jackson, Henry Clay of Kentucky, and treasury secretary William H. Crawford of Georgia. When none of the candidates obtained a majority of the electoral vote, the election went to the House of Representatives. On February 9, 1825, the House surprised almost everyone by settling the matter on the first ballot: it elected Adams, making him the first son of a president to obtain the nation's highest office.

Legend has it that JQA obtained his victory after Congressman Stephen Van Rensselaer prayed for divine guidance in casting his vote and, upon opening his eyes, saw a ballot for Adams at his feet, which he took as a sign to select him. Van Rensselaer's decision then threw New York to Adams and helped give him the victory. In reality, Adams's lobbying of congressmen, including Van Rensselaer, proved more important, as did Clay's decision to have his congressional supporters vote for the secretary of state.

No divine intervention quelled the enormous outcry over Adams's election. Andrew Jackson had received the highest popular vote, and he and his supporters claimed that in electing Adams as a minority president, Congress had cheated them and thwarted the popular will. Adding to JQA's woes, his election as a National Republican came with the party in disarray, a problem made worse by his never having strongly identified with it.

Adams pushed the outcry to higher decibels when he chose Henry Clay as secretary of state. The appointment shocked Congressman Robert Y. Hayne of South Carolina, who said the two men had entered into a "monstrous union." Jacksonians charged Adams with a "corrupt bargain," saying he and Clay had reached a deal where Clay would support Adams for president and Adams would appoint Clay to the politically powerful secretary's job. Andrew Jackson believed Clay would use the position to grab the presidency.

In truth, Henry Clay never had to ask John Quincy Adams specifically to make him secretary of state, for in the closeted political world of Washington, where politicians knew exactly where to scratch to get a desired reaction, nothing needed to be said directly. Clay disliked Adams, but he disliked Jackson even more, so in December he sent an emissary to speak to the New Englander. For his part, Adams despised Clay and expressed his feelings in his diary. Yet according to historian Robert V. Remini in *Henry Clay: Statesman for the Union,* Adams decided he would place his personal dislike aside, thinking "if that was the price of the presidency, so be it. He would pay it. [He] was just as ambitious as Henry Clay."

In early January, Adams met with Clay at the Kentuckian's request. JQA's diary leaves much unsaid about the meeting, but the New Englander notes about Clay: "He wished me . . . to satisfy him with regard to some principles of great public importance, but without any personal considerations for himself. In the question to come before the House between General Jackson, Mr. Crawford, and myself, he had no hesitation in saying that his preference would be for me." Whatever transpired between the two men, Clay's appointment smelled so suspect that it ruined his chances of reaching the White House.

Because the Clay deal was one of several Adams made to collect votes in the House for his election to the presidency, he began his term sullied and distrusted and never recovered from his inauspicious start. In late 1825, on the heels of the Clay controversy, he backed John W. Taylor of New York for Speaker of the House because Taylor had supported him in the congressional vote for president. Taylor won by a narrow majority, but Adams antagonized the South with his support, for Taylor strongly opposed slavery. The president stumbled again when he chose Tobias Watkins to be his contact person with politicians, newspapermen, and office-seekers. Watkins had few political connections and only limited talent.

Throughout his public life, Adams had been a strong nationalist, whether it was in supporting Jefferson's purchase of Louisiana or in arranging for the acquisition of Florida. He combined this nationalism with his passion for books and learning and his faith in reason to introduce a nationalist program. It was so strong in its call for an activist federal government that his opponents condemned him for trying to be "another Caesar." He wanted the government to take responsibility for the nation's cultural, scientific, and general welfare, a radical concept back then. He called for roads and canals to be built, geographic exploration expanded, and a national university founded, all through congressional legislation. He even called for a national astronomical observatory, a project critics thought as starry-eyed as its advocate. Adams's own cabinet considered his proposals excessive. At that point he could have compromised, but instead he held stubbornly to his agenda. "He made himself ludicrous," says biographer Paul Nagel. As it turned out, Congress passed little of the program, choosing to fund only piecemeal internal improvements, such as money to repair the

Cumberland Road, which stretched from Maryland into the Midwest.

Another fight developed when Congress resisted naming delegates to the Pan-American Conference meeting in Panama. Southerners feared slavery would be discussed there, or even worse, the meeting might lead to relations with the black republic of Haiti. By the time Congress relented, the conference was nearly over, and it was too late to send the delegates.

All the fighting and back-stabbing caused JQA to suffer insomnia and indigestion and to lose weight. To relieve the pressure he took daily four-mile walks, swam in the Potomac River—in a fitting metaphor for his presidency, he once almost drowned in the currents—and began gardening, occasionally greeting callers at the White House in dirt-covered clothes.

Another issue for Adams involved Indian-occupied land. Early in his presidency he signed a treaty with the Creek in Georgia requiring them to cede their lands. Congress ratified it, but the treaty had been negotiated with a small minority of Creek; when Adams discovered this, he reconsidered the deal. During a cabinet debate on the issue Henry Clay said, "It is impossible to civilize Indians. . . . I do not think them, as a race, worth preserving. . . . Their disappearance from the human family will be no great loss to the world." Under a second treaty, the Creek retained land west of the Chattahoochee River. But when Congress balked, yet a third treaty again confiscated all the Creek land. Years later, in a general observation, Adams claimed: "We have done more harm to the Indians since our Revolution than had ever been done to them by the French and English nations before. . . ."

If Adams found Congress uncooperative early in his presidency, he found it more so after 1826, the year his political opponents captured control of the House under the banner of the new Democratic Party. General Jackson and his supporters organized the Democrats with the express purpose of winning the presidency in 1828. When the House met in March 1827, it ousted John Taylor as Speaker, causing Adams's influence to hit rock bottom. The president lost all support in the South in 1828 when he signed the so-called Tariff of Abominations, passed by Congress to raise taxes to their highest level yet on imports. Southerners applied this name to the tariff because they considered it to be oppressive in its potential to stifle their economy.

In the 1828 presidential contest Andrew Jackson used innovative campaign tactics, such as avoiding issues, telling voters what they wanted to hear, and staging huge rallies. Jackson's supporters attacked Adams for having bought a billiard table for the White House and for having bargained with Henry Clay in the previous election to win the presidency.

Adams's supporters gave as good as they got. They smeared Jackson by charging him with adultery for having married his wife before she had finalized her divorce with her first husband. Jackson considered it a vicious attack and blamed Adams for it, to which the president said, "I have not been privy to any publication in any newspaper against either himself or his wife." Modern campaigning had arrived.

Jackson easily defeated Adams with 56 percent of the popular vote and a tally of 178 to 83 in the electoral college. As Adams's term ended he said, "The greatest change in my condition occurred . . . which has ever befallen me—dismission from the public service and retirement to private life."

Depression overwhelmed him. He took his defeat hard and believed his life worthless. To make matters worse, his son George, for years an alcoholic, committed suicide. "I have no plausible motive for wishing to live," Adams said.

His spirits lifted when political leaders in Massachusetts asked him to run for the House of Representatives. He agreed, for here was a way for him to salvage some dignity from his defeat and maybe get back at those who had opposed him. In November 1830 he became the first, and as of 2000 still only, former president to serve in Congress. Adams cheerily proclaimed: "No election or appointment conferred upon me ever gave me so much pleasure."

Adams combined political activity with writing poetry but suffered more depression in 1834 after his work in the House grew tedious and his son John, like George an alcoholic, died. His spirits again revived in 1835 when he found, as he put it, a cause. Adams strenuously opposed the gag rule, adopted by Congress in 1836, that forbade the House from considering any petitions dealing with slavery. He had long hated slavery; in 1820 he said that it "polluted" the nation. He therefore saw the gag rule as another example of slavery's corrupt influence, in this case blinding Americans to a republican principle—namely, the right to petition.

Early in 1837 Adams moved to present 21 antislave petitions to the House, some purportedly from the slaves themselves. Congress tried, but failed, to censure him, while southern congressmen shouted "Expel him! Expel him!"

Adams angered Southerners even more with his prominent role in the *Amistad* case. Slaves aboard the Cuban schooner *Amistad* mutinied in 1839 and tried to sail back to Africa, but their white navigators misled them, causing them to land near Long Island. A federal court ruled the slaves had been seized illegally from Africa and must be released. To avoid angering Southerners, however, President Van Buren appealed the case to the Supreme Court. In 1841 Adams made a closing statement before the Court on behalf of the slaves. In an impassioned eight-hour speech he called human liberty more important than maritime laws and property rights. The Supreme Court agreed with him and ruled that the slaves had been illegally smuggled from Africa and must be freed. The decision made Adams a hero in the North.

In 1846 Adams suffered a paralytic stroke that kept him from his duties in the House for four months and impaired his speech. Good news soon came with the repeal of the gag rule. Meanwhile, Adams continued his long-held opposition to the U.S.-Mexican War, which he considered a fight to gain more territory for slavery. On February 21, 1848, he voted against a measure to commend the war's veterans. He then rose on the floor of Congress to address the Speaker, but upon getting up his face grew flushed and he started to fall. A colleague caught him, and he was carried to a sofa in the Speaker's private chamber. At one point Henry Clay came to visit him and wept at his side. Adams died in the chamber two days later, on February 23, 1848, at 7:15 P.M.

Some fellow congressmen claimed that as JQA collapsed in the House he said, "This is the last of earth—I am composed." His equanimity may have come from the realization he had achieved the goal of service to society instilled in him by his parents and adopted by him as his guiding light. In the case of the presidency, however, such service damaged his reputation. His ineptness in appointing Henry Clay to his cabinet and his failure to achieve any effective working relationship with Congress has relegated his tenure to the list of failed chief executives.

CHRONOLOGY

1767 Born July 11

1778 Sails to France with father

1779 Attends school in Amsterdam

1781 Enters Leyden University

Travels to St. Petersburg, Russia, as secretary to American minister

1783 Resumes studies at The Hague

Accompanies father to Paris

1785 Returns to United States

1787 Graduates from Harvard

1790 Admitted to the bar

1794 Appointed minister to the Netherlands

1797 Marries Louisa Johnson in London

Named minister to Prussia

1801 Returns to United States

1802 Elected to Massachusetts senate

1803 Elected to U.S. Senate

1805 Appointed professor at Harvard

1808 Resigns from U.S. Senate

1809 Named minister to Russia

1814 Signs Treaty of Ghent

1815 Appointed minister to Britain

1817 Named secretary of state

1818 Settles northwest boundary with Canada

1819 Negotiates Adams-Onís Treaty

1823 Helps draft the Monroe Doctrine

1825 Elected president by House of Representatives

Proposes internal improvements

1826 Nominates delegates to Panama Congress

1828 Signs Tariff of Abominations

Defeated for reelection

1830 Elected to U.S. House of Representatives

1836 Opposes gag rule

1841 Argues *Amistad* case before Supreme Court

1846 Suffers paralytic stroke

1848 Dies February 23

FURTHER READING

Bemis, Samuel Flagg. *John Quincy Adams and the Foundations of American Foreign Policy.* New York: Alfred A. Knopf, 1949.

———. *John Quincy Adams and the Union.* New York: Alfred A. Knopf, 1956.

Brookhiser, Richard. *America's First Dynasty: The Adamses, 1735–1918.* New York: Free Press, 2002.

East, Robert A. *John Quincy Adams: The Critical Years, 1785–1794.* New York: Bookman Associates, 1962.

Ford, Worthington C., ed. *The Writings of John Quincy Adams*, 7 vols. New York: Macmillan, 1913–1917.

Hargreaves, Mary W. M. *The Presidency of John Quincy Adams.* Lawrence: University Press of Kansas, 1985.

Hecht, Marie B. *John Quincy Adams: A Personal History of an Independent Man.* New York: Macmillan, 1972.

Nagel, Paul C. *John Quincy Adams: A Public Life, A Private Life.* New York: Alfred A. Knopf, 1997.

Nevins, Allan, ed. *The Diary of John Quincy Adams, 1794–1845.* New York: Longman, Green and Co., 1929.

Remini, Robert V. *John Quincy Adams.* New York: Times Books, 2002.

Richards, Leonard L. *The Life and Times of Congressman John Quincy Adams.* New York: Oxford University Press, 1986.

Russell, Greg. *John Quincy Adams and the Public Virtues of Democracy.* Columbia: University of Missouri Press, 1995.

Weeks, William Earl. *John Quincy Adams and American Global Empire.* Lexington: University Press of Kentucky, 1992.

ANDREW JACKSON (1767–1845)

Seventh President, 1829–1837

ANDREW JACKSON
(Library of Congress)

"It will be my sincere and constant desire to observe toward the Indian tribes within our limits a just and liberal policy, and to give that humane and considerate attention to their rights and their wants which is consistent with the habits of our Government and the feelings of our people."

—Inaugural words, first term, March 4, 1829

No previous president so strongly appealed to the average voter as did Andrew Jackson. Others tried in a limited way—John Adams when he addressed large gatherings in 1800, and more so Thomas Jefferson with his talk about fighting an entrenched elite and his display of everyman's attire at the presidential residence, where he sometimes answered the door in his bathrobe. But Jackson reached deep into a changing political system built in homage to the common person. In his lifetime "democracy" became all the rage and with it came policies enveloped by controversy that matched Jackson's own strident, volatile, dynamic personality. By the time his administration ended, he had created a presidency much stronger than the one he had found.

Andrew Jackson was born on March 15, 1767, somewhere in the southern backwoods. The exact location remains in dispute because Jackson's father, a Scotch-Irish immigrant also named Andrew, died two weeks before his son's birth, and his mother, Elizabeth, sought help from relatives in delivering the baby. One likely location was the James Crawford cabin in South Carolina, but she may have gone to the McCamie farmhouse in North Carolina, both places located in the Piedmont, the rolling hill country between the coastal plains and the Appalachian Mountains. Born of humble origins, Andrew was thus a child of the frontier and would carry its influence with him throughout his life.

Elizabeth wanted Andrew to enter the ministry, so she enrolled him in a frontier school so he could first obtain his basic education. Surrounded by a forest and log cabins from which smoke rose lazily into the air, he learned to read, write, and cipher, and he studied Latin and Greek. He was, however, never attracted to academics and knew little history, literature, or science. As a result, he learned only a few fundamentals. As a child he liked games and wrestling and would stand up to anyone, no matter how big. Mischievous, irascible, strong-willed, easily offended, and sometimes a bully, he frequently found himself in scrapes with other boys.

When the American Revolution broke out, Andrew supported the Patriot cause. Although just entering his teens, he joined a militia and learned how to drill. His primary duty was to carry messages, but in one incident he fought to defend the house of a Patriot captain, only to be captured by redcoats. When a British officer demanded that Andrew clean his boots, the youngster defied him, at which point the officer swung his sword in anger. Andrew blunted the blow with his hand, but the blade left a gash on his head and fingers. He carried the resulting scars as reminders of British cruelty.

While they were prisoners of war, Andrew and his brother Robert contracted smallpox. After their release Elizabeth cared for both boys, but she was unable to save Robert. With Andrew well on his way to recovery, Elizabeth went to Charleston, South Carolina, to nurse war prisoners held aboard ships in the city's harbor. Tragically, cholera felled her, and she died in the fall of 1781.

For Andrew the war had brought much suffering—his mother and brother dead, his own body wracked by disease. He felt deserted and alone. But the Revolution also left him with deep patriotic feelings and a fervid attachment to his new nation that would make nationalism among his strongest values.

Soon after Elizabeth's death, Andrew Jackson studied law at Salisbury, North Carolina. In 1788 he set out across the Appalachian Mountains and through Indian country for Nashville, located in the Western District of North Carolina (now Tennessee). There he joined a small group of settlers who lived in blockhouses to protect themselves from Indian raids. While practicing law, Jackson lived in the blockhouse occupied by the widow Donelson, whose daughter, Rachel, had recently separated from her husband, Lewis Robards.

A messy episode followed when Robards tried to reconcile with Rachel and accused Jackson of having made advances toward her. Jackson challenged him to a duel, but he refused. Jackson subsequently moved out of the blockhouse, and soon after, Robards took Rachel with him to Kentucky. In 1790, the same year Jackson was appointed attorney general for the Tennessee region, he heard stories that Rachel again wanted to leave Robards. He therefore rode to Kentucky and took her back to Nashville. Lewis Robards soon filed for divorce, and in August 1791 Jackson married

Rachel. He did so, however, before the divorce had been granted, making the couple's marriage an invalid union and forcing them to restate their vows three years later.

The marriage improved Jackson's social standing because the Donelsons were a leading family in Tennessee. The couple lived on a small plantation along the Cumberland River while he practiced law and acquired tracts of land as payment for his services. By age 30 he had amassed tens of thousands of acres and had expanded his activities to include a trading business and a store.

Tennessee entered the Union in 1796, and Jackson was elected to the U.S. House of Representatives as the state's first congressman. One story tells of the frontiersman-turned-lawmaker arriving in the national capital at Philadelphia dressed in buckskin, his scraggly hair tied into a queue with eel skin and draped down his back. As picturesque and rustic as the story sounds—or frightening to a refined Easterner of the day—it was told by an enemy of Jackson and likely holds little truth. The Tennessean had visited large cities before and knew how men dressed in formal settings.

More startling to some was Jackson's vote against a resolution praising President George Washington on his retirement from office. Jackson disliked what he considered to be Washington's lenient treatment of Indians and his pro-British foreign policy, and he let his feelings on those two subjects override Washington's accomplishments. Opposed by few, the resolution passed, and Jackson's futile vote exposed him to criticism, even ridicule, for having disrespected the nation's founding hero.

Jackson was elected to the Senate in 1797 and served one year before resigning to sit on the Tennessee superior court. As a judge he sided consistently with large landholders and creditors, much the same people he had represented as a lawyer. Accepted into Tennessee's inner circle, Jackson showed in his rise from poverty the mobility possible in frontier society but also its inequality.

When President Thomas Jefferson purchased Louisiana from France in 1803, Jackson tried to convince the president to appoint him the territory's governor. He was devastated and angry when Jefferson chose someone else, and he reacted by supporting the more radical states' rights wing of the Republican Party. In 1804 he resigned his judgeship to concentrate on his law practice and business dealings.

Jackson continued his heavy investments in land, helping to found several towns, including Memphis, Tennessee. He raised cows and mules and bred horses for racing. He loved to bet on horse races and won thousands of dollars that way. He also enjoyed cockfighting. He entered his birds in the bloody contests, collected bets on them, and cheered for them.

With more money and land, Jackson expanded his slaveholdings. In 1798 he owned 15 slaves. A few years later the number had risen to 44, and by the time he reached the presidency, more than 100. He pledged himself to treat his slaves kindly, and in many ways he did. But on numerous occasions he punished them with severity. When his wife Rachel told him one slave, Betty, was behaving disrespectfully, he ordered the offender whipped in full view of the other slaves, a bloody spectacle from which the only sure outcome was humiliation.

The frontier and Jackson's character worked together like fuel poured on fire. He needed to dominate, much as backwoods settlers fought to rule the wilderness and bend the land to their desires. He remained supremely self-confident, emotional, and short-tempered. His violent explosions—some observers say they were more planned than spontaneous—often cowed opponents into submission.

Jackson brawled and dueled his way through several confrontations. One duel resulted after he and Charles Dickinson, a wealthy "dandy," exchanged insults in a dispute over notes to be used in paying off a gambling debt. The verbal war intensified when Dickinson said in a letter to Jackson: "I shall be very glad when an opportunity serves to know in what manner you give your anodines and hope you will take in payment one of my most moderate cathartics." Jackson said in a newspaper article referring to Dickinson: "[You are] a worthless, drunken, blackguard scoundrel." Dickinson replied in a newspaper article referring to Jackson: "[You are] a worthless scoundrel, a poltroon and a coward. . . ."

With hard feelings made public and honor besmirched, the two men scheduled a duel for May 30, 1805, across the state line in Kentucky. Many people in Nashville, welcoming a diversion from cockfights, bet on the outcome.

Dickinson fired first and hit Jackson in the chest, but the wounded man clenched his teeth and stood still. His reaction stunned Dickinson, who thought he had missed. Dickinson was ordered to stay at his mark, at which point Jackson raised his pistol, squeezed the trigger, and . . . nothing; it had stopped at half cock. Jackson pulled back the hammer, again carefully aimed at his target, and fired. He hit Dickinson just below the ribs, wounding him so severely that he died.

Jackson left the duel with blood dripping into his boots from Dickinson's bullet, which had lodged near his heart. Too close to be removed, it caused the Tennessean pain for years to come. He suffered damage to his reputation as well when many in the state called him a murderer and "a fearful, violent, vengeful man."

Andrew Jackson was nothing less than ambitious. He wanted to carve his name in American history as a military leader and found his opportunity in the War of 1812. That year he organized 2,000 Tennessee volunteers to fight the British. During a particularly arduous journey with his men, one soldier remarked that he appeared "tough as hickory," giving Jackson his nickname, Old Hickory.

In 1813 Jackson fought the Creek Indians after they attacked a stockade north of Mobile, Alabama, and killed 250 non-Indians. The Creek had received help from Spanish and British agents who had encouraged them to take up arms. Old Hickory believed the Creek attack had to be answered. By 1814 he had totally crushed and humiliated the Indians. The Creek would never recover, and their loss signaled doom for all Indians in the South—an end that Jackson desired. Like many Americans he viewed Indians as inferior to whites and as barbaric, simpleminded, and backward. Historian Robert Remini calls Old Hickory "a fire-breathing frontiersman obsessed with the Indian presence and the need to obliterate it."

After subduing the Creek, Jackson decided to attack Pensacola, then located within Spanish Florida. British agents ran spy operations out of Pensacola, and British ships anchored in its harbor. Old Hickory believed he could disrupt the enemy's operations in the South. Acting without President James Madison's explicit approval, in November 1814 he captured Pensacola with little problem.

Jackson's success forced the British to look farther west in their plan to invade the United States along the Gulf Coast. Late in 1814 a British fleet laden with soldiers bore down on New Orleans. Jackson, who had earlier been commissioned a major general in the U.S. Army, readied several thousand troops under his command. In mid-December the enemy ships arrived at Lake Borgne and defeated an American fleet, setting the stage for a land invasion. On December 24 negotiators from Britain and the United States, meeting in Europe, signed the Treaty of Ghent to end the war. News of its signing, however, would not reach Jackson for weeks.

On January 8, 1815, the British troops began their final assault. Their failure to capture several American batteries left them exposed, and from behind fortifications fronted by a canal and flanked by the Mississippi River, woods, and swamps, Jackson's men annihilated them. British casualties exceeded 2,000, with nearly 300 killed, while the Americans lost only 13 dead and 39 wounded. According to one eyewitness, the ground was "covered with dead and wounded laying in heaps," leaving the soil "completely red." There were so many bodies near the canal "you could have walked a quarter of a mile to the front" on them.

From the carnage, Old Hickory emerged a national hero. When he entered New Orleans as a savior, artillery blasts saluted him and a laurel crown was placed on his head. Although Jackson's victory did not affect the Treaty of Ghent, had the British won at New Orleans they may well have obtained the Louisiana Purchase territory, since the treaty contained no provisions protecting it for the United States. In that way Jackson's victory secured America's hold on Louisiana.

One provision in the Treaty of Ghent, Article IX, angered Jackson: It said the United States agreed to restore to the Indians the territory he had won from them in the Creek War. For Jackson this was untenable, and as commander of the southern division of the army, he ignored the provision. The Creek complained, but President Madison wanted expansion and was unwilling to discipline the enormously popular hero. The British, meanwhile, backed away from enforcing Article IX because they feared if they antagonized the United States, Canada's security would be jeopardized.

Over the next few years Jackson, in his position as commander, signed treaties with several other tribes, acquiring land covering one-third of Tennessee, three-fourths of Alabama, and more. He was given yet another opportunity to fight the Indians and display his bravado when President James Monroe ordered him to secure the border with Spanish Florida and put an end to raids by tribes using that territory as a base. In 1818 Old Hickory marched into Florida, where he killed and captured Seminole Indians and punished runaway slaves who were hiding there. (Southern slaveowners could no more tolerate a haven for runaways than they could a staging ground for Indian raids.) In Spanish East Florida, he hanged two British citizens whom he had accused of fomenting Indian attacks. Then he marched to Pensacola and reprised his attack from the War of 1812. Jackson claimed he acted in response to "helpless women" killed along the frontier and babies in cradles "stained with the blood of innocence." Yet expansion was his zest; he even told Monroe that he was ready to conquer Cuba.

By hanging Britons and violating Spanish territory, Jackson risked provoking a war. The president, his cabinet, and Congress all debated what to do about Old Hickory. The House of Representatives moved to censure him, but his popularity prevailed and no reprisal was ever issued. Indeed, as much as Monroe criticized Jackson, he coveted Florida. He was familiar with Jackson's temperament and views before sending him on the sensitive frontier mission, and Jackson's invasion served the president's purpose by hastening Spain's agreement in 1819 to sell Florida to the United States.

In the wake of Jackson's triumph, crowds feted him in New York City, Baltimore, and elsewhere. In 1821 Monroe appointed him governor of Florida, but he served only four months before returning to Tennessee.

Because Jackson was a national hero, political leaders wanted him to run for president in 1824. At first he demurred, thinking his talents more military than presidential and longing for rest because he still suffered from his bullet wound, along with dysentery incurred during the Creek War. But in 1823 he returned to the U.S. Senate and set his sights on the presidency.

America had entered a new era, labeled the Age of the Common Man. All through the 1820s restrictions on voting by adult white males diminished as property qualifications were removed. As more people could vote, politicians used open conventions rather than closed caucuses to choose candidates. A competitive party system emerged as many voters tired of the dominant National Republicans, who had adopted the policies of the dying Federalists—namely, protective tariffs, a national bank, and a system that served an elite more than it did the common folk. Politicians ceased to distance themselves and actually campaigned; they shook hands, spoke at rallies, and coined slogans.

Historian Frederick Jackson Turner, writing in the late 1800s, attributed this democratic upsurge to the frontier, where elitist trappings gave way to egalitarian practices in a shift from finery to buckskin. Yet Jackson's wealth and that of other large landholders belied such an egalitarian image, and ambition revealed another feature of democracy: For every democratic idealist in tune with the people there existed a practical opportunist in tune with a self-serving agenda. The new system allowed for demagoguery and an upper class who controlled the emerging political parties and manipulated the voters. Historian Edward Pessen claims politics was "marked by extravagant campaign techniques, sordid manipulation, brilliant organization, [and] marvelous rhetorical flourishes."

Enter Andrew Jackson. He ran for president in 1824 as a Washington outsider in a four-way race, after the National Republicans shattered into factions. He finished first in both the popular and electoral vote, but he lacked a majority. Consequently, the election went to the House of Representatives, which chose John Quincy Adams to be president after one of the other candidates, Speaker of the House Henry Clay, threw his support to Adams. The new president then appointed Clay secretary of state.

Although no hard proof of a deal existed between Adams and Clay, Jackson cried foul, and his supporters called the Adams-Clay arrangement a "corrupt bargain." The people—the masses brought to life by democratic reform—had been denied their choice. Over the next four years Jackson's supporters, chief among them New York Senator Martin Van Buren, worked in Congress to block Adams, embarrass him, and elevate Jackson to the White House. They built the Democratic Party to accomplish their goal.

The 1828 presidential race produced more mud than a frontier downpour. The Adams campaign portrayed Jackson as uncouth and illiterate and they dredged up the old story that he had married Rachel before her divorce from Lewis Robards had been finalized. The scandalmongers called Rachel an adulteress, and the couple had to endure national exposure of an embarrassing moment in their lives.

For their part, the Jacksonians portrayed Adams as a procurer of women for the Russian czar when he was a minister to that country and as a profligate president who squandered the public's money on a billiard table for the White House, both blatantly false charges. The candidates avoided serious issues, but Jackson appealed to those who supported states' rights and limited government, important principles to the Democratic Party, though his record in Congress included support for a higher tariff and federal funding for roads and canals.

Old Hickory won with an electoral vote of 178 to 83. The election stimulated voter interest: 36.8 percent of those qualified to cast ballots did so in 1824, but 57.6 percent did so in 1828. Jackson saw his victory as expressing the will of the people, and he considered himself to be their direct representative. Consequently, he would speak for the entire nation.

Seeking loyalty, Jackson began appointing Democrats to federal jobs. Although previous presidents had also based their appointments on party allegiance and Jackson filled only about 20 percent of all government positions, his opponents derisively called his action the "spoils system," after a phrase used by New York Senator Marcy Tweed. Old Hickory defended his tactic, saying rotation in office prevented development of an entrenched bureaucracy unresponsive to the people.

Those who saw barbarity and vulgarity in Jackson believed they were justified when he appointed John Eaton secretary of war. Eaton was a wealthy lawyer who had served on Old Hickory's staff during the War of 1812 and had helped organize his presidential campaign. According to gossip, Eaton's wife, Margaret "Peggy" O'Neale, was nothing less than a harlot. In the years before her marriage to Eaton, this beautiful daughter of a boardinghouse keeper supposedly had engaged in sexual liaisons with several congressmen, after which, at age 16, she married John Timberlake, a navy purser. When Timberlake went to sea, John Eaton became Margaret's guardian, and soon the Washington rumor mill began spreading stories about the couple's affair. In 1828, after hearing the gossip, Timberlake died aboard ship. Some reports said he killed himself, but the cause of his death remains unclear.

John Eaton and Margaret married on January 1, 1829, well before the end of the traditional one-year grieving period. With Eaton's appointment as secretary of war, fellow cabinet members and their wives, horrified by Peggy's background, snubbed her—except, notably, for Secretary of State Martin Van Buren.

The imbroglio concerned more than morality; the Eaton affair involved an intense power struggle within the Jackson administration. For obscure reasons, Jackson blamed Vice President John C. Calhoun for attacking Eaton. Thus, those who condemned the secretary of war were considered to be pro-Calhoun. On the other side, those who defended him were considered pro-Van Buren. Because both Calhoun and Van Buren aspired to the presidency, whichever man emerged from the Eaton affair on top would be in a strong position to succeed Jackson.

It was Van Buren who determined a way to end the dispute and damage Calhoun. In 1831 he resigned, whereupon Eaton did the same. This allowed Jackson to dismiss his entire cabinet, ridding himself of the Calhoun allies who had opposed Eaton. Van Buren sailed to London as minister to Britain, while Calhoun watched his relations with Jackson sour, even more so after he led the Senate in rejecting Van Buren's appointment and forcing him to return to the United States.

When a dispute erupted over internal improvements, President Jackson appeared committed to states' rights. In 1830 Henry Clay wanted Congress to fund the Maysville Road, which would stretch from Maysville to Lexington in Kentucky, his home state. After Congress passed the bill in May, Jackson vetoed it. He did so less from a principled stand than a practical one: Although he called it wrong for Congress to finance an internal improvement that resided exclusively in one state, he wanted mainly to contain Clay's power and defeat a project coveted by his political opponents.

The president's veto may have emboldened John C. Calhoun, making him think Jackson would hold steadfastly to states' rights. In any event, Jackson and Calhoun tangled again, this time over an issue that threatened the country's survival. After Congress passed a high tariff, extreme states' righters in South Carolina, led by Calhoun, declared the act unconstitutional and claimed their state could nullify it. This, directly challenged Jackson's nationalist sentiments; he called nullification "abominable" and added that it "strikes at the root of our Government and the social compact, and reduces every thing to anarchy." Union would be impossible if every state could decide which federal laws to accept or reject.

Jackson decided on a two-pronged response: He pushed Congress to lower the tariff, while at the same time he readied the army and navy for a show of force against South Carolina. These measures, he believed, would discourage other states from joining the protest. When a new tariff reduced some of the rates but left South Carolina dissatisfied and a special state convention declared collection of the tariff duties illegal, he was convinced the intransigence had less to do with principle than with Calhoun's opportunism.

In December 1832, the same month Calhoun resigned as vice president to become senator from South Carolina, Jackson called for an additional tariff revision. At the same time, he issued a proclamation that called nullification a violation of the Constitution and declared the Union perpetual. He also guided the Force Bill through Congress, a symbolic measure that reaffirmed the president's right to use the military to quell any insurrection.

The crisis eased in January 1833 when South Carolina's political leaders announced postponement of nullification while Congress worked on the tariff revision. Calhoun, whom author Harriet Martineau called "the cast iron man who looks as if he had never been born, and never could be extinguished," joined Kentucky Senator Henry Clay to produce a compromise tariff, which Jackson signed on

March 1. That same day he signed the Force Bill. Years later Jackson said he wished he had hanged Calhoun for treason. "My country would have sustained me in the act," he said, "and his fate would have been a warning to traitors in all time to come."

This crisis revealed Andrew Jackson's strong attachment to a united nation. "I will die with the Union," he once said. He remained in favor of states' rights, but only up to a point, and South Carolina had exceeded that point. As his administration continued, he became more supportive of a stronger national government, perhaps in part because of his experience in the nullification showdown.

In championing the people's rights, Jackson took aim at the national bank, which he believed favored the powerful and the wealthy. With Jackson's reelection approaching in 1832, Nicholas Biddle, president of the bank, pushed Congress to issue a recharter four years ahead of schedule and make the institution a referendum in the election. After a heated debate, Congress obliged and sent a recharter bill to Jackson, who fumed about it. To Van Buren he said: "The bank . . . is trying to kill me. *But I will kill it!*" A few days later he vetoed the bill and Congress upheld him. If the bank had been allowed to continue, Jackson said, it would "make the rich richer and the potent more powerful." One Massachusetts congressman accused the president of engaging in class warfare; the veto, he said, "is found appealing to the worst passions of the uninformed part of the people, and endeavoring to stir up the poor against the rich."

Jackson went on to win reelection, though the bank issue may have cost him as many votes as it gained. At that point Old Hickory could have let the bank expire with the end of its charter in 1836, but he decided to kill it early. "The hydra of corruption," he said, "is only *scotched, not dead.*" After firing two treasury secretaries before finding a third, Roger Taney, who would follow his order, he removed all government funds from the bank. His action stirred outcries in Congress from those who thought Jackson had violated the Constitution. That a president could arbitrarily manipulate federal deposits, critics said, smacked of monarchy. Consequently, the Senate censored Jackson, but two years later the censure was expunged from the record.

Nicholas Biddle fought back. He tightened credit and called in loans to cause an economic panic and demonstrate the bank's power. This, he believed, would make Jackson back down. Biddle's tactic, however, ruined some of the bank's strongest supporters and forced *him* to back down. In the end, Jackson placed government funds in selected state banks—critics called them "pet banks"—in a move that loosened credit and produced inflation.

On the issue of Indians, President Jackson supported states' rights. After the Cherokee in northwest Georgia adopted white practices and a constitution in which they declared themselves a sovereign and independent nation, the state legislature decided it could no longer tolerate them. In December 1828, Georgia extended its jurisdiction over the Cherokee.

As a result, in his 1829 message to Congress Jackson presented a proposal to move the Indians to the West. He said, "I informed the Indians inhabiting parts of Georgia and Alabama, that their attempt to establish an independent government would not be countenanced by the Executive of the United States; and advised them to emigrate beyond the Mississippi, or submit to the laws of those States." Of course, to submit would mean the end to Indian culture. Settlers in Georgia wanted the Cherokee land, particularly since gold had been discovered on it. That they would never allow the Cherokee to govern themselves was evident in state laws that took all power from the chiefs and prohibited Indians from voting or even testifying in court.

Congress supported Jackson in 1830 by passing the Indian Removal Act. After the Supreme Court upheld Cherokee treaty rights to their southern homeland, Jackson declared that the Court "must not be permitted to control the Executive." He then ignored the ruling, and the removal began in 1832, first with the Creek Indians. Over six years more than 10,000 died from accidents, starvation, and freezing cold. In 1838 the military rounded up 17,000 Cherokee, evicted them from their homes at bayonet point, and sent them west along the "Trail of Tears." The removal killed about 25 percent of the Indians.

By then Andrew Jackson had left the presidency. During his last few days in office, in March 1837, he extended recognition to the Republic of Texas, which had won its independence from Mexico several months earlier. Ever the expansionist, he looked forward to the United States one day annexing Texas and acquiring more slave territory. Later that month he attended the inauguration of his hand-picked successor, Martin Van Buren. He then retired to his plantation home, The Hermitage, near Nashville, Tennessee. He still remained involved in politics, supporting Van Buren and later arranging for his protégé, James K. Polk, a fellow nationalist and expansionist, to obtain the Democratic presidential nomination in 1844. Jackson died on June 8, 1845.

Andrew Jackson's beloved Union suffered enormous pressure over the next few years, and the nullification doctrine he battled against found renewed popularity. But the democratized political system continued as a monument to the Age of the Common Man and the president who embodied its spirit. His legacy included the greater powers he assumed for the presidency by making himself the spokesperson for the people. In defending the popular will, Jackson vetoed more bills, 12 of them, than any previous president and used the threat of vetoes to shape legislation. These acts strengthened the executive branch at the expense of Congress.

Old Hickory's most prominent biographer, Robert V. Remini, says in *Andrew Jackson:* "It was Jackson who first explored the full dynamic potential of the American government. That potential largely depends on the initiative and aggressiveness of the chief executive, and none of the previous presidents had sought this kind of leadership while in office. Jackson was different."

Chronology

1767 Born March 15

1781 Captured by the British

1784 Begins law study

1788 Established law practice in Nashville

1790 Appointed attorney general of Western District of North Carolina

1791 Marries Rachel Robards

Appointed judge advocate of Davidson County militia

1796 Elected to U.S. House of Representatives

1797 Elected to U.S. Senate

1798 Elected judge of Tennessee superior court

1802 Elected major general of Tennessee militia

1804 Resigns judgeship

1806 Shot and wounded in duel

1812 Organizes volunteers to fight British and Indians

1814 Commissioned major general of U.S. Army

1815 Defeats British at Battle of New Orleans

1817 Commands forces in First Seminole War

1818 Captures St. Marks and Pensacola in Spanish East Florida

1821 Appointed governor of Florida territory

1823 Elected to U.S. Senate

1824 Loses presidential election

1828 Elected president

1829 Begins spoils system

1830 Vetoes Maysville Road Bill

Signs Indian Removal Act

1831 Breaks with John C. Calhoun over Eaton Affair

Reorganizes cabinet

1832 Vetoes bill for U.S. Bank recharter

Reelected president

1833 Approves Force Bill

Removes deposits from Bank of the United States

1835 Escapes assassination

1836 Backs Martin Van Buren as presidential candidate

1837 Recognizes Texas

Retires to The Hermitage in Nashville

1844 Backs James K. Polk for presidency

1845 Dies June 8

Further Reading

Cole, Donald B. *The Presidency of Andrew Jackson.* Lawrence: University Press of Kansas, 1993.

Ellis, Richard E. *The Union at Risk: Jacksonian Democracy, States' Rights, and the Nullification Crisis.* New York: Oxford University Press, 1987.

Latner, Richard B. *The Presidency of Andrew Jackson: White House Politics, 1829–1837.* Athens: University of Georgia Press, 1979.

Marquis, James. *The Life of Andrew Jackson.* Indianapolis, Ind.: Bobbs-Merrill, 1938.

Meyers, Marvin. *The Jacksonian Persuasion: Politics and Belief.* Stanford, Calif.: Stanford University Press, 1957.

O'Brien, Sean Michael. *In Bitterness and in Tears: Andrew Jackson's Destruction of the Creeks and Seminoles.* Westport, Conn.: Praeger, 2003.

Pessen, Edward. *Jacksonian America: Society, Personality, and Politics.* Homewood, Ill.: Dorsey Press, 1969.

Remini, Robert V. *Andrew Jackson.* New York: Harper and Row, 1966.

———. *Andrew Jackson and the Course of American Democracy, 1833–1845.* New York: Harper and Row, 1984.

———. *Andrew Jackson and the Course of American Empire, 1767–1821.* New York: Harper and Row, 1977.

———. *Andrew Jackson and the Course of American Freedom, 1822–1832.* New York: Harper and Row, 1981.

———. *Andrew Jackson and His Indian Wars.* New York: Viking, 2001.

———. *The Legacy of Andrew Jackson: Essays on Democracy, Indian Removal, and Slavery.* Baton Rouge: Louisiana State University Press, 1988.

Schlesinger, Arthur M., Jr. *The Age of Jackson.* Boston: Little, Brown, 1953.

Van Deusen, Glyndon G. *The Jacksonian Era, 1828–1848.* New York: Harper and Brothers, 1959.

Wallace, Anthony F. C. *The Long, Bitter Trail: Andrew Jackson and the Indians.* New York: Hill and Wang, 1993.

Watson, Harry L. *Liberty and Power: The Politics of Jacksonian America.* New York: Hill and Wang, 1990.

Martin Van Buren (1782–1862)

Eighth President, 1837–1841

Martin Van Buren
(engraving by Currier & Ives, Library of Congress)

"The . . . perhaps . . . greatest of the prominent sources of discord and disaster supposed to lurk in our political condition was the institution of domestic slavery. Our forefathers . . . treated it with a forbearance so evidently wise that in spite of every sinister foreboding it never until the present period disturbed the tranquility of our common country. . . . Have not recent events made it obvious to the slightest reflection that the least deviation from this spirit of forbearance is injurious to every interest, that of humanity included?"

—Inaugural words, March 4, 1837

"The Flying Dutchman," "The Red Fox," "The Little Magician"—Martin Van Buren went by several nicknames attesting to his character, astute and perceptive to some, sly and deceptive to others. Before becoming president, Van Buren reshaped American politics by promoting political parties and making the Democrats into a modern campaign organization. His appeal to the masses through populist tactics and his building of loyalty through a spoils system resulted, under Andrew Jackson, in a more powerful presidency than ever before. Van Buren's opportunism, however, made his own presidential administration weak and provided the blueprint used by his opponents to prevent his reelection.

Martin Van Buren's birth on December 5, 1782, to Abraham Van Buren and Maria Hoes Van Alen Van Buren in the Dutch town of Kinderhook, New York, made him the first president to be born after America's declaration of independence from Britain. His ancestors were indentured servants from the Netherlands, and his father a farmer and tavern keeper.

Martin attended local schools until age 14 and then studied law, first in Kinderhook, where he clerked in the firm of Francis Silvester, and then in New York City. As he developed an interest in politics, he supported the Republican Party and in 1800 campaigned for its presidential candidate, Thomas Jefferson, who attacked the opposition Federalists for being more concerned with serving the wealthy than the nation as a whole. Although far from a modern mass party, the Republicans hinted at the future with their appeal to a broad following, and Van Buren learned from their tactics.

Martin Van Buren was admitted to the bar in 1803 and began his law practice in Kinderhook as the partner of James Van Allen. He described himself as a lightweight intellectually, more inclined to political action. In 1807 he married a distant cousin, Hannah Hoes. They had four sons, but their marriage was cut short by Hannah's death in 1819.

Van Buren held a local office and won election in 1812 to the state senate on a platform criticizing the national bank, a recurring theme in his political career. He supported the War of 1812 and New York's building of the Erie Canal and sponsored a bill to abolish imprisonment for debt, a progressive measure opposed by many creditors. While continuing in the state senate, he served as attorney general from 1816 to 1819, at which time he prosecuted General William Hull for neglect of duty in surrendering Detroit to the British during the war. Although Van Buren won his case, President James Madison overturned Hull's sentence.

Van Buren aligned himself with the Bucktail faction among the Republicans and supported Jeffersonian principles based on limited government while opposing those in the party who compromised with the Federalists. At the same time he built a powerful political machine, known as the Albany Regency, which set party policy, managed campaigns, and maintained discipline through patronage. This meant government workers had to adhere to the party line or lose their jobs. Van Buren later applied these tactics to national politics. No more powerful a politician could be found in populous New York than the Dutchman from Kinderhook.

In 1821 Van Buren served as a delegate to the New York State constitutional convention, and the legislature elected him to the U.S. Senate. Three years later he managed Georgian William H. Crawford's unsuccessful campaign for the presidency. The race stimulated Van Buren and convinced him he could be a "president maker." He believed the answer to winning four years later and unseating John Quincy Adams lay in the organizational structure he had learned in New York and therefore in forming a cohesive political party.

Although political parties existed before Van Buren began his career, by the 1820s the Federalists had dissolved. This left only the National Republicans, who had fallen prey to factional squabbles so severe that John Quincy Adams, only a nominal Republican to begin with, presided over a weak, ineffectual party. Van Buren saw an opportunity. Unlike many Americans, including past presidents George Washington and Thomas Jefferson, who thought political parties evil or at best a necessary evil, Van Buren saw them as quite the opposite. "With fairness and moderation," he said, "the very discord which is . . . produced may . . . be conducive to the public good."

Particularly after the 1820 Missouri crisis, when Northerners and Southerners differed over whether that territory should be allowed to enter the Union as a slave state, Van Buren believed parties could maintain national unity by bringing sections of the country together while keeping slavery out of politics. He pointed out that "formerly attacks upon Southern Republicans were regarded by those of the north as assaults upon their political brethren & resented accordingly. This all powerful sympathy has been much weakened, if not, destroyed by the amalgamating policy of Mr. Monroe" and the demise of a two-party system. In other words, Northerners and Southerners together in the same party would refrain from attacking each other over slavery, or any other issue, for fear of tearing the party apart.

Reelected to the Senate in 1827, Van Buren pledged himself to "protect the remaining rights reserved to the states by the federal constitution [and] to restore those of which they have been divested by construction." He then applied his political insight and helped put together an effective coalition for the upcoming 1828 presidential contest, the Democratic Party. He wanted the Democrats to unite southern planters with "plain Republicans" in the North.

Historian Robert V. Remini observes that "The making of the Democratic Party . . . was largely the work of Martin Van Buren. . . . It was Van Buren who joined together the different sections of the country and united the followers of [John C.] Calhoun and [William] Crawford with the Jacksonians. It was he who tried to draw the East and West closer together. It was he who renewed the alliance between the North and South that lasted until 1860." Van Buren toured the South in 1827, where his meeting with prominent politicians solidified the alliance he sought.

The Democrats attached themselves to Jeffersonian principles and embraced a limited national government. This was in stark contrast to the highly nationalistic program advocated by John Quincy Adams, who wanted the federal government to fund projects as wide-ranging as canals and astronomical observatories. To a certain extent, Van Buren's party chose opportunism over principles. Van Buren wanted Andrew Jackson to be its standard bearer more because of his popular appeal as a military hero from the War of 1812 than his stand on any issues. Yet too much can be made of this. Van Buren would never have supported or promoted Jackson if the general had shown himself opposed to Jeffersonian ideas. According to Remini, Van Buren turned to Jackson "because he could use the General to . . . eliminate Federalist principles from the national government"—principles that advanced federal power over that of the states.

The Democrats worked to build mass support at a time when the removal of property qualifications meant that most adult white males could vote. Rallies, parades, and slogans became their tools, as did mud-slinging when they portrayed John Quincy Adams as a president intent on raiding the public treasury. The Adams campaign retaliated by presenting Jackson as an illiterate adulterer.

To help Andrew Jackson win New York, Van Buren relinquished his Senate seat in 1828 and ran for governor, placing his name, with its strong appeal in his home state, on the Democratic ticket alongside Jackson's. Van Buren's tactics carried the day, and Jackson was elected president. A new era began in politics as the appeal to the common folk unlocked the door to the White House. Others would soon copy the Democrats.

Van Buren served as governor for only two months in 1829 before Jackson named him secretary of state. He received widespread acclaim when he negotiated a settlement with Britain over trade in the West Indies and obtained an agreement with Turkey granting America access to the Black Sea.

Van Buren's prominence within Jackson's administration came from his close relationship with the president. He worked indefatigably behind the scenes for Jackson and outdistanced all others in the cabinet and among the president's advisers in influence. One observer commented about Van Buren: "He glides along as smoothly as oil and silently as a cat, managing so adroitly that nobody perceives it." With his cautious and often compromising ways, Van Buren counterbalanced Jackson's impetuous and stubborn character.

The New Yorker strengthened the Democratic Party and Jackson's administration by developing the spoils system, under which appointment to office depended in large measure on party loyalty. Critics called it corrupt, but Van Buren defended it, saying that it ensured Jackson's administration would be responsive to the people.

Martin Van Buren displayed his political cunning in a crisis called the Eaton Affair, which threatened to destroy Jackson's presidency and Van Buren's own hopes of succeeding to the White House. After Jackson appointed John Eaton secretary of war, all other cabinet members, except Van Buren, decided to snub Eaton's wife, Peggy, for a supposedly checkered sexual past. Those who ostracized Peggy were linked with Vice President John C. Calhoun, who, like Van Buren, wanted to become president. To end the dispute and weaken Calhoun, Van Buren resigned in 1831. This allowed Jackson to ask for resignations from all his department heads, purge the Calhoun faction, and appoint a new cabinet.

President Jackson then made Van Buren minister to Britain. Calhoun struck back, however, when he broke a tie in the Senate over whether to confirm the New Yorker's appointment by voting nay. Calhoun thought he had ruined Van Buren's political career, but he reappeared when Jackson, angered by Calhoun's action, chose Van Buren to be his running mate in 1832. As vice president, Van Buren resumed his advisory role to Jackson and presided over the same body, the Senate, that had denied him his ministerial appointment. When the smoke of the political battle with Calhoun had cleared, Van Buren was in an even stronger position to become the next president.

With Andrew Jackson's full support, Martin Van Buren obtained the Democratic nomination for president in 1836. Opponents of Jacksonian democracy tried to prevent his ascension by forming the Whig Party and running three candidates for president: westerner William Henry Harrison, New Englander Daniel Webster, and Southerner Hugh L. White, each with a strong following in his own geographic section. They called Jackson "King Andrew I" and claimed Van Buren would simply be the outgoing president's puppet.

During the campaign, Van Buren criticized the national banks and opposed federal funding for internal improvements, which he thought best left to the states. He stood against the abolition of slavery in Washington, D.C., unless the South agreed to it and against ending slavery where it already existed. Together the Whig candidates polled 739,795 popular votes, but Van Buren obtained 765,483, along with a majority of the electoral vote. The result revealed two political parties closely matched rather than a resounding triumph for Jackson's policies.

Opinions about the new president corresponded to the prevailing sharp differences in politics. John Quincy Adams, long a critic of Jackson and Van Buren, once stated: "There are many features in the character of Mr. Van Buren strongly resembling that of Mr. [James] Madison—his calmness, his gentleness of manner, his discretion, his easy and conciliatory temper. But Madison had none of his obsequiousness, his sycophancy, his profound dissimulation and duplicity."

Andrew Jackson observed quite differently: "Instead of his being selfish and intriguing, as has been represented by some of his opponents, I have found him frank, open, candid, and manly. As a Counsellor he is able and prudent . . . and one of the most pleasant men to do business with I ever saw." Critics claimed Van Buren was ineffective in controlling subordinates;

supporters called him skillful in managing others. All agreed that the short, plump, balding man, known as an exquisite dresser and connoisseur of fine wine, presented a cheerful countenance and a firm attachment to Jacksonian politics.

At his inauguration Van Buren reiterated his campaign position on slavery, stressed the importance of national unity, and described the United States as enjoying a prosperity "surely not elsewhere to be found." As it turned out, economic issues vexed his presidency after a severe depression hit in 1837. The causes of the downturn were several. First, an economic collapse in England lowered the overseas demand for American cotton and dropped prices from 17.5 cents per pound to 13.5 cents, devastating not only the South but also the North and West, whose economies were linked to southern commerce. Second, excessive speculation in land and in stocks on Wall Street encouraged unsound economic practices.

Finally, Jacksonian policy contributed to the collapse. Andrew Jackson had destroyed the national bank, and with this controlling influence gone, state banks made risky loans at high interest rates that caused inflation. As prices climbed 50 percent in the 1830s, President Jackson tried to dampen inflation and speculation by having Congress pass the Specie Circular, which said the federal government would only accept gold and silver in payment for public land. Although the circular reduced speculation as intended, it made land more difficult for common people to buy and became the most unpopular Jackson program.

Now Van Buren reaped the impact of his predecessor's policies and inherited an economic mess. Yet he had supported Jackson and in particular had endorsed the president's decision to kill the national bank.

As the depression worsened, President Van Buren called a special session of Congress, which met in September 1837. In his message to those assembled he called for action but then laid out his belief in limited government. He said, "All communities are apt to look to government for too much. Even in our own country, where its powers and duties are so strictly limited, we are prone to do so, especially at periods of sudden embarrassment and distress." He went on to say that government should not be considered a source of relief from the depression and added the founding fathers had "wisely judged that the less government interferes with private pursuits the better for the general prosperity."

The Whigs were perplexed and thought his argument contorted and limited. Senator Daniel Webster said, "I feel as if I were in some other sphere, as if I were not at home, as if this could not be America when I see schemes of public policy proposed, having for their object the convenience of Government only, and leaving the people to shift for themselves."

The president did propose to change the banking system when he asked Congress to establish an Independent Treasury so the federal government could deposit its money in its own vaults rather than in selected state banks. Van Buren believed this would protect federal funds from those state banks that were using the money for speculative purposes. The Whigs opposed him; they claimed the plan would make recovery more difficult by taking specie out of circulation and making loans and credit tighter. To them Van Buren seemed to be straddling the fence, trying to correct the bad policy that had destroyed the national bank but failing to develop a proposal that honestly admitted the mistake and completely corrected it. They wanted the national bank restored.

Many conservative Democrats broke with Van Buren on the issue for another reason: They wanted the federal government to continue using the state banks. This faction combined with the Whigs to defeat the Independent Treasury in the House by a vote of 120-106. Whig leader Henry Clay then tried to reestablish the national bank but failed.

The depression encouraged factional fighting among Democrats—a constant hindrance for Van Buren—and provided the Whigs with political ammunition. They made large gains in the 1837 elections, and in Van Buren's home state of New York they won control of the assembly.

In foreign affairs President Van Buren skillfully handled two disputes with Britain. In 1837 dissidents in Canada revolted against British rule. Those Americans who wanted Canada to become a part of the United States sympathized with the rebels; some even formed clubs to support them with arms and men. In December 1837 Canadian militia attacked a private American ship, the *Caroline,* used in smuggling military supplies. This resulted in the death of an American. During the following year Canadian rebels launched several raids against the British from American soil. Van Buren cooled Britain's anger by making it clear that Americans had no right to invade Canada, and that those who did would receive no help from their government if they were captured.

At the same time a dispute involving the border between Maine and Canada nearly erupted into fighting. The 1783 Treaty of Paris, by which Britain recognized America's independence, had left the border unclear. At stake was about 12,000 square miles of valuable timber land in the Aroostook region. After the United States refused to accept a decision arbitrated by the Netherlands, residents of Maine and the Canadian province of New Brunswick began arming themselves, and Congress allocated $10 million for defense while authorizing the president to call up 50,000 volunteers.

Working with General Winfield Scott, who was appointed as an emissary, Van Buren convinced the governor of Maine to withdraw his militia from the Aroostook, and when New Brunswick agreed to restrain itself, the tension lessened. In 1842, after Van Buren left the presidency, the Webster-Ashburton Treaty established a compromise line by which Maine received 7,000 of the 12,000 square miles in dispute.

Although the economy improved in 1838 after repeal of the Specie Circular, in 1839 it took another plunge and would remain depressed for five years. Cotton prices hit new lows, textile mills in Lowell, Massachusetts, stood idle, and an estimated 50,000 unemployed in New York City sank into poverty. Civic leader Philip Hone observed: "Business of all kinds is completely at a stand, and the whole body politic sick and infirm, and calling aloud for remedy."

The Whigs demanded a protective tariff, federal funding for internal improvements, and expansion of the banking system. In those states where they governed, they increased the number of banks and enlarged the supply of paper money.

In Washington, Van Buren finally convinced Congress in 1840 to establish his Independent Treasury. The measure produced neither relief nor disaster. According to historian Glyndon G. Van Deusen, it "made no fundamental contribution either to financial stability or to the search for a uniform currency."

As much as Van Buren thought a political party system would foster national unity by making it unwise to touch the sensitive slave issue and risk alienating voters, events worked to heighten sectional tension. After the House of Representatives passed five gag rules in the late 1830s and 1840s (the last one being repealed in 1844) that prohibited Congress from considering any petitions dealing with slavery, abolitionist protests grew louder and stronger. Southerners reacted with an uncompromising defense of slavery made more strident when the Underground Railroad continued to transport runaway slaves from the South and when the state of New York refused to extradite three African Americans accused of stealing slaves.

Because of the heated atmosphere, Van Buren tried to avoid antagonizing Southerners. He condemned the continued illegal importation of slaves from Africa but did little to stop it. When the Cuban ship *Amistad* arrived near Long Island, New York, bearing mutinous slaves under transport from Africa to the Caribbean, he instructed the government to argue in district court that the slaves should be returned to their owners. The court, however, ordered the slaves released. Van Buren appealed the decision to the Supreme Court but lost again, and the Africans were set free.

Much as Van Buren had plotted in the 1820s to deny John Quincy Adams reelection, the Whigs plotted in the 1830s to deny the same to him. They copied Van Buren's tactics with precision. They accused him of living in luxurious splendor at the taxpayers' expense. One Whig congressman said the president used finger bowls to dip his "pretty tapering soft, white lily fingers, after dining on fricandaus de veau and omelet soufflé." Where the Democrats had charged Adams in 1828 with buying a billiard table for the White House, the Whigs charged Van Buren with spending $1,000 on a gardener's salary. That a heating system was installed in the drafty White House during Van Buren's presidency, along with copper bathtubs, lent credence to the Whig attack.

Much as the Democrats had turned to a frontier military hero, Andrew Jackson, as their presidential candidate in 1828, the Whigs selected William Henry Harrison, famous for his victory over the Indians at Tippecanoe. They selected Virginian John Tyler as his running mate, leading to the slogan "Tippecanoe and Tyler Too!" Although the Whigs refused to write a campaign platform, they stood for federal funding of internal improvements, protective tariffs, and a national bank, while Van Buren opposed them on these issues and defended the Independent Treasury.

The election relied mainly on creating simple images. Harrison was portrayed as close to the people and as a common frontiersman. (He actually lived on a large plantation.) The Whigs said Martin Van Buren should more accurately be called Martin Van Ruin, in light of the economic depression. They also accused the president of being a fence sitter, demonstrated by his refusal to take controversial stands so he could maintain political coalitions.

Harrison won easily, carrying 19 of the 26 states. Van Buren tried again for the Democratic nomination in 1844 but blundered and lost to James K. Polk when he angered Andrew Jackson by opposing the annexation of Texas. Four years later Van Buren voiced his opposition to slavery and ran for president as the candidate of the Free Soil Party. He won no electoral votes, but by splitting the Democratic Party in New York, he helped elect Zachary Taylor, the Whig nominee.

In his later years, Van Buren oversaw his Lindenwald estate in New York and traveled to Europe, where he bought fine clothes and presumably ate omelet soufflés without recrimination. After the Civil War began, he expressed support for Abraham Lincoln, but he died before the war ended, on July 24, 1862. Although as president he proved weaker and less popular than Andrew Jackson and lived in his predecessor's shadow, he left an enduring legacy in building the Democratic Party, stimulating a competitive two-party system, and developing the techniques of modern campaigning.

Chronology

1782 Born December 5

1796 Becomes clerk in law firm of Francis Silvester

1801 Works in New York law office as a clerk

1803 Admitted to the bar

Becomes law partner of James Van Allen

1807 Marries Hannah Hoes

1812 Elected to New York state senate

1816 Reelected senator

Chosen attorney general of New York

1821 Attends third New York State constitutional convention

Elected to U.S. Senate

1824 Backs William H. Crawford for president

1827 Reelected senator

1828 Backs Andrew Jackson for president

Elected governor of New York

1829 Appointed secretary of state

1831 Resigns as secretary of state

1832 Appointment as minister to Britain rejected by Senate

Elected vice president

1836 Elected president

1837 Proposes Independent Treasury

Lessens tension over *Caroline* incident

1839 Sends General Winfield Scott to Maine to negotiate truce

1840 Signs Independent Treasury bill

Loses reelection

1841 Retires to Kinderhook

1844 Loses bid for Democratic presidential nomination

1848 Runs unsuccessfully for president on Free Soil ticket

1862 Dies July 24

Further Reading

Benson, Lee. *The Concept of Jacksonian Democracy: New York as a Test Case.* Princeton, N.J.: Princeton University Press, 1961.

Cole, Donald B. *Martin Van Buren and the American Political System.* Princeton, N.J.: Princeton University Press, 1984.

Curtis, James C. *Andrew Jackson and the Search for Vindication.* Boston: Little, Brown, 1976.

———. *The Fox at Bay: Martin Van Buren and the Presidency 1837–1841.* Lexington: University of Kentucky Press, 1970.

Gunderson, Robert G. *The Log Cabin Campaign.* Lexington: University of Kentucky Press, 1957.

Niven, John. *Martin Van Buren: The Romantic Age of American Politics.* New York: Oxford University Press, 1983.

Remini, Robert V. *Martin Van Buren and the Making of the Democratic Party.* New York: Columbia University Press, 1959.

Van Deusen, Glyndon G. *The Jacksonian Era, 1828–1848.* New York: Harper, 1959.

Widmer, Ted. *Martin Van Buren.* New York: Times Books, 2005.

Wilson, Major. *The Presidency of Martin Van Buren.* Lawrence: University Press of Kansas, 1984.

William Henry Harrison (1773–1841)

Ninth President, March–April 1841

William Henry Harrison
(Library of Congress)

> *"It may be observed . . . that republics can commit no greater error than to adopt or continue any feature in their systems of government which may be calculated to create or increase the lover of power in the bosoms of those to whom necessity obliges them to commit the management of their affairs. . . . I . . . [renew] the pledge heretofore given that under no circumstances will I consent to serve a second term."*
>
> —Inaugural words, March 4, 1841

When William Henry Harrison ran for president in 1840 his campaign stimulated more excitement than any previous one. Parades, slogans, whiskey, and songs rallied voters who saw in him a common man risen to the ranks of a military hero. On election day more than 80 percent of all eligible voters turned out, and in a close popular vote they chose him over the incumbent, Martin Van Buren. They had high hopes that Harrison would lead America out of a deep economic depression and speak for the common folk more forcibly than did established politicians. Those hopes were quickly dashed when, one month after his inauguration, he died. "In memory of President Wm. H. Harrison," a funeral ribbon said, "Deeply lamented by 16 millions of people."

William Henry Harrison's heritage was far different from the image of him as a simple farmer presented to the public in 1840. He was born on February 9, 1773, to Benjamin Harrison and Elizabeth Bassett Harrison at a manor house called Berkeley on the James River in Virginia, 24 miles east of Richmond. The distinguished Byrd family's Westover mansion stood nearby, and on the opposite side of the James stood the Brandon mansion, occupied by others in the Harrison family. The Harrisons played an important role in Virginia's settlement, some having served in the House of Burgesses. William's father, Benjamin, owned thousands of acres and many slaves. When the colonies moved toward revolution, Benjamin Harrison served in the Continental Congress and signed the Declaration of Independence.

With his father active on the Patriot side, William met the marquis de Lafayette and George Washington when they stayed at Berkeley. In 1781, at age nine, he watched British troops as they marched through his father's plantation, burning furniture and destroying other property. Soon after, Benjamin Harrison fought with the Virginia militia in the defeat of the British at Yorktown. After the Revolution, the elder Harrison served three terms as governor.

William's early education consisted of tutoring before he attended Hampden-Sidney College in the Blue Ridge Mountains. He left there in 1789 to study medicine under Dr. Benjamin Rush, the nation's leading physician, in Philadelphia. This choice, though, was more his father's than his own, and soon after Benjamin Harrison died in April 1791, the affable young man decided to join the army. As a lieutenant on duty in the Northwest Territory he directed the building of two forts in 1793–94, and under General Anthony Wayne he fought at Fallen Timbers against a combined force of British troops and about 1,000 Indians, helping to achieve an important American victory.

In 1795 Harrison married Anna Tuthill Symmes, daughter of a prosperous local farmer and judge. They had 10 children. Harrison resigned from the army in 1798 and accepted appointment as secretary of the Northwest Territory, a rugged frontier region under constant turmoil from battles between Indians and non-Indians. One year later he was elected the territory's first delegate to Congress.

Although it was a nonvoting position, a territorial delegate could make recommendations, and in December 1799 Harrison suggested a study of the land distribution system important to the Northwest. Congress agreed, and he chaired a special committee that recommended land be sold in small plots to reduce the role of speculators and enhance the individual's opportunity to own a homestead. Where the Land Act of 1796 had stipulated that 50 percent of the territory's land be sold in tracts of 5,770 acres and the rest in tracts of 640 acres, Harrison's bill allowed land to be sold in tracts of 320 acres at just $2 an acre. Northwesterners applauded this substantial reform, modified slightly by the Senate on its way to passage. At the same time Harrison helped Congress devise a plan to divide the Northwest Territory in two, creating the Indiana (comprising present-day Indiana, Illinois, Michigan, and Wisconsin), and Ohio territories.

In recognition of his prominent role in developing the Northwest, in 1800 Harrison was appointed governor of Indiana Territory, a position he held for 12 years. With the governorship came substantial power to formulate policy, and Harrison had the difficult task of maintaining peaceful relations with the Indians while acquiring more land from them for white settlement. He often disliked the way whites treated Indians and said if he were an Indian he would be resentful. Nevertheless, he skillfully negotiated treaties that resulted in the territory obtaining millions of acres, as was the case with the 1809 Treaty of Fort Wayne, signed with the Miami, Potawatomi, and Lenni Lenape (Delaware) tribes.

This treaty and the continuing white intrusion onto Indian lands angered two Shawnee brothers, Tecumseh and Tenskwatawa (known as the Prophet), who united several tribes in a confederation. Tecumseh refused to recognize the Fort Wayne treaty and told Harrison that if he entered Indian Territory it would result in "bad consequences."

The consequences soon followed. In spring 1811 Harrison began training more than 1,000 volunteer and regular soldiers. He was subsequently appointed general, and that August he received orders to march north through the Wabash River Valley. He was told to meet with the Indians and try to arrange a peaceful settlement; if the Indians refused, he was to attack and destroy their confederation. With Tecumseh away, Harrison led his men toward the Prophet's encampment. On November 6 he negotiated an armistice with the Prophet's messenger and camped out along the Tippecanoe River.

Early the following morning, with the sky still dark, the Indians attacked; Harrison's men barely withstood the assault. A bullet went through the general's hat, and another grazed his skull. "Indians were in the Camp before many of my men could get out of their tents," he later reported. "Confusion for a short time prevailed, but aided by the great activities of the officers, I was soon enabled to form the men in order. . . ." Harrison repelled the attack with a bayonet charge, and swords, tomahawks, muskets, and battle axes all clashed in a fierce engagement. The following day his men entered the Prophet's encampment and burned it.

The victory, which dealt the Indian confederation a mortal blow, cost Harrison 188 casualties. At the time it raised questions as to whether he had blundered; as the years passed and white settlers overran more Indian land, the battle at Tippecanoe assumed epic proportions, with Harrison a heroic leader.

Tippecanoe won William Henry Harrison a powerful supporter in Washington: Kentucky congressman Henry Clay. When the War of 1812 began, Clay obtained for Harrison a commission as brigadier general in the regular army, and later general commander of the army of the Northwest. After Oliver Hazard Perry's fleet defeated the British on Lake Erie, Harrison marched north and encountered a combined British-Indian army, with the Indians led by Tecumseh, at the Thames River on October 15, 1813. Tecumseh was killed during the battle, a rare victory for the Americans in a war mostly known for its botched military strategy.

When the War of 1812 ended, Harrison returned to his farm near Cincinnati, Ohio, and in 1816 he won election to the U.S. House of Representatives. He served one term and then was elected to the Ohio senate in 1819. After he was defeated for reelection, he again went back to his farm. In 1825 he won election to the U.S. Senate, where he supported federal funding of internal improvements. He argued for extending the Cumberland Road, which began in Maryland and traversed the Appalachian Mountains, saying it would benefit the entire nation. In fall 1827 he called for a protective tariff and supported the nationalist president, John Quincy Adams, for reelection. His service in the Senate provided an outline for his later presidential agenda: an activist national government committed to promoting business interests and economic expansion.

Harrison's Senate term was cut short when, with the help of Henry Clay, he was appointed minister to Colombia in 1828. Clay acted partly from friendship, but mainly from an ulterior motive: Harrison wanted to be John Quincy Adams's running mate that year, and if that happened and Adams won, it would position Harrison for the presidency. Clay, however, coveted the White House for himself and by sending Harrison to Colombia he hoped to thwart him. As it turned out, John Quincy Adams lost the 1828 election.

During the 1820s American politics underwent great change. The lowering of property qualifications for voting meant nearly all adult white males could cast ballots. This encouraged an opportunistic system geared to winning the popular vote, as first developed by the Democratic Party. Using such tactics, the Democrats ran Andrew Jackson for the presidency in 1828 and won. By the mid-1830s, however, Jackson's policies had antagonized those who thought the presidency too strong and who for a variety of reasons—everything from seeing their hopes for appointment to political office ruined to having their principles violated—disagreed with Jackson's policies.

These dissatisfied political leaders formed the Whig Party to oppose the Democrats and win the presidency. The Whigs were a curious combination. Many were refugees from the fading National Republican Party who wanted a federal government that would charter a national bank, fund internal improvements, and support a protective tariff as measures to help business and expand the economy. Others were states' righters who thought President Jackson had sold them out with his stand against South Carolina's nullification principle, and still others were Democrats disgruntled with Jackson's destruction of the national bank. Despite its internal differences, the Whig Party's dislike for Jackson held it together. Whigs especially opposed his accretion of power at the expense of Congress, as well as his attempt to form a coalition of northern businessmen and southern planters to govern America.

Although the Whigs distrusted the masses, they concluded that to win office they had to copy the populist Democratic tactics. In 1836 they decided to run three candidates for the presidency, thinking they could defeat Democratic nominee Martin Van Buren, Jackson's vice president, by preventing any one person from gaining a majority in the electoral college. This would throw the election into the House of Representatives, where they expected to broker a victory. Consequently, they ran Hugh L. White of Tennessee, Daniel Webster of Massachusetts, and William Henry Harrison, at that time holder of a minor political office, clerk of the Cincinnati Court of Common Pleas. Their strategy failed, but Harrison won 73 electoral votes, far more than the other Whig candidates.

President Van Buren encountered serious political problems when an economic depression began soon after his inauguration. As the 1840 election approached, the Whigs sensed they had a good chance for victory. Henry Clay, then a senator, fully expected to win the Whig nomination and reside the following year in the White House. He wrote to a friend: "Our cause everywhere is making sure and certain progress, my *particular* cause could hardly be improved."

But many Whigs worried about nominating Clay. In political parlance, they thought he came with too much "baggage." His outspoken call for a new national bank antagonized too many people; his ownership of slaves displeased Northerners critical of the practice; his defeat in the 1832 presidential election made him appear to be a loser.

When Daniel Webster threw his support for the presidential nomination to William Henry Harrison, Clay's candidacy faltered. Then New York political boss Thurlow Weed began working for Harrison's nomination. At the Whig national convention in Harrisburg, Pennsylvania, in December 1839, Clay commanded a plurality of the delegates, but Weed slyly maneuvered a change in the voting procedure that gave Harrison the advantage and the victory.

Neither Weed nor any other Harrison backer thought much about the general's views, as long as they fit what the Whigs wanted. They chose Harrison precisely because few people knew where he stood—a shift away from Clay's baggage to no baggage at all—and because they thought they could promote him as a military hero and frontiersman, just as the Democrats had done with Andrew Jackson. One Whig leader said, "Let no Committee, no convention, no town meeting, ever extract from him a single word about what he thinks now or what he will do hereafter."

Parades, rallies, and songs saturated the Harrison campaign. These devices were used to avoid the issues and make "Old Tip," as newspapers called him, a folk hero. "Tippecanoe and Tyler, Too!" Whigs chanted to remind voters of Harrison's greatest military victory and of his running mate, John Tyler of Virginia. One image for the campaign actually came from a Democratic newspaper that scoffed at the idea of the general becoming president: "Harrison for President! Why, he's just a backwoodsman. He eats corn pone and drinks cider. His mother still lives in a log cabin." Harrison's promoters jumped on the statement and gleefully portrayed him as a hard cider and log cabin man, completely submerging his aristocratic origins and his wealth.

Everywhere it could, the Harrison campaign draped its man in the symbols of the frontier. At one rally, a speaker sitting with the candidate on a platform rose and said:

> Log cabins, sirs, were the dwelling places of the founders of our Republic! It was a log cabin that sheltered the daring pioneers of liberty. . . . It was in view of the rock of Plymouth, my friends, that the Puritans of New England first erected the log cabins which sheltered the mothers and fathers of a race which now overspreads a continent.

The crowd hooted and cheered: "Tippecanoe and Tyler, Too!"

For his part, Harrison contributed to the image making. He wrote in 1840: "I would have preferred to remain with my family in . . . *our log cabin* . . . rather than become engaged in political or other disputes." As Tippecanoe clubs sprang up around the country, E. G. Booz, a Philadelphia distiller whose name soon would be indelibly attached to liquor, distributed whiskey in cabin-shaped bottles. Log cabins, whiskey, frontier masculinity . . . all of this contrasted Harrison with the incumbent Democrat Martin Van Buren, and a Whig song brought the differences to life:

> *Let Van from his coolers of silver drink wine,*
> *And lounge on his cushioned settee,*
> *Our man on a buckeye bench can recline,*
> *Content with hard cider he.*

While Van Buren explicitly opposed nationalistic projects such as internal improvements and argued against any interference with slavery, the Whigs never even bothered writing a platform. One Democrat compared the Whigs to the image of Nebuchadnezzar, "made of clay and brass and various materials, a single stone must shatter it to pieces."

As the Democrats and Whigs sidestepped the issue of slavery, those who considered human bondage morally reprehensible formed the Liberty Party and ran James G. Birney for president. Birney won few votes, but the party's appearance signaled an abolitionist storm brewing on the political horizon.

In the huge turnout of more than 80 percent of all eligible voters, Harrison polled 1,275,612 votes, a narrow margin over Van Buren's 1,130,033. But in the electoral college Harrison won handily, with 234 votes to Van Buren's 60. Harrison had once said, "To be esteemed eminently great it is necessary to be eminently good." He would now try to apply that maxim to the country's highest office.

At age 67 the oldest man ever to be elected president, Harrison headed east for Washington in the spring of 1841 on a grueling trip made more difficult when crowds greeted him with ringing bells, receptions, and nearly endless dinners. He had shaken thousands of hands during the campaign, and he shook many more in the days before his inauguration.

Former president and congressman John Quincy Adams, frequently critical of others, said about Harrison: "His popularity is all artificial. There is little confidence in his talents or firmness." If by *artificial* Adams meant an appeal to the masses as opposed to an educated elite, he had assessed the situation accurately. The enthusiasm surrounding Harrison's inauguration reached feverish heights; frequent ceremonies and a constant flow of office seekers besieged the president-elect. In an expression of cordiality, President Van Buren invited Harrison to the White House for dinner and subsequently said about his successor: "He talks and thinks with . . . much ease and vivacity. . . . He is as tickled with the Presidency as is a young woman with a new bonnet."

The activity took its toll, though, and wore Harrison down. On March 4, 1841, without an overcoat and hat, Old Tip rode on horseback to his inauguration on a gray, rainy, and raw day. He presented his address to the largest inauguration crowd ever, more than 50,000 people, and spoke for longer than 90 minutes.

In his speech he offered an idea of how his administration would operate. He said executive power would be wielded sparingly, and he vowed to serve only one term. The president, Harrison cautioned, should never intrude on Congress, and while he would recommend legislation written by others, he would never be the source of it. In a rebuke to Andrew Jackson's arbitrary removal of federal funds from the national bank, he insisted Congress should control revenues.

In another contrast to Jackson, he promised to use the veto sparingly, mainly to protect against violations of the Constitution. He criticized the spoils system, by which government bureaucrats were appointed according to their party loyalty, and in another dig at Jackson who had removed two treasury secretaries in his effort to kill the national bank, Harrison promised never to remove a treasury secretary without a full accounting to Congress.

Harrison's emphasis on congressional power reflected Whig principles and, combined with his friendly personality, made it appear he could be easily pushed around. Some said the real president would be powerful Kentucky senator Henry Clay. Harrison contributed to this view and displayed considerable diffidence when he said shortly before entering the White House that if the Constitution allowed it, he would be happy to relinquish the presidency to Clay and return to his farm.

Clay indeed tried to exert control when he told Harrison whom to appoint as treasury secretary, but Old Tip rebuffed him and in a heated exchange supposedly said to the Kentuckian: "Mr. Clay, you forget that *I* am the President." When Clay pressed Harrison to call a special session of Congress to consider economic issues that would ease the depression, the president at first refused. He may have realized that a special session would put Clay in the limelight. To Clay's protests he said, "You are too impetuous." But after a report from the treasury revealed a looming revenue shortfall, Harrison changed his mind and called the session for May.

The Whigs planned for Harrison's cabinet to govern in concert with Congress, in effect making the president a mere single vote among many. By late March, though, Harrison was having trouble with this arrangement and showed signs of wanting to take greater control.

Then, as the crush of office seekers continued to sap his energy, he caught a cold, one that may have festered since his inauguration, and in the closing days of March it turned to pneumonia. The treatment he received almost assured he would die. To the consternation of more progressive physicians, the attending doctors bled the president; then they fed him opium, camphor, brandy, and Serpentaria, the root of the Virginia snake weed. His death came a few hours after midnight on April 4, 1841. His last spoken words were reported to be: "I wish you to understand the true principles of the government. I wish them carried out. I ask nothing more."

For the first time, America faced the crisis of a president's death in office. In choosing John Tyler to be Harrison's running mate, the Whigs had hardly considered his suitability for the presidency. They had picked him because he came from a populous state, Virginia, and because his states' rights views and ownership of slaves appealed to the more conservative wing of the party. Now their choice would resound in ways never expected.

William Henry Harrison occupied the White House for too short a time to leave a notable presidential legacy, but his 1840 campaign continued the popularization of politics begun under Andrew Jackson and refined modern campaign tactics. Even more, it demonstrated the growing tendency of the masses in a democratic country to consider themselves the makers, or breakers, of their presidents.

Chronology

1773 Born February 9

1787 Enters Hampden-Sidney College

1789 Studies medicine under Dr. Benjamin Rush

1790 Enlists in U.S. Infantry

1795 Marries Anna Symmes

1798 Resigns from army
Appointed secretary of Northwest Territory

1799 Elected U.S. representative from Northwest Territory
Proposes changes to Northwest Territory land system

1802 Granted power to make treaties with Indians

1809 Negotiates Treaty of Fort Wayne

1811 Defeats Indians in Battle of Tippecanoe

1812 Appointed supreme commander in the Northwest

1813 Wins Battle of the Thames

1816 Elected to U.S. House of Representatives

1819 Elected to Ohio senate

1825 Elected to U.S. Senate

1828 Named minister to Colombia

1836 Defeated for president

1840 Elected president

1841 Dies April 4

Further Reading

Cleaves, Freeman. *Old Tippecanoe: William Henry Harrison and His Time.* New York: Scribner's, 1939.

Green, James A. *William Henry Harrison and His Times.* Richmond, Va.: Garrett and Massie, 1941.

Gunderson, Robert G. *The Log Cabin Campaign.* Lexington: University of Kentucky Press, 1957.

Peterson, Norma Lois. *The Presidencies of William Henry Harrison and John Tyler.* Lawrence: University Press of Kansas, 1989.

JOHN TYLER (1790–1862)

Tenth President, 1841–1845

JOHN TYLER
(Library of Congress)

"I can never consent to being dictated to."
—John Tyler to Secretary of State Daniel Webster, 1841

Some of John Tyler's contemporaries called him inflexible, stubborn, and obstinate. A more complete description may have added "beleaguered." He was the first president to obtain office because his predecessor had died. Without support from his own political party, without much support in Congress, and operating under the derisive label "His Accidency," Tyler found he had to fight hard to make others understand he was the legitimate president. He told the cabinet that he inherited from William Henry Harrison: "I am very glad to have . . . such able statesmen as you. But I can never consent to being dictated to as to what I shall or shall not do. . . . I am the President. . . . When you think otherwise, your resignations will be accepted." Despite his determination, many leading politicians spurned him and set out to destroy him.

John Tyler came from a wealthy family, part of Virginia's plantation elite. He was born on March 29, 1790, in Charles County to John Tyler, a planter and judge, and Mary Marot Armistead Tyler, who died when young John was only seven. Judge Tyler's estate, located along the James River, encompassed 12,000 acres and 45 slaves. Young John received an education from tutors before entering the College of William and Mary in 1802. After graduating in 1807, he lived in Richmond with his father, who had just been elected governor, and studied law. In 1809 he was admitted to the bar and went on to specialize in criminal justice.

Tyler entered politics two years later, when he won election to the state House of Delegates. In March 1813 he married Letitia Christian, the daughter of a planter. They had four daughters and three sons. The marriage solidified his social ties with the state's leading plantation families.

John Tyler was elected to the U.S. House of Representatives in 1816. There he applied his belief in states' rights and a strict reading of the Constitution. In 1819 his conservative views caused a split between him and General Andrew Jackson when he denounced Jackson's seizure of Pensacola in Spanish Florida during a war against the Indians. Tyler argued that Jackson had exceeded his constitutional authority in trespassing on foreign soil. His criticism of the immensely popular general has been described by a biographer, Oliver Perry Chitwood, in *John Tyler: Champion of the Old South,* as "exhibiting a courage and disinterestedness that have been only too rare in the history of American statesmanship."

Tyler insisted the power of the Union flowed not from the people but from the states and that all sovereignty rested in the states. Although he praised the Union, he recognized a state's right to secession. In 1820, when Congress debated whether to allow Missouri into the Union with slavery intact, he argued that every state had the right to determine its own institutions and that the federal government should impose no restrictions. He added that slavery's growth in Missouri and its spread elsewhere would cause the demand for slaves to outstrip the supply and, as a consequence, benefit all slaves by making them more valuable and encouraging their owners to treat them more kindly.

That same year Tyler opposed a higher protective tariff passed by Congress, saying it would reduce imports and result in fewer agricultural exports. His stand revealed a Jeffersonian agrarianism that complemented his states' rights ideology. Tyler never abandoned this outlook, for it emanated from Virginia's planter class as strongly as did wealth, and over the years he showed a steadfast attachment to it—either through grit or stubbornness—that belied a gentle character others mistook for weakness.

Tyler served in the Virginia House of Delegates from 1823 to 1825 and then was elected governor. His term proved uneventful. He then won election to the U.S. Senate in 1827. He again expressed his states' rights position during the nullification crisis of the early 1830s when South Carolina said it would prohibit collection of the federal tariff within its borders. Tyler disliked South Carolina's decision but strenuously opposed Andrew Jackson's Force Bill, which reasserted the president's right to send troops into a rebellious state. When the bill passed Congress he said it "swept away the barriers of the Constitution and [gave] us in place of the Federal government, under which we had fondly believed we were living, a consolidated military despotism." Determined to defuse the crisis and keep the Union together, Tyler worked behind the scenes to help craft a compromise in 1833 that modified the tariff. Still, the dispute made him uneasy about the Democratic Party, which he had joined because of its commitment to states' rights.

Although Tyler could agree with Andrew Jackson's dismantling of the national bank, an institution the Virginian considered an excessive use of federal authority, he thought the president was hungry for power and unpredictable.

In 1834 he called Jackson a "man who on all his proceedings appears to be more the creature of passion than of judgment."

Tyler's Senate career came to an abrupt end in a collision between his steadfast attachment to principle and a political ploy by the Democrats. In 1835, two years after the Senate had censored Jackson for arbitrarily removing federal funds from the national bank, the president's supporters pushed to have the censorship expunged from the records. Tyler opposed the move, both because it went against his earlier vote to censor Jackson and because he thought it unconstitutional, but Virginia Democrats convinced the state legislature to instruct him and fellow senator Benjamin Leigh to vote for expunction. They believed neither man would agree with the instructions and both would resign, allowing them to appoint loyal Democrats in their stead. Leigh, however, ruined their plan by deciding to ignore the instructions. Leaders of the emerging Whig Party, who at the time were attracting Tyler to their cause, urged him to do the same so his seat would be protected and he and Leigh could present a united front, but Tyler refused. He called it unprincipled to reject instructions sent by the people through their legislature. Instead, in February 1836 he resigned.

Despite his decision, the Whigs nominated Tyler that year to run for vice president with two of the three candidates they offered for the White House, William Henry Harrison and Hugh L. White. All the Whig candidates lost, but in 1838 Tyler returned to public office when he once more won election to the Virginia House of Delegates.

In 1840 the Whigs again nominated William Henry Harrison for president, this time as their sole candidate. A military hero known for his battle against the Indians at Tippecanoe in Indiana, Harrison appealed strongly to westerners and Northerners. He also appealed to the nationalistic wing of the Whig Party, who supported federal funding of internal improvements and the restoration of a national bank. To balance the ticket and appeal to Southerners and states' righters, the Whigs nominated John Tyler for vice president. By and large, contemporaries considered his selection unimportant; vice presidents wielded little power, and no one expected him to become president. Although at odds with Harrison and other leading Whigs on several issues, Tyler said little during the campaign, and the Whigs went on to win the election. He and Harrison were sworn into office in March 1841.

Then the unexpected happened. On April 4, 1841, President Harrison died from pneumonia. A messenger notified Tyler of Harrison's death, and Tyler rushed to Washington to assume the presidency on April 6. Uncertainty and controversy over his official status surfaced immediately. The Constitution was unclear on whether, in the event of the president's death, the vice president became acting president or president outright—that is, whether the duties of the office or the office itself devolved on the vice president. Some legal scholars such as Joseph Story had written that a vice president becomes president and remains so until the next election, but others dissented.

Needing a quick decision, Harrison's cabinet met with Tyler soon after he arrived. The Virginian insisted he was president in office as well as in name. After some discussion, the cabinet agreed and decided to have Tyler take the oath of office, a move that reaffirmed their decision and set an important precedent.

Few Whigs expected any problems with John Tyler. A party newspaper, the *National Intelligencer,* stated on April 7: "President Tyler is a Whig—a true Whig, and we risk nothing in expressing our entire confidence that he will fulfill in all their extent, the expectations of the People. . . ." Although Tyler quickly put the cabinet in line when he said he would refuse their dictation, he believed, as did other Whigs, in limited executive power and said the president should never remove from office those entrusted with handling federal moneys—a reference to Andrew Jackson's firing of two treasury secretaries. Further, by keeping Harrison's cabinet intact, he affirmed continuity with

Whig policies. At the same time, many states' righters expressed confidence in Tyler based on his previous record.

A close observer, however, would have found differences between Tyler and many Whigs. Most important, he objected to what the Whigs had intended for Harrison—that the president be little more than a figurehead, with the real power wielded by Congress. Tyler may have opposed Jacksonian-style executive authority, but he also opposed letting Congress prevail over the presidency; in his view a middle ground worked best, and he intended to pursue it.

This stance brought him into conflict with one of the most ambitious politicians in Washington: Henry Clay. The Kentuckian intended to rule the nation from the Senate and would tolerate no opposition from Tyler. Clay reportedly declared: "Tyler dare not resist; I will drive him before me."

Simply put, Clay wanted to be president. He expected to win the office in 1844. Toward that end he and other Whigs had convinced President Harrison to serve only one term. But Tyler made no such promise, and if "His Accidency" were a successful and widely popular president, he might ruin Clay's plan. That was all Clay needed to decide that the president, Whig or not, had to be destroyed.

Tyler faced numerous obstacles in meeting Clay's challenge or exerting any substantial power. For one, he had never held a leadership position in the Whig Party or established close ties to its leaders. For another, his reserved temperament made him unable to appeal directly to the people, as had Andrew Jackson, and thus denied him a possible weapon in circumventing Clay. Finally, many Northerners distrusted Tyler's Virginia plantation background.

In May 1841 Tyler and Clay engaged in a pitched battle during a special session of Congress that had been called in March by President Harrison to handle a severe economic depression. Clay intended to win approval for a national bank. Tyler opposed the bank, saying it would be an unconstitutional extension of federal power. Both men fought for principles—Clay for nationalism, Tyler for states' rights. Both men also looked toward 1844 and the presidential election.

Even before Congress met, Tyler indicated to Clay that he would veto any bank bill. Clay's friends advised him to proceed with caution to avoid tearing the party apart, but he ignored them. When the session began, most Whigs in the Senate wanted a strong national bank, but the party held only a slight majority over the Democrats, leaving little room for dissension. After Tyler indicated he would be willing to sign a bill establishing a national bank if its branches were opened only in those states that permitted them, Clay responded that the federal government should determine where its bank's branches should be placed, and he would settle for nothing less. To allow the states to influence any of the bank's operations, he said, would be disastrous. Clay clearly had politics on his mind; he believed if Congress accepted a compromise plan, Tyler would be recognized as a great conciliator, and that could only boost the president's prestige and popularity.

Congress eventually sent Tyler legislation closest to Clay's proposal. After the president vetoed it, Clay unleashed a venomous speech. He accused the president of operating from excessive pride, vanity, and egotism and of being unable to "see beyond the little, petty, contemptible circles of his own personal interests." He said Tyler had usurped Congress and denied the will of the people, as expressed in the Whig victory of 1840. His statement failed to mention that the Whigs had refused to write a party platform that year, believing a stand in favor of a national bank would cost them the election.

Clay continued the hunt. According to historian Norma Lois Peterson in *The Presidencies of William Henry Harrison and John Tyler*, the Kentuckian "exerted extreme pressure on Whigs who even dared hint that Tyler . . . was due at least a modicum of consideration. More than Clay wanted a bank, he wanted to bring down Tyler. . . ." Congress passed a second bank bill after Tyler initially indicated he might sign it, but he instead used his veto.

With that, five of the six members of his cabinet resigned, encouraged to do so by Clay. Harsh editorials condemned the president; he was burned in effigy in many cities and received hundreds of assassination threats.

On September 13, 1841, a caucus of Whig congressmen declared they could no longer be responsible for Tyler's actions; in effect, they booted him from the party. The president had actually supported much Whig legislation, but the bank bill, Clay's ambition, and Tyler's unwillingness to let Congress dominate the executive persuaded the Whigs to act.

From that point on, the Whig congress rejected nearly all of John Tyler's domestic proposals. Nevertheless, in 1842 the much-maligned president showed considerable tact in handling a rebellion in Rhode Island led by Thomas W. Dorr. Dorr had declared a separate state government after the legislature refused to reform the state constitution to end property qualifications for voting and for holding office. When the governor asked Tyler to send in troops, the president advocated restraint and refused to act without evidence of a violent insurrection. After Dorr's followers seized state office buildings, Tyler warned them to disband within 24 hours or face military reprisal. The rebels surrendered without bloodshed.

President Tyler's achievements in foreign affairs rivaled those of any previous administration. In 1842 his secretary of state, Daniel Webster, reached an agreement with Britain over the boundary between Canada and Maine, after Tyler stepped in at a crucial moment and saved the talks. Under the Webster-Ashburton Treaty, the United States obtained 7,000 of the 12,000 square miles of rich timberland under dispute. The two sides agreed as well to patrol the African coast jointly in an effort to disrupt the illegal transatlantic slave trade. The treaty passed Congress easily, despite the Whig dislike of Tyler, and earned widespread praise. During a Whig dinner in New York City, a toast to Lord Ashburton evoked approval, while one to Tyler met with silence. Thousands of New Yorkers subsequently protested what they rightly considered a snub of the president.

In December 1842 Tyler presented Congress with a Webster-composed message that extended the Monroe Doctrine to Hawaii. The Tyler Doctrine, as it was called, noted that since nearly all ships in Hawaiian harbors were American and that the Hawaiian monarchy was weak, the United States would disapprove of any nation trying to exert control over the islands.

As Britain expanded its exclusive trading rights in China during the early 1840s, Tyler worried that Asian ports would be closed to the United States. As a result, in 1844 he signed the Treaty of Wanghia with China, which granted America most-favored-nation trading privileges.

The greatest controversy in foreign affairs, and one that had serious domestic implications, involved Texas, the slave-permitting republic established by American settlers after they had won their independence from Mexico. In the 1840s Texans sought to be annexed by the United States, but many Northerners opposed the move, considering it nothing less than a plot to expand America's slave territory.

Intrigue permeated the dispute. While President Tyler moved slowly on the issue, Sam Houston and other Texas leaders flirted with Britain as a means to pressure the United States. According to rumors, Britain would soon provide money to Texas so the Lone Star Republic could end its slavery and serve as a haven for runaways from the South. This would satisfy British abolitionists and help the British weaken the United States by disrupting its economy. The money would also draw Texas and Britain closer together in an alliance that would threaten America's southwestern border.

Tyler inadvertently intensified the Texas controversy in 1844 when he appointed John C. Calhoun as secretary of state to succeed Abel Parker Upshur, who had died in a tragic accident. Calhoun came from South Carolina, and his strident proslavery advocacy made the debate more sectional by shifting attention away from annexation of Texas as beneficial to the entire nation to annexation of Texas as beneficial to the South.

On April 12, 1844, the United States signed a treaty with Texas to annex it as a territory and promised to defend it against any attack by Mexico. At the same time Calhoun sent a long letter to the British government in which he said the United States must annex Texas both to protect its own happiness and prosperity and to protect slavery. He presented a discourse on race, in essence an international primer, in which he said blacks could never survive without the kindly paternalism of their masters. There were more deaf, dumb, blind, insane, and idiot blacks in the North than in the South, he said, because free blacks lived under conditions more horrible than bondage.

President Tyler held milder views about slavery. Although he owned slaves, he disliked the institution and refrained from promoting a proslave philosophy. On the other hand, he never freed his own slaves, nor did he try to end slavery. Instead, he disliked abolitionists for making dangerous statements that could cause a slave rebellion; he hoped slavery would just fade away. Irrespective of Tyler's views, to many Northerners Calhoun's letter amounted to an incitement.

The annexation of Texas along with the possible American acquisition of Oregon dominated presidential politics in 1844. In May that year, Tyler tried to form a third party consisting of conservative states' rights Democrats and disaffected Whigs. As the Democrats convened in Baltimore to nominate a presidential candidate, the Tylerites met nearby, and with chants of "Tyler and Texas!" they chose him to run. Tyler held little hope of beating the Democrats and Whigs. He really wanted to pressure the Democrats into accepting annexation; they did so when they followed former president Andrew Jackson's advice and rejected front-runner Martin Van Buren in favor of a committed expansionist, James K. Polk.

In June the Senate defeated the annexation treaty, and Tyler forged ahead with his presidential campaign. This caused Democrats to fear he would drain votes from Polk and throw the election to Whig candidate Henry Clay. After the Democrats assured Tyler they would support Texas annexation and would provide federal jobs to his supporters, he withdrew from the race and backed Polk.

With Polk's victory in November, President Tyler proposed annexing Texas as a state rather than a territory. This meant that instead of a treaty requiring a two-thirds vote in the Senate, a resolution could be passed by a majority vote in Congress as a whole. Tyler expected the measure to win approval based on the earlier commitment he had received from Democrats to support annexation, and it passed despite continued northern opposition and considerable debate over whether a foreign nation could be annexed as a state. Tyler signed the bill on March 1, 1845, with just three days remaining in his term. According to the resolution, he still had to decide whether to begin immediate annexation or opt for new negotiations with Texas. At first he thought the decision should be left to the incoming president, James K. Polk, but his cabinet, and especially Calhoun, urged him to act. On March 2, therefore, he annexed Texas.

Massachusetts congressman John Quincy Adams, a former president and foe of slavery, reacted by calling Tyler's action "the heaviest calamity that ever befell myself and my country. . . . I regard it as the apoplexy of the Constitution." But Tyler considered it a monumental achievement, one that would rescue his presidency from historical oblivion.

After Polk's inauguration, Tyler retired to Sherwood Forest, his plantation in Virginia. He took with him a new bride, Julia Gardiner, many years his junior, whom he had married in June 1844 after the death of his first wife; they would have seven children. In 1861 Tyler presided over a peace conference intended to avoid civil war. That November he won election to the Confederate House of Representatives, but on January 12, 1862, he suffered a stroke. He died six days later, on January 18.

When John Tyler left the White House, he firmly believed he was leaving the country in better shape than when he had come into office.

The economy was rebounding, in part owing to increased trade with the Far East; states' rights had been successfully defended, though with some concessions to nationalists; the dispute with Britain over Canada had been resolved; and Texas had been annexed. The *Richmond Enquirer* said about Tyler: "Erroneous as his policy may have been in several particulars, yet his presidency was responsible for a number of brilliant events. Posterity at least will do him justice in these respects, if the present age denies it."

Posterity, though, has been harsh. Most historians rank his presidency as mediocre; many others rank it much lower. Few Americans today know of Tyler, except perhaps as the first "president by accident." Yet his administration reveals the mix between principle and opportunism in American politics, both in his actions and those of his opponents who tried so hard to destroy him.

CHRONOLOGY

1790 Born March 29

1807 Graduates from College of William and Mary

1809 Admitted to the bar

1811 Elected to Virginia House of Delegates

1813 Marries Letitia Christian

1816 Elected to U.S. House of Representatives

1827 Elected to U.S. Senate

1829 Attends Virginia constitutional convention

1833 Opposes Force Bill
Helps draft tariff compromise

1836 Resigns Senate seat
Renounces Democratic Party
Runs for vice president as a Whig
Loses vice presidential race

1838 Elected to Virginia House of Delegates

1840 Elected vice president

1841 Becomes president
Vetoes bank bill
Kicked out of the Whig Party

1842 Signs Webster-Ashburton Treaty
Announces Tyler Doctrine

1844 Calls for annexation of Texas
Marries Julia Gardiner

1845 Signs Texas annexation bill
Retires to Virginia

1861 Presides over Washington peace conference between North and South
Elected to the Confederate House of Representatives

1862 Dies January 18

FURTHER READING

Chitwood, Oliver Perry. *John Tyler: Champion of the Old South.* 1939. Reprint, Newton, Conn.: American Political Biography Press, 1990.

Merk, Frederick. *Fruits of Propaganda in the Tyler Administration.* Cambridge, Mass.: Harvard University Press, 1971.

Monroe, Dan. *The Republican Vision of John Tyler.* College Station: Texas A&M University Press, 2003.

Morgan, Robert J. *A Whig Embattled: The Presidency Under John Tyler.* Lincoln: University of Nebraska Press, 1954.

Peterson, Norma Lois. *The Presidencies of William Henry Harrison and John Tyler.* Lawrence: University Press of Kansas, 1989.

Seager, Robert, II. *And Tyler Too: A Biography of John and Julia Gardiner Tyler.* New York: McGraw-Hill, 1963.

Tyler, Lyon G., ed. *The Letters and Times of the Tylers,* 3 vols. 1884–1896. Reprint, New York: Da Capo Press, 1970.

*J*AMES K. POLK (1795–1849)

Eleventh President, 1845–1849

JAMES K. POLK
(Library of Congress)

"Our title to the country of the Oregon is 'clear and unquestionable,' and already are our people preparing to perfect that title by occupying it with their wives and children. . . . The world beholds the peaceful triumphs of the industry of our emigrants. . . . The . . . benefits of our republican institutions should be extended over them in the distant regions which they have selected for their homes."

—Inaugural words, March 4, 1845

Near the end of his presidency, James K. Polk ordered that a statue of Thomas Jefferson be moved from the Capitol rotunda to the lawn directly in front of the White House. There it stood for 27 years. Polk admired Jefferson for his states' rights views, principles that he adopted and applied to his own administration. But he might just as well have drawn a connection between Jefferson's purchase of Louisiana and his own striving for territory. His acquisition of Oregon and California—one through negotiation, the other through conquest—brought America to the Pacific Ocean, the end point of Jefferson's Lewis and Clark expedition more than 40 years earlier.

James Knox Polk was born on November 2, 1795, to Samuel Polk and Jane Knox Polk in Mecklenburg County, North Carolina, a region known for its independent spirit and dislike for government interference. His father was a prosperous farmer who, when James was 11, moved the family to middle Tennessee, just south of Nashville. When James was growing up, his parents presented a contrast in beliefs. Samuel was critical of religion, to the point of arguing with the minister at James's baptism and preventing its consummation. Jane, on the other hand, was a pious woman who raised her children as devout Presbyterians.

Frail and sickly, young James preferred bookish activities. He obtained his early schooling at an academy in Murfreesboro, Tennessee, where he earned a reputation for discipline and hard work. He entered the University of North Carolina at Chapel Hill in 1816, excelled at debate, and graduated two years later. He then returned to Tennessee to pursue the study of law under Felix Grundy, a leading attorney.

Polk experienced his first taste of politics in 1819, when Grundy won election to the state legislature and helped him obtain the position of senate clerk in the state capital at Murfreesboro. Polk was admitted to the bar in 1820 and served as senate clerk a second time in 1821.

James K. Polk looked at law as a route to elective politics, and he worked hard to win public office. He advanced rapidly, with so much success it appeared he would never experience failure. In 1823 he won election to the state legislature and displayed his family's independent political spirit by siding with democratic reformers while supporting Andrew Jackson, a states' rights advocate, for the U.S. Senate. The following year Polk married Sarah Childress, the attractive, well-educated, and self-assured daughter of a leading Murfreesboro family; he also won election as a Jacksonian to the U.S. House of Representatives.

While he identified with the emerging Democratic Party, Polk's appointment to the Ways and Means Committee in 1832 put him at the center of issues he considered critical to America's development: the national bank, tariff, and internal improvements, all of which would later confront him during his presidency. On each he tried to limit the power of the national government. In 1833 he gained more influence when he was elected chairman of the committee. Soon after, he supported President Andrew Jackson's removal of federal funds from the national bank in order to destroy it and won the president's praise when he shaped a report on the bank agreeable to the White House.

In 1835 Polk was elected Speaker of the House over a candidate from the Whig Party. He earned a reputation as an opinionated and principled leader but also a secretive and untrustworthy one, prone to deceit. He managed the House with efficient zeal, though he was thwarted in his efforts to win passage of a bill to establish President Van Buren's Independent Treasury and was dismayed by an increasingly bitter fight over several gag rules, passed to prevent discussion of petitions relating to slavery.

When a severe economic depression hit America in the late 1830s, Polk thought it more advantageous to leave the Washington political scene and return home to Tennessee. Consequently, in 1839 he ran for governor and won, bucking a strong Whig Party movement among Tennesseans and throughout the nation. Polk knew that the governorship, restricted by the state constitution, would allow him little chance to exert power. But he was more interested in using the office as a base from which to seek the vice presidency in 1840. Unfortunately for his plans, the Democrats failed to nominate him. The following year, he sought reelection to the governor's office, but he was defeated by a folksy candidate, "Lean Jimmy" Jones. It was the first time in his career that he had lost an election.

Polk and Jones contended for the same office once more in 1843 in a campaign devoid of issues and known for its homespun stories and slogans. Polk again lost, and the defeat devastated him. In previous years hard work had usually brought success; now his perseverance seemed futile. He went into seclusion, confused and dejected, with his political career apparently at an end.

Then the unexpected happened: The front-runner for the 1844 Democratic presidential nomination, Martin Van Buren, stumbled when he announced his opposition to the annexation of Texas, angering the nation's expansionists in an era when Americans thirsted to push westward. He particularly angered the most powerful Democrat in the country, Andrew Jackson, who retained considerable popularity from his presidency a decade earlier.

When the Democratic convention met in May 1844, the delegates went through seven ballots and eventually deadlocked between Van Buren and Michigan senator Lewis Cass. In a quandary, the convention turned to a dark-horse candidate promoted by Jackson—namely, James K. Polk. Although he was much less known than several Whigs and Democrats such as Cass, James Buchanan of Pennsylvania, or John C. Calhoun of South Carolina, the expansionists respected him.

That the Jackson-Polk friendship, which reached back to Polk's early political career, had paid off startled Polk. He had been vying for the vice presidency, but he came up with the big prize. "Young Hickory"—so called by his supporters to reinforce his connection with Jackson, long known as "Old Hickory"—threw himself into the race with as much determination as he had applied to his earlier campaigns. He called himself a strong expansionist and supported both the annexation of Texas and the acquisition of Oregon. He proposed policies with geographic appeal: a low tariff for Southerners, an independent treasury for northeastern Democrats, and cheap land and expansion for westerners.

After winning the nomination, Polk promised to serve only one term as president. This, he believed, would soothe those within the Democratic party still licking their wounds from the tough nomination battle, mainly the Cass and Van Buren camps, and would stress his populist appeal by placing him on the side of those who favored the frequent rotation of officeholders. But this decision turned out to be a mistake, since it encouraged fellow politicians to spend too much time and energy and engage in too much intrigue in jockeying for position as his successor.

For all his expansionist credentials, Polk's race against his Whig opponent, Kentucky senator Henry Clay, nearly resulted in his third election defeat. Clay hurt himself, however, by waffling on expansion. He first opposed annexing Texas and then moderated his position. In the end Clay lost the election because a third-party candidate, James G. Birney of the antislavery Liberty Party, attracted enough votes from the Whigs to allow Polk to win narrowly in New York. Had Clay been victorious in that state, he would have been president, since Polk's count in the electoral college topped the Kentuckian's by only 170 to 105. Polk won 15 states to Clay's 11, but the Tennessean lost his home state by about 200 votes.

Although he had been a dark horse who had barely won the election, James K. Polk made it clear that he would continue the Jacksonian commitment to a vigorous presidency and exert firm leadership. He noted that if a president "entrusts the details and smaller matters to subordinates, constant errors will occur. I prefer to supervise the whole operations of Government myself." He watched over the bureaucracy so closely that, according to historian Charles A. McCoy in *Polk and the Presidency*, "He established for the first time the right and the duty of the president to control personally the departmental activity of the executive branch."

According to historian Allan Nevins, soon after entering the presidency Polk met with his secretary of the navy, George Bancroft, and in a strong tone, his hand hitting his thigh for emphasis, he declared: "There are four great measures which are to be the measures of my administration: one, a reduction of the tariff; another the independent treasury; a third, the settlement of the Oregon boundary question; and, lastly, the acquisition of California."

Polk went to work. In his first annual message to Congress, he devoted four pages to the tariff issue. He opposed the protective tariff passed in 1842, saying that while it promoted manufacturing it hurt farmers, who were forced to pay more for products made in this country and for those imported from abroad. Further, he believed the high tariff favored the industrializing North and hurt southern development.

This was not a new position for him; he had supported a lower tariff while in Congress, and when he first ran for governor of Tennessee, he said a protective tariff was intended "to take the property of one man and give it to another, without right or consideration. It was to depreciate the value of the productive industry of one section of the Union and transfer it to another—it was to make the rich richer and the poor poorer." Polk wanted a moderate tariff intended only to raise revenue. In 1846 Congress agreed and enacted a bill outlined by Secretary of the Treasury Robert J. Walker.

Like President Martin Van Buren, Polk sought to establish an independent treasury to keep federal funds in the government's own vaults rather than in a national bank or in state banks. A national bank, he believed, favored the wealthy, and state banks used funds recklessly. Congress had founded an independent treasury in 1840, but a Whig majority dismantled it the following year. Polk wanted it back, and just two days after Congress enacted the Walker Tariff, it complied with his demand.

The president also entered into an ongoing debate over internal improvements. In keeping with his states' rights principles and his beliefs in a strict interpretation of the Constitution, he fought any federal funding of canals, roads, and other similar projects. Whigs in Congress overwhelmingly supported the funding and were joined by some western Democrats, who wanted work done on harbors and rivers. That coalition resulted in Congress passing an internal improvements bill in 1846, but Polk vetoed it. Another harbor-and-rivers bill passed the following spring, but that was also vetoed.

In his veto message to Congress, Polk referred to limited government, pointed to precedent in Andrew Jackson's Maysville Road veto, and claimed that funding internal improvements would drain the treasury. He said about the 1847 legislation, "Let the imagination run along our coast from the river St. Croix to the Rio Grande and trace every river emptying into the Atlantic and Gulf of Mexico to its source; . . . let it pass to Oregon and explore all its bays, inlets, and streams . . . and the mind will be startled at the immensity and danger of the power which the principle of this bill involves."

American minds indeed passed to Oregon, as they had for several years. They looked toward the verdant, fertile Pacific Northwest with its harbors beckoning ships from the East Coast and pointing enticingly at Asia and determined they wanted it. They embraced Manifest Destiny, the belief God intended America to spread its "superior civilization" westward. Not everyone agreed with this, but enough did to make it the zeitgeist, or spirit of the times.

When James K. Polk entered the White House carrying his expansionist banner, several thousand Americans were living in Oregon, and more kept immigrating to the distant land. Oregon was then under joint control of Britain and the United States, but Polk's predecessor, John Tyler, had tried to reach an agreement to divide the territory, and Congress even debated a bill to organize a territorial government and build several forts.

These actions left unresolved a major question: How much of Oregon should the United States procure? Radicals, called the "All Oregon men," wanted the vast territory into present-day Canada, to latitude 54° 40', even if it meant war. Their shouts of "Fifty-four forty or fight!" resonated across expansionist America. Polk at first sided with this faction, though unenthusiastically, and in a message to Congress in December 1845 he invoked the Monroe Doctrine, warning against European plans to colonize any part of the Americas. He asked Congress to notify Britain formally, as it could under the existing treaty, that the United States was ending the joint occupation of Oregon. Congress agreed, though only after five months of debate. Soon after, Britain expressed its willingness to settle the boundary at the 49th parallel, with Vancouver Island remaining British territory. Polk consulted with the Senate, which indicated that it would support the arrangement. He then signed a treaty, which the Senate ratified on June 18, 1846, by a vote of 41-14. The All Oregon men fell short, but the president acquired a verdant and valuable land, a treasure for Manifest Destiny.

As evidence of the nation's expansionist fervor, at the same time President Polk dealt with Oregon, he pursued the Mexican territories of California and New Mexico to the point that he provoked a war. Relations with Mexico had begun worsening considerably in the late 1830s when American settlers in the Mexican province of Texas won their independence and asked the United States to annex their Lone Star Republic. President Tyler, Polk's predecessor, hesitated at first but then decided to take action after Polk won the presidency on the Democrat's expansionist platform in fall 1844.

As Congress debated annexation in February 1845, Polk arrived in Washington and expressed conflicting views about the various proposals then under debate, though he still supported expansion. On March 2, after Congress acted, Tyler officially annexed Texas as a state, just two days before he left the White House. Texas, though, had yet to agree to the measure.

Although Tyler's move stole some of Polk's thunder, the incoming president may have welcomed it, for the proposal to annex the Lone Star Republic was more controversial than the one to acquire Oregon. Since slavery existed in Texas, many Northerners considered its annexation nothing less than a southern plot to expand an oppressive institution.

Yet other Northerners supported annexation precisely because Texas had slavery. They believed that slaves would be drawn away from border states near the North, and this would lessen the threat of blacks migrating into their region in large numbers. It little mattered as Texas annexation and Manifest Destiny carried the day.

Two days after Polk was inaugurated, the Mexican envoy to the United States resigned in protest over the new president's support of Tyler's annexation measure. Texas itself was still undecided on the issue, as some Texans wanted to remain independent. Yet there was a strong sentiment to join the United States, and Polk sent agents west to reinforce those views by promising money for harbors, forts, and lighthouses—an interesting offer from a president who opposed the federal funding of internal improvements. One of his agents was Commodore Robert F. Stockton, who stirred up Texans with stories of an imminent Mexican invasion. When former Texas president Sam Houston announced his support of the annexation measure, the opposition collapsed.

Mexico, though, was deeply unhappy. Not only had the United States made Texas a state, but it had also set the Rio Grande as its southern boundary. Mexico insisted the boundary ended farther north at the Nueces River. When President Polk heard rumors that a Mexican army was marching toward the Rio Grande, he told General Zachary Taylor, whose troops were already in Texas, that any attempt by the Mexicans to cross the river would be considered an act of war. Although the rumors proved false, the president kept Taylor's army ready for battle.

In November 1845 Polk sent former congressman John Slidell to Mexico on a secret mission to resolve the Texas boundary dispute, settle debts owed to the United States, and acquire California, where Captain John C. Frémont was already fomenting rebellion among the American settlers. Mexico had every reason to be suspicious of Slidell's mission, given Tyler's army in Texas and Frémont's aggression in California. Adding to the tension, a rebellion broke out in Mexico that brought General Mariano Paredes to power, and he refused to even meet with Slidell. Paredes opposed giving any territory to the United States or doing anything that might make it appear to the Mexican people that he had sold out his country.

Polk still held out hope for a peaceful settlement, but after learning in late April that Slidell's mission had failed, he now wanted war. At first he moved cautiously to avoid upsetting the debate then underway in Congress over the Oregon issue. His hope was that the Mexican army would attack Taylor's troops, thus providing him with the justification he needed to fight. When the Mexicans apparently failed to attack, he met with his cabinet on May 9, 1846, and told them there already existed "ample cause of war."

Four hours after the cabinet meeting adjourned, Polk received news that the Mexican and American armies had clashed near the Rio Grande. On May 13 Congress declared war by an overwhelming margin. Later the president asserted:

> The existing war with Mexico was neither desired nor provoked by the United States. . . . After years of endurance of aggravated and unredressed wrongs on our part, Mexico, in violation of solemn treaty stipulations and of every principle of justice recognized by civilized nations, commenced hostilities, and thus by her own act forced the war upon us.

President Polk devised a strategy to conquer California, New Mexico, and northern Mexico using a volunteer army. He wrote in his diary on May 16: "During the sitting of the Cabinet I submitted to them the distribution among the States of the 50,000 volunteers authorized to be raised. A portion of this force was assigned to each State and Territory in the Union, so as to make each feel an interest in the war."

In the summer of 1846 Polk made what would prove to be a controversial decision when he sent a delegate to Havana, Cuba, to meet with an exiled Mexican general, Antonio Lopéz de Santa Anna. The delegate offered to guarantee Santa Anna's safe return to Mexico as long as the general promised that once he gained power he would accede to American terms. Santa Anna agreed, and the U.S. Navy carried him home. But after the general captured the Mexican presidency, he changed his mind. Polk's blunder likely resulted in extending the duration of the war because Santa Anna proved to be a tenacious leader.

Compounding the president's problems, the U.S.-Mexican War agitated the slavery issue. In August 1846 Democratic congressman David Wilmot of Pennsylvania offered an amendment to an appropriations bill that stipulated slavery be banned from any territory acquired from Mexico. An intense debate followed over the Wilmot Proviso; the House finally passed it, but the Senate rejected it. Polk, himself a slaveholder, reacted to the controversy with a prescient assessment: "The movement . . . will be attended with terrible consequences to the country, and cannot fail to destroy the Democratic party, if it does not ultimately threaten the Union itself." The president believed Congress should settle the issue of slavery in the territories through compromise. To one congressman preparing to attend a southern political conference he said, "The agitation of the slavery question is mischievous and wicked and proceeds from no patriotic motive by its authors . . . And this they seem willing to do even at the hazard of disturbing the harmony if not dissolving the Union itself."

Although in the spirit of Manifest Destiny most Americans supported the U.S.-Mexican War and volunteers filled the army's ranks, they expected a quick victory and grew disenchanted when fighting continued into the fall. As a result, the Democrats suffered substantial losses in the 1846 midterm elections.

Some of the newly elected Whigs opposed to slavery condemned the war. One of them, Congressman Abraham Lincoln of Illinois, introduced resolutions asking the president to name the exact spot on which American blood had been shed in the clash between armies near the Rio Grande. Lincoln hoped to expose Polk as the aggressor. But most Whigs tempered their criticism by supporting appropriations for the war and remaining in agreement with America's expansionist zeal.

Meanwhile, the American army had scored an impressive victory in September 1846 when Monterrey fell to Zachary Taylor's troops after they overcame heavy resistance in the city's fortified streets. Then in 1847 an army under General Winfield Scott broke through the walls of Mexico City and captured the capital.

With these victories, the president's representative in Mexico, Nicholas Trist, negotiated the Treaty of Guadalupe Hidalgo, even though Polk had ordered his recall over a policy dispute. Referring to a dispatch written by Trist in which the emissary refused to return home, Polk called it "arrogant, impudent, and very insulting to his Government, and even personally offensive to the President." Nevertheless, Polk opposed those who wanted to reject the treaty in favor of more land (among them his secretary of state, James Buchanan). He therefore submitted it to the Senate, where it was ratified in March 1847 by a vote of 38-14. Under the treaty's terms, the Texas border was fixed at the Rio Grande, and Mexico ceded New Mexico and California to the United States for $15 million. American war casualties amounted to 1,721 killed in battle, 11,155 dead from disease, and 4,102 wounded.

True to his word, President Polk refused to seek reelection and retired from office in March 1849. Just three months later, he died at his home in Nashville, Tennessee, worn down by his constant attention to detail and the dramatic events that marked his presidency.

James K. Polk once said, "The acquisition of California and New Mexico are results . . . of greater consequence . . . than any . . . since the adoption of the Constitution." He meant it in terms of an expansion of the republican Union, but others may just as well have pointed to the republic bringing slavery into lands where, under Mexican rule, it had been prohibited and to the controversy slave expansion would generate—an explosive issue threatening to tear the nation apart.

Chronology

1795 Born November 2

1806 Moves to Tennessee

1818 Graduates from University of North Carolina

1820 Admitted to the bar

Serves as Tennessee state senate clerk

1821 Again chosen to serve as Tennessee senate clerk

1823 Elected to the Tennessee legislature

1824 Marries Sarah Childress

Elected to U.S. House of Representatives

1832 Named to House Ways and Means Committee

1833 Selected to chair House Ways and Means Committee

1835 Chosen Speaker of the House

1839 Elected governor of Tennessee

1841 Defeated in bid for reelection as governor

1843 Loses race for governorship

1844 Elected president

1845 Sends Slidell Mission to Mexico

Recommends tariff revision

1846 Reestablishes Independent Treasury

Signs Walker Tariff

Signs Oregon treaty with Britain

Asks Congress to declare war on Mexico

1847 Send Nicholas Trist to negotiate peace with Mexico

Signs Treaty of Guadalupe Hidalgo

1848 Signs bill establishing territorial government for Oregon

1849 Retires to Nashville, Tennessee

Dies June 15

Further Reading

Bauer, K. Jack. *The Mexican War, 1846–1848.* New York: Macmillan, 1974.

Bergeron, Paul H. *The Presidency of James K. Polk.* Lawrence: University Press of Kansas, 1987.

Dusinberre, William. *Slavemaster President: The Double Career of James Polk.* New York: Oxford University Press, 2003.

Haynes, Sam W. *James K. Polk and the Expansionist Impulse.* New York: Longman, 1997.

McCoy, Charles A. *Polk and the Presidency.* 1960. Reprint, New York: Haskell House, 1973.

Merk, Frederick. *Manifest Destiny and Mission in American History: A Reinterpretation.* New York: Alfred A. Knopf, 1963.

———. *The Oregon Question: Essays in Anglo-American Diplomacy and Politics.* Cambridge, Mass.: Harvard University Press, 1967.

———. *Slavery and the Annexation of Texas.* New York: Alfred A. Knopf, 1972.

Nevins, Allen, ed. *Polk: The Diary of a President, 1845–1849.* New York: Longmans, Green and Company, 1929.

Schroeder, John H. *Mr. Polk's War: American Opposition and Dissent, 1846–1848.* Madison: University of Wisconsin Press, 1973.

Seigenthaler, John. *James K. Polk, 1845–1849.* New York: Times Books, 2003.

Sellers, Charles G., Jr. *James K. Polk, Jacksonian.* Princeton, N.J.: Princeton University Press, 1957.

ZACHARY TAYLOR (1784–1850)

Twelfth President, 1849–1850

ZACHARY TAYLOR
(The White House)

"I this day . . . proclaim my fixed determination to maintain to the extent of my ability the Government in its original purity and to adopt as the basis of my public policy those great republican doctrines which constitute the strength of our national existence."
—Inaugural words, March 4, 1849

Dressed in baggy cotton pants, a plain coat, and a wide-brimmed straw hat, and seated sideways on his horse Old Whitey, Zachary Taylor looked anything but a famous general. Yet that is what he had become in the early stages of the U.S.-Mexican War, and as he watched his men prepare for battle amid the arid terrain and looming mountains at Monterrey, he could already hear the drumbeat from those back in the states who wanted him to run for president. He neither encouraged them nor craved the office. He was, at heart, a career military man who had never voted, and who, in fact, never would vote, not even when his own name appeared on the ballot next to the word *president.*

Zachary's father, Richard Taylor, owned a prosperous farm in Virginia and fought in the Continental Army during the American Revolution. In October 1783 he received a large grant of land in Kentucky as reward for his service. He thereupon decided to take his family west. During the move, his wife, Sarah Dabney Strother Taylor, gave birth to Zachary on November 24, 1784, on a plantation in Orange County, Virginia.

Richard Taylor built his new farm on the Muddy Fork of Beargrass Creek, five miles east of the frontier outpost called Louisville. There young Zachary grew up and played childhood games, while Indians lurked in the woods and the howling of wolves filled the night. He received little formal education and throughout his life read little and spelled poorly in a nearly indecipherable handwriting.

When Congress increased the size of the U.S. Army in 1808 in response to a crisis with Britain, 24-year-old Zachary Taylor joined as a first lieutenant with the Seventh Infantry. This began his career with the military, which would last until his election as president. In 1810 Taylor married Margaret Mackall Smith, whose father owned a plantation in Calvert County, Maryland. They had six children, only three of whom reached adulthood.

Zachary received 324 acres along Beargrass Creek from his father for a homestead but soon sold the property for a profit. Throughout the years he combined his military career with land speculation and farming. His friends later said he was always more comfortable discussing crops than current events. Over time, farmer Taylor amassed thousands of acres and hundreds of slaves but was involved in so many military campaigns he had to have others manage his property.

Taylor experienced his first battle during the War of 1812, distinguishing himself with his defense of Fort Harrison in Indiana Territory in September of that year. The fort, a small stockade overlooking the Wabash River near Vincennes, came under attack from Indians allied with the British. After they set fire to a blockhouse, the flames spread to the barracks and nearly caused Taylor to evacuate. Taylor recalled: "Most of the men immediately gave themselves up for lost, and I had the greatest difficulty in getting my orders executed—from the raging of the fire—the yelling and howling of several hundred Indians—and cries of nine women and children." But the young officer repulsed the attack and saved the fort at the cost of two of his men killed and two wounded.

Taylor's soldiers liked him. He was unpretentious and friendly (though short tempered), and he cared about their welfare. Never a brilliant tactician, he nevertheless won the respect of his men, and they would do almost anything for him. In the late 1830s, during the second Seminole War, he earned the nickname "Old Rough and Ready" for his disheveled appearance and toughness. He was considered among the most determined of Indian fighters. His work with the army in commanding numerous posts and in building roads, bridges, and forts helped open the West to non-Indian settlement. By 1844 he was a brevet brigadier general and the commanding officer of the U.S. Army First Department at Fort Jessup, Louisiana. Although his large head and torso were mismatched with his short legs and he much preferred his common clothes to his military attire, an observer said "he looked like a man born to command," and his direct style communicated confidence and authority.

Zachary Taylor's renown as a general came as a result of the prominent role he played in the outbreak of the U.S.-Mexican War. After the United States annexed Texas in 1845, tension mounted with Mexico over the state's southern boundary. President James K. Polk claimed it extended to the Rio Grande, but Mexico claimed it ended farther north, at the Nueces River. Polk determined to put pressure on Mexico to settle the boundary dispute and to sell California. He did this by strengthening naval squadrons in the Gulf of Mexico and the Pacific Ocean and by sending Zachary Taylor's army into Texas.

In January 1846 Taylor received instructions "to advance and occupy . . . positions on or near the east Bank of the Rio del Norte as soon as it can be conveniently done with reference to the Season and the routes by which your movement must be made." He was not to interfere with shipping along the Rio Grande, but if attacked he was to respond aggressively. On March 29, 1846, with his army near the river, Taylor notified Washington that "the attitude of the Mexicans is so far decidedly hostile."

And understandably so. With Mexico refusing to sell California, Polk wanted war. Taylor consequently directed the building of Fort Texas at Matamoros, along the Rio Grande and within the disputed terrain between it and the Nueces. Mexico considered the United States the inciter and invader, and on April 4 Major General Mariano Arista received orders from his superiors to attack. While a tense quiet continued, on April 14 Taylor blockaded the Rio Grande. Ten days later Arista sent 1,600 men across the river, west of Matamoros.

Two companies of Americans clashed with the Mexicans on April 25, at which point Taylor declared "hostilities may now be considered commenced"—words of great relief to Polk, who was prepared to have Congress declare war without an armed battle but wanted one in order to portray Mexico as the aggressor. While the Mexican infantry laid siege to Fort Texas, Taylor's main army fought Arista's men at Palo Alto, along a strategic road that ended at Port Isabel on the Gulf Coast. The Mexicans suffered from a shortage of weapons and bad powder; their cannonballs skipped along the ground so slowly Americans could easily dodge them. Taylor's victory resulted in 92 Mexicans killed and 116 wounded versus nine Americans killed and 44 wounded.

Arista's army retreated from Palo Alto on May 9, but unwilling to surrender the road, they fortified themselves at a shallow ravine, Resaca de la Palma. Taylor asked his officers if he should continue along the road to Fort Texas before receiving reinforcements. They said no, but he rejected their advice with the words "I shall go to Fort Texas or stay in my shoes," meaning he would prefer to die in the attempt.

Astride Old Whitey, Taylor unleashed infantry attacks that eventually sent the hard-fighting Mexican army in flight across the Rio Grande, with some soldiers panicking and drowning in the river's current. Taylor, however, showed a conservative streak that appeared often in his battles; he refused to pursue Arista's army and let it slip into northern Mexico. Yet his victory meant he controlled the lower Rio Grande Valley and could strike across the river. At first unknown to Taylor, his success also elevated him to heroic status in the United States. Modern technology had arrived, and for the first time the telegraph was used to report battles and other wartime events. Americans followed the news closely, and Taylor's reputation as a brave commander spread quickly.

In September 1846 General Taylor marched toward the most important city in northern Mexico—Monterrey. A citadel defended Monterrey from the north, and the imposing peaks of the Sierra Madre bordered the city on the south. Taylor decided to approach from the plains along the eastern end of the city and have part of his army attack the heights in the west. Given his preference for conservative strategy, this bold move more likely came from his officers rather than from Taylor himself. In any event, forces under General William J. Worth attacked Federacion, a fortified Mexican post in the heights. After winning there they attacked a second post, Independencia, where they clawed their way up a steep hillside and engaged in hand-to-hand combat before subduing the enemy. The Americans now controlled the western heights.

At the same time Taylor led an inept attack on the eastern part of Monterrey. His men were unused to fighting in narrow city streets and were unprepared for the house-to-house combat required when the entrenched Mexicans fought from rooftops. The poor placement of field batteries further weakened the effort, but Worth came to Taylor's rescue when he advanced from the west. In all, 394 Americans were killed or wounded before the Mexican army surrendered. Taylor agreed to an eight-week armistice, a plan that was later criticized since it allowed the Mexicans to regroup; but it also allowed his own army, tired and suffering from dwindling supplies, a respite.

He later said, "These terms were liberal but . . . it was thought it would be judicious to act with magnanimity towards a prostrate foe, particularly as the president of the United States had offered to settle all differences between the two countries by negotiation. . . ." The armistice was sorely tested by American troops, particularly Texas soldiers, who engaged in atrocities against the Mexicans, but Taylor made it clear he considered such acts reprehensible.

With the general's military victories, his political star began lighting the Whig Party. The Whigs were searching for a presidential candidate, and newspaper editor Thurlow Weed, a party leader, championed Taylor's cause, even though Old Rough and Ready had declared no party preference. Rallies at several locations, including the Revolutionary War battlefield at Trenton, New Jersey, fueled the Taylor mania. The general reacted, however, by saying the prospect of his candidacy "seems to me too visionary to require a serious answer. Such an idea never entered my head, nor is it likely to enter the head of any sane person."

After the battle at Monterrey, relations between President Polk and Zachary Taylor soured, partly because Polk thought the armistice was wrong and partly because he feared the enthusiasm for Taylor would damage his own Democratic Party's prospects. He said, "Gen'l Taylor, I fear, is not the man for command of the army. He is brave but he does not seem to have resources or grasp of mind enough to conduct such a campaign." In January 1847 the president ordered most of Taylor's units to the Mexican coast to serve under General Winfield Scott, a Whig whose popularity paled next to Taylor's.

Taylor was incensed. Polk's maneuver was aimed at pressuring him to quit, but resigning would make it look like he was deserting his men. Old Rough and Ready dug in his heels, and in February 1847 his outnumbered army confronted a huge Mexican force under the command of General Santa Anna at Buena Vista. Santa Anna told Taylor: "You are surrounded by twenty thousand men and cannot in any human probability avoid suffering a rout. . . . I wish to save you from a catastrophe, and for that purpose give you this notice, in order that you may surrender at discretion."

Taylor rejected the note, and a battle ensued during which he supposedly had this exchange with a battery firing on Santa Anna's men:

> *"What are you using, Captain, grape or canister?"*
> *"Canister, General."*
> *"Single or double?"*
> *"Single."*
> *"Well, double-shot your guns and give 'em hell!"*

On February 24 the Mexican army retreated. Taylor once again failed to pursue his enemy, but the victory at Buena Vista secured northern Mexico and made him the undisputed leader for the Whig presidential nomination.

More Whigs than ever before wanted him to run, and after his falling out with Polk he became receptive to their overtures. By the spring of 1847 he was telling a friend: "I will not say I would not serve if the good people of the country should think it proper to elect me." In October 1847 Taylor asked for and received a leave of absence from the army. Although he maintained a nominal command in Mexico, his career in the military was nearing an end.

Some Whigs, however, opposed Taylor. Abolitionists in the party condemned him for owning slaves. One said he "raises babies for the market and makes merchandize of his fellow men! . . . He furnishes creole virgins for the 'hells' of New Orleans, and riots on the ruins of souls for whom the Man of Sorrows died." Kentucky senator Henry Clay, long frustrated in his bid for the White House, started his own candidacy, a move that caused Taylor finally to declare his party allegiance in May 1848: "I am a Whig," he said, "but not an ultra Whig." He added, "If elected . . . I would endeavor to act independent of party domination & should feel bound to administer the Government untrammeled by party schemes. . . ."

His words fell far short of a ringing endorsement of the Whig Party, and they would return to hurt his presidency. Nevertheless, in June 1848 the Whigs nominated him for president and chose Millard Fillmore, former chair of the House Ways and Means Committee and a candidate for the vice presidency in 1844, as his running mate. At the Whig National Convention, Ohio delegates signaled a major problem resulting from the U.S.-Mexican War and foreshadowed the intense crisis that would face Taylor's presidency when they introduced a resolution affirming the right of Congress to control slavery in the territories. The convention rejected it.

When Taylor decided to refrain from campaigning, many Whigs breathed a sigh of relief, for his comments often contained political gaffes. To avoid divisive issues, the Whigs refused to write a platform. On November 7, 1848, for the first time in a presidential race, all the nation's voters went to the polls on the same day. Turnout lagged behind recent elections—77 percent of the eligible voters turned out, with Taylor among those staying home—but Old Rough and Ready won with 163 electoral votes, compared to 127 for Democrat Lewis Cass of Michigan. Free Soil candidate Martin Van Buren, who ran on a platform opposed to slavery in the territories, failed to win a single state, but the votes he captured in New York threw that state to Taylor and assured the general's victory.

Political pundits thought Zachary Taylor would be a figurehead president. His detachment from Washington and his immersion in a military life led some to conclude he didn't know what was going on. Outgoing President Polk called him "wholly unqualified for the station." Adding to the doubts, Taylor stressed a traditional Whig attachment to a weak presidency and strong Congress.

The general's inexperience showed from the start. He sincerely believed he could be a president above party. This outlook, combined with political ineptness, caused him to ignore building good relations with the Whigs in Congress. Henry Clay said, "I have never before seen such an Administration. There is very little co-operation or concord between the two ends of the avenue. There is not, I believe, a prominent Whig in either House that has any confidential intercourse with the Executive."

But no one could doubt President Taylor's commitment to national unity. He fought for it his entire life, and more than any other issue or principle, he believed in a strong Union. As president, he concluded, he must turn back sectionalism. His weak party relations combined with his unionist beliefs to produce a peculiar reaction to the hottest issue facing America after the war: slavery in the territories acquired from Mexico—namely, California and New Mexico.

In January 1848 John Marshall, a mechanic building a sawmill on Johann Sutter's land, discovered gold in California, near Sacramento. By the end of 1849 more than 100,000 Americans had moved into the territory, and Californians petitioned for statehood with an antislave constitution. At the same time a border dispute erupted between New Mexico and Texas, when Texas claimed a huge chunk of eastern New Mexico, reaching to Santa Fe. The dispute grew so acrimonious that armed conflict loomed. Many Northerners believed Texas wanted the land in order to expand its slave domain. Taylor believed the same and committed himself to upholding the New Mexican boundary as it existed under Mexico and as stipulated in the Treaty of Guadalupe Hidalgo, which had ended the U.S.-Mexican War.

Southerners opposed California's entry into the Union as a free state, for it would give the nonslave states a majority in the U.S. Senate, then evenly divided at 15 free states and 15 slave states. They feared the new majority would allow the North to pass legislation levying a protective tariff and keeping slavery out of the territories, or maybe ending it altogether. In 1849 one-third of the Southerners in Congress signed South Carolina senator John C. Calhoun's "Address," which portrayed the Northwest Ordinance of 1789, the Missouri Compromise of 1820, and the refusal of Northerners to return fugitive slaves as "acts of aggression" against the South.

While sectionalism intensified, President Taylor insisted that because Californians had written an antislavery constitution, they should be admitted as a free state. He also believed New Mexico should obtain statehood as a way to force resolution of its border dispute with Texas. As a result, he sent agents to Santa Fe, and in short order New Mexico readied its petition to enter the Union as a free state.

In December 1849 President Taylor released his annual message to Congress in which—in a passage added to answer John C. Calhoun—he warned against sectionalism and defended the Union. "Upon its preservation must depend our own happiness and that of countless generations to come," he said. "Whatever dangers may threaten it, I shall stand by it and maintain it in its integrity to the full extent of the obligations imposed and the powers conferred upon me by the Constitution."

Taylor found enough time during the domestic crisis to negotiate the Clayton-Bulwar Treaty, in which Britain and the United States agreed never to claim exclusive control over an isthmian canal in Central America and promised to guarantee the neutrality and security of such a canal. They promised also to ensure peace in Central America and never to colonize or occupy any part of the region. The Senate passed the treaty in April by a vote of 42-10.

But the domestic crisis still held center stage, and to many it looked as if the quarrel over California and New Mexico would end the Union. With the crisis worsening, Henry Clay introduced into Congress several compromise resolutions. They provided for admission of California into the Union as a free state; the organization of New Mexico as a territory, with the issue of slavery left to the residents to vote on; a resolution of the Texas–New Mexico boundary dispute; an assumption by the United States of the Texas debt; an end to the slave trade in the District of Columbia; a strong provision for the return of fugitive slaves to their owners; and a declaration that Congress lacked any authority to interfere with the slave trade among the states.

The resolutions sparked a great debate led by the Senate's aging but renowned trio of Clay, Calhoun, and Daniel Webster of Massachusetts. Clay called for moderate tempers and compromise, while Calhoun insisted the South must have equal rights with the North in any territory. Webster began his speech with the eloquent words "I wish to speak today, not as a Massachusetts man, nor as a Northern man, but as an American. . . . I speak today for preservation of the Union. Hear me for my cause."

A Senate committee subsequently decided to combine the resolutions covering territorial organization into an omnibus bill and thus allay southern fears that Taylor would sign legislation dealing with California but veto all else. But the president opposed the compromise outright. For one, he thought that in such form it would never pass Congress; for another, he wanted New Mexico admitted as a state to resolve the slave issue and avoid compromising its boundaries.

As the debate in Congress continued, Taylor concluded the South was too obstinate and its leaders too eager for secession. He was increasingly convinced he must ally with Northerners in order to save the Union. His own hardening position presented an obstacle: Any bill passed needed his signature; should he use his veto, the divisiveness in Congress assured it would never be overridden. At the same time, his poor relations with Capitol Hill made it difficult for the two sides to work together.

On July 4, 1850, Taylor attended an Independence Day celebration at the unfinished Washington Monument. The day was hot, and when he returned to the White House he drank iced water and chilled milk and ate cherries and perhaps some vegetables. He fell seriously ill, and on July 7 a fever wracked his body. Two days later, on July 9, he was dead from an intestinal disease. His last words were recorded as "I have always done my duty. I am ready to die. My only regret is for the friends I leave behind me." Clay's resolutions, known as the Compromise of 1850, passed Congress later that year under President Millard Fillmore.

Zachary Taylor's presidency showed the dangers of inexperience in the White House in the near paralysis of government that followed the inability of Congress and the executive to cooperate or, for that matter, to even communicate. On such ground compromise over the territorial crisis nearly failed. But his presidency also displayed commitment to the Union that under a less resolute chief executive might have collapsed in 1850.

CHRONOLOGY

1784 Born November 24

1808 Appointed first lieutenant, Seventh Infantry

1810 Appointed captain

1811 Marries Margaret Smith
Takes charge of Fort Knox

1812 Defends Fort Harrison against Indians

1814 Commissioned major

1815 Receives honorable discharge

1816 Reinstated as major, Third Infantry

1819 Appointed lieutenant colonel, Fourth Infantry

1832 Appointed colonel
Fights in Black Hawk War

1837 Named a brigadier general

1838 Commands Department of Florida

1844 Assumes command of Fort Jessup

1845 Commands army of occupation on Mexican border

1846 Fights at Matamoros
Defeats Mexicans at Palo Alto
Defeats Mexicans at Resaca de la Palma
Becomes major general
Captures Monterrey

1847 Fights General Santa Anna at Buena Vista

1848 Nominated for president by Whig Party
Elected president

1849 Resigns from army
Inaugurated as president

1850 Threatens to veto Compromise of 1850
Dies July 9

FURTHER READING

Bauer, Karl Jack. *Zachary Taylor: Soldier, Planter, Statesman of the Old Southwest.* Baton Rouge: Louisiana State University Press, 1985.

Dyer, Brainerd. *Zachary Taylor.* Baton Rouge: Louisiana State University Press, 1946.

Hamilton, Holman. *Zachary Taylor: Soldier of the Republic.* Indianapolis, Ind.: Bobbs-Merrill, 1941.

Nichols, Edward J. *Zach Taylor's Little Army.* Garden City, N.Y.: Doubleday, 1963.

Smith, Elbert B. *The Presidencies of Zachary Taylor and Millard Fillmore.* Lawrence: University Press of Kansas, 1988.

MILLARD FILLMORE (1800–1874)

Thirteenth President, 1850–1853

MILLARD FILLMORE
(lithograph by Currier & Ives, Library of Congress)

> *"I have to perform the melancholy duty of announcing to you that it has pleased Almighty God to remove from this life Zachary Taylor. . . . I propose this day at twelve o'clock . . . in the presence of both Houses of Congress, to take the oath prescribed by the Constitution."*
>
> —Millard Fillmore to Congress, July 10, 1850

Writing in 1888, the Briton James Bryce noted that in the United States the vice presidency was usually given to a "man in the second rank" and as a result "if the President happens to die, a man who may . . . be of no great personal account steps into the chief magistracy of the nation." Such seemed to be the case in 1841 when John Tyler succeeded William Henry Harrison, and it seemed true when Millard Fillmore succeeded Zachary Taylor.

But such a conclusion ignores Fillmore's valuable contributions: He was instrumental in preventing a civil war in 1850, in arranging a compromise between North and South that same year, and in expanding American overseas trade. In a life that took him from a hardscrabble farm in New York to the White House and a career that spanned three political parties, he developed a reputation for dignity, intelligence, and selflessness that made him a credit to the presidency.

Millard Fillmore was born on January 7, 1800, to Nathaniel Fillmore and Phoebe Millard Fillmore in Cayuga County, located in west-central New York. There he grew up on his father's farm, contributing backbreaking work as the elder Fillmore struggled in poverty. Millard obtained little formal education. Later he recalled "an old deserted log house, which had been furnished with a few benches without backs, and a board for writing upon. In this school I learned my alphabet, at the age of six or seven. . . . I learned to plow, to hoe, to chop, to log and clear land, to mow, to reap."

At age 14 Millard apprenticed to a cloth maker and then soon after to a textile mill. While working at the machines he taught himself to read, using a small dictionary he had bought. After a Quaker judge, Walter Wood, recognized the young man's talent and drive, he convinced Millard to study law. In 1822 Fillmore began clerking in a Buffalo law office. At age 24 he was admitted to the bar, and in 1826 he married Abigail Powers, the daughter of a minister. They had two children.

Fillmore was a strikingly handsome man, an impeccable dresser, good-tempered and intelligent, and committed to making sure he never again lived in poverty. He developed a prosperous practice while dedicating himself to helping Buffalo grow and was one of the leaders in improving the terminal facilities of the Erie Canal.

Fillmore saw politics as a way to climb further from his impoverished roots and serve the larger community. In the 1820s he first identified with the Antimasonic Party, which condemned secret societies, especially the Freemasons. Subsequently, as a proponent of federal funding for internal improvements, he allied with the National Republicans after Thurlow Weed, a newspaper editor and power broker, merged that party with the Antimasons. Fillmore supported John Quincy Adams for reelection as president in 1828 and himself ran for the state legislature. He won despite a huge victory for the Democrats that swept Adams from the White House and brought in Andrew Jackson.

In the assembly Fillmore worked to reform the legal system and to abolish imprisonment for debt. He established a relationship with Thurlow Weed best described as a working one rather than a close one. Over the years Weed promoted and supported Fillmore when it was politically beneficial to himself. Fillmore never trusted him, a wise move borne out by Weed's later treachery.

Millard Fillmore won election to the U.S. House of Representatives from western New York in 1832, and two years later, as the National Republicans dissolved, he joined Weed in organizing the Whig Party. Through his hard work, the Whigs built a strong organization in western New York, attracting many former Antimasons. Among his many projects, Fillmore converted the *Commercial Advertiser* into an influential Whig newspaper.

Fillmore's preoccupation with building a political party and his desire to be at home with his wife, who disliked Washington and insisted on staying in Buffalo, caused him to leave Congress in 1834. Two years later, however, he accepted the Whig nomination from his district and defeated his Democratic opponent to return to the House of Representatives. Fillmore's victory was all the more impressive because he bucked a Democratic landslide in New York.

Back in Washington, Fillmore opposed President Martin Van Buren's plan to establish an independent treasury consisting of federal depositories that would hold government money separate from state and private banks. Fillmore had previously criticized the destruction of the national bank by President Andrew

Jackson and thought the independent treasury would do nothing more than lock away funds that could be used for economic investment. He preferred what he called a "free-banking system" whereby federal funds would be deposited in state banks, similar to the method then being used, but one devoid of political influence. He said, "I . . . hope to see the day when . . . the moral pestilence of political banks and banking shall be unknown."

A severe economic depression in 1837 led to the Whigs gaining control of the New York legislature. At the same time, Fillmore and Weed had a falling out when the congressman rejected Weed's entreaties to run for state comptroller. Further worsening relations, Fillmore disliked Weed's choice for governor, William H. Seward, who won the office in 1838.

After the Whigs and William Henry Harrison captured the White House in 1840, Millard Fillmore ran for Speaker of the House against Kentuckian Henry Clay. He had long been at odds with Clay, particularly since Clay's slaveholding antagonized the increasingly strident abolitionist movement in western New York, and he wanted to diminish his fellow Whig's influence. Although Fillmore lost, as a reward for finishing second in the balloting he obtained the powerful position of chairman of the Ways and Means Committee. In that role Fillmore crafted Whig legislation meant to deal with the depression and supported a bankruptcy act that allowed businesses to have their old debts forgiven. On a more controversial issue, he promoted a higher tariff that would protect industries from foreign competition. Most Southerners opposed such legislation, for it would mean higher prices on manufactured goods they either purchased from the North or imported from overseas. To circumvent them Fillmore promoted a bill that would distribute the federal income from the sale of public lands on a proportional basis to the states. He argued that this would help the state treasuries then being emptied by the depression.

But Southerners suspected that northern Whigs wanted to lower funds in the national treasury so they could then argue the tariff needed to be increased to replenish the money lost. They were right; this had been Fillmore's plan all along. Despite southern objections, his distribution bill passed Congress, though it was modified to provide a cap on the amount of land-sale money that could be transferred to the states.

When the bill reached President John Tyler, he vetoed it. Fillmore then worked to write a compromise, which Tyler signed after it passed Congress in 1842. The bill gave Fillmore and the protectionist Whigs almost everything they wanted: It stopped the downward trend in the tariff and boosted it to the 30 percent level; it taxed some imports at 40 percent, even 50 percent; and it protected woolen textile manufacturers and pig-iron producers by rates that jumped from 20 percent to 40 percent. Fillmore's victory was great enough to antagonize the South. The *Charleston Mercury* in South Carolina said Whigs "carry their reason, patriotism, conscience and religion in their purses . . . and . . . know no other voice but that of Mammon."

Just as Fillmore's political star reached new heights, he surprised many in 1842 by again retiring from Congress in order to return to Buffalo. In 1844 Thurlow Weed met with Fillmore and promised to support him for that year's Whig vice-presidential nomination. Horace Greeley, editor of the *New York Tribune* and a prominent Whig himself, pronounced the arrangement sealed when he placed Fillmore's name on his newspaper's masthead. Weed, however, reneged on his promise, and Fillmore lost to Theodore Frelinghuysen of New Jersey.

Then Weed decided that, given the surging antislavery views in New York and Fillmore's own dislike for slavery, the former congressman would make a formidable candidate for governor. Fillmore's presence on the Whig ticket, he reasoned, would help Henry Clay, the party's presidential candidate. Although Fillmore disliked Clay and distrusted Weed for his maneuver with Frelinghuysen, he reluctantly agreed to run for governor as a way to help the party. On hearing about his nomination he said, "So I am in for it and there is no escape."

As it turned out, Clay lost the presidency, and Fillmore lost the governorship to Democrat Silas Wright. Accustomed as he was to winning office, the defeat stunned Fillmore. He resumed his lucrative law practice but remained in public view, particularly with his criticism of President James K. Polk's war against Mexico. Fillmore considered the conflict part of a plot by Southerners to grab more land for slavery. His stand was popular in western New York, where antislavery sentiment continued to strengthen.

The tortuous relationship between Millard Fillmore and Thurlow Weed continued. In 1846 Fillmore acted to contain Weed's power by using his influence to get the Whigs to nominate a gubernatorial candidate Weed opposed. The following year, Fillmore won election as New York comptroller with Weed's support, a powerful post that put him in charge of the state's finances. He superintended New York's banks, wrote a new banking code, and developed a state currency system.

As the 1848 elections approached and the Whigs seemed likely to nominate General Zachary Taylor, hero of the U.S.-Mexican War, as their presidential candidate, talk circulated that Millard Fillmore would make an attractive running mate. Whigs—especially New York Whigs—who were suspicious of Taylor's background as a slaveholder believed Fillmore would add much-needed balance to the ticket. To many the New Yorker's candidacy was essential to keep the party's two main factions, southern planters and northern industrialists, together.

Thurlow Weed thought differently. He wanted the second spot for former New York governor William H. Seward, who was securely in his grasp. For his part, Fillmore had little interest in the nomination but wanted to help achieve a Whig victory. At the party convention, backers of Henry Clay for president (who failed to win the nomination) threw their support behind Fillmore for the vice presidency, as did Weed's political enemies. Fillmore won on the second ballot, frustrating Weed.

Fillmore knew little about the presidential candidate, Zachary Taylor, other than his military exploits. Undoubtedly Taylor knew even less about Fillmore. The New Yorker sent Taylor a letter. "Although I have never had the pleasure of a personal acquaintance," he wrote, "nor can I flatter myself that you have ever heard of me before the late convention, yet as I feel quite acquainted with you from a general knowledge of your widely extended reputation, and as our fellow citizens have seen fit to associate our names for the next presidential contest, I take the liberty by introduction of enclosing a copy of my acceptance of the nomination. . . ."

The Taylor-Fillmore team went on to defeat Democrat Lewis Cass of Michigan. Fillmore's presence on the ticket proved crucial when it convinced many New York Whigs to accept Taylor rather than bolt the party for another candidate. As a result, he delivered New York's electoral votes, the winning margin in the race.

Fillmore entered the vice presidency opposed to slavery but unwilling to abolish it where it already existed. Whether slavery should continue, he believed, was best left to the states to decide. He told the South: "[I have always] regarded slavery as an evil, but one with which the National Government had nothing to do. That by the Constitution of the United States the whole power over that question was vested in the several states where the institution was tolerated."

In 1850 a sectional crisis steeped in slavery threatened to tear the nation apart. California and New Mexico, two territories acquired during the U.S.-Mexican War, wanted to enter the Union with antislavery constitutions. At the same time New Mexico and Texas approached armed conflict after Texas claimed a sizable part of New Mexico's territory. Congress reacted by debating a series of resolutions, written primarily by Henry Clay. These would provide a compromise where California would enter the Union as a free state, while New Mexico would organize a territorial government and resolve its slave issue later by a vote of its residents. The compromise would also settle the border dispute, prohibit the slave trade in Washington, D.C., and establish a stronger law for the return of runaway slaves to their masters. As the debate continued, a Senate committee decided to combine the measures dealing with California and New Mexico into one omnibus bill.

President Taylor opposed the bill, mainly because he wanted New Mexico to enter the Union as a state so its territory could be more assuredly protected from Texas. Many Northerners condemned the compromise as a sellout to the "slaveocracy." They wanted California and New Mexico both in the Union as free states. They also believed the Texas land claim was nothing less than an attempt to expand slave territory, and they despised the fugitive slave law. The compromise was so unpopular that Massachusetts Senator Daniel Webster saw his political support plummet when he joined with Clay to push the legislation.

The crisis confronted Vice President Fillmore with the possibility of having to break a tie vote in his role as president of the Senate. As much as Fillmore disagreed with slavery, he thought a compromise crucial in keeping the Union together. At the same time he wanted to avoid rupturing the Whig Party by opposing President Taylor. After much consideration, Fillmore informed the president that he would vote his conscience. "If I should feel it my duty to vote for it, as I might," he later said, "I wished him to understand, that it was not out of any hostility to him or his Administration, but the vote would be given, because I deemed it for the interests of the country."

Fillmore never was required to cast the vote. While he was working on correspondence late Tuesday evening, July 9, 1850, someone knocked on his door. He opened it to find a messenger, excited and pale, who told him that President Taylor, taken ill a few days earlier, had died. Fillmore met with Taylor's cabinet and said, "I have no language to express the emotions of my heart. The shock is so sudden and unexpected that I am overwhelmed." The next day he took the oath of office making him president.

Millard Fillmore asked Taylor's cabinet members to stay on the job for a month; they agreed only to one week, forcing him to move quickly in forming his administration. More than anything else, the sectional crisis shaped his cabinet choices, and he selected those who supported some form of compromise. His appointments included Daniel Webster as secretary of state.

Like Taylor, Fillmore opposed the omnibus bill. By now Congress had changed it, much to his dismay. An amendment added in the Senate left the border dispute between New Mexico and Texas unresolved while prohibiting New Mexico from forming a territorial government in the disputed land—an arrangement that would allow Texas to exert its authority and perhaps obtain all it was demanding.

While moving to kill the omnibus bill, Fillmore added 750 men to the U.S. Army in Texas and in a message to Congress warned: "If Texas militia . . . march into any one of the other States or into any territory of the United States, there to execute or enforce any law of Texas, they become at that moment trespassers." In response, several southern newspapers vilified Fillmore. One said, "Why should the sword . . . be brandished with something like a menace over a State?"

Along with the sword, though, Fillmore sought compromise, and as a result Congress wrote a bill that gave Texas 33,000 square miles, about one-third of the land it had claimed from New Mexico, mainly in the panhandle, leaving New Mexico with the area it most wanted. The Texas and New Mexico Act, as it was called, organized New Mexico as a territory but left the slavery issue to popular sovereignty, meaning a vote by the local residents. The act stated "that, when admitted as a State, the said territory, or any portion of the same, shall be received into the Union, with or without slavery, as their constitution may prescribe at the time of their admission."

All the other resolutions passed Congress in September and were signed by Fillmore. Together they made up the Compromise of 1850. The resolutions "were not in all respects what I could have desired," he later said, "but they were the best that could be obtained after a protracted discussion that shook the Republic to its very foundation."

In hindsight the compromise appears an ill-fated attempt to save the Union, but at the time many Americans believed it would work. Certainly President Fillmore's firm stand toward Texas on the boundary issue prevented civil war in the year 1850. Had he led Texas to believe the national government would do nothing in the event of an armed attack on New Mexico, in all likelihood Texans would have invaded. That would have sparked a war with New Mexico, and from there North and South would likely have chosen sides, leaving no alternative but a larger conflict.

Later that year, recognizing as he did the importance of foreign trade to national prosperity and hoping that by developing it the Union would be made more secure, President Fillmore sent a mission to Japan. Commodore Matthew Perry arrived there in 1851 with four ships and presented the Japanese emperor with a note from the president. "Great and good friend," it read, "I send you this letter . . . to bear to you my greeting and good wishes, and to promote friendship and commerce between [our] two countries. . . . We wish that our People may be permitted to trade with your People. . . ." The peaceful greeting combined with the show of force left its impression; after Fillmore retired from the presidency, trade with Japan began.

Well before the presidential election of 1852, Millard Fillmore let it be known that he would not seek another term. Wearied by the sectional crisis and never desirous of the presidency to begin with, he wanted to return to Buffalo. But the Whig Party was moving toward self-destruction with the increasing possibility it would nominate General Winfield Scott, who was much disliked in the South for his friendship with the antislavery New Yorker William H. Seward. Scott's selection would tear the party apart. Realizing this, Fillmore's supporters promoted him for president, and he reluctantly postponed any formal announcement of his retirement.

As Fillmore's friends beseeched him to seek the nomination and save the Whig Party, he relented and allowed his name to be entered at the national convention in June 1852. On the first ballot he won more votes than Scott, with solid support from the South. A third candidate, Daniel Webster, prevented anyone from receiving a majority. The voting continued until the exhausted delegates chose Scott on the 53rd ballot. As predicted, the Whig Party shattered when its southern members refused to support the nominee. In the general election Democrat Franklin Pierce won the presidency.

The breakup of the Whigs and turmoil among the Democrats over slavery left an opening for third parties to gain power, and in 1852 the National American Party was formed. More popularly called the Know-Nothing Party, after the practice of its members to use the phrase "I know nothing" as a secret password, within two years it gained a considerable following. The Know-Nothings stood for nativism, an anti-immigrant stand that called for all Catholics and foreigners to be excluded from public office and for an extended 21-year residence before immigrants could qualify for citizenship.

In January 1855 Millard Fillmore made himself available as the Know-Nothing candidate for president. He said, "I have for a long time looked with dread and apprehension at the corrupting influence which the contest for the foreign vote is exciting upon our elections." He believed America should be open to settlement by immigrants but that its public offices should be restricted to the native-born. Then the man who years earlier had criticized secret societies as an Antimason joined the secretive Order of the Star Spangled Banner to qualify him for party membership.

In the ensuing presidential campaign, Fillmore said little about nativism and instead emphasized his strong commitment to the Union. While insisting he would side with neither North nor South, he charged the Democrats and the new Republican Party with being under the control of sectional interests. "When I left the Presidential chair, the whole nation was prosperous and contented," he said. "But where are we now? Alas! Threatened at home with civil war. . . ."

Sectionalism doomed Fillmore's candidacy when dramatic events in 1856 made slavery the leading issue. In May proslavery settlers attacked antislavery settlers in Lawrence, Kansas; a few days later violence hit Kansas again when abolitionist John Brown hacked five proslavery men to death. Soon after that, Representative Preston Brooks of South Carolina caned Senator Charles Sumner of Massachusetts in Congress while Sumner sat in the Senate chamber.

Republican newspapers subsequently launched an unremitting attack on the "slaveocracy." With emotions running so strong, the Know-Nothings appeared too mild and too irrelevant; many Democrats who liked Fillmore decided to stay with their party in order to turn back the Republicans. On election day 1856, the New Yorker finished third behind Democrat James Buchanan, who won, and Republican John C. Frémont. Fillmore captured just eight electoral votes, all from the state of Maryland.

Defeated, Millard Fillmore retired from seeking political office. A widower since 1853, he married wealthy widow Caroline McIntosh in 1858. When the Civil War began he helped recruit volunteers for the Union army. He grew disenchanted with Abraham Lincoln, however, for what he called "military despotism," and in 1864 he supported Democrat George McClellan for president. McClellan lost the race and Fillmore lost much respect in New York, where some questioned his patriotism. In April 1865, though, he headed a committee that escorted Lincoln's funeral train as it entered Buffalo.

Millard Fillmore died on March 8, 1874, shortly after suffering a stroke. Although not ranked among the greatest presidents, he exceeds James Bryce's depiction of the typical vice president elevated by death to the White House. His devotion to the Union and his ability to compromise in order to save it kept the peace, albeit a short and uneasy one.

Chronology

1800 Born January 7

1814 Works in a clothier's mill

1818 Becomes law clerk

1823 Admitted to the bar

1826 Marries Abigail Powers

1828 Elected to New York state assembly

1832 Elected to U.S. House of Representatives

1834 Helps organize Whig Party in New York

1840 Becomes chairman of House Ways and Means Committee

1844 Loses race for governorship of New York

1848 Elected vice president

1850 Becomes president
Signs Compromise of 1850

1852 Loses Whig presidential nomination

1854 Joins Know-Nothing Party

1856 Loses race for president
Retires from seeking public office

1858 Marries Caroline McIntosh

1864 Supports Democrat George McClellan for president

1874 Dies March 8

Further Reading

Grayson, Benson Lee. *The Unknown President: The Administration of Millard Fillmore.* Washington, D.C.: University Press of America, 1981.

Rayback, Robert J. *Millard Fillmore: Biography of a President.* Buffalo, N.Y.: Henry Stewart, 1959.

Scarry, Robert J. *Millard Fillmore.* Jefferson, N.C.: McFarland, 2001.

Smith, Elbert B. *The Presidencies of Zachary Taylor and Millard Fillmore.* Lawrence: University Press of Kansas, 1988.

Van Deusen, Glyndon. *Thurlow Weed, Wizard of the Lobby.* Boston: Little, Brown, 1947.

Franklin Pierce (1804–1869)

Fourteenth President, 1853–1857

Franklin Pierce
(Library of Congress)

"I believe that involuntary servitude, as it exists in [the] different States . . . is recognized by the Constitution. I believe that it stands like any other admitted right, and that the States where it exists are entitled to efficient remedies to enforce the constitutional provisions."

—Inaugural words, March 4, 1853

Shortly before Franklin Pierce became president, the writer Nathaniel Hawthorne said about him, "He is deep, deep, deep. . . . Nothing can ruin him." But it seemed everything conspired to do just that. No previous president was so overwhelmed by events and so incompetent to handle them. As his inauguration approached, he and his wife were horrified when, during a trip near Boston, the train in which they and their 11-year-old son Bennie were riding overturned, crushing Bennie to death. Pierce never recovered from the tragedy, and the dark pallor that cloaked the White House replicated that which spread across the nation as sectional strife moved Americans closer to civil war.

Pierce came from a frontier community in New Hampshire. He was born on November 23, 1804, in his family's log house along a branch of the Contoocook River in Hillsborough County. His father, Benjamin Pierce, served in the militia, fought in the Revolutionary War, and rose from local sheriff to become governor of the state in the 1820s. His mother, Anna Kendrick Pierce, was kind, outgoing, and a hearty drinker. Pierce later said, "She was a most affectionate and tender mother, strong in many points and weak in some but always weak on the side of . . . deep affection. . . ."

Soon after Franklin's birth, Benjamin Pierce moved into a bigger house along a highway and opened a tavern. In this countryside of hills, hollows, and deep forests, with short summers and long winters, Franklin took to hunting, fishing, and swimming in the local ponds. After obtaining some education at a nearby one-room schoolhouse, he enrolled at an academy in Hancock. He graduated from Bowdoin College in 1824, studied law, and was admitted to the bar in 1827.

Two years later Pierce won election to the state legislature, with the spotlight on him as the governor's son, and in 1831, at age 26, he was chosen speaker of the house. By then the senior Pierce had left the governorship, but father and son continued to reinforce each other's beliefs as staunch Jacksonian Democrats. For Franklin, the party became central to his life, a fraternity from which there could be no deviation, and he compiled one of the strongest voting records in support of Jacksonian programs.

Pierce won election to the U.S. House of Representatives in 1832 and then unhesitatingly supported Andrew Jackson in the president's war against the national bank. He voted early in 1834 to endorse Jackson's removal of government funds from the bank, and like most Democrats he opposed federal funding of internal improvements. Pierce's biographer Ron Franklin Nichols has said the congressman held President Jackson in such high regard he "was a devout hero worshipper."

Also in 1834, Franklin Pierce married Jane Means Appleton, daughter of the president of Bowdoin College. They had three children: one who died in infancy; Frank Robert, who died at age four; and Benjamin, or Bennie, who died in the train wreck. Withdrawn and deeply religious, Jane never considered Pierce's family her equal and never liked his political endeavors. Despite her feelings and the brooding atmosphere from the tragedies in their lives, Franklin developed a close attachment to her.

In 1835 Pierce first confronted the issue of slavery, which would help ruin his presidency, when the House of Representatives received a petition to make the "peculiar institution" illegal in Washington, D.C. A few weeks earlier, Pierce had written a friend that in New Hampshire there existed overwhelming sentiment against "fanatics" who disturbed tranquility by promoting opposition to slavery. Such rabble-rousers, he said, succeeded at exciting only a few villages. Speaking in Congress he noted there was "not one in a hundred" in his home state "who does not entertain the most sacred regard for the rights of their Southern brethren—nay not one in five hundred who would not have those rights protected at any and every hazard."

In the Senate, John C. Calhoun of South Carolina criticized Pierce for portraying the abolitionist movement in New Hampshire as smaller than it actually was, to which the congressman stood his ground and replied that when he had used the figure "one in five hundred" he excluded women and children. These were the people, he said, who were at the heart of the abolitionist movement and were the ones signing the antislavery petitions submitted to Congress. With his remarks Pierce made his stand: He hated abolitionists and ridiculed them as "women and children," he believed slavery best left to the states to handle, and he expressed strong sympathy for the South. Much as with his Jacksonian beliefs, he never deviated from these ideas.

In 1836 the New Hampshire legislature elected Pierce to the U.S. Senate, making him the youngest man serving in that body. Some two years later, a close friend said about him: "With no very remarkable talents, he at the age of 34 fills one of the highest stations in the nation."

As senator, Pierce voted to receive a petition criticizing slavery, not because he sympathized with it, but because he believed if the Senate refused to hear it, the abolitionist cause would use the vote as ammunition against the slave interests. In casting his vote he sided with the Whig Party, one of the few instances in which he broke ranks with his fellow Democrats.

Soon after this, he voted for resolutions introduced by John C. Calhoun stating that any decisions regarding slavery were to be made by the states and that any attempt to abolish slavery in the territories or in the nation's capital would be an attack against the South. Pierce said he supported Calhoun "to preserve inviolate the public faith and the provisions of the Constitution under which we have so long lived in prosperity." The Senate adopted the resolutions.

Pierce's service in the House and the Senate caused him great personal damage. Attracted to the conviviality of his colleagues and to the swirl of parties, he drank heavily. Knowledge of his alcoholism spread, and although he later abstained and joined the temperance movement—some historians claim he gave up drinking around 1840—evidence indicates he returned to the bottle while president, and most certainly in his later years. Some rumors claimed his drinking muddled his mind. Whatever the case, it certainly proved a hardship on his family.

Largely for that reason he quit the Senate in 1842, resumed his law practice, and hoped that in New Hampshire he could escape the temptations of drink. In addition, his wife hated politics, hated Washington, and wanted to return home.

When the U.S.-Mexican War began in 1846, he volunteered for the army and served first as a private, then as a colonel, and finally as a brigadier general. In this role he led 2,500 men from Veracruz to Mexico City and along the way repulsed six attacks. Misfortune struck, though, during one battle when his horse threw and injured him. He returned to duty only to be injured again, at which point General Winfield Scott thought him incompetent. Pierce came home from the U.S.-Mexican War with combat experience but without the glory he desperately wanted.

He received national political attention when, after serving as president of the New Hampshire constitutional convention in 1850, he led a successful effort to replace his party's antislavery gubernatorial candidate with one more sympathetic to the South. In June 1852 he benefited from a deadlock at the Democratic National Convention at Baltimore. Amid stifling heat and short tempers, the delegates went through ballot after ballot unable to decide on a presidential candidate among front-runners Lewis Cass of Michigan, Stephen Douglas of Illinois, and James Buchanan of Pennsylvania. Into the frustration stepped Pierce's supporters, who insisted their man would unite the party and give offices to all the factions that supported him. The delegates chose Pierce on the 49th ballot.

Franklin Pierce never expected the nomination and reacted in disbelief. Here was a man who had been out of Congress for a decade; now he was running for president of the United States. Jane Pierce fainted when she heard the news.

Yet Pierce's relative obscurity pleased most Democrats. They believed they could effectively sell to the voters someone who had been largely removed from the sectional firestorm that surrounded the Compromise of 1850, which had alienated Northerners and Southerners alike with its various provisions.

In a peculiar twist, Pierce ran against his former commanding general in the U.S.-Mexican War, Winfield Scott, the Whig candidate. By most accounts the election generated little interest. One anti-Pierce newspaper said, "In our recent travels in New York and New England we should not have known from any indication of popular feeling, that a Presidential election was pending." Some controversy erupted when newspapers reported remarks Pierce had made months earlier in which he called the Fugitive Slave Law immoral but said it must be enforced to maintain the Compromise of 1850. His words were repeated by those who wanted to drive a wedge between him and the South. Pierce sidestepped the issue by calling the news reports distorted. For its part, Scott's campaign focused on Pierce's character and released a book ostensibly about the Democrat's heroism. Small in size, it contained nothing but blank pages.

On election day, with the turnout down slightly from the presidential contest of 1848, Pierce won 254 electoral votes to Scott's 42. The loss greatly weakened the Whig Party.

The year 1853 should have been a celebratory one for the start of Pierce's presidency, but nothing went right. First came the death of Bennie, a tragedy that sent Pierce into depression and stole his confidence. To a friend he said, "How I shall be able to summon my manhood to gather up my energies for the duties before me, it is hard for me to see." Jane Pierce became a semirecluse who spent much of her time writing letters to her dead son. One visitor to the White House remarked, "Everything in that mansion seems cold and cheerless. I have seen hundreds of log cabins which seemed to contain more happiness."

Then, soon after Pierce's inauguration, Senator Charles G. Atherton of New Hampshire died. Pierce had expected Atherton to be his spokesman in the Senate. More turmoil came on April 19 when Vice President William R. King died while in Cuba seeking to restore his health.

To add to the president's miseries, he stirred opposition from almost every quarter when he put together a cabinet that reflected diverse opinions—from Free Soilers to southern rights advocates. In trying to please everyone, he pleased no one (though the cabinet remained intact and functioned reasonably well). At the same time, sectional discord within Congress ended any hope that divisive issues could be avoided, and rumors circulated that the president was drinking again. By the end of Pierce's first year, one Democratic leader was lamenting that a great mistake had been made in placing him in the White House.

A strong states' rights supporter, with few exceptions President Pierce opposed federal funding of internal improvements. In fighting a public domain land grant to a railroad he said, "Is it not the better rule to leave all these works to private enterprise, regulated and, when expedient, aided by the cooperation of the State?"

Much as Pierce wanted the nation to avoid sectional issues, primarily the emotion-laden one of slavery, almost everything Americans did in the 1850s raised that specter, even in the building of railroads. Slavery's effect on the Union was evident in a proposal by Illinois senator Stephen A. Douglas, a Democrat and ardent expansionist, who wanted a railroad built from Chicago to the Pacific Coast. His hope was to boost his state's economy, that of the nation, and the value of land in which he had invested. He wanted to act quickly in order to stop a move by Southerners, backed by President Pierce, to build a transcontinental line along a route connected to the South. Douglas asked: "How are we to develop, cherish and protect our immense interests and possessions on the Pacific with a vast wilderness fifteen hundred miles in breadth; and filled with hostile savages, and cutting off all direct communication?" The answer: Organize the western territories to encourage settlement and provide stable government.

As chair of a Senate committee, Douglas wrote a bill in January 1854 to establish a territorial government in Nebraska, with slavery to be determined by popular sovereignty, meaning by a vote of the people living there. Southerners objected; they said if a vote resulted in favor of slavery it would still be prohibited by the Missouri Compromise of 1820, which made the peculiar institution illegal in the western territories north of latitude 36°30'. They wanted the compromise repealed. Northerners, however, considered the compromise a sacred trust, and Douglas realized that if he supported repeal there would be a huge protest. Nevertheless, he wanted the railroad built. Thus, he revised his measure to divide Nebraska into two territories, Kansas and Nebraska, and to declare the Missouri Compromise "inoperative and void."

Unfortunately for President Pierce, Senator Douglas's bill soon became his, as did all the criticism it carried. Pierce disliked the Missouri Compromise but thought that overturning it would only rekindle the slavery controversy. As a result, he first regarded the Kansas-Nebraska Act with disfavor. Then Douglas and several other senators met with him and applied pressure; so did Secretary of War Jefferson Davis, a Southerner. They then arranged a deal whereby the senators agreed to support Pierce's candidate for the position of collector at the Port of New York, and Pierce agreed to support Douglas's bill.

The outrage from the North and its intensity and fury stunned even Douglas. James G. Blaine of Maine later said of the Kansas-Nebraska Act: "It produced a frenzy of wrath on the part of thousands and tens of thousands in both old parties who had never before taken any part whatsoever in antislavery agitation." Several Democratic leaders condemned the measure and called it the work of a conspiracy among slaveholders. The entire furor surrounding the act split the Democratic Party and helped give rise to the Republicans and their Free-Soil platform that opposed slavery in any of the western territories.

Despite the uproar, in March 1854 the Senate approved the Kansas-Nebraska Act by a vote of 37-14, with Democrats overwhelmingly supporting it. The fight in the House lasted longer, but the measure passed in May, 159-75. Elections in the fall were disastrous for the Democrats. With the Whig Party dissolving and the Know-Nothing Party gaining strength, about 115 congressmen who opposed the Kansas-Nebraska Act won election. Faced with this outcome, many Democrats concluded that Pierce was a liability.

Another controversy shook the nation in March 1855 when northern newspapers published the Ostend Manifesto, which had been signed by three U.S. diplomats in Europe in October 1854. The document proposed offering Spain $130 million for Cuba, which was declared to be indispensable for the security of American slavery. The manifesto also recommended that if Spain refused to sell the island, the United States should take it by force. As Northerners pointed to the manifesto to prove Pierce was in league with proslavery Southerners, he backed away from it. The document, however, angered Spain and other countries, turning it into a foreign policy blunder.

Nevertheless, Pierce made some diplomatic progress during his presidency. Late in 1853 he obtained what is today southern New Mexico and Arizona, including Tucson, in the Gadsden Purchase from Mexico, and in 1854 Commodore Matthew C. Perry signed a treaty of peace, friendship, and commerce with Japan that opened two of that nation's ports to American trade.

The storm over the Kansas-Nebraska Act and the Ostend Manifesto having extracted a heavy toll on political civility, it took the House 133 ballots over nine weeks in 1855 to choose a Speaker—and then only by a three-vote margin. As that mess unfolded, Pierce took the unprecedented step of releasing his annual message before the Speaker was chosen. In a second message he blamed the troubles over Kansas on northern agitators.

Certainly northern opinion had shifted markedly. Work by abolitionists and Free-Soilers intensified the opposition to slavery's expansion; then the Kansas-Nebraska Act seemed to confirm the warnings about a slaveholders' conspiracy. Where once there existed only minor opposition to the Fugitive Slave Law, it now spread across the region. President Pierce never understood this depth of feeling. He insisted the Fugitive Slave Law must be enforced and southern property rights in slaves protected.

The Kansas controversy overwhelmed Pierce. After the federal government opened the territory for settlement in May 1854, a mad scramble for land ensued and settlers arrived from both the North and the South. Many who came from neighboring Missouri, a slave state, were intent on making sure Kansas formed a proslavery government. Tension between them and the Free-Soilers quickly escalated, made all the worse by Pierce. In 1855 he appointed Wilson Shannon, a proslavery politician from Cincinnati, as governor. Free-Soilers reacted by forming their own territorial government with a constitution that excluded blacks from settling in Kansas. This revealed the Free-Soiler belief that slavery should be restricted mainly to protect lands for white settlement.

In January 1856 President Pierce said he preferred a proslavery government and would enforce all laws passed by the territorial legislature to protect slavery. He also called the Free-Soilers troublemakers. Anyone familiar with Pierce's long-held ideas could have predicted the stand he would take. He believed the South had been wronged by the North and that slavery should be left alone. In his view Congress lacked any authority to restrict slavery while a territory was organizing to become a state. He once wrote: "While the people of the Southern States confined their attention to their own affairs, not presuming officiously to intermeddle with the social institutions of the Northern States, too many of the inhabitants of the latter . . . organized in associations to inflict injury on the former by wrongful acts."

In May 1856 violence flared in Kansas when a proslavery mob attacked a Free-Soil settlement at Lawrence. The mob caused no deaths, but they burned the Free State Hotel to the ground, pillaged several houses, and destroyed two newspaper presses. Northern newspapers excited passions with sensationalist stories about what they called the "Sack of Lawrence."

A few days later, a fanatical abolitionist, John Brown, accompanied by six followers, massacred five proslavery settlers in Kansas at Pottawatomie Creek. Guerrilla fighting then erupted throughout the territory—a civil war in what was called "Bleeding Kansas." During that same month, the violence in Kansas spilled into Congress. After Senator Charles Sumner of Massachusetts presented a vitriolic speech in which he condemned a "slave oligarchy" and insulted several southern congressmen, representative Preston S. Brooks of South Carolina responded by smashing him over the head with a cane in the Senate chamber. Southerners applauded Brooks, while Northerners expressed outrage. Several congressmen started carrying knives and pistols for protection.

In September peace was restored in Kansas after Pierce appointed a new governor, John W. Geary, a moderate determined to suppress the violence. Yet the damage had been done. "Bleeding Kansas" came to symbolize the failure of Pierce's administration. He understood neither compromise nor how to achieve it. Biased against the North, unable to grasp the magnitude of what was happening, he reacted to sectional disputes defensively. The proslavery element could do no wrong, the antislavery element no right. According to Larry Gara in *The Presidency of Franklin Pierce,* when the president presented his final message to Congress he permeated it with his belief "that all the sectional troubles stemmed from northern interference and aggression. . . ."

Although southern Democrats supported Pierce in 1856, hardly anyone else did. As a result, when the Democratic Party met that June in Cincinnati for its national convention, the delegates refused to renominate him. After 15 ballots the president withdrew his candidacy. Because the delegates wanted to avoid anyone tainted by the Kansas-Nebraska Act, they turned to James Buchanan.

After Pierce left office, he and his wife traveled in Europe for two years. In 1860 Abraham Lincoln won the presidency as a Republican, a party Pierce hated for its appeal to northern sectional interests. Near the time Lincoln was elected, northern newspapers intercepted and printed a letter written by Pierce to his friend Jefferson Davis. In it the former president said, "If I were in the Southerners' places, after so many years of aggression, I should probably be doing what they are doing. If our fathers were mistaken when they formed the Constitution, then the sooner we are apart the better."

On July 4, 1863, Pierce spoke at a Democratic rally in Massachusetts and condemned the Civil War. A few hours later, news came of the North's victory at Gettysburg. With his letter and speech—and with the turn of events in the war pointing to a southern defeat—Pierce became reviled in the North. After his wife passed away later that year, he took again to heavy drinking. He died on October 8, 1869, abandoned by most everyone, his name seldom recalled, not even in New Hampshire.

Most likely no president could have survived the sectional tempest of the 1850s unscathed. But Franklin Pierce's limited talent and bad decisions assured his failure. Historian Eugene H. Roseboom has called his decision to repeal the Missouri Compromise "one of the costliest blunders in White House history." Certainly it darkened the national mood and hastened America's movement toward civil war.

CHRONOLOGY

1804 Born November 23

1824 Graduates from Bowdoin College

1827 Admitted to the bar

1829 Named to the New Hampshire legislature

1831 Chosen speaker of the state legislature

1832 Elected to U.S. House of Representatives

1834 Marries Jane Means Appleton

1836 Elected to U.S. Senate

1842 Resigns from Senate

1847 Commissioned brigadier general of volunteers

Marches to Mexico City with Winfield Scott's army

1848 Resigns from the army

1850 Elected president of New Hampshire constitutional convention

1852 Elected president

1853 Completes Gadsden Purchase

1854 Signs Kansas-Nebraska Act

Signs commercial treaty with Japan

1856 Supports proslavery government in Kansas territory

1857 Retires from presidency

Travels to Europe

1859 Returns to United States

1863 Denounces North in Civil War

1869 Dies October 8

FURTHER READING

Gara, Larry. *The Presidency of Franklin Pierce.* Lawrence: University Press of Kansas, 1991.

Hawthorne, Nathaniel. *Life of Franklin Pierce.* Boston: Ticknor, Reed and Fields, 1852.

Nichols, Ron Franklin. *Franklin Pierce: Young Hickory of the Granite Hills.* 1931. Reprint, Philadelphia: University of Pennsylvania Press, 1958.

JAMES BUCHANAN (1791–1868)

Fifteenth President, 1857–1861

JAMES BUCHANAN
(lithograph by Currier & Ives, Library of Congress)

"A difference of opinion has arisen in regard to the point of time when the people of a Territory shall decide this question [of slavery] for themselves. . . . It is a judicial question, which legitimately belongs to the Supreme Court of the United States, before whom it is now pending, and will, it is understood, be speedily and finally settled. To their decision, in common with all good citizens, I shall cheerfully submit, whatever this may be. . . ."

—Inaugural words, March 4, 1857

By late 1860 many Northerners believed James Buchanan supported the southern states in their drive toward secession. Numerous critics went so far as to consider him a traitor. Buchanan reacted with consternation and professed a strong attachment to the Union—though one in which slavery would be protected as a property right in the western territories. His reaction to secession when it finally came reinforced northern skepticism; for the most part, he simply stood back and watched.

Maybe political leader William H. Seward was right. An "irrepressible conflict" had been reached that no president, in fact no human being, could settle without bloodshed. But Buchanan's sectional bias and strained legalism made war all the more likely and assured that when Southerners gathered arms, confiscated forts, and declared their own independent nation in his last weeks as president, the federal government would act with meekness rather than strength.

James Buchanan was born on April 23, 1791, in a one-room log cabin near Mercersburg, Pennsylvania, where hills, oak groves, and farms dominated the landscape. He was one of 11 children. His father, also named James, had emigrated from Ireland and operated a trading post where he earned a reputation as a canny and arrogant businessman. In contrast, his mother, Elizabeth Speer Buchanan, embraced a modest, Christian life, dedicating herself to deciphering God's will and making it to heaven.

The elder Buchanan moved his family to town when James was six, buying a two-bedroom brick house that served as both home and business for his mercantile trade. Young James attended school at the local Old Stone Academy, where he studied Latin and Greek. In 1807 he enrolled at Dickinson College in Carlisle, Pennsylvania. At first he tended to his studies; then, in an effort to become more popular, he began smoking, carousing, and drinking heavily. He later said, "Without much natural tendency to become dissipated, and chiefly from the example of others, and in order to be considered a clever and spirited youth, I engaged in every sort of extravagance and mischief."

The college reacted by expelling him, perhaps more in the hope of shocking him into changing his ways than preventing him from returning. If that was the intent, it worked. After James promised to temper his social life and tend to his studies, the college readmitted him, and he graduated in 1809 with a reputation for ambition, if not also the arrogance found in his father.

He went on to study law, and in 1812 he began his practice in Lancaster. That same year the United States went to war against Britain, and during the conflict James Buchanan decided he would help defend Baltimore. He joined a volunteer regiment and headed south, but the only duty he saw was to confiscate horses for use by the army.

After returning home, Buchanan ran for the state legislature in 1814 as a Federalist and won. He retired after two terms to concentrate on his law career and by age 27 amassed considerable wealth. In 1818 he fell in love with Ann Coleman, daughter of an iron-mill owner in Lancaster, and proposed marriage. She accepted, but her parents disapproved. They thought Buchanan wanted to marry their daughter for one reason: money. As a result, Ann broke off the engagement. She then slid into a depression and soon after died under mysterious circumstances. Town rumors said she committed suicide, but that was never proven. The Colemans blamed Buchanan for her death and barred him from the funeral. He never fully recovered from the emotionally racking experience and never married.

Buchanan returned to public office in 1820 when he won election to the U.S. House of Representatives. With the Federalist Party dying and his own ambition thriving, in 1824 he announced his support of Andrew Jackson in the presidential race. Jackson lost, but Buchanan took the lead in creating an "amalgamation" of Federalists and Jacksonians in western Pennsylvania. In 1828 he forcefully expressed his attachment to the new alliance when he verbally attacked incumbent president John Quincy Adams as despotic, immoral, and corrupt. He then devoted his efforts to obstructing the Adams program in Congress as a way to boost another presidential run by Jackson.

His support for Jackson, who won the presidency that fall, made for a case of strange bedfellows. The two politicians differed on several issues. Buchanan, for example, wanted a high protective tariff, a policy Jackson never subscribed to, though while serving in Congress he did vote to increase rates on several occasions. Further, the Jacksonians appealed to the masses, while the Federalists distrusted them. Yet both men believed in a vigorous executive branch. Buchanan also often disregarded issues in finding a vehicle that would advance his career. Some called him a blatant opportunist, moving in whatever direction the political weather vane pointed.

That he won reelection to Congress in 1828 under the banner of the new Democratic Party testified both to his hard work in building an organization to replace the Federalists and to his political agility. Four years later, President Jackson appointed him minister to Russia. Buchanan accepted though with disappointment, for he wanted a more prestigious position and hoped to become Jackson's running mate in the fall election. He set sail for the Russian capital of St. Petersburg in the spring of 1832 on a mission, he said, "in which my heart never was: to leave the most free and happy country on earth for a despotism more severe than any which exists in Europe."

For all his reluctance he achieved a diplomatic victory when he arranged America's first trade agreement with Russia. The treaty provided for reciprocity, meaning the ships of each country would receive treatment equal to that received in the ports of the other. In practice, the treaty benefited the United States most, for the number of American ships visiting Russian ports far exceeded those sailing the other way, and Russian regulations were more burdensome than American ones.

Buchanan returned from Russia in 1833 and won election to the U.S. Senate in 1834, where he served 11 years. Known as a conservative Democrat with a reputation for caution, he chaired the Foreign Relations Committee, and on several occasions he criticized the expanding activities of abolitionists.

James Buchanan wanted the presidency in 1844, and several leading Democrats promoted him. But the party turned instead to Andrew Jackson's choice, the expansionist James K. Polk of Tennessee. Buchanan worked hard for the nominee, and Polk rewarded him by appointing him secretary of state. The cabinet position was considered a stepping-stone to the White House and certainly encouraged Buchanan's own ambition. In 1846 he won praise from expansionist Americans for negotiating the acquisition of Oregon with Britain.

Polk and Buchanan, however, fought almost constantly over important issues. The president grew exasperated with the Pennsylvanian's frequent changes of position, changes that convinced him Buchanan thought only about what could get him elected president. In one incident after the U.S.-Mexican War had begun, Buchanan argued that the president should renounce any territorial ambition. Polk refused.

Later, with victory for the United States in sight, Buchanan advised the president to acquire as much territory as possible. Polk recorded in his diary: "I cannot help laboring under the conviction that the true reason of Mr. Buchanan's present course is that he is now a candidate for the Presidency, and he does not wish to incur the displeasure of those who are in favour of the conquest of all Mexico." In fact, those who wanted more land were Southerners, the very constituent group Buchanan closely identified with when he became president.

Polk was correct about his secretary of state: Buchanan was indeed maneuvering for the White House in 1848, but he lost the Democratic nomination to Lewis Cass of Michigan. He subsequently retired to an estate he had recently purchased outside of Lancaster, named Wheatland, with spacious rooms, broad lawns, and towering oaks. There he lived as a country squire.

He tried a third time for the presidential nomination in 1852, but Franklin Pierce, a largely unknown politician from New Hampshire, defeated him. In spring 1853 Pierce appointed Buchanan minister to Britain.

At any other time the appointment may have ended his domestic political career, taking him far from the public stage and making him forgettable. But in the mid-1850s the appointment helped him, for it removed him from the vicious sectional battles then being fought in Congress and elsewhere over whether to extend slavery into the western territories. His assignment across the Atlantic also kept him distant from the unpopular Pierce administration and its many blunders.

Yet Buchanan did not escape every mistaken policy, and he actually contributed to one that helped ruin Pierce's presidency. In October 1854 he and two other American ministers, Pierre Soulé and John Y. Mason, met in Belgium to formulate a policy toward Spain over the slave island of Cuba. They wrote the Ostend Manifesto, in which they recommended the United States try to buy Cuba or, if Spain refused to sell the island, to take it forcibly. Pierce never accepted the recommendation, but in March 1855 the manifesto was published in newspapers and greatly angered Northerners. The emerging Republican Party pointed to it as proof Pierce wanted more slave territory to placate the South.

Buchanan's involvement in the Ostend Manifesto worked to his benefit, however, by raising his standing among Southerners. As a result, when the 1856 Democratic National Convention met, his diplomatic experience helped him in two ways. First, many delegates from the North and West supported him for president because he had been away from the heated debate over the Kansas-Nebraska Act, while southern delegates supported him because he seemed sympathetic toward slavery. Two other candidates for the nomination, President Pierce and Senator Stephen A. Douglas of Illinois, had made enemies over the Kansas issue. As a result, after 15 ballots the convention nominated Buchanan for president.

Buchanan ran against John C. Frémont of the Republican Party and former president Millard Fillmore of the Know-Nothing Party. In November the Pennsylvanian won less than 50 percent of the popular vote but a majority in the electoral college, with 174 votes to Frémont's 114 and Fillmore's 8.

As Buchanan's inauguration neared, the nation prepared for another explosion over slavery. The Supreme Court had before it a suit by Dred Scott, a slave who was claiming his freedom because at one point, from 1834 to 1838, his master had taken him into Illinois and into Wisconsin Territory, both of which forbade slavery. The court could rule for or against Scott, or it could take another route and refuse to rule at all. Buchanan wanted a decision, one that would resolve the issue of slavery in the territories. The five southern justices on the court stood ready to rule against Scott, but without support from a northern justice they hesitated, lest their decision appear completely sectional. With the case in the balance, Buchanan secretly contacted one of the justices, Robert C. Grier of Pennsylvania, and pressured him to join his southern colleagues. Grier wrote back to the president-elect: "We fully appreciate and concur in your views as to the desirableness . . . of having an expression of the opinion of the Court on this troublesome question."

Buchanan's contact with Grier violated court ethics. He and Grier were close friends and political allies, and Buchanan well knew the justice's sympathy for the South. According to historian Roy F. Nichols, "Buchanan always had desired to be a member of the Supreme Court; in this instance he practically participated in their deliberations and influenced their judgment." That the president-elect ever thought the North would accept a decision against Scott testifies either to his misreading of the political crisis or how far he was willing to go to protect southern interests.

At his inauguration Buchanan pledged himself to one term as president; then, knowing the Supreme Court decision would come at any moment and would likely favor the South, he said he would abide by whatever ruling the Court chose to issue. Belying the crisis, the capital was filled with revelers, who at his inaugural ball consumed 500 gallons of oysters,

800 chickens, and 100 gallons of ice cream, along with venison, beef, turkey, pheasants, ham, and lobster.

Just two days after the celebration, the Supreme Court made its decision public: As a slave, Dred Scott was not a citizen of the United States; his temporary residence in free territory had not ended his bondage; and the Missouri Compromise of 1820 prohibiting slavery in most of the Louisiana Purchase territory was unconstitutional because it deprived persons of their property without due process of the law. In effect, the decision prohibited Congress from preventing slavery in the western territories.

No other decision could have caused greater outrage in the North. Theoretically, at least, the Court was saying slavery could even expand into the free states—no law could stop it. As a result, Buchanan began his administration with sectional animosities increasing rather than lessening and with many Northerners suspecting he had some involvement in the *Dred Scott* case. Making his standing worse, a financial panic in 1857 damaged the economy. That the downturn was more severe in the North than in the South only caused Southerners to say it showed northern depravity and the superiority of the southern economy.

Buchanan's greatest challenge—the very survival of his administration, if not the nation—came in Kansas. Under President Pierce, proslavery and antislavery (Free-Soil) settlers had established separate governments in the territory. James Buchanan, however, appointed a new governor, Robert J. Walker, to resolve the crisis. Walker, a former secretary of the treasury, hailed from Mississippi but was a strong unionist. Before he could arrive in the beleaguered territory, the proslavery government in the Kansas town of Lecompton called for a convention to write a constitution and proceeded to schedule an election to choose delegates for it. Free-Soil leaders in nearby Lawrence called the election procedure rigged, saying it ignored the free-state residents, who by then composed a clear majority in the territory.

The balloting for delegates was held in June 1857. The rules established at Lecompton kept half the Free-Soilers from voting, while the other half staged a boycott. Consequently, the Lecompton convention met in October and wrote a constitution filled with proslavery provisions, including prohibiting the freeing of slaves already in Kansas—numbering 200—and strict enforcement of the federal Fugitive Slave Law. The convention scheduled a popular vote for December 21, whereby residents could decide for the "Lecompton constitution" with or without slavery, but if the "without slavery" version were chosen, it would only prohibit the introduction of new slaves and do nothing about the slavery that already existed. In addition, the balloting was to be supervised by the proslavery government.

Northerners branded the arrangement fraudulent. Democratic leader Stephen A. Douglas, who in the 1850s promoted popular sovereignty—the right of the residents in a territory to vote whether or not to permit slavery—found himself under pressure from his constituents in Illinois and from newspapers to oppose the Lecompton constitution. Thus, for both political reasons and because he thought the arrangement in Kansas an affront to popular sovereignty, he met with President Buchanan and announced his opposition to the document.

Buchanan responded by saying he believed the Lecompton constitution was legitimate. He added that Kansas must be admitted into the Union quickly to defuse the sectional crisis and weaken the new Republican Party, which with its free-soil platform was gaining strength from the Kansas controversy. Buchanan warned Douglas: "I desire you to remember that no Democrat ever yet differed from an Administration of his own choice without being crushed." In reference to the weakened state of the presidency compared to years earlier, Douglas replied: "Mr. President, I wish you to remember that General [Andrew] Jackson is dead."

Due to its divided condition, Kansas held two votes on the Lecompton constitution. The one arranged by the proslavery government ended in 6,143 ballots for the document with slavery and 569 against it—but most Free-Soilers refused to participate, and in any event the tally included many fraudulent votes. The Free-Soil government held a referendum in which the constitution was soundly defeated—a more accurate reflection of opinion given the greater number of antislavery settlers in the territory.

In February the U.S. Senate approved the Lecompton constitution and slavery for Kansas by a vote of 33-25. That result came only after much wheeling and dealing by President Buchanan, including both threats and promises of higher office.

When approval of the constitution stalled in the House, Buchanan was forced to propose a compromise, finalized by others, whereby Kansans would vote on a proposed federal land sale that at the same time would allow them to accept or reject the Lecompton constitution. In August 1858 the constitution went down to defeat by a large margin, 11,812 to 1,926.

The Kansas debacle destroyed Buchanan. Southerners accused him of allowing Yankee politicians such as Stephen Douglas to engage in sneaky maneuvering that stole the election from the proslavery settlers. Northerners condemned him for siding with the Lecompton constitution. Added to this, the controversy helped the Republicans by allowing them to assume the mantle of democracy, based on their attacks against the proslavery government in Kansas.

In the 1858 congressional elections, candidates who opposed the Lecompton constitution swept to victory. The Republican Party gained more seats, though Abraham Lincoln lost his senate race to Douglas, who publicized his stand against President Buchanan. No one could deny Buchanan's humiliation, and for the remainder of his presidency he was nothing more than a figurehead.

In 1859 John Brown staged his dramatic but failed raid on the federal arsenal at Harper's Ferry, Virginia, in an attempt to incite a slave uprising. Passions flared again as Northerners hailed him as a hero and Southerners portrayed him as the vanguard of an abolitionist-led crusade to end slavery through bloodshed. As the 1860 presidential election approached, the Democratic Party split, torn asunder by Northerners and Southerners unable to compromise their sectional hatreds.

In that setting the Republican candidate, Abraham Lincoln, won the presidency, although he had a minority of the popular vote, and his name was kept off the ballot in the South. Southerners in the Deep South had threatened to secede should the winner be Lincoln, a man they believed to be nothing less than an abolitionist who would destroy their civilization. They now intended to carry out their threat.

In a message to Congress in December 1860, Buchanan placed blame for the sectional crisis on northern antislavery agitators. But he also advised caution and said Lincoln would respect the Constitution rather than usurp it and that, in any event, his power would be checked by the other branches of government. Buchanan wanted Congress to affirm the right of slavery in the territories, with popular sovereignty to be used whenever any territory petitioned for statehood. He also wanted action to strengthen the right of masters to their runaway slaves. Despite his message, the Deep South seceded; South Carolina left before Christmas Day, followed by Mississippi, Florida, Alabama, Georgia, Louisiana, and Texas.

As Southerners seized federal arsenals and forts, President Buchanan was confronted with the need to show decisiveness; instead he showed timidity. Although he declared secession unconstitutional, he said the federal government had no authority to use force against the rebellious states. Buchanan obviously faced a conundrum: Should he do nothing, the South would grow more emboldened; should he use the military—itself in a weak state—he would ignite a full-scale war before Lincoln even set foot in the White House. To make matters worse, the incoming president rejected Buchanan's overtures for a meeting between them to develop a policy—understandably so from Lincoln's view, because he wanted to avoid any association with the discredited chief executive.

When Buchanan refused to reinforce the federal forts at Charleston, South Carolina, Secretary of State Lewis Cass resigned in protest. His departure from the cabinet stunned the president because Cass represented the moderate wing of the Democratic Party. Cass, however, had concluded Buchanan was too pro-southern.

After Lincoln's inauguration in March 1861, Buchanan retired to Wheatland, leaving the unresolved crisis in the new president's hands. During the Civil War he supported Lincoln and said he would have reacted to the firing on Fort Sumter in the same way that Lincoln did. But most Northerners denigrated him. One said, "Buchanan is . . . as truly a traitor as was Benedict Arnold himself."

In his memoirs, James Buchanan expressed his strong feelings about the differences between North and South, saying: "The Constitution . . . expressly recognizes the right to hold slaves as property in states where slavery exists. . . . The southern states have rights guaranteed to them, and these rights I determined to maintain, come weal, come woe." He added, "The abolitionists . . . scattered throughout the slave holding states pamphlets, newspapers and pictorial representations . . . calculated . . . to excite the wild and brutal passions of the slaves to cut the throats of their masters."

Shortly before his death on June 1, 1868, Buchanan insisted, "I have always felt and still feel that I discharged every public duty imposed on me conscientiously. I have no regret for any public act of my life, and history will vindicate my memory." By then the Civil War had ended—a conflict that took more American lives than any other.

Chronology

1791 Born April 23

1809 Graduates from Dickinson College

1812 Admitted to the bar

1814 Elected to Pennsylvania legislature

1816 Returns to law practice

1820 Elected to U.S. House of Representatives

1822 Reelected to U.S. House of Representatives

1824 Reelected to third term in Congress

1826 Reelected to fourth term in Congress

1828 Reelected to fifth term in Congress, this time as a Democrat

1832 Appointed minister to Russia

1834 Elected to U.S. Senate

1844 Defeated in bid for Democratic presidential nomination

1845 Appointed secretary of state

1846 Negotiates Oregon treaty with Britain

1848 Loses bid for Democratic presidential nomination

1850 Opposes Compromise of 1850

1852 Loses bid for Democratic presidential nomination

1853 Appointed minister to Britain

1854 Helps draft Ostend Manifesto

1856 Elected president

1857 Upholds Lecompton convention in Kansas

1858 Submits Lecompton constitution to Congress

1861 Refuses to reinforce Fort Sumter

Retires to Wheatland

1868 Dies June 1

FURTHER READING

Baker, Jean H. *James Buchanan.* New York: Times Books, 2004.

Binder, Frederick M. *James Buchanan and the American Empire.* Selinsgrove, Pa.: Susquehanna University Press, 1994.

Birkner, Michael, ed. *James Buchanan and the Political Crisis of the 1850s.* Selinsgrove, Pa.: Susquehanna University Press, 1996.

Klein, Philip Shriver. *President James Buchanan: A Biography.* University Park: Pennsylvania State University Press, 1962.

Moore, John B. *The Works of James Buchanan.* New York: Antiquarian Press, 1960.

Smith, Elbert B. *The Presidency of James Buchanan.* Lawrence: University Press of Kansas, 1975.

ABRAHAM LINCOLN (1809–1865)

Sixteenth President, 1861–1865

ABRAHAM LINCOLN
(National Archives)

With malice toward none; with charity for all; with firmness in the right, as God gives us to see the right, let us strive on to finish the work we are in; to bind up the nation's wounds; to care for him who shall have borne the battle, and for his widow, and his orphan—to do all which may achieve and cherish a just, and a lasting peace, among ourselves, and with all nations.

—Inaugural words, second term, March 4, 1865

Among all presidents, Americans rank Abraham Lincoln at or near the top; they have done so for a long time. Lincoln's life intrigues people, perhaps because he rose from backwoods obscurity to lead the Union in the Civil War. In summer 1999 a writer for *American Heritage* magazine asked a number of prominent people what attracted them to Lincoln. They responded:

> "I suppose part of the fascination is that [he] started from the bottom, and I started from the bottom," said Mario M. Cuomo, former governor of New York.
>
> "[Lincoln once] said that 'if the Negro is a man, is it not to that extent a total destruction of self-government to say that he too shall not govern himself?' That is the Lincoln . . . when I found him, I was happy to meet . . .," said John Hope Franklin, an African-American historian.
>
> "When people in my business would complain to me about how tough things were, I'd say: 'Wait a minute! You got it easy, kid! Try to grow up in a lean-to, like Lincoln. Try to grow up in the life of Lincoln!'" said David L. Wolper, movie producer.

Lincoln the self-made man; Lincoln the democrat; Lincoln the determined. These qualities stand out. Being human, Abraham Lincoln never acted perfectly, nor did he lack flaws, but throughout his presidency he provided leadership that was strong, compassionate, and sure.

Abraham Lincoln was born on February 12, 1809, not quite in the "lean-to" described by David Wolper, but in a one-room log cabin with a dirt floor on his family's Sinking Spring Farm near Hogdenville, Kentucky. When Abe was two years old his father, Thomas Lincoln, moved him; his mother, Nancy Hanks Lincoln; and his sister, Sarah, to another farm near Knob Creek, Kentucky. Five years later he moved the family to Pigeon Creek in southern Indiana where Abe helped him build a log house deep in the woods, a "wild region," Lincoln later recalled, "with many bears and other wild animals. . . ." In 1818 Nancy Hanks died, leaving Abe motherless. The following year Thomas married Sarah Bush, a widow with three small children. She immediately won Abe's affection by bringing the two families together with kindness, and as she and Abe developed a strong bond, he called her "mama." Sarah later said about her stepson, "Abe never gave me a cross word or look and never refused in fact, or even in appearance, to do anything I requested him. I never gave him a cross word in all my life."

Sarah fed Abe's already developing appetite for books. He read *The Pilgrim's Progress* and later adopted John Bunyan's cadences for his speeches. He also read *Aesop's Fables,* from which he learned about the strength of union, a lesson he would remember as president: "Three bulls for a long time pastured together. A Lion lay in ambush in the hope of making them his prey, but was afraid to attack them while they kept together. Having at last by guileful speeches succeeded in separating them, he attacked them without fear as they fed alone, and feasted on them one by one at his own leisure."

Young Abe emerged as a leader in school, and the students liked his storytelling and his jokes. But his bookish ways caused problems with his father, an uneducated frontiersman who thought Abe lazy. Perhaps for this reason Lincoln seldom mentioned him in favorable terms and in his late teens wanted desperately to get away from home.

Abe got his first taste of a larger world in 1828, soon after his sister's death. As a 6'4" skinny adolescent—so thin he had a "spidery look"—he accompanied the son of a store owner on a trip to New Orleans. They sailed down the Mississippi River on a flatboat laden with cargo, and when they reached their destination Lincoln saw for the first time a large number of slaves. At the docks the blacks worked in bondage amid a thousand other flatboats, loading and unloading carts and wagons, while a few blocks away whites bought and sold more of them—mere property auctioned under conditions fit more for farm animals than human beings. The sight shocked the young man, and he remembered his father's dislike of slavery. As a Separate Baptist, the elder Lincoln thought slavery was morally wrong.

When Abe Lincoln returned home, he gave his father the $25 he had earned. In 1830 he helped his family move to central Illinois, where they started a farm 10 miles west of Decatur.

The following year he set out on his own and, after a second trip to New Orleans, settled in New Salem, an Illinois frontier town founded just two years earlier. There he clerked in a store and showed his physical strength when he beat the champion of a nearby settlement in a wrestling match. His neighbors thought him principled and later praised him; one said, "He was attentive to his business—was kind and considerate to his customers and friends and always treated [them] with great tenderness . . . and honesty." New Salemites often turned to Lincoln for legal advice, and he drafted deeds and other basic forms for them, even though he was not then a lawyer.

His budding interest in law coincided with an interest in politics, but before he ran for office, he volunteered in 1832 to join the military and fight against the Indians in what was called the Black Hawk War. His fellow soldiers elected him militia captain—"A success which gave me more pleasure than any I have had since," he wrote in 1859—but he saw no combat and few Indians. He did, however, stumble across five dead white men, each with "a round, red spot on top of his head," he said, indicating the Indians had scalped them. About his war adventure he once joked: "I had a good many struggles with the musquetoes." He was honorably discharged later in the year.

Lincoln's military experience helped him politically by putting him in contact with men from around the state. In fall 1832 he ran for the Illinois legislature but lost when he finished eighth out of 13 candidates—though he won nearly every vote in New Salem.

Lincoln next entered into a partnership and bought a general store. Because so few customers came in, he spent much of his time reading and studying grammar. As New Salem stagnated and its economy suffered, Lincoln's store began failing, and in 1833 it collapsed. He subsequently took to splitting rails to make money before he was appointed the town's postmaster. In that job he often went out of his way to serve people, walking several miles, for instance, to take mail to those who would forget to pick it up. He delivered many newspapers and read most of them, thus broadening his knowledge. To help make ends meet, he became a county surveyor, a job that required hacking through bushes and trees.

In 1834 Lincoln ran for the legislature a second time and won as a Whig. When a resolution was introduced to condemn abolitionist societies and confirm that the Constitution guaranteed slavery, Lincoln stood among the few who opposed it. Yet though he called slavery unjust, he said the abolitionists only made it worse by angering Southerners and causing them to defend it.

While in the legislature he started studying law and also fell in love with Ann Rutledge. They would likely have married, but in 1836 she died, probably from typhoid. The loss devastated Lincoln. He shook off this blow by running for another legislative term later that year. During the campaign, he and 16 other candidates rode on horseback from town to town, enduring saddle sores and inclement weather to speak at meetings. Lincoln called for the state to fund internal improvements, especially railroads, and with that stand he won.

Back in office, he led a successful effort to move the state capital from Vandalia to Springfield, a town of about 1,500 people in Sangamon County. Then, with New Salem continuing to decline, in April 1837 he settled in Springfield, law license in hand, and formed a partnership with John Todd Stuart, a successful attorney. The legislature met in the county courthouse, one of the town's few brick buildings. Log cabins lined most of the streets, and unpaved roads turned to mud in the rain and dust most other times, but here Lincoln built his clientele and expanded his political horizons.

An amusing incident earned him renown, though not necessarily the kind he wanted. Near the end of the 1840 legislative session, Democrats sought to destroy the state bank by ending the suspension of specie payments as soon as the legislature adjourned, a move that would drain money from the vaults. Lincoln and other Whigs attempted to stop them with their own tactic: They would prevent a quorum from voting for adjournment by leaving the floor of the legislature. When they tried to exit, however, they found the doors bolted. Not to be outsmarted, they jumped out a second-story window. Their ploy failed when the legislature voted to adjourn anyway. Later, newspapers ridiculed Lincoln, with one saying he had never really jumped; he merely stretched his long legs from the second floor to the ground below.

In addition to long legs, Abraham Lincoln had cold feet. In 1840 he and Mary Todd, a stubborn and spirited woman from a large, slave-owning Kentucky family, considered becoming engaged. Lincoln felt at ease with Mary. Like him, she read poetry, and like him, she identified with the Whigs. But marriage frightened him, so he broke off their relationship.

Forlorn, he sank into a deep depression, causing his friends to worry he might kill himself. A few weeks later, Mrs. Simeon Francis, the wife of a Lincoln friend, intervened and reunited the couple. After seeing the happiness enjoyed by a recently wed friend, Lincoln married Mary in November 1842. Over the years they had four children and many tempestuous days. Mary felt ignored when her husband wanted to read or relax after his work in court, and as a result they often quarreled. She also tried his patience with her extravagant taste for clothes. Yet she championed him, and they remained strongly devoted to each other, though historians debate whether Lincoln was, like his friend, ever truly happy in marriage.

Abraham Lincoln moved from the state legislature to the U.S. Congress after he defeated Peter Cartwright, a Democrat and Methodist preacher, in 1846. He recorded the largest victory margin in the history of the Seventh District, which included Springfield.

The Illinoisan stirred controversy in December 1847 when he replied to President James K. Polk's annual message by criticizing the U.S.-Mexican War. Most of the fighting in the war had ended, but Lincoln still wanted to discredit Polk, a Democrat. With his Spot Resolutions he wanted the House to demand from Polk "all the facts which go to establish whether the particular spot of soil on which the blood of our *citizens* was so shed, was, or was not, *our own soil.*" He supported a Whig resolution claiming Polk had "unnecessarily and unconstitutionally begun" the war. Lincoln said the United States had wronged Mexico by engaging in combat around the Rio Grande, a region that had never submitted to American rule. He called Polk's insistence that Mexico was to blame for the war "the half-insane mumbling of a fever-dream" and described the president as "bewildered, confounded, and miserably perplexed."

Lincoln's proposals never passed Congress, but they raised controversy in Illinois. Some Whigs cheered him; other voters questioned his patriotism. Years later, when he ran for president in 1860, Lincoln found himself having to defend his war stand by saying that despite his criticism he had "voted for all the supply measures which came up, and for all the measures in any way favorable to the officers, soldiers, and their families. . . ."

To avoid dividing the Whig Party, Lincoln refrained from debating the Wilmot Proviso, a bill to ban slavery in the lands acquired from Mexico, though he voted in favor of it. He firmly supported Free-Soil, meaning he opposed allowing slavery in the West, and believed if slavery were contained where it already existed, it would die.

By prior agreement with his Whig colleagues in Illinois, Lincoln served only one term in Congress. Disappointed with fellow Whig Zachary Taylor's presidency, Lincoln concentrated on his law practice and for the moment turned his back on politics.

Few persons with a political conscience could avoid the growing crisis between North and South, least of all Abraham Lincoln. He expressed his views on several occasions. In 1854 he spoke out against the Kansas-Nebraska Act that repealed the Missouri Compromise and allowed the settlers in Kansas territory to follow popular sovereignty, which allowed them to vote on whether to permit slavery. The act violated Lincoln's Free-Soil principles. He criticized Illinois senator Stephen Douglas for writing the bill and stressed an important difference between them: Where Douglas considered blacks to be less than human, Lincoln believed them to be entitled to the republican rights enjoyed by all Americans. He did agree, however, that blacks were intellectually inferior to whites.

Lincoln said he hated the "covert zeal for the spread of slavery." He added: "I hate it because of the monstrous injustice of slavery itself." Yet he worried that blacks and whites could never live peacefully together, and since the 1840s he had supported overseas colonization for blacks. He believed that Southerners would be more willing to free their slaves if they knew they could avoid having to live next to them and that Northerners would more strongly support ending slavery if they knew blacks would migrate to foreign lands rather than into the North in search of jobs. At the same time, colonization would help blacks by showing they could stand on their own. Rather than forcing their removal, Lincoln wanted voluntary emigration.

In 1855, one year after the Kansas-Nebraska Act, Lincoln ran for the U.S. Senate but lost. The following year he helped organize Republicans in Illinois and supported John C. Frémont's bid for the presidency, a move that solidified his allegiance to the new party.

Lincoln disagreed sharply with the Supreme Court's ruling in the 1857 *Dred Scott* case, in which the justices said that when a master takes his slave into free territory, the slave remains in bondage. The justices added that the Missouri Compromise was invalid because it deprived persons of their property without due process of the law.

The ruling struck hard at the Republicans, for it made it impossible to enforce the Free-Soil policy they promoted. To Lincoln, slavery went against all that his party stood for: self-help, social mobility, and economic independence. The Illinoisan strongly disagreed with Chief Justice Roger Taney's argument that neither the Declaration of Independence nor the Constitution applied to blacks. Lincoln said it was true that when the founding fathers declared all men equal, they never meant all men were equal in intellectual and physical attributes, but they "did consider all men created equal—equal in 'certain inalienable rights, among which are life, liberty, and the pursuit of happiness.'" Soon he worried there might be "a new *Dred Scott* decision to bring slavery up into the very heart of the free North."

In May 1858 Lincoln showed his legal prowess when he won acquittal for a murder defendant by using the almanac to shatter the testimony of an important witness as to the height of the moon at the time of the victim's death. He then set his sights on winning the U.S. Senate seat from Democrat Stephen Douglas. That June he accepted the Republican nomination for the office with his "House Divided" speech, which crystallized ideas he had held for at least two years:

> "A house divided against itself cannot stand."
>
> I believe this government cannot endure, permanently half *slave* and half *free*. . . .
>
> Either the *opponents* of slavery, will . . . place it where the public mind shall rest in the belief that it is in the course of ultimate extinction; or its *advocates* will put it forward, till it shall become alike lawful in *all* the States, *old* as well as *new*—*North* as well as *South*.

Autumn 1858 brought the famous Lincoln-Douglas debates, seven of them in all. Lincoln appeared in his ill-fitting clothes, looking as if he had just slept in them. To a question posed by Lincoln, Senator Douglas announced his Freeport Doctrine. He claimed that people of a territory can prevent slavery from taking root by refusing to enact the laws necessary to protect it. Lincoln had known that Douglas would likely answer this way, which would anger many fellow Democrats by saying, in effect, that slavery could be prevented from expanding.

When Douglas charged Lincoln with supporting racial equality and promoting intermarriage between whites and blacks, Lincoln answered by saying he had never favored such a thing. Further, he said, he was not in favor "of making voters or jurors of negroes, nor of qualifying them to hold office, nor to intermarry with white people."

After Lincoln lost the election, he thought his political career over. But the debates had earned him national prominence, and some Illinois newspapers said he should run for president. To someone who suggested the same, Lincoln said: "I admit the force of much of what you say, and admit that I am ambitious, and would like to be President." Yet to someone else he said, "I do not think myself fit for the Presidency." Instead, he indicated he would run against Douglas again in 1864.

As the election of 1860 approached, the White House reentered Lincoln's mind. That February he traveled to the northeast, where he delivered an impressive speech at Cooper Institute in New York City. He offered no new ideas, but summarized his thoughts succinctly and passionately. He stated:

> If any man at this day sincerely believes that a proper division of local from federal authority . . . forbids the Federal Government to control as to slavery in the federal territories, he is right to say so. . . . But he has no right to mislead others, who have less access to history, and less leisure to study it, into the false belief that 'our fathers, who framed the Government under which we live,' were of the same opinion. . . .

Addressing the South, he stated:

> You charge that [Republicans] stir up insurrections among your slaves. We deny it; and what is your proof? Harper's Ferry! John Brown!! John Brown was no Republican; and you have failed to implicate a single Republican in his Harper's Ferry enterprise.

He asked what it was that Southerners wanted and provided his own answer:

> This, and this only: cease to call slavery *wrong*, and join them in calling it *right*, And this must be done thoroughly—done in *acts* as well as in *words*.

He concluded:

> LET US HAVE FAITH THAT RIGHT MAKES MIGHT, AND IN THAT FAITH, LET US, TO THE END, DARE TO DO OUR DUTY AS WE UNDERSTAND IT.

As a snowstorm swirled outside, the crowd of about 1,500 interrupted him several times with cheers. In the following days northern newspapers praised him. The speech boosted his presidential standing—as he intended—by showing him committed to principle while also reflective and reasonable. Lincoln wrote his wife in a pleased but tempered tone: "The speech at New-York, being within my calculation before I started, went off passably well, and gave me no trouble whatever."

Lincoln's supporters burnished his image with America's love for the frontier. They stressed his log-cabin roots—this despite Lincoln's own desire to forget his impoverished past—and presented him as a rail-splitter. In campaign literature he stood alongside the common man, despite his work as a prosperous lawyer representing corporations.

Lincoln entered the Republican National Convention at Chicago as an appealing candidate who could carry both the Northeast and the Midwest. He won on the third ballot. As befitting a deeply divided country, in the general election four candidates ran for president. Lincoln made only one campaign appearance, at a rally in Springfield, but his supporters staged marches throughout the North, carrying torches and rails (to represent the "rail splitter"). In the balloting Lincoln won slightly less than 40 percent of the popular count, with 180 votes in the electoral college, compared to 72 for John Breckenridge, 39 for John Bell, and 12 for Stephen A. Douglas. Denied a spot on the ballot in the South, he received no votes there.

Southerners considered Lincoln's victory abominable. Since as Free-Soilers the Republicans wanted to contain slavery in order to strangle it, the South called Lincoln an abolitionist. To have him serve as president would mean an end to slavery and to "southern civilization." For his part the president-elect never thought the South would leave the Union; nationalist sentiment, he predicted, would keep the radicals contained. That view proved misguided when in late 1860, before he even set foot in the White House, several Deep South states, led by South Carolina, seceded.

Lincoln condemned the Southern action and strongly defended the Union. While in principle he supported the people's right to revolt, he insisted it must be for a morally just cause, and the South had no such cause. As some Americans looked to him for a compromise, Lincoln refused to waver on the issue of slavery in the territories. The central plank of the Republican platform, he said, could not be ripped away. He told several congressmen: "By no act or complicity of mine, shall the Republican party become a mere sucked egg, all shell and no principle in it."

In March 1861 Lincoln headed for Washington and his inauguration with assassination threats all around him. To foil any attempt he departed his hotel in Harrisburg, Pennsylvania, at night, with a coat draped over his shoulders and his arms concealed to make him seem shorter than he actually was. To complete the camouflage he donned a soft felt hat rather than the stovepipe one he usually wore. Lincoln boarded a special train with a guard and rode in a berth reserved for an "invalid passenger," though the only invalid was the Union, crippled by secession and President James Buchanan's failure to do anything about it. At Baltimore, Lincoln transferred to another train and then continued to Washington. He arrived there without incident, only to find several newspapers questioning his courage.

In his inaugural speech Lincoln shifted the responsibility for rebellion to the South. "In *your* hands, my dissatisfied countrymen, and not in *mine,* is the momentous issue of civil war," he said. "The government will not assail *you.* You can have no conflict, without being yourselves the aggressors. *You* have no oath registered in Heaven to destroy the government, while *I* shall have the most solemn one to 'preserve, protect and defend' it."

If there were to be a war, Lincoln wanted Southerners to fire the first shots. That happened on April 12, 1861, when he tried to provision federal troops at Fort Sumter, South Carolina, and Confederate troops opened fire. Lincoln thereupon called for 75,000 volunteers to defend the Union and ordered a blockade of the South. Consequently, Virginia, Arkansas, North Carolina, and Tennessee joined the seceded states.

On July 21 Confederate forces defeated Union troops at Bull Run (Manassas), causing Lincoln to replace his field commander with General George B. McClellan. A few weeks later he promoted McClellan to general-in-chief in charge of all the Union forces.

By mid-July 1862 Lincoln was leaning toward freeing the slaves as a way to boost Northern morale in a war that had gone badly and to strike a blow for the North on the side of freedom and liberty. Yet he wanted to withhold emancipation until the North scored a victory, otherwise the Union might look desperate. His opportunity came when, on September 17, McClellan's army met Robert E. Lee's Confederates at Antietam, near Sharpsburg, Maryland, and forced Lee to pull back to Virginia.

Four days later Lincoln issued his preliminary Emancipation Proclamation (to take effect January 1, 1863). The proclamation was a limited measure, freeing slaves only in those states in rebellion and not in those still in the Union, and thus it immediately freed hardly anyone because the federal government had no authority in the Confederacy. Nevertheless, Lincoln saw it as an effective measure to help save the Union by disrupting the Southern economy. He knew slaves in the South would hear about it, and he believed this would encourage them to defy their masters and rally around the Union troops as they penetrated the Confederacy. "I can only trust in God I have made no mistake," Lincoln said. "It is now for the country and the world to pass judgment on it. . . ."

At the same time the president moved toward emancipation, he and other Northerners debated using African Americans in the army. Any decision to enlist them would be a big step, one that would indicate a willingness to accept blacks as responsible human beings, perhaps even brave and courageous ones. Speaking in 1862 Frederick Douglass, an abolitionist and former slave, derided Lincoln's reluctance: "Colored men . . . were good enough to help win American Independence, but they are not good enough to help preserve that independence against treason and rebellion." One contemporary African American recalled: "Most observing and thoughtful people concluded that centuries of servitude had rendered the Negro slave incapable of any civil or military service. . . . Some [army] officers talked of resigning if Negroes were to be called upon to fight the battles of a free republic."

Soon after Lincoln agreed to use African-American troops, the *New York Times* observed: "There has been no more striking manifestation of the marvelous times that are upon us than the scene in our streets at the departure of the first colored regiments." By the end of the Civil War, approximately 190,000 African Americans had served in the United States military.

Despite the victory at Antietam, Lincoln grew disgusted with McClellan, who consistently failed to take the offensive. When in late October 1862 McClellan again refused to pursue Lee because of insufficient supplies, the president said to his general, "Will you pardon me for asking what the horses of your army have done since the battle of Antietam that fatigue anything?" A few days later he replaced McClellan with Ambrose E. Burnside.

The year 1862 also presented Lincoln with personal catastrophe when his 11-year-old son, Willie, died from a fever. The loss devastated Lincoln, and Mary went into mourning for almost two years. She held seances in the White House to make contact with her dead son and said to her half sister, "Willie . . . comes to me every night and stands at the foot of the bed with the same sweet adorable smile he always has had. . . ."

Because the war went no better in the first half of 1863, Lincoln again changed military commanders. After Lee defeated the Union army at Fredericksburg, Maryland, the president replaced Burnside with General Joseph Hooker. When Hooker faltered, he was replaced by General George Meade. While making these changes, Lincoln expanded his practice of suspending the writ of habeas corpus, and the government jailed and held without trial several hundred persons suspected of being traitors. To critics who claimed he had exceeded his authority, he said the Constitution provided for extraordinary measures in time of rebellion.

Good news finally came in July 1863 when General Ulysses S. Grant captured Vicksburg, Mississippi, and blocked Confederate traffic along the Mississippi River. This split the western from the eastern Confederacy. Meanwhile, in Pennsylvania the Union army defeated General Lee after three days of battle, from July 1 through July 3, at Gettysburg. Lee withdrew on July 4, only to find his retreat south blocked by the flooded Potomac River. Lincoln ordered General Meade to pursue the enemy, but Meade hesitated, and once the Potomac subsided Lee escaped. An angry Lincoln said, "Our army held the war in the hollow of their hand and they would not close it."

In November Lincoln traveled to Pennsylvania to present his Gettysburg Address. According to his law partner, William Herndon, the president "saw all things through a perfect mental lens. There was no diffraction or refraction there. He was not impulsive, fanciful, or imaginative; but cold, calm, and precise. In the search for words Mr. Lincoln was often at a loss . . . because there were, in the vast store of words, so few that contained the exact coloring, power, and shape of his ideas."

True to his nature, Lincoln crafted the Gettysburg Address to be concise and strong. More than limiting his words, he mastered the art of finding powerful ones, of mining those potent enough to say a great deal in a few syllables. In *Lincoln at Gettysburg,* Garry Wills says the president's address revolutionized writing and "anticipated the shift to vernacular rhythms that Mark Twain would complete twenty years later." Wills claims that Lincoln's words reflected the quickened pace of a world influenced by the telegraph and that the president used carefully interlocked and balanced sentences. "Four score and seven years ago our fathers brought forth on this continent, a new nation, conceived in Liberty and dedicated to the proposition that all men are created equal," Lincoln began. He ended: "It is . . . for us to be here dedicated to the great task remaining before us . . . that we here highly resolve that these dead shall not have died in vain—that this nation, under God, shall have a new birth of freedom—and that government of the people, by the people, for the people, shall not perish from the earth."

It became increasingly clear in 1864 that Lincoln intended no Union soldier should die in vain. Impressed with Ulysses S. Grant's victories in the West, he made him general-in-chief of the armies. Lincoln liked Grant's direct language, his Illinois background, his down-to-earth character, and his willingness to press on against the Confederates at nearly all costs. The president believed Northern generals had relied too heavily on complicated strategy; he wanted an unremitting assault against the Confederates, and on this point Grant agreed. Heeding Lincoln's demand, the new commander unleashed simultaneous attacks against Mobile in Alabama, Atlanta in Georgia, and Petersburg and Richmond in Virginia.

As the war seemed unending, Abraham Lincoln entered the 1864 election convinced he would lose. Everywhere, his critics vented their fury. Some called him too lenient toward the South; others called him too harsh. In Congress, Republicans considered his reconstruction plan too forgiving. Tension between Lincoln and Capitol Hill grew worse when he pocket vetoed the Wade-Davis Bill, which would have set more stringent rules for the South to regain its normal standing in the government and would have put reconstruction largely in congressional rather than presidential hands.

Throughout the North, protests expanded as war casualties mounted. Grant's tactic of taking heavy losses to wear down the Confederates unnerved many, while Lincoln's insistence that any settlement with the South include an end to slavery caused Democrats to ridicule him as fighting for blacks.

Lincoln felt so sure he would be defeated that he wrote to a friend in August: "You think I don't know I am going to be beaten, *but I do* and unless some great change takes place *badly beaten.*" He even faced a movement among radical Republicans to dump him as the party nominee.

But the Democrats had their own problems. In August they nominated George McClellan, only to have him turn around and renounce the party platform as a surrender to the South. Then in September news spread throughout the North of the capture of Atlanta and, soon after that, of Mobile, the last major Confederate port along the Gulf Coast. Abraham Lincoln had turned from an apparent loser to a definite winner. His reelection disappointed the South, where newspapers called him a dictator and a "vulgar buffoon."

After the election Lincoln struck another blow against slavery when he used patronage to cajole Congress to pass the Thirteenth Amendment, which banned the peculiar institution. On April 3, 1865, the Confederate capital of Richmond fell to the North. Six days later General Lee surrendered to General Grant at Appomattox Court House. Lincoln then prepared to turn from making war to making peace.

Others, however, were preparing to kill him. Threatening letters arrived at the White House in ever greater numbers, yet he ignored them and did nothing to boost security. John Wilkes Booth, a stage actor, originally schemed to kidnap Lincoln and tried on March 17,

1865, but the president, riding in a carriage, took an unexpected route.

After listening to Lincoln address a crowd on April 11, when he said that some blacks should be given the right to vote, Booth decided the president should be killed. He reacted to Lincoln's comments by saying, "That means nigger citizenship;" and he said about the president, "That is the last speech he will ever make."

The Lincolns planned to see the play *Our American Cousin* at Ford's Theater in Washington on the night of April 14. As the time to leave approached, Mary said she had a headache and wanted to stay home. Lincoln insisted they must go, that he had promised too many people he would be there; therefore they went. Later that evening, after finishing a drink at a nearby bar, Booth entered the theater, made his way into the president's box, and aimed a derringer at the president's skull, three inches behind the left ear. "*Sic semper tyrannis!*" ("Thus always to tyrants"—the Virginia state motto) he cried after he fired the pistol and leaped from the president's box onto the stage below.

Conspirators working with Booth also planned to kill Vice President Andrew Johnson and Secretary of State William Seward but failed, though one assailant entered Seward's home and knifed and badly bloodied him. Lincoln, meanwhile, was carried across the street to a boardinghouse and laid diagonally across a bed too small for his long frame. Mary watched in shock, and Lincoln's son Robert stood vigil. Shortly after 7 A.M. on April 15, as rain fell, Lincoln died. One of those at his bedside, Secretary of War Edward Stanton, said, "Now he belongs to the ages."

In the 1999 *American Heritage* article, businessman Lewis Lehrman commented: "I learned that the untutored chief magistrate of a great nation could be the unsurpassed master of his enemies, above all the master of himself. There for the first time I sensed the meaning of true American statesmanship." This comment and the others recorded by the magazine show the continuing respect Americans have for Lincoln nearly 150 years after his death, a grand and eloquent monument to his strong, compassionate, and often wise leadership.

CHRONOLOGY

1809 Born February 12 in Kentucky

1816 Moves with family to Indiana

1828 Sails to New Orleans

1830 Moves with family to Illinois

1832 Serves as volunteer in Black Hawk War

Loses bid for seat in the Illinois legislature

1833 Appointed postmaster for New Salem

Appointed deputy county surveyor

1834 Elected to Illinois general assembly

1836 Reelected to Illinois general assembly

Admitted to the bar

1837 Moves to Springfield

1842 Marries Mary Todd

1846 Elected to U.S. House of Representatives

1847 Introduces Spot Resolutions in Congress

1848 Campaigns for Zachary Taylor for president

1854 Condemns Kansas-Nebraska Act

1855 Loses bid for U.S. Senate

1857 Opposes *Dred Scott* ruling

1858 Delivers "House Divided" speech

Debates Stephen A. Douglas during unsuccessful campaign for U.S. Senate

1860 Elected president

1861 Orders Fort Sumter reprovisioned

Calls for 75,000 volunteers

Orders blockade of South

1862 Issues Preliminary Emancipation Proclamation

Removes George B. McClellan as commander of Union army

1863 Issues Emancipation Proclamation
Delivers Gettysburg Address

1864 Appoints Ulysses S. Grant as general-in-chief of Union army
Reelected president

1865 Visits Richmond
Shot by John Wilkes Booth
Dies from bullet wound April 15

Further Reading

Beveridge, Albert J. *Abraham Lincoln, 1809–1858,* 2 vols. Boston: Houghton Mifflin, 1928.

Donald, David Herbert. *Lincoln.* New York: Simon & Schuster, 1995.

———. *We Are Lincoln Men: Abraham Lincoln and His Friends.* New York: Simon & Schuster, 2003.

Farber, Daniel. *Lincoln's Constitution.* Chicago: University of Chicago Press, 2003.

Fehrenbacher, Don E. *Abraham Lincoln: Speeches and Writings, 1859–1865.* New York: Library of America, 1989.

Holzer, Harold. *Lincoln at Cooper Union: The Speech That Made Abraham Lincoln President.* New York: Simon & Schuster, 2004.

Keneally, Thomas. *Abraham Lincoln.* New York: Viking, 2002.

Klingaman, William K. *Abraham Lincoln and the Road to Emancipation.* New York: Viking, 2001.

Luthin, Reinhard H. *The Real Abraham Lincoln.* Englewood Cliffs, New Jersey: Prentice Hall, 1960.

Mearns, David C., ed. *The Lincoln Papers,* 2 vols. Garden City, N.Y.: Doubleday, 1948.

Neely, Mark E., Jr. *The Last Best Hope of Earth: Abraham Lincoln and the Promise of America.* Cambridge, Mass.: Harvard University Press, 1993.

Nicolay, John G., and John Hay. *Abraham Lincoln: A History,* 10 vols. New York: Century Company, 1890.

Oates, Stephen B., *With Malice Toward None: The Life of Abraham Lincoln* New York: New American Library, 1977.

Paludan, Phillip S. *The Presidency of Abraham Lincoln.* Lawrence: University Press of Kansas, 1994.

Randall, J. G. *Lincoln the President,* 4 vols. New York: Dodd, Mead, 1945–1955.

Sandburg, Carl. *Abraham Lincoln: The Prairie Years,* 2 vols. New York: Harcourt, Brace, 1926.

———. *Abraham Lincoln: The War Years,* 4 vols. New York: Harcourt, Brace, 1939.

Thomas, Benjamin P. *Abraham Lincoln: A Biography.* New York: Alfred A. Knopf, 1952.

Wills, Garry. *Lincoln at Gettysburg: The Words That Remade America.* New York: Simon & Schuster, 1992.

Winik, Jay. *April 1865: The Month That Saved America.* New York: HarperCollins, 2001.

Andrew Johnson (1808–1875)

Seventeenth President, 1865–1869

Andrew Johnson
(Library of Congress)

"Are those who want to destroy our institutions . . . not satisfied with the blood that has been shed? . . . Does not the blood of Lincoln appease the vengeance and wrath of the opponents of this government?"

—Andrew Johnson comments
to a political rally, 1866

Harsh words filled the Senate chamber in April 1868 when Andrew Johnson stood trial as the first president ever impeached. One senator called him an "ungrateful, despicable, besotted, traitorous man . . . a dictator . . . a genius in depravity . . . perfidy and treachery and turpitude unheard of in the history of the rulers of a free people."

The country watched, riveted. Crowds packed the Senate gallery; tickets were hard to come by; some frustrated enthusiasts even beseeched Johnson himself for help in obtaining them. In the end the president remained in office, but as a weak and discredited figure. Years later, some observers blamed the impeachment fight on congressional Radicals who wanted to get Johnson at any cost. But through obstinate behavior and a desire for battle, the president contributed greatly in taking America into dangerous political waters.

Andrew Johnson was born on December 29, 1808, in Raleigh, North Carolina, then a small settlement with 726 whites and about 300 black slaves. He endured poverty from the beginning of his life. His father, Jacob Johnson, was landless and illiterate; his mother, Mary McDonough Johnson, was a seamstress and laundress who townspeople called "Polly the Weaver." When Andrew was three, his father died in an accident, leaving the family in difficult straits. The town elite considered Andrew "poor white trash," and he bore the brand deep in his soul. Looking up from the bottom, he saw a bleak picture but determined to improve his lot.

At age 14 Andrew apprenticed to a tailor. He obtained no schooling but learned to read from a book of orations given him by a friend. After fleeing his harsh work, he moved to Carthage, North Carolina, then on to other towns: Laurens, South Carolina, for two years; back to Raleigh briefly; then to Tennessee, where a tailor in Columbia employed him. After another return to Raleigh, in 1826 he settled in Greeneville, Tennessee, population 500, with his mother and stepfather, whom he brought with him, also poor and landless. There in the state's eastern mountains he again worked for a tailor, met Eliza McCardle, and in May 1827 married her. They had five children.

After his marriage, Andrew Johnson opened his own shop in the front part of his house. While he mended and made clothes, Eliza encouraged him to expand his reading, which he did. Before long he was debating public issues with Greeneville's residents. As his speaking ability improved, in 1828 he won election to the Board of Aldermen. In 1830 they chose him to serve as town mayor. Five years later he won a campaign for the state House of Representatives. Although he had earlier backed Jacksonian Democrats in their push for a new state constitution, he remained unsettled in his party allegiance and in 1836 supported a Whig candidate for president. Johnson suffered his first political setback in 1837 when he lost his bid for another term, largely because he had voted against developing railroads in eastern Tennessee.

He returned to the legislature in 1839 after announcing his support for South Carolina senator John C. Calhoun's strong states' rights ideas and the Democratic Party. From then on he remained a Democrat, even after joining Abraham Lincoln's Republican presidential ticket. In 1841 Johnson was elected to the state senate; he soon sold his tailor's business in order to concentrate on politics and real estate. As senator he supported a conservative Democratic agenda, opposed government interference in business, and wanted economy in the state budget.

With his poverty behind him, Johnson, like many a successful Southerner, bought slaves and eventually owned several. He never freed them and never considered slavery wrong. Whatever his later differences with secession and the southern aristocracy, Johnson firmly believed in white supremacy.

In 1843 the *Nashville Union,* a Democratic newspaper, said of Johnson: "We consider him . . . as decidedly among the first men of the State. He is just the *man* for a crisis. Bold, prompt, and energetic, no responsibility can intimidate, and no obstacles discourage him." That same year he won a seat in the U.S. House of Representatives.

Pugnacious and fiery, dressed plainly in black, and with dark, piercing eyes, Andrew Johnson developed a speaking style that appealed to the Tennessee frontier stump. His voice was loud, his language blunt, and encouraged by whooping crowds, he knew nothing of the refined speaking found back east or among more educated men. This was demonstrated when on the floor of the House he castigated fellow congressman Jefferson Davis for an unintended aspersion against tailors. Johnson launched into a long speech in which he asked his listeners to remember the humble backgrounds of Jesus Christ, a carpenter, and Ben Franklin, a painter, and he disparaged the elite as an "illegitimate, swaggering, bastard, scrub aristocracy, who assumed to know a good deal" but actually knew little.

Johnson's words reflected his advocacy for the lower class. He believed in land for the landless, and with an attachment to agrarian ideas he considered farmers noble, cities evil, and government dangerous. Soon after taking office he introduced a homestead bill that he would spend years fighting for. Johnson wanted lands to be given to farmers who settled and improved tracts on the public domain. His proposal stirred resistance from many Southerners, who feared it would lower revenue from land sales and pressure Congress into raising tariffs to replenish the treasury. In 1852 his bill passed the House only to languish in the Senate.

Showing defiance toward party discipline, Johnson criticized Democratic president James K. Polk for denying him several patronage appointments. Bad feelings between the two men actually dated back to Johnson's discontentment with Polk's candidacy in 1844 and to Polk's concurrent discomfort with Johnson's agrarian extremism. The president now believed Johnson wanted to present himself as a victim of the administration so he could play the role of demagogue back home.

Yet Johnson supported the U.S.-Mexican War and criticized those who argued that the president had started it only to expand slave territory. When the war stirred a sectional crisis over whether to allow slavery in the West, Johnson urged compromise. But as part of any deal he advocated a stronger fugitive slave law and the placement of the District of Columbia under the authority of Maryland so that state, rather than the federal government, could determine whether slavery should continue in the nation's capital.

Johnson applied himself vigorously to amending the Constitution. He wanted to require the direct election of senators and the president and to restrict judges to 12 years in office—proposals his Democratic colleagues found mystifying but that complemented his agrarian radicalism and populist roots. In 1852 Whigs in the Tennessee legislature acted against Johnson when they changed boundary lines to eliminate his First District in a ploy known as gerrymandering. "I have no political future," the maverick congressman lamented, "my political garments have been divided and upon my vesture do they intend to cast lots."

He sought revenge in 1853, running for governor as the "Mechanic Statesman," a slogan meaning he represented the common folk. He frustrated the Whigs by winning, and in his inaugural address he angered the state's elite with his ringing endorsement of popular power. "Democracy is a ladder," he said, "corresponding in politics, to the one spiritual which Jacob saw in his vision: one up which all, in proportion to their merit, may ascend." Few of his proposals, however, passed the legislature.

Johnson was reelected in 1855. Two years later his political career advanced again when the state legislature chose him to serve in the U.S. Senate. As the sectional crisis over slavery deepened out West, the Tennessean voted in favor of admitting Kansas into the Union under the proslavery Lecompton constitution. At the same time he continued to push his homestead bill and in 1860 finally convinced the Senate to pass it. The bill allowed every head of a family who settled in certain parts of the public domain to receive 160 acres, though it required them to pay 25 cents per acre. This provision met the demand by many southern senators that some charge be levied. Yet all of Johnson's efforts again proved futile when President James Buchanan vetoed the bill, and Congress failed to override him. (A similar version finally was enacted in 1862.)

The Tennessean thought he stood a chance for the Democratic presidential nomination in 1860, but his hopes ended when the party split into warring sectional groups. In that year's presidential contest, he supported John Breckinridge, the candidate of the southern Democrats.

With Abraham Lincoln's election to the White House as a Republican and Southerners considering both him and his party anathema, several states in the Deep South, led by South Carolina, seceded. Johnson reacted in December 1860 by declaring his commitment to the Union:

> I will not give up this Government that is now called an experiment. . . . No, I intend to stand by it, and I entreat every man throughout the nation who is a patriot . . . to come forward . . . and rally around the altar of our common country . . . and swear by our God, and all that is sacred and holy, that the Constitution shall be saved, and the Union preserved.

For all his nationalism, Johnson classified himself a Southerner. He defended slavery, and he believed the South had been wronged. But he equated secession with treason, and in an emotional speech to the Senate in February 1861 he said that on his death he wanted "no more honorable winding sheet than that brave old flag, and no more glorious grave than to be interred in the tomb of the Union."

With the firing of the Civil War's first shots at Fort Sumter, South Carolina, in April 1861, Johnson encountered hostile crowds. Shouts of "Hang the traitor!" spread through western Tennessee and echoed among the state's central hills; they could even be heard in heavily Unionist towns such as Greeneville. On a trip back from Washington, Johnson drew his pistol when secessionists boarded his railroad car and one pulled his nose. Another mob in Bristol, Tennessee, threatened to lynch him until Confederate president Jefferson Davis ordered the train be allowed to take him home. After Tennessee voted to secede in June 1861, Johnson fled the state for his own safety, barely escaping arrest on his way to Kentucky.

Early in 1862 General Ulysses S. Grant conquered Nashville and part of western Tennessee for the Union. President Lincoln thereupon appointed Johnson military governor of the state. Johnson had to wait another year, however, before Union forces could clear out enough remaining Confederate troops for him to exert substantial control. In 1863 he reversed his previous stand and supported Lincoln's freeing of the slaves in rebel states. He may have been thinking this change would win him supporters in the North, or he may have believed victory for the Union required ending slavery to eliminate a divisive issue and hurt the Confederate economy. He once said that if either the government or slavery must go, he preferred it to be slavery.

Johnson even cooperated with Lincoln in raising black troops for service in Tennessee. Yet he still considered African Americans inferior and assured people in the state they would remain that way. He hoped all blacks would one day be exiled, perhaps to Mexico.

When the Republicans nominated Lincoln for a second term in 1864, they wanted to campaign under the National Union Party banner and promote themselves and the war as being above partisan differences. Consequently, they reached into the Democratic Party for a vice-presidential candidate and chose Andrew Johnson. A strong unionist and a military governor preferred by Lincoln, he met all their requirements, though one Republican congressional leader asked the president's advisers, "Can't you get a candidate for Vice President without going down into a damned rebel province for one?" The ticket's victory in November brought the Tennessean into the vice presidency.

Had Johnson tried, he could not have done more harm to himself than he did at his inauguration on March 4, 1865. Before entering the Senate chamber to take his oath, he drank three glasses of whiskey that mixed with an illness to make him drunk. He presented an embarrassing speech, and after placing his hand on the Bible, he held it up and said loudly, "I kiss this Book in the face of my nation of the United States." Democrats blistered him, newspapers slammed him as a sot. Johnson liked to drink, but seldom, if ever, to excess, yet he now carried a damning label into national office.

Just 41 days later, and only one week after the South surrendered at Appomattox, John Wilkes Booth assassinated Abraham Lincoln. His conspirators intended to kill Johnson, too, but failed. On the morning of April 15, Andrew Johnson—former tailor, staunch unionist, and states' right Democrat—took the presidential oath of office at his hotel, Kirkwood House. The country still faced wounds as fresh as the graves dug for its war dead and waited to see how the Tennessean proposed to heal them and restore the Union.

In the months prior to Congress convening in December, Johnson developed a reconstruction plan based on his belief that the Southern states had never seceded and should establish governments quickly with little punishment. Consequently, he offered amnesty to all rebels, except for those owning taxable property valued at more than $20,000. He also appointed governors—some Democrats, some who had been Whigs, but all who were unionists. They, in turn, held elections for the state legislatures. Many Republican congressmen pleaded for the president to call a special session of Congress. They believed that the same politicians who had once led the South to secede would regain power, that the former slaves would be abused, and that since blacks would now be counted in full to determine congressional representation, southern Democrats would gain more seats and make the Republicans a minority party. Johnson rejected the Republican pleas.

In reaction to the president's reconstruction plan, John Sherman, a Republican senator, said, "Never by my consent shall these rebels gain by this war increased political power and come back [to Congress] to wield that power in some other form against the safety and integrity of the country." Southerners, however, hailed Johnson's plan and called his gubernatorial appointments the best ones possible. A Tennessean wrote the president: "Our *Southern* brothers are beginning to know that you are their friend, their protector, and to *feel* that 'in thy hands a nation's fate lies circled.'"

They praised Johnson for good reason. Although southern state conventions recognized slavery's end, nullified the secession ordinances, and repudiated Confederate debts, the president failed to ensure that these measures were always carried out. Making matters worse, the southern states sent to Congress four Confederate generals, five colonels, and Alexander Stephens, the former vice president of the Confederacy, while conservatives and secessionists filled the legislatures.

Southerners made it clear that with slavery gone, a new system would oppress African Americans—namely, black codes. Southern legislatures considered these necessary to bring order to a chaotic labor system. The black codes allowed freedmen to hold and sell property but prohibited them from serving on juries, testifying against whites in court, and, in South Carolina, from engaging in anything except farm labor, unless exempted by a special license. In Mississippi the black codes prohibited freedmen from buying farmland, and most southern states passed laws stating that blacks arrested as vagrants could be hired out to landowners.

Johnson saw nothing wrong with the black codes nor with the decision by southern states to exclude freedmen from voting, and he did nothing when Mississippi refused to ratify the Thirteenth Amendment, which outlawed slavery. (The state would not ratify it until 1995.) He still thought of blacks as inferior to whites. When he heard that his home in Greeneville had been used by African-American troops, he exploded: "The negro soldiery . . . have even gone so far as to have taken my own house and converted it into a rendez-vous for male and female negroes . . . in fact making it a common negro brothel."

Writing in *Andrew Johnson: A Biography,* Hans L. Trefousse concludes that Johnson "put into operation policies that were in accordance with his deeply felt views on states' rights. At the same time, however, he reanimated Southern resistance and fatally undermined efforts to integrate the freedmen into society." Northern congressmen fumed about the rebels back in power, the resistance reborn, the black codes passed. When Congress met in December 1865, they determined to take charge, and as a first step they barred congressmen elected under Johnson's plan.

Historians have called 1866 the "critical year" when President Johnson could have built a bridge to Congress, then dominated by moderates, if he had only been willing to compromise. But the Tennessean refused; reconstruction would be accomplished his way. His obstinacy allowed a group of congressmen, called Radicals, to work skillfully and gain the upper hand for their agenda—namely, a more punitive reconstruction of the South, combined with asserting Republican power and advancing the rights of blacks, all directed by Congress rather than the president.

Johnson first showed his inflexibility when he vetoed a bill to extend the Freedmen's Bureau, which supervised labor contracts for the former slaves, fixed wages and terms of employment, established schools, and protected civil rights. Moderates saw the bureau as a way to help southern blacks without trampling the president's reconstruction plan. At this time a group of African Americans led by Frederick Douglass went to see Johnson and asked him to support black suffrage. The president refused, and after the blacks left, he told his private secretary, "Those d——d sons of b——s thought they had me in a trap. I know that d——d Douglass; he's just like any nigger, and he would sooner cut a white man's throat than not."

When the president rejected the Freedmen's bill, he said that the former slaves had enough safeguards and that the legislation would extend military authority where civil courts should properly operate. His veto caused many moderates to rally behind the Radicals. An even larger number turned against the president when he vetoed a civil rights bill, despite his entire cabinet's advising him to sign it. Johnson said the bill violated states' rights. His rapidly weakening status became apparent when moderates and the Radicals voted together to override his veto.

Congress then sent the Fourteenth Amendment to the states to be ratified. Moderates prevented the Radicals from including a proposal to guarantee black suffrage, but the amendment stipulated that "No state shall . . . deprive any person of life, liberty, or property, without due process of the law. . . ." Johnson could not veto a constitutional amendment, but he encouraged the southern states to reject it, and when they did, the amendment stalled. Moderate and radical Northerners alike, in and outside Congress, berated this intransigence and the president's part in it.

Johnson's attempt to portray his reconstruction plan as working smoothly received a sharp setback in July 1866 when a race riot erupted in New Orleans. After someone fired a shot outside a meeting hall where African Americans had gathered for a suffrage rally, police fired through the windows of the building and then rushed it. Once inside they again opened fire, and as the crowd fled, the police shot at them. In all, 37 blacks were killed, along with three of their white supporters; 119 blacks and 17 whites were injured.

As the bloodshed in New Orleans combined with the plight of the Fourteenth Amendment to create the leading issue for the 1866 congressional races, Johnson embarked on a speaking tour intended to rally support for his candidates. He thought he could replicate his success on the Tennessee stump, but crowds heckled him, and he responded with intemperate speeches that made him seem crude. The

Republicans carried all the Union states except Delaware, Kentucky, and Maryland, and they increased their majority to more than two-thirds in both the House and the Senate. A Radical-dominated Congress now seized full control of reconstruction; it determined which states could be represented and as a result set the requirements for rebuilding the Union.

The Radicals divided the South into five military districts under federal commanders and stipulated that blacks be allowed to vote in choosing delegates to state constitutional conventions. Additionally, they said that any new constitution must protect the black franchise and disqualify Confederate leaders from voting and that the state legislature must ratify the Fourteenth Amendment. Congress might then allow a state to regain its representation.

Johnson vetoed all the Radical bills; in each instance Congress overrode him. He was so unyielding that he even vetoed a bill to extend suffrage to African Americans in the District of Columbia—this despite Congress's right to legislate for the capital. He argued that Congress must first consult the people in the district, much as a legislature must consult the people of a state. The president taunted Congress late in 1867 when he appointed conservative generals to head the military governments in the South and removed those who enforced radical measures. Gone were John Pope, who presided over Georgia and Alabama, and O. C. Ord, who presided over Arkansas and Mississippi; in their places were George Mead, a conservative, and Alvan C. Gillem, an archconservative. The *Boston Commonwealth* said about Johnson: "The work of reconstruction, at very short intervals, receives from him a staggering blow. . . . While Congress is passing acts to reconstruct the South, the President is driving a carriage and six through them."

Angered by the president's actions, Congress decided to seek his impeachment. Although some of the Radicals eagerly sought to destroy Johnson, most congressmen approached the showdown reluctantly. As it turned out, the Tennessean provided his enemies with their fire power when he first suspended and then, in February 1868, removed Secretary of War Edward Stanton. In so doing Johnson violated the Tenure of Office Act, passed months earlier, that required the president to obtain approval of the Senate before discharging a cabinet secretary (or certain other officeholders). Stanton defiantly refused to leave his post and barricaded himself in his office for two months. The Tenure of Office Act, of dubious constitutionality, had been passed by the Radicals to restrict Johnson's power and protect Stanton, one of their sympathizers. Stanton's firing convinced even the moderates that Johnson should be impeached and tried in the Senate.

In a highly irregular procedure, the House first declared the president would be impeached for high crimes and misdemeanors and then subsequently decided to find something he could be charged with. Early in 1868 the House sent to the Senate 11 articles, eight of which dealt with the removal of Stanton and one of which accused the president of having brought Congress into disrepute with his various speeches.

When the trial began, newspapers and magazines covered almost every word. Johnson refused to appear and left his defense to his attorneys. During the proceedings he met with several moderate senators and assured them that he would appoint a secretary of war all Americans could support and that he would confer more closely with his cabinet. He complied with a request from one senator that he accept newly written radical constitutions in two states and send them quickly to Congress. With his political neck on the line, he was finally showing some willingness to compromise.

Such anti-Johnson publications as *Harper's Weekly* defended the Tenure of Office Act and the charges brought under it. "It was passed in precise conformity with the Constitution," the magazine said, "and declares that its violation shall be deemed a high misdemeanor. The President is brought, therefore, within its provision, and, when the attending circumstances are considered, the violation should be treated as willful." Others saw the president as an embattled hero, defending the Constitution against a power grab by the legislative branch. As the trial continued, some in and out of Congress worried about a presidency under Ben Wade, the Radical Senate president who would succeed Johnson if he were removed. Others grew weary of the trial, and several who at first supported Congress changed their minds. *The Nation* wrote: "We shall . . . hear no more of impeachment, and we are glad of it."

Johnson escaped removal by a single vote, that of Senator Edmund G. Ross, a moderate Republican from Kansas. The president, holding a cabinet meeting at the time, was reported to have "received . . . congratulations . . . with the same serenity and self possession which have characterized him throughout this terrible ordeal."

Andrew Johnson finished his term ignored and largely forgotten. When he left the White House in March 1869, *Harper's Weekly* called him "a President who will be remembered for not one wise work or one truly honorable action." Again seeking revenge, Johnson ran for the Senate from Tennessee in 1874 and won. When he returned to Washington the following March for a special session of Congress, applause greeted him as he entered the Senate chamber and found his desk covered with flowers. But his term ended quickly: While in Tennessee he died of a stroke on July 31, 1875.

Despite his domestic struggles, President Johnson achieved some success in foreign policy, mostly thanks to the work of his secretary of state, William H. Seward. After invoking the Monroe Doctrine, in the spring of 1867 Johnson forced France to remove troops it had sent to Mexico. And in March of that year the Senate ratified a treaty negotiated by Seward under which Russia sold Alaska to the United States for $7,200,000.

As a result of Johnson's domestic troubles, his modern biographer, Hans L. Trefousse, describes his presidency as "a disaster." The Tennessean thought that with his lenient plan for reconstructing the South, he was continuing the work of Abraham Lincoln. But where Lincoln had showed compassion toward Southerners, Johnson showed vindictiveness toward those who opposed him. And where Lincoln could compromise and grow, even on the issue of black civil rights, Johnson could do neither. He saw himself as an outsider battling great odds, and he felt most effective under siege, an attitude that did much to bring on his impeachment. Although Andrew Johnson avoided removal from office, Trefousse's assessment stands as the most widely accepted one and the most accurate.

Chronology

1808 Born December 29

1822 Becomes tailor's apprentice

1826 Moves to Greeneville, Tennessee

1827 Marries Eliza McCardle

1828 Elected alderman

1830 Elected mayor of Greeneville

1835 Elected to Tennessee House of Representatives

1837 Loses bid for reelection

1839 Declares himself a Democrat

Returns to Tennessee House of Representatives

1841 Elected to Tennessee state senate

1843 Elected to the first of five terms in the U.S. House of Representatives

1852 Gerrymandered out of office

1853 Elected governor of Tennessee

1855 Reelected governor

1857 Elected to U.S. Senate

1860 Supports John Breckenridge for president

Opposes secession of Southern states

1862 Appointed military governor of Tennessee

1864 Elected vice president

1865 Becomes president

Offers amnesty to ex-Confederates

Clashes with Congress over Reconstruction

1866 Vetoes new Freedmen's Bureau bill

Orders U.S. troops to Mexican border

Urges defeat of Fourteenth Amendment

Vetoes Civil Rights Act

1867 Vetoes first Reconstruction Act

Authorizes purchase of Alaska

1868 Tries to remove Secretary of War Edward Stanton

Impeached by the House of Representatives

Acquitted by the Senate

1869 Retires to Tennessee

1874 Elected to U.S. Senate

1875 Dies July 31

FURTHER READING

Benedict, Michael Les. *The Impeachment and Trial of Andrew Johnson*. New York: W. W. Norton, 1973.

Hearn, Chester G. *The Impeachment of Andrew Johnson*. Jefferson, N.C.: McFarland, 2000.

McKitrick, Eric L., ed. *Andrew Johnson: A Profile*. New York: Hill and Wang, 1969.

———. *Andrew Johnson and Reconstruction*. New York: Oxford University Press, 1960.

Riddleberger, Patrick W. *1866: The Critical Year Revisited*. Carbondale: Southern Illinois University Press, 1979.

Sefton, James E. *Andrew Johnson and the Uses of Constitutional Power*. Boston: Little, Brown, 1980.

Trefousse, Hans L. *Andrew Johnson: A Biography*. New York: W. W. Norton, 1989.

Williams, Frank Broyles. *Tennessee's Presidents*. Knoxville: University of Tennessee Press, 1981.

ULYSSES S. GRANT (1822–1885)

Eighteenth President, 1869–1877

ULYSSES S. GRANT
(Library of Congress)

"Throughout the war, and from my candidacy for my present office in 1868 to the close of the last Presidential campaign, I have been the subject of abuse and slander scarcely ever equaled in political history, which to-day I feel that I can afford to disregard in view of your verdict, which I gratefully accept as my vindication."

—Inaugural words, second term, March 4, 1873

For more than 40 years Ulysses S. Grant knew failure on intimate terms. He excelled in the army his first time around but quit amid rumors about his drunkenness; he tried farming, but harvested more calluses than crops; he tried his hand as a rent collector but had no liking for the job; he worked at his family's store as a clerk but showed little desire to stay with it. Then the Civil War came, and he found his calling and accomplishment. Later, his heroic military record swept him into the White House. He had reached the pinnacle of

American politics, only to find himself crashing down again when his personal shortcomings exposed his presidency to graft. As it turned out, in government Grant trusted too much and commanded too little.

Ulysses S. Grant was born Hiram Ulysses Grant on April 27, 1822, in Point Pleasant, Ohio. Within a few years he would reverse his first and middle names to keep his initials from spelling "H.U.G.," which he felt invited ridicule. When at West Point he discovered he had been admitted as Ulysses S. Grant, he accepted it as his new name. "What does the S stand for in Ulys.'s name?" he would later ask his wife about his newborn son. "In mine you know it does not stand for anything!"

Grant's father, Jesse, was a tanner who as a Whig frequently expressed his political views in letters to local newspapers. His mother, Hannah Simpson Grant, came from a farming family and was known for her strong character. When Ulysses was 18 months old, the Grants moved to Georgetown, Ohio, where Jesse could find plenty of tanning bark in the deep midwestern forest. The Grants lived in a small brick house close to the tannery, and the stench from slaughtered animals and processed hides filled Ulysses' bedroom. He grew to hate the noisome air and the blood.

Although Jesse provided well for his family, he feared slipping into poverty, a fear his son inherited and constantly fought as an adult. Ulysses attended public schools in Georgetown before enrolling at the Richardson and Rand Academy in Maysville, Kentucky, in 1836 and then transferring to a school in Ripley, Ohio, in 1838. He was a mediocre student who preferred horseback riding to scholarship.

Jesse Grant worried about his son's indifference toward school and dislike for the tannery. Without telling Ulysses, he decided to ask his local congressman to appoint the youngster to West Point. The congressman agreed, and when Ulysses got the news, he accepted it with only mild protest. Even though he had no burning desire to join the military, he saw the appointment as a means to get away from home.

Ulysses arrived at West Point in 1839, a 5'1" 17-year-old with sandy brown hair and freckled skin. He easily passed the entrance exam, and as a student he presided over the cadet literary society. He showed his talent with horses when he set an academy equestrian high-jump record that stood for 25 years.

His casual manner—he disliked discipline—resulted in several demerits for slovenly dress and tardiness. He graduated in 1843 ranked 21st in a class of 39 and was named brevet second lieutenant in the Fourth U.S. Infantry stationed at Jefferson Barracks near St. Louis, Missouri.

In St. Louis, Grant met Julia Dent, the daughter of a plantation owner. Strong-willed and physical, she liked to fish, hunt, and ride horseback as much as he did. She looked homely—Grant once said he found her crossed eyes attractive—but they fell in love and were soon engaged. They waited to marry, however, while Grant served at army posts in Louisiana and Texas and then in the U.S.-Mexican War.

On May 3, 1846, Ulysses S. Grant heard his first shots of battle when, some 25 miles distant from where he was stationed, Mexican artillery fired on American troops north of the Rio Grande, and the Americans responded in kind. Grant thought the U.S.-Mexican War was a mistake, a result of American greed to obtain land for slavery. In referring to the role played by the army to make Mexico look like the aggressor, he said in his memoirs: "We were sent to provoke a fight, but it was essential that Mexico should commence it." He once referred to the American Civil War as punishment for the way the United States had hurt Mexico.

For all his misgivings, he compiled an admirable war record. At Resaca de la Palma he led an assault, even though as a quartermaster he had no company to command. He participated in another assault at Monterrey before proceeding to Mexico City, where he and a few other men set up a howitzer in a bell tower near the town's gates.

Grant's service in the U.S.-Mexican War ended in 1848. That year Grant and Julia married, concluding their long engagement and their long time away from each other. Over the years, any lengthy separation caused them both to suffer (and often drove Ulysses to drink). A strong family man, Grant lavished love on his wife and their four children.

The army next stationed Grant at Sackets Harbor, New York, before sending him to the West Coast. During that trip, while still serving as a quartermaster, he led a regiment across the Isthmus of Panama in 1852. When many of his men died of yellow fever, the *Panama Herald* excoriated him. "*With Quartermaster GRANT, we have not done,*" the paper said. "*Unfitted by either natural ability or education for the post he occupied, he evinced his incapacity at every movement.*" Grant made no public response to the *Herald*'s exaggerated attack.

He served at Fort Vancouver in the northwest and then at Fort Humboldt in California, an isolated outpost that, combined with an intolerable commander, made him miserable. Grant's distance from Julia and his children, Fred and baby Ulysses, whom he had not yet seen, depressed him. He wrote his wife: "I am almost crazy sometimes to see Fred," and, "I dreamed of you and our little boys the other night. . . ." He turned to the bottle, and when he resigned from the army in 1854 after receiving a promotion to captain, rumors attributed his departure to heavy drinking. Yet no notice of drunkenness ever appeared on his official record.

Jesse Grant desperately tried to convince the army to reject his son's resignation, for he feared, and rightly so, that Ulysses would be lost—what could he possibly do for a living? For a short time he worked as a farmer on land near St. Louis owned by his brother-in-law. In 1855 he built his own home, a log house he called Hardscrabble. Although he used slave labor (he owned one slave, his wife owned four, and he borrowed others), he experienced only hardship. In 1858 he gave up the farm to work as a rent collector in St. Louis for one of Julia's cousins. Temperamentally unfit for the job, he failed again.

Thirty-seven years old and desperate, he was forced to ask Jesse Grant for help. In summer 1860 Ulysses Grant moved to Galena, Illinois, where he clerked in his father's leather goods store. Eventually Grant may have become a partner, and at one point he even said, "Our business here is prosperous and I have evry [*sic*] reason to hope, in a few years, to be entirely above the frowns of the world, pecuniarily." But in truth he disliked his job. According to a Grant biographer, William S. McFeely, townspeople talked about his "vacant expression as he went down the long, long flight of stairs to work and climbed back up them to his house at the end of the day."

War saved Grant. Though he never praised or extolled it, he knew warfare gave his life meaning and raised him above the ordinary. After the South fired on Fort Sumter in April 1861, Galena's residents chose Grant to preside over their town meeting. His vacant expression disappeared, and one neighbor said: "I saw energies in Grant. . . . He dropped a stoop shouldered way of walking, and set his hat forward on his forehead in a careless fashion."

He began enlisting men as volunteers to fight in the war and then drilled them. Although he refused to seek a commission aggressively, he did contact some officers he had known in the army, and through the help of his local congressman, Elihu B. Washburne, he obtained rank as a colonel.

In summer 1861 Ulysses S. Grant led the 21st Illinois Regiment into Missouri, a strategically important state with its border on the Mississippi River and its commercial center at St. Louis. Early in February 1862 Grant joined his force, numbering 17,000 men, with the U.S. Navy for a successful assault on Fort Henry, Kentucky, along the Tennessee River.

Soon after, he attacked Fort Donelson in Tennessee, where he trapped 11,500 rebels. When the Confederate commander asked for terms of surrender, Grant replied: "Sir: Yours of this date proposing an armistice and appointment of Commissioners to settle terms of capitulation is just received. No terms except an unconditional and immediate surrender can be accepted. I propose to move immediately upon your works." With that tough stand Grant earned a nickname. His first and middle initials, "U" and "S," said newspaper stories, stood for "Unconditional Surrender."

As Grant continued to march through Tennessee, General Henry Halleck thought him too independent and in spring 1862 stripped him of his command. Although he had good reason to criticize Grant, who distrusted almost everyone but himself in battle, Halleck's complaint came more from jealousy than anything else; he feared his colleague might surpass him and be appointed commander in the West. After Congressman Washburne interceded on Grant's behalf and President Lincoln appointed Halleck to the post he desired, Grant was reinstated. "Instead of relieving you," Halleck wrote Grant, "I wish you, as soon as your new army is in the field to . . . lead it on to new victories."

In April 1862 Grant commanded his men in battle at Shiloh, Tennessee. Historian Bruce Catton has said, "The entire war had no fighting more terrible than the fighting which took place here." Shiloh resulted from a Confederate assault that took Grant off guard, and the two days of combat produced no real changes to the military map. It did, however, leave behind a bloody legend: 1,723 Southern soldiers dead, 1,754 Northern soldiers dead, and more casualties than in the Revolutionary War, War of 1812, and U.S.-Mexican War combined. Shiloh convinced Grant the war would be a long one and that the North would have to destroy the Confederate army completely to win. After critics blamed him for losing so many men, he commented, "I have been so shockingly abused that I sometimes think it almost time to defend myself." But he said little and believed his record should speak for itself.

Despite the criticism, he emerged from Shiloh a hero. Northern newspapers called Grant a great general, for unlike other Union military leaders, he stubbornly resisted the Confederates, and he exuded noble qualities: calmness, self-control, and fortitude under fire.

After Shiloh, other battles followed in which Grant humbled the Confederates by hitting them with his massive army. So many injuries and deaths swept through his ranks that some said his battles resembled charnel houses (places where dead bodies are deposited). Even Gideon Wells, Lincoln's navy secretary and a Grant supporter, said that while Northerners had great confidence in the general, "the immense slaughter of our brave men chills and sickens us all."

Grant employed a bold strategy against Vicksburg, the vital Mississippi town located on a bluff overlooking the mighty river. He attacked in April 1863 by going around it and approaching it from the south. Other generals called the move risky, but he argued that the North needed a quick victory to boost its morale. Anxiety must have gripped Grant, for he knew that if he failed he would be ruined.

Rather than a quick victory, after two unsuccessful assaults, both in May and both resulting in massive carnage, he had to settle for a weeks-long siege. Finally, on July 3 the rebels hoisted white flags. As historian Shelby Foote has written, "It was indeed a Glorious Fourth, from the northern point of view." The conquest along the Mississippi River, completed on July 9 with the surrender of Port Hudson in Louisiana, split the western from the eastern Confederacy.

After Grant won a crucial contest over the Confederates at Chattanooga, Tennessee, in November 1863, President Lincoln appointed him supreme commander of the entire Union army with the rank of lieutenant general. In May 1864 Grant led his men into the Wilderness, a dense forest near Richmond, Virginia. There he tried but failed to break Robert E. Lee's defenses. Chaos exploded; cannon and guns turned the trees blood red; a forest fire burned alive many of the wounded. Grant kept marching, though, and fought another frustrating battle at Spotsylvania—five days of trench warfare with more butchery. "I propose to fight it out along this line if it takes all summer," he said.

In June Grant failed to break through Confederate lines at Cold Harbor in Virginia; he later ranked the assault among his most "useless." The rebels suffered little, but Grant lost 12,000 men in one day alone. From there he moved on to Petersburg and began the longest siege of the war. In early April 1865 Lee abandoned the city and a few days later surrendered at Appomattox Courthouse.

Although Grant's victory came in part from the superior numbers of men he could employ in battle, it also stemmed from a careful strategy to keep Lee tied down with constant attacks so that the Confederate general would be prevented from sending his men elsewhere, and a resolve to keep fighting seldom before exhibited by other Union commanders. While Grant battered Lee from the east, he sent General Philip Sheridan into the Shenandoah Valley with orders to make it a "barren waste." General William Tecumseh Sherman was sent into Georgia, where he burned Atlanta and swept through the state to Savannah and then into the Carolinas, his army an inferno on caissons that consumed factories, warehouses, railroads, and bridges.

As Northerners celebrated their victory, Grant narrowly escaped death in April 1865, when President Lincoln invited him and Julia to see a play at Ford's Theater. Grant agreed to go, but Julia, who disliked Mrs. Lincoln, convinced him to change his mind. As a result, John Wilkes Booth, who planned to kill both Grant and Lincoln, found only one of his targets present.

Grant developed an ambivalent relationship with the new president, Andrew Johnson. In 1866 Johnson commissioned him general of the army, and in 1867, after the president removed Edward Stanton as secretary of war, he chose Grant for the job. For unclear reasons, Grant accepted and stepped into a messy political battle as Johnson and Congress fought over whether the president had the authority to remove Stanton. Eventually the dispute figured prominently in Johnson's impeachment: It was the major justification for his impeachment.

Grant initially supported Johnson, but in late summer 1867 he quit his post, infuriating the president, who thought the general had agreed to remain in office while the fight with Congress continued. Johnson's enemies, the Radicals within the Republican Party, now considered Grant a friend. Although Grant sympathized with the Radicals, he also differed with them on several issues and received his strongest boost for the presidency from moderates. His supporters included the *New York Times,* which portrayed him as a sympathetic and just leader. After the Democrats won more seats in Congress in 1867, many Republicans boosted Grant as the weapon needed to stop the opposing party's advance.

When the Republican National Convention opened in Chicago in 1868, it displayed all the trappings of the Civil War. A hero at Gettysburg, General Daniel E. Sickles, led the procession into the Crosby Opera House. In such an atmosphere, who else but Grant could be nominated for president?

That fall Grant faced Horatio Seymour, the wartime governor of New York, as his Democratic opponent. Grant took no prominent stand on the issues and remained largely silent during the campaign. His supporters, though, rallied Americans around a banner of loyalty and portrayed the Democrats as the party of secession. "Vote As You Shot," they urged. Few doubted Grant would win, but his popular-vote margin turned out surprisingly small, and because the white vote had divided nearly evenly, his victory was heavily reliant on the ballots of African Americans.

At his inauguration in April 1869, Ulysses S. Grant alluded to Southern assaults on blacks when he called for the government to protect life and property throughout the country. A proponent of rights for African Americans, he urged the states to ratify the Fifteenth Amendment, which prohibited denying persons the right to vote based on their color, and he asked Congress to reform the treatment of Indians.

Grant soon disappointed those who expected him to exert firm leadership. He filled his first cabinet largely with friends and cronies, nearly all of whom lacked talent, except in their ability to deceive the president and promote their own interests. And although he called for civil service reform, he hardly pushed for it.

He tenaciously fought for one project, though, when he proposed to annex the Dominican Republic to the United States. He thought that by so doing Americans would enhance their trade with the Caribbean and that the acquired land would serve as a frontier—a sort of Dakotas with mountains and palm trees—where blacks could settle and escape racism. He pursued his goal into 1870. That December he described the Dominican Republic to Congress as a "weak power, numbering probably less than 120,000 souls, and yet possessing one of the richest territories under the sun, capable of supporting a population of 10,000,000 people in luxury."

Grant's proposal caused a rift within the Republican Party, and he pressured the Senate to remove Charles Sumner, a vindictive and obstructionist Radical, from the chairmanship of its foreign relations committee. His attempted land grab revealed a characteristic that stamped Grant's presidency: corruption. Evidence indicated that his chief aide, Orville Babcock, had pushed hard to annex Santo Domingo because he had been given land there which, should the deal be approved, would appreciate considerably and bring him a handsome profit. The Dominican president would also fill his pockets with money from the sale of his country to the United States.

Santo Domingo consumed Grant's first term as president. A fellow Republican, Carl Schurz, met with him at the White House, and as they sat together on a sofa he told the president all the reasons why he opposed annexation. "At first the President listened to me with evident interest," Schurz later reported. "But after a little while I noticed that his eyes wandered about the room, and I became doubtful whether he listened to me at all." Try as Grant did, by spring 1871 his Santo Domingo project was dead.

Corruption spread quickly through Grant's presidency, showing itself in the audacious Credit Mobilier scandal, which began before Grant reached the White House. Businessmen established the Credit Mobilier Company to sell materials to firms building the Pacific railroad. They then charged inflated prices in order to reap huge profits and distributed the haul to the company's stockholders, including congressmen who had been sold shares at bargain rates to assure their support. Although Grant had no involvement with the underhanded dealings, when the scandal broke in 1872 it mixed with other stories about greedy politicians to make his presidency appear dishonest.

Some thought that corruption in America came with the Gilded Age, an era of gaudy materialism. Everything seemed to be for sale, and in Grant the purveyors of riches had a compliant president who little understood or cared about financial matters, and who believed the executive branch should accede to Congress.

Two of the biggest speculators in America, James Fisk and Jay Gould, beguiled Grant. They wined and dined him aboard their yacht and tried to convince him the government should hold onto its gold reserves. Fisk and Gould wanted to corner the market for gold and knew that if the government sold its holdings the price for the precious metal would be driven down, rather than up as they desired. They went so far as to insinuate themselves with the president's sister and established contacts within the treasury department. To Grant's credit he defied the two manipulators and ordered the government to sell some of its gold. He did so, though, only after others exposed the plot. To many, Grant looked like a fool, or worse, his family looked like grafters.

Scandal also enveloped the New York Customhouse. Its collector, Thomas Murphy, presided over a system whereby importers paid one month's rent for one day's storage and the excess money found its way into private pockets. As Congress began to investigate, Grant dismissed Murphy but praised him for his "honesty."

While immersed in the scandals, Grant showed his impulse toward justice when he appointed Amos T. Akerman, a crusader for African-American civil rights, to the post of second attorney general in 1870. In 1871 Akerman convinced Grant to support the Ku Klux Klan Act then being considered by Congress. The act gave the president power to deploy the army and suspend the writ of habeas corpus should Southerners defy court rulings meant to protect black rights. Grant used the act in October when terrorists ran rampant in South Carolina, but that December he fired Akerman after some political leaders complained that Akerman's efforts to crush the Ku Klux Klan were merely reopening Civil War wounds.

President Grant achieved a diplomatic victory in 1871 when his secretary of state, Hamilton Fish, ended a dispute with Britain over damage done to American property by ships the British had provided to the Confederate navy. Under the Treaty of Washington, a tribunal awarded the United States more than $15 million.

Grant's scandalous first term repulsed some Republicans. Carl Schurz derided the presidency as a "train of officers and office-mongers," and in 1872 he and fellow liberals bolted the party and joined the Democrats in supporting Horace Greeley, a cantankerous newspaper editor, for president. The Liberal Republicans wanted civil service reform, free trade, limited government, and more lenient treatment of the South.

For Grant, reelection became another Vicksburg—he had to prove himself or face ruin. He never liked the reformers and concluded they were out to get him. As he ran for a second term, he told his supporters that the Liberal Republicans appeared stronger than they were; he compared them to "the deceptive noise made in the West by prairie wolves," who sounded like many but turned out to be few.

According to historian Eugene H. Roseboom, "Never in American history have two more unfit men been offered to the country for the highest office." Greeley lacked presence; Grant lacked sound judgment. But the Republicans hid Grant's faults behind his heroic image, and he won by a much bigger margin than in 1868. He carried the entire North and even several states in the South.

The president felt vindicated, but more criticism soon followed. In 1873 he signed a bill that raised congressional pay, gave each congressman a bonus, and doubled his own annual salary. So many protests descended on Washington that Congress rescinded the act in 1874. Grant's readiness to sign the original bill, though, made him look greedy.

Soon after that episode, stories circulated that his secretary of war, William W. Belknap, had received kickbacks from a contract he had granted for operating a post at Fort Sill in the Indian territory. As Congress investigated, Belknap resigned to thwart his impeachment. After the House impeached him anyway, the Senate refused to convict him because he had already left office. The evidence against Belknap was massive, and many congressmen believed Grant had planned Belknap's resignation as a way to save his associate from greater embarrassment.

Yet another scandal dwarfed Belknap's graft. Well before Grant entered the White House, whiskey distillers started paying bribes to government agents to avoid the revenue tax. After 1870, 12 to 15 million gallons of whiskey avoided the levy. In February 1875 the *St. Louis Democrat* broke the story about a notorious Whiskey Ring—a chilling name given Grant's problems with the bottle—and Secretary of the Treasury Benjamin H. Bristow investigated the matter. John McDonald, appointed by Grant as collector of internal revenue for the St. Louis district, turned out to be the lead culprit.

McDonald—who in 1874 presented President Grant with a "valuable pair of horses"—first confessed his role to Bristow but then became closemouthed after it appeared indictments would be handed down.

As the investigation continued, Grant's private secretary, Orville E. Babcock, himself intimately involved in the Whiskey Ring, continuously fed information to McDonald. In May 1875, the government arrested 350 government employees and businessmen.

Babcock was among those arrested, but he avoided jail largely because Grant perjured himself in a court deposition when he attested to his friend's innocence, even though he knew Babcock was guilty. Nothing indicated that Grant was involved in the graft, but he called reformers "narrow-headed men" with eyes so close together "they can look out of the same gimlet hole without winking." In June 1876 he fired treasury secretary Bristow and several others in the department, a clear insult to those who had uncovered the Whiskey Ring. The entire episode sullied Grant and caused people to lose confidence in him.

As the scandals worsened, the economy collapsed. Unemployment reached 1 million, families crowded together in tenements, and long lines formed at soup kitchens. Between 1873 and 1876 daily wages for city workers fell 25 percent; a 5 percent drop in food prices alleviated the hardship only slightly while hurting farmers. Wheat prices fell from $1.57 a bushel in 1867 to 77¢ in 1876. Corn prices followed a similar plunge.

During the crisis, Grant sided with businessmen rather than the workers, whose votes he had earlier courted by calling himself their friend. As unions lost members, down from 300,000 in 1872 to 50,000 in 1878, he hoped for their demise, since he thought them antagonistic. In April 1874 Congress sent him a bill that many thought would help farmers and laborers by allowing the government to issue an unlimited amount of paper money, called greenbacks. But conservative business interests pressured him to veto it, and he did. According to William S. McFeely, with Grant's act the Republican Party "was the party not of the working class but of those who were or aspired to be the capitalists."

In May 1874 Grant and his wife arranged an elaborate White House wedding for their daughter, Nellie. The food, the presents on display, the eight bridesmaids, the marine band, and the bridal gown of white satin and lace bedazzled the press and public.

Capitalizing on the scandals and the economic collapse, the Democrats gained power in several large states in 1874 and swept that year's elections for the House of Representatives. Yet Grant and his supporters entertained thoughts about his running for an unprecedented third term in 1876, until the House, in a 234-18 vote, resolved that such a move would be "unwise, unpatriotic and fraught with peril to our free institutions."

After Grant left the presidency, he took a lengthy overseas tour, the spectacular success of which served to erase the dark memories of his years in the White House. He dined with Queen Victoria at Windsor Castle and met with Bismarck in Germany. He sailed the Nile on the khedive's own ship, obtained an audience with Pope Leo XIII at the Vatican, and dined with the czar in St. Petersburg. The Japanese emperor presented him and Julia with lacquer sitting-room furniture. When Grant returned to the United States in 1879, his friends again promoted him for the White House, but he lost the 1880 Republican nomination to James A. Garfield.

Grant faced economic ruin in 1884 when he lost all his money to a brokerage firm. He refused all offers to pay off his debt and instead raised funds by writing his memoirs. A few months after beginning the project, he felt a sharp pain in his throat that turned out to be cancer, likely caused by his prodigious cigar smoking. Barely able to eat, he kept writing, often while sitting on his front porch bundled against the wind. His handwriting reduced to a scrawl, his voice gone, he finished the manuscript on July 16, 1885—295,000 words that reviewers later called masterful. Within two years the memoirs earned $450,000 for Julia and their children, as he had hoped. Grant never saw the money; he died on July 23, 1885.

Ulysses S. Grant was buried on New York's Riverside Drive in a tomb bearing his famous utterance, "Let us have peace." Yet success for Grant depended on war; in peace he proved incompetent, both as a businessman and a president. In politics he trusted too much those who pretended to be his friends but who wanted only to fill their own pockets; and when reformers exposed treachery, he reacted by defending the treacherous.

The scandals and greed that swamped Grant's presidency came as much from the decadent society around him as from his own failings. Walt Whitman wrote: "I say that our New World democracy, however great a success in uplifting the masses . . . is so far an almost complete failure . . . in really grand religious, moral, literary and esthetic results." He said that with territorial growth America was "being endowed with a vast and more thoroughly appointed body" but "left with little or no soul." To a large extent, Grant's presidency left grand moral designs in tatters and the national soul empty.

Chronology

1822 Born April 27

1839 Enters U.S. Military Academy

1843 Serves as second lieutenant in Fourth Infantry

1846 Serves in U.S.-Mexican War

1847 Made brevet captain for gallantry at Chapultepec

1848 Marries Julia Dent

1852 Moves with regiment to Pacific Coast

1854 Resigns from army
Works as farmer and bill collector

1860 Works in father's store in Galena, Illinois

1861 Appointed colonel of 21st Illinois Volunteers
Named brigadier general

1862 Captures Fort Henry and Fort Donelson

1863 Captures Vicksburg
Wins Battle of Chattanooga

1864 Appointed general-in-chief of Union armies
Fights at the Wilderness, Spotsylvania, and Cold Harbor

1865 Captures Petersburg
Accepts Lee's surrender at Appomattox Courthouse

1866 Commissioned general of the army

1867 Serves as interim secretary of war

1868 Elected president

1869 Attempts to annex Dominican Republic

1871 Suspends writ of habeas corpus in several South Carolina counties

1872 Reelected president

1873 Signs "Salary Grab" Act

1875 Refuses to condemn grafters in Whiskey Ring

1877 Begins world tour

1880 Fails to win presidential nomination

1884 Bankrupted by unwise investments
Discovers he has throat cancer

1885 Finishes writing memoirs
Dies July 23

FURTHER READING

Barber, James G. *U.S. Grant: The Man and the Image.* Carbondale: Southern Illinois University Press, 1985.

Bunting, Josiah. *Ulysses S. Grant.* New York: Times Books, 2004.

Catton, Bruce. *Grant Takes Command.* Boston: Little, Brown, 1968.

———. *U.S. Grant and the American Military Tradition.* New York: Grosset and Dunlap, 1954.

Long, E. B., ed. *Personal Memoirs of U.S. Grant.* New York: Da Capo, 1982.

McFeely, William S. *Grant: A Biography.* New York: W. W. Norton, 1981.

Perret, Geoffrey. *Ulysses S. Grant: Soldier and President.* New York: Random House, 1997.

Simpson, Brooks, *Let Us Have Peace: Ulysses S. Grant and the Politics of War and Reconstruction, 1861–1868.* Chapel Hill: University of North Carolina Press, 1991.

———. *Ulysses S. Grant: Triumph over Adversity.* Boston: Houghton Mifflin, 2000.

Smith, Jean Edward. *Grant.* New York: Simon & Schuster, 2001.

*R*UTHERFORD *B. H*AYES (1822–1893)

Nineteenth President, 1877–1881

RUTHERFORD B. HAYES
(Library of Congress,
Brady-Handy Collection)

"I ask the attention of the public to the paramount necessity of reform in our civil service . . . a reform that shall be thorough, radical, and complete; a return to the principles and practices of the founders of the Government. They neither expected nor desired from public officers any partisan service. They meant that public officers should owe their whole service to the Government and to the people."

—Inaugural words, March 5, 1877

In 1876, during its centennial year, the United States displayed a new era of industry and technology when the International Exposition and World's Fair opened in Philadelphia. Visitors could see the first telephone, a slice of the cable the Roebling brothers would use in building the Brooklyn Bridge, and the gigantic Corliss Steam Engine that powered 13 acres of machinery. For all its modernity, its Philadelphia site connected the exposition to the founding fathers, who in that city 100 years earlier had declared America's independence from Britain on high principle. The exposition seemed to say, "Here on our country's moral foundation is being built a splendorous society infused with the goodness and rectitude of the past."

In that year's presidential contest, however, another historical legacy, the convulsive Civil War, reasserted itself to mock such moral pretense and produce a tainted and controversial result. Consequently, Rutherford B. Hayes, who won as a reformer promising greater integrity in government, faced the taunts of "His Fraudulency" and "Rutherfraud." How he would reconcile his election with his promise, and the new America with the old, became the challenge for his presidency.

In 1817 Rutherford Hayes, the father of the future president, moved his family from Vermont to a farm north of the village of Delaware, Ohio. Five years later he died, leaving behind a son, Lorenzo; a daughter, Fanny; and his pregnant wife, Sophia Birchard Hayes. On October 4, 1822, Sophia gave birth to Rutherford Birchard Hayes, affectionately called Rud. After Lorenzo drowned while skating on an icy pond, Sophia kept Fanny and Rud close to home as she tried to protect them from danger. As a result, the two children developed a strong bond—some called them inseparable, especially given Fanny's tomboy ways. Rud was outgoing and loved to play in the woods. He also liked sliding in the snow, and he hunted, fished, rowed, sailed, and swam. He even took up ice skating to conquer the fear he felt after hearing stories about Lorenzo's death.

The youngster developed a strong self-assurance, and once he made up his mind, he stuck with his decisions in the full confidence that he was right. Rud would carry this trait with him into the White House, as he would a strong patriotism. He extolled George Washington as a hero, dreamed of becoming a military leader, and memorized parts of patriotic speeches, especially Daniel Webster's "Reply to Robert Y. Hayne": "Liberty *and* Union, now and for ever, one and inseparable!"

Rud's Uncle Sardis acted as his surrogate father, and he and Sophia determined that Fanny and Rud would both obtain excellent schooling. At age 13 Rud went to Norwalk Seminary in Norwalk, Ohio, near his home, and soon after enrolled at Webb's Preparatory School in Middletown, Connecticut. After graduating from Webb's, he returned to Ohio and in 1838 entered Kenyon College. At first he complained about Kenyon; when Fanny urged him to like his teachers, he replied: "Well, I do like them—a great ways off." But by the following year he was content as he made friends and became more serious about his studies. He read history, biography, fiction, and poetry, and checked out more books from the library than any other student.

Soon after graduating from Kenyon in 1842, Hayes decided to attend Harvard Law School, where he could study under a distinguished faculty that included U.S. Supreme Court justice Joseph Story. In the fall of 1844, during his last term at Harvard, he said, "I hardly have time to think of politics." Nevertheless, in that year's presidential race he supported the Whig candidate, Henry Clay. On New Year's Day of 1845 Hayes wrote in his diary: "The rudeness of a student must be laid off, and the quiet, manly deportment of a gentleman put on." A few months later he returned to Ohio, law degree in hand, and began his practice in Lower Sandusky (today called Fremont).

In 1849 Hayes moved to Cincinnati, where he would prosper. Before long, he met Lucy Ware Webb, a student at Wesleyan Female College, whom he described as beautiful and intelligent, with a mind able to assess people and events quickly. In December 1852 they married and went on to raise a large family, with eight children in all.

Sadly for Hayes, in 1856 his sister Fanny died after giving birth. "Oh what a blow it is!" he wrote to a friend. "During all my life she has been the dear one. . . ." One week later, Hayes pasted in his diary a woodcut of Republican presidential candidate John C. Frémont. "Not a good picture," he wrote, "but will do to indicate my politics this year. For free States and against new slave States." His act reflected his departure from the disintegrating Whig Party and move to the Republican Party with its Free-Soil platform, which opposed expanding slavery into the western territories.

As Hayes's legal renown spread, Republicans began talking about his entering politics. In December 1858, when the solicitor of Cincinnati was killed in an accident, the city council chose Hayes to fill the remaining term. He called it a good job with an acceptable salary. His step into public office led to a pattern in his career: He always seemed to be in the right place at the right time. But according to Ari Hoogenboom in *Rutherford B. Hayes: Warrior and President,* while the Ohioan's advance appeared to come easily, he actually worked hard to shape developments that made his success more likely.

Hayes won election to a full two-year term as city solicitor in 1859. As the crisis between North and South intensified the following year, and as the Deep South sped toward secession, he firmly supported the Union, though he believed that if Southerners wanted to leave, they should be allowed to. "If the threats are meant," he said, "then it is time the Union was dissolved or the traitors crushed out." He opposed any compromise that would result in continuing slavery for a long time.

After Abraham Lincoln was elected president in November 1860, Hayes praised him and attended his visit to Cincinnati the following March. But many others in town thought the Republican Party too extreme and blamed it for moving America toward war. As a result, the Democrats swept Cincinnati in the 1861 elections, and Hayes lost his office.

He resumed his law practice on April 9, 1861. Three days later, rebel forces attacked Fort Sumter in South Carolina, beginning the Civil War. In May Hayes wrote about the conflict: "*I would prefer to go into it if I knew I was to die or be killed in the course of it, than to live through and after it without taking any part in it.*" One month later he joined the 23rd Regiment of Ohio Volunteers as a major.

Hayes was convinced that winning the war required striking at the Southern economy through its labor system; consequently, he advocated slavery's end in all the states under rebellion. As an officer he engaged in several battles, including one in which he was injured. In September 1862, while commanding the 23rd during an assault at Turner's Gap in South Mountain, Maryland, a musket ball fractured his left arm. Bleeding and feeling weak, he lay down on the ground. As the battle shifted, he found himself at one point pinned down between his troops and the rebels, with musket balls whizzing about him. He occupied his time speaking with a wounded Confederate soldier nearby and thinking about death. His men, however, rescued him, and the Battle of South Mountain turned into a Union victory.

Hayes soon advanced to brigadier general, and in 1864 the Republicans chose him to run for Congress. Although he refused to campaign while still in the military, he won the election. After being promoted to major general, he resigned from the army and in 1865 he took his seat in Congress. In the showdown between House Radicals and President Andrew Johnson, Hayes sided with the Radicals, though he had little enthusiasm for the fight. He was reelected in 1866, but the following year he returned home to run for governor. During the campaign he called on voters to ratify an amendment to the state constitution that would permit African Americans to vote. Although the amendment went down to defeat and the Democrats captured many offices, Hayes won his race by 3,000 votes.

As governor he supported establishing a state civil service system, regulating railroads, writing a safety code for mines, and improving prisons and mental hospitals. A conservative in finances, he urged the federal government to oppose issuing more paper money that might cause inflation. This mix of social reform and economic conservatism would appear again in the White House, as would his commitment to honesty and a vibrant executive branch.

Hayes won a second term as governor in 1869. Three years later he agreed to run again for Congress. This time he lost, a victim less of his own campaign than of the public disgust with the Republicans and the scandalous presidency of Ulysses S. Grant. Hayes subsequently bought his uncle's estate in Lower Sandusky and moved there. He reentered politics in 1875 after the Republicans nominated him for governor a third time.

A tough fight awaited him. The Republican Party was unpopular for several reasons. Fraud within the state organization and a national economic depression had hurt the party. So, too, had the 1875 Civil Rights Act passed by Congress that made it illegal to segregate railroads, hotels, and places of amusement and protected the right of blacks to serve on juries. Many Ohioans thought the act went too far in promoting social integration. Hayes himself expressed discomfort with it—though he supported African-American political rights, he opposed any type of racial mixing.

Despite these obstacles, Hayes won the governorship, defeating William Allen, the Democratic incumbent, by 5,500 votes. Ohio newspapers immediately touted Hayes for president. This was just the response he thought his victory would bring and one he welcomed. He had once again created a setting favorable to his advancement.

In March 1876, as a winter snowstorm gripped Ohio, Hayes wrote in his diary that many counties had elected delegates to the forthcoming state convention who were favorable to his seeking the presidency. "I feel less diffidence in thinking of this subject than perhaps I ought," he admitted. "It seems to me that good purposes, and the judgment, experience and firmness I possess would enable me to execute the duties of the office well. I do not feel the least fear that I should fail!"

When the Republican National Convention met in Cincinnati in June, Hayes was one of six prominent candidates for the presidential nomination. Representative James G. Blaine of Maine, Speaker of the House, led the field, but he came to town with a liability: Opponents in Congress had charged him with receiving money in a suspicious stock deal involving a railroad that he was in a position to help him politically. Blaine denied the charge but never convincingly, and in a year when scandal in the Grant presidency made Republicans skittish about signs of dishonesty, some delegates thought they should look elsewhere. Blaine obtained the most votes on the first roll call, but Hayes, known for his honesty and reform, won on the seventh ballot.

There followed the controversial election of 1876, peculiar and complex because of its relationship to southern reconstruction. Few believed Hayes would defeat the Democratic candidate, New York governor Samuel J. Tilden, who was well known for chasing crooks out of the state government, including a notorious political ring that had bilked funds intended for canal improvements.

The Republicans suffered from the continuing scandals that rocked President Grant, such as the indictment of his private secretary for defrauding the treasury and the impeachment of his secretary of war for shady deals involving the Indian territories. Although both men were acquitted, the White House and the party seemed sordid to the public. Furthermore, the economic depression hurt, as did the largely successful efforts by southern whites to prevent African Americans, most of whom were Republicans, from voting.

Yet Hayes did win support from liberal Republicans who had bolted the party in 1872 to protest Grant's renomination. He managed this with his call for a complete reform of the spoils system, under which Congress and the president customarily filled jobs based on political loyalty rather than professional talent.

As was customary for presidential candidates of that time, Hayes stayed largely at home rather than take to the campaign stump. He did, however, make a trip in October to the International Exposition in Philadelphia, where sizable crowds came to see him, and he marveled at the inventions.

Despite his reluctance to travel, Hayes participated in campaign strategy. He insisted that to rally Republicans and get them to the polls, reform had to be made a secondary issue and the "bloody red shirt" waved—meaning, Republicans needed to remind Northerners that should the Democrats win, ex-Confederates would likely gain power in the government. He said, "*The danger of giving the Rebels the Government,* is the topic people are most interested in."

By mid-November the election returns showed Tilden with about 200,000 more popular votes than Hayes out of more than 8 million cast. The electoral vote also looked to be Tilden's as he apparently swept the South, won his home state of New York, and beat Hayes in Indiana, Connecticut, and New Jersey.

In his diary, Rutherford Hayes attributed the Democratic victory in several southern states to the plight of African Americans who intended to vote. With defeat in mind, he claimed:

> History will hold that the Republicans were by fraud, violence and intimidation, by a nullification of the 15th amendment, deprived of the victory which they fairly won. But we must . . . prepare ourselves to accept the inevitable. I do it with composure and cheerfulness. To me the result is no personal calamity. . . . In the old slave States . . . if there had been neither violence nor intimidation, nor other improper interference with the rights of the colored people, we should have carried enough Southern States to have held the country, and to have secured a decided popular majority in the Nation.

Several weeks remained, however, before the electors would meet to cast their votes, and William E. Chandler, New Hampshire committeeman for the Republican Party and a leader in Grant's campaigns, pursued a plan. In three southern states—South Carolina, Florida, and Louisiana—Republican reconstruction governments remained in power. He and several colleagues arranged to have each state's returning board, which validated ballot counts and were, like the state governments, Republican-controlled, review the votes cast. If enough Democratic ballots could be tossed out, Hayes would carry those states and win the presidency.

Even before the canvas, late returns showed Hayes had won in South Carolina by 600-1,000 votes, so there was little worry for the Republicans there. In Florida he trailed Tilden by 94 votes, a margin that could be changed with little effort. But Louisiana posed a big problem—Hayes had lost by 6,300 votes.

There was no doubt that Democratic efforts to keep African Americans from the polls cost Hayes many votes in Florida and Louisiana (as well as in other southern states). Yet both sides had used trickery and stuffed ballot boxes. On top of all that, while many blacks stayed away from voting in Louisiana because whites intimidated them, others did so because of bickering factions within the Republican Party.

Hayes told his supporters, "We are not to allow our friends to defeat one outrage and fraud by another. There must be nothing crooked on our part." Nevertheless, Republicans and Democrats alike used bribery to sway the returning boards. On December 5, the board in Louisiana disqualified 15,000 votes, 13,000 of them Democratic, and declared Hayes the winter by 3,000 votes. The following day the board in Florida declared Hayes the winner by 900 votes. Hayes reacted by telling a friend: "I have no doubt that we are justly and legally entitled to the presidency."

At the same time, a dispute erupted in Oregon. Hayes carried the state, but after a Republican elector resigned, the governor appointed a Democratic replacement. When electors met across the country on December 6 to cast their ballots, the Democrats in Louisiana, Florida, South Carolina, and Oregon submitted results that challenged the Republican tallies. In all, there were 184 votes for Tilden and 165 for Hayes, with 20 in dispute. Congress, therefore, would have to settle the disputed votes. Should it award all 20 to Hayes, he would be the winner.

As it happened, the House was Democratic and the Senate Republican. Congress decided to appoint a commission of five senators, five representatives, and five Supreme Court justices, evenly divided between the two parties, except for the fifth justice, David Davis of Illinois, who was to be an independent.

But another problem arose when the Tilden camp, in a tactical error, supported Davis for a seat in the Senate. When he won, they thought he would stay on the commission and return their favor by supporting them. Davis, however, said that because he was beholden to the Democrats, he would resign his seat. He was replaced by Justice Joseph P. Bradley, a Republican, thus giving the Republicans an 8-7 majority.

In each disputed state, the commissioners voted 8-7 in favor of Hayes. As a result, Hayes defeated Tilden in the electoral college, 185 to 184. The Democrats subsequently decided to filibuster the outcome. With Hayes's inaugural date fast approaching, they hoped to pressure him to remove the last Union troops in the South, those in South Carolina and Louisiana, which would enable them to wield unhindered white Democratic power. Hayes refused any specific promise, but since he believed the Reconstruction governments in those states had outlived their effectiveness, he implied there would be change.

Then in late February, two Republican congressional leaders signed a statement with Democrats at Washington's Wormley Hotel committing Hayes to home government in South Carolina and Louisiana in return for a promise to guarantee all citizens their political and civil rights. Although arranged without Hayes's approval, this Compromise of 1877 ended the filibuster. Hayes was officially declared the winner in the electoral college on March 2; he took the oath of office on March 3.

In his inaugural address the following day, Rutherford B. Hayes called for civil service reform—"thorough, radical, and complete"—saying federal appointments should be made based on ability rather than partisanship. He blamed economic problems on paper money and said he wanted greenbacks redeemed for gold coin to fight inflation and make credit sound. A crowd of 30,000 cheered, among them his wife, Lucy, who sat with him on the speakers' platform. The press would call her "Lemonade Lucy" for prohibiting alcohol in the White House, but more notably she was the first of the first ladies to hold a college degree. She also strongly supported women's suffrage, though she generally kept her belief private out of respect for her husband. Many Americans, meanwhile, began attaching the nickname "Rutherfraud" to the president for the controversial way in which he won the White House.

Among Rutherford Hayes's immediate problems was what to do about federal troops in South Carolina and Louisiana. Despite his own racial prejudice, he wanted to protect the rights of African Americans. (Privately, he headed the Slater Fund, which raised funds to educate blacks in the South.) Yet he realized the Democrats in Congress would block money for the army, and the military presence was only making southern whites more antagonistic toward blacks. "The real thing to be achieved is safety and prosperity for the colored people." he wrote in his diary. "Both Houses of Congress and the public opinion of the Country are plainly against the use of the army. . . . The wish is to restore harmony and good feeling between Sections and races."

He withdrew the troops from South Carolina in early April after receiving assurances from the governor that the constitutional rights of African Americans would be upheld. Later that month he did the same in Louisiana after its governor announced the state would accept the three constitutional amendments generated by the Civil War and promote friendship between the races.

Hayes entered the White House when the piston was beginning to overtake the plow in America's economy. Industry expanded in tandem with internal improvements, most notably the building of railroads, to produce a wrenching change, belied by the seemingly unfettered displays at the Philadelphia exposition. Industrial growth brought uneven benefits and numerous problems, and in 1877 they boiled over when several railroads sought to boost their profits by increasing shipping rates and cutting wages. This ignited a widespread strike that disrupted rail service. Hayes sided with the companies when he said the strikers had no right to prevent others from working; yet he recognized that the workers had legitimate complaints, and he resisted pressure to intervene as a strike-breaker or to smear the movement as a communist conspiracy, a tactic used by several newspapers.

Violence marred the strike. In Baltimore a mob attacked the militia, which reacted by opening fire, killing 10 men and boys. Then 15,000 rioters burned railroad cars and part of a depot. The governor requested that Hayes send in troops, but the turmoil ended before the president could act. Hayes eventually deployed troops in Indiana, however, to keep the railroads there open, and he prodded judges to find the strikers in contempt of court. Still, his overall restraint meant few federal troops ever entered the dispute. While the public deplored the violence, they thought the railroads had brought it on, and they supported Hayes in his moderate response.

President Hayes made it clear he would restore some of the power and independence that the executive branch had lost under Andrew Johnson and Ulysses S. Grant. He began by appointing a cabinet without respect to what some leading Republicans in Congress wanted. His secretary of state, William Evarts, ranked among the most talented lawyers, and his secretary of the interior, Carl Schurz, brought with him a record as a vigorous reformer.

Then in June 1877 Hayes attacked the corrupt spoils system when he issued an executive order prohibiting federal civil servants from taking part "in the management of political organizations, caucuses, conventions, or election campaigns" and making illegal any requirement that they contribute money to candidates. Later that year Hayes engaged in a bitter fight with Senator Roscoe Conkling, a fellow Republican, over the New York City Customhouse. Conkling treated the customhouse as his personal fiefdom; 75 percent of the country's tariff revenue was collected there, and his handpicked workers funneled some of the money to his political machine.

Hayes sided with reformers in the New York Republican Party in September when he announced the removal of collector Chester A. Arthur and his associate, Alonzo Cornell. The president noted in his diary: "I am now in a contest on the question of the right of Senators to dictate or control nominations. Mr. Conkling insists that no officer shall be appointed in New York without his consent . . . . This is the first and most important step in the effort to reform the Civil Service. . . . None who are opposed . . . on this important question are to be regarded as Republicans in good standing."

Conkling retorted about the reformers: "[They] forget that parties are not built up by deportment, or by ladies' magazines, or gush." Republican Stalwarts in Congress—those who supported the spoils system—sided with Conkling against the president. They thought Hayes had conceded too much to southern Democrats, they disliked his appointment of Schurz, and they wanted no weakening in congressional power over patronage. With Conkling as chair, the Senate Commerce Committee rejected the president's appointments to replace Arthur and Cornell. Hayes reacted by saying, "In the language of the press 'Senator Conkling has won a great victory over the Administration' . . . But the end is not yet. I am right, and shall not give up the contest."

He kept his word. In July 1878 he suspended Arthur and Cornell after Congress adjourned. By the time the Senate considered his new appointees, he had rallied enough support among Republicans and Democrats to defeat Conkling. Hayes later said about his rival: "His treachery stopped short of results only because he lacked the back bone required to make it notorious and effective." Looking back on his victory, he observed: "The great success of [my] Administration . . . was in getting the control of the New York custom House and in changing it from a political machine for the benefit of party leaders into a business office for the benefit of the public."

While Hayes was doing battle with Conkling, in February 1878 Congress passed the Bland-Allison Act, which instructed the treasury to purchase silver and convert it into standard dollars. The intended effect of this act was to lessen the nation's reliance on gold. Farmers and some labor interests wanted more paper money circulated as the best means to raise prices for foodstuffs and industrial wages. Hayes, however, exerted his sound money view and vetoed the act. Although Congress overrode the president, the act gave him the authority to instruct the secretary of the treasury to limit silver purchases, which was done.

In 1879 President Hayes vetoed an appropriations bill containing a rider that would have repealed the law giving the army power to maintain peace at the polls, a measure used to protect blacks voters in congressional elections. Congress decided to relent and drop the rider. That same year Hayes vetoed a bill restricting Chinese immigration to the United States, claiming it violated an earlier treaty that provided for free movement between the two countries. He thus avoided a crisis with China. In November 1880, however, he negotiated a new treaty that allowed the United States to impose some limits.

When Hayes won the presidency, he promised to serve only one term. Consequently, he retired from office in March 1881. He died on January 8, 1893, at his home in Fremont, Ohio.

An honest man, Rutherford B. Hayes struggled throughout his presidency with the tainted 1876 vote. Despite that encumbrance, he brought a modicum of reform to the civil service, and although Congress retained much of the power it had acquired when Andrew Johnson and Ulysses S. Grant occupied the White House, his showdown with Conkling and his determined but judicious use of vetoes restored some authority to the executive branch.

Chronology

1822 Born October 4

1836 Enters academy at Norwalk, Ohio

1838 Enters Kenyon College

1843 Enters Harvard Law School

1845 Admitted to the Ohio bar

1849 Moves to Cincinnati

1852 Marries Lucy Webb

1858 Named Cincinnati city solicitor

1859 Wins election as Cincinnati city solicitor

1861 Joins Union army as a major

1862 Wounded in Battle of South Mountain

1864 Promoted to brigadier general

1865 Promoted to major general
Begins term in U.S. House of Representatives

1866 Reelected to Congress

1867 Elected governor of Ohio

1869 Reelected governor

1872 Loses congressional election

1875 Elected governor of Ohio

1876 Named Republican nominee for president

1877	Declared president by Electoral Commission with approval of Congress
	Withdraws federal troops from South Carolina and Louisiana
	Issues executive order to limit spoils system
1878	Vetoes Bland-Allison bill
	Suspends Chester A. Arthur as New York customs collector
1879	Vetoes Chinese immigration bill
1881	Retires to Fremont
1893	Dies January 17

Further Reading

Barnard, Harry. *Rutherford B. Hayes and His America.* Indianapolis, Ind.: Bobbs-Merrill, 1954.

Davison, Kenneth E. *The Presidency of Rutherford B. Hayes.* Westport, Conn.: Greenwood Press, 1972.

Hoogenboom, Ari. *Rutherford B. Hayes: Warrior and President.* Lawrence: University Press of Kansas, 1995.

Polakoff, Keith Ian. *The Politics of Inertia: The Election of 1876 and the End of Reconstruction.* Baton Rouge: Louisiana State University Press, 1973.

Trefousse, Hans. *Rutherford B. Hayes, 1877–1881.* New York: Times Books, 2002.

Williams, T. Harry, ed. *Hayes: The Diary of a President, 1875–1881.* New York: David McKay, 1964.

Woodward, C. Vann. *Reunion and Reaction: The Compromise of 1877 and the End of Reconstruction.* Garden City, N.Y.: Doubleday, 1956.

JAMES A. GARFIELD (1831–1881)

Twentieth President, March–September 1881

JAMES A. GARFIELD
(Library of Congress, Brady-Handy Collection)

"The elevation of the negro race from slavery to the full rights of citizenship is the most important political change we have known since the adoption of the Constitution of 1787. No thoughtful man can fail to appreciate its beneficent effect upon our institutions and people."

—Inaugural words, March 4, 1881

Two men who believed strongly in destiny met at a Washington train station in 1881. Ever since converting to the Disciples of Christ years earlier, President James A. Garfield thought God was directing his life. Likewise, Charles Guiteau, a deranged lawyer and public-office seeker, saw divine guidance in his own actions. On July 2 Guiteau fired two bullets at Garfield, one of which lodged in the president's back. Garfield fell to the ground. "Oh my God!" he said. Two months later, he died.

Following a route taken by many other New Englanders, in the late 1820s James A. Garfield's father, Abram Garfield, moved to the Midwest in search of opportunity. Once in Ohio, he invested his savings in a canal company that failed. Then, with his remaining money, he bought a farm in Orange township near Lake Erie, where in 1829 he settled down with his wife, Eliza Ballou Garfield, and their two children. In a short while, Abram and Eliza joined the Disciples of Christ, a religious sect separated from the Baptists. The Disciples called for adherence to the commandments as originally stated in the Bible. In that sense they were fundamentalists, though rational rather than emotional ones.

On November 19, 1831, James Abram Garfield was born to Abram and Eliza in a log cabin built by his father. Just two years later the elder Garfield died from a fever, leaving James's upbringing to Eliza. She was described as a "bright, cheerful woman," who created a happy atmosphere for her children. James loved to hunt and to read; he especially liked studying the American Revolution and delving into fiction. The farm, however, occupied much of his time, as from an early age he helped his mother in a struggle that, despite their efforts, left them mired in poverty.

In 1848, at age 17, Garfield decided to take to the sea, but got no farther than a nearby canal. For six weeks he worked on a barge and made several trips from Cleveland to Pittsburgh, first as a driver then as bowman, with the responsibility of preparing the locks along the route. Soon after an illness forced him to return home, he resumed the schooling he had disrupted earlier. At first unconcerned with religion, in 1850 he was baptized into the Disciples of Christ and from then on saw God's will in almost everything, including his own life. He remarked, "Thus by the providence of God I am what I am and not a sailor. I thank him."

In 1851 Garfield enrolled in a new Disciples school, the Western Reserve Eclectic Institute (later Hiram College), where he earned a reputation as a serious student, well-liked for his friendly and kindly manner, and discovered his talent as an orator. The Ohioan initially looked at life as rewarding, but after a love affair turned sour, he said, "To the first view . . . the world and society seem pleasant and alluring, but when their depths are penetrated, their secret paths trod, they are found hollow, soulless, and insipid." From then on he went through bouts of depression and confusion that sometimes caused indecision.

In 1852 Garfield obtained a job teaching at the institute, and after saving his money he enrolled in 1854 at Williams College in Massachusetts as a junior. After graduating, he returned to Ohio and in 1857 became president of Hiram. He also began preaching; his open-air orations were described by one observer as inducing tranquility among listeners, making it seem they had been taken to a "beautiful region of heaven." The following year he married Lucretia Rudolph after a long courtship, filled with much self-doubt on his part. They had seven children, one of whom died in childhood.

Garfield soon grew tired of educators, finding the petty bickering among the faculty to be insufferable, and he searched for an alternative career. In 1859 he decided his future pointed to politics. That August he ran for the state senate as a Republican and won—beginning his remarkable record of never losing a political campaign. He owed his success largely to Harmon Austin, a banker who became his lifetime campaign manager. Austin's adept tactics made it appear that office sought Garfield, rather than the other way around, and as a result preserved Garfield's belief in destiny—an objective observer would call it a manufactured destiny—and the aura that came with it. "His desire to manage people and their affairs is very marked," Garfield said about Austin, "and though I like him very much indeed and accept his admonitions . . . I can't say they are entirely reasonable or pleasant." Austin saw politics as a sport. He said, "I have such a horror of being whipped that I cannot let it alone."

Garfield's speeches on the stump in his state senate campaign dealt mainly with slavery, then an issue tearing the country apart. He condemned the practice while praising the Republican Party for protecting free labor.

The following year Garfield spoke throughout Ohio in support of Abraham Lincoln's presidential campaign; he attracted large audiences and much acclaim. When the Deep South moved toward secession in late 1860, he opposed all efforts at forming a peace mission and was one of only three senators in his state legislature who voted against negotiating with southern leaders. As a strong unionist, he called the secessionists traitors and thought they should be hanged.

To James Garfield the Civil War was nothing less than a crusade for union and against slavery. "The sin of slavery," he said, "is one of which it may be said that 'without the shedding of blood there is no remission.'" In 1861 he became colonel of an Ohio regiment and rallied his troops with oratory and patriotic fervor. Knowing nothing about strategy, he studied training manuals and the accounts of European military leaders, particularly Napoleon. In January 1862 he achieved one of the rare Union victories at that time when he defeated a Confederate force at Middle Creek, Kentucky.

With his battlefield prestige, powerful oratory, and commanding presence—he was six feet tall and broad-shouldered—Garfield won the notice of Republican leaders, and in September 1862 they selected him to run for the U.S. House of Representatives. After his election victory, he absented himself from Congress so he could continue serving in the army. In August 1863 General W. S. Rosecrans attacked the Confederates at Chickamauga in Tennessee. After the general made a strategic mistake, Garfield prevented defeat by riding along the battlefront and redirecting the army. The fight, which ended in a draw, resulted in criticism of Rosecrans but praise for Garfield, though he may well have been culpable in planning the botched effort.

The Ohioan retired from the army in December 1863 and took his seat in Congress, where his colleagues placed him on the Military Affairs Committee. He later served on the Appropriations Committee and the Ways and Means Committee and exerted considerable influence on both. He ranked among the hardest workers in Congress, and though never known as an intellectual, he read extensively and owned a 3,000-volume library.

Garfield's ardor for Lincoln cooled as the Civil War continued. He criticized the president for failing to win the conflict sooner and for being too lenient with the South. Although he supported Lincoln for reelection in 1864, he let it be known that he did so reluctantly. Garfield wanted the total defeat of the South, including the seizure of large plantations and an end to slavery. He said: "This is an abolition war."

After Lincoln's assassination, Garfield tried to establish cordial relations with the new president, Andrew Johnson. But he later broke with Johnson over Reconstruction policy and sided with the Radicals who sought to punish the South. Garfield wanted the Confederate leaders either exiled or shot. He insisted: "Let no weak sentiments of misplaced sympathy deter us from inaugurating a measure which will cleanse our nation and make it the fit home for freedom and a glorious manhood." As part of that freedom, he advocated equal rights for African Americans.

Yet by the early 1870s the Ohioan began changing his views. He concluded that much of Reconstruction had failed, and he disliked Republican policy as thoroughly as he did that of the southern Democrats. He was appalled, for example, when in 1875 federal troops expelled several Democrats from the Louisiana legislature so it could organize under the Republicans. He realized, too, that northern public opinion no longer supported large-scale federal intervention in the South. Northerners wanted their political leaders to spend more time tackling the severe economic depression that was hurting almost every American. Garfield believed that with the Fifteenth

Amendment, which protected black suffrage, the federal government had done all it could for the former slaves. The amendment, he said, "confers upon the African Race the care of its own destiny. It places their fortune in their own hands." They would have to fend for themselves and, as he put it, show their manhood and worthiness by their achievements.

On several other issues then before Congress, Garfield sided with conservatives. He disliked the Grange, an organization of farmers devoted to ending monopolies and setting railroad shipping rates, calling it a form of communism. He opposed unions and believed the federal government should use troops to break up strikes, and he opposed the large-scale immigration of Eastern Europeans, fearing they would corrupt politics.

Yet he supported civil service reform, though with greater restraint than some in the Republican Party. Where many reformers considered the spoils system crude for its appeal to political favoritism and wanted to end it in order to add dignity to government, Garfield mainly wanted to alleviate the pressure on officeholders, particularly congressmen being badgered for jobs. He said, "I should favor the Civil Service if for no other reason [than] of getting partially rid of the enormous pressure for office."

During the disputed presidential election of 1876, Garfield organized congressmen to support the Republican candidate, Rutherford B. Hayes, and served on the special Election Commission that voted to make Hayes president. After Hayes entered the White House and chose Ohio Senator John Sherman as his secretary of the treasury, Garfield appeared ready to obtain Sherman's seat in the Senate. Hayes, however, asked the congressman to remain in the House, where as minority leader he could fight for the president's programs, and Garfield agreed. An opportunity to enter the Senate presented itself again in January 1880 when the Ohio legislature met to fill a vacancy for the following year, but the unexpected struck—namely, the Republican nomination for president.

Garfield entered that year's national convention in Chicago supporting Sherman for the White House. He did not particularly like his fellow Ohioan, nor did he expect him to win, but he wanted to stop Ulysses S. Grant's campaign. Grant, whose renown as the hero of Appomattox partly erased from the public mind the scandals during his two terms in the White House, came to the convention with a substantial following. As reformers within the party searched for someone who could beat him, they turned to Garfield. He rejected their pleas, though, saying that as Sherman's campaign manager he might be accused of impropriety should he seek the nomination. Yet as much as Garfield neither craved the presidency nor expected to obtain it, he realized a deadlocked convention could turn to him.

New York senator Roscoe Conkling, leader of the Stalwarts, who opposed the reformers, placed Grant's name into nomination in what has been called "one of the most brilliant speeches in convention history," but also one controversial for its sharp attack on the general's critics. Conkling said:

> Vilified and reviled, ruthlessly aspersed by unnumbered presses, not in other lands, but in his own, assaults upon him have seasoned and strengthened his hold on the public heart. Calumny's ammunition has all been exploded; the powder has all been burned once—its force is spent—and the name of Grant will glitter a bright and imperishable star in the diadem of the Republic when those who have tried to tarnish it have moldered in forgotten graves; and when their memories and their epitaphs have vanished utterly.

With Conkling's speech, delegates shouted and cheered. Then Garfield strode to the platform and presented Sherman's name. His booming voice and impassioned call for harmony slowed Grant's momentum. Speaking extemporaneously, Garfield said,

> Not here, in this brilliant circle where fifteen thousand men and women are gathered, is the

destiny of the republic to be decreed for the next four years. Not here . . . but by four millions of Republican firesides, where the thoughtful voters, with wives and children about them, with the calm thoughts inspired by love of home and country, with the history of the past, the hopes of the future, and reverence for great men who have adorned and blessed our nation in days gone by, burning in their hearts—*there* God prepares the verdict which will determine the wisdom of our work tonight.

Despite these words, his successful fight to stop a change in rules turned out to be more crucial. The Stalwarts wanted each state to cast its vote as a unit—that is, to give all of its votes to the one candidate leading in the state. They knew that such a change would assure Grant's nomination. The Stalwarts were defeated, however, when about 60 delegates from New York, Pennsylvania, and Illinois broke with their colleagues and cast their votes individually.

Grant took the early lead in the balloting but barely so. On the first roll call he won 304 votes to Maine senator James G. Blaine's 284 and Sherman's 93, with scattered votes for others but none for James Garfield. Thirty-three roll calls later, little had changed. Then the Blaine and Sherman forces agreed to back Garfield. On the 34th ballot the Wisconsin delegation voted for him. "I rise to a point of order," Garfield protested. "No man has a right, without the consent of the person voted for, to announce that person's name and vote for him in this convention. Such consent I have not given." The delegates rejected his argument. On the 35th roll call he won 50 votes, and on the 36th he won the nomination.

For the convention to adjourn united, the Conkling forces would have to be appeased; the delegates therefore agreed to make Chester A. Arthur the vice-presidential candidate. Arthur, former head of the New York Customhouse, once known for its corruption and attachment to Conkling's political machine, had linked his career to the Stalwarts. Conkling, however, never promoted Arthur for the vice presidency since he thought it to be an insignificant post. In fact, he urged Arthur to reject the nomination, but the New Yorker decided to accept it anyway.

As it turned out, Arthur helped the ticket immensely by using his influence to raise money from government office holders, squeezing so much from them that even old-time political pros marveled at his deed. The spoils system thus benefited a ticket promoted by reformers. The campaign, though, produced little excitement. The Republicans attacked the Democratic candidate, General Winfield S. Hancock of Pennsylvania, for his political inexperience. A man who looked imposing at 240 pounds, Hancock possessed little knowledge of government.

Garfield campaigned for sound money, a moderate tariff, pensions for veterans, and limits on Chinese immigration. Although he called for civil service reform, he did so without enthusiasm. In New York City in August 1880, he met with the Stalwarts, and though the record is murky, he likely promised an important job to one of them and agreed to consider all factions in making appointments.

The biggest campaign controversy emerged just days before the election when a New York newspaper, *Truth,* published a letter alleged to have been written by then-Congressman Garfield to "H. L. Morey of the Employers' Union, Lynn, Massachusetts," in which he approved of Chinese immigration. "I take it that the question of employes is only a question of private and corporate economy," the letter stated, "and individuals or companys have the right to buy labor where they can get it cheapest."

Garfield called the letter a forgery, and the misspellings in it—for he was an impeccable speller—bore him out. The Democrats hoped that given Garfield's campaign pledge, the letter would portray him as a hypocrite on the Chinese issue and excite western voters to side with Hancock. The ploy failed, however, and on election day Garfield carried nearly the entire North and West. He finished with 214 electoral votes to Hancock's 155, though with a popular vote plurality of less than 10,000. As president the Ohioan would face a divided Congress—a Republican majority in the House, but a deadlock in the Senate, where two independents held the balance of power.

James A. Garfield came into office seeking to make government appointments unfettered by certain congressional restrictions and to select men of quality. He aimed to challenge the custom that the senior senator in a state should approve major appointments in the state involved. He called it "one of the most corrupt and vicious practices of our time."

Much as had happened with his predecessor, Rutherford B. Hayes, Garfield's determination brought him into conflict with Roscoe Conkling. When the president removed Edwin A. Merritt as collector of the port of New York by naming him consul-general to London and appointed William H. Robertson to the collector's post, he defied Conkling and his fellow New York senator, Thomas C. Platt, both of whom supported Merritt. Garfield called the impending fight one that would "settle the question whether the President is registering clerk of the Senate or the Executive of the United States."

Although on the surface Garfield seemed to be crusading only for civil service reform, he was also fighting for presidential prerogative and trying to build an organization in New York that could weaken Conkling. Newspapers overwhelmingly supported the president, and Conkling's abrasive style won him few supporters in the Senate. In a gamble, Conkling and Platt decided to resign their Senate seats and then win immediate reelection as a way to show that New York stood behind them. But after they quit, the Senate on May 18 quickly confirmed Robertson's appointment as collector. A few weeks later, the New York legislature refused to send Conkling and Platt back to the Senate, choosing instead two moderates to replace them.

President Garfield faced a scandal soon after entering the White House. The *New York Times* had uncovered fraud in the Post Office Department, the government's largest bureaucracy, which employed more than 50 percent of all federal workers. Years earlier the department had established Star Routes, whereby it entered into contracts with private horse, stagecoach, and wagon companies to deliver mail to remote settlements. The *Times* found that several companies had received overpayments, some of them thousands of dollars yearly, to make no more than three mail deliveries. Garfield ordered Postmaster General Thomas L. James to investigate the charges, and when the inquiry implicated his own campaign manager, Harmon Austin, he told James to forge ahead and take the investigation wherever it might go.

James found that contracts had been awarded to companies closely associated with leaders in previous Republican administrations. The inquiry would continue beyond Garfield's presidency and force the second assistant postmaster general to resign, along with the secretary of the Republican national committee, and encourage civil service reform.

Unknown to Garfield, a lawyer named Charles Guiteau began calling at the White House, looking for a job; at one point he even crashed a reception. Guiteau wrote to the president:

> I called to see you this A.M., but you were engaged. . . . What do you think of me for Consul-General at Paris? I think I prefer Paris to Vienna, and if agreeable to you, should be satisfied with the Consulship at Paris . . . I claim to be a gentleman and a Christian.

At one time an itinerant preacher, Guiteau believed God worked through him. He began stalking Garfield and first thought about assassination in late June 1881 when he found the president walking with James G. Blaine, but he lost his nerve. Then on the morning of July 2 he hunted Garfield down at the Baltimore and Potomac Station in Washington. The president was walking to his railroad car, preparing to leave for his alma mater, Williams College, where he planned to deliver the commencement address. One of the two shots Guiteau fired from his pistol grazed Garfield's arm; the other lodged in his back near his spinal column. "His death was a political necessity," Guiteau wrote in a letter prior to the assassination. "I am a lawyer, theologian, and politician. I am a Stalwart of the Stalwarts. . . ."

The president lingered in pain for weeks while doctors tried to locate the bullet. They thought it might be in his lung or liver. They even brought in Alexander Graham Bell to use his electric device, an experimental model of a metal detector, to locate it. The attempt failed, however, when metal coils in the president's mattress interfered with the machine. The country followed the president's battle for life closely; one railroad even issued progress charts to its riders, presenting the fallen leader's "pulse, temperature, and respiration."

Meanwhile, the public looked more closely at Vice President Chester A. Arthur and found him wanting. His long friendship with Conkling made many fear for the integrity of the presidency, badly damaged a few years earlier under Grant. Newspapers told about Arthur's shady deals, and the *Nation* said, "It is out of this mess of filth that Mr. Arthur will go to the Presidential chair in case of the President's death." During the campaign, the same publication had discounted Arthur's threat to clean government, saying that as vice president he would have no influence.

For his part, Arthur genuinely wanted no higher office than the vice presidency, and he reacted to the shooting of Garfield with stunned disbelief. In September aides took the president to the seaside village of Elberon, New Jersey, where he could breathe the ocean air as a tonic. Quite possibly the contaminated instruments used by his doctors to probe for the bullet did the most harm, and had he been left alone, he would have lived. But on September 19, 1881, after saying, "My work is done," he died. When notified later that day, Arthur cried; on September 20 he took the oath of office.

Guiteau's trial began in November 1881 and lasted until March 1882. His attorneys entered a plea of insanity, and most historians today believe Guiteau was deranged. A jury, however, found him guilty of murder, and on June 30, 1882, he was hanged at the District of Columbia jail.

Americans went into deep mourning over Garfield's death. His body lay in the Capitol rotunda for two days, during which time 100,000 people filed past the casket. Since James A. Garfield had held the presidency only six months, a mere four actively, he had little chance to set policy or leave a lasting presidential legacy. Yet in his rise from poverty to the White House Americans saw the opportunity their society provided for advancement; it encouraged them to believe that if he could do it, so could they. As a result, Guiteau's assault seemed as much an attack on someone who represented their cherished values as on a man who served as president.

Chronology

1831 Born November 19

1850 Joins Disciples of Christ

1851 Enters Western Reserve Eclectic Institute

1854 Enters Williams College

1856 Graduates from Williams College

1857 Appointed president of Hiram College

1858 Marries Lucretia Randolph

1859 Elected to Ohio state senate

1861 Commissioned lieutenant colonel in Ohio volunteers

Promoted to colonel

1862 Defeats Confederates at Middle Creek, Kentucky

Promoted to brigadier general

Commands brigade at Shiloh

Elected to U.S. House of Representatives

1863 Fights at Chickamauga

Begins term in Congress

1871 Appointed chairman of House Committee on Appropriations

1876 Becomes minority leader in House

1880 Elected president

1881 Clashes with Senator Roscoe Conkling over patronage

Approves investigation of Star Route frauds

Shot by Charles Guiteau

Dies of gunshot wound on September 19

Further Reading

Doenecke, Justus D. *The Presidencies of James A. Garfield and Chester A. Arthur.* Lawrence: University Press of Kansas, 1981.

Peskin, Allan. *Garfield.* Kent State, Ohio: Kent State University Press, 1978.

Schlesinger, Arthur M., Jr., Fred L. Israel, and William P. Hansen, eds. *History of American Presidential Elections, 1789–1968,* vol. II. New York: McGraw-Hill, 1971.

Taylor John M. *Garfield of Ohio: The Available Man.* New York: W. W. Norton, 1970.

CHESTER A. ARTHUR (1829–1886)

Twenty-first President, 1881–1885

CHESTER A. ARTHUR
(lithograph by Currier & Ives, Library of Congress)

"For the fourth time in the history of the Republic, its Chief Magistrate has been removed by death. . . . Men may die, but the fabrics of our free institutions remain unshaken."

—Chester A. Arthur address to the public, September 1881

When James A. Garfield died on September 18, 1881, and Chester A. Arthur took the oath of office the following day, reformers were shocked. Andrew Dickson White, an educator and diplomat, remarked: "It was a common saying of that time among those who knew him best, 'Chet' Arthur President of the United States. Good God."

Throughout the 1870s America had suffered one scandal after another. Corruption ruled from New York City, with Mayor Boss Tweed, to the White House, with President Ulysses S. Grant. Then Arthur became president, a political boss whose friendly demeanor masked his calculating work for one of the country's more corrupt machines. The presidency seemed headed for its greatest debasement yet—until Arthur surprised almost everyone.

Chester Alan Arthur was born on October 5, 1829, to William Arthur and Malvina Stone Arthur at Fairfield, Vermont. William had joined the Baptist clergy in 1827 and relocated to a church in Fairfield the following year. Known as "Elder Arthur," he was a staunch abolitionist. He moved his family often as he served in several different parishes. When Chester was nine, the family settled in Union Village, New York, where he attended school. After Elder Arthur moved yet again and took his family to Schenectady, Chester entered that town's Union College in 1845. He graduated in 1848 and soon began studying law while teaching school.

Arthur moved to New York City in 1853 to join the law office of E. D. Culver, a friend whose abolitionist views reinforced those the young man had learned from his father. There he clerked and studied law, and in 1854, after gaining admission to the bar, he became a partner in the firm, renamed Culver, Parker, and Arthur.

A hardworking lawyer, over the years Chester Arthur developed a solid, if unspectacular, track record. His one notable case occurred in 1855, when he represented Elizabeth Jennings, an African American who had been assaulted after refusing to leave a streetcar reserved for whites. He won the suit for her by arguing that her treatment violated a recently enacted law that forbade the expulsion of "colored persons" from public vehicles. She received $225, but more important, as a result of the trial New York City enforced the law and integrated its streetcars.

In 1859 Arthur married Ellen Lewis Herndon, a Virginian and the daughter of a navy hero. They had three children, one of whom did not live past childhood. The couple had a strained relationship; his absences were so frequent while he pursued politics that she talked about divorcing him. Nevertheless, after Ellen died in 1880, Arthur mourned his loss and claimed he no longer had a passion for life.

When the Civil War erupted in 1861, the governor of New York appointed Arthur as assistant quartermaster general. This put him in charge of feeding, housing, and equipping the many volunteers arriving in New York City from throughout the northeast to fight the Confederates. He worked so effectively that the governor promoted him to quartermaster general for the entire state, a post he held until he resigned in late 1862.

Arthur returned to his law practice, and his business flourished as his political contacts expanded. He soon became chairman of the state Republican executive committee, and he supported Ulysses S. Grant for president by heading the Central Grant Club of New York. Grant's victory in 1868, combined with the earlier election of Roscoe Conkling to the U.S. Senate, boosted Arthur's political standing. In 1871 Grant needed a competent loyalist to take over the New York Customhouse as collector to replace Thomas Murphy, recently exposed as corrupt. Conkling recommended Arthur, and Grant appointed him.

Despite his campaign work, at age 42 Arthur was largely unknown. Yet when he strode into the customhouse, a huge, solid granite building—complete with a vast rotunda and marble columns—that fronted Wall Street, he entered an important and lucrative job. The customhouse collected about 75 percent of all trade revenues flowing into the country and housed about 1,000 workers. As collector he earned more than $50,000 annually, the highest pay in the federal government, and he wielded power surpassing that of most persons in the president's cabinet. Arthur's job was to make appointments and removals and to supervise political assessments—that is, collect money from the workers to support the Republican

Party. The assessments provided Republicans with $36,000 annually, much-needed fodder for campaign treasuries.

The customhouse workers liked Arthur. His sophisticated manners and learning stood out among the local politicians, and he cared about their welfare, fighting hard to protect their salaries against budget-cutters in Washington.

Chester A. Arthur thrived in the spoils system that had first emerged several decades earlier under President Andrew Jackson. Federal jobs typically went to party loyalists, who reciprocated with their "donations" and work for candidates. Each election year, hordes of job seekers descended on Washington, besieging congressmen and presidents. Most went away disappointed, while others latched onto their jobs like parasites.

Reformers thought the spoils system disgusting. In particular, dissident Republicans, known as Mugwumps, wanted a bureaucracy filled with professionals, largely from the educated elite, and removed from the tawdry reliance on political hacks and retainers—the result, they believed, of a democratic system gone rotten.

Stalwarts such as Arthur scoffed at the reformers; one observer said the New Yorker treated reform "with a jocular indulgence as the temporary essay of a few well-meaning visionaries with no practical sense of political needs." He collected high marks from many Republican leaders. Chauncey DePew called him "one of the most rigid of organization and machine men. . . ." As with other politicians who worked behind the scenes, few outsiders saw Arthur's activities, and few realized that his power extended well beyond the customhouse as a leader in the Grant-Conkling wing and a faithful Conkling lieutenant.

When a new civil service rule in 1872 made it illegal to require government workers to pay into campaign coffers, Arthur ignored it. This resulted in a reprimand from the chairman of the civil service commission. Arthur's cunning reply was coated with defiance: "Until after the receipt of your letter none of these facts were known to me. Since they became known, I have not thought it either my duty or my right to interfere with such contributions or solicitations, or the use which my subordinates voluntarily make of their own money."

Scandal embroiled the customhouse in 1873. After Phelps, Dodge, and Company used duplicate invoices that undervalued its imports and reduced its tax bill, customhouse detectives told William E. Dodge he had to pay $271,000 to avoid a court battle over the illegal act. Dodge did as instructed but then discovered the invoices totaled much less than the detectives had reported. In short, the bamboozler had been bamboozled, and he denounced the customhouse so vehemently that Congress investigated. Arthur professed ignorance, which was a highly unlikely story, and manipulated his political contacts to avoid testifying before a committee. The scandal, however, led to a law that ended the system whereby informers and customs officials shared in fines or penalties obtained when investigators uncovered fraud. Consequently, Arthur's income declined.

President Grant reappointed Arthur in 1875, and thanks to Conkling's pull, the Senate confirmed him without dissent. The *Northern Budget* of Troy, New York, said, "Gen. Arthur has brought so much suavity, good nature, skill, executive ability, and general fairness and uprightness into the discharge of official duties that he has fully disarmed . . . his political opponents."

When Republicans needed money in 1876, Arthur again obliged with funds from customhouse workers. That year he wrote checks to party leaders amounting to $72,000. Yet he prided himself in never engaging in graft to fill his own pockets and in keeping his word and remaining dignified. Many called him the "gentleman boss."

In 1877 Secretary of the Treasury John Sherman investigated several customhouses, including Arthur's. Sherman uncovered widespread illegal acts, ranging from bribes paid by passengers to get their baggage checked quickly to money paid by companies to avoid duties. When Arthur testified before Congress, he offered a contradictory story, calling the practices that had been revealed commonplace while also saying the charges lacked proof.

After a report criticized Arthur and other officials for allowing inefficiency and graft under their watch, and after Arthur's colleague Alonzo Cornell defied an order that no workers be forced to participate in partisan campaigns, President Rutherford B. Hayes, a fellow Republican but a reformer engaged in a power struggle with Conkling, removed the two men. Conkling exerted his influence, and Congress refused to support Hayes, at which point Arthur wrote his friend: "I cannot tell you how gratified I am at the splendid victory you have won—apart from & way beyond any personal considerations of my own. The whole town is excited by the event & the current of popular feeling is all with you."

Popular feeling actually moved opposite to Arthur's assessment, and on a second try in 1878 Hayes fired Arthur and Cornell and, with congressional approval, replaced them with reformers. The following year Arthur led the state Republican campaign as chairman of the New York City central committee and the state committee. With Alonzo Cornell chosen to run for governor, Conkling's Stalwart machine confronted the Democrats. Cornell won, though narrowly. Conkling then thought Arthur would make a good U.S. senator for the next open seat in 1881.

That opportunity never came. Instead, in 1880 the Republicans turned to Arthur as a running mate for their presidential candidate, James A. Garfield. A reformer from Mentor, Ohio, Garfield, along with his supporters, thought Arthur would keep the Stalwarts in line and attract New York's large popular and electoral vote. Conkling, embittered over Garfield having defeated his favorite, Ulysses S. Grant, at the convention, advised Arthur to reject the vice presidential nomination. "Well, sir, you should drop it as you would a red hot shoe from the forge," he told Arthur. A heated exchange then followed:

> "I sought you to consult—" Arthur said.
>
> "What is there to consult about?" Conkling said. "This trickster of Mentor will be defeated before the country."
>
> "There is something else to be said," Arthur replied.
>
> "What, sir, you think of accepting?" Conkling asked.
>
> "The office of the Vice-President is a greater honor than I ever dreamed of attaining. A barren nomination would be a great honor. In a calmer moment you will look at this differently," Arthur said.
>
> "If you wish my favor and respect, you will contemptuously decline it," Conkling retorted in a huff.
>
> "Senator Conkling," Arthur said, "I shall accept the nomination and I shall carry with me the majority of the delegation."

With that, Arthur defied Conkling, but the wounds healed quickly, and the senator subsequently campaigned for the ticket. Arthur provided crucial support in the campaign. He planned a Midwestern speaking tour for Conkling and Grant, and he collected money from state workers so effectively that it may have been key to the defeat of Democratic presidential candidate Winfield S. Hancock—who lost by fewer than 10,000 votes out of more than 9 million cast nationwide.

Although Arthur surprised many during the campaign when he expressed his support for civil service reform, he entered the vice presidency in 1881 committed to Conkling and the Stalwart agenda. He excited public disgust when, before his inauguration, he spoke at a dinner to honor an Indiana Republican. After a few drinks, he said the recent campaign had been won in that state "by close and perfect organization and a great deal of—" at which point the crowd chanted "Soap! Soap!" a euphemism among Republican workers for money. "I don't think we had better go into the minute secrets of the campaign because I see the reporters are present," he laughed. "If I should get to going about the secrets . . . there is no saying what I might say." Arthur's allusion to the Indiana vote having been bought produced enormous criticism.

He committed another mistake after his inauguration when he went to Albany, New York, and lobbied state legislators to reelect Thomas Platt, a Conkling Stalwart, to one of the U.S. Senate seats Platt and Conkling had recently quit. The legislators refused, and many newspapers condemned the vice president for diving so directly into a tawdry state political battle.

While Arthur was in Albany, on July 2, 1881, Charles Guiteau shot President Garfield. "It cannot be," the vice president said. "I hope, my God, I do hope it is a mistake." Arthur rushed back to Washington amid news Garfield might die within hours. As it turned out, Garfield clung to life for weeks. Arthur never wanted more than the vice presidency and followed every report about the president's health with an anxiety that caused him to lose weight and withdraw from his friends. When it looked like Garfield might live, Arthur said, "As the President gets better I get better, too."

Newspapers praised the way Arthur handled himself, how he refused to take over temporary powers while Garfield lay ill or to even speculate about a possible Arthur presidency. The *New York Times* said, "He has effaced himself after a fashion as manly as it was statesmanlike."

When Chester A. Arthur took the presidential oath the day after Garfield's death, Stalwarts salivated over their prospects. But they found the White House door to be more ajar than wide open. The new president wanted a dignified legacy for his presidency and decided the office required better behavior from him. He often refused requests from Conkling's cronies for jobs, and though he appointed Stalwarts, sometimes to prominent posts, he removed fewer of the existing bureaucrats than Conkling and others expected. One Conkling partisan said, "We thought he would throw in our direction enough of the patronage to make our work less onerous. On the contrary, he has done less for us than Garfield, or even Hayes."

Arthur distanced himself from the Stalwarts when he supported a continuing probe to uncover graft involving Star Routes in the post office. In the 1870s Congress had begun investigating the routes, established when the government signed contracts with private horse, stagecoach, and wagon companies to deliver mail to remote settlements. Several of the companies, linked to Republican leaders, charged outlandishly high rates for their services. In April 1881 Congress presented President Garfield with evidence of widespread fraud.

Arthur ordered the investigators to continue their work and declared no person would be exempt from the probe. He removed from office several federal employees implicated in wrongdoing. Several weeks later the attorney general prosecuted Stephen Dorsey, a former Republican senator from Arkansas (his term had ended in 1879), and Thomas J. Brady, second assistant postmaster general, both charged with conspiracy to defraud the government. The *New York Times* reported that the "Stephen W. Dorsey gang" had pocketed over $400,000. Defense lawyers prolonged the trial in an attempt to exhaust and confuse the jury, which heard from 150 witnesses.

Arthur suffered embarrassment when three letters released to newspapers showed his close relationship with Dorsey and Conkling. According to Thomas C. Reeves in *Gentleman Boss: The Life of Chester Alan Arthur,* nothing in the trial likely surprised the president—he had worked closely with Dorsey and Brady in the past and in 1880 had even collected $40,000 from Dorsey for the Republican Party.

The trial, concluded in September 1882, resulted in guilty verdicts for two minor figures charged along with Dorsey and Brady but a hung jury for the prominent defendants. A second trial followed, lasting from December 1882 until June 1883 and producing 4,481 pages of testimony. The verdict of not guilty stunned Americans. Millions of dollars had been stolen from the national government, with hardly anyone convicted. Evidence indicated the defense had tampered with the jury, but the government failed to prove it. Arthur called the inquiry and trial beneficial for having reformed the post office, but the embarrassing letters had made him appear tawdry. The Democrats also pointed out that the scandals had happened under Republican rule.

While the Star Route trials were underway, Arthur damaged his presidency in March 1882 when he nominated Roscoe Conkling to serve on the Supreme Court. Arthur acted out of friendship for Conkling; he wanted to see his mentor's career capped with a veneer of dignity. The Senate easily confirmed Conkling, but newspapers condemned the president. The Youngstown *News Register* said, "Better for Conkling that he pass at least a decent probation in the seclusion of private life, and better for Arthur not to force under the nostrils of the American people an unsavory smelling object." Conkling turned down the judgeship, however, in order to stay with his lucrative law practice.

When it came to reforms, President Arthur seemed to take two steps forward and one step back—admittedly an advance where earlier in his career there had been none, but one so frustrating as to anger those who wanted a much cleaner government. He stunned many observers when he took a step forward and announced his support for the Pendleton Act, then being considered by Congress to reform the civil service. Senator George Hunt Pendleton, an Ohio Democrat known more for his groomed beard, meticulous clothes, and polite manners than for any expertise in government, sponsored the act. Arthur said he opposed one part of the proposal that provided for civil service exams but would accept them if Congress wanted them.

At first Congress wanted nothing, and the Pendleton Act stalled as the politicians refused to relinquish their grip on patronage. But the 1882 elections changed the picture when reform Democrats badly beat the Republicans. Arthur thereupon reversed himself and said he wanted civil service exams, and Congress finally passed Pendleton's bill, which the president signed in January 1883. The act established a five-member civil service commission to be appointed by the president and gave it the power to make rules and begin competitive exams.

The Pendleton Act applied only to a limited list of jobs in Washington and only to major customhouses and post offices elsewhere—about one-tenth of the total number of federal employees—but Stalwarts still hated it. Looking back on the national reform movement, George W. Plunkitt, a political boss at New York's Tammany Hall, commented, "You hear of this thing or that thing goin' wrong in the nation, the State or the city. Look down beneath the surface and you can trace everything wrong to civil service. . . . This great and glorious country was built up by political parties; . . . parties can't hold together if their workers don't get the offices when they win; . . . if the parties go to pieces, the government they built up must go to pieces, too; . . . then there'll be h—to pay."

Reformers hailed the Pendleton Act and applauded President Arthur when he took another step forward and appointed one of their own as chair of the civil service commission. Yet reformers howled in protest when he took a step back and nominated a Grant crony to be the commission's chief examiner. Eventually they forced Arthur to withdraw the name. Despite the president's mixed record, historians believe he handled himself respectably in administering the Pendleton Act.

Historians continue to debate the president's commitment to African Americans. Some say he did little for the race. For example, when the Supreme Court ruled the 1875 Civil Rights Act unconstitutional and Republicans in Congress introduced five bills to save most of it, Arthur supported none of them, causing them to die.

Other historians emphasize that Arthur supported southern politicians who defended black suffrage and that in his call for federal aid to schools he stressed the need to fight back illiteracy. Further, he appointed several African Americans to significant government posts and risked his political future by taking an unpopular stand in criticizing the Supreme Court for negating the civil rights act. He went so far as to declare his desire for a new bill and said he would approve anything that strengthened "the guaranties which the Constitution affords for the equal enjoyment by all the citizens of the United States by every right, privilege, and immunity of citizenship. . . ." Nearly every black newspaper supported Arthur and looked forward to his reelection.

The president avoided a foreign crisis and stood against nativism when he vetoed a bill that prohibited Chinese laborers from entering the United States for 20 years and that denied citizenship to resident Chinese. He noted that the bill violated an 1880 treaty with China, and he called its section on citizenship undemocratic. Chinese immigrants, he reminded Americans, had contributed mightily to building the transcontinental railroad and developing the West. Yet he soon gave in to nativistic pressure and signed a revised bill that substituted 10 years for the 20-year ban.

Arthur tried hard to lower tariffs and open new markets overseas. His tariff commission proposed a downward adjustment in rates, but Congress opposed it. Likewise, his reciprocal trade treaties with other nations, which would have meant more reasonable tariffs, won little support.

Despite an honest presidency with achievements that surpassed his most recent predecessors, Arthur found little enthusiasm for his reelection in 1884. His erratic stand on reform and his appointment of Stalwarts, albeit seldom Conkling ones, dampened any support from reformers. At the same time, his backing of the Star Route probe and the Pendleton Act caused the Stalwarts to reject him. Most Americans considered his presidency a mere interregnum between Garfield and the next leader. In short, neither the Republican Party nor the country as a whole rallied around him.

For his part, Arthur did not want another term. One observer said about him: "He is a sensitive, almost a timid man, I mean with reference to his responsibilities. He is also a moody man." His moodiness passed into lethargy, and for good reason: Arthur had been stricken with a serious illness, Bright's disease. Bright's infects the kidneys; often fatal, it makes a person nauseous, depressed, and listless. Since the symptoms usually appear well after the infection, Arthur likely contracted it before he entered the White House. On a visit to New York in 1883, he looked ill. "He has grown thin and feeble looking," said an observer. "His cheeks are emaciated, and he has aged in appearance."

Some newspapers reported the illness, but Arthur never commented on it directly. Quite likely Bright's contributed to his distaste for the presidency and his desire to return home. Instead of Arthur, the Republican Party nominated Benjamin Harrison for the presidency. Arthur died in New York City on November 18, 1886, a mere 20 months after leaving the White House.

No one can mistake Chester A. Arthur for a bold president. Despite differences with Conkling over appointments, he never renounced him or completely broke with the Stalwarts. But he prosecuted the Star Route case, administered the Pendleton Act reasonably well, respected African-American rights, and showed a firm grasp of foreign policy. His record surprised many who thought he would be nothing more than an unredeemed Stalwart, and it makes the cry "Chet Arthur President . . . Good God," more exaggerated than justified.

Chronology

1829 Born October 5

1844 Enters Lyceum School in Schenectady, New York

1845 Enters Union College as a sophomore

1848 Graduates from Union College

1851 Teaches school in Vermont

1852 Becomes school principal in Cohoes, New York

1853 Studies law and is admitted to the bar

1854 Becomes partner in law firm

1855 Represents Elizabeth Jennings in suit over racial segregation

1859 Marries Ellen Lewis Herndon

1861 Appointed assistant quartermaster general of New York State

1862 Commissioned quartermaster general of New York State

1871 Named collector of customhouse for the Port of New York

1875 Reappointed collector of customs

1878 Removed as collector

1880 Elected vice president

1881 Becomes president

Supports investigation of Star Route fraud

1883 Signs Pendleton Act

1885 Retires to New York City

1886 Dies November 18

Further Reading

Doenecke, Justus D. *The Presidencies of James A. Garfield and Chester A. Arthur.* Lawrence: University Press of Kansas, 1981.

Howe, George Frederick. *Chester A. Arthur: A Quarter-Century of Machine Politics.* New York: Frederick Ungar, 1935.

Karabell, Zachary. *Chester Alan Arthur.* New York: Times Books, 2004.

Reeves, Thomas C. *Gentleman Boss: The Life of Chester Alan Arthur.* Newtown, Conn.: American Political Bibliography Press, 1991.

Grover Cleveland (1837–1908)

Twenty-second President, 1885–1889

Twenty-fourth President, 1893–1897

Grover Cleveland
(Library of Congress)

"Vital to our supremacy as a nation and to the beneficent purposes of our Government [is] a sound and stable currency. Its exposure to degradation should at once arouse to activity the most enlightened statesmanship, and the danger of depreciation in the purchasing power of the wages paid to toil should furnish the strongest incentive to prompt and conservative precaution."

—Inaugural words, second presidency, March 4, 1893

Nothing less calamitous than a clash between capital and labor revealed a predicament in Grover Cleveland's two presidencies. He desired limited government but reacted to the Pullman Strike of 1884, when railroad workers walked off their jobs, by sending troops into Illinois, where the governor did not want them. Down went several railroad cars when a mob overturned them; in came Cleveland's soldiers, an army employed to enforce court orders and get the trains running again; and up went the power in the White House. Whatever his philosophy about limited government, Cleveland believed in a vibrant presidency and insisted labor unrest must be controlled and the corporate economy protected.

—∾—

Stephen Grover Cleveland was born on March 18, 1837, in Caldwell, New Jersey, the fifth of nine children in the family of Richard Cleveland, a Presbyterian preacher, and his wife, Ann Neal Cleveland. In 1841 Richard moved his family to Fayetteville, New York, near Syracuse. They moved again in 1850, this time to Clinton, New York, where he worked as director of the American Home Missionary Society.

By that time Grover wanted to attend Hamilton College, but his father was struggling to make ends meet and asked the youngster to take a job at a general store in Fayetteville. Grover agreed and worked for $50 a year. He lived over the store in a stark room, his one piece of furniture a bed. In 1853 Richard Cleveland accepted a pastorate in Holland Patent, New York, but he soon died, leaving his family nearly penniless. Grover then worked as an assistant teacher at the New York Institution for the Blind, where his brother taught. In 1854 he returned to Holland Patent.

Unable to find a job, Grover borrowed $25 and headed for the city of Cleveland, Ohio, where he intended to start over. On his way he stopped to see his uncle, Lewis F. Allen, in Buffalo, New York. Allen, a wealthy businessman, thought Grover bright and liked the young man's willingness to work hard. In 1855 he arranged for his nephew to study law at Rogers, Bowen, and Rogers, a local firm.

Grover Cleveland was admitted to the bar in 1859 and continued to work at the law firm while engaging in minor political activities. He labored long hours and liked his books as well as socializing in saloons, where he could smoke and drink and drop his courtroom demeanor for hearty talk. Although he enjoyed hunting and fishing with his friends, Cleveland traveled little and preferred staying in Buffalo. He liked male companionship and independence, and he never planned to marry, let alone assume the responsibility of being president of the entire country.

Cleveland identified with the Democratic Party despite Buffalo's loyalty to the Republicans and his uncle's work for them. He may have thought the North too overbearing in the sectional crisis with the South and the Republicans too antagonistic toward slavery, but whatever the case, he opposed the election of Abraham Lincoln as president. His politics upset his uncle, who hated the Fugitive Slave Law, engaged in antislavery work, and thought the Democratic Party represented the "slaveocracy."

When war came Grover Cleveland supported the Union cause, though not as a soldier. After his two brothers enlisted in the army, he decided to take over the support of his mother and sister. Thus, rather than fight he paid a substitute to take his place, at that time a legal and common practice.

Cleveland first sought elective office at the citywide level in 1865, when he ran for district attorney. He lost, however, and returned to practicing law. Three years later he served as a delegate to the state Democratic convention and formed two law partnerships, first with Isaac K. Vanderpoel and then with A. P. Laning and Oscar Folsom. In 1870 he ran for sheriff of Erie County and won, but two years later he refused to seek another term. For nearly a decade thereafter, Cleveland participated little in politics but tended to his legal business instead. By 1881 he had accumulated considerable money and earned renown for his dependable work.

That same year the Democrats nominated him to run for mayor of Buffalo. The city had suffered from a corrupt administration, and the Democratic Party wanted a new face, someone untainted by scandal. Cleveland filled the bill; he used as his campaign slogan, "A public office is a public trust."

Cleveland won the mayoralty and went to work battling graft. He exposed a fraudulent street-cleaning contract and placed a new sewage system under professional managers, rather than cronies. He frequently used his veto power—Buffalonians called him the "veto mayor"—to reject wasteful spending proposed by the city council.

With his reputation for honesty and commitment, Grover Cleveland earned a name for himself well beyond Buffalo, and in 1882 the Democrats nominated him for governor. In New York City, the political machine at Tammany Hall, where spoilsmen ruled, supported him only reluctantly. Still, he defeated his Republican opponent. At his inauguration on January 1, 1883, Cleveland promised integrity and economy and said he would apply business principles to government.

Unwilling to delegate duties, Governor Cleveland worked 14-hour days. He sometimes acted independently of party and public wishes, as when he vetoed the popular "five-cent fare bill" intended to lower the charge on elevated railroads in New York City from ten to five cents. Even though he despised the owner of the railroads, the unscrupulous Jay Gould, he said the bill violated contract rights protected by the Constitution. Surprisingly, the public accepted his veto with little protest after concluding he had reached his decision honestly.

His preference for independence and integrity revealed itself again when he refused to appoint Tammany Hall candidates to state offices. In this he also considered politics when he calculated that his stand would play well with voters disgusted by Tammany's corrupt practices.

Cleveland's rapid rise—just three years removed from mayor of Buffalo—continued in 1884 when he won the Democratic nomination for president on the second ballot. His victory resulted largely from the work of Daniel Manning, who headed a political machine in Albany and used his influence to overcome Tammany Hall's resistance. Little that was reformist touched Manning; his wheeling and dealing took Cleveland to the top, aided by the understanding among the convention delegates that to win the presidency Democrats needed to carry New York. For that reason Cleveland would make a strong candidate. According to one story, Cleveland was putting in another long day at the governor's office in Albany when he heard the sound of cannon. An aide who was with him observed, "That means you are the nominee," to which Cleveland replied, "Do you think so? Well, anyway, we have to finish up this work."

Cleveland's candidacy came amid scandal in the national government and turmoil in the Republican Party. Although outgoing president Chester A. Arthur and his predecessors, James Garfield and Rutherford B. Hayes, had brought some reform to politics, continuing stories of graft sullied the Republicans. Their standing suffered again when they chose James G. Blaine, a congressman from Maine, to run for president. Blaine had stirred mistrust when, as speaker of the House, he ruled favorably on legislation affecting a railroad company and later received a handsome profit by selling railroad bonds. When the Republicans nominated Blaine, reformers within the party, called Mugwumps, bolted. This small group included prominent leaders such as Charles W. Eliot, president of Harvard University, and Edwin L. Godkin, editor of the *Nation*.

Many Americans disliked the Mugwumps for their intellectual snobbery and self-righteousness. For their part, the Mugwumps disliked many Americans for their crass materialism and repulsive politics. The Mugwumps hated political machines and the plying of the masses with patronage. They wanted honest leadership and efficient government under an educated elite.

As the campaign got underway, Cleveland once again claimed, "A public office is a public trust." His honesty stood in sharp contrast to Blaine, and his obscurity allowed Democrats to unite a party still deeply divided between Northerners and Southerners.

But a dirty campaign unfolded. The Democrats attacked Blaine for political sleaze, and letters written by James Mulligan added to their assault. A bookkeeper at the railroad that had benefited from Blaine's rulings in the House, Mulligan had tried to blackmail the congressman over the previous bond deal. When his letters appeared in the press, they raised more doubts about Blaine's integrity.

Additional damage came with another letter, written months earlier by Blaine to a Boston broker, Warren Fisher, with advice to copy it and present it as Fisher's own to clear the congressman of any wrongdoing in selling the railroad bonds. On the back, in Blaine's handwriting, appeared the words "Burn this letter." One political cartoonist left a lasting picture in the public's mind when he presented Blaine as the "tattooed man" with etchings on his body such as "Bribery" and "Mulligan Letters."

The Republicans stewed and then launched a vicious attack. They uncovered a 10-year-old story about Cleveland's relationship with Maria Halpin. Maria, who had once lived near Cleveland's apartment, claimed she had given birth to his child. Although she lacked irrefutable evidence, Cleveland agreed the child should be named Oscar Folsom Cleveland, and he agreed to support him. Soon after, Maria suffered a mental breakdown, and he arranged for the child to be adopted. She later brought suit for the boy's return but lost. Cleveland never hid his problems with Maria, and the story was well known to Buffalonians.

Now the entire nation knew. Republicans called Cleveland "immoral" and said he had acted cruelly by not raising the boy himself. Smearing him, they claimed he had sent Maria to an insane asylum to hide her and the entire relationship. One reverend wrote "A Terrible Tale," claiming that Cleveland kept a harem and preyed on women throughout the city of Buffalo. To vote for Cleveland, insisted the reverend, would be to vote for the brothel over the family.

When news of the scandal first broke, Cleveland sent a telegram to his supporters, instructing them to "tell the truth." Its appearance in newspapers boosted his standing and reinforced his image as a forthright leader. Still, Republicans chanted:

Ma! Ma! Where's my pa?
Gone to the White House.
Ha! Ha! Ha!

Just days before the vote, Democrats held a huge rally in New York City in which marchers chanted "Blaine, Blaine, James G. Blaine, the Monumental Liar from the State of Maine," and "Burn this letter, burn this letter," while holding lighted matches aloft.

Despite the attacks on Blaine and the Mugwump portrayal of the Democratic nominee as "Grover the Good," the contest was extremely close. Cleveland finished ahead of Blaine by about 30,000 votes nationwide and by fewer than 1,200 in New York. If the public wanted reform, it did so by the narrowest of margins. Yet the Democrats still bore the odious label of the "party of secession," and though the Civil War no longer burned as a leading issue, Cleveland had to overcome that stigma. With that challenge he became the first Democratic president in 24 years.

He was also the heaviest man yet to enter the White House, for his beer drinking and perpetual eating had ballooned his portly body to about 240 pounds, causing his topcoat buttons to bear an unreasonable strain—a big man soon to face some big problems. By the 1880s industry and business had dwarfed the White House in prestige and influence. Andrew Carnegie built the world's largest steel mill; John D. Rockefeller organized Standard Oil into the nation's first great trust; and railroads stretched from coast to coast, with more miles of track than in all of Europe. In 1860, 4.3 million Americans worked in industry; by 1900 that number would rise to 20 million. Exploitive conditions led to unrest and the formation of workers' unions, such as the American Federation of Labor in 1886. Strikes, sometimes violent, added to the turmoil that accompanied change.

America boasted several cities of more than 500,000 people and three—New York, Chicago, and Philadelphia—with more than a million each. Their growth came mostly from rural folk moving to find jobs in new industries and from a surge in foreign immigrants who came from Poland, Russia, Italy, and other countries in eastern and southern Europe. Approximately 6 million foreigners entered the United States between 1877 and 1890.

Grover Cleveland distrusted both unions and big businesses and found the corrupt practices among railroads distasteful, but he wanted Washington to stay out of the economy as much as possible. As labor disputes intensified, however, in 1886 he proposed to Congress that it establish a voluntary arbitration board. In his request he revealed his spread-the-blame philosophy: "The discontent of the employed is due in a large degree to the grasping and needless exactions of employers and the alleged [government] discrimination in favor of capital," he said, before adding, "the laboring men are not always careful to avoid causeless and unjustifiable disturbance." Congress passed his proposal, though in a limited form, applying it only to railroad disputes and requiring that the arbitration boards be staffed by railroad employees and managers, rather than by the government officers the president wanted.

Cleveland opposed demands by labor groups that Congress investigate and regulate business, saying a stronger national government might later use its power for reform to grant favors to corporations. Yet after the Supreme Court ruled in 1886 that a state had no authority to regulate railroad traffic that went beyond its borders, the president joined those who pushed for legislation to remedy the problem. Congress already had a bill before it, and when in 1887 the Interstate Commerce Act reached Cleveland's desk, he signed it. The act required railroad rates be reasonable and just, and it established the Interstate Commerce Commission (ICC), the nation's first regulatory commission. Before court rulings weakened the ICC, it had the power to investigate railroad management, and many Americans considered the act a step forward in industrial reform.

Another economic issue generated debate: whether the national government should mint more silver coins. Farmers in particular tended to favor silver over gold since, being of lesser value, silver stimulated inflation and raised the price of foodstuffs. Some labor groups sided with the farmers, thinking inflation would boost wages, and silver mining companies obviously desired more silver coins. The business community, however, was divided on the issue.

For his part, President Cleveland believed cheap silver dollars would drive away gold, unreasonably increase prices, and ruin the nation's credit. He wanted Congress to repeal the Bland-Allison Act, which required the treasury to buy between $2 million and $4 million worth of silver each month. Even though the government made only the minimum purchase, Cleveland still thought the act was harmful. Congress rejected his request, but it also rejected demands for the unlimited coinage of silver.

As the treasury accumulated a surplus, President Cleveland addressed the divisive tariff issue when he devoted his entire annual message to it in December 1887. He argued that high tariffs, favored by the Republicans, hurt consumers by raising prices on domestic goods. He claimed the tariff amounted to unacceptable government favoritism toward business. Cleveland said, "The simple and plain duty which we owe the people is to reduce the taxation to the necessary expenses of an economical operation of the government. . . ." With the Democrats divided on the issue and the Republicans opposed to lowering rates, Congress moved slowly.

Disdainful of fraud, Cleveland acted to eliminate it in the West, where large companies violated land laws by hiring or enticing cowboys and lumberjacks to file homesteads for them.

Inaccurate surveys also threatened the public domain, as did cattlemen who illegally fenced in public land. At the same time, other exploiters out West made crooked deals with Indian tribes to use reservation land. Cleveland reduced homestead abuses, ordered the fences pulled down, and ended the bribing of Indian leaders.

The president took his role as protector of the Indians seriously. He considered them childlike and vulnerable to greedy predators. In 1885 he revoked an order issued by President Chester A. Arthur to open two reservations in South Dakota to white settlement, and the following year he vetoed a bill granting railroads a right-of-way through Indian lands in northern Montana.

Cleveland believed Indians should be assimilated into white society and backed the Dawes Act, which passed Congress in 1887. Under this act, the president could allot reservation land to individual Indians, with remaining land to be bought by the federal government and made a part of the public domain. The act intended to end tribes as legal entities and make Indians individual landholders, just like non-Indians. Cleveland and Congress considered the Dawes Act a reform measure, but over time it subverted Native American culture and disrupted Indian life.

Amid politics, a festive atmosphere prevailed at the White House on June 2, 1886, when the 49-year-old bachelor president married 21-year-old Frances Folsom. Cleveland had been her guardian after her father died, and she had recently graduated from Wells College near Ithaca, New York. The wedding took place in the Blue Room, where bright flowers gathered from the conservatory bedecked the chandelier, and John Philip Sousa directed the Marine Corps band. Most Americans admired the new first lady for her beauty, intelligence, and wit, and her cheerfulness counterbalanced her husband's irascible nature. The couple had five children, including the first baby born in the White House.

As president, Cleveland brought renewed vigor to the office. His fight against silver and for tariff reform, his changes in land practices, and his Indian policy revealed his activism, as did his use of the veto—304 times, more than all previous presidents combined. Foremost in reviving the presidency, early in his term he wrested more authority over appointments from Congress when he fought against the Tenure of Office Act. Passed under Andrew Johnson (and modified under Ulysses S. Grant), this act forbade the president from removing certain officials without Senate approval. Republicans, anxious to expose what they called Cleveland's hypocrisy in portraying himself as a civil service reformer but making many appointments based on party loyalty, refused to confirm his nominees unless he gave the Senate all documents relating to why he had removed previous officeholders. Cleveland's response was that those papers were confidential, and he said the president must determine appointments in the executive branch. In a showdown over his removal of a U.S. attorney in southern Alabama, Cleveland insisted that the Senate's demand interfered with his duty to see that the "laws be faithfully executed." After the press and public largely supported him, the Senate backed down, and in March 1887 it repealed the Tenure of Office Act.

For a man allied with a political party that many Northerners still held suspect, even the slightest controversy could cost the votes needed for another term. Thus, Cleveland's fight against the tariff hurt more than helped him. As the 1888 presidential contest approached, the House finally passed a bill to lower the tariff slightly, but it stalled in the Senate. When the Republican National Convention met, it made clear its support for high tariffs, saying they protected jobs by discouraging Americans from buying foreign goods and encouraging them to buy goods made in their country. The Republicans declared: "We are uncompromisingly in favor of the American system of protection. We protest against its destruction, as proposed by the President and his party. They serve the interests of Europe; we will support the interests of America."

The Republican delegates chose Benjamin Harrison, a senator from Indiana, as their nominee. The "tariff campaign," as the contest between the two candidates was called, had an unusual ending. Cleveland defeated Harrison by a margin of about 100,000 popular votes, but Harrison defeated Cleveland in the electoral count, 233 to 168, and as a result won the presidency. As the Clevelands prepared to leave the White House, Frances told the staff to take care of the furniture—she and Grover would be back, she said.

Cleveland then moved to New York City and joined Bangs, Stetson, Tracy, and McVeagh, a law firm that primarily handled cases for big business. He largely avoided politics, but in 1891 he wrote his "silver letter," in which he criticized silver coinage. The following year he again ran for president. The contest repeated the one in 1888 by emphasizing the tariff—and by again facing off Cleveland against Benjamin Harrison.

Cleveland criticized the McKinley Tariff, which Congress passed under Harrison to boost rates. By and large, though, the campaign excited few people. Historian Eugene H. Roseboom claims, "Honest bearded Benjamin Harrison confronting honest mustached Grover Cleveland in a tariff debate was a repeat performance that did not inspire parades with torches or the chanting of campaign ditties." The race, he says, "was the dullest in many years."

This time Cleveland won easily, by a margin of nearly 400,000 popular votes and by 277 to 145 electoral votes. He became the only president ever elected to nonconsecutive terms. For the New Yorker, though, the second time around proved bittersweet: Just weeks after his inauguration, the industrial economy collapsed in a depression second in its severity only to the one that came in 1929. Overproduction, problems in agriculture, and the treasury's declining gold reserve all led to the collapse.

To revive the economy, Cleveland decided he would get Congress to repeal the Sherman Silver Purchase Act. As a successor to the Bland-Allison Act, it required greater purchases of silver by the government. But as he readied for battle, doctors told him they had discovered cancer in his left jaw. Fearing that news of his illness would cause a financial panic, he kept his disease secret. In the summer of 1893 he boarded a yacht, the *Oneida,* purportedly to begin a vacation. Instead, a team of five doctors and dentists sailed with him. They strapped him to a chair against the mainmast, anaesthetized him with ether and nitrous oxide, and operated for 41 minutes. Later they fitted him with an artificial jaw.

To hide his impaired speech, Cleveland saw no one except a few advisers until late August, by which time he had largely recovered. He then explained away his remaining discomfort by saying a dentist had removed some of his teeth. Except for rumors, Cleveland's ordeal remained secret until it was revealed in 1917.

In fall 1893 the monetary fight hit full stride. Because most Republicans favored gold, the president received their support, but the issue divided Democrats, and repeal of the Sherman Silver Purchase Act eluded Cleveland until he threatened to suspend all patronage appointments. At that point, in October, the Senate ended the act by a vote of 48-37.

Yet the gold reserve continued to shrink, forcing Cleveland to raise money by selling bonds. In a widely criticized move, he sold a large number at a high interest rate to the Morgan-Belmont syndicate, for whom the bonds later made a $7 million profit. Many thought this reliance on wealthy financiers was demeaning to the government, especially given questions about J. P. Morgan's character.

Cleveland's close relationship with the corporate world appeared evident during two showdowns with workers in 1894. That spring Jacob Coxey led an "industrial army" of unemployed from Massillon, Ohio, to Washington. When the marchers reached their destination, Cleveland ordered the national guard to end the protest. At the Capitol, where spectators greatly outnumbered Coxey's bedraggled followers, the authorities arrested him for trespassing after he tried to read a petition demanding the government issue unlimited amounts of paper money. His protest ended, he spent 20 days in jail. Critics subsequently called Cleveland insensitive to the unemployed and a president willing to heed businessmen while eager to silence the poor.

Coxey's Army was only a gnat on an elephant compared to a strike at George Pullman's company in Chicago, where workers built railroad cars. As the depression worsened, Pullman tried to protect his profits by cutting wages 25 percent while maintaining the rents he charged for company housing. This left the workers with less than a dollar a day for food and clothing.

After the Pullman workers struck, Eugene V. Debs's American Railway Union supported them by boycotting all railroads using Pullman cars. By early July, traffic in and out of Chicago, America's railroad hub, had declined 90 percent. With the *Chicago Tribune* labeling Debs an anarchist, Attorney General Richard Olney obtained a court injunction forbidding interference with rail traffic. Before entering the president's cabinet, Olney had worked as a lawyer for several railroad companies, and soon after the strike began he allied himself with the General Managers Association, a group of leaders from 24 railroads. The association even paid the salaries for hundreds of U.S. special marshals who acted as strikebreakers.

When a mob rioted near Chicago and overturned railroad cars and stabbed a deputy, Olney persuaded the U.S. attorney in the district to request federal troops to enforce the court injunction. Grover Cleveland received the request and deployed the army, despite protests from Governor John Altgeld that he not do so. With this action Cleveland became the first president to send troops into a state without a governor's request and support. He so acted despite his states' rights ideology and despite his fear the federal government would grow too powerful. By deploying the troops, he assumed police powers previously left to state and local governments. In Cleveland's struggle between ideology and his desire to exert authority, authority won.

With troops on the scene, violence spread. Rioters burned several buildings at the Chicago World's Fair, and a battle between soldiers and a mob sympathetic to the railroad strikers resulted in seven deaths. In July the government indicted Debs and 70 union members for violating the court injunction. This crushed the union, and with the protection from Cleveland's troops, the railroads began running again.

Although Cleveland spent more time on domestic than foreign policy, pressure from expansionists caused him to act in Samoa during his first presidency and in Hawaii during his second. Because an earlier treaty gave the United States, Britain, and Germany trading rights in Samoa, he sent warships to the Pacific when the Germans tried to take over the islands, while telling them the dispute should be negotiated. Germany eventually agreed, and after Cleveland left office, the three countries established a Samoan protectorate.

From Benjamin Harrison, Grover Cleveland inherited a problem involving Hawaii. Back in 1893, American planters, with the help of the U.S. minister to the islands, overthrew the Hawaiian monarchy and declared a republic. They then asked Harrison to annex Hawaii as a territory within the United States. He agreed and sent a treaty to the Senate. Cleveland, however, recalled the treaty. He rightly suspected the new government had been forced on the Hawaiian people, and he believed they opposed annexation. He said, "If a feeble but friendly state is in danger of being robbed of its independence and its sovereignty by a misuse of the name and power of the United States, [we] cannot fail to vindicate its honor and its sense of justice by an earnest effort to make all possible reparation."

When expansionists pushed harder to acquire Hawaii, he turned the problem over to Congress, and when it passed a resolution saying the United States should recognize the government established by the planters,

Cleveland agreed. From then on he called the Hawaiian president, Sanford Dole, his "Great and Good Friend."

In 1895 President Cleveland invoked the Monroe Doctrine against Britain when that country threatened to use force in a border dispute between British Guiana and Venezuela. His sharp criticism nearly pulled the United States into a war. After tempers cooled, relations with Britain improved so markedly that the foundation was laid for the close ties that would prevail between the two powers in the 20th century.

Cleveland's handling of the Pullman Strike earned him the enmity of many workers and those sympathetic to labor, and the devastating depression hurt his popularity. In the 1894 midterm elections, the Democrats lost 113 seats in Congress. Cleveland decided not to seek another term as president in 1896, and most Americans welcomed his departure from the White House.

In 1897 Cleveland settled in Princeton, New Jersey. He involved himself in the development of Princeton University and in 1901 became a trustee. Beginning in 1905, he was active in the insurance industry, helping to reorganize one company and lobby for another. After suffering from heart and kidney ailments, he died on June 24, 1908.

When Grover Cleveland left the White House, the Democratic Party was in shambles, deeply divided over his tariff and monetary policies and shaken by his attitude that when it came to disputes he should command rather than conciliate. So intense had differences become that when the Democrats nominated the silver advocate and silver-tongued orator William Jennings Bryan for president in 1896, Cleveland refused to support him. Yet for all his failings, Grover Cleveland had dominated the national political scene for a decade and regained some of the power lost by the presidency in the years immediately after the Civil War.

CHRONOLOGY

1837 Born March 18

1853 Teaches at New York Institution for the Blind

1859 Admitted to the bar

1863 Appointed assistant district attorney of Erie County, New York

1865 Loses election for district attorney

1870 Elected sheriff of Erie County

1881 Elected mayor of Buffalo

1882 Elected governor of New York

1884 Elected president

1886 Advocates reduced tariff

Proposes labor-management arbitration board

Marries Frances Folsom

1887 Obtains repeal of Tenure of Office Act

Signs Interstate Commerce Act

Supports the Dawes Act

1888 Loses bid for reelection

1891 Writes "silver letter"

1892 Elected president

1893 Pushes for repeal of Sherman Silver Purchase Act

Hides operation for cancer

Defeats treaty for Hawaiian annexation

1894 Disperses Coxey's Army

Sends troops into Pullman strike

1895 Invokes Monroe Doctrine in border dispute between British Guiana and Venezuela

Makes deal with J. P. Morgan to resolve treasury crisis

1897 Retires to Princeton, New Jersey

1901 Becomes Princeton University trustee

1905 Helps reorganize insurance company

1908 Dies June 24

Further Reading

Graff, Henry F. *Grover Cleveland*. New York: Times Books, 2002.

Jeffers, H. Paul. *An Honest President: The Life and Presidencies of Grover Cleveland*. New York: Morrow 2000.

McElroy, Robert. *Grover Cleveland: The Man and the Statesman*, 2 vols. New York: Harper & Bros., 1923.

Merrill, Horace Samuel. *Bourbon Leader: Grover Cleveland and the Democratic Party*. Boston: Little, Brown, 1957.

Nevins, Allan. *Grover Cleveland: A Study in Courage*. New York: Dodd, Mead, 1933.

Tugwell, Rexford G. *Grover Cleveland*. New York: Macmillan, 1968.

Welch, Richard E., Jr. *The Presidencies of Grover Cleveland*. Lawrence: University Press of Kansas, 1988.

BENJAMIN HARRISON (1833–1901)

Twenty-third President, 1889–1893

BENJAMIN HARRISON
(National Archives)

"I look hopefully to the continuance of our protective system and to the consequent development of manufacturing and mining enterprises in the States hitherto wholly given to agriculture as a potent influence in the perfect unification of our people."

—Inaugural words, March 4, 1889

The governor of Ohio had come to the White House seeking a favor, but as he stood in front of Benjamin Harrison, the president's gaze seemed distracted—or maybe not, since Harrison could be looking at a person but appear to be looking somewhere else. The president pointed to a stack of reports on his desk. "I've got all these papers to look after," he said in a soft but firm and impatient voice, "and I'm going fishing at two o'clock." A chill filled the room. Yet the governor felt nothing more than almost everyone else did when they met Harrison. "For God's sake, be human," a friend once told the president. "I tried it, but I failed," he responded. "I'll never try it again."

Sandwiched between the two dominating features of his personality, distant and frigid, and the two presidencies of Grover Cleveland, by most accounts Harrison forged a forgettable term in office, one whose end even his fellow Republicans welcomed. Still, he recorded at least two notable deeds when he protected the environment and built a stronger navy.

Benjamin Harrison was born on August 20, 1833, on his grandfather's estate at North Bend, Ohio, near Cincinnati. He came from a long line of political leaders. His great-grandfather, also named Benjamin Harrison, had signed the Declaration of Independence; his grandfather, William Henry Harrison, had served as president, though for only one month before he died; and his father, John Scott Harrison, had been elected to Congress. John and his wife, Elizabeth Irwin Harrison, raised Benjamin on their farm, called The Point, at the confluence of the Miami and Ohio rivers. There the youngster hunted, fished, and helped raise corn and wheat. From his front porch he could see the rough-hewn flatboats, arks, and skiffs floating down the Ohio laden with men, women, animals, and household goods, all destined to build the American West.

Benjamin obtained an education from private tutors and from the local country school before enrolling at Farmers' College in Cincinnati in 1847. He later transferred to Miami University, where he met and fell in love with Caroline Scott. As graduation neared in 1852, Benjamin remained uncertain about his future work. He felt pulled toward the ministry by his parents' religiosity, his attendance at revivals, and his recent acceptance of the Presbyterian faith.

Yet throughout his life he carefully weighed alternatives. He would allow no one to pressure him and gave as much thought to the law as he did the church. While considering his options, he observed: "That all rogues are lawyers may in some sense be true, but that all lawyers are rogues, no syllogistic reasoning can prove. Where is the justice in denouncing the whole profession on account of the unworthy conduct of some of its members?" That said, he decided to follow the legal route and in 1852 moved to Cincinnati to study with a law firm. The following year he married Caroline, and in 1854 they left Ohio and settled in Indianapolis. For all of his legal training, he remained devoutly religious and joined the city's First Presbyterian Church, where he served first as deacon and then nearly 40 years as an elder.

Reserved and studious, Harrison worked hard to advance his career. In 1855 William Wallace, a young lawyer, approached him about forming a partnership, and he agreed. Within months their firm's business surpassed all others in Indianapolis. As Harrison's contacts expanded, he ran for Indianapolis city attorney as a Republican in 1857 and won. Three years later he was elected state supreme court reporter.

Then the Civil War interceded. In July 1862 Governor Oliver P. Morton asked Harrison to recruit men for the 70th Indiana Volunteers. He agreed, and as a colonel he led his regiment on a mission to guard the Louisville and Nashville Railroad in Kentucky. Realizing that his men had little discipline and even less military knowledge, he imposed stern training. His cold personality and abrupt manner made him unpopular, yet he whipped his regiment into a fighting force and compiled a commendable record.

In 1864, the 70th took part in the Union army's Georgia campaign. To his wife, Harrison offered a revealing self-portrait:

> Behind my saddle I have a comfort rolled up in my rubber coat . . . strapped as small as possible. In front of my saddle I have my blue coat rolled up and strapped on. The small cavalry saddle bags are filled to their utmost capacity . . . my little tin bucket for making tea,

> swings clattering by my side. About my person I have my sword and belt. . . . The bundle behind my saddle is so large that it is a straining effort to get my leg over it in getting on or off and when in the saddle I feel like one who has been wrapped up for embalming . . . it is *very* disagreeable.

At the town of Resaca, Harrison led a charge that his commander, General Joseph Hooker, called "brilliant." After the battle, Harrison's soldiers gave him the nickname "Little Ben," in salute to his courage and in reference to his size—just five feet, six inches tall. He led the 70th in another charge at Golgatha Church near Kenesaw Mountain. "My Regiment was advanced without any support to within three hundred yards of a strong rebel breastwork . . . ," he reported. "We stood there fighting an unseen foe for an hour and a half without flinching, while the enemy's shells and grapes fell like hail in our ranks, tearing down large trees and filling the air with splinters. Two or three of my men had their heads torn off close down to the shoulders and others had fearful wounds."

As injuries mounted, he took to the operating table. "Our Surgeons got separated from us," he said, "and putting our wounded in a deserted house, I stripped my arms to dress their wounds myself. Poor Fellows! I was but an awkward surgeon . . . but I hope I gave them some relief."

With such service he earned his men's respect, and if Harrison is to be believed, his aloofness melted. He said: "I have got to love them for their bravery and for dangers we have shared together. I have heard many similar expressions from the men towards me."

Harrison was promoted to brigadier general before leaving Georgia in September 1864 and returning home. He resumed his law practice and campaigned successfully throughout the state for the Republican gubernatorial candidate and for his own candidacy as state supreme court reporter, a post taken from him two years earlier by the Democrats.

But Harrison waited several years for greater political prominence. After hoping for, but failing to get, the Republican nomination for governor in 1872, he obtained it in August 1876 when the party nominee was forced to withdraw from the race amid charges of corruption. Harrison had little time to campaign, yet he waged a strong fight against the Democrat James Douglas Williams, who won by a narrow margin.

In 1880 Harrison chaired the Indiana delegation to the Republican National Convention and delivered 27 important votes to James A. Garfield for president. After Garfield won the White House that fall, he offered Harrison a cabinet post, but the Indianan had been elected to the Senate and decided to serve there.

Although independent in thought, Harrison aligned himself with the Republican moderates who supported a limited protective tariff and laws to regulate railroads and provide pensions to veterans. Harrison lost his Senate seat in 1886 after Democrats in the state legislature gained a majority and replaced him with one of their own.

When Republicans considered the 1888 presidential campaign, they thought little about Harrison but much about James G. Blaine, the former Speaker of the House who had run against Grover Cleveland, the incumbent president, four years earlier. Blaine, however, refused another try, and other Republicans thought the party needed to put forward an honest politician with a clean record if they were going to win against Cleveland, who was known for his reform programs. They began looking at Harrison.

The Indianan at first expressed reluctance about running for the White House and refused to make himself available. When the national convention met that summer in Chicago, the delegates cast seven ballots without reaching an agreement. They anxiously awaited word from Blaine, hoping the former standard bearer would change his mind and run after all. Finally a friend of Blaine's, industrialist Andrew Carnegie, sent the delegates a telegram: "Blaine immovable. Take Harrison and Phelps." The convention took Harrison, but for vice president it rejected William Walter Phelps, a former congressman, and instead selected Levi Morton, a Wall Street banker.

Many wealthy businessmen liked Benjamin Harrison's pro-tariff stand, and after department-store magnate John Wanamaker rallied industrial leaders behind him, Harrison's campaign raised more money than any previous one in American history. The Indianan traveled little but gave 94 front-porch speeches. His criticisms of the opposition included the following:

> There are two very plain facts that I have often stated—and others more forcibly than I—that it seems to me should be conclusive with the wage-earners of America. The policy of the Democratic party— . . . a revenue-only tariff, or progressive free trade—means a vast and sudden increase of importations. Is there a man here so dull as not to know that this means diminished work in our American shops?

In an unusual result, Harrison lost the popular tally to Cleveland by a plurality of about 10,000 votes but won in the electoral college 233 to 168, thus capturing the White House. He ran strong in northern New York and carried that state with its rich vein of electoral votes by a plurality of just 13,002 ballots out of 1,315,409 cast. He won his home state by an even slimmer margin of 2,348 ballots out of 536,964 cast, yet he lost Indianapolis. "Now I walk with God," he said.

After a rain-swept inauguration, President Harrison opened the White House doors to the usual barrage of office seekers, for despite civil service reform many jobs depended on presidential appointment. He disliked the pleading and the hours taken from his day for this chore and he hoped Congress would expand the merit system. As with most of his decisions, when it came to naming officeholders he took a middle ground, trying to avoid anyone corrupt but generally making party loyalty the critical credential. When his first assistant postmaster general, James S. Clarkson, swept Democrats from smaller post offices and gained renown for "decapitating a fourth-class postmaster every three minutes," newspapers harped on this point rather than Harrison's support for the civil service. Yet he earned praise when he named two reformers, Hugh S. Thompson and Theodore Roosevelt, to the civil service commission.

Although Harrison protected presidential power, he believed Congress should lead the country. He did, however, offer his opinions about measures under consideration, and as a way to shape bills he sometimes threatened to wield his veto power. He refused to use patronage as a way to gain congressional support, and in several instances his appointments so angered Republican leaders that he won their lasting enmity.

Harrison quickly revealed himself to be an ineffective party leader. One sympathetic observer said, "He loved politics but disliked politicians; he possessed a fine sense of humor but kept it a carefully guarded secret; and he displayed a superb ability in the analysis of problems but none in the management of men." That he often failed to make his desires known when talking to congressmen, and that he appeared arrogant made him unpopular with many in his own party.

In July 1890, Congress responded to public discontent with big business when it passed the Sherman Antitrust Act, the first major law under Harrison's presidency. In more than one instance, Harrison had called trusts harmful, but he had little to do with the act as it was largely written by two of his friends, Senators George E. Edmunds of Vermont and George F. Hoar of Massachusetts. It declared illegal "every contract, combination in the form of trust or otherwise, or conspiracy, in restraint of trade or commerce among the several states, or with foreign nations. . . ." Later, critics said the law's vague wording made it ineffective, and the Supreme Court ruled it could be applied to labor unions—hardly the restraint on big business reformers wanted. In any event, Harrison showed his indifference to the issue when under his presidency the government filed only seven antitrust suits, and those originated not from the White House but primarily from ambitious district attorneys.

As with the trust controversy, the initiative for changing the tariff came from Congress. Late in 1889, William McKinley, chair of the House Ways and Means Committee, offered a bill that raised rates. Harrison disliked the proposal and worked behind the scenes to change it. He wanted Congress to establish reciprocity, an idea pushed by Secretary of State James G. Blaine, under which the United States would adjust its rates with other countries provided they did likewise. Harrison's effort, along with public anger over yet another tariff hike, caused Congress to amend the bill. The McKinley Tariff raised rates on average by 49.5 percent, but it gave the president authority to arrange lower duties with foreign governments. Harrison eventually negotiated 12 reciprocal agreements.

In a compromise deal involving those who backed the McKinley Tariff, Congress acted on another economic issue in 1891 when it passed the Sherman Silver Purchase Act. Early in his presidency, Harrison wrote: "I have been an advocate of the use of silver in our currency. We are large producers of that metal, and should not discredit it." The act required the treasury to buy 4.5 million ounces of silver each month, roughly the amount coming from the country's mines. Under the law Harrison could use gold to redeem treasury certificates and hold down inflation, so he did. He thus once again showed his desire to take a moderate path, in this case between those who supported silver and those who supported gold.

From the start of his presidency, Harrison defended black voting rights. In his first message to Congress in December 1889, he said: "The colored people did not intrude themselves on us; they were brought here in chains and held . . . by a cruel slave code. . . . When and under what conditions is the black man to have a free ballot? When is he in fact to have those full civil rights which have so long been his in law?" After a bill to provide for federal supervision of congressional elections that was introduced by Congressman Henry Cabot Lodge became bogged down, Harrison urged Congress to pass it. Although the Senate reacted by killing the bill in 1891, the president's stand earned him much praise from African Americans.

Harrison wasted no time in using a new power given him by Congress in March 1891 when it passed the Land Revision Act. The act included Section 24, which enabled the president to set aside public forestlands as reservations. A year earlier Harrison had asked Congress to take adequate steps "to prevent the rapid destruction of our great forest areas and the loss of our water supplies." He now established America's first forest reserve, adjacent to Yellowstone Park in Wyoming (first set aside as "a public park or pleasuring ground" by President Ulysses S. Grant in 1872) and followed that with 14 reserves in several western states, encompassing 22 million acres.

When Secretary of State James G. Blaine fell ill in March 1891, reportedly from a nervous collapse, President Harrison took over foreign affairs. (Blaine continued in office until June 1892.) Here he displayed toughness and set the stage for Teddy Roosevelt's display of bravado some 10 years later. When running for president, Harrison had presented himself as a strong nationalist who disliked England; now he wanted to show that America was every bit a power on the international scene, as was Britain.

Harrison's first test came in October 1891, when the captain of the *Baltimore*, a U.S. ship, granted his crew shore leave in Chile despite a rebellion there that had made relations with the United States tense. When a bar fight broke out between the Americans and a gang of Chileans and several of the sailors were wounded and two of them killed, the captain of the ship claimed that Chilean police had fired on his men and jabbed them with bayonets.

In December Harrison insisted Chile must agree to a settlement. The following month he began preparing for war and readying ships for the Chilean coast. He considered this action necessary to exert pressure on Chile. On January 21, 1892, he gave the Chilean leaders an ultimatum, and Blaine sent them a note equating the attack on the sailors with an attack on the U.S. Navy. Four days later, Harrison presented Congress with the story and urged it to take whatever action it deemed best. "The evidence of our sailors shows," he said, "our men were struck and beaten by police officers before and after arrest." The American display of power forced Chile to admit its liability and to make a complete apology. It also showed that the United States would assert its expanding military might in Latin America.

Harrison simultaneously extended U.S. power into the Pacific. In 1889 the white ruling class in Hawaii, largely prosperous sugar and fruit planters, proposed a treaty whereby the United States would establish a protectorate over the islands. Many Hawaiians protested the move, and Harrison deployed marines to restore order and stationed a ship off the coast.

Two years later, Queen Liliuokalani proclaimed a new constitution that took power from the white elite and restored it to native Hawaiians. The whites reacted by forming a provisional government, and the American minister provided them with soldiers. On January 17, 1893, the planters declared a new government under Sanford Dole. The American minister sent a message to Harrison: "The Hawaiian pear is now fully ripe and this is the golden hour to pluck it."

The president, who earlier had told Blaine, "The necessity of maintaining and increasing our hold and influence in [Hawaii] is very apparent and very pressing," now forwarded a treaty to the Senate calling for annexation of the islands. "The overthrow of the monarchy was not in any way promoted by this Government," he claimed. His words displayed American machismo stripped bare when he called the Hawaiian monarchy "effete" and "weak." In just two days the Foreign Relations Committee sent Harrison's treaty to the Senate floor, but Democrats rallied against it and prevented it from passing; later, President Grover Cleveland revoked it.

In another Pacific adventure, the United States joined Britain and Germany in establishing a protectorate over Samoa. Harrison took an active role in writing the agreement, which frustrated efforts by Germany to gain complete control of the islands. He believed that increased trade in the Pacific and the prospect of a canal across Central America made Samoa valuable to the United States.

Exerting power required more weapons, and President Harrison enthusiastically backed his secretary of the navy, Benjamin F. Tracy, who wanted bigger, more modern ships. Harrison called for more steel cruisers and said, "The construction of a sufficient number of modern warships and of their necessary armament should progress as rapidly as is consistent with care and perfection."

In 1892 Congress agreed to build two additional ships, including America's first battleship, the *Iowa*. Despite the small number built, Harrison said shortly before leaving office: "The wholesome influence for peace and the increased sense of security which our citizens . . . in other lands feel when these magnificent ships . . . appear is already most gratefully apparent."

Money for the navy, along with generous pensions given Civil War veterans, produced the "billion-dollar Congress" that spent much of the treasury surplus. Voters so disliked the high tariff and massive spending, however, that they elected a Democratic House in 1890 and sent a warning message to the Republicans for the next presidential campaign.

Benjamin Harrison originally decided he would serve only one term, but his enemies raised his ire. In 1892 Thomas B. Reed, a powerful congressman and former Speaker of the House, Pennsylvania Senator Matthew S. Quay, and ex-New York Senator Thomas Platt, all fellow Republicans, organized a "dump Harrison" campaign. They disliked him personally and disliked his patronage appointments. The president reacted by declaring, "No Harrison has ever retreated in the presence of a foe without giving battle, and so I have determined to stand and fight."

Harrison's opponents could find no one to seek the nomination except Blaine; still in poor health, he really did not want it. As a result, at the national convention in Minneapolis, Harrison won on the first ballot. Platt quickly wrapped himself in an overcoat, scurried from the convention hall, and boarded the first train for New York.

Benjamin Harrison once more faced Grover Cleveland. During the campaign, Harrison's wife took seriously ill, and in October 1892 she died. The blow hurt him, and he lost interest in the political fight. Both he and Cleveland ignored the Populists, largely discontent farmers who wanted reform (though Republicans and Democrats fused with Populist groups on the local level), and as the election neared, labor strikes and violence rocked the country. Yet the campaign aroused little excitement, and Cleveland defeated Harrison by 277 to 145 electoral votes. The voter discontent expressed in the 1890 congressional elections had doomed the colorless Indianan.

In March 1893 Benjamin Harrison left the White House and returned to his law practice in Indianapolis. Three years later, he married Mary Scott Lord Dimmick, a 38-year-old niece of his deceased wife, and in 1898 they had a daughter. The union, however, estranged him from his two children by his previous marriage.

In addition to his work as a lawyer, Harrison wrote several articles on politics for the *Ladies' Home Journal*, and in 1899 he represented Venezuela in a boundary dispute with Britain. Benjamin Harrison died on March 13, 1901, after catching pneumonia. In later years few remembered his term in the White House except as an interlude between Grover Cleveland's more forceful presidencies.

Chronology

1833 Born August 20

1847 Enters Farmers' College

1850 Transfers to Miami University in Ohio

1852 Graduates from Miami University

1853 Marries Caroline Scott

1854 Admitted to the bar
Moves to Indianapolis

1855 Becomes law partner of William Wallace
Becomes notary public
Appointed commissioner for the court of claims

1856 Joins Republican Party

1857 Elected city attorney

1860 Elected state supreme court reporter

1862 Commissioned second lieutenant
Promoted to captain
Commissioned a colonel

1864 Fights at Nashville, Tennessee

1865 Promoted to brigadier general

1867 Returns to law practice

1876 Loses gubernatorial race

1881 Elected to U.S. Senate

1886 Loses reelection

1888 Elected president

1892 Asks Congress to take action against Chile
Caroline Harrison dies
Defeated for reelection

1893 Sends Senate treaty to annex Hawaii
Returns to Indianapolis

1896 Marries Mary Dimmick

1901 Dies March 13

FURTHER READING

Hedges, Charles. *Speeches of Benjamin Harrison.* 1892. Reprint, New York: Kennikat Press, 1971.

Sievers, Harry J. *Benjamin Harrison: Hoosier Warrior, 1833–1865.* Chicago: Henry Regnery, 1952.

———. *Benjamin Harrison, Hoosier Statesman: From the Civil War to the White House, 1865–1888.* New York: University Publishers, 1959.

———. *Benjamin Harrison, Hoosier President: The White House and After.* Indianapolis, Ind.: Bobbs-Merrill, 1968.

Socolofsky, Homer E., and Allan B. Spetter. *The Presidency of Benjamin Harrison.* Lawrence: University Press of Kansas, 1987.

William McKinley (1843–1901)

Twenty-fifth President, 1897–1901

William McKinley
(Library of Congress)

"War should never be entered upon until every agency of peace has failed; peace is preferable to war in almost every contingency."
—Inaugural words, first term, March 4, 1897

The sinking of the battleship *Maine* in Havana harbor in 1898 outraged Americans. They accused Spain, then fighting a war against Cuban rebels seeking independence for their island, of having staged the attack. The *New York World* declared: "The DESTRUCTION OF THE MAINE BY FOUL PLAY should be the occasion of ordering our fleet to Havana and *demanding proper amends within forty-eight hours under the threat of bombardment.*" Soon a chant spread across the country:

Remember the Maine!
To hell with Spain!

More than any other single event, the crisis with Spain defined William McKinley's presidency. He had to answer the pressure to act, and when he did he pointed the United States toward war and empire.

—~—

William McKinley was born on January 29, 1843, in Niles, Ohio, a tree-shaded midwestern hamlet with several clapboard houses, a small church, and a bridge that crossed a meandering creek. His father, also named William McKinley, was a worker in an iron foundry who once described Niles as a town with "no railroads, no canals, and [with] terribly poor, wild country roads." Young William's strong-willed mother, Nancy Allison McKinley, provided most of his guidance. In growing up, he played the usual childhood games for that time, fished some (though he did not much like it), and worked hard at school, which he enjoyed. Never a brilliant student, he preferred the practical to the speculative; his schoolmates found him convivial and friendly, and from an early age he could judge people quickly.

When he was 17, William entered Allegheny College in Meadville, Pennsylvania, but health problems and his family's tight finances forced him to leave after one year. He then clerked for a short while at the post office in Poland, Ohio, after which he taught school. "My parents . . . lived only three miles from the schoolhouse," he later recalled, "and . . . most of the time I stayed with them and walked to school and back every day."

His midwestern tranquility was soon shattered by the Civil War, and in spring 1861 he joined the Union army. He compiled a commendable record in several battles and won particular praise for his role as a commissary sergeant at Antietam, when he risked his life to bring food to the front lines. The slaughter in combat, however, appalled him and later, when he served as president, he opposed war except as a last resort.

McKinley left the military in 1865 as a brevet major and would be known as "the Major" throughout his public life. He returned to Ohio, studied law there and at a law school in Albany, New York, and began his legal practice in Canton in 1867. That year he campaigned for Rutherford B. Hayes, the Republican candidate for governor. He quickly earned a reputation as an effective speaker—and an attractive one, given his good looks. Two years later he won election as prosecuting attorney of Stark County.

Soon after his election, he met Ida Saxton, the daughter of a leading Canton family. She was nervous and possessive, but he fell deeply in love with her. "Oh, if you could have seen what a beauty Ida was as a girl," he told a friend years later. For her part, Ida liked McKinley's charm, his graceful manners, and his reserved but firm character. They married on January 24, 1871, and their first child, Katherine, was born on Christmas Day.

But tragedy soon struck, and it devastated Ida. First, early in 1873, her mother died. Then that spring the couple's second child died in infancy. Ida sank into a deep depression. Her nervousness intensified, and she became short-tempered and extremely jealous of anyone who occupied her husband's time.

Making matters worse, Katherine died in 1875. Ida thought God was punishing her, and according to historian H. Wayne Morgan, "her obsessive love for [her husband] became a fixation as she . . . pitifully forbade him to leave her side." Ida began to have epileptic convulsions and sometimes lost consciousness—a malady she endured all her life. At home she plastered a wall with pictures of McKinley, and acting out of his love for her and his desire to be loved by her, he did most everything she wanted.

Politics provided an outlet for the Major, and his public career moved forward. In 1876 he won election to the U.S. House of Representatives as a Republican and carved out a moderate stand on the leading issues. He supported civil service reform and voting rights for African Americans. Foremost in importance to him, though, was the tariff, one of the biggest problems facing America in a time of rapid industrial growth and business expansion. McKinley wanted a high tariff, one that would increase the prices of imported goods and protect American companies from foreign competition. He thought this would boost profits and help workers keep their jobs. The McKinley Tariff, passed by Congress in 1890, placed high rates on farm products and manufactured goods, providing a triumph for protectionism.

Although the tariff generated controversy, with opponents charging that it hurt consumers, it made McKinley a national figure. Two years earlier he had blocked a move by those who wanted to promote him as the Republican presidential candidate, but as his name spread, he received support from Marcus Alonzo Hanna, a leading businessman, who was determined to direct McKinley into the White House.

Hanna had built his fortune in the Cleveland coal and iron business and had also helped establish the Union National Bank. He owned the *Cleveland Herald* and controlled the city's street railway system. Like many other businessmen, he was a protectionist, and the McKinley Tariff of 1890 only intensified his enthusiasm for his fellow Ohioan.

McKinley suffered a political setback in 1890 when he lost his congressional seat after Democrats gerrymandered his district. Nevertheless, he recovered the next year by winning the governorship, with his campaign financed by Hanna.

McKinley devoted considerable time to Ida. Every workday afternoon he stood by his office window and waved a handkerchief to her as she watched from their nearby home. She accompanied McKinley to social functions but often experienced epileptic attacks that forced him to cover her face with a handkerchief and take her out of the room. The seizures embarrassed McKinley's friends, but he seemed unshaken by them.

A serious threat to McKinley's political future appeared in 1893 when a friend, Robert Walker, lost all his money during a massive economic depression, declared bankruptcy, and revealed that the governor had signed notes to secure the debt, which amounted to $150,000. McKinley never realized he had committed himself to backing Walker so extensively; now he faced embarrassment over his carelessness and, even worse, faced financial and political ruin. He feared people would conclude that his inability to manage his own finances bespoke an inability to manage the responsibilities that came with being president. In short, the White House seemed out of reach.

Yet newspapers sympathized with him. One in Columbus said, "The financial troubles of Governor McKinley will be learned with deep regret not only in Ohio but all over the country. He has been a liberal, kind hearted man and has always done more for others than for himself." When Ida McKinley heard the news, she rallied behind her husband and offered him her property. To critics she answered: "My husband has done everything for me all my life. Do you mean to deny me the privilege of doing as I please with my own property to help him now?"

As the crisis deepened, one of McKinley's friends commented, "I am inclined to think . . . that his many and wealthy friends will look after his interests fully." He was right. Marcus Hanna stepped in, set up a trust fund to help the governor, and raised money from industrialists. Small contributors also lent a hand, sending McKinley everything from nickels to dollars. He survived the storm and kept his sights on the White House.

Since the Midwest provided the country with several presidents in the late 1800s—namely, Ulysses S. Grant, Rutherford B. Hayes, James A. Garfield, and Benjamin Harrison—anyone who held the Ohio governorship could expect to be mentioned in talk for the country's highest office, McKinley included. With Hanna's backing and with reelection behind him in 1893, the Major maneuvered toward the 1896 presidential nomination. After Hanna withdrew from his businesses in 1895, he launched an expensive preconvention campaign for McKinley, to which he contributed most of the money. All their careful planning succeeded:

The Republicans nominated William McKinley on the first ballot.

In the general election the Major faced the great orator William Jennings Bryan, whom the Democrats chose as their silver candidate. This meant that Bryan advocated the unlimited coinage of silver as a way to make money more available to workers and farmers and produce inflation that would benefit both groups by boosting wages and the prices for agricultural goods. As a nationwide economic depression continued, the silver message held a strong appeal, particularly in the West where farmers distrusted eastern bankers. In a thundering speech, Bryan told how he and his supporters would respond to those who opposed them: "Having behind us the producing masses of this nation and the world, supported by the commercial interests, the laboring interests and the toilers everywhere, we will answer their demand for a gold standard by saying to them: You shall not press down upon the brow of labor this crown of thorns, you shall not crucify mankind upon a cross of gold."

Many "gold Democrats" refused to support Bryan; this worked to McKinley's advantage, for he stood by the existing gold standard. Yet "silver Republicans" left his party, and his planned strategy fell apart: He had wanted to emphasize the tariff issue and instead found himself forced to discuss monetary policy.

For Hanna and many eastern bankers and businessmen, McKinley's campaign amounted to a crusade. Bryan must be stopped, they reasoned, or else his radical monetarism would ruin the country. Many of his supporters were farmers and factory workers, a number of them from the Populist Party, considered by the industrialists and bankers to be filled with troublemakers.

Hanna raised money from the same business groups that had helped McKinley through his financial crisis a few years earlier. Life insurance companies gave liberally, as did large corporations. Standard Oil, for one, contributed $250,000. In all, Hanna collected $3.5 million, a record for a presidential campaign, while Bryan raised considerably less.

As a dynamic speaker, Bryan attracted huge crowds; they jammed Madison Square Garden in New York City, and they turned out in droves in small towns from Nebraska to Maine. He traveled more than 18,000 miles and made some 600 speeches. All the while McKinley stayed in Canton, conducting a front porch campaign. Over several weeks hundreds of thousands made the pilgrimage to his home.

As it turned out, the continuing economic depression hurt the Democrats, as did a rift between their party and the Populists, some of whom supported Bryan while others supported their own presidential candidate, Tom Watson. On top of this, many Republican businessmen coerced their workers, telling them if Bryan won they would be fired. On election day McKinley polled about 7,100,000 votes to Bryan's nearly 6,500,000. He also won in the electoral count, 271 to 176.

As president, McKinley cautioned those who wanted an American empire. "We want no wars of conquest," he said in his inaugural speech. "We must avoid the temptation of territorial aggression." But in 1895 an uprising in Cuba seduced America when rebels on the Caribbean island attacked their Spanish rulers. Unintentionally, a tariff levied in the United States helped ignite the rebellion when it placed higher rates on sugar imported from Cuba and hurt the island's economy. Yet Cuban disgust with Spanish rule dated back many years, and the rebellion amounted to the rebirth of an earlier uprising that had lasted from 1868 to 1878. This time around the rebels attacked economic targets, such as crops, to foment popular discontent and keep Spanish troops occupied. Within the United States, the rebels obtained money and weapons and launched an effective propaganda campaign to influence public opinion.

Americans sympathized with them. They disliked Spain's continued presence so close to the United States, and atrocities committed by Spanish troops horrified them. Economics also mattered: Businessmen with property in Cuba wanted their holdings protected, and others wanted order on the island as a prerequisite to making additional investments there and throughout Latin America. Added to these influences, the *New York Herald* and the *New York Journal* printed sensational, embellished stories about atrocities committed by the Spanish against the Cubans.

Yet an even deeper spirit moved America: the desire for conquest. By the late 1800s leading Americans such as Admiral Alfred Mahan and Theodore Roosevelt were calling for an empire. They wanted the United States to rule the oceans and dominate trade. Although anti-imperialists fought against them, they were losing ground.

President McKinley faced this crescendo with his usual deliberative manner, refusing to be rushed into anything, let alone war, a bitter memory that lingered from his days as a soldier. Besides, although some businessmen rattled their bayonets, many others thought differently and believed war risked more economically than it could possibly gain.

Still, McKinley's policy toward Cuba differed greatly from Grover Cleveland's. Whereas Cleveland had wanted Spain to retain the island, McKinley wanted Cuban independence, which he hoped could be accomplished peacefully. With Spain suffering high losses among its troops, he thought this a real possibility.

The Spanish government seemed to be following this path in October 1897, when it granted Cuba more autonomy, but after mobs led by Spanish officers rioted against the change, it became clear that meaningful autonomy remained elusive. Then on February 9, 1898, the *New York Journal*, under the headline WORST INSULT TO THE UNITED STATES IN ITS HISTORY, published a confidential letter written by Dupuy de Lome, the Spanish ambassador to the United States, in which he described McKinley as "weak and a bidder for the admiration of the crowd, besides being a would-be politician who tries to leave a door open behind himself while keeping on good terms with the jingoes of his party."

That passage angered Americans, but McKinley was much more disturbed by another that showed Spain engaging in stalling tactics over a commercial treaty then being negotiated. To the president it proved the Spanish could not be trusted.

A few weeks earlier McKinley had sent the battleship *Maine* to Havana to protect Americans in Cuba and make a show of strength, to which the wife of one naval officer said, "You might as well send a lighted candle on a visit to an open cask of gunpowder." On February 13 an explosion destroyed the ship and killed more than 200 of its sailors. Americans started blaming Spain for a barbaric act, and Congress pressured McKinley to declare war. Instead, he appointed a naval board to investigate, saying to a friend, "I shall never get into a war until I am sure that God and man approve. I have been through one war; I have seen the dead piled up; and I do not want to see another." Critics called him a coward, and fellow Republican Theodore Roosevelt declared the president had "no more backbone than a chocolate éclair!"

To this day no one is sure what caused the *Maine* to blow up, but evidence points to a spontaneous combustion in the boiler room—in short, an accident. The naval board, however, blamed Spain, and McKinley placed pressure on that country to make concessions.

In early April Spain agreed to suspend hostilities in Cuba, end its policy of placing suspected rebels in concentration camps, and submit the *Maine* incident to arbitration. But how long the armistice would last was left up to the commander in Cuba. McKinley believed this stipulation was a maneuver to buy time to prepare for war.

On April 11, 1898, as more congressmen beat their battle drums and threatened to act without the president, he sent a war message to Capitol Hill in which he stressed the need to bring order to Cuba, protect American property and trade, and help the Cuban people. As Congress debated, tempers flared. The *London Times* reported that on the floor of the House, "Men fought; 'Liar,' 'Scoundrel,' and other epithets were bandied to and fro; there were half-a-dozen personal collisions; books were thrown;

members rushed up and down the aisles like madmen, exchanging hot words, with clenched fists and set teeth. . . ." On April 19, after congressmen broke out singing "The Battle Hymn of the Republic," they passed a resolution declaring Cuba free. Six days later McKinley signed the declaration of war against Spain.

America's army entered the Spanish-American War poorly prepared. A debate among congressmen over how much to rely on regular troops and how much to use volunteers—they eventually decided to use both—delayed mobilizing the forces. So many volunteers wanted to fight that one official described the war department building as "filled daily so that both sides nearly bulge out with a steaming, surging and sometimes nasty crowd who are insisting for places." With the mobilization, supplies lagged. For example, the military needed 5,000 wagons to move men and supplies but had only 1,200; it also needed many more bullets than it had. Most of the problems were soon corrected, but the public remembered the initial chaos and shortages and held the army in low esteem.

McKinley, meanwhile, set up a war command office in the White House, where a switchboard and 20 telegraph wires were installed. He was connected to French, British, and American cable lines that went to Cuba and enabled him to exchange messages with his commanders in less than 20 minutes. The president took charge of war strategy, often writing directives on the backs of envelopes but also using the recently invented graphaphone, a device similar to a dictaphone. Fifteen telephone lines in the White House ran directly to the executive departments and to the House and the Senate.

Unlike the army, which was bedeviled by early problems, the navy scored a quick victory when Admiral Dewey defeated the Spanish fleet at Manila Bay in the Philippines on May 1, 1898. In a stunning feat, he sank seven Spanish ships while losing none of his own. Legend has it that Dewey launched his attack at the insistence of Theodore Roosevelt, then serving as assistant secretary of the navy. But McKinley's naval board had recommended back in 1897 that should war with Spain break out, the Spanish Philippines should be attacked as a way to exhaust the enemy's resources and help the insurgents battling Spanish rule in those islands. Thus on April 24 the president himself gave the final order for Dewey to attack.

With Dewey's easy victory, the nature of the war changed. Some Americans looked toward acquiring the Philippines as a way to expand trade in Asia and support a bigger navy in the Pacific that could protect American merchant ships. From early May onward, McKinley wanted to take over at least part of the Philippines, and when he committed additional troops to those islands he moved the United States ever closer to grabbing them. That America wanted to expand its presence in the Pacific became clearer when McKinley pressured Congress to annex the Hawaiian Islands, and after much debate the Senate agreed.

In June McKinley expressed his hope that an arrangement could be reached with the rebels in the Philippines who had fought against Spanish rule. He wanted a trade: They would get American protection and America would get Manila. But in a note he added: "If . . . as we go on it is to appear desirable that we should retain all, then we will certainly do it." After American troops reached the Philippines on June 30, almost everyone with any political knowledge in Washington was predicting McKinley would settle for nothing less than the entire archipelago.

Back in the Caribbean, the U.S. Navy demolished the Spanish fleet at Santiago de Cuba while the American "Rough Riders" led by Theodore Roosevelt charged up San Juan Hill and captured it. They suffered heavy losses, but their victory weakened Santiago's defenses. The Spanish-American War officially ended on August 12, 1898, less than four months after it had begun, with Spain agreeing to negotiate a treaty that would end its rule over Cuba and determine the future of the Philippines.

Throughout the war, Ida McKinley attended social functions at the White House. She believed that by staying at her husband's side she was helping him. Yet luncheons and receptions were interrupted by her seizures, and at official dinners the president broke with custom and had her sit next to him so he could take care of her in the event of an attack. Fellow Republican William Howard Taft recalled a meeting with McKinley during which Ida made a "peculiar hissing sound." The president, according to Taft, covered her face but kept right on talking. When her seizure ended, she joined in the conversation as if nothing had happened.

On the Philippine front, McKinley worried that either Germany or Japan would grab the islands, and as talks with Spain neared he made patriotic statements about acquiring the entire archipelago. "Territory sometimes comes to us when we go to war in a holy cause," he said, "and whenever it does the banner of liberty will float over it and bring, I trust, blessings and benefits to all the people."

On October 28, 1898, he sent word to the American peace negotiators meeting with Spain: Demand all the Philippines. This occurred well before he supposedly told a group of visitors from the Methodist Episcopal Church that he prayed about the Philippines and that God had told him to take the islands. McKinley's decision, then, had less to do with religion than with demands from Congress and people across the country to expand beyond Hawaii.

The Treaty of Paris, signed on December 10, 1898, officially ended Spain's rule over Cuba, and for $20 million Spain transferred the Philippines, Puerto Rico, and Guam to the United States. Despite the strong pro-expansion sentiment in America, antiexpansionists fought the treaty, and it was far from certain the document would be ratified. That the Senate finally approved it—and then by only one vote more than the two-thirds required—owed much to McKinley's strong lobbying efforts. Writing in *The Presidency of William McKinley*, historian Lewis L. Gould claims: "The president made the difference. From Dewey's victory onward, he guided events so that American acquisition of the Philippines became logical and, to politicians and the people, inevitable."

With the Philippines came problems when in 1899 insurgents led by Emilio Aguinaldo rebelled against American rule. A brutal war raged in which the United States committed 70,000 troops and during three years lost more men than in the entire conflict with Spain. Both sides engaged in atrocities, with the Americans requiring Filipinos to dig their own graves, then stand in front of them and be shot. One American general said, "It may be necessary to kill half the Filipinos in order that the remaining half be advanced to a higher plane of life."

At the same time, relations with Cuba suffered. In 1901 the United States forced the Cuban government to accept the Platt Amendment, allowing America to intervene in the island "for the preservation of Cuban independence and the maintenance of stable government"—meaning, for almost any reason. Cubans protested, but they had no choice, and until the measure was repealed in 1934, it served as a sore point in relations between the two countries.

By the time the Platt Amendment had been forced on Cuba, President McKinley had won reelection, buoyed by the victory over Spain, the passage of the Gold Standard Act that made gold the only standard of currency, and economic recovery. "Do you smoke?" a McKinley campaign button asked, meaning not "do you smoke tobacco" but "do you support the industrial smokestacks of McKinley prosperity?"

Enormously popular, McKinley went on a tour in 1901, and on September 5 he appeared at the Pan-American Exposition in Buffalo, New York, where he laid out an important economic goal. "Commercial wars are unprofitable," he said. "A policy of goodwill and friendly trade relations will prevent reprisals. Reciprocity treaties are in harmony with the spirit of the times; measures of retaliation are not."

The next afternoon he headed for the Temple of Music, where he was scheduled to shake hands for 10 minutes. His chief aide argued against going, saying it posed a security risk. McKinley thought otherwise: "No one would wish to hurt me," he said.

The temple was decorated for the president's appearance with potted palms and flowers, and as a huge pipe organ provided soft music and three bodyguards stood nearby, he began shaking hands. Only two or three minutes remained in the event when an anarchist, Leon Czolgosz, approached him. From his bandaged hand Czolgosz pulled a gun and fired twice at McKinley. One bullet bounced off a button; the other went into the president's stomach. As the crowd wrestled Czolgosz to the ground, McKinley asked that his assailant, "some poor, misguided fellow," not be hurt.

Over the following week the president talked and joked and seemed to be recovering. But his wound had never been properly cleaned, and gangrene set in. On September 13 he told those standing near his bed: "Good-bye, good-bye all. It is God's way. His will, not ours, be done." Then he whispered the words of "Nearer My God to Thee." On September 14 he died. Months later, Ida McKinley, suffering in grief, wrote a friend: "I am more lonely every day I live." She died six years after her husband.

As much as William McKinley hated war, he remains best remembered as the president who deepened American power in the Caribbean and the Pacific and brought the country into the 20th century era of empire. "Isolation is no longer possible or desirable," McKinley said. "The period of exclusiveness is past."

CHRONOLOGY

1843 Born January 29

1860 Enters Allegheny College

1861 Enlists in army

1862 Fights at Antietam
Promoted to first lieutenant

1865 Promoted to brevet major

1866 Enters Albany Law School
Moves to Canton, Ohio

1868 Elected county prosecuting attorney

1871 Marries Ida Saxton

1876 Elected to U.S. House of Representatives

1878 Votes for Bland-Allison Bill

1880 Reelected to Congress

1889 Becomes chairman of House Ways and Means Committee

1890 Sponsors McKinley Tariff

1891 Elected governor of Ohio

1893 Reelected governor

1896 Elected president

1897 Signs Dingley Tariff

1898 Declares war with Spain
Convinces Congress to annex Hawaii
Demands cession of Philippines

1899 Fights Filipino insurgents

1900 Wins second term

1901 Forces Platt Amendment on Cuba
Shot September 6
Dies September 14

FURTHER READING

Gould, Lewis L. *The Presidency of William McKinley*. Lawrence: University Press of Kansas, 1980.

Leech, Margaret. *In the Days of McKinley*. New York: Harper & Bros., 1959.

Morgan, H. Wayne. *William McKinley and His America*. Syracuse, N.Y.: Syracuse University Press, 1963.

Olcott, Charles S. *Life of William McKinley*, 2 vols. Boston and New York: Houghton Mifflin, 1916.

Phillips, Kevin. *William McKinley.* New York: Times Books, 2003.

Rauchway, Eric. *Murdering McKinley: The Making of Theodore Roosevelt's America.* New York: Hill and Wang, 2003.

THEODORE ROOSEVELT (1858–1919)

Twenty-sixth President, 1901–1909

THEODORE ROOSEVELT
(Library of Congress)

"Never before have men tried so vast and formidable an experiment as that of administering the affairs of a continent under the forms of a Democratic republic. The conditions which have told for our marvelous material well-being, which have developed to a very high degree our energy, self-reliance, and individual initiative, have also brought the care and anxiety inseparable from the accumulation of great wealth in industrial centers."

—Inaugural words, March 4, 1905

When he was a little boy Theodore Roosevelt—Teedie as his family called him—stood on one leg, bent his other in front of him so as to form a flat surface, and placed his book there to read. He liked *Boy Hunters* by Captain Mayne Reid, an adventure story filled with alligators, buffalo, and grizzly bears. Early in the story, Reid describes a house in which a hunter lived:

In the great hall or passage . . . a singular picture presented itself. Along the walls, on both sides, were suspended . . . rifles, shot guns, pouches, flasks, hunting knives, and, in short, every species of trap, net, or implement, that could be devised for capturing the wild denizens of the earth, air, and water. . . .

Were we to enter and examine the inside of the house, we should find three or four good-sized rooms . . . all stocked with the subjects of natural history, and implements of the chase. In one of the rooms we should see a barometer and thermometer hanging against the wall, an old clock over the mantel-piece, a sabre and pistols, and a bookcase containing many choice and valuable books.

Such a picture could easily describe Sagamore Hill, the home where Roosevelt lived later in his life. Located at Oyster Bay, New York, this museum-as-house displayed rifles, animal heads mounted on walls, and bear rugs spread on the floors. They reflected Roosevelt's lifelong interest in big-game hunting—and his equally vigorous and unwavering pursuit of politics.

From the moment of his birth in New York City on October 27, 1858, Theodore Roosevelt was surrounded by wealth. Earlier in the century, his grandfather Cornelius Van Schaack Roosevelt had amassed a fortune through investments that placed him alongside Cornelius Vanderbilt and William B. Astor. His father, Theodore Roosevelt, Sr., succeeded as a glass importer and banker. The Roosevelt house at 28 East 20th Street looked out not at tenements or hungry-eyed immigrants, but grand facades on one side and a pleasant garden on the other.

Roosevelt's mother, Martha Bulloch Roosevelt, came from a prominent family in Georgia. She was, according to historian Edmund Morris, "a lady about whom there always clung a hint of white columns and wisteria bowers."

Teedie was a frail and sickly child. He suffered from bronchial asthma and experienced regular attacks so severe they threatened his life, racking his body, making him feel as if he were drowning. The attacks were physiological in origin, likely caused by airborne allergens, but derived as well from psychological influences.

Teedie loved books. "I was nervous and timid," he later recollected. "Yet from reading of the people I admired—ranging from the soldiers of Valley Forge, and Morgan's riflemen, to the heroes of my favorite stories—and from hearing of the feats performed by my Southern forefathers and kinsfolk, and from knowing my father, I felt a great admiration for men who were fearless and could hold their own in the world, and I had a great desire to be like them."

His father, an energetic, outgoing man who made friends easily, took Teedie on a family trip to Europe in 1869 and the following year told him what he would need to hold his own in the world: "Theodore, you have the mind, but you have not the body, and without the help of the body the mind cannot go as far as it should. You must *make* your body."

There followed a regimen of working out in the gym and pulling himself up on parallel bars. His sisters recalled watching him "widening his chest by regular, monotonous motion—drudgery indeed." He took to horseback riding and swimming, too. At the same time, he learned English, French, German, and Latin from private tutors.

During a trip to the Adirondacks and the White Mountains in 1871, Teedie studied wildlife. The following year he learned taxidermy and received his first shotgun. While with his family in Egypt in 1872, he shot many birds and carefully preserved them.

At age 17 the young man who "never seemed to know what idleness was" entered Harvard. His fellow students were fascinated by his frenetic pace, his fast talk chopped by large white teeth, his New York accent. Some students purposely drew him into arguments so they could hear his rapid-fire words. He was a joiner. He joined the Hasty Pudding Club, the Rifle Club, the Art Club, and the Glee Club; he served on the editorial board of the undergraduate magazine; he rowed and boxed, though he never excelled at any sport. Where other students took their time in getting from place to place, he scurried; where other students sat quietly in class, he spoke out, his high-pitched voice cutting through inattention.

He socialized mainly with Boston's old elite Brahmin families and, according to Edmund Morris, showed "the self-protective instinct of a born snob" when he "carefully researched the 'antecedents' of potential friends." Although in later life Roosevelt remembered Harvard primarily as a place where he had a good time, his record shows that he worked hard, usually studied about 40 hours a week, and earned solid grades.

During his sophomore year, tragedy struck when his beloved father died. Not long after he returned to college he met Alice Lee, a 17-year-old girl with honey-blonde hair, deep blue eyes, and a personality described by most everyone as bright, cheerful, and high spirited. Roosevelt fell in love with her. He later told a friend that he had spent his last two years at Harvard in "eager, restless, passionate pursuit of one all-absorbing object." Early in 1880 Alice agreed to marry him, and he wrote in his diary: "I do not think ever a man loved a woman more than I love her; for a year and a quarter now I have never (even when hunting) gone to sleep or waked up without thinking of her." Alice wrote a friend that she loved Teddy "deeply." In October 1880 she and Roosevelt were pronounced man and wife at a gala wedding ceremony in downtown New York.

Roosevelt graduated from Harvard the same year as his marriage and enrolled at Columbia Law School, but disturbed by what he considered to be the greedy values of corporate law and drawn to politics, he soon quit. He spent time completing his *Naval History of the War of 1812*, which he had started in college. One of several books he wrote over the years, it went through three editions, and reviewers praised it.

Roosevelt said he entered politics as his civic duty, but clearly he wanted power and prominence. His father had been involved politically in the 1870s when he sided with Republican reformers repulsed by the corruption in Ulysses S. Grant's presidency. Still, a curious mix surrounded young Theodore's political birth. Many in the upper crust abhorred office-seeking as degrading and urged him to stay away from it, while others backed him, among them J. P. Morgan, Elihu Root, and Joseph M. Choate. Displaying an equally curious mix of social adaptability, Roosevelt was comfortable both in smoke-filled rooms where precinct men worked the voters and at exclusive restaurants, such as Delmonico's, where New York's finest gathered in white tie and tails to fete him.

In 1881 he won election to the state assembly as a Republican and caused a stir when he entered the legislative chamber dressed, as was typical for him, as a dandy. He burst through the door and deliberately paused long enough for others to notice him. One observer recollected, "He had on a cutaway coat with one button at the top, and the ends of its tails almost reached the tops of his shoes. He carried a gold-headed cane in one hand, a silk hat in the other, and he walked in the bent-over fashion that was the style with the young men of the day. 'Who's the dude?' . . . was [the question] being put in a dozen different parts of the hall."

Theodore Roosevelt—TR, as he was often called— thought little of his fellow assemblymen, having judged many of them to be crooked. Of one he said, "He [has] . . . the same idea of public life and civil service that a vulture has of a dead sheep." In a time when corrupt political machines controlled the legislature, Roosevelt advocated reform. He did not stand alone—as governor of New York and later as president, Democrat Grover Cleveland also fought graft—but he certainly stood on a dangerous ledge from which the bosses eventually plotted to push him to his political ruin.

Two events affected him greatly: a cigar bill and a scandal. In 1882 the assembly considered a bill to make illegal the manufacturing of cigars at home. Each year poor immigrants made thousands of cigars in their New York City tenements. TR at first opposed the bill, but when he investigated, what he saw shocked him. Much later he still recalled a tenement in which children, men, and women were crowded together in one room, and how "the tobacco was stowed about everywhere, alongside the foul bedding, and in a corner where there were scraps of food." He changed his mind and supported the bill, which passed the legislature (only to be ruled unconstitutional by a state court).

The scandal involved Theodore Westbrook, a state supreme court judge, whom Roosevelt discovered was making decisions to benefit Jay Gould, a notorious businessman known for bribing legislators. TR stunned the assembly when he stood up, recited his suspicions about a Gould-Westbrook connection, and called Gould a "swindler." He demanded an investigation, and newspapers covered his assault so extensively that the legislators could only agree. Even though a judiciary committee cleared Westbrook, Roosevelt earned widespread acclaim as a brave reformer. In 1882 he won reelection, upon which fellow Republicans chose him to serve as House minority leader.

Roosevelt's natural enthusiasm met a sharp challenge in February 1884 when his mother and his wife died within hours of each other. Typhoid fever claimed his mother, and Bright's disease claimed his wife just two days after she gave birth to a daughter. "When my heart's dearest died," he said about Alice, "the light went out from my life for ever."

Yet politics still beckoned as an escape and as a forum for exerting his will. Early in June he attended the Republican National Convention in Chicago and promoted a reform candidate, James G. Blaine, for president against the front-runner, Grover Cleveland. TR lost his battle, but unlike those who bolted the party rather than have anything to do with Blaine, he stayed with it and protected his Republican credentials.

Still beset with grief from the deaths of his mother and his wife, Roosevelt headed for South Dakota, where he hoped strenuous outdoor pursuits would ease his pain. He had invested in the Elkhorn Ranch in 1883, and there he branded steers and broke stampedes. Although the ranch hands at first derided him as a tenderfoot, they changed their minds when they saw his energy and fortitude. At one point he encountered a nine-foot, 1,200-pound grizzly. He later wrote in his diary: "As I pulled the trigger I jumped aside out of the smoke, to be ready if he charged; but it was needless, for the great brute was struggling in the death agony . . . the bullet hole in his skull was as exactly between his eyes as if I had measured the distance with a carpenter's rule." He had stepped into the Captain Mayne Reid stories that he had read as a boy.

October 1884 found Roosevelt back in New York, aiming at Democrats in a failed attempt to win the White House for Blaine. In 1886 he ran for mayor of New York City but lost. That same year he married his childhood sweetheart, Edith Kermit Carow, with whom he would have five children.

From 1889 until 1895, TR served on the United States Civil Service Commission, a job that might have consigned others of lesser ambition and energy to obscurity. Roosevelt, however, exposed graft in the New York Customhouse and shifted thousands of federal jobs from appointments made through political patronage to ones earned through merit.

The newspapers covered TR's every move, and given his renown as a reformer, New York Mayor William L. Strong appointed him police commissioner in 1895. In the city, shops and businesses typically greased the palms of patrolmen for favors, and brothels paid bribes to stay open. In short, corruption ruled the police department. TR aimed to root out the grafters. He made headlines early in his term when he fired the police chief and the inspector. He even walked the streets at night in a campaign against laziness; as one newspaper declared: "He Makes the Night Hideous for Sleepy Patrolmen." Not surprisingly, graft declined and efficiency increased.

In 1897 President William McKinley appointed TR assistant secretary of the navy under

John Long. TR's bluster unnerved Long, as did his crusade for an American empire. Roosevelt embraced the ideas of Alfred Thayer Mahan and others who advocated a strong navy and overseas territory. As war with Spain over Cuba loomed, he itched for the fight to begin.

War finally came, and President McKinley ordered three volunteer regiments formed of frontiersmen. TR was asked to command the first regiment, but he deferred to the more experienced Leonard Wood and served as second in command. Despite Wood's higher rank, the men of the First U.S. Volunteer Cavalry—the "Rough Riders"—looked to TR as their forceful leader.

On July 1, 1898, Roosevelt led his men up Kettle Hill and then San Juan Hill at Santiago, a port city along Cuba's southeast shore. Bullets whizzed by him and one grazed his elbow, but with his revolver he shot a Spaniard 10 yards from him. The assault up the hills resulted in 89 casualties among the Rough Riders. Roosevelt's men nonetheless broke through the enemy defenses, their effectiveness causing him to exult, "Look at all these damned Spanish dead!" Roosevelt's victory along with that of the U.S. Navy forced Spain's navy to flee Santiago harbor.

TR returned home in the fall of 1898 as a colonel and a hero. Even Thomas Platt, a political boss who hated him, agreed that for the Republicans to win the New York governorship, TR must run. Roosevelt crisscrossed the state in a vigorous and victorious campaign.

Platt thought he might be able to contain Roosevelt's reform instinct, but the new governor used publicity to an extent previously unknown in the state. He opened his office to reporters and used the newspapers as his "bully pulpit," rallying the people behind his programs to make government more responsive and democratic. He triumphed when he got the legislature to pass a tax on corporations franchised by the state; these businesses, he said, should pay a fair percentage of their profits. Platt at first opposed the bill, but TR forced it to the floor of the legislature, bringing it to the public's full view. With pressure to pass it mounting, Platt fell in line, and Roosevelt scored one of the greatest victories for reform in New York history.

He kept fighting, eventually obtaining a civil service bill stronger than in any other state; a bill to improve working conditions in sweatshops; another limiting the maximum hours that could be worked by women and children; and yet another that established the eight-hour workday for state employees. Time and again he consulted extensively with union leaders and showed a willingness to support labor.

As the 1900 election approached, Republicans talked about making TR President McKinley's running mate. Roosevelt said it was "about the last thing for which I would care." Shortly before the national convention, he angered Platt by forcing the state's corrupt insurance superintendent from office, despite Platt's threats of political retribution. TR told a friend: "I have always been fond of the West African proverb: 'Speak softly and carry a big stick; you will go far.'"

As a result, Platt and other business leaders decided to end TR's gubernatorial career and consign him to political oblivion by helping to elect him vice president. Platt's effort, coupled with a genuine desire by many Republicans to see TR run with McKinley, made the New Yorker his party's vice-presidential candidate. One political boss who opposed the scheme cried out: "Don't any of you realize there's only one life between this madman and the Presidency?"

The "madman" soon ascended. In September 1901 Roosevelt went hiking through the Adirondacks with his wife and a group of friends. On September 13, as he climbed down Mount Marcy, the highest peak in the mountain chain, a ranger came running up to him with a telegraph message in hand. President McKinley, the note said, had died from an assassin's gunshot wound. TR hurried quickly through the night, traveling along rutted mountain roads on a buckboard. On September 14 he reached Buffalo, where he took the oath of office as the 26th president.

Roosevelt announced he would continue McKinley's policies, but his temperament and national developments bespoke change. His desire to command coupled with his disdain for capitalist excesses meant that where McKinley acted cautiously, Roosevelt would act boldly. All around him the Progressive movement was gaining momentum as middle-class Americans demanded reform. They recoiled at the abuses pouring from the new industrial, corporate economy—the immigrant slums, the unsafe working conditions, the contaminated food, the bought and sold votes, the venal and corrupt politicians. TR embraced the Progressive movement and established himself as its leader. He determined to shift power from corporate boardrooms to the White House, or at least let it be known the president would be no mere puppet, his strings pulled by money makers.

When a conservative Congress obstructed Progressivism, Roosevelt acted. In a battle against what he called the "criminal rich," he pursued Northern Securities, a huge holding company that had established a near monopoly over railroads in the northwest and charged shippers high rates. In 1902 he surprised the country when he announced the federal government would sue Northern Securities for violating the Sherman Antitrust Act and for restraining trade. A year later a federal court ordered Northern Securities dissolved, a ruling upheld by the Supreme Court.

TR never saw "trust busting"—forcing big businesses to break into smaller units—as the primary way to control corporate abuses. Instead, he favored regulation by a powerful national government. Nevertheless, trust busting captured the public imagination, and TR realized he could use the courts to restrain capitalists who threatened the country's welfare.

Back in the 1890s, Roosevelt had expressed conservative views toward labor, saying about the Pullman Strike, "I like to see a mob handled by regulars, or by good State-Guards, not over-scrupulous about bloodshed." But he moderated his views while governor of New York, and now he shifted further into labor's camp as a way to counteract corporate power. This was demonstrated during the anthracite coal strike of 1902 when more than 50,000 miners walked out on their jobs. They wanted their union recognized, an eight-hour day, fringe benefits, and a 10 to 20 percent increase in pay. The railroads that owned the mines refused to even talk to the strikers. One industry executive, George F. Baer, said that God had placed large-scale property rights exclusively in the hands of capitalists. His comment angered a public already upset with the rigidity of the railroads.

TR considered the owners arrogant, and he prepared to send 10,000 federal troops into Pennsylvania to run the mines—quite a change from previous presidents, who used troops to crush strikes. The owners reacted by agreeing to submit the dispute to arbitrators appointed by TR. The arbitrators granted recognition to the union, reduced the weekly work hours, and awarded a 10 percent raise, while permitting the companies to raise coal prices by 10 percent. "My business," Roosevelt said, "is to see fair play among all men, capitalists or wage-workers." He wanted "to see to it that every man has a square deal, no more and no less." According to historian George Mowry, "The government had become . . . a third force and partner in major labor disputes."

With the strike settled, in February 1903 Congress established a Bureau of Corporations to investigate businesses engaged in interstate commerce. That same month The Elkins Act, meant to eliminate shipping rebates, became law.

Quite likely no greater domestic issue stirred Roosevelt the hunter and outdoorsman than conservation. He looked with disgust at the raid on resources that was then destroying the landscape. Encouraged by a myth of superabundance—the belief that America's natural resources would never run out—and by economic development, lumber companies clear-cut forests, mining companies stripped bare entire mountainsides with high-pressure water hoses, and petroleum companies allowed oil to gush unstopped from wells.

While preservationists such as John Muir demanded that the national government set aside sites to protect their natural beauty from commercial development, and TR sometimes agreed with him, the president more often agreed with Gifford Pinchot, his chief forester. Pinchot wanted companies to use natural resources but use them carefully. He wanted the national government to set aside forests where scientific principles would prevail. Under an act passed by Congress in 1891, presidents Benjamin Harrison, Grover Cleveland, and William McKinley had set aside 50 million acres as forest reserves. TR began setting aside much more; all told he would convert 150 million acres into reserves. To a group of foresters, he declared: "I hate a man who skins the land."

Roosevelt also set aside game reserves, and in 1902 he signed the Reclamation Act, which authorized the national government to build flood control and irrigation projects in the West. At one point, when a speculator wanted to build tourist businesses along the rims of the Grand Canyon, TR reacted by declaring the site a national monument—a move that required him to loosely interpret existing law. In all, while he occupied the White House, TR created 138 national forests in 21 states, four large wildlife refuges, 51 smaller reserves, and 18 national monuments.

In matters of foreign policy, Roosevelt consulted Congress only when absolutely necessary. Many Progressives wanted a vibrant national government to not only advance reform at home but also advance humanity and extend liberty around the globe, a view with which Roosevelt agreed. He saw the world in three tiers: At the top stood a few powerful civilized nations, in the middle stood the smaller civilized countries of Europe, and at the bottom stood all others. The United States ranked in the first tier and had the responsibility to use its power to benefit humankind.

With TR's expansionist drive wrapped in such moral platitudes, he acted to build a canal in Central America. After Congress passed a bill authorizing him to negotiate with Colombia for land in its territory of Panama, he arranged a treaty whereby the United States would be granted sovereignty in perpetuity over a three-mile strip; Colombia would get $10 million and an annual rent. But the Colombian senate outraged TR when it refused to ratify the treaty and instead demanded more money. He called it blackmail and let it be known that he would welcome a revolution in Panama. American newspapers and magazines soon started talking about the possibility of a Panamanian secession from Colombia.

In 1903 Panama revolted, and the American warship *Nashville* prevented Colombian troops from entering the isthmus to restore their government's authority. Money raised in the United States by Phillipe Bunau-Varilla, who was a French engineer associated with a canal company, financed the revolt. In a treaty signed between Washington and Panama, the United States obtained its canal zone for $10 million. TR at first claimed he had acted constitutionally, but in 1911 he told an audience, "I took the Canal Zone." When it was completed in 1914, the 40-mile long Panama Canal made the United States a formidable sea power in the Pacific.

Roosevelt again displayed American might when the Dominican Republic defaulted on its foreign debts, and Britain, Germany, and Italy threatened to collect the money owed them by sending in their navies. The President reacted in 1904 by announcing the Roosevelt Corollary to the Monroe Doctrine, stating the United States would intervene in the affairs of Western Hemispheric countries where there has been wrongdoing or "an impotence." Then, without congressional approval, he appointed an American as collector of customs in the Dominican Republic, with orders to rearrange the country's finances and pay its debts.

While that event unfolded, Roosevelt sought a second term in the White House. Voters identified him with progressivism and his Democratic opponent, the staid judge Alton Parker, with conservatism. While the Democrats criticized excessive executive power, imperialism, and the protective tariff, Roosevelt's policies met with widespread approval and his strong leadership with acclaim. He won easily, by a margin of nearly 2 million popular votes and by 356-140 in the electoral college.

TR's high-spirited style in the White House continued. He rose early for push-ups, boxed almost every day, and played football on the White House lawn. He led a Boy Scout troop at Oyster Bay, Long Island, and continued to write books, such as *Winning the West*. The public watched with fascination as his daughter Alice, at age 20, acted the emancipated woman with her social life and her cigarette-smoking, and as his little boys frolicked with a bear and sneaked the family pony into the White House.

At his inaugural in March 1905, Roosevelt warned about the danger from great industrial wealth. When Congress again convened, he renewed his reform crusade. The biggest clash occurred between him and a conservative Senate over the Hepburn Bill, which gave the Interstate Commerce Commission the power to fix railroad rates. After a prolonged struggle in which TR made only minor concessions, the bill passed, a tribute to his progressive economic record.

Meanwhile, Roosevelt continued to expand America's role in foreign affairs. In 1904, as Japan and Russia waged war, he worried that the Japanese, emerging victorious, would grab land. He pressured both sides to talk, and in 1905 he mediated a conference at Portsmouth, New Hampshire, that ended the war and guaranteed Manchuria would remain within China. For his effort he received the Nobel Peace Prize.

TR involved himself in Europe in 1906, after differences intensified between Germany and France over Morocco. He arranged a meeting of several European nations, along with delegates from the United States, that convened at Algeciras, Spain, and reached an agreement that affirmed Morocco's independence and stabilized its finances.

That same year, in another domestic reform, he signed the Pure Food and Drug Act, prohibiting the manufacture, sale, or interstate transport of adulterated food, drugs, medicine, or liquor. The act required all ingredients to be labeled accurately. In addition, the Meat Inspection Act passed Congress after Upton Sinclair's factually based novel, *The Jungle*, exposed unsanitary conditions in Chicago's meat-packing industry.

TR returned to his conservation crusade in 1907 when he appointed a commission to study inland waterways and declared in his annual message to Congress: "We are prone to speak of the resources of this country as inexhaustible; this is not so . . . . " He went so far as to declare the conservation of natural resources to be "the fundamental problem which underlies almost every other problem of our national life." In essence, his message was: Respect the land, treat the land honestly and through democratic means, and the same will be done for society at large.

He followed his speech with the White House Conservation Conference in May 1908, a gathering of cabinet members, Supreme Court justices, congressmen, and the governors of 34 states. Never before had the environmental movement been given such publicity. The conference resulted in a widening land ethic, an assault on the myth of superabundance and, more specifically, the founding of the National Conservation Commission, chaired by Gifford Pinchot. This group studied America's mineral, water, forest, and soil resources, marking the first attempt to inventory them.

In a move that displayed TR's political tact as well as his commitment to conservation, he outsmarted Congress when conservatives teamed with lumber interests to attach a rider to a funding bill that would prohibit him from setting aside new forest reserves in several western states. He needed the bill and so could not veto it. But for a time he let it sit on his desk while he created more reserves, after which he signed the appropriations bill. Critics called his action "arrogant," yet they could do nothing about it.

As Roosevelt's second term entered its final year, he arranged the Root-Takahira agreement by which Japan promised to honor open trade in China and respect China's territorial integrity. That same year, TR had sent 16 battleships on a journey around the world to display American power; this "Great White Fleet" stopped in Japan, where it received a warm welcome. Two years later, despite Root-Takahira, Japan and Russia divided North China, Mongolia, and Korea into spheres of influence.

At the Republican National Convention in 1908, TR secured the presidential nomination for his friend, Secretary of War William Howard Taft, whom he expected would continue progressive reform. After Taft won the White House, TR embarked on a safari to Africa, where he killed hundreds of animals—elephants, rhinoceroses, hippopotamuses, zebras, giraffes, and buffalo. He portrayed his activities as pursuing scientific research, but in fact he enjoyed the hunt. His safari never quite meant "roughing it": He stayed in a comfortable tent that included a bath and tea served hot, and he visited at the homes of wealthy Britons.

When Roosevelt returned to New York in 1910, more than half a million people showered him with a boisterous ticker tape parade. He was, according to one observer, "second in interest only to Niagara Falls among American natural phenomena." Before long, differences between TR and President Taft made them enemies. Progressives criticized Taft's support for the Payne-Aldrich tariff, his use of injunctions in strikes, and his digression from Theodore Roosevelt's programs. For his part, TR wanted to return to the White House and renew his fight for reform.

After losing a bitter battle with President Taft for the Republican nomination in 1912, TR ran as a third-party candidate under the Progressive banner, often called the Bull Moose Party (after his comment that he felt as fit as a bull moose). In pronouncing a "New Nationalism," he advocated a bigger and more activist national government to control corporations and to remove politics from the special interests. He never thought big business to be bad, for it brought many economic benefits, but he believed it must be regulated, and he insisted that property be subject to the community's right to manage it for the public good. Much to the dismay of conservatives, he advocated that decisions by state courts nullifying social legislation be subject to a popular vote, and he promoted such measures as workmen's compensation, child labor laws, and a minimum wage for women workers as part of a bold social welfare program.

On October 14, 1912, while on his way to deliver a speech, in Milwaukee, Wisconsin, Roosevelt was standing in an automobile and waving to a crowd when a would-be assassin shot him. The bullet went through TR's jacket and a 50-page folded manuscript before hitting his metal eyeglass case and striking his body. Although the bullet landed near his heart, the objects had blunted its impact. After stating to his doctor, "I will make this speech or die," Roosevelt entered the auditorium, dramatically opened his coat, and showed the shocked audience his blood-stained shirt.

Roosevelt finished ahead of Taft by almost 632,000 votes, but the Democratic candidate, Woodrow Wilson, won the presidency. Roosevelt had failed to win over the progressive Democrats whom he needed.

In 1914 TR joined an expedition and traveled a previously uncharted tributary of the Amazon, the River of Doubt, which was renamed the Theodore Roosevelt River. On his return to the United States, the former president, his voice weakened by jungle fever, spoke about "the mosquitoes, the poisonous ants, the maribondo wasps" that he had encountered. Even his later life was wrapped in Captain Mayne Reid's adventures.

Despite his illness, when World War I began, Roosevelt demanded that Wilson let him form a regiment to fight Germany. The president refused, sending TR into a rage—a characteristic of his whenever someone denied him what he desperately wanted. On January 6, 1919, while Republicans thought about convincing Roosevelt to again seek the White House, he died of a coronary occlusion.

To this day, historians debate whether TR advocated radical reform. He angered many businessmen, but several of his closest advisers came from their ranks, such as George W. Perkins of the House of Morgan and James Stillman of the Rockefeller interests. While Roosevelt pursued reform, he also wanted to maintain the corporation capitalism that had emerged in the late 1800s. Historian Gabriel Kolko believes Roosevelt primarily sought to protect the capitalist system from the challenge presented by socialists. If capitalism failed to show that it could produce modest reforms to alleviate injustices, then socialism would gain power. As such, TR's efforts represented a fine tuning of the system, much as a person would eliminate static from one of the radios then being developed—not by throwing the set out, but by adjusting it.

Another historian, Richard Hofstadter, has called Roosevelt a master at taking popular discontent and channeling it into moderate change. Hofstadter claims that in 1912 TR used the Progressives "for the purposes of finance capital." Some businessmen, in fact, may have feared William Howard Taft more than Roosevelt, given Taft's penchant for trust busting. With socialism on his mind, TR once told Taft: "The dull, purblind folly of the very rich men; their greed and arrogance . . . and the corruption in business and politics, have tended to produce a very unhealthy condition of excitement and irritation in the popular mind, which shows itself in the great increase in the socialistic propaganda."

Whatever the historians' verdict, Roosevelt headed a progressive march that moved the country left of center and produced reforms desperately needed to correct abuses. Few doubted TR's sincerity when he said, "If on this new continent we merely build another country of great but unjustly divided material prosperity, we shall have done nothing; and we shall do as little if we merely set the greed of envy against the greed of arrogance, and thereby destroy the material well-being of all of us."

Chronology

1858 Born October 27

1880 Graduates from Harvard
Marries Alice Lee
Enrolls in law school

1881 Elected to New York state assembly

1884 Alice Roosevelt dies
Martha Bulloch Roosevelt dies

1886 Loses race for mayor of New York City
Marries Edith Carow

1889 Appointed U.S. civil service commissioner

1895 Appointed president of New York City Board of Police Commissioners

1897 Appointed assistant secretary of the Navy

1898 Organizes the Rough Riders
Commands forces at Kettle Hill and San Juan Hill
Elected governor of New York

1900 Elected vice president

1901 Becomes president
Signs Hay-Pauncefote Treaty

1902 Forces arbitration of anthracite coal strike
Instructs federal government to sue Northern Securities Company

1903 Directs negotiations for Panama Canal Zone

1904 Announces corollary to the Monroe Doctrine
Elected president

1905 Mediates Russo-Japanese peace treaty
Wins Nobel Peace Prize

1907 Sends U.S. Navy on voyage around the world

1908 Calls White House conservation conference

1909 Leaves White House
Embarks on African safari

1912 Runs for president on Progressive Party ticket
Loses presidential race

1913 Journeys to South America

1917 Request to raise voluntary division for World War I refused

1919 Dies January 6

Further Reading

Auchincloss, Louis. *Theodore Roosevelt.* New York: Times Books, 2002.

Beale, Howard K. *Theodore Roosevelt and the Rise of America to World Power.* Baltimore: Johns Hopkins University Press, 1956.

Blum, John Morton. *The Republican Roosevelt.* Cambridge, Mass.: Harvard University Press, 1954.

Brands, H. W. *T. R.: The Last Romantic.* New York: Basic Books, 1997.

Collin, Richard H. *Theodore Roosevelt's Caribbean: The Panama Canal, the Monroe Doctrine and the Latin American Context.* Baton Rouge: Louisiana State University Press, 1990.

Cutright, Paul R. *Theodore Roosevelt: The Making of a Conservationist.* Urbana: University of Illinois Press, 1985.

Dalton, Kathleen. *Theodore Roosevelt: A Strenuous Life.* New York: Alfred A. Knopf, 2002.

Gould, Lewis L. *The Presidency of Theodore Roosevelt.* Lawrence: University Press of Kansas, 1991.

Grondahl, Paul. *I Rose Like a Rocket: The Political Education of Theodore Roosevelt.* New York: Free Press, 2004.

Hofstadter, Richard. *The American Political Tradition and the Men Who Made It.* New York: Vintage Books, 1973.

McCullough, David. *Mornings on Horseback.* New York: Simon & Schuster, 1981.

Morris, Edmund. *Theodore Rex.* New York: Random House, 2001.

———. *The Rise of Theodore Roosevelt.* New York: Ballantine Books, 1979.

Mowry, George E. *The Ear of Theodore Roosevelt and the Birth of Modern America.* New York: Harper & Row, 1958.

Pringle, Henry F. *Theodore Roosevelt.* New York: Harcourt, Brace, 1956.

Roosevelt, Theodore. *The Naval War of 1812: Or, The History of the United States Navy During the Last War with Great Britain.* New York: Putnam's Sons, 1882.

———. *The Winning of the West,* 4 vols. New York: Putnam's Sons, 1889–1896.

———. *Rough Riders.* New York: Scribner's Sons, 1899.

———. *History as Literature, and Other Essays.* New York: Scribner's Sons, 1913.

Watts, Sarah. *Rough Rider in the White House: Theodore Roosevelt and the Politics of Desire.* Chicago: University of Chicago Press, 2003.

William Howard Taft (1857–1930)

Twenty-seventh President, 1909–1913

William Howard Taft
(Library of Congress)

"I have had the honor to be one of the advisers of my distinguished predecessor, and, as such, to hold up his hands in the reforms he has initiated. I should be untrue to myself, to my promises, and to the declarations of the party platform upon which I was elected to office, if I did not make the maintenance and enforcement of those reforms a most important feature of my administration."

—Inaugural words, March 4, 1909

Almost everyone who knew William Howard Taft described him as friendly, gregarious, and jovial. He smiled frequently and laughed heartily. But for all that, he endured a miserable presidency. He hated criticism, yet politics meant there would be no escape from it; he disliked pressuring Congress to enact his policies, yet without doing so he crippled his power; he trusted widely, yet often found his trust betrayed.

Some two years into the Taft presidency, essayist William Allen White wrote: "It was evident that the army of progress that had been moving along with President Roosevelt was camped under President Taft." When the "army" received so many contradictory signals that it stayed encamped, the same voters who in 1908 had given Taft one of the biggest victories in presidential history turned against him in 1912 and saddled him with a humiliating defeat.

William Howard Taft was born on September 15, 1857, in Cincinnati, Ohio to Alphonso and Louisa Torrey Taft. Alphonso, a lawyer, had married Louisa two years earlier, after the death of his first wife. Intellectual, energetic, and determined to have more in her life than a husband and children, Louisa founded a local book club, organized a local art association, and campaigned for kindergartens in the public schools. She instilled her ambitious drive in her children, most especially William, with whom she remained close, giving him career advice until her death, shortly before he won the presidential nomination.

William was a chubby boy from birth, and his mother wrote to a friend: "He has such a large waist, that he cannot wear any of the dresses that are made with belts." In grammar school other children called him "Lub" and "Lubber." William graduated from Woodward High School in 1874, upon which he enrolled at his father's alma mater, Yale University. "If you work hard for an examination and do your best in it and get fifty, you will have my sympathy," the elder Taft advised him. "But if you get ninety-five, when you *can* get one hundred, I tell you, I am thoroughly ashamed of you."

Alphonso Taft served as secretary of war in 1875 and then attorney general in 1876 under President Ulysses S. Grant. His son, meanwhile, excelled at college, finishing second in his class. After he graduated in 1878, William began studying law in his father's office and enrolled in the Cincinnati Law School. Two years later he participated in his father's Republican campaign for governor. Alphonso lost, but in 1881 President Chester A. Arthur appointed him ambassador to Austria-Hungary.

In 1883 William Howard Taft also received an office from the president when Arthur named him district collector of internal revenue. This was his second appointive post, his first having been assistant prosecutor in Hamilton County. Taft remarked later in his life that when it came to getting government jobs he was always in the right place at the right time, a record he began straight out of law school. Still, after only one year as collector, he quit in a political dispute with Arthur.

In June 1886 Taft married Helen "Nellie" Heron, whose ambition mirrored his mother's. Nellie was the daughter of John Williamson Herron, a prominent Cincinnati lawyer, former Republican state senator, and friend of President Rutherford B. Hayes. At age 17, Nellie spent several weeks in the White House. That experience, along with her upbringing in a political family, made her want to marry a man who would become president. She constantly pushed Taft toward the White House, even after he insisted he wanted nothing more than to be a judge.

Taft discovered how much he liked serving on the bench in 1887 when he was appointed to the Ohio Superior Court. He felt so right for such a career that he talked about one day serving on the U.S. Supreme Court. Just two years later, he pressured the Ohio governor to intercede with President Benjamin Harrison to get him such an appointment, but Harrison rightly thought Taft too inexperienced and instead named him solicitor general, the federal government's attorney before the Supreme Court. Although Taft hesitated about moving to Washington, Nellie convinced him to accept the post, believing it would drive her husband from the Ohio backwater to the country's political hub.

Yet another appointment came Taft's way after Congress created new appeals courts. In

1892 President Harrison offered him a judgeship on the sixth circuit, covering Ohio, Kentucky, Michigan, and Tennessee. The prospect excited Taft, for here at last he could preside over a federal court. Nellie, however, thought differently and worried that the return to Cincinnati would derail him politically. She warned: "If you get your heart's desire . . . it will put an end to all the opportunities you now have of being thrown with the bigwigs."

Nevertheless Taft accepted, and through the remainder of the 1890s he earned a reputation as a conservative judge. He disliked labor strikes and favored property rights. He hated socialists, and when the Pullman Strike erupted in Chicago, he expressed in private letters his hope that the federal troops stationed there would crush the workers. "There are a lot of sentimentalists who ought to know better," he said, "who allow themselves to sympathize with the wild cries of socialists." About the troops he said, "They have killed only six of the mob as yet. This is hardly enough to make an impression."

Yet he tempered his conservatism and spoke in favor of unions in a case involving a labor leader in the Pullman upheaval. He declared: "It is of benefit to . . . the public that laborers should unite in their common interest and for lawful purposes. They have labor to sell." When he went on to say that a "peaceable strike" would have been acceptable, he advanced the first judicial argument for the right of workers to strike. In 1898 he showed he would protect consumers when he used the Sherman Antitrust Act to rule against the Addyston Pipe and Steel Company for conspiring with other firms to fix the prices of cast-iron pipes.

In 1900, President William McKinley surprised Taft when he asked him to head a commission to govern the recently annexed Philippines. Taft agreed to serve, this time with Nellie's unhesitating support, for although the Philippines were far from Washington, she thought her husband would gain invaluable executive experience.

And he did. While an ongoing Filipino revolt challenged American rule, he followed McKinley's orders to guide the islands to peace and bring the indigenous people into the government. When he was asked about reports that American soldiers had treated Filipinos cruelly, he said the press had greatly exaggerated the situation. Privately, he called American treatment of the rebels too mild.

Taft desired an island economy that would help the Filipinos materially while expanding schools and public services. At the same time, the United States would obtain raw materials. Criticism by anti-imperialists and by one reporter who accused Taft of "great incapacity and great insincerity" puzzled and angered him. Yet his job satisfied him because it allowed him to plunge into the legal issues at which he excelled.

In 1901 McKinley appointed Taft as the first civil governor of the Philippines. The Ohioan envisioned the day the archipelago would be self-governing, but in 1904, when Filipinos demanded more power, he thought them precipitate and claimed they lacked the experience and knowledge needed for sensible politics. Despite McKinley's orders, Taft actually brought few Filipinos into the colonial government.

President Theodore Roosevelt twice offered Taft an appointment to the Supreme Court, but both times he refused, insisting much work remained to be done on the islands. Taft finally left the Philippines in 1904, after Roosevelt made him secretary of war.

The two men, already friends from Taft's days as solicitor general, developed a close relationship. At one point, the Ohioan even handled presidential duties while Roosevelt vacationed. But nothing prepared Taft for Roosevelt's next offer: to make him president.

Theodore Roosevelt was so popular with the voters and so powerful within the Republican Party in 1908 that he could dictate who would succeed him. And he picked Taft. He liked the Ohioan personally—his insight, his friendliness, his honesty—and he believed Taft would support progressive reform. President Roosevelt had assumed the leadership of progressivism, making the national government bigger and more powerful in order to attack industrial capitalism's worst abuses. He set aside national forests, sued corporations for monopolistic restraints on trade, and railed against purveyors of greed.

In the November 1908 election Taft defeated his Democratic opponent, William Jennings Bryan, by more than a million votes. Roosevelt subsequently wrote, "Taft will carry on the work substantially as I have . . . he will do all in his power to further . . . the great causes for which I have fought and . . . he will persevere in every one of the great governmental policies in which I most firmly believe."

Taft quickly disappointed nearly every progressive, foremost among them Roosevelt. Warning signs appeared when the new president appointed five corporation lawyers to his cabinet. He said such legal minds were needed to continue reform without injuring business. Then he tackled an issue his predecessor had avoided for its explosive nature: the tariff. Taft wanted rates revised downward; at his inauguration he called for a special session of Congress to deal with them. But in a subsequent message on the topic he never specifically demanded lower duties, and when the debate began on Capitol Hill he offered little direction. He said about the congressmen, "I am trusting a great many of them, and I may be deceived."

So he was, for they hoodwinked him. After both houses passed somewhat different tariff bills, Speaker Joseph Cannon and Senator Nelson Aldrich packed the ensuing conference committee with those who wanted not a downward adjustment but an upward boost. Big business sought higher rates to protect domestic industries, and they saw the tariff as symbolic, affirming their power; to roll back the rates would be to retreat before a reformist horde.

As the Payne-Aldrich tariff evolved, it raised the duties on more than 600 imports. When Progressives complained, Taft promised he would veto the bill. Then he changed his mind, saying that the bill reduced tariffs on iron ore, scrap iron, coal, and oil and that it provided for a corporate income tax that he liked.

When Taft signed the bill in August 1909, widespread protest erupted, and progressive Republicans deserted him. To make matters worse, on a trip to Minnesota, where progressivism ran strong, he declared: "I am bound to say that I think the Payne Tariff Bill is the best tariff bill that the Republican party ever passed and therefore the best tariff bill that has been passed at all." The *New York Times* reacted by saying, "He no longer apologizes. He accepts, he defends, he is enthusiastic."

Progressives never forgave him for the way he handled the tariff. During the most crucial moments in Congress, when the bill's fate hung in the balance, Taft played golf, his favorite pastime, rather than supply leadership. Then he broke his promise, praised the bill they hated, and on top of that tried to pass off his remarks in Minnesota as hastily written when, in fact, he repeated his statement at a dinner in New York City. His alliance with conservatives indicated trouble for reform; to progressives and many others, his waffling bespoke weakness. Harold J. Laski, writing in his classic work *The American Presidency*, observes that "There is a sense in which the more positive and independent the affirmations of the president, the more, so to say, the springs of his policy are in himself, rather than shared with others, the profounder will be the impact he makes upon the national life. A president who is believed not to make up his own mind rapidly loses the power to maintain that hold." Taft drifted.

He showed little more political savvy in a showdown with Progressives over conservation when Louis Glavis, an investigator for the General Land Office, uncovered evidence damaging to Richard A. Ballinger, secretary of the interior. While serving as commissioner of the land office in 1907, Ballinger had validated land claims made by a group of his friends on the national domain in Alaska. These friends had intended to transfer the land to the Morgan-Guggenheim syndicate and would have done so had not Ballinger been ordered to reverse his action. Now that Ballinger was secretary of the interior, in 1909 he removed Glavis from his continuing investigation. At the same time, Ballinger and Taft agreed that, as president, Theodore Roosevelt had gone too far in planning future environmental works to be completed by the Bureau of Reclamation. Taft said the bureau had been commandeered by "transcendentalists."

Gifford Pinchot, chief forester in the national government and a prominent conservationist and close friend of Roosevelt, forwarded the findings of Glavis's aborted investigation to President Taft. Pinchot intended to use the controversy over Ballinger's background to rally support for protecting the environment and getting Ballinger removed. He supplied information to magazines so they could publish articles critical of Ballinger.He then tested Taft's resolve by having a senator publicly read a letter in which Pinchot praised Glavis, attacked Ballinger, and admitted supplying the damaging information to the press.

Taft knew that if he fired Pinchot for insubordination, Progressives would howl. He could, of course, fire Ballinger at the same time and quiet any protest, but he decided to remove only Pinchot. The progressive outcry rang in his ears. Later, a congressional committee dominated by conservatives exonerated Ballinger of any wrongdoing. The hearings, however, revealed the secretary of interior's opposition to bold environmental reform.

Despite the Ballinger mess, Taft compiled a substantial conservation record. By the end of his term, he had set aside nearly as much public land for protection as had Roosevelt, and in the last year of his presidency he finally dismissed Ballinger and replaced him with Walter L. Fischer, a strong environmentalist.

Still disgusted with Taft over the tariff and the Ballinger-Pinchot fight, Progressives committed themselves to defeating him in the next presidential contest. That the public at large opposed Taft was shown in 1910 when Democrats swept Congress and turned a large Republican majority in the House into a minority.

Taft blundered throughout most of 1910. His anxiety over his failures resulted in an expanding waistline as he hit 355 pounds. Workers installed a new bathtub for him in the White House amid rumors he had gotten stuck in the old one. As he consumed more food, he fell asleep at meetings and social gatherings; once he dozed off while the Speaker of the House was leaning over his chair and talking to him. That Taft golfed almost every day—and would let nothing disturb his game—made him look lazy and detached. He certainly lacked Roosevelt's energy, and on more than one occasion he admitted his inability to keep up with paper work. Although he joked about his weight, he was sensitive to criticism about it, as he was to almost all criticism. He often used his smile and hearty laugh to divert reporters from questions that made him uncomfortable.

Beginning late in 1910, Taft recorded several accomplishments in domestic policy. He backed the Mann-Elkins Bill, written by Progressives in Congress. When it passed, it gave the Interstate Commerce Commission the power to suspend railroad rate hikes for 10 months while reviewing them and to either approve the new rates or reject them.

At Taft's request, Congress created the Commission on Economy and Efficiency to study budgets in the government's departments. This led to a unified budget office after Taft's departure from the White House and shifted the control of financial policy from Congress to the president.

Under Taft, Arizona and New Mexico joined the Union, though he forced Arizona to remove provisions in its proposed constitution pertaining to the recall of judges. In addition, two amendments to the federal constitution passed during Taft's presidency: the Sixteenth, which allowed for an income tax; and the Seventeenth, which stipulated the direct election of senators. Taft, however, expressed little enthusiasm for either.

A new law established the eight-hour workday for government workers, and another established safety regulations for the country's mines. Taft strongly supported civil service reform and extended the merit system to include 35,000 postmasters and 20,000 workers in the naval yards. In all, though, when it came to domestic policy, Congress took the lead, with progressive Republicans and Democrats working together to shape legislation. Taft believed in congressional initiative, and Capitol Hill obliged him.

Beginning in 1910, President Taft's justice department sued several trusts for restraining trade, most notably American Tobacco, Standard Oil, and United States Steel. The government accused the steel company of monopolistic behavior when it bought Tennessee Coal and Iron. Taft's decision to pursue the steel giant infuriated Theodore Roosevelt, who had approved the Tennessee Coal deal in 1907 and now considered the suit a personal affront.

Throughout his presidency, Taft worked to expand overseas trade. He said he wanted to see "the American commercial flag . . . made to wave upon the seas as it did before the Civil War." He so aggressively encouraged bankers and industrialists to invest in foreign lands that observers dubbed his policy "Dollar Diplomacy."

The president supported an Open Door policy in China so the United States could expand its markets, and he forced American entry into a foreign consortium, building a railroad there. He particularly tried to spread American capital in the Caribbean and push out investments by other countries. This, he believed, would help both the United States and Latin America economically, and by expanding American power it would protect the Panama Canal from European interference. Because he believed the United States should supervise the finances of Latin American governments, Taft caused much ill will between those countries and Washington. In 1911 he signed arbitration treaties with Britain and France that called for reviewing any disputes that might lead to war, but the Senate gutted them, and as a result he never concluded their ratification.

As Taft struggled to establish a credible presidency even as found himself isolated from Progressives and unable to excite the public—he once confided to a reporter that he was a dull chief executive—Theodore Roosevelt returned from an African safari to a five-mile-long ticker tape parade in New York City. From there he toured 16 western states, gave over 100 speeches, and addressed more than 250,000 people. He proclaimed a New Nationalism—his program to eliminate special interests from politics, establish direct primaries, and expand the federal government to advance social and economic reforms. He wanted to make the courts subservient to Congress and to the president, with the chief executive the "steward of the public welfare," as he put it.

Taft informed friends and newspaper reporters numerous times that he wanted nothing more than to leave the White House. In 1911 he told one reporter he desired to "go back to private life with no heart burnings." But as Roosevelt publicly aired his differences with the president and determined to capture the Republican nomination in 1912, Taft changed his mind. "I am content with one term and get through with it," he said, "but if they do not look out . . . they may drive me into a second term against their will." He worried about TR's politics, declaring: "He has gone too far. He will either be a hopeless failure if elected or else destroy his own reputation by becoming a socialist, being swept there by force of circumstances just as the leaders of the French Revolution were swept on and on, all their individual efforts failing to stem the tide until it had run itself out."

For the first time, direct presidential primaries were held in 10 states before the national convention. Roosevelt won nearly all of them while viciously attacking his former friend. In one speech he said the president meant well "but he means well feebly." At other times TR called Taft a "puzzlewit," "fathead," and a "man with brains of about three guinea-pig power."

The national convention exposed a Republican Party torn between conservatives and progressives. Delegates engaged in fistfights, extra security patrolled the floor, and barbed wire surrounded the speaker's platform. When

Senator Warren G. Harding nominated Taft with the words, "President Taft is the greatest progressive of his time," Roosevelt's supporters retorted with loud boos.

Had it been left to the party rank-and-file to choose a presidential nominee, Roosevelt would likely have been the one. But the bosses controlled the convention, and after a tough battle with the Progressives, they obtained the nomination for Taft.

Roosevelt then announced he would run as a third-party candidate under the Progressive Party banner. At first he attacked mainly Taft, but when the president failed to fight back, he turned his guns on the Democratic candidate, Woodrow Wilson. Demoralized, Taft campaigned little and golfed more. He told friends he was running only to defeat "socialists"—an inaccurate portrayal of Roosevelt's ideas—and in letters he called Roosevelt a "fakir" who ranked in the same class as the leaders of religious cults.

In the election Wilson won a convincing 435 electoral votes; Roosevelt won 88, while Taft came away with just eight. "Roosevelt was my closest friend," Taft said to a reporter during the campaign . . . and then cried.

In March 1913 Taft returned to private life and accepted the Kent Chair of Constitutional Law at Yale University, where he taught for eight years. Finally, in 1921 President Warren G. Harding appointed him to the post he had long coveted: Chief Justice of the United States. As head of the Supreme Court he wrote the majority opinion in *Myers v. United States* which protected the president's right to remove executive appointees without the advice and consent of the Senate. His conservative decisions in labor cases made unions liable to suits, and in *Bailey v. Drexel Furniture Company* (1919) he ruled unconstitutional an attempt by Congress to tax interstate products made by child labor.

Taft was comfortable on the Supreme Court. His weight went down, and his laugh expressed happiness. He wrote in 1925: "The truth is that in my present life I don't remember that I ever was president." In February 1930 a heart ailment forced him to retire. He died on March 8.

On his election defeat in 1912, Taft said, "I am content to retire from [the presidency] with a consciousness that I have done the best I could. I have strengthened the Supreme Bench, have given . . . a good deal of new . . . legislation, have not interfered with business, have kept the peace, and on the whole have enabled people to pursue their various occupations without interruption." In all, these stand as modest accomplishments from a president who never understood his office, never felt right in performing its duties, and found his greatest joy in his nine years on the Supreme Court, where he could forget that he ever lived in the White House.

CHRONOLOGY

1857 Born September 15

1870 Enters Woodward High School

1878 Graduates from Yale University

1880 Graduates from Cincinnati Law School

1881 Becomes assistant prosecutor of Hamilton County, Ohio

1882 Appointed district collector of internal revenue

1886 Marries Helen Herron

1887 Appointed to Ohio Superior Court

1890 Become U.S. solicitor general

1891 Appointed judge of U.S. circuit court of appeals

1896 Becomes president of Philippine Commission

1901 Appointed civil governor of the Philippines

1904 Appointed secretary of war

1908 Elected president

1909 Proposes reduced tariff rates
Begins "Dollar Diplomacy"

1910 Supports Richard A. Ballinger in conservation controversy

Appoints Commission on Efficiency and Economy

Strengthens Interstate Commerce Commission

Advocates arbitration treaties with France and Britain

1911 Breaks American Tobacco and Standard Oil trusts

1912 Theodore Roosevelt challenges him for Republican presidential nomination

Loses bid for reelection

1913 Appointed Kent professor of constitutional law at Yale University

1918 Appointed chairman of National War Labor Board

1921 Appointed chief justice of the United States

1926 Upholds power of the president to remove appointees

1930 Retires as chief justice

Dies March 8

FURTHER READING:

Anderson, Donald F. *William Howard Taft: A Conservative's Conception of the Presidency.* Ithaca, N.Y.: Cornell University Press, 1968.

Anderson, Judith Icke. *William Howard Taft: An Intimate History.* New York: W. W. Norton, 1981.

Butt, Archibald W. *The Letters of Archie Butt,* 2 vols. Garden City, N.Y.: Doubleday, Page, 1924.

———. *Taft and Roosevelt: The Intimate Letters of Archie Butt, Military Aide,* 2 vols. Garden City, N.Y.: Doubleday, Doran, 1930.

Coletta, Paolo E. *The Presidency of William Howard Taft.* Lawrence: University Press of Kansas, 1973.

Mowry, George E. *The Era of Theodore Roosevelt and the Birth of Modern America, 1900–1912.* New York: Harper & Row, 1958.

Pringle, Henry. *The Life and Times of William Howard Taft,* 2 vols. New York: Farrar & Rinehart, 1939.

*W*OODROW *W*ILSON (1856–1924)

Twenty-eighth President, 1913–1921

WOODROW WILSON
(Library of Congress)

"We are provincials no longer. The tragic events of the thirty months of vital turmoil through which we have just passed have made us citizens of the world. There can be no turning back. Our own fortunes as a nation are involved whether we would have it so or not."

—Inaugural words, second term, March 5, 1917

When Woodrow Wilson was a child, a cousin spotted him looking at a portrait of an old man. "Who is that?" the cousin asked. "That," Wilson replied, "is the greatest statesman who ever lived, Gladstone, and when I grow up to be a man I mean to be a great statesman too."

Wilson long remembered that portrait. Everything he did seemed poised for the day when through force of speech, strength of mind, and purity of virtue he would change a country, even the world. Indeed, in several ways his political career mirrored that of William Ewart Gladstone. A renowned English prime minister, Gladstone changed his beliefs from conservatism to liberalism, stunned audiences with his oratory, and stood adamantly if not stubbornly by his principles.

—∞—

Woodrow Wilson grew up in a family where Presbyterian rectitude meant almost everything. He was born Thomas Woodrow Wilson on December 28, 1856, in Staunton, Virginia, a town surrounded by farms and rolling hills and anchored by a county courthouse and several churches. His father, Joseph Ruggles Wilson, was the minister at the First Presbyterian Church and directed a women's seminary. His mother, Jessie Woodrow Wilson, was the daughter of another Presbyterian minister.

A little more than a year after Woodrow's birth, his father moved to a pastorate in Augusta, Georgia. Woodrow and his two sisters lived there for 12 years, and though for a while he attended a private school, he received most of his education at home. Joseph Wilson was so enthusiastic about learning that he used reference books at evening meals to stimulate debate over current topics. He supported the Confederacy in the Civil War, making Woodrow proud of southern culture. He later said, "The only place in the world where nothing has to be explained to me is the South."

In 1870 Joseph Wilson moved his family again when he accepted a professorship at a theological seminary in Columbia, South Carolina. There Woodrow saw the ravages of the South's lost cause: Union troops had burned the city, and on many streets there stood only skeleton buildings, crumbling walls, and charred chimneys and pillars—forlorn sentries guarding a Southern culture both decimated and defiant.

Three years later Woodrow Wilson joined the Presbyterian church and enrolled at Davidson College near Charlotte, North Carolina. Nervous indigestion forced him to leave the school after his first year, and when he returned home, his family moved once more, this time to Wilmington, North Carolina. In 1875 he resumed his studies when he entered Princeton University in New Jersey.

Over four years, the studious Wilson ranked near the top of his class. He read much and found himself attracted to the study of government and the lives of statesmen. He formed a debating club, penned political works, and made several close friendships. Wilson's essay "Cabinet Government in the United States," which he wrote as a senior, argued that Congress should invigorate its debates by providing cabinet members with nonvoting seats. He earned acclaim in academic circles when the *International Review* published his work.

Wilson graduated from Princeton in 1879 and enrolled at the University of Virginia to study law. "Dry dust," he called it, but he thought it would prepare him for his future as a statesman. Acclaim came his way again in March 1880 when his speech on John Bright, an English politician and orator, attracted a standing-room-only crowd and when the college magazine published an article he wrote about Gladstone. In it he said great men need a moral quality to distinguish them from the commonplace.

Illness forced Wilson to withdraw from the university before receiving his degree. He continued to study law on his own, though, and in 1882 he was admitted to the bar and opened a practice with a partner in Atlanta, Georgia.

Wilson hated the glad-handing required to obtain legal business and wanted a career that would gratify his interest in politics and history while leading him to greater accomplishments. He wanted, he said, to reshape political thought. Consequently, in fall 1883 he entered graduate school at Johns Hopkins University in Baltimore.

By then he was engaged to Ellen Louise Axson of Rome, Georgia. After his book *Congressional Government* received strong reviews in 1885, making his academic career all the more promising, he wrote her: "[It] succeeds because I have taken the lead; and now, the opening having been made, I must come up to my opportunities and be worthy of them. That is enough to sober—as well as enough to inspire—anyone!"

In June 1885, he married Ellen, and that fall he began teaching at Bryn Mawr College, a woman's school, in Pennsylvania. The following June, with his book accepted as his thesis, Johns Hopkins awarded him a Ph.D. According to historian John Morton Blum in *Woodrow Wilson and the Politics of Morality*, the future president sought in his studies to reinforce his ideas rather than challenge them, and in his conservatism he believed in the superiority of the British political system and in American history as an extension of British history.

Beginning in 1888, Woodrow Wilson taught at Wesleyan University in Middletown, Connecticut. Two years later he received a much-desired appointment: full professor of jurisprudence and political economy at his alma mater, Princeton. His reputation spread with his scholarly record; by 1902 he had published five books—including a textbook on comparative government and a history of the Civil War—and numerous articles. Throughout these years, he held many conservative ideas: He opposed restrictions on corporations, criticized labor protests, and supported the gold standard and states' rights.

Three times at the University of Virginia, officials offered him the college presidency, and three times he declined it. He again waited for the call from his alma mater, and again it came—this time in June 1902, when Princeton's board of trustees elected him president.

When Wilson took command, Princeton was facing numerous problems: Too many professors coasted through their work, the curriculum creaked from stagnation, and student social clubs prevailed over academics. Ever the Anglophile, he looked at British educational practices and desired to model Princeton after them.

Wilson tightened standards so much that 25 percent of the class of 1902 quit the college, and entering classes grew smaller. When alumni complained about the declining enrollment, he insisted Princeton needed to stay focused on the long-term benefits that would come from its enhanced prestige.

In 1905, Wilson founded a program using young assistant professors as preceptors who would invigorate learning. The preceptors lived in dorms and met with the students in small conference groups rather than in classes. Wilson encouraged testing students on what they read rather than what their teachers told them, and he discouraged the use of syllabi, saying they resulted in spoon feeding.

In another reform he worked with the faculty to group related academic departments into divisions, the way nearly all colleges are organized today. This allowed Princeton to revise its curriculum so students could spend their first two years in a common program and their last two in their major discipline.

As other colleges adopted Wilson's reforms, his reputation extended well beyond Princeton. Late in 1906, however, he ignited a controversy when he proposed ending upperclass eating clubs, groups similar to fraternities. These clubs split students between those who were offered membership and those who remained outside the clubs. Wilson wanted to build an intellectual environment by having students live together in quadrangles, with each unit largely run by them, and with a shared eating hall and two or three preceptors to guide the group and encourage thoughtful debate. His proposal divided professors and angered alumni. In the end he lost, defeated in part by his imperious manner when he refused to discuss details of his plan with the faculty. Wilson thought about quitting, but he stayed on and quipped, "I didn't get the quads, but I got the wrangles."

While presiding over Princeton, Wilson continued to teach classes in political science and history and used his lectures to try out phrases and develop ideas. At first conservative in his economic views and protective of trusts, he began, by 1910, to condemn excessive concentrations of wealth. Wilson still longed to be a statesman and knew his academic prominence attracted Democratic leaders who thought he might be the right man to win the New Jersey governorship. They liked his wit, his profundity, and his talent for being a good listener. They also liked his scholarly look, though he appeared a bit too stern with his jutting jaw. They overlooked his compulsive and supremely self-righteous character—attributes that made him so stubborn he would sometimes rather suffer defeat than concede a principle. On a personal level Wilson—who dreamed that great speeches "would move people, parliaments, and parties,"—was distant, cold, and aloof and generated more respect than love, or even fondness.

Beyond his desire to achieve reknown as a statesman, Wilson became more receptive to leaving Princeton after he lost a battle with a fellow administrator, Andrew F. West, over where to locate a new graduate school. Meanwhile, George Harvey, publisher of *Harper's Weekly*, began promoting Wilson for public office in 1906, suggesting in an article that the college president would one day make a good United States president. As the 1910 gubernatorial election approached, he brought Wilson together with New Jersey's political bosses. They told him that they wanted to lead him into the White House, and that if he won the governor's office they would support him for the presidential nomination in 1912.

By the time Wilson met with the bosses, his views had changed. Greatly influenced by President Theodore Roosevelt's progressive programs, though opposed to Roosevelt's style, Wilson moderated his conservatism and advocated liberal reform. But the bosses cared nothing for his ideas, wanting only to protect their power. They therefore extracted from him a promise that he "would not set about fighting and breaking down the existing Democratic organization." Wilson desired the White House, the ultimate statesman's job, and he knew what beckoned. "The question of my nomination for the governorship," he wrote a friend, "is the mere preliminary of a plan to nominate me in 1912 for the presidency."

When Wilson ran for governor in 1910, the bosses thought they could control him, while he thought he could outsmart them and advance a righteous cause. "We are witnessing a renaissance of public spirit . . . ," he proclaimed, "a revival of the power of the people . . . that makes our thought hark back to the great age in which democracy was set up in America." Progressives criticized Wilson for the company he kept, but he mollified them when he accepted the Democratic gubernatorial nomination: "I shall enter . . . office . . . with absolutely no pledges of any kind to prevent me from serving the people."

Woodrow Wilson presented himself as a committed progressive, declaring: "I am and always have been an insurgent." However inaccurate that statement regarding the past may have been, as governor-elect Wilson earned his progressive credentials when the Democratic machine pressured the New Jersey legislature to name James Smith, Jr., as the state's next U.S. senator. Progressive Democrats wanted James Martine, who had been chosen in a nonbinding preferential vote. With a constitutional amendment soon to provide for the direct election of senators, the Progressives thought it only fair that popular votes count this time around, and they lobbied Wilson to back their choice. When Wilson agreed, the political bosses realized they would be unable to control the man they had promoted for governor.

Between January and May 1911, the legislature approved Wilson's entire reform program: a law that made city governments more responsive to the people, another that provided for workmen's compensation, and another that gave the Public Service Commission power to set utility rates. His program cost him supporters from the Old Guard, and even George Harvey cooled on the governor. But Wilson rallied Democratic reformers, and as the party's 1912 national conclave neared, he said, "The . . . convention is to be a convention of progressives."

Wilson knew that if he won the presidential nomination, he would likely win the White House because the Republican Party had been shattered by a fight between the incumbent president, William Howard Taft, and his predecessor, Theodore Roosevelt, who had bolted the Republicans and joined the Progressive Party.

Wilson won the Democratic nomination, but it took 43 ballots over nearly seven days before the delegates chose him. On the campaign trail, he and Roosevelt fought hard against each other, while Taft sat on the sidelines. When Roosevelt proposed a social welfare program that included a minimum wage for female workers and a child labor law, Wilson called it paternalistic and went so far as to say that the power his opponent advocated would destroy liberty. Influenced by lawyer and economist Louis D. Brandeis, Wilson said he wanted to protect free enterprise by ending special privileges for business.

As Wilson campaigned from the rear platform of a train and voters shouted "Give it to 'em, Doc," he rallied the Progressives and won, with 435 electoral votes to Roosevelt's 88 and Taft's 8. In a joking mood Wilson wrote to a friend: "It is a fine system where some remote, severe schoolmaster may become president of the United States." Wilson owed his election in part to the work of William F. McCombs, national chairman of the Democratic Party and a conservative, along with other prominent political strategists. Yet, with all seriousness, he told a political leader: "Remember that God ordained . . . I should be the next president of the United States."

Woodrow Wilson considered high tariffs a prime example of a "special privilege;" in preventing lower-priced foreign goods from entering the country, the rates encouraged monopolies and hurt consumers. He wanted the duties lowered, so on April 7, 1913, he called Congress into special session. Wilson presented his request in person, making him the first president since John Adams to speak before Congress. He said he wanted to show that the president could speak with his own voice.

His appearance implied that he, rather than Congress, was representing the people and that they must be heard. He determined to set the national agenda and awaken the presidency from William Howard Taft's lethargy. According to historian Arthur S. Link, "Wilson's strengthening and extension of the presidential powers constituted perhaps his most lasting contribution to American political practice."

One month after his speech, the House passed the Underwood Tariff, which the Senate approved in September 1913. The tariff lowered rates while compensating for any revenue loss by providing for an income tax (as permitted by a recently enacted constitutional amendment).

When Wilson entered the White House, America lacked a coordinated banking system that could bring greater stability to the economy. As a result, conservatives wanted to establish a central bank under private control. Liberals, however, insisted there must to be some form of government oversight. Wilson agreed, and in June 1913 he backed Progressive congressmen who wrote the Owen-Glass Act, which formed district banks supervised by a federal reserve board. Each district bank served as a depository for the national banks and for the state banks.

The Federal Reserve Board could influence the country's credit supply by raising or lowering rediscount rates at the district banks. In addition, the federal reserve banks could issue notes to circulate as part of the money supply, and the number of notes could be expanded or contracted as economic conditions required. Historian John Morton Blum has called the Owen-Glass Act "the most significant piece of domestic legislation of [Wilson's] administration."

To achieve another Progressive goal, President Wilson requested a law to prohibit interlocking directorates (in which board members of one company sat on the boards of other companies), and as a result Congress wrote the Clayton Antitrust Act. Although the act contained several provisions that outlawed specific practices in restraint of trade and gave the Federal Trade Commission power to issue cease-and-desist orders, it was watered down before it passed and only prohibited those interlocking directorates harmful to competition. Progressive Senator James A. Reed of Missouri claimed the Clayton Act had "degenerated to a tabby cat with soft gums, a plaintive mew, and an anaemic appearance."

When it came to African Americans, President Wilson's progressivism left him. At a time when whites flocked to see *Birth of a Nation*, a movie that extolled white supremacy, Wilson's postmaster general, Albert S. Burleson, racially segregated his department (as did other department heads in the federal government) and allowed the postmaster in Atlanta, Georgia, to fire 35 black workers with the claim that persons of their race had no place in the government. Angry African Americans protested, and Booker T. Washington wrote: "I have never seen the colored people so discouraged and bitter as they are at the present time."

Wilson supported Burleson, saying that mixing the white and black races only caused animosity between them. He insisted, "I would say that I do approve of the segregation that is being attempted in several of the departments." When African-American leader William Monroe Trotter met with Wilson at the White House in 1915, the president rejected Trotter's argument that segregation humiliated black workers. The *New York Times* carried the headline, "President Resents Negro's Criticism," while several other northern newspapers criticized the president.

Wilson considered blacks to be politically incompetent and the Fifteenth Amendment, which extended voting rights to them, to be poisonous to southern civilization. He thought the Ku Klux Klan had gone too far with its tactics, but he supported its goal of preventing African Americans from voting.

The moralistic zeal that infused Wilson's domestic reform carried into his foreign policy, called Missionary Diplomacy to distinguish it from President Taft's Dollar Diplomacy. Although Wilson encouraged bankers to invest overseas as a way to extend American influence, he insisted, "The force of America is the force of moral principle."

The president believed in bringing Anglo-Saxon culture to other lands. At one point he said to a British visitor, "I am going to teach the South American republics to elect good men!" Under Wilson the United States intervened in Latin American countries more often than it had under Theodore Roosevelt or William Howard Taft. Wilson sent troops into Santo Domingo and turned Haiti into an American protectorate. To enable the United States to intervene in Nicaragua any time it wanted, he tried to revise a treaty negotiated with that country by Taft, which gave the United States two Caribbean islands and an exclusive option to a canal route for $3 million. After the Senate rejected Wilson's addendum but accepted the rest of the treaty, the *New York Times* called it a bargain so incredibly dirt cheap that dollar diplomacy was being replaced by "ten-cent diplomacy."

When conservatives in Mexico under Victoriano Huerta staged a coup in 1913 and murdered the country's ruler, Wilson withdrew diplomatic recognition and funneled weapons to Venustiano Carranza, the leader of rebel forces. Then, in April 1914—before Congress could give its approval—Wilson ordered the U.S. Navy to seize the port city of Veracruz to prevent German arms from falling into Huerta's hands. The ensuing battle (which began after the House of Representatives finally approved Wilson's armed intervention) resulted in 126 Mexicans and 19 Americans killed. With war looming, and with widespread protests against Wilson's actions, he finally accepted mediation of the dispute.

But the Mexican adventure soon resumed. In August 1914 Carranza overthrew Huerta, an event Wilson welcomed until Carranza said he wanted the United States to mind its own business. Wilson then backed another rebel, Pancho Villa, who subsequently tried to drag the United States into war with Carranza by killing a group of Americans. When Carranza failed to do anything about the murders, Wilson sent 12,000 troops under General John J. Pershing to track down Villa. They entered Mexico, and once again it looked like war would erupt. Villa raided across the U.S. border, but Wilson eventually withdrew the American troops, ending the intervention so he could prepare for war with Germany. His meddling did little more than sour relations with Mexico for years to come.

When World War I began in Europe in August 1914, Wilson declared the United States would be neutral in thought and deed, and most Americans applauded his stand. In an editorial the *New York Sun* said, "There is nothing reasonable in such a war . . . and it would be folly for the country to sacrifice itself to the frenzy of dynastic policies and the clash of ancient hatreds." The *Literary Digest* said with obvious relief, "Our isolated position and freedom from entangling alliances inspire our press with the . . . assurance that we are in no peril of being drawn into the European quarrel."

While Wilson confronted the foreign crisis, his wife Ellen died from a kidney ailment in August 1914. Although he had engaged in an affair with Mary Hulbert Peck from 1908 until 1910, he had since reconciled with Ellen and strengthened their marriage. About her death he said, "God has stricken me beyond what I can bear." He went into a prolonged depression, which hindered him in dealing with the European war.

In the spring of 1915 he met Edith Galt, a 43-year-old Washington widow whom he called "a special gift from Heaven." As newspapers covered their courtship, he proposed marriage in May, and in December they were wed in a quiet ceremony at her home in Washington, D.C.

From the outset of the world war, Wilson found it difficult to maintain his declared neutrality. Germany's invasion of Belgium, which violated a treaty it had signed to respect that country's border, convinced many Americans that the Germans had started the conflict, and many political leaders believed that should Germany win, its navy would threaten U.S. interests in the Caribbean and the Pacific.

Like Wilson, most of his advisers greatly preferred British culture. This was especially true of Colonel Edward M. House, a wealthy Texan who, despite holding no government post until after the war, exerted more influence over the president than any other person. "Mr. House is my second personality," Wilson said. "He is my independent self. If I were in his place I would do just as he suggested." House considered Germany a militaristic threat to world peace.

Wilson's favoritism toward Britain was evident in his reaction when the warring countries violated America's rights as a neutral nation. Late in 1914 Britain announced a naval blockade of Germany. Wilson protested, but mildly. The *New Republic* said that "a benevolent American government did not intend to cause the Allies any serious embarrassment." The president's response resulted in part from America's limited trade with Germany, in contrast to its extensive trade with Britain.

When Britain announced it had placed mines in a zone in the North Sea, a strategy that risked blowing up neutral ships, Wilson again said little. But after Germany reacted to the mining by declaring a submarine zone around the British Isles, Wilson replied that if a U-boat should hit an American ship, it would be deemed a "flagrant violation of neutral rights."

Germany's belligerence increased in May 1915 when one of its submarines sank the British passenger ship *Lusitania* causing the deaths of 1,200 people, among them more than 100 Americans. Although urged by several political leaders to declare war, Wilson initially took a moderate stand and continued to pursue diplomatic negotiations. In March 1916, however, a German submarine attacked the *Sussex*, a French passenger steamer, injuring four Americans. Wilson reacted to the incident by calling submarines "incompatible with the principle of humanity," and he threatened to cut diplomatic relations with Germany if submarine warfare continued. The Germans subsequently issued the Sussex Pledge, in which they promised to suspend attacks made without warning but reserved the right to resume them should the

United States fail to get Britain and the other allied countries to abide by international law.

President Wilson accepted the first part of the Sussex Pledge while ignoring the second and headed into the 1916 presidential campaign with the statement "I am not expecting this country to get into war." He won a second term by a razor-thin margin of 277 to 254 electoral votes over former Supreme Court Justice Charles Evans Hughes, who had attracted the support of many Progressives.

Wilson tried to negotiate an end to the war while continuing to follow his uneven policy toward the British and the Germans. Then, on January 31, 1917, a German diplomat handed Secretary of State Robert Lansing a note that said his government would begin unrestricted submarine warfare. A few weeks later the British released the text of a telegram they had intercepted that had been sent by German foreign secretary Arthur Zimmerman to the Mexican government. In his telegram, Zimmerman proposed that should America go to war with Germany and then Germany and Mexico should form an alliance to help Mexico recover land it had lost to the United States in the 1800s. With these developments, Wilson asked Congress for permission to arm American merchant ships for self-defense. When opponents in the Senate began a filibuster, he ordered the ships to be armed anyway.

After Germany attacked three American ships, Wilson asked Congress to declare war. He declared: "The world must be made safe for democracy." With that moral crusade as its banner, the Senate voted for war, 82-6, on April 4, followed by the House, 373-50, on April 6. To keep American forces independent from European command, the United States entered the fight as an associate, not as an ally.

In January 1918 Wilson announced his Fourteen Points, which he hoped would be the basis of international reorganization and world peace. They called for reduced armaments; freedom of the seas; self-determination for all peoples; and foremost, "a general association of nations . . . for the purpose of affording mutual guarantees of political independence and territorial integrity to great and small states alike." In the meantime, Germany nearly defeated the Allies with several offensives until, in the summer of 1918, U.S. troops secured a victory.

That fall President Wilson urged Americans to show their support for him by electing Democrats to Congress. The result embarrassed him when Republicans gained control of both the House and the Senate. A few days later he signed an armistice with Germany, and in a bold move he announced that he would sail to Paris and lead the American delegation at the scheduled peace conference. Never before had a sitting president visited Europe, and Wilson risked damage to his prestige should the conference disintegrate into petty squabbles. He immediately raised a controversy and weakened his entire effort when he failed to appoint any prominent Republicans to his negotiating team.

In Europe huge crowds greeted him, hailing him as a savior and the prince of peace. Typical of the prevailing sentiments, one French woman exclaimed, "You have saved our fiancés; love blooms again, Wilson, you have saved our children. Through you evil is punished. Wilson! Wilson! Glory to you, who, like Jesus, have said: Peace on Earth and Good Will to Men!"

Wilson tried to get the leaders from Britain, France, and Italy to adopt his Fourteen Points as the basis of his postwar settlement, but he was largely ignored. The Treaty of Versailles ceded lands to France, Japan, and Italy, leaving self-determination badly damaged; much to Wilson's dismay, the Allies sought revenge and punished Germany with harsh reparations, while forcing the vanquished country to accept full responsibility for the war.

The negotiations tore the American diplomatic team apart when Wilson and Edward House disagreed over several terms in the settlement. Wilson also recoiled at how Europeans referred to House as the American "prime minister." Influenced by Edith Wilson, who was jealous of House, the embittered president ended his friendship with his longtime colleague.

Wilson sacrificed nearly all his Fourteen Points by making concessions to obtain what mattered most to him: the League of Nations and in particular Article X of its charter, which committed the signatories "to respect and preserve" the territories and independence of all League member states. On one level the League reflected the president's idealistic hopes for global peace and his belief that the world body could solve all international problems. On another it reflected his realistic response to a revolution then underway in Russia in which the communists blamed the world war on capitalism and urged Europeans to overthrow the economic system. With the League, Wilson wanted to show that capitalism could reform itself; in effect, he wanted to apply progressivism to the world scene.

Wilson fought communism in another way when he ordered American troops to join those of Britain, France, and Japan in invading Russia. In late summer 1918, about 9,000 Americans landed at Vladivostok in Siberia and another 5,000 at Murmansk. Wilson sent the troops for several reasons, among them to help the Czech army make its way back to Europe and to keep Russian weapons from falling into German hands; another goal was the disruption of the Bolshevik government. The invasion accomplished little, however, and he withdrew American forces in July 1919.

At home Wilson's peace plan ran into opposition from Republicans and others who feared the League of Nations Charter would drag the United States into foreign wars or that Article X (which stated that member nations would defend each other) would be used by other countries to invade America. Wilson refused to compromise his moral crusade and set out to secure public support. Beginning in September 1919, he traveled thousands of miles and delivered more than 40 speeches to rally support for the treaty. Exhausted, on September 25 at Pueblo, Colorado, he suffered a slight stroke.

Wilson canceled the remainder of his trip and returned to Washington. On October 2 he suffered a second stroke that left him partially paralyzed. For the next seven months he lived as a recluse, his judgment so impaired that his private secretary, Joseph Tumulty, and Edith Wilson conducted presidential business.

When Henry Cabot Lodge, a powerful Republican senator from Massachusetts, agreed to vote for the treaty but with changes, Wilson rejected them. In November 1919 the president's treaty, and with it his League of Nations, went down to defeat. Despite the loss, Wilson received the Nobel Peace Prize for his work.

Eventually the president's health became so impaired that on March 4, 1921, he was able to attend Warren G. Harding's inauguration only after being bodily lifted into the car that took him to the Capitol. He lived the remaining three years of his life in continued seclusion and died on February 3, 1924, after having said his last word: "Edith."

Under President Warren G. Harding, Congress passed a joint resolution officially declaring hostilities with Germany to be at an end. As for the Treaty of Versailles, although some scholars blame Republican obstruction for its defeat, others blame Wilson's obstinacy. Whatever the verdict, history remembers Wilson less for his educational reforms at Princeton, his progressive reforms in the White House, or even his success in leading his country to victory in a world war than for the tragedy that befell him when he refused to compromise on the League of Nations. That he "won the war but lost the peace" haunts his legacy.

Chronology

1856 Born December 28

1873 Enters Davidson College

1875 Enters Princeton

1879 Studies at University of Virginia law school

1882 Admitted to the bar

1883 Enters Johns Hopkins University graduate school

1885 Publishes *Congressional Government*
Marries Ellen Axson
Teaches at Bryn Mawr

1886 Receives Ph.D. from Johns Hopkins

1888 Teaches at Wesleyan

1890 Appointed professor at Princeton

1902 Named president of Princeton

1910 Elected governor of New Jersey

1912 Elected president

1913 Proposes lower tariff rates to Congress
Signs Owen-Glass Act establishing Federal Reserve System

1914 Gets Congress to establish Federal Trade Commission
Orders troops to occupy Veracruz, Mexico
Proclaims American neutrality in European war
Ellen Wilson dies

1915 Marries Edith Galt

1916 Sends troops across Mexican border
Reelected president

1917 Breaks diplomatic relations with Germany
Asks Congress to declare war on Germany

1918 Issues Fourteen Points
Sails to France to attend peace conference

1919 Helps draft Treaty of Versailles and League of Nations Covenant
Tours country to promote Treaty of Versailles and League of Nations
Crippled by stroke
Awarded Nobel Peace Prize

1921 Retires to private life

1924 Dies February 3

FURTHER READING

Auchincloss, Louis. *Woodrow Wilson.* New York: Viking Press, 2000.

Baker, Ray Stannard. *Woodrow Wilson: Life and Letters,* 8 vols. New York: Doubleday, Doran, 1927–1939.

Blum, John Morton. *Woodrow Wilson and the Politics of Morality.* Boston: Little, Brown, 1956.

Brands, H. W. *Woodrow Wilson, 1913–1921.* New York: Times Books, 2003.

Heckscher, August. *Woodrow Wilson: A Biography.* New York: Scribner's, 1991.

Knock, Thomas J. *To End All Wars: Woodrow Wilson and the Quest for a New World Order.* New York: Oxford University Press, 1992.

Levin, Phyllis Lee. *Edith and Woodrow: The Wilson White House.* New York: Scribner, 2001.

Link, Arthur S., ed. *The Papers of Woodrow Wilson.* Princeton, N.J.: Princeton University Press, 1966–1994.

———. *Woodrow Wilson and the Progressive Era, 1910–1917.* New York: Harper & Brothers, 1954.

———. *Woodrow Wilson and a Revolutionary World, 1913–1921.* Chapel Hill: University of North Carolina Press, 1982.

Macmillan, Margaret. *Paris 1919: Six Months That Changed the World.* New York: Random House, 2002.

Smith, Daniel M. *The Great Departure: The United States and World War I, 1914–1920.* New York: Alfred A. Knopf, 1965.

Smith, Gene. *When the Cheering Stopped: The Last Years of Woodrow Wilson.* New York: Morrow, 1964.

Tribble, Edwin, ed. *A President in Love: The Courtship Letters of Woodrow Wilson and Edith Bolling Galt.* Boston: Houghton Mifflin, 1981.

Unterberger, Betty Miller. *The United States, Revolutionary Russia, and the Rise of Czechoslovakia.* Chapel Hill: University of North Carolina Press, 1989.

Walworth, Arthur. *Wilson and His Peacemakers: American Diplomacy at the Paris Peace Conference.* New York: W. W. Norton, 1986.

———. *Woodrow Wilson*, 2nd ed. Boston: Houghton Mifflin, 1965.

Warren G. Harding (1865–1923)

Twenty-ninth President, 1921–1923

Warren G. Harding
(Library of Congress)

"Service is the supreme commitment of life. I would rejoice to acclaim the era of the Golden Rule and crown it with the autocracy of service. I pledge an administration wherein all the agencies of Government are called to serve, and ever promote an understanding of Government purely as an expression of the popular will."

—Inaugural words, March 4, 1921

Over the 20 years before Warren G. Harding was elected president, Americans had fought in the Philippines against rebels, sent troops into Mexico, and battled in the "war to end all wars," World War I. Their economic base had changed quickly and dramatically from farms to factories—a fitful development filled with strikes, violence, and doubts about how an industrial society should be governed. They had crusaded for reform, with the Progressive movement leading the way in attacking the worst economic and social abuses.

Now Americans longed for quiet. Their international foray in World War I had turned out disappointing, their domestic overhaul exhausting. Into that atmosphere appeared Harding with the words, "I do not believe that anywhere in the world there is so perfect a democracy as in the village."

If the village meant probity, stability, and trust, Americans would be disappointed again. Harding's presidency exposed probity to graft, stability to tumult, and trust to lies. The greed that corrupted Harding's friends and the deceit with which they worked destroyed his administration, broke him, and maybe even killed him. Coupled with his own limited talent and limitless incompetence, they made for what many consider to be the worst presidency in America's history.

Warren Gamaliel Harding, the oldest of eight children, was born on November 2, 1865, in Blooming Grove, located in north-central Ohio, to George Tryon Harding and Phoebe Dickerson Harding. Over the years, his father worked at several different jobs—farming, teaching, and practicing medicine—while dabbling in real estate speculation. Always closer to financial ruin than success, he was still able to maintain his family in a middle-class setting.

Warren Harding attended the local rural school. Never possessed of a brilliant mind, he preferred play to study. In 1879 his parents sent him to Ohio Central College with the hope he would become a minister. He joined the school band, occasionally entered debates, and served as the yearbook editor.

On graduating in 1882, Harding taught school. He later called it the hardest job he ever had. He did not like having to discipline the children, nor did he like the rumors that followed him into the classroom and that the students whispered—that he was part black, an ancestral trait supposedly dating back to the 18th century. After one term he quit teaching and moved to Marion, a farming town then attracting small manufacturing businesses, where his father had relocated his family.

For several months Harding drifted. He studied law but found it too boring; then he sold insurance. In 1884 he worked as a reporter for the *Marion Democratic Mirror* at $1 per week, but when he supported the Republican presidential candidate, James G. Blaine, the paper fired him. He believed, however, that he had found an occupation he liked. Late in 1884 he raised $300 and, with two partners, bought the *Marion Star*. This failing newspaper struggled to generate an income, and in short order Harding's partners sold out to him. Still, he gradually built its circulation, and along with the daily *Star* he printed the *Weekly Star*, an openly Republican paper intended to attract advertising revenues from political candidates.

Like many a small-town publisher, the usually genial Harding attacked his opponents with gusto. When a competing editor accused him of abandoning his principles in order to fill his wallet with Republican money, Harding retaliated: "This Crawford . . . foams at the mouth whenever his sordid mind grasps anything done without his counsel. This sour, disgruntled, and disappointed old ass [is] an imbecile whose fits will make him a paralytic, then his way of spitting venom will end."

Harding found it hard to say no to anyone, and in 1891, in an unlikely match, he married Florence Kling De Wolfe. A 31-year-old widow with a son, she pursued the handsome Harding, then only 26, with a vengeance. The more he rebuffed her, the more she went after him, showing up at his office, greeting him at the train station, and chasing him down when he tried to sneak away from her. She was far from beautiful, and the couple was far from being in love. Why they married remains puzzling. Because she came from Marion's leading family, she brought some wealth to the partnership, but her father, a real estate agent and banker, had a falling out with her shortly before she married Harding, so the money may not have amounted to much.

From the start, Florence Harding dominated her husband. She took over the newspaper and revitalized it—a much-needed move as he preferred playing poker to working. "She makes life hell for me," Harding once said and only half in jest called her "Duchess."

To some extent Warren Harding entered politics to get away from his wife. But he also genuinely liked the political world. In 1892 the Republicans asked him to run for county auditor, and he agreed, knowing full well he would lose to the much stronger Democratic machine. Long involved in civic clubs, Harding traveled the state, and as his newspaper grew in size and prominence, he spoke at Republican meetings. He was proud of his speaking skill, and many a listener agreed that with his oratory and good looks, he could win public office.

Harding ran for state senate in 1898 in the district comprising Hardin, Logan, Union, and Marion counties and won. He enjoyed the conviviality he found in the legislature—being away from home, hanging around with the boys, and playing poker. Two years later he was reelected.

While Harding served in the legislature, Harry M. Daugherty took notice of him. A shrewd political boss and lobbyist, Daugherty looked at Harding's appearance and manners and, thinking in grand terms, concluded his fellow Ohioan would make a great president. In 1902 he convinced Harding to run for lieutenant governor. Harding won, but bickering within the Republican Party caused him to refuse reelection.

Harding returned to his newspaper while factional fights among Republicans continued, and the Democrats dominated the state. In 1910 Daugherty ran Harding for governor. Although Harding lost, he received a boost in 1912 when President William Howard Taft selected him as his nominating speaker at the Republican National Convention. Later that year he again ran for governor—and again lost.

At that point he thought about quitting politics for good, but in 1914 Daugherty convinced him to seek the U.S. Senate. This time he won. Much as he had in the Ohio legislature, Harding enjoyed serving in the Senate. He went to the horse track, played golf, and sat down with his buddies for endless hands of poker. With such a schedule he answered only 50 percent of the roll calls, and no one ranked him higher than mediocre in ability, but he made many friends.

Harding seldom took a stand on issues, yet he opposed measures that regulated industry, disliked the Prohibition amendment—though he voted for it after he saw it would pass—and supported President Woodrow Wilson's war effort. By and large, other senators found Harding outgoing and completely harmless.

Without Daugherty, and without the changing times, Harding's career would have amounted to little more than being an obscure senator. He showed no burning desire to reach the White House and several times said the presidency required more talent than he could possibly muster. Nevertheless, in 1916 Daugherty arranged for Harding to serve as the keynote speaker at the Republican National Convention, a prelude to a greater moment. Two years later World War I ended, and Americans were soon expressing deep regret over their involvement in it. Bickering among European nations that wanted retribution against Germany bespoke the same old world rather than the new harmonious one promised by Wilson.

Americans also grew tired of progressive domestic crusades, as well as with the strife and problems associated with industry. Many waxed nostalgic and longed for a supposedly simpler past, when their country avoided foreign involvement and rural villages encouraged community.

Harding came from a small town, and his statements were in accord with this nostalgia. Where progressives questioned society, Harding reassured Americans that their modern economic system produced more good than bad. "American business is not a monster," he said. "It is the guardian of our happiness."

In summer 1919 Pennsylvania senator Boies Penrose, another Republican boss, joined Daugherty in backing Harding for the presidency.

Harding ran in three primaries, winning one narrowly and losing the other two handily, but because there were few such contests back then and because they lacked the influence they have today, it was Daugherty's dealing that would make the difference in whether Harding got the nomination. To reporters Daugherty predicted the Republicans would make their choice not on any convention floor, but hidden away in a hotel room in the early morning hours.

At the 1920 Republican National Convention in Chicago—the first one where women attended as delegates—a deadlock developed between the two front-runners: General Leonard Wood, backed by soap manufacturer William Cooper Procter, and Frank Lowden, governor of Illinois. The political bosses, however, distrusted Wood as too reform minded and distanced themselves from Lowden after newspapers revealed that his supporters used money to convince delegates to vote for him. The bosses wanted someone with a spotless record and someone they could control.

Meeting at two o'clock in the morning, in a since-legendary smoke-filled room at the Blackstone Hotel, 15 Republican leaders decided to anoint Warren G. Harding, knowing full well that almost anyone they picked would ride the wave of public discontent with the Democrats into the White House. First, however, they met with Harding and asked him if there might be anything in his past that would cause embarrassment. He thought about it for awhile and then said no.

Harding won on the 10th ballot. The longtime poker player said, "I feel like a man who goes in on a pair of eights and comes out with aces full." Only six months earlier he had told a friend, "The only thing I really worry about is that I might be nominated."

Boies Penrose, on his deathbed, advised his fellow Republicans to keep Harding quiet for fear the candidate would blow the election. As a result, party leaders devised a front-porch campaign where Harding mainly stayed at home, though he did make a few public speeches and campaigned on a limited whistle-stop tour. As photographers crowded around Harding, his wife protected his image. "Just let me catch him lighting a cigarette where any hostile eye might see him!" Florence Harding said. "He can't play cards until the campaign is over, either."

Harding stuck to broad generalities, but at various times he called for a high tariff, the creation of a public welfare department, and restrictions on immigration. At Cleveland, Ohio, he said, "I want my chance to lead in making America a land where men and women place the welfare of America above their own selfish interests; where no class contentions can arise because men's minds understand other men's hearts and aspirations; where the strong serve all of us to the end that all of us may serve the weak."

As victory neared, Harding grew more confident. A friend, Evalyn Walsh McLean, recalled: "The constant adulation of the people was beginning to have an effect on Senator Harding. He was more and more inclined to believe in himself. He cherished an idea that when a man was elevated to the presidency his wits by some automatic mental chemistry were increased to fit the stature of his office."

Harding reaped the benefits of the front-porch strategy and the desire of voters to oust the Democrats. Voters responded enthusiastically when he said, "America's present need is not heroics, but healing; not nostrums, but normalcy; not revolution, but restoration." He defeated his opponent, James M. Cox, a self-made millionaire and progressive reformer, by a margin of 404 to 127 electoral votes.

President Harding appointed several men with outstanding backgrounds to his cabinet, including Charles Evans Hughes as secretary of state, Herbert Hoover as secretary of commerce, and Henry Wallace as secretary of agriculture. Later in 1921 he named former president William Howard Taft to the Supreme Court as Chief Justice of the United States.

Other appointments caused dismay, most notably Albert B. Fall as secretary of the interior and Harry Daugherty as attorney general. Fall held strong anticonservation views and angered environmentalists. Daugherty's qualifications amounted to little more than a law degree and many years as a backroom political manipulator. To critics Harding responded, "Harry Daugherty has been my best friend from the beginning of this whole thing. He tells me he wants to be attorney general, and by God he will be attorney general."

Early in 1922 President Harding invited the world's powers to the Washington Armament Conference. He appointed Charles Evans Hughes, Elihu Root, Henry Cabot Lodge, and Oscar Underwood to the American delegation. The countries signed nine different treaties. In one, the United States, Britain, France, Italy, and Japan agreed to a 10-year moratorium on the building of warships displacing more than 10,000 tons. In another, all those present guaranteed China's territorial integrity. Although the U.S. Senate ratified the treaties, it expressed its continued postwar hostility to foreign entanglements when it insisted "there is no commitment to armed force, no alliance, no obligation to join in any defense."

During his first year in office, Harding ignored the advice of Republican leaders and pardoned socialist Eugene V. Debs, a family friend then in jail for having violated the Sedition Act during World War I. He appointed Charles G. Dawes to reform the budget process, a move that led to more responsible accounting. In 1922 he signed the Fordney-McCumber Act, which established the highest tariff yet, while he vetoed a bill to provide a bonus for war veterans, saying the government lacked the money to pay for it.

Writing in *American Heritage* magazine in July 1998, Carl S. Anthony emphasizes Harding's commendable qualities and his laudable accomplishments on the domestic scene. He notes, for example, that Harding stood up for laborers when he backed collective bargaining and pressured businesses to reduce the typical 12-hour day as a way to lessen injuries in factories and mines. The president showed his support for technology when he promoted the 1921 Federal Highway Act, a bill that provided $75 million for building a national highway system.

Unusual for the times, Harding showed no racial or ethnic bias. He went against society's widespread anti-Semitism and appointed his good friend Albert Lasker, a Jew, to head the Shipping Board. While speaking in the South, the president advocated black civil rights and called for equality in education, employment, and politics. Although he tempered his remarks by saying whites and blacks should remain separate socially, he challenged practices that white supremacists considered essential, and he introduced into Congress an antilynching law, which the Senate rejected.

Yet according to William Howard Taft, Harding expressed racial views that corresponded with popular prejudice. When Taft urged Harding to protect Republicans in the South by appointing only whites to offices there, the president agreed and, Taft noted, "said sarcastically that this was a matter he must of course give attention to because of his reputed ancestry. . . . He said he believed in a Lily White Republican party and not a Black and Tan."

Whatever Harding's accomplishments, he thought Congress should take the lead on most matters, and when he disagreed with Capitol Hill he usually conceded his point. More damning, corruption ruined his presidency. As with Ulysses S. Grant, known for the most scandalous White House prior to Harding's, the president trusted others too much.

From the beginning of Harding's tenure, a poker-playing friend, Charles Forbes, accepted kickbacks as head of the Veterans' Bureau when he sold "surplus material" at prices well below what they cost the government. In one instance he unloaded 84,000 unused bedsheets, for which the government had paid $1.37 each, for 26¢ each. At other times Forbes bought items at inflated prices. In another scheme he received money in exchange for fixing bids on hospital construction projects. President Harding learned about his friend's conduct in 1922, called him to the White House, yelled at him, and shoved him against a wall. Early in 1923 Harding fired Forbes.

In March, Charles F. Cramer, attorney for the Veterans' Bureau, shot himself to death after writing several letters to Harding, all unsent. Stories circulated that the letters told about more graft. But they mysteriously disappeared, likely picked up and destroyed by William J. Burns, head of the federal government's Bureau of Investigation.

Harding probably heard about other scandals. One in particular involved another of his friends, Jesse Smith, a loud-mouthed and, to many, obnoxious man who was Harry Daugherty's close companion. Since the beginning of Harding's tenure, Smith, Daugherty, and the rest of their "Ohio Gang" had sold government jobs from their "Little Green House" on K Street in Washington. Although Harding knew nothing about the payoffs, he approved the appointments. Smith made more money when he issued government licenses to distillers so they could sell liquor "for medicinal purposes" during Prohibition. In March 1923, Harding advised him to avoid an investigation by leaving town. Soon after, Smith was found dead with a .32-caliber revolver in his hand. Evidence showed he had been burning his correspondence. An inquiry ruled his death a suicide, but many suspected he had been murdered to keep him quiet.

Harding's job genuinely baffled him. To one friend he said, "I listen to one side and they seem right, and then—God!—I talk to the other side and they seem just as right, and here I am where I started. I know somewhere there is a book that will give me the truth, but hell!—I couldn't read the book." To another he said, "I knew that this job would be too much for me." And to journalist William Allen White he said, "My God, this is a hell of a job! I have no trouble with my enemies. I can take care of my enemies all right. But damn my friends, my God-damn friends, White, they're the ones that keep me walking the floor nights!"

To escape his troubles—most still hidden from public view—he decided to tour the West, but escape proved elusive. While in Kansas City, the wife of interior secretary Albert Fall visited him. After their conversation, Harding appeared more troubled than ever. By the time he reached the Pacific Coast, he was openly talking about betrayal. At one point he called Herbert Hoover into his shipboard cabin and asked him, "If you knew of a great scandal in our administration, would you for the good of the country and the party expose it publicly, or would you bury it?" Hoover advised him to expose it.

Harding traveled to Alaska and then arrived in Seattle, where he fell ill from eating bad crabmeat. He improved and continued his trip but in San Francisco he caught pneumonia. Headlines in the *San Francisco Chronicle* revealed a rapid change. "PRESIDENT RAPIDLY IMPROVING," one said, only to be followed by another just a day later: "HARDING DEAD." Doctors believed a blood clot killed him on August 2, 1923, but Florence Harding, who had been with him on the trip, refused to allow an autopsy. Soon rumors circulated: The president, depressed over scandals yet to be revealed, killed himself; or Florence Harding, angered by her husband's affairs with several women, killed him. In truth, Harding had suffered from high blood pressure and other problems before the trip, and stress over the unfolding scandals may have contributed to his death.

The country saw Harding as a decent man who stood above graft, and so it mourned him. Then the Teapot Dome scandal broke, and it became difficult to find anyone who would even attend the interment of his body in his tomb, built several months after his death. A Senate committee, led by Democrat Thomas J. Walsh of Montana, began hearings in October 1923. Walsh found that Albert Fall, who had retired from the cabinet in March, had accepted $400,000 from two millionaires: E. L. Doheny of the Pan-American Petroleum Company and Harry F. Sinclair of the Mammoth Oil Company. The two had paid the money to gain control over government oil fields held in reserve for the navy, one at Elk Hills, California, and the other at Teapot Dome, Wyoming. In 1921 Harding had approved transferring these oil fields from the navy department to the interior department. Half of the $400,000 payment—which Harding was unaware of at the time—had gone to the Republican Party.

The Senate continued to investigate and exposed other scandals so extensive that the phrase *Teapot Dome* came to mean more than the graft involving Fall (much as in the 1970s the word *Watergate*, under President Richard Nixon, came to mean more than the break-in at the Watergate complex). Subsequently, several officials in the Harding administration were brought to trial. Albert Fall was convicted of bribery and sentenced to one year in prison. Charles Forbes received a two-year prison term for bribery and conspiracy. Harry Daugherty, who resigned as attorney general at President Calvin Coolidge's request in March 1924, was tried for conspiracy in a case involving the transfer of German assets seized during World War I. He was eventually acquitted, but one of his associates was found guilty.

As the public learned about these scandals, it began learning about Harding's numerous extramarital affairs. He had had a long relationship with Nan Britton, a native of Marion, Ohio, who lived in New York City. The affair had begun in 1916 when she was 20 years old and was continuing at the time he told the political bosses he knew of nothing in his past that could cause embarrassment. In 1927 Britton claimed Harding was the father of her daughter.

Harding had also been involved in a relationship with a woman named Carrie Phillips, shortly before 1920. Phillips had blackmailed Harding; his campaign managers had paid $20,000 to keep her quiet during the presidential race and an additional $2,000 per month while he served in the White House. Harding had engaged in at least two other affairs, one in which he had paid for an abortion and another with Grace Cross, his presidential secretary.

Florence Harding had known about her husband's amorous escapades and once caught him in a tryst in the White House. At the time of his death, she knew also about the political scandals brewing. As a result, before leaving Washington she collected papers from the Oval Office and from Harding's study and burned them. At one point she took a black suitcase loaded with bundles of papers and threw it on to a fire.

But she destroyed only part of the historical record. Committee hearings and trial transcripts remained and exposed a president who, though personally not involved in graft, lacked the talent, courage, and strength to control it. Americans in the 1920s had looked back toward the village and found their heritage had been robbed by greed.

CHRONOLOGY

1865 Born November 2

1879 Enters Ohio Central College

1884 Purchases *Marion Star* with two partners

1891 Marries Florence Kling De Wolfe

1898 Elected to Ohio state senate

1902 Elected lieutenant governor of Ohio

1910 Loses election for Ohio governorship

1912 Nominates William Howard Taft for president at Republican convention

Loses second bid for Ohio governorship

1914 Elected to U.S. Senate

1916 Votes against confirmation of Louis D. Brandeis to Supreme Court

1920 Speaks against U.S. membership in League of Nations

Elected president

1922 Calls together Washington Armaments Conference

Signs Fordney-McCumber Act

Scandal in Veterans' Bureau unfolds

1923 Takes trip out West

Dies August 2

Further Reading

Dear, John W. *Warren G. Harding*. New York: Times Books, 2004.

Ferrell, Robert H. *The Strange Deaths of President Harding*. Columbia: University of Missouri Press, 1996.

Murray, Robert K. *The Harding Era: Warren G. Harding and His Administration*. Minneapolis: University of Minnesota Press, 1969.

———. *The Politics of Normalcy: Government Theory and Practice in the Harding-Coolidge Era*. New York: W. W. Norton, 1973.

Russell, Francis. *The Shadow of Blooming Grove: Warren G. Harding and His Times*. New York: McGraw-Hill, 1968.

Sinclair, Andrew. *The Available Man: The Life Behind the Mask of Warren Gamaliel Harding*. New York: Macmillan, 1965.

Traina, Eugene, and David L. Wilson. *The Presidency of Warren G. Harding*. Lawrence: University Press of Kansas, 1977.

*C*ALVIN *C*OOLIDGE (1872–1933)

Thirtieth President, 1923–1929

CALVIN COOLIDGE
(Library of Congress)

"I favor the policy of economy, not because I wish to save money, but because I wish to save people. The men and women of this country who toil are the ones who bear the cost of the Government. Every dollar that we carelessly waste means that their life will be so much the more meager. Every dollar that we prudently save means that their life will be so much the more abundant. Economy is idealism in its most practical form."

—Inaugural words, March 4, 1925

On August 2, 1923, Vice President Calvin Coolidge, tired from a day of haying, was asleep in the house in which he had grown up at Plymouth Notch, Vermont, when his father awakened him. The elder Coolidge told his son that President Warren G. Harding had died; then he called Calvin "Mr. President." Shocked, Calvin Coolidge dressed hurriedly and, with his wife Grace beside him, knelt down and prayed. His spirit soothed, he typed out the presidential oath, based on a copy of the Constitution he found in a book, and gave it to his father, a notary public. In the sitting room shortly after 2 A.M., by the light of an oil lamp that cast shadows on faded wallpaper, and as Grace and six men looked on, his father administered the oath of office. Coolidge then signed it.

Soon thereafter, Calvin Coolidge left the tiny village tucked in the state's Green Mountains and headed for Washington. He carried with him the simplicity of his home. Uncomplicated, dour, and unfailingly honest, he produced a presidency that on the one hand contrasted sharply with the poker-playing, scandal-soaked Harding era but on the other hand fitted well with his predecessor's conservatism and the cautious policies Americans desired. For Coolidge, business should run the country, Congress should run the federal government, and the president should stand back and let events take their course.

John Calvin Coolidge was born in Plymouth Notch, Vermont, on July 4, 1872. Named after his father, he went by his middle name to distinguish himself from the elder Coolidge, who ran a store, farmed, and served three times in the Vermont House and once in the Vermont Senate. Calvin's mother, Victoria Josephine Moor Coolidge, died when he was only 13.

Calvin grew up a farm boy, obtaining his early education at the local one-room schoolhouse. In 1885, the year his mother died, he was sent to Black River Academy, a private school in Ludlow, 12 miles from his home. Although never outstanding in his studies, he earned solid grades.

In fall 1891 Calvin entered Amherst College in western Massachusetts, where for three years he compiled a mediocre classroom record. Shy and laconic, he played no sports, but as a senior he blossomed both academically and socially. In 1895 he graduated *cum laude*. He was greatly influenced by one of his professors, who emphasized the superiority of Congregationalism, with its emphasis on hard work, community service, and godliness.

A photograph of Calvin Coolidge at college shows him dressed respectably with hat and topcoat and holding a cane tucked smartly beneath his arm. He displays the granitelike expression which millions of people came to know during his years in the White House. One contemporary later described him as "colorless" with "a tight-shut, thin-lipped mouth, very chary of words, but with a gleam of understanding in his . . . keen eye."

After graduation, Coolidge settled in nearby Northampton, Massachusetts, and began studying law at the office of John C. Hammond and Henry P. Field. He plunged into politics when he campaigned in 1895 for Hammond, who won election as district attorney, and for Field, who won as mayor. The following year Coolidge displayed his conservatism when he wrote an essay for the Northampton newspaper that defended the gold standard against farmers and others who were advocating the increased coinage of silver.

In 1897 Coolidge worked as a local committeeman for the Republican Party and, after being admitted to the bar, began his law practice. He preferred reading to socializing, and like his father he said little. One episode among many over the years showed his taciturn character: Calvin once took a boat ride with the elder Coolidge, and for a long time they sat near each other, looking at the scenery along the river and saying nothing. Then Calvin, staring at the water, said to his father, "How is the sheep business?" A long pause followed. "Good," his father replied, and silence returned. With that, they exhausted their conversation.

Yet Coolidge was witty. At Amherst he had presented the Grove Oration, the yearly humorous speech, and he was forever known for his wisecracks. When a dinner guest told him that she had bet she could engage him in a conversation for five minutes, he responded: "You lose."

Many in Northampton thought Calvin Coolidge odd, yet he gained a reputation for honesty and ambition. He once said that he entered politics to serve the community and help his law career, but he soon showed that he wanted public office for himself and enjoyed the power it conferred.

In 1898 Coolidge won election to the Northampton common council and the following year was elected city solicitor. After a hiatus from politics, he ran for the school board in 1905 but lost—the only time he ever lost an election. That same year he married Grace Anna Goodhue, who was as open and lively as he was closed and quiet. Grace helped her husband learn to socialize. Ever since childhood, he feared meeting strangers, and though he would forever be uncomfortable in the company of those he hardly knew, she made him a bit more approachable. They had two sons: John, born in 1906, and Calvin, Jr., born in 1908.

Although Calvin and Grace Coolidge developed a strong bond in their marriage, Grace admitted to friends she more than once thought about leaving him. His introverted manner made her believe he was ignoring her, and he was often mean toward her as he vented his frustrations in private. Yet he liked to tease her and his sons, all of whom he deeply loved.

Coolidge's ambition intensified after he won the mayor's office in 1910. He began to believe he could, and should, go further in politics. As mayor he raised the pay of teachers and lowered the city debt. From city hall he went to the Massachusetts state senate in 1911, and in 1914 his fellow legislators chose him to be senate president. During most of his time in the legislature, Coolidge supported progressive reform. He voted to provide pensions for the families of schoolteachers, lower railroad fees for workingmen, and reduce the workweek from seven to six days. From his own modest background, he identified with the common people. Later in his legislative career, however, he veered away from progressivism, most likely because his basically conservative nature took hold and he thought reform had gone too far.

With his enhanced stature, Coolidge won election as lieutenant governor in 1916 and then as governor in 1918. While serving in these offices and working in Boston, he stayed at the Adams House, a rundown hotel, where he occupied a dreary, tiny room for $1 a night. Penurious almost to a fault, Coolidge refused to live beyond his means or indulge in comforts he considered wasteful.

As governor, Coolidge vetoed a pay raise the legislature voted for itself in June 1919; he described sitting in the House or Senate as a "voluntary public service" and firmly stated: "Men do not serve here for pay." To make government more efficient and to save money, he consolidated 118 departments into 18, a significant reform but also politically dangerous because it meant reducing the number of state workers.

Despite his achievements, few people beyond Massachusetts knew about Coolidge until a showdown with labor grabbed national headlines in 1919. In the months after World War I, strikes spread across the country as workers protested wages that lagged behind inflation. A general strike erupted in Seattle, Washington; elsewhere, carpenters and machinists struck, and construction workers walked off their jobs. The strikes shocked many Americans, who saw them as threats to order and evidence that radical "communism" had infiltrated the labor movement.

But nothing so rattled the public as the police strike in Boston. Police in that city suffered from low pay and poor working conditions as station houses, badly neglected, fell apart. Unable to make progress in getting the city to act, the police unionized under the American Federation of Labor. Police Commissioner Edwin U. Curtis insisted that no policeman could effectively do his job while holding union membership, and he subsequently suspended several of the organizers, forcing a showdown with labor. As the mayor pleaded for help, Governor

Coolidge did nothing, leaving the entire crisis to Curtis, whom he backed. Donald R. McCoy, writing in *Calvin Coolidge: The Quiet President*, says "the governor's aloofness was inexcusable."

Finally, on September 9, 1919, all except a handful of the Boston police went out on strike. That night, robberies surged and riots flared. Newspapers called the strikers "Bolsheviks." On September 10 the mayor activated the State Guard. A few more riots followed, and when guardsmen fired into a crowd, they killed two men. At that point the mayor and labor leaders proposed a compromise, but Curtis rejected it.

Governor Coolidge at last acted on September 12, when he ordered additional state guardsmen to patrol Boston's streets, but by then conditions had improved. Curtis then fired the striking police and broke the union. In the aftermath, people forgot that Coolidge had acted reluctantly, late, and minimally. Instead he emerged a hero, a defender of the public order and the public good against labor radicals. Democrats and Republicans alike supported him. President Woodrow Wilson called the strike "a crime against civilization," and one U.S. senator said about Coolidge, "It is to such men that we must look for the preservation of American institutions."

An exchange of messages with union leader Samuel Gompers further boosted Coolidge's standing. In one of them he said, "There is no right to strike against the public safety by anybody, anywhere, any time." Yet Coolidge's remark came less from a sense of victory than from fear he would lose his bid for reelection that fall. He thought there would be a backlash in Massachusetts, a strong labor state. As it turned out, he won by a landslide. His campaign was assisted by Frank W. Stearns, the rotund, wealthy owner of a Boston dry-goods business, who circulated a book titled *Have Faith in Massachusetts*, a collection of Coolidge's speeches with their no-nonsense statements.

Stearns went on to promote Coolidge for the 1920 Republican presidential nomination as a law-and-order candidate, and he sent every delegate a copy of the book. Few of them supported the governor, however, and when the convention deadlocked, the party's bosses turned to Ohio senator Warren G. Harding as the standard bearer. Having dictated who the presidential nominee would be, the bosses tried to do the same for the vice presidency, pushing for Wisconsin Senator Irvine L. Lenroot. This time the delegates rebelled; they wanted to show some independence. When Oregonian Wallace McCamant nominated Coolidge, they remembered the governor's stand in the police strike and cast their votes for him. He beat Lenroot, 674.5 votes to 146.5, a margin that stunned the bosses.

Coolidge, sitting with Grace in his sparse room at the Adams Hotel, received a phone call from the convention. After hearing the news, he turned to his wife.

> "Nominated for vice president," he said.
>
> "You aren't going to take it, are you?" she asked.
>
> "I suppose I'll have to," he replied.

Some historians have wondered whether Coolidge accepted the nomination in the belief that Harding would likely die in office, for politicos were whispering that the presidential candidate, by all appearances fit, suffered from dangerously high blood pressure. If Coolidge knew this, he remained as tight-lipped as ever.

The Harding-Coolidge ticket rode a conservative tide that decimated the progressive reformers; they won with over 60 percent of the popular vote. As vice president, Coolidge registered close to zero on the Washington awareness scale. He seldom appeared at club meetings, and much as he had in Boston, he lived in a hotel. During these months he received the nickname "Silent Cal," not from any reluctance to speak officially but from his terse comments. Coolidge actually held regular press conferences and gave numerous speeches at luncheons and dinners. When asked why he went to them, he responded, "Got to eat somewhere."

President Harding permitted Coolidge to sit as an official member of his cabinet, an innovation in governance; yet here again the New Englander said little and contributed nothing worthwhile. Coolidge thus perfected the state previous vice presidents had complained about: anonymity.

Many Republicans doubted Coolidge would even be renominated for vice president in 1924. Then came the shocking tragedy of Harding's death, and suddenly Silent Cal was president.

On arriving in Washington from Plymouth Notch, Coolidge met with Secretary of the Treasury Andrew Mellon. The two men discussed economics, the very endeavor Coolidge believed made or destroyed presidents. He considered economics to be concrete—something voters felt and experienced every day and which they would most remember when it came time to cast ballots.

Mellon came away from their meeting impressed with Coolidge's grasp of issues. This was a revealing assessment, given nearly everyone else's belief—and Coolidge's own insistence on several occasions—that the president little understood the economic system. When Mellon offered his resignation in order to allow the new president to choose his own cabinet, Coolidge refused to accept it and announced he would keep Harding's cabinet intact.

Calvin Coolidge entered the White House during an economic boom, and as the country's industrial engine kicked into higher gear, he took pride in what commentators called "Coolidge Prosperity." National income jumped from $71.6 billion in 1923 to $81.7 billion in 1928. Mergers quickened so that between 1919 and 1930 some 8,000 businesses disappeared when they were swallowed by their competitors. In that regard, by the decade's end four companies produced 90 percent of all cigarettes, and almost every pill Americans downed came from Drug, Incorporated, or one of the firms it owned.

Advertisers assaulted the traditional Puritan value of thrift. Just a couple of decades earlier, most Americans considered debt something to avoid at all costs. Now they bought on credit to satisfy the wants created by Madison Avenue. When in 1929 Helen and Robert Lynd completed their study of Muncie, Indiana, titled *Middletown*, they found almost no families who were debt-free.

Calvin Coolidge embraced this materialistic ethic. He admired industrialists such as Charles Schwab, who built Bethlehem Steel into a giant (and who lived lavishly, invested unwisely, and in the 1930s went bankrupt). Coolidge said, "Beginning as he did, with no property and with meager opportunities, [Schwab] has developed a great manufacturing plant for the service of the people of America and is doing considerable business abroad."

Quite possibly to accept materialism, Coolidge molded it to his Congregational beliefs in piety and community welfare. In so doing, he faced a conflict, one that remains curious, between his own Calvinistic-infused, rural upbringing with its tightwad habits and the consumer-extravagant urban economy he revered and championed, leading him to declare: "The chief business of the American people is business." He even likened the factory to a temple and those who worked there to worshipers.

Despite the conflicts, for Coolidge, the material and the spiritual blended. As Charles R. Kesler states in *Coolidge and the Historians*, this characteristic appeared in the New Englander's largely probusiness statements. Coolidge said on various occasions:

> "The accumulation of wealth cannot be justified as the chief end of existence. But we are compelled to recognize it as a means to well-nigh every desirable achievement. So long as wealth is made the means and not the end, we need not greatly fear it."

> "We live in an age of science and abounding accumulation of material things. These things did not create our Declaration [of Independence]. Our Declaration created them. The things of the spirit come first. Unless we cling to that, all our material prosperity, overwhelming though it may appear, will turn to a barren scepter in our grasp."

> "We want idealism. We want that vision which lifts men and nations above themselves. These are virtues by reason of their own merit. But they must not be cloistered; they must not be impractical; they must not be ineffective."

Coolidge wanted business to run the country; he wanted fewer government regulations, higher tariffs, lower taxes, and a reduced federal debt. He favored business not because he hated labor, but because he thought the president should reflect the popular will, and the people wanted business to operate largely unfettered.

As an administrator, President Coolidge delegated almost everything. He said, "In the discharge of the duties of the office there is one rule of action more important than all others. It consists in never doing anything that someone else can do for you." As a result, when a coal strike threatened in September 1923, he left it to be resolved by Pennsylvania governor Gifford Pinchot, Secretary of Commerce Herbert Hoover, and various bureaucrats.

He trusted his cabinet as well. When the Teapot Dome scandals of the Harding administration roiled the country, he rejected Senate pressure to fire Attorney General Henry Daugherty, a central figure in the controversy, saying there needed to be more proof of his guilt. He eventually removed Daugherty, though only after the besmirched politician refused to let Senate investigators search his files.

Coolidge gave Herbert Hoover enormous power to remake the Commerce Department. Hoover converted the Bureau of Standards, which was under his authority, into a research agency for industry and through various programs promoted individualism. Hoover had so many interests and gained such widespread authority that people referred to him as "secretary of commerce and under-secretary of everything else."

President Coolidge voiced no objections when businesses began taking over the regulatory agencies founded by progressive reformers over the previous two decades. As a result, the Federal Trade Commission pursued few antitrust cases, and rather than begin its own investigations, it waited for others to file complaints. According to Robert H. Ferrell in *The Presidency of Calvin Coolidge*, it was the silent New Englander "who turned the FTC into a shell of a regulatory body."

In line with his own Spartan habits, Coolidge considered the national debt evil, much as Thomas Jefferson had more than a hundred years earlier, and he worked to lower the deficit. Between 1923 and 1929, the national debt dropped from $22.3 billion to $16.9 billion. The government, he said, should live within its means.

As the 1924 election neared, the Coolidges suffered a grievous loss when their youngest son, Calvin, Jr., died. Only 16, the youngster had developed a blister on one of his toes that became infected and caused blood poisoning. During the illness, the president tried to conduct business as usual, but whenever possible he joined Grace at their son's bedside. He later recalled how Calvin, Jr., "in his suffering . . . was asking me to make him well. I could not." According to Robert E. Gilbert in *The Mortal Presidency: Illness and Anguish in the White House*, the youngster's death sent Calvin Coolidge into a deep depression, robbing him of his enthusiasm for politics and life itself. Withdrawn, he slept longer at night and took daytime naps. Gilbert believes that Coolidge's reaction to his son's death dampened his willingness to act on public matters.

Yet he pressed forward toward reelection in 1924, and with the economy showing no signs of slowing, he easily defeated the Democratic candidate, John W. Davis. The president continued to favor business and pursued deeper tax cuts, which he believed would lessen the burden on individuals and fuel the economy. He endorsed Andrew Mellon's program, passed through Congress in 1926 (followed by a second one in 1928), that lowered surtaxes for the wealthy, reduced corporate rates, and increased tax exemptions for married couples. Thus, by 1927 few Americans paid any income tax.

Acting from his belief in individualism and a limited budget, Coolidge vetoed the McNary-Haugen Farm Relief Bill in February 1927, which would have allowed the government to buy surplus commodities and keep them off the market until their prices rose. As such, it was intended to help farmers who suffered throughout the decade from declining incomes. Although "Coolidge Prosperity" had largely bypassed rural America, the president insisted farmers should stand up for themselves.

President Coolidge showed little interest in foreign policy and obtained few triumphs in that area. Under the Dawes Plan in 1924, the United States loaned $2.5 billion to Germany to help its economy. He supported involvement in some activities sponsored by the League of Nations and wanted the United States to join the Permanent Court of International Justice, but the Senate rejected his idea. In 1928 he became the first president to travel to Cuba when he spoke at the Sixth Inter-American Conference at Havana. That same year the United States and several other nations, eventually 61 in all, signed the Kellogg-Briand Pact outlawing war. All show and no substance, the pact had no enforcement provision.

At least as early as 1926, Coolidge Prosperity began to show signs of weakness. Underconsumption was dragging down the economy, as few Americans could afford the goods being produced by industry. A study by the Brookings Institute in 1928 revealed that 60 percent of American families earned less than the $2,000 annual income needed to afford basic necessities. While average per capita disposable income rose about 9 percent in the 1920s, most of that increase came from the income of the wealthiest 1 percent, which rose 75 percent. As for production, the automobile industry clearly showed the effects of underconsumption: By the late 1920s only 50 percent of all families owned cars, and between 1926 and 1929 the industry operated at less than four-fifths capacity. Yet Coolidge, along with most of the country's economists, failed to see underconsumption as a problem.

The president did receive direct warnings, however, about excessive stock speculation and dangerous banking activities. Herbert Hoover even asked for more control over banking, but Coolidge ignored him. Worse yet, by expressing optimism in the stock market, he encouraged reckless speculation. The *New York Times* said the president's remarks made the market "a lively buoyant affair."

Nor did he do anything about the Federal Reserve Board, whose practices encouraged risky economic behavior. Time and again the president told reporters the economy was "a matter that I wouldn't happen to know anything about" (though he knew enough to tell Americans they should keep buying stocks). Maybe Coolidge understood more than he let on—in 1926 he had said privately the stock market was rigged—but wanted to avoid taking action.

Even though Coolidge insisted in 1927 that "I do not choose to run for president in 1928," some Republicans pushed him to run for another term. But he had no heart for it. He still mourned Calvin, Jr.'s death, and he may have realized that Coolidge Prosperity would soon end. Just seven months after he left office in March 1929, the stock market crashed, and the Great Depression began.

Calvin Coolidge retired to Northampton, where he wrote a newspaper column, magazine articles, and his autobiography. Though he supported Herbert Hoover, he felt tired and believed the times had passed him by. Franklin Roosevelt's landslide win in 1932 befuddled him.

Throughout that year, Coolidge suffered from indigestion and bronchitis. During the morning of January 5, 1933, he went to his kitchen for a glass of water and then down to the cellar, where he checked on the furnace before going upstairs to his room. There he stretched out on his bed and died of a coronary thrombosis. He was buried in the Coolidge family plot at Plymouth Notch, Vermont, back in the tiny village that had shaped his conservatism. His ideas are still praised by those who prefer minimal government interference in business and are still criticized by those who prefer an activist government engaged in social reform.

Chronology

1872 Born July 4

1886 Enters Black River Academy

1891 Enters Amherst College

1895 Graduates cum laude

1897 Admitted to the bar

1899 Elected Northampton, Massachusetts city solicitor

1905 Marries Grace Goodhue

Loses election to Northampton School Board

1910 Elected mayor of Northampton

1911 Elected state senator

1914 Becomes president of Massachusetts state senate

1915 Elected lieutenant governor of Massachusetts

1918 Elected governor of Massachusetts

1919 Ends Boston police strike

Reelected governor

1920 Elected vice-president

1923 Succeeds to the presidency after the death of Warren G. Harding

1924 Elected president

1927 Refuses to seek another term as president

1928 Issues statement endorsing activities on stock market

Attends Sixth Inter-American Conference in Havana, Cuba

1929 Leaves the presidency

Finishes autobiography

1930 Writes occasional newspaper column

1932 Endorses reelection of Herbert Hoover as president

1933 Dies January 5

Further Reading

Coolidge, Calvin. *Autobiography of Calvin Coolidge.* New York: Cosmopolitan, 1929.

Ferrell, Robert H. *The Presidency of Calvin Coolidge.* Lawrence: University Press of Kansas, 1998.

Gilbert, Robert E. *The Mortal Presidency: Illness and Anguish in the White House.* New York: Basic Books, 1998.

McCoy, Donald R. *Calvin Coolidge: The Quiet President.* New York: Macmillan, 1967.

Sobel, Robert. *Coolidge: An American Enigma.* Washington, D.C.: Regnery Publishing, 1998.

Herbert Hoover (1874–1964)

Thirty-first President, 1929–1933

Herbert Hoover
(Library of Congress)

"The larger purpose of our economic thought should be to establish more firmly stability and security of business and employment and thereby remove poverty still further from our borders."
—Inaugural words, March 4, 1929

When Herbert Hoover graduated from Stanford University in 1895, he obtained a job at the Reward Mine in Nevada City, California, as a laborer—work filled with heat, dirt, and the ever-present acrid smell of explosives; work that devoured 10 hours a day, seven days a week while it spit back a few dollars. Soon, activity at the mine declined, and Hoover lost his job. He recalled: "I then learned what the bottom levels of real human despair are paved with. That is, the ceaseless tramping and ceaseless refusal at the employment office. . . ."

Years later, millions of Americans tramped to employment offices, hoping to find work while a great depression devoured the economy during Hoover's presidency. As men tried to earn money by selling apples on street corners, as soup lines lengthened and children cried from want of food, many Americans thought Hoover uncaring; they believed he had forgotten his own experience at "the bottom levels of real human despair."

—✿—

Herbert Clark Hoover was born on August 10, 1874, at West Branch, Iowa, to Jesse Clark Hoover, a blacksmith, and Hulda Minthorn Hoover. Just six years later Herbert's father died from heart trouble, and little more than two years after that, in February 1883, his mother died from pneumonia complicated by typhoid fever. Orphaned (along with his brother and sister), young Herbert lived briefly with relatives in Iowa before being sent by them in 1885 to live with John and Laura Minthorn, his uncle and aunt, at Newberg, Oregon.

Like his parents, the Minthorns were Quakers, and they impressed upon him the values of community service and hard work. He cleared land and chopped wood while attending the Friends Pacific Academy, where Laura Minthorn taught the elementary grades.

In 1888 Hoover helped his uncle open a land sales office in nearby Salem and worked there as a bookkeeper. Three years later he enrolled at Stanford University, which began classes for the first time that fall. He majored in geology, and in order to make enough money for expenses he operated a laundry and worked at various jobs, including waiter and handyman. Hoover served as student treasurer and in that role eliminated a deficit and put into place reforms that prevented fraud. He graduated in 1895 with $40 in his pocket. Desperate for work, he landed the job at the Reward Mine.

But the mine declined, and Hoover was hired by the firm of Bewick, Moreing, and Company, based in London, to investigate gold deposits that had been discovered in Western Australia. Hoover arrived at the town of Coolgardie, which he described as filled with "red dust, black flies, [and] white heat." On his advice, Bewick, Moreing bought the Sons of Gwalia mine for $1 million. Located 130 miles north of the already productive Kalgoorlie mines, the Sons of Gwalia earned many times its cost, proving Hoover's sound judgment.

While at Stanford, Hoover had started dating Lou Henry, a banker's daughter and fellow geology major. He proposed to her in a telegram he sent from Australia, and they were married in California in February 1899. They had two sons, Herbert Clark and Allan Henry. A licensed mining engineer and lover of the outdoors, Lou Hoover accompanied her husband on many trips.

Soon after their marriage, the couple traveled to China, where Herbert Hoover discovered coal deposits in Chihli Province. After he secured a deed to several mining properties for Bewick, Moreing, they made him a junior partner. While in China, he privately expressed his disappointment with the people. He said, "The simply appalling and universal dishonesty of the working classes, the racial slowness, and the low average of intelligence, gives them an efficiency far below the workmen of England and America."

At Tientsin (Tianjin), Lou and Herbert Hoover, along with other foreigners, found themselves besieged during the Boxer Rebellion of 1900 in which Chinese rebels fought against colonial powers. As troops from other countries battled the rebels, the Hoovers helped defend the city. Herbert took charge of building barricades made of sacks filled with rice, sugar, and grain. Lou supervised a dairy and worked in a hospital, while carrying a pistol and guarding their house at night.

Over the next several years, Herbert Hoover traveled the world, displaying his engineering and business prowess when he found silver, lead, and zinc in Burma; zinc in Australia; and copper and oil in Russia. In the process he accumulated both wealth and prestige. After 1908 he owned his own firm, which helped rescue financially troubled mining companies. By 1913 his net worth had reached $4 million.

In 1909 Hoover wrote *Principles of Mining*, which was widely used as a textbook. *Principles* went beyond technical matter and discussed business ideas that showed that its author supported reform. He called unions beneficial and insisted they would eventually contribute to harmony in the workplace. "The time when the employer could ride roughshod over his labor is disappearing with the doctrine of 'laissez-faire' on which it was founded," he said. "The sooner the fact is recognized, the better for the employer."

When World War I broke out, Hoover was in London, and he looked for ways he could help alleviate suffering. First he established the American Citizens' Relief Committee to help Americans fleeing the continent for England. Then he headed a private charitable group, the Commission for the Relief of Belgium (CRB). As in all his endeavors, Hoover worked tirelessly, raising funds from the British, French and, later, American governments. He bought wheat from overseas and shipped it to Belgium, where it was sold to millers, who in turn sold it as flour to bakers, all at controlled prices.

Brand Whitlock, the mayor of Toledo, Ohio, who accompanied Hoover to Europe, expressed the thoughts of many Americans when he said, "I was proud . . . to think that my country was doing this noble work amidst all this rage, this brutal and ignorant destruction." According to David Burner in *Herbert Hoover: A Public Life*, the CRB "*was* Hoover," and as director "he manipulated the British, the Germans, the Americans . . . just as he had earlier . . . brooked no interference when running great mining enterprises."

After the United States entered the war, President Woodrow Wilson brought Hoover to Washington in 1917 when he appointed him food administrator. Although on principle Hoover opposed price fixing, as an emergency measure he set the price of wheat in order to prevent excess profits. When profits still rose, he supported taxing them. He worked to prevent waste and encouraged Americans to conserve food.

Hoover returned to Europe in November 1918, this time to head the Inter-Allied Food Council and provide postwar relief. He persuaded Congress to make available to the Allies $100 million in credits, a not entirely disinterested act because the United States needed other countries to buy its food surpluses. He guided its expenditure through his role as director general of the American Relief Administration, a public group that turned private in 1919. That fall he began providing food to Germany. When those who wanted to punish rather than help America's wartime enemy criticized him, he said, "The United States is not at war with German infants."

Hoover did more than provide food; he led in rebuilding the wrecked European economies. Through his efforts, rivers were cleared, railroads repaired, and communications restored. As Bolshevism festered in the rubble, the American wanted a strong capitalism to resist it.

Did Hoover use his relief efforts as a blunt weapon against the rise of communism? Some observers at the time thought so, as have some historians since. But the evidence says otherwise. For example, after a communist revolution in Hungary, Hoover ordered that food shipments to that country continue. "The provisioning of Hungary should go on," he said, "as long as no excesses are committed by the Government."

In 1919 President Wilson appointed Hoover vice chairman of the Second Industrial Conference in Washington. The group's final report, written largely by Hoover, called for several progressive reforms, among them greater equity between profits and wages, the establishment of a minimum wage law, equal pay for men and women, and a 48-hour workweek.

Hoover sought the Republican presidential nomination in 1920 but had little support among the convention delegates; the party leaders decided on Ohio senator Warren G. Harding. After Harding won the presidency, he selected Hoover to serve as secretary of commerce.

Herbert Hoover took a lethargic and uncoordinated department and made it vibrant and powerful. He applied scientific management, reduced bureaucratic waste, and developed services to assist business and strengthen the economy. He relied heavily on national conferences where leaders gathered facts, discussed ideas, and developed plans of action. The conferences operated, some observers said, much like Quaker meetings, with participants searching for consensus.

In 1922 Hoover began a series of conferences on the new technology of radio that resulted in his regulating broadcast hours of operation and issuing licenses to assigned frequencies. This was followed by the Radio Act of 1927 that, in line with Hoover's desire for minimal government control, prohibited censorship except for obscenity.

While serving as commerce secretary, Hoover acted as head of the American Relief Administration. In 1921 he responded to a famine in Russia by sending food there with no political strings attached. The first shipment, 700 tons of rations, arrived at Petrograd (Saint Petersburg) in September. To someone who complained to Hoover that he was only bolstering the communist regime, he replied: "Twenty million people are starving. Whatever their politics, they shall be fed!" Of course, food sent to Russia helped American farmers when Congress provided money for the shipments, but historian David Burner concludes that Hoover acted mainly from "conscience, compassion, workmanship, and pride."

In 1922 Herbert Hoover published his book *American Individualism*, in which he defended civil liberties, extolled scientific progress, and criticized those who advocated laissez-faire economics. Above all, he called for individual sacrifice, rather than government programs, to help Americans.

Yet he was not adverse to all public works projects, and he pushed for the building of a dam along the Colorado River that would generate hydroelectric power. Toward that end, he formed the Colorado River Commission and worked to rally southwestern states behind the project. After much delay, Congress passed the Boulder Canyon Project Act that authorized the building of Boulder (today Hoover) Dam.

In 1927 Hoover directed relief efforts after that year's Mississippi flood. The acclaim he received for this latest project, and his years of work as the "Great Humanitarian," made him a front-runner among Republicans for the presidency. After Calvin Coolidge decided in 1927 to forego another term in the White House, Hoover won his party's nomination the following year. He ran against Democratic New York Governor Alfred E. Smith, a Catholic in an era when most Americans thought only Protestants fit to be chief executive. Hoover called for expanding prosperity through greater productivity. In August he declared:

> We in America today are nearer to the final triumph over poverty than ever before in the history of any land. The poorhouse is vanishing among us. We have not yet reached the goal, but given a chance to go forward with the policies of the last eight years, we shall soon with the help of God be in the sight of day when poverty will be banished from this nation.

Hoover's words belied reports that showed a majority of American families struggling to afford basic necessities. Yet with "Coolidge Prosperity" generating high profits and ever higher returns on stocks, he won the White House with 444 electoral votes to Smith's 87.

In June 1929 Hoover convinced Congress to pass the Agricultural Marketing Act—some historians consider it his greatest presidential achievement—which provided a fund to encourage farmers to form cooperatives and gave a farm board the power to enter the commodities market and keep prices from falling. Throughout the year, the board maintained the prices of wheat, cotton, and other crops.

Just seven months after Herbert Hoover entered the White House, economic trouble mocked his campaign statement about being near "the final triumph over poverty." On October 24, 1929, panic swept the New York Stock Exchange, as nearly 13 million shares changed hands. Wall Street recovered briefly after big investors shored up prices, and a couple of days later Hoover insisted, "The fundamental business of the country, that is production and distribution of commodities, is on a sound and prosperous basis." But on Tuesday, October 29, the market plunged—a collapse that announced the beginning of the Great Depression.

President Hoover acted quickly. On November 19 he began meeting with industry leaders, a reprise of his conference strategy from his days as secretary of commerce. A series of meetings ended in pronouncements that employment and investments would be maintained. Yet when the leaders left Washington and returned home, they invariably encountered declining profits and the need to cut spending and, with that, jobs.

No one knew the depression would last a decade; most thought it would last only a few months. As a result, when the stock market rebounded in early 1930 and reached levels nearly as high as those before the crash, Hoover concluded the worst was over. He told the public that "with continued effort we shall rapidly recover." Even the American Economic Association predicted recovery by June of that year. Yet the rise in stock prices failed to correspond to the activity in industry. Consumers still lacked the money needed to buy more of what factories produced.

Making matters worse, in June 1930 Congress passed the Smoot-Hawley Tariff, which Hoover endorsed. Tariff rates on agricultural raw materials jumped from 38 percent to 49 percent and on most other items from 31 percent to 34 percent. These high rates, meant to protect domestic industry, made it difficult for Europeans to trade with the United States and contributed to the collapse of their economies, which in turn hurt American exports. The tariff engulfed both continents in a circle of poverty and despair.

By September 1931 manufacturing volume in the United States had declined 50 percent from before the crash, and steel plants were operating at only 11 percent of capacity. Despite such dire developments, many experts within and outside the White House believed that once the economy hit bottom, it would recover and that the government should wait rather than begin bold reforms.

Hoover encouraged more construction to boost employment, but neither the private nor the government sectors could afford many projects. Conceivably, the federal government could have launched additional building projects if it resorted to deficit spending. The president, however, insisted the budget must be restrained and that a large deficit spelled trouble.

While dealing with the depression, Hoover faced an aggressive Japan. In 1931 the Japanese invaded Manchuria and established the puppet state of Manchukuo. Secretary of State Henry L. Stimson urged military intervention and economic sanctions, but Hoover settled for a verbal rebuke.

As pressure built on the president to provide some kind of relief for Americans, he resisted any form of dole or public assistance, saying it would ruin initiative. Most people agreed with him. They pointed to the British experience, where the dole had been started at the end of World War I and had since bred dependency on handouts. New York Governor Franklin Roosevelt condemned such relief, as did liberal newspapers.

Yet for many, Hoover went too far in 1931 when he vetoed the Norris Dam project for its supposedly dolelike characteristics. The bill, sponsored by Tennessee senator George Norris, provided for the government to expand its power plant at Muscle Shoals, along the Tennessee River, and sell power directly to consumers. Although the dam's construction would have created many needed jobs, Hoover said the project would lose money, and, inexplicably, he complained that the paychecks workers would receive amounted to a handout. He also noted that, unlike the Colorado River Project, all the power would be under government control. These complaints appeared petty, since the line of difference between the Colorado and Tennessee projects was thin. Norris called the veto unfathomable and became Hoover's resolute enemy.

As the depression showed no signs of easing, Hoover increasingly placed the blame for it on Europe. Weak markets overseas, he said, held back American recovery. More accurately, the Smoot-Hawley Tariff continued to work its damage, and with the subsequent decline in trade, the tariff made it impossible for other countries to repay their war debts to the United States. Late in 1931 Hoover declared an 18-month moratorium on those debts.

In February 1932 the president established the Reconstruction Finance Corporation, authorized by Congress to provide loans for businesses and banks. A writer in the liberal magazine *New Republic* praised it, saying, "There has been nothing quite like it. . . . In the face of a crisis, it amazes me that it should be going through Congress with so little modification and amendment." The RFC authorized $1.2 billion in loans to about 5,000 companies. Favoritism appeared, however, when some of the loans were given to banks on which two members of the RFC served as directors, and many people disliked the disparity between Hoover's help for business and his reluctance to provide more direct relief to unemployed workers.

Hoover projected a cold image. In comments he made to reporters, in the way his voice sounded over the radio, and in the way he appeared before newsreel cameras, the Great Humanitarian, who started his career alongside the common workers in the mine shafts of California, came across as snobby, inept, and uncaring. Everywhere, people derided him. The unemployed called their shantytowns "Hoovervilles," the homeless called newspapers under which they slept "Hoover blankets," and the president lost all credibility.

Hoover worked 18-hour days and took more emergency economic action than had any previous president, but he relied too heavily on the pattern that had worked for him so well earlier: voluntarism, but he called for more charity while the crisis overwhelmed the charities. Nothing in his past—not even the ravages of world war—and nothing in America's past had prepared him for a catastrophe this big.

As the 1932 election neared, he acted again. In February Congress passed the Glass-Steagall Act which made $750 million in gold available to businesses to counteract the nation's contracted credit. That spring he attacked the unequal distribution of wealth as a cause of America's economic collapse, saying, "In every society there will always be at the bottom a noxious sediment and at the top an obnoxious froth." He called for an increase in excise taxes on luxuries and said about the income tax, "My view is that we should raise the upper brackets . . . to 45 per cent, as compared to the present 23 per cent. " In June 1932 he signed the progressive Revenue Act that increased estate, corporate, and excise taxes and shifted some of the burden to the wealthy.

Nothing he did, however, would ever erase from people's minds what happened that summer when about 20,000 veterans from World War I marched on Washington while Congress was considering a Bonus Bill to advance the payment of money promised them for 1945. The veterans, who gathered together as the "Bonus Army," and many other Americans wanted the money paid immediately to alleviate hardship.

Because Hoover opposed the Bonus Bill, and the Senate rejected it, some of the veterans, led by Roy W. Robertson of California, walked for three days and four nights around the Capitol Building in a "Death March." Other veterans took over the Capitol steps and forced frightened congressmen to use underground passageways.

When a number of veterans sought shelter by occupying abandoned government buildings in the downtown business district, police tried to clear them out. On July 28 a riot ensued and one veteran was killed. At that point President Hoover ordered General Douglas MacArthur to remove all veterans from the buildings and force them back to their temporary camps. He explicitly ordered MacArthur to do no more than that, but MacArthur moved against the ragged veterans with a vengeance. Cavalrymen used drawn sabers, and infantrymen used tear gas. Six tanks joined the fray, and Major George S. Patton, Jr., chased down marchers in the last mounted charge of the U.S. Cavalry. After removing the veterans from the buildings, MacArthur's soldiers went into the camps, where the veterans, acting in anger, set their own huts on fire.

MacArthur's treatment of the Bonus Army shocked Colonel Dwight Eisenhower, one of his aides, who later told of "a pitiful scene, those ragged, discouraged people burning their own little things." The excessive use of force, especially by an army against men who had fought for their country, disgusted most Americans. When Democratic presidential hopeful Franklin Roosevelt heard about the attack, he said, "This will elect me." Hoover further damaged his standing when he derided the bonus marchers as rabble and refused to criticize MacArthur publicly. The entire fiasco sealed the president's election defeat.

Every economic development worked against Hoover in 1932: Unemployment, under 2 million in 1929, neared 13 million. In Chicago, people foraged in garbage trucks for food; across the country, about 270,000 families were evicted from their homes; between 1 and 2 million people wandered the land in search of jobs and shelter.

The contrast between Republican Herbert Hoover and his Democratic opponent, Franklin Roosevelt, could not have been greater. Where Hoover sounded disheartened, Roosevelt sounded inspired; where Hoover appeared distant, Roosevelt appeared intimate; where Hoover defended his past record, Roosevelt looked to the future. The Republican lost in a landslide, and the Democrats rode Roosevelt's coattails to gain control of Congress.

Hoover left the White House an embittered man. He thought Roosevelt dangerous and warned in 1934 that the New Deal would lead to a fascist state. In his postpresidential years he lived in Palo Alto, California, and with his wife worked for the Hoover Institute on War, Revolution and Peace, which he had founded in 1919 at his alma mater, Stanford. Until Japan attacked Pearl Harbor, Hoover opposed American entry into World War II, arguing that to side with Russia's Joseph Stalin would be no better than siding with Germany's Adolf Hitler.

After the war, Hoover helped President Harry S. Truman distribute food in Europe. In 1947 Truman appointed him head of a commission to reorganize the executive branch and reduce waste. He led a second commission with that same purpose in 1953, under President Dwight Eisenhower. Meanwhile, in 1951 Hoover published his memoirs, followed in 1958 by his book, *The Ordeal of Woodrow Wilson*. He died at the age of 90 on October 20, 1964.

In Herbert Hoover's later years, Americans considered him an elder statesman and recalled his sacrifices in helping others in war-torn Europe. Yet they never forgot his failure as president—a failure born from his own inability to handle the economic crisis that confronted him, made all the more miserable by the promise his presidency once held. "We were in a mood for magic," journalist Anne McCormick said about Hoover's inauguration. "We had summoned a great engineer to solve our problems for us; now we sat back comfortably and confidently to watch the problems being solved." After the stock market crash, however, the answers and the promise vanished.

CHRONOLOGY

1874 Born August 10

1884 Moves to Newberg, Oregon

1891 Enters Stanford University

1895 Graduates from Stanford University

1899 Marries Lou Henry

1900 Besieged by Boxer Rebellion

1914 Forms American Citizens' Relief Committee in London

1915 Serves as chairman of Belgian Relief Commission

1917 Appointed U.S. food administrator

1919 Serves as vice chairman of Second Industrial Conference

1921 Appointed secretary of commerce

Directs food relief to Russia

1928 Elected president

1929 Holds national conference to address the depression

1930 Signs Smoot-Hawley Tariff

1931 Vetoes Norris Dam proposal

Protests Japanese invasion of Manchuria

Establishes Reconstruction Finance Corporation

1932 Signs Glass-Steagall Act

Uses army to disperse bonus marchers

Loses reelection

1933 Retires to Palo Alto, California

1944 Lou Hoover dies

1946 Serves as coordinator of Food Supply for World Famine

1947 Chairs Commission on Organization of the Executive Branch of the Government

1951 Publishes *Memoirs*

1952 Heads second commission to reorganize executive branch

1958 Publishes *The Ordeal of Woodrow Wilson*

1964 Dies October 20

FURTHER READING

Best, Gary Dean. *Herbert Hoover: The Post-presidential Years, 1933–1964.* Stanford, Calif.: Hoover Institution Press, 1983.

———. *The Politics of American Individualism: Herbert Hoover in Transition, 1918–1929.* Westport, Conn.; Greenwood Press, 1975.

Burner, David. *Herbert Hoover: A Public Life.* New York: Alfred A. Knopf, 1979.

Lisio, Donald J. *The President and Protest: Hoover, MacArthur, and the Bonus Riot.* 2nd ed. New York: Fordham University Press, 1994.

Nash, George H. *Herbert Hoover and Stanford University.* Stanford, Calif.: Hoover Institution Press, 1988.

———. *The Life of Herbert Hoover.* New York: W. W. Norton, 1983.

Romasco, Albert U. *The Poverty of Abundance: Hoover, the Nation, the Depression.* New York: Oxford University Press, 1965.

Wilson, Joan Hoff. *Herbert Hoover: Forgotten Progressive.* Boston: Little, Brown, 1975.

Franklin Delano Roosevelt (1882–1945)

Thirty-second President, 1933–1945

Franklin Delano Roosevelt
(Library of Congress)

"In Washington's day the task of the people was to create and weld together a nation.
In Lincoln's day the task of the people was to preserve that Nation from disruption from within.
In this day the task of the people is to save that Nation and its institutions from disruption from without."

—Inaugural words, third term, January 20, 1941

Anyone watching Franklin Delano Roosevelt as he neared middle age would have no reason to suspect he would ever enjoy anything less than a favored life, one cushioned by the intelligence, good looks, and wealth bestowed on him at birth. He moved through childhood pampered and as a young man obtained an education from the best schools. He glided into politics, lifted by the right contacts, experiencing only slight turbulence, landing, almost always, gently.

All of that changed during a vacation in August 1921 when in a single day he exerted himself fighting a forest fire, then cooled off by swimming in a lake, then jogged, and then dove into the frigid Bay of Fundy, after which he sat in his wet bathing suit for half an hour and caught a chill. The next day pain shot through his back and legs, accompanied by a fever. Two days later, a doctor diagnosed his illness as polio.

Paralyzed, for weeks he could barely move. His wife, Eleanor, tended to his needs while he sank into a deep depression. Gradually, however, he began to exercise and strengthen his upper body. He wintered in Florida, where he swam long distances, his arms pulling his deadened legs, and crawled along deserted beaches. Six years into his illness, he still expressed hope he would one day walk.

But he never did. Throughout the rest of his life, Roosevelt remained a paraplegic. He had to be lifted out of bed each day by a valet. Even with heavy braces he could move only jerkily, perilously close to toppling over. Although his aides, helped by a cooperative press, hid his handicap so effectively that many Americans never realized the extent of his condition, it was always there, a constant challenge that some observers thought affected his personality, making him not angry or mad but patient and confident.

Rather than languish in self-pity, Roosevelt pushed himself harder to become governor of New York and president of the United States. According to historian Doris Kearns Goodwin, he "had such inner elan, such confidence, such sparkle that to be around him was like opening your first bottle of champagne." He communicated that quality to Congress and to the public, and through the difficult years of the Great Depression and the darkest years of World War II, his fortitude remade American society and saved it from Nazi conquest.

Franklin Delano Roosevelt was born on January 30, 1882, at Springwood, his family's home located at Hyde Park, a village in upstate New York. His father, James Roosevelt, came from a long line of wealthy Roosevelts whose involvement in West Indian trade and real estate investments, along with strategic marriages, made them prosperous. His mother, Sara Delano Roosevelt, was James's second wife. Rebecca Brien Howland, whom he had married in 1853, died from a heart attack in 1876 and was buried at the Roosevelt home in Hyde Park.

Like James Roosevelt, Sara Delano came from wealth. Her father, Warren Delano, was descended from an old family accustomed to fine houses and exclusive schools. Warren Delano had added to his inherited fortune through his merchant trade with China.

Springwood, Franklin Roosevelt's birthplace, was a large clapboard house on 110 acres (later expanded to 1,000) that overlooked the Hudson River. Some 30 years before Franklin's birth, essayist Nathaniel Parker Willis said, "The Hudson at Hyde Park is a broad, tranquil, noble river. . . . The shores are cultivated by the water's edge, and lean up in graceful rather than bold elevations; the eminences around are crested with the villas of the wealthy. . . ." None of that had changed by 1882. James Roosevelt, who invested in various businesses, pictured himself a country gentleman and embellished his home's address with a British-sounding name, "Hyde Park on the Hudson."

While growing up, Franklin Roosevelt spent much time at his family's second home in New York City and traveled overseas with his parents. Hyde Park, however, was special. Here, as an only child, he lived in a protected world. Both of his parents loved him; his mother doted on him, constantly watching him and following him. She planned his every day: awake at seven in the morning, breakfast at eight, school lessons with a private tutor from nine until noon, play from noon until one, and so on. Not until age nine did he take a bath on his own, and she picked his playmates, invariably from the nearby homes of other wealthy people.

Her apron strings loosened a bit in 1896 when Franklin, then 14 years old, entered Groton School in Massachusetts, two years later than when boys normally did. "James and I feel this parting very much," Sara wrote in her diary. "It is hard to leave my darling boy."

Nine out of 10 of Groton's students came from families listed on the social registers of major cities. Franklin found his days at Groton as regimented as those his mother had planned for him but without the warmth. Groton provided its boys an austere atmosphere with its strict dress codes, cold showers, and bare rooms, each six by nine feet with a bed, bureau, and chair.

Franklin found his budding snobbishness reinforced at Groton—he threw his head back and looked down his nose at those he spoke to—yet he learned about social commitment and attended lectures given by prominent reformers. In one year alone he heard Jacob Riis, the progressive photographer and writer, and Booker T. Washington, the African-American leader. More than once he heard his fifth cousin, Theodore Roosevelt, then assistant secretary of the navy and soon to be governor of New York.

For Franklin, though, social consciousness would await another day, for when he entered Harvard in 1900 he stuck with the Groton crowd, dined with Boston's elite Beacon Hill families, and showed more interest in conforming to his upper-crust peers than in excelling at academics. In 1902, soon after his father died, his mother rented an apartment near the Harvard campus. Franklin spent much time there and escorted her to the theater and other events, while she frequently entertained his friends.

In his junior year he began dating a distant cousin, Anna Eleanor Roosevelt. Although Eleanor lacked beauty, her intelligence and sympathy attracted him; they had both grown up largely in the company of adults and had both led pampered and sheltered lives. When they decided to marry, Franklin's mother opposed their engagement and insisted they keep it secret for several months until they could be sure they wanted to spend their lives together. They agreed, and as Sara Roosevelt adjusted herself to the prospect of losing her son, he wrote her: "I am so glad, dear Mummy, that you are getting over the strangeness of it all—I knew you would, and that you couldn't help feeling that not only I but you also are the luckiest & will always be the happiest people in gaining anyone like E. to love and be loved by."

Franklin graduated from Harvard in 1903 and the following year entered Columbia Law School in New York City. He and Eleanor married on March 17, 1905. Eleanor immediately found herself subject to Sara's commands. She also acquiesced in Franklin's desire for a large family—five children in all, born between 1906 and 1916.

Franklin Roosevelt passed his bar exam in 1907. He then practiced law as a well-heeled attorney commuting between Hyde Park and New York and vacationing at his family's large "cottage" on Campobello Island, off the coast of Maine. Nothing he did indicated he wanted to pursue a career in politics. He stayed away from civic clubs and had no contact with political bosses or their machines. Instead, in 1910 the Democratic Party came to him, its leaders anxious to capitalize on the Roosevelt name, made nationally prominent when Franklin's cousin, Theodore, won the White House. They recruited him to run for the state senate in the traditionally Republican district that included Hyde Park.

FDR, as he came to be known, enjoyed the challenge. He campaigned in a Maxwell car that was painted red and adorned with flags, and he quickly honed his oratory, using the phrase "my friends" to reach out to his listeners. Taking advantage of a year in which the Republicans suffered from infighting, he surprised almost everyone by winning.

In the legislature, Roosevelt caused turmoil by defying the political bosses and opposing the candidate picked by Tammany Hall for the U.S. Senate. "The Democratic Party is on trial," he said, "and having been given control of the government chiefly through up-State votes, cannot afford to surrender its control to the organization in New York City." He joined the insurgents, as they were called, and although the bosses forced them to compromise and accept another Tammany-endorsed candidate, he and his colleagues won national acclaim for their reformist crusade.

In 1912 Roosevelt supported Woodrow Wilson, a progressive Democrat, for president and played an important role in getting the New York delegation to vote for him on the 46th ballot. That fall, while Wilson won the presidency, Roosevelt won reelection to the state senate. After Wilson appointed Josephus Daniels as secretary of the navy, Daniels asked Roosevelt to join his department. The New Yorker quickly agreed, and in 1913 he arrived in Washington as assistant secretary of the navy, the exact position held some 15 years earlier by his cousin, Theodore.

When World War I began in 1914, Franklin Roosevelt advocated that America enter the fight against Germany, and he pushed for military preparedness. He even fed information to the Republicans about the navy department so they could attack Josephus Daniels for moving too slowly. That same year he ran unsuccessfully for the U.S. Senate, upon which he returned to his post in the navy department. In fall 1916 Roosevelt said impatiently to Daniels, "We've got to get into this war." That he saw pre-Hitler Germany as a threat to American power suggested how he would see Germany in the 1930s, under a Nazi dictator.

After the United States entered the war in 1917, Roosevelt compiled a plan for naval action, coordinated ship deployments with Britain and France, and supervised the building of more battleships. Most notably, he advocated a mine field between Scotland and Norway in order to keep Germany's submarines in port. The scheme was so complex that Britain initially objected to it, but improved technology, along with Roosevelt's continued pressure, brought it to reality.

In 1918 Eleanor's life crumbled when she discovered her husband's affair with Lucy Mercer, a pretty young woman Eleanor had hired as her social secretary. Eleanor offered Franklin an amicable divorce, but neither he nor his mother wanted to see the marriage end in disgrace and ruin his political future. Instead, Franklin temporarily distanced himself from Lucy and remained with Eleanor. He still looked elsewhere for companionship, however, and in 1920 he began a close friendship with his secretary Missy LeHand, though it remains uncertain as to whether they had an affair.

At the 1920 Democratic convention the delegates chose James M. Cox of Ohio to run for president and tried to make the ticket more glamorous by picking Roosevelt as his running mate. FDR campaigned vigorously for Cox and defended outgoing President Woodrow Wilson's League of Nations, but the Democrats stood no chance of winning. Americans wanted to retreat from overseas involvement, much as they wanted to retreat from domestic reform. The Republican ticket, led by Warren G. Harding, who promised "normalcy" and a return to traditional values, won in a landslide.

Roosevelt returned to his law practice. The following year, 1921, he contracted polio. As he fought his disease and reached the point where he could sit up and move his upper body, he rejected his mother's pressure to live at Hyde Park as an invalid and instead reentered politics. Having received therapy in 88° waters at Warm Springs, Georgia, he led Governor Alfred E. Smith's New York campaign for the Democratic presidential nomination in 1924. Smith lost, but Roosevelt earned respect for his appearance at the state convention when he made his way to the speaker's rostrum hobbled by pain and metal braces strapped to his legs—and then flashed his famous grin.

When Alfred E. Smith won the presidential nomination a second time around, in 1928, he urged FDR to run for governor of New York to attract Democratic voters. Roosevelt at first refused, but when the New York state convention nominated him anyway, he changed his mind. Republicans questioned whether FDR's polio would impair him, but he engaged in a vigorous campaign to dispel any doubts. He won by a slim margin, while Smith lost the state in the presidential contest.

Just a few months into his term, in October 1929, the stock market crashed and New York's once prosperous economy collapsed. To meet the crisis, FDR advanced innovative ideas and practices that he later applied to his presidency. He won reelection in 1930 by 725,000 votes, taking nearly every county with a margin of victory greater than that for any other Democratic candidate in the state.

At Roosevelt's urging, in 1931 the New York legislature passed a bill limiting the workweek for women and children to 48 hours. Another act expanded workmen's compensation. In his boldest move, FDR began the Temporary Emergency Relief Administration, funded with $30 million to help the jobless and needy. According to historian James MacGregor Burns in *Roosevelt: The Lion and the Fox*, "The governor possessed the indispensable quality of accepting the need for change, for new departures, for experiments." As the depression continued, FDR began broadcasting his "fireside chats" on radio and so raised people's spirits.

In such a devastating economic crisis, the national government needed to act boldly, something President Herbert Hoover found difficult to understand. As FDR felt the country's discontent with the president and studied his own ambition for higher office, he decided to seek the White House.

He entered the Democratic National Convention in June 1932 about 100 votes short of the number he needed to win the presidential nomination. He collected the remainder on the fourth ballot after promising to make John Nance Garner of Texas, then Speaker of the House, his running mate.

Roosevelt broke with tradition and traveled to Chicago to accept his nomination in person. At the end of his speech he proclaimed: "I pledge you, I pledge myself, to a new deal for the American people." The press picked up on his phrase *new deal*, and it became the label attached to his reform programs.

In the campaign against Herbert Hoover, FDR offered few specifics—though he did stress the need for unemployment relief, the repeal of Prohibition, and lower tariffs. He largely attacked Hoover for encouraging the speculation and overproduction that had caused the depression and said he opposed letting powerful interests exploit the people.

FDR again showed his remarkable physical stamina when he pursued a coast-to-coast campaign covering 27,000 miles across 41 states. His message of hope contrasted with Hoover's defensive speeches, just as his warm voice and broad smile contrasted with Hoover's stilted and wooden manner. Roosevelt won in a landslide, capturing all but six states.

FDR almost never saw the White House. When he visited Miami, Florida, in February 1933, an unemployed bricklayer, Giuseppe Zangara, tried to kill him. After shouting, "Too many people are starving to death," Zangara opened fire, but a bystander knocked his gun upward and the bullets meant for Roosevelt struck others, among them Chicago Mayor Anton Cermak, who was killed.

As FDR prepared to begin his presidency, he selected his cabinet, including Cordell Hull as secretary of state, Henry Morgenthau, Jr., as secretary of the treasury, and Frances Perkins, the country's first female cabinet member, as secretary of labor. Outside the cabinet, he surrounded himself with experts, financiers, union leaders, and college professors whom newspapers started calling a "brain trust."

Roosevelt's voice resonated with firmness and command when he delivered his inaugural address on March 4, 1933. "This great Nation will endure as it has endured, will revive and will prosper . . .," he said. "Let me assert my firm belief that the only thing we have to fear is fear itself—nameless, unreasoning, unjustified terror which paralyzes needed efforts to convert retreat into advance."

That Roosevelt would act quickly, supported by an overwhelmingly Democratic

Congress, became clear at the very start of his term. On March 5 he declared a four-day bank holiday (though most banks were already closed) to prevent people from withdrawing money and to stop the carnage of bank failures. On March 8 he held his first press conference and displayed an openness and warmth unknown during the presidencies of Calvin Coolidge and Herbert Hoover. Unlike his predecessors, he let reporters ask questions off the cuff rather than submit them in advance.

On March 12, 1933, FDR made the first of his presidential fireside chats, in which he explained the problems facing America's banks. He talked with such confidence and clarity that people quickly gained trust in his leadership and in the banking system itself. Congress soon provided insurance for depositors through the Federal Deposit Insurance Corporation, along with federal assistance that made banks stronger.

Given public discontent and Roosevelt's backing in Congress, he could have nationalized all banks but refused to do so. The way he approached banking typified how he intended to battle the depressed economy—namely, with moderation rather than radicalism. Roosevelt's main strategy was to experiment. The New Deal never developed from a grand plan; it was always a laboratory where formulas sometimes mixed well and sometimes poorly and where he was less the master strategist than the seasoned politician taking the details drawn up by his aides, smoothing them over, and getting them through Congress.

The legislation passed during Roosevelt's first 100 days in office emphasized relief and recovery. The Economy Act, passed on March 20, aimed at balancing the budget and reorganizing government agencies to reduce costs. The Beer and Wine Revenue Act legalized and taxed wine, beer, and ale.

Concerned about the natural environment and about putting people to work, FDR convinced Congress to establish the Civilian Conservation Corps (CCC) . Some 250,000 young men went into forests and parks to plant trees, build roads, and work to control floods. On May 12 Congress created the Federal Emergency Relief Administration (FERA) and provided it with $500 million to help the states establish programs for the unemployed.

The controversial Agricultural Adjustment Act (AAA) sought to boost prices for corn, cotton, wheat, rice, hogs, and dairy products by paying farmers a subsidy for reducing their production. But the AAA hurt poor farmers when the wealthy ones used the government money they received to buy machinery and evict sharecroppers and tenants from their lands. "Tractored out," these people, and others dislocated by exhausted soils, joined the ranks of hollow-eyed migrant workers wandering the countryside in search of low-paying jobs picking fruits and vegetables.

In the boldest legislation of his first 100 days, Roosevelt worked with Senator George W. Norris to establish the Tennessee Valley Authority (TVA) and save the region from its chronic poverty while protecting its natural resources. Roosevelt wanted a comprehensive plan that would include power development, flood control, land reclamation, projects to stop soil erosion, and enticements to attract industry. The bill gave the TVA authority to build dams and power plants and to make and distribute fertilizers. Between 1933 and 1944, the government constructed nine main dams and several smaller ones and generated electricity at prices that attracted industry. Conservatives protested, claiming only private business should operate electric plants. As a result of TVA, the Tennessee Valley entered a modern era of scientific land use, industry, and electricity.

Passage of the National Industrial Recovery Act (NIRA) on June 16, 1933, caused yet more controversy. This bill sought to reduce unemployment by encouraging businesses to collude in fixing prices and wages, while through Section 7A it guaranteed labor's right to bargain collectively. Roosevelt reasoned that if businesses set prices to keep them from falling, profits would be maintained and jobs saved, but in the long run the NIRA failed.

When FDR presented his inaugural address in March 1933, he said he would dedicate America "to the policy of the good neighbor—the neighbor who resolutely respects himself and, because he does so, respects the rights of others." He particularly directed his remarks at Latin America, where Woodrow Wilson had on several occasions intervened militarily. At a conference in Montevideo late in 1933, Secretary of State Cordell Hull signed a document declaring no state had the right to intervene in the affairs of another.

Consequently, while Roosevelt pursued his domestic New Deal, he applied the Good Neighbor Policy to the Western Hemisphere. In 1934 the United States agreed to end the Platt Amendment which had given it nearly absolute authority to send troops into Cuba. That same year, Roosevelt withdrew American troops that had been stationed in Haiti. As war threatened in Europe, he wanted the Good Neighbor Policy to foster inter-American unity. He therefore presented a speech to the Buenos Aires Conference in which he warned aggressors from outside the Western Hemisphere that should they attack, they would find the Americas united in their defense.

Roosevelt changed his domestic course in 1935 and shifted, as he put it, "a little left of center." Several developments led to his Second New Deal. For one, attacks by big business angered him. When members of the U.S. Chamber of Commerce denounced the New Deal, he said that their criticism failed to take "the human side, the old-age side, the unemployment side."

For another, Roosevelt felt emboldened by Democratic gains in the 1934 congressional elections. He also feared that continued high unemployment might mean his defeat in 1936 and cause Americans to embrace radical leaders, such as Louisiana Senator Huey Long, who promoted his plan to limit wealth and assure everyone a guaranteed annual income of $2,500.

FDR stunned Washington when he ordered Congress into special session for the summer of 1935 to consider proposals aimed mainly at reform. One of the most important established a social security system to provide retired persons with a small pension, ranging from $10 to $85 a month, from moneys paid into a fund by employers and employees.

The National Labor Relations Act, also called the Wagner Act, created the National Labor Relations Board (NLRB), which had the power to supervise elections called by workers to determine collective bargaining units. The NLRB could also hear testimony about unfair employment practices and issue orders to stop them. Notably, it could act against companies that fired workers for engaging in union activities. Historian Walter E. Leuchtenburg has called the Wagner Act with its pro-labor content "one of the most drastic legislative innovations of the decade." The act had languished until FDR supported it, leading one observer to recall, "We who believed in the Act were dizzy with watching a 200-to-1 shot come up from the outside."

The Emergency Relief Appropriation Act that passed in April 1935 established the Works Progress Administration (WPA), a large-scale program to employ the jobless. (In 1939 the name was changed to Works Projects Administration.) Roosevelt saw the WPA as a way to get money both into the pockets of workers and flowing through the economy. Between 1935 and 1943 the WPA employed 8.5 million workers at a cost of $11 billion. Critics called it wasteful and pointed to those on the government payroll whose jobs consisted of little more than "busy work" to kill time. Undoubtedly, waste occurred, but the WPA produced some outstanding results: paintings, public buildings, playgrounds, and some of the finest state histories ever written. WPA workers built more than 650,000 miles of highways and built or improved more than 120,000 bridges, 8,000 parks, and 850 airport runways. Teachers taught the mentally handicapped, and musicians played to community audiences for pay that averaged $55 a month.

By executive order President Roosevelt established the Resettlement Administration to help poor farmers ignored by the Agricultural Adjustment Act. He also founded the Rural Electrification Administration, which encouraged farmers to form nonprofit cooperatives and obtain low-cost government loans to bring electricity into rural America. In 1935 few farms had electricity; by 1941, four out of every 10 had it.

No single measure more strongly stirred America's well heeled into contempt for the New Deal than the Revenue Act of 1935, passed by Congress after FDR criticized America's "unjust concentration of wealth and economic power." Along with increases in estate and gift taxes, the government increased the surtax rate on individual incomes over $50,000 and imposed a 75 percent tax rate on incomes over $5 million.

With the New Deal, Roosevelt attempted to build a welfare state with corporate capitalism as its foundation, meaning he wanted the federal government to help those Americans that business could not or would not help. He rejected socialism and other radical ideas and thought his programs would save capitalism. But conservatives considered him an extremist, a threat to free enterprise and the profit motive.

In the 1936 presidential campaign, about 70 percent of the newspapers in America's 15 largest cities supported FDR's Republican opponent, Alfred M. "Alf" Landon. Nevertheless, Roosevelt won the biggest victory in the electoral college since James Monroe's first-term triumph in the early 1800s, and he collected nearly 61 percent of the popular vote as the working class cast its ballots for him. Economic conditions helped FDR with more than 6 million new jobs created since 1933.

More than any presidential election since 1896, the vote divided along class lines, with big business backing Landon and unions backing Roosevelt. Critics assailed FDR for stirring class animosities. They pointed to his statement in October 1936 calling for an end to "the glaring inequalities of opportunity and security which, in the recent past, have set group against group and region against region," as well as his declaration: "Government by organized *money* is just as dangerous as Government by organized *mob.*" In *Freedom From Fear: The American People in Depression and War, 1929–1945*, David M. Kennedy agrees with FDR's critics and says that for all Roosevelt's good qualities, he could call out the worst in people and did so when he exploited class resentments.

Franklin Roosevelt's coattails proved so strong in 1936 that Democrats captured 334 seats in the House of Representatives compared to only 89 for Republicans, while in the Senate they held a 75-17 advantage. FDR cemented an emerging coalition of Southern Democrats, urbanites, labor, and African Americans. Blacks, who had traditionally voted Republican, benefited from the relief programs that uplifted all lower-income groups, such as the WPA, 20 percent of whose jobs went to African Americans. Roosevelt, though, refrained from pushing a strong civil rights program that would antagonize the southern white congressmen whose support he needed for his New Deal.

Despite the Democratic election sweep, the New Deal lost its momentum when Roosevelt attacked the Supreme Court, whose conservative justices had ruled several of his programs unconstitutional, among them the NIRA and the AAA. The justices also struck down a New York law establishing a minimum wage, which they said interfered with the right of workers to negotiate contracts. In February 1937, FDR announced he would ask Congress to allow him and future presidents to appoint a new justice to the Supreme Court for each one that remained on the bench after age 70, up to a total of six. Called by critics a "court-packing bill," it was intended to let Roosevelt appoint enough justices sympathetic to the New Deal so they could outvote the conservatives.

Many Americans agreed with Roosevelt's criticism that the Court intended to gut the New Deal, but they considered his proposal too radical. FDR lost the fight, and the entire episode emboldened conservatives and others who warned about dictatorial tendencies in the White House. Yet as congressmen debated the

Court-packing bill, the Supreme Court began finding New Deal programs constitutional; they approved the Wagner Act in April 1937 and the Social Security Act a short time later.

FDR endangered the New Deal again in 1937 when he reacted to an economic upturn by cutting federal programs quickly and severely to achieve a balanced budget. He slashed WPA rolls by 50 percent, and as the Federal Reserve Board tightened credit, unemployment returned to its pre-1935 level. The president took a different course in 1938 when he increased spending, but the economy remained weak. In elections that year Republicans gained 13 governorships, eight Senate seats, and 81 House seats.

From then on, Roosevelt was unable to convince Congress to pass most of the reform legislation he wanted. As the New Deal lost its vitality, in many ways it left America unchanged: It had failed to end the depression or to compensate for declines in private investment, and it had failed to shift the distribution of wealth or income significantly. Yet FDR strengthened the presidency by exerting stronger leadership and wielding more power than his predecessors, Harding, Coolidge, and Hoover, and the federal government entered people's lives more extensively than ever.

Historians still debate how innovational FDR was with his New Deal. John A. Garraty, for example, sees Roosevelt as merely reflecting efforts then underway to reform the European economies, and Arthur Schlesinger, Jr., believes that America was moving toward a new era of reform even before the Great Depression began. FDR's response to the economic crisis, he says, "was controlled and tempered by the values of traditional American experimentalism."

As Adolf Hitler built his war machine in Germany, Americans wanted to avoid entry into another world war. Consequently, Congress passed a series of Neutrality Acts in the 1930s, including one that placed an embargo on arms shipments to belligerents. These, however, limited FDR's power to act against aggression in Europe and the threat from Japan in the Pacific.

When Hitler invaded Poland on September 1, 1939, igniting war with Britain and France, Roosevelt responded: "It's come at last. God help us all." He convinced Congress to repeal the 1935 Neutrality Act and allow the United States to export arms to belligerent powers, provided they pay cash for the supplies and carry them in their own ships. In June 1940 France surrendered to Germany, leaving Britain as the last western defense against Hitler. By that time FDR openly favored the Allies, and while isolationists warned that he was pulling the United States into war, he signed a deal that transferred 50 old destroyers to Britain in exchange for leases on British bases in the Western Hemisphere.

In the 1940 election, FDR ran for an unprecedented third term against Indiana lawyer and utilities executive Wendell Willkie. Both men favored an international role for the United States while advocating the avoidance of war. Roosevelt talked about the economy and said, "This year there is being placed on the tables of America more butter, more cheese, more meat, more canned goods—more food in general than in that luxurious year of 1929." He also promised the voters: "Your boys are not going to be sent into any foreign wars," and added, "It is for peace that I have labored; and it is for peace that I shall labor for all the days of my life." Yet after his victory, events combined with his own actions to take the United States deeper into the conflict. In December 1940 he declared that America must defend freedom overseas by becoming an "arsenal of democracy."

When Britain could no longer afford to pay for arms, Roosevelt obtained congressional approval in March 1941 for a lend-lease deal whereby the British (and other countries) promised to return weapons lent to them. In May a German submarine downed the American merchant ship *Robin Moor* near the coast of Brazil. When Hitler attacked the Soviet Union in June, FDR extended lend-lease to that country.

In August Roosevelt and British prime minister Winston Churchill signed the Atlantic Charter, committing their countries to a list of "Four Freedoms" that FDR had expressed earlier: freedom of speech and expression, freedom of worship, freedom from want, and freedom from fear. The charter renounced territorial ambition and pledged support for people to choose their own form of government.

In September the American ship *Greer* provoked a German submarine into attacking it. FDR then announced that American destroyers would shoot German and Italian ships on sight in a zone that extended to Greenland and Iceland. When in October the Germans sank the American destroyer *Reuben James*, killing more than 100 sailors, Congress permitted the shipment of weapons to England on armed American merchant ships.

While confronting the European crisis, Roosevelt also had to deal with Japan. After the Japanese occupied French Indochina in July 1941, he prohibited shipments of scrap iron and oil to them and froze their credit in the United States. Diplomatic talks followed, but when he insisted the Japanese get out of China, they decided to attack the United States at Pearl Harbor. The surprise bombing on December 7, 1941—"a date which will live in infamy," FDR intoned—destroyed 19 ships, most of the U.S. Pacific fleet, and killed 2,400 Americans. After the United States declared war on Japan, Germany and Italy declared war on the United States.

For the most part, Roosevelt left battlefield strategy to his generals and delegated the job of mobilization to the War Production Board, which faced the challenge of rapidly converting industries from civilian to military use. The change happened so quickly that one observer called it an "economic revolution."

FDR generally respected civil liberties, except in one notable instance when he approved the internment of 120,000 Japanese Americans—77,000 of whom were native-born citizens of the United States—in "relocation centers." They were imprisoned because the army thought all Japanese, whether they were American or not, were "an enemy race" that threatened national security.

The United States quickly mobilized its armed forces in 1942 and entered the war in the Pacific, European, and Mediterranean theaters. As the Japanese advanced throughout the Netherlands East Indies, Major General James Doolittle led a fleet of B-25 bombers on a raid of Tokyo in April. In May there occurred the Battle of the Coral Sea and in June the Battle of Midway, which was the first major defeat of the Japanese navy. In August, American forces began their offensive at Guadalcanal in the Solomon Islands, leading to a decisive naval victory that November. The United States launched its first independent bombing attack in Europe in August with a raid on railroad yards near Rouen, a city in northern France. That November, General Dwight D. Eisenhower and British admiral Sir Andrew Cunningham unleashed Operation Torch, an amphibious assault in North Africa.

As the war continued to expand, Roosevelt adeptly handled the difficult diplomacy necessary to coordinate plans with Britain and the Soviet Union. In January 1943 he conferred with Winston Churchill at Casablanca, Morocco, and they agreed to a strategy whereby Allied troops would attack Hitler's army from the Mediterranean and from the west through France. The two leaders also declared they would demand Germany's unconditional surrender.

In November 1943 Roosevelt met with Churchill and Soviet communist dictator Joseph Stalin at Tehran, Iran. At the meeting Stalin expressed his fear that Britain would delay launching the planned western assault through France as a way to bleed his country in a prolonged fight with Germany. After prodding from Roosevelt, Churchill mollified Stalin by agreeing to launch Operation Overlord—the invasion of France by allied troops—in May 1944.

Roosevelt thought that by charming Stalin, he could loosen him up. He started cracking jokes about Churchill, telling Stalin one morning that the British prime minister was cranky because "he got up on the wrong side of the bed." FDR later recounted:

> A vague smile passed over Stalin's eyes, and I decided I was on the right track. I began to tease Churchill about his Britishness, . . . about his cigars, about his habits. . . . Winston got red and scowled, and the more he did so, the more Stalin smiled. Finally Stalin broke out into a deep, heavy guffaw . . . . I kept it up until Stalin was laughing with me, and it was then that I called him "Uncle Joe."

In August 1944, the tide of battle having turned in their favor, the Allies met at Dumbarton Oaks, near Washington, D.C., to structure a new international peacekeeping organization, the United Nations. That fall, Roosevelt turned back the challenge from another Republican presidential candidate, New York governor Thomas E. Dewey, and won reelection to an unprecedented fourth term.

In February 1945 FDR again met with Stalin and Churchill, this time at Yalta in the Crimea. They gathered at a former summer retreat for the Russian czars—with 50 ornate rooms, gardens, and trees—while Allied troops from the west and Soviet troops from the east advanced toward Berlin. As Hitler's end neared, they discussed policies for postwar Europe. Stalin wanted Germany punished; Churchill wanted to ensure that Germany would be left strong enough to resist Soviet aggression. They ultimately decided to divide Germany into occupation zones, one each for the United States, Britain, and the Soviet Union (with France to be given a zone carved from the British and American ones, and all four countries to govern Berlin).

The biggest sticking point involved Poland. Both FDR and Churchill wanted Polish exiles in London to form a government in Warsaw. But Stalin insisted on maintaining the Soviet-backed government already in Poland and headquartered in Lublin. The three leaders eventually reached a compromise whereby the Soviets obtained territory in eastern Poland and promised to hold free elections throughout the country after the war. The agreement, however, left this last point vague, and in the long term, the elections were never held.

In the Far East, FDR wanted Stalin to join the war against Japan. Uncle Joe agreed, but for a price: The Soviet Union would be given the Kuril Islands, Sakhalin Island, the port of Darien, and control over a railroad in Manchuria.

Critics later charged FDR had abandoned eastern Europe to the Soviets and their communist system. In truth he could do little against Stalin's army, which occupied Poland and most of eastern Europe, and little more without risking Stalin's refusal to participate in the United Nations, which FDR considered crucial to any postwar peace. FDR knew full well the Soviet dictator could not be trusted. In March 1945 he said to a friend, "We can't do business with Stalin. He has broken every one of the promises he made at Yalta."

In recent years a few historians have criticized Roosevelt for failing to prevent Hitler from slaughtering European Jews during World War II. They claim he should have ordered the bombing of Auschwitz and of railroad lines leading to other death camps. But Lucy Dawidowicz and other historians reject the idea that Roosevelt cared little about the Jews and insist that by diverting air strikes away from military installations, he would have prolonged the war and its horrible Holocaust.

At the Yalta Conference, Roosevelt looked pale and drawn; Churchill later said, "I felt that he had a slender contact with life." In late March he went to Warm Springs, Georgia, to rest. While there he drafted his Jefferson Day speech, in which he said about World War II, "We must go on to do all in our power to conquer the doubts and the fears, the ignorance and the greed, which made this horror possible."

Roosevelt had begun seeing Lucy Mercer again. On April 12 he was speaking with her and her friend, Madame Shoumatoff, an artist painting his portrait, when he complained of a severe headache and suddenly slumped over, unconscious. His aides carried him to his bed, where he lay in a coma. Realizing what propriety required, Lucy left the scene. At 3:35 P.M. on April 12, 1945, Franklin Delano Roosevelt died from a massive cerebral hemorrhage. Americans deeply mourned the death of a president who had led them through depression and war.

That in meeting these challenges Roosevelt conquered his own physical handicap makes his accomplishments all the more momentous. Historian Doris Kearns Goodwin recalls that whenever FDR had trouble sleeping at night, he would think back to his boyhood when he would jump on his sled and fly down a hill, reach the bottom, then go back up, over and over again. "This man is the most powerful man in the world, and yet he's imagining . . . —and getting solace from—the idea that he can run, sled, walk again. . . ." Americans also sought solace and found it in Franklin Roosevelt's leadership.

CHRONOLOGY

1882 Born January 30

1896 Enters Groton School

1900 Enters Harvard University

1903 Graduates from Harvard

1904 Enters Columbia Law School

1905 Marries Anna Eleanor Roosevelt

1907 Admitted to the New York bar

1910 Elected to the New York state senate

1912 Helps Woodrow Wilson win the Democratic presidential nomination

Reelected state senator

1913 Appointed assistant secretary of the navy

1914 Loses bid for U.S. Senate seat

1920 Nominated for vice-president to run with James M. Cox

Cox-Roosevelt ticket loses

1921 Stricken with polio

1924 Nominates Al Smith for president at Democratic National Convention

1928 Elected governor of New York

1930 Reelected governor of New York

1931 Establishes New York Temporary Emergency Relief Administration

1932 Wins Democratic presidential nomination

1933 Escapes assassination in Miami, Florida

Inaugurated as president

Declares four-day bank holiday

Calls Congress into special session to consider New Deal legislation

Begins fireside chats

Establishes National Labor Relations Board

First Hundred Days legislation establishes New Deal

Recognizes Soviet Union

1935 Proposes Second New Deal that emphasizes social reform

Begins Works Progress Administration

Signs Wagner Act

Establishes social security system

Proposes Revenue Act

1936 Reelected president

Attends Inter-American Conference in Buenos Aires, Argentina

1937 Fails to expand size of Supreme Court

1938 Campaigns unsuccessfully against conservative Democratic congressmen

1939 Proclaims U.S. neutrality in World War II

Recommends "cash and carry" export of arms to belligerents

1940 Sends destroyers to Britain in exchange for leases on naval bases

Reelected president for unprecedented third term

1941 Announces Four Freedoms

Proclaims national emergency

Extends aid to Soviet Union

	Confers with Winston Churchill and announces Atlantic Charter
	Asks Congress to declare war on Japan
1942	Signs United Nations Declaration
	Establishes War Production Board
	Orders internment of Japanese Americans
1943	Meets with Winston Churchill at Casablanca
	Attends Tehran Conference with Churchill and Joseph Stalin
1944	Reelected president
1945	Confers with Churchill and Stalin at Yalta
	Dies April 12

FURTHER READING

Abbott, Phillip. *The Exemplary Presidency: Franklin D. Roosevelt and the American Political Tradition.* Amherst: University of Massachusetts Press, 1990.

Badger, Anthony J. *The New Deal: The Depression Years, 1933–1940.* Basingstoke, England: Macmillan, 1989.

Beschloss, Michael R. *The Conquerors: Roosevelt, Truman and the Destruction of Hitler's Germany, 1941–1945.* New York: Simon & Schuster, 2002.

Black, Conrad. *Franklin Delano Roosevelt: Champion of Freedom.* New York: Public Affairs, 2003.

Brinkley, Alan. *The End of Reform: New Deal Liberalism in Recession and War.* New York: Alfred A. Knopf, 1995.

———. *Voices of Protest: Huey Long, Father Coughlin, and the Great Depression.* New York: Vintage Books, 1982.

Burns, James MacGregor. *Roosevelt: The Lion and the Fox.* New York: Harcourt, Brace & World, 1956.

———. *Roosevelt: The Soldier of Freedom.* New York: Harcourt, Brace, Jovanovich, 1970.

Conkin, Paul. *The New Deal.* Rev. ed. New York: Crowell, 1975.

Dallek, Robert. *Franklin D. Roosevelt and American Foreign Policy, 1932–1945.* New York: Oxford University Press, 1995.

Davis, Kenneth S. *FDR: The Beckoning of Destiny.* New York: Putnam, 1972.

———. *FDR: The New Deal Years, 1933–1937.* New York: Random House, 1979.

Freidel, Frank. *Franklin D. Roosevelt,* 4 vols. Boston: Little, Brown, 1,952–1,973.

———. *Franklin D. Roosevelt: A Rendezvous with Destiny.* Boston: Little, Brown, 1990.

Goodwin, Doris Kearns. *No Ordinary Times: Franklin and Eleanor Roosevelt, The Home Front in World War II.* New York: Simon & Schuster, 1994.

Jenkins, Roy. *Franklin Delano Roosevelt.* New York: Times Books, 2003.

Kennedy, David. *Freedom from Fear: The American People in Depression and War, 1929–1945.* New York: Oxford University Press, 1999.

Kimball, Warren F., ed. *Churchill and Roosevelt: The Complete Correspondence,* 3 vols. Princeton, N.J.: Princeton University Press, 1984.

Lash, Joseph P. *Eleanor and Franklin: The Story of Their Relationship Based on Eleanor Roosevelt's Private Papers.* New York: New American Library, 1973.

Leuchtenburg, William E. *The FDR Years: On Roosevelt and His Legacy.* New York: Columbia University Press, 1995.

———. *Franklin D. Roosevelt and the New Deal, 1932–1940.* New York: Harper & Row, 1963.

McJimsey, George. *The Presidency of Franklin Delano Roosevelt.* Lawrence: University Press of Kansas, 2002.

Meacham, Jon. *Franklin and Winston: An Intimate Portrait of an Epic Friendship.* New York: Random House, 2003.

Robinson, Greg. *By Order of the President: FDR and the Internment of Japanese Americans.* Cambridge, Mass.: Harvard University Press, 2001.

Schlesinger, Arthur M., Jr. *The Age of Roosevelt.* 3 vols. Boston: Houghton Mifflin, 1957–1960.

Ward, Geoffrey C. *Before the Trumpet: Young Franklin Roosevelt, 1882–1905.* New York: Harper & Row, 1985.

*H*ARRY S. TRUMAN (1884–1972)

Thirty-third President, 1945–1953

HARRY S. TRUMAN
(Library of Congress)

"Communism is based on the belief that man is so weak and inadequate that he is unable to govern himself, and therefore requires the rule of strong masters."

—Inaugural words, January 20, 1949

Few Americans had seen a mushroom cloud before 1945. Then atomic bombs were dropped on Hiroshima and Nagasaki, and so many pictures of nuclear explosions followed that most people soon readily equated the phrase *mushroom cloud* with the bomb.

Few Americans could locate Korea on a map before 1950. Then the United States went to war against communist aggression on the Korean Peninsula, and Americans quickly learned about Pusan, Inchon, and the Yalu River.

Americans also learned that Korea and the mushroom cloud—and the frightening prospect of a world war that could destroy the Earth—were knotted to each other and to their president, Harry S. Truman. For when in the short time span between 1945 and 1950 he decided to employ both the bomb and the troops, he brought together the fear and firmness that became the chief weapons in a cold war against communism. This, much more than any domestic policy, was his greatest legacy.

Harry S. Truman was born on May 8, 1884, in Lamar, Missouri, to John Anderson Truman and Martha Ellen Young Truman. (The initial "S" in Truman's name was not an abbreviation of any name but was supposedly chosen to avoid showing favoritism between his paternal grandfather's name, which was Shippe, and his maternal grandfather's name, which was Solomon.) In 1885 Truman's father bought a farm near Harrisonville, where Harry spent his next six years. A friendly boy, his outdoor activities were handicapped by poor eyesight, and he became a curiosity to his neighbors when he began wearing thick glasses at age five; they had never seen eyeglasses worn by anyone at such a young age.

In 1890 the Trumans moved to Independence, Missouri, a town of 6,000 people more southern than midwestern in character. There Harry could receive better schooling, and his father could work as a stock trader. Harry was a voracious reader, a habit encouraged by his parents, who kept many books at home. When he was 10, he read the multivolume *Great Men and Famous Women*, an anthology of articles from American and British magazines written at an adult level that left an impression on him so strong that he later called it an important influence on his life.

The stories showed him the power of the human will. About the American revolutionary-era naval hero John Paul Jones, one story said: "He was one of nature's self-made men; that is, nature gave the genius, and he supplied the industry, for he knew how to labor and . . . exerted himself to secure the attainments which he possessed." Truman later wrote: "It takes men to make history, or there would be no history. History does not make the man."

Neighborhood children considered Harry different, but they respected his seriousness, and despite his bookish behavior he remained sociable. Early on, he developed the knack of observing other people. He later said, "I used to watch my father and mother closely to learn what I could do to please them, just as I did with my schoolteachers and playmates."

In addition to reading, he liked to play the piano, and he practiced two hours a day with the hope of becoming a concert pianist. Politics piqued Harry's interest when his father took him to the Democratic National Convention in Kansas City in 1900. The youngster ran errands for delegates and reveled in the charged atmosphere.

Just weeks after Harry graduated from high school in May 1901, his father went broke over bad investments and was forced to move his family to Kansas City, where he could get a job. Harry's idyllic boyhood in Independence had ended.

Harry wanted to attend college, but finances prevented it. To earn money he began laying track for the Santa Fe Railroad. For several years, beginning in 1903, he worked as a bank clerk and a teller; after that he helped his father farm land at Grandview. He hated farming, however, and talked disparagingly about shucking corn.

Despite his struggling economic prospects, in 1913 he became engaged to his childhood friend, Elizabeth "Bess" Wallace. Marriage, however, was delayed by his continuing economic problems and by World War I when, in 1917, the national guard unit he had joined was mobilized. The bespectacled, farsighted Truman, already in his thirties, served as an artillery officer in France.

In letters home Truman showed uncertainty about his future, yet revealed his first serious consideration of politics when he wrote about running for public office. He called Missouri "God's country" and said to Bess, "I love you as madly as a man can." He thought constantly about settling down. "We'll be married anywhere you say at any time you mention," he said. "And if you want only one person or the whole town I don't care as long as you can make it quickly after my arrival."

Truman returned from France in 1919 to a triumphant parade in Kansas City. He and other officers rode on horseback, their procession surrounded by flags and bunting on buildings and by cheers from a big crowd. In June he married Bess; they would have one child, Margaret. That November he and a partner opened Truman & Jacobson, a haberdashery in Kansas City that sold men's shirts, socks, ties, belts, underwear, and hats. The store started strong, but with the recession of 1921 it struggled, and in 1922 it closed its doors.

While he was still in business, Truman met Mike Pendergast, father of an army buddy of his from World War I. Mike and his brother Tom were political bosses in Kansas City, and Mike asked Truman to run for district judge, technically an administrative post rather than a judicial one, as part of their Democratic machine. Truman immediately agreed. Later he explained he needed the job, but clearly his latent liking for politics mattered as well. He wrote a friend: "They are trying to run me for Eastern Judge, out in Independence, and I guess they'll do it before they are through." He won election to the office in 1922 and controlled county spending on many projects.

Truman lost his bid for reelection in 1924, but Tom Pendergast decided to run him for presiding judge over all of Jackson County, which included Kansas City. This time he won, and he served from 1927 until 1935. While in that office in 1933, President Franklin Roosevelt appointed him director of the federal reemployment service for Missouri. With his frequent trips to Washington to meet with government officials, he soon thought about running for Congress. In May 1934 Tom Pendergast surprised Truman by asking him to seek the U.S. Senate. Truman said he would, unaware at the time that he was actually Pendergast's third choice and that many of Pendergast's friends considered the former haberdasher a political lightweight.

Harry Truman hit the stump as an honest, down-to-earth country boy who spoke his piece in plain words. He traveled by car from one county courthouse to another, and after winning a tough primary battle he beat his Republican opponent by a large margin. Yet he went to Washington bearing an odious label: the stooge of a political boss. Critics said he would not have won without Pendergast's support—likely true, but the Great Depression had swept most Democratic candidates into office—and rather than call him the "Senator from Missouri" they called him the "Senator from Pendergast." Truman gave his critics more ammunition when he maintained his close ties to the Kansas City machine and placed in the reception area of his office a framed portrait of none other than Tom Pendergast.

Though Truman thought liberals arrogant, he supported Franklin Roosevelt's New Deal to help the common folk during the economic crisis of the 1930s. In his most notable early speech, presented in December 1937, he attacked corporate greed and blamed unemployment on a high concentration of economic power, stating: "It is a pity that Wall Street, with its ability to control all the wealth of the nation and to hire the best law brains in the country, has not produced some . . . men who could see the dangers of bigness and of the concentration of the control of wealth. Instead of working to meet the situation, they are still employing the best law brains to serve greed and self interest."

Despite Truman's opposition to social equality between whites and blacks, and his private references to African Americans as "niggers," he strongly supported civil rights legislation. He voted for a bill to end the discriminatory poll tax, and in 1938 he tried, but failed, to break the filibuster of an antilynching bill.

In time Harry Truman earned the respect of fellow senators who no longer looked at him as a mere Pendergast puppet. But his prospects for reelection in 1940 dimmed when Franklin

Roosevelt opposed his bid for another term, and when the Pendergast machine collapsed after Tom Pendergast was found guilty of income-tax evasion. Still, Truman beat the odds against a Republican opponent and won a narrow victory.

In his second term he obtained national prominence by fighting waste in government. He began his crusade after he heard about cost overruns in the building of Fort Leonard Wood in his home state. He then drove several thousand miles throughout the South, checking federal military installations. In February 1941 his findings convinced him to propose a special committee to probe military spending. The Senate agreed and created the Committee to Investigate the National Defense Program, more often called the Truman Committee.

The White House at first disliked the committee, for any problems it uncovered implied Democratic mismanagement. But as Truman expanded his investigation, he obtained such favorable press coverage that Franklin Roosevelt embraced him. As the United States fought in Europe against Hitler and in Asia against Japan, *Time* magazine called Truman's committee "the watchdog, spotlight, conscience and spark plug to the economic war-behind-the-lines." The committee saved taxpayers billions of dollars, but it went beyond cutting costs, exposing defective airplane engines and poor-quality steel, and proposing design changes that improved military equipment.

During his investigation Truman stumbled across the Manhattan Project, the government's top-secret program to develop an atomic bomb. Although the exact nature of the weapon was kept from him, he did learn there would be a powerful new device, and in July 1943 he wrote to a former senator about the government's purchase of land at Hanford, Washington: "I have been informed that it is for the construction of a plant to make a terrific explosion for a secret weapon that will be a wonder."

Truman completely backed Franklin Roosevelt in World War II, and he fully believed stories about the Holocaust. In a speech presented in 1943, he said, "No one can any longer doubt the horrible intentions of the Nazi beasts. We know that they plan the systematic slaughter throughout all of Europe, not only of the Jews but of vast numbers of other innocent peoples."

When President Franklin Roosevelt sought a fourth term in 1944, fellow Democrats pressured him to drop Vice President Henry Wallace from the ticket for his strident liberalism and sympathetic remarks about Russia. The party's national chairman, Robert Hannegan, wanted either William O. Douglas, the Supreme Court justice, or Harry Truman to run with Roosevelt, but neither man desired the nomination. As recounted by David McCullough in his book *Truman*, Hannegan called Truman into his office, and as the senator stood there, Hannegan picked up the phone and held it away from his ear so Franklin Roosevelt's commanding voice could be heard from the other end.

> "Bob," Roosevelt said, "have you got that fellow lined up yet?"
>
> "No," Hannegan said, "he is the contrariest goddamn mule from Missouri I ever dealt with."
>
> "Well, you tell the senator that if he wants to break up the Democratic party in the middle of the war, that's his responsibility."
>
> "Well, if that's the situation," Truman said to Hannegan, "I'll have to say yes. But why the hell didn't he tell me in the first place?"

Having been picked by the Democratic Party's political bosses and anointed by President Roosevelt, Truman accepted the nomination, and the ticket went on to win in November 1944. With Roosevelt's health in decline, however, the Missourian and other Democratic insiders knew that the president would likely die in office. "I did not want to think about the possibility." Truman recalled. "The rumors were widespread but not publicly discussed." About a talk with Roosevelt, Truman wrote: "I met with the president [in late

February 1945] and was shocked by his appearance. His eyes were sunken. His magnificent smile was missing from his careworn face. He seemed a spent man."

Roosevelt died on April 12, 1945. Harry Truman thereupon inherited a war nearly over in Europe—Germany's surrender was just days away—but still being fought vigorously in Asia, as Japan resisted the advancing American forces. To quickly learn about Roosevelt's war policies, he studied the correspondence between his predecessor and America's allied leaders, Winston Churchill of Britain and Joseph Stalin of the Soviet Union, and also gathered information from his own advisers. Truman concluded that Stalin was breaking promises he had made at the Yalta Conference earlier that year and that after the war the Russian communist regime would pose a danger to American security.

As a result, on April 23, 1945, Truman met at the White House with Soviet Foreign Minister Vyacheslav Molotov and demanded that Russia abide by the Yalta agreement to hold free elections in Poland. When Molotov tried to say the Poles were undermining the Red Army, Truman interrupted him and firmly stated he wanted Molotov to tell Stalin to keep his word. According to Truman, Molotov said, "I have never been talked to like that in my life." Truman responded, "Carry out your agreements and you won't get talked to like that." Another observer at the meeting remembered the words as being less dramatic, but whatever the case, the exchange amounted to a tense confrontation.

Soon after, the Russians made a minor concession when they allowed a few noncommunist Poles into the government. The United States then agreed to allow Poland into the newly formed United Nations.

One day after Truman met with Molotov, Secretary of War Henry L. Stimson told the president about the government's A-bomb project. In a note he said, "Within four months we shall in all probability have completed the most terrible weapon ever known in human history, one bomb of which could destroy a whole city." Truman then read a lengthy report on the bomb and formed a committee to study how it might affect society.

In July 1945 he met with Churchill and Stalin at Potsdam, Germany. (Churchill was replaced in midconference by Britain's new prime minister, Clement Attlee.) On July 16 the president's advisers told him the United States had completed a successful test of the A-bomb. He decided to inform Stalin in cryptic language that America now possessed a weapon of mass destruction. When he did, Stalin merely said, "Good, I hope the United States will use it." According to Molotov,

> Truman decided to surprise us. . . . He took Stalin and me aside and—looking secretive—informed us they had this secret weapon of a wholly new type, an extraordinary weapon. . . . It's difficult to say what he was thinking, but it seemed to me he wanted to throw us into consternation. Stalin, however, reacted to this quite calmly, and Truman decided he hadn't understood. The words "atomic bomb" hadn't been spoken, but we immediately guessed what was meant.

And well they should have, for the Russians had their own A-bomb research underway, and physicist Klaus Fuchs, working at the American nuclear site in Los Alamos, New Mexico, was passing secrets to them.

While at Potsdam on July 25, Truman decided to use the A-bomb against Japan unless that nation surrendered by August 3. The following day, the American, British, and Chinese governments issued the Potsdam Declaration calling for Japan to give up or face "utter destruction."

The Japanese likely would have surrendered if they had been provided assurances that they could keep their emperor. But Truman faced intense pressure from his advisers to accept nothing less than unconditional surrender. Furthermore neither he nor most other Americans felt any compassion toward the Japanese after their sneak attack at Pearl Harbor and their atrocities against American soldiers. Truman also believed that if he ordered a ground invasion of Japan, American troops would suffer horrific losses from an enemy determined to fight to the bitter end.

The president wrote in his memoirs: "On July 28 Radio Tokyo announced that the Japanese government would continue to fight. There was no formal reply to [the Potsdam Declaration]. There was no alternative now." America's commanding general in Europe, Dwight D. Eisenhower, thought differently. He later said he told Stimson of his "grave misgivings, first on the basis of my belief that Japan was already defeated and that dropping the bomb was completely unnecessary, and secondly because I thought our country should avoid shocking world opinion by the use of a weapon whose employment was, I thought, no longer mandatory as a measure to save American lives."

On August 6, 1945, a B-29 aircraft, the *Enola Gay*, dropped the A-bomb on Hiroshima. Heat from the blast melted roof tiles, charred telegraph poles, and obliterated human bodies, leaving only shadows etched on concrete. As many as 100,000 civilians died immediately. More than two miles away from the blast, people had their skin burned and peeling from their bodies. Radiation poisoned the air and would cause more deaths for years to come.

On August 8 Stalin declared war on Japan, sending Soviet troops into the Asian fight. On August 9 the United States dropped an A-bomb on Nagasaki, and on August 10 Japan surrendered. Truman said the emperor could remain, a preservation of an ancient regime as the modern atomic age began. Had Truman dropped the bomb to frighten Russia as well? He never said so, but many analysts thought he did, and numerous historians since then have concluded that was one of his objectives.

Despite the euphoria surrounding the end to World War II, Truman's public support plummeted as domestic problems mounted. Through his Fair Deal program he tried to pursue numerous reforms, but inflation caused workers to strike for higher wages. In 1946 John L. Lewis led the United Mine Workers (UMW) in a walkout that closed soft-coal mines. In May, Truman seized the mines and forced a settlement that the UMW condemned but accepted.

When railroad workers called a strike for later that month, Truman seized the railroads and prepared to ask Congress for the power to draft the laborers into the army and force them back to their jobs. With that threat hanging over their heads, the union reached a settlement.

As the cost of living continued to rise, Truman's popularity dropped, and with congressional elections approaching in 1946, only 32 percent of the public supported him. That fall the Republicans won both houses of Congress for the first time in more than 15 years. Over the following months, discontent with labor reached a fever pitch, culminating in the passage of passed the antiunion Taft-Hartley Act in June 1947. Although Truman vetoed it, saying it imposed "harsh restrictions on the hard-won rights of labor," Congress overrode him.

Meanwhile, relations with the Soviet Union worsened. Stalin wielded an iron hand in Eastern Europe and refused to remove Soviet troops from Iran, at least until Truman strongly protested. At the same time, the president worried about Greece. Communist rebels had gained power over much of the country during World War II, and in 1947 the British, who had committed themselves to restoring the Greek monarchy but were financially strapped, decided give up the fight. Truman feared that if Greece fell to communism, so too would Turkey and the rest of the eastern Mediterranean. He mistakenly believed Stalin supported the rebels, and he decided in March to scare the hell out of the American public about the threat. In his Truman Doctrine of May 1947, he said the United States would help peoples facing "attempted subjugation by armed minorities or by outside pressures."

Truman subsequently wrote his daughter Margaret: "The attempt of Lenin, Trotsky, Stalin, et al., to fool the world and the American

Crackpots Association, represented by . . . Henry Wallace, [Congressman] Claude Pepper and the actors and actresses in immoral Greenwich Village, is just like Hitler's and Mussolini's so-called socialist states. Your pop had to tell the world just that in polite language." Truman's speech announcing the doctrine stressed a simplistic view: a fight between good and evil, with the United States all good. After the speech, by a vote of 67-23 in the Senate and 287-107 in the House, Congress approved aid to Greece and Turkey, and the communist rebels were soon defeated. The phrase *cold war* began appearing, referring to the rapidly emerging conflict between the United States and the Soviet Union for world influence, waged largely through arms buildups, economic pressure, overseas intervention, espionage, and propaganda.

Later in 1947 Secretary of State George Marshall announced a plan to give economic aid to war-torn Europe. Originally Truman had intended the aid to be made available to the Soviet Union as well, but no one expected the Soviets to accept it (and in fact they refused), and the president really meant it as another weapon against communism. Marshall and Truman believed that making Europe prosperous again would make it less prone to left-wing movement. Congress at first balked at the cost, until communists took over in Czechoslovakia and Truman went to Capitol Hill to denounce the Soviets as ruthless. In April 1947 Congress voted $4 billion for the program.

To Americans it looked like communism might conquer the world, and as rebellions flared, they refused to believe that anyone would willingly embrace the Red ideology. Many concluded that communism's success came from Moscow directing revolutions and from traitors operating within the federal government. Consequently, in the late 1940s America plunged into a Red Scare—a hunt for communists and radical influences throughout American society. The hunt took place in Washington, in Hollywood movies, in television, in classrooms, and in literature. Joseph McCarthy, a Republican senator from Wisconsin, soon led the charge, using smear tactics that involved lies, guilt by association, and falsified evidence. Investigations did uncover spies, and without a doubt there were communists living in America, but McCarthy's broad brush painted many innocent people Red and ruined their careers.

Truman hated McCarthy but said little about him, believing the senator would dig his own political grave, which he eventually did. In 1948, however, the president tired of McCarthy's attacks on Secretary of State Dean Acheson and in a bold public statement called McCarthy "the greatest asset that the Kremlin has."

In summer 1948 Stalin blockaded Berlin in retaliation for American and British plans to recognize West Germany. Truman then ordered a massive airlift of food and fuel that broke the blockade. Where Stalin believed he had acted defensively to prevent the rise of a strong Germany that would again threaten the Soviet Union, world opinion judged him to be both aggressive and brutal in his efforts to starve a city into submission.

Truman's breaking of the blockade displayed his commitment to the containment of communism. A top official within the State Department, George Kennan, had advanced the idea of containment in an article he wrote for the journal *Foreign Affairs* in July 1947. Kennan said that although the Russians did not want war, they wanted to destroy capitalism. He advocated using mainly political and economic weapons, but also military ones, to keep communism within its current borders. In this way, he said, the communist system within Russia would eventually collapse.

When Truman sought election to the White House in 1948, most political pundits thought he would lose. Inflation remained a problem, liberals considered him too conservative, and white Southerners disliked his civil rights proposals. In February Truman recommended to Congress that a civil rights commission be established, and in July he ordered the armed forces to end their racial segregation. Angry conservatives bolted the Democratic Party to form the Dixiecrat, or States' Rights Party and some liberals joined the Progressive Party.

After the Republicans chose Thomas Dewey, governor of New York, as their presidential candidate, Truman led a rousing whistle-stop campaign against what he called the "do-nothing Eightieth Congress." On the night of the election, he went to bed thinking he had lost—the *Chicago Daily Tribune* blared a heavy black headline, "Dewey Defeats Truman"—but he awoke with later returns showing him the winner. He had pulled off a stunning upset.

The Cold War dominated Truman's second term. In his inaugural address he called for a Point Four Program that would provide money and technical assistance to underdeveloped nations. He insisted that if these countries conquered poverty, communism would have no ground on which to grow. Several months later Congress appropriated $34.5 million for the program. A couple of years after that it provided substantially more.

In January 1949 President Truman announced military aid for Western Europe, and in April he signed documents that formed the North Atlantic Treaty Organization (NATO), which joined the United States, Canada, and 10 Western European nations in a military alliance. Later that year containment suffered a devastating blow when communist revolutionaries under Mao Tse-tung gained power in China.

Early in 1950 Truman adopted a policy paper written by his national security council titled "NSC-68." Historian Walter LeFeber has called it "one of the key historical documents of the Cold War." NSC-68 advocated a quick, large-scale military buildup to prevent further Soviet expansion. The document stated: "The whole success [against communism] hangs ultimately on recognition by this government, the American people and all the peoples that the cold war is in fact a real war in which the survival of the world is at stake." In short, America would have to act as a world policeman.

The cop's beat, though, toughened on June 25, 1950, when North Korea's communist army, supported with supplies from the Soviet Union, invaded South Korea. Few American leaders thought the Korean Peninsula strategically important, but if Truman were to let the area fall to the communists, he would risk legitimizing his conservative critics, who considered him and the Democratic Party weak on communism. In addition, if he stood firm, Congress would likely appropriate the money he needed to activate NSC-68 and strengthen NATO.

With the backing of the United Nations, Truman provided weapons and air support to the South Koreans. When this proved insufficient, on June 30 he sent the U.S. Army into battle, without any formal declaration of war or even extensive consultation with Congress. His action displayed the growth of presidential power in foreign affairs.

Under General Douglas MacArthur, famous for leading the defeat of Japan in World War II, the Americans turned back the North Koreans. But Truman then committed a grave mistake. Despite warnings from the People's Republic of China that U.S. troops should stay away from the Yalu River, the president told MacArthur to continue north and conquer North Korea (though he also told the general to deploy South Korean rather than American troops near the river). As MacArthur's forces neared the Yalu in October 1950, the Chinese army poured down the peninsula and routed the Americans, forcing them to retreat below the 38th parallel, which divided North Korea from the South. Early in 1951 MacArthur fought his way back to the parallel, though his troops suffered heavy losses.

At that point Truman wanted to negotiate, but MacArthur demanded an unconditional surrender and sent a letter to a congressman, which was read on the floor of the House, in which he called for unifying Korea and hitting

China with nuclear bombs. It was clear that MacArthur was disobeying Truman and trying to make foreign policy. Consequently, Truman fired MacArthur. As he explained in his memoirs: "If there is one basic element in our Constitution, it is civilian control of the military. Policies are to be made by the elected political officials, not by generals or admirals."

Truman privately called MacArthur a "play actor" and con man, but the general returned home to a hero's welcome as Americans overwhelmingly supported him. Public opinion changed, however, when hearings in the Senate revealed that MacArthur's actions risked war with China and Russia and amounted to insubordination toward the president.

Truman decided against seeking another term in 1952. Republicans nevertheless attacked his administration for its corruption, though the transgressions involved only a few lower-level officials. Truman left the White House in January 1953 and returned to Independence. There he started a library dedicated to maintaining his papers, and he wrote his memoirs published in 1955 and 1956. He died from lung congestion and other complications on December 26, 1972.

In the years after his death, Americans remembered Truman for his resolve in dropping the A-bomb and for his firmness in dealing with the Soviet Union. They also remembered him as an honest leader who spoke his mind and stood by his decisions. "The buck stops here," the Missourian firmly believed. Where other politicians shifted responsibility away from themselves or waffled on issues, Truman met them directly—a quality Americans longed for in subsequent times when presidential image often prevailed over substance.

Chronology

1884 Born May 8

1890 Moves to Independence, Missouri

1901 Graduates from high school

1903 Begins work as bank clerk and teller

1906 Works on father's farm

1917 Fights in France during World War I

1919 Marries Bess Wallace

Opens haberdashery

1922 Elected judge of county court for Eastern District, Jackson County, Missouri

1924 Loses bid for reelection

1926 Elected presiding judge of county court, Jackson County, Missouri

1934 Elected to U.S. Senate

1940 Reelected to U.S. Senate

1941 Appointed chairman of Senate Committee to Investigate the National Defense Program

1944 Elected vice president

1945 Becomes president

Attends Potsdam Conference

Orders atomic bombs dropped on Hiroshima and Nagasaki

1946 Intervenes in railroad and mining strikes

1947 Issues Truman Doctrine

Supports Marshall Plan

1948 Elected president

1950 Sends U.S. troops to Korea to fight communist invasion

1951 Relieves General Douglas MacArthur of Far East command

1953 Retires to Independence, Missouri

1955 Publishes first volume of memoir

1956 Publishes second volume of memoirs

1957 Presents Truman Library to the National Archives

1972 Dies December 26

Further Reading

Beschloss, Michael R. *The Conquerors: Roosevelt, Truman and the Destruction of Hitler's Germany, 1941–1945.* New York: Simon & Schuster, 2002.

Donovan, Robert J. *Tumultuous Years: The Presidency of Harry S. Truman.* New York: W. W. Norton, 1982.

Ferrell, Robert H. *Harry S. Truman: A Life.* Columbia: University of Missouri Press, 1994.

Hamby, Alonzo. *Man of the People: A Life of Harry S. Truman.* New York: Oxford University Press, 1995.

Jenkins, Roy. *Truman.* London: Collins, 1986.

McCoy, Donald R. *The Presidency of Harry S. Truman.* Lawrence: University Press of Kansas, 1984.

McCullough, David. *Truman.* New York: Simon & Schuster, 1992.

Miller, Richard Lawrence. *Truman: The Rise to Power.* New York: McGraw-Hill, 1986.

Pemberton, William E. *Harry S. Truman: Fair Dealer and Cold Warrior.* Boston: Twayne, 1989.

Truman, Harry S. *Memoirs.* 2 vols. New York: Doubleday, 1955–1956.

Truman, Margaret. *Harry S. Truman.* New York: Morrow, 1973.

DWIGHT DAVID EISENHOWER (1890–1969)

Thirty-fourth President, 1953–1961

DWIGHT DAVID EISENHOWER
(Library of Congress)

"Freedom is pitted against slavery; lightness against the dark."
—Inaugural words, first term, January 20, 1953

As much as the 1950s has produced images of suburbs, rock music, sock hops, and happy families, the decade was in many ways a troubling time. Over it loomed the threat of nuclear war, as children ducked under their desks at school to practice for possible A-bomb attacks and adults worried that communists lurked everywhere.

When Dwight Eisenhower ran for president in 1952, he projected the confident side of post–World War II society and the desire of many Americans for a reassuring voice in the nuclear darkness. Eisenhower's role as commander of the European theater in World War II made him the most famous man in America, perhaps in the entire world. Many compared him to George Washington, with his status as a military hero and father figure. Like Washington,

Eisenhower inspired trust. "I'm going to try to be as truthful as I can be," he said. Unlike Washington, however, he refused to take a public stand on moral issues—a fault that compromised his presidency.

—~—

Dwight David Eisenhower was born in Denison, Texas, on October 14, 1890, the third son of David and Ida Stover Eisenhower. In 1891 his father moved to Abilene, Kansas, and Dwight, called "Little Ike," grew up in a small, two-story, white frame house. The elder Eisenhower, a failed shopkeeper, worked as a mechanic at a creamery. Both he and Ida were devout Mennonites and pacifists. She had an enormous influence on Ike through her enthusiasm for life and her preaching in favor of worldly success and divine spirituality.

In Abilene, a small town with fewer than 4,000 people, Ike imbibed mainstream values, among them patriotism and conservative politics; almost everyone in town voted Republican. He later recalled that as a boy he got caught up in the town's political excitement: "The earliest national election I can recall is that of 1896, in which William McKinley opposed William Jennings Bryan. I . . . helped campaign that year by marching in a nighttime parade with a flaming torch made of a rag and soaked in coal oil."

Ike had a terrible temper as a child and fought to control it throughout his life; yet he was outgoing and friendly and flashed a grin that disarmed intimates and later charmed the voting public. In school he liked spelling and math, and in his teens he played football and baseball and organized the Abilene High School Athletic Association to promote games. Enthralled with military history, he sometimes ignored his chores and schoolwork while he pored over the pages of a book.

Young Eisenhower wanted to attend the University of Michigan, but in 1910 a friend, Everett "Swede" Hazlett, convinced him to take the service academy exam. Ike's score failed to qualify him for the Naval Academy, but it did qualify him for West Point. He entered the military academy in 1911, much to the regret of his mother, who abhorred war and any kind of violence.

An average student and something of a nonconformist who occasionally disobeyed rules, Ike excelled at football. A writer for the *New York Times* extolled his potential, but a knee injury ended his playing days, after which he became a cheerleader and coach of the junior varsity.

Eisenhower graduated from West Point in 1915 and was assigned as a second lieutenant to Fort Sam Houston in San Antonio, Texas. Just a few days later, he met the daughter of a successful Denver meatpacker, 18-year-old Mary Geneva Doud (called "Mamie,") and began courting her. She thought him "the handsomest male I have ever seen." He later recalled that she "was a vivacious and attractive girl . . . saucy in the look about her face and in her whole attitude." They married in July 1916 and had two sons, Doud Dwight, born in 1917, and John Sheldon, born in 1922. Doud died at age four from scarlet fever.

When the United States entered World War I, Eisenhower yearned to join the fight but never got his opportunity. In San Antonio he trained the 57th Infantry so effectively his superiors promoted him to captain and sent him to Camp Colt in Gettysburg, Pennsylvania, an abandoned facility that he converted into a bustling tank training center. There he combined strict discipline with empathy to earn the respect of his men and the loyalty of his fellow officers. Still he felt disappointed about missing combat, and he told a friend, "I suppose we'll spend the rest of our lives explaining why we didn't get into this war. By God, from now on I am cutting myself a swath and will make up for this."

Between the two world wars, Eisenhower served in several different military posts. From 1922 to 1924 he worked as executive officer under Brigadier General Fox Conner in the

Panama Canal Zone. Ike developed a friendship with his commander and later called his time in Panama "a sort of graduate school in military affairs." Conner helped him enter the army's command and general staff school at Leavenworth, Kansas. Applying himself diligently and plunging into a pressure-packed atmosphere that others found exhausting but that to him was exhilarating, Eisenhower graduated first in his class in 1926. After a year at the Army War College, he went to France, where he researched the role played by the American army in World War I and wrote a guide to French battlefields.

Eisenhower returned to the United States in 1929, and after serving on the staff of the assistant secretary of war, in 1932 he joined the new Chief of Staff, General Douglas MacArthur, as an aide. He spent several years with MacArthur. Though Eisenhower found the general too flamboyant and disagreed with him on some issues, including the way he handled the Bonus Army protest in Washington during the Great Depression, Ike learned much and developed a good rapport with the general. MacArthur called Eisenhower "the best officer in the Army." From 1935 until Hitler invaded Poland in 1939, Ike servedas MacArthur's assistant in the Philippines, helping to reorganize the army in the archipelago.

By 1941 Eisenhower had attained the rank of full colonel and was named chief of staff for the Third Army. His impressive victory over the Second Army in a mock battle earned him promotion to the temporary rank of brigadier general and caught the attention of General George C. Marshall. After Japan attacked Pearl Harbor in December 1941, Marshall called Ike to Washington to serve as his assistant chief of staff. World War II revived Eisenhower's military career at a time when he was nearing retirement, and an inglorious one at that, with a small pension and without an outstanding record.

After Eisenhower had helped to develop strategy for the Pacific, Marshall placed him in charge of the Philippines and Far Eastern Section of the War Plans Division. In February 1942, he was made head of the Operations Division, in which role Ike and his staff planned an attack by American and British forces against the Germans from the west, along the French coast. Pleased with Eisenhower's work, Marshall appointed him commander of the European Theater of Operations in June 1942.

Ike showed at least one of the qualities needed for seeking public office when he established an excellent rapport with the press. He looked like a commander, and many reporters liked his warmth and sense of humor. The American public also liked what it saw, as newspaper photographs revealed a sometimes pensive, sometimes smiling general.

President Roosevelt soon chose Eisenhower to command the western attack on Germany, called Operation Overlord, and the general worked grueling hours to finish and coordinate the plan. But before Overlord could begin, two problems had to be dealt with: First, he adeptly handled a controversy that erupted when General George Patton slapped a private in a hospital. Ike could have dismissed Patton but instead convinced reporters who had heard of the incident to keep it quiet. Second, he expertly commanded the conquest of Morocco, Algeria, Tunisia, Sicily, and southern Italy. Although his victory hurt the Germans, they continued to control most of Europe.

Eisenhower launched Operation Overlord on June 6, 1944. American, Canadian, and British troops arrived at the beaches of Normandy, where they confronted the German army's formidable defensive line. The Allied attack used the largest air and sea armada in history. Under Ike's plan, aircraft struck the French railway system and damaged Germany's ability to transport its troops.

Eisenhower encountered numerous problems, primarily from giving too much authority to his battlefield commanders, who failed to capture Antwerp quickly and end the war before winter. He also misread the German willingness to counterattack at the Battle of the

Bulge, though he recovered by quickly moving reinforcements into place and turning the enemy back.

The fighting men liked Ike. While other officers saw their recruits as soldiers, he saw them as civilians in uniform, engaged in a difficult, dirty, and unwanted war. He saw in their faces wheat fields and picket fences, and he recognized in them the heart and soul of small-town America, places like Abilene, his hometown.

Operation Overlord collapsed Germany's western front and forced that country's inevitable surrender in May 1945. That December Truman appointed Eisenhower chief of staff of the U.S. Army, in which post he supervised the demobilization of troops.

Even during the war, talk circulated about Ike as a candidate for president. "The possibility that I might one day become a candidate for the presidency was first suggested to me about June 1943," he wrote in his diary. "My reaction was of course completely negative. . . . The hard military campaigns of the war were at that time obviously still ahead of us, and my diverting of our attention to political matters would have been more than ridiculous."

The talk intensified in 1947, and Ike responded by saying, "I say flatly, completely, and with all the force I have—I haven't a political ambition in the world. I want nothing to do with politics." He disliked the idea of going after votes and playing partisan games.

In time, however, his views about running for president shifted, especially after the Republican candidate, Thomas E. Dewey, failed to unseat President Harry Truman in 1948. Ike's written statements at a later date show his change in attitude:

> About his refusing to run in 1948, he said, "I felt that I had removed myself from the political scene for once and all."
>
> Reflecting on the year 1951, he said, "I think the argument that began to carry for me the greatest possible force was that the landslide victories of 1936, 1940 and 1944 and Truman's victory . . . in 1948 were all achieved under a doctrine of 'spend and spend, and elect and elect.' It seemed to me that this had to be stopped or our country would deviate badly from the precepts on which we had placed so much faith. . . ."

Reflecting on the year 1952, he said, "Always with friends I brought out [the points why I should not run]; always they were brushed aside by people who had become in some instances almost fanatical in their conviction as to my duty to become a candidate for the presidency."

While he was changing his views about running, Ike wrote his war memoirs, *Crusade in Europe*; left the army in 1948 so he could serve as president of Columbia University in New York City, and was recalled into the army in 1950 by President Truman to help organize the military forces for the North Atlantic Treaty Organization.

In January 1952 Eisenhower declared himself a Republican, and soon after that he entered the race for the presidential nomination, saying he opposed a centralized government and high taxes and wanted a stronger policy toward communist expansion than that provided by the Democrats. At the Republican National Convention he supported a platform that called for the "independence of . . . captive people" in Eastern Europe, meaning people under Soviet control. This became a clarion call in the fall campaign.

Ike chose a young California senator, Richard Nixon, as his running mate. Together they tapped the cold war fear of communism, though Nixon hit the Democrats much harder on the issue, and his name-calling made it a bitter campaign. As Americans warmed to the "I Like Ike" campaign slogan, the former general's popularity, combined with a widespread public desire for change, meant that in November 1952 he easily defeated Adlai Stevenson, 442 electoral votes to 89.

The only major campaign problem involved Richard Nixon, when the *New York Post* provided evidence that he had accepted secret contributions totaling $18,000 from several California supporters. Ike's advisers urged him to dump Nixon from the ticket, but after the senator defended himself in a nationally televised speech, the general decided to keep him. Their relationship, however, never recovered, and neither one liked or trusted the other.

Prior to taking his presidential oath of office, in December 1952 Eisenhower made good on a campaign promise and flew to Korea, where American and communist troops were locked in battle. He spent three days looking at conditions and several months later arranged a truce agreement ending the Korean War.

When Ike's presidency began in 1953, Senator Joseph McCarthy of Wisconsin was leading a campaign to purge society of communists and their influence. Though many Americans supported McCarthy, Eisenhower disliked his smear tactics. Yet in what several analysts today consider a failure of moral leadership, he refrained from criticizing the senator.

Under pressure from McCarthy, the State Department began burning "liberal" books in its overseas libraries; Eisenhower mentioned the purge in a speech at Dartmouth College, saying he hoped the students would never become book burners, but he rejected suggestions that restrictions at the libraries be lessened. Eisenhower believed he needed to say little about McCarthy because the senator would eventually self-destruct. That is what happened, but the president's silence smacked of a political cowardice quite different from the image many people held of him as another George Washington.

In 1953 Eisenhower appointed Earl Warren as chief justice of the United States, only to hear conservatives criticize him for picking a liberal activist. When that same year the Supreme Court considered the case of *Brown v. Board of Education*, which would determine the issue of racial segregation in public schools, Ike invited Warren to the White House, where he said a few words to him about Southerners: "These are not bad people. All they are concerned about is to see that their sweet little girls are not required to sit in school alongside some big overgrown Negroes."

Eisenhower obviously supported segregated schools, but he refused to give the South any advice about how to respond when the court made such segregation illegal, saying he would uphold the decision. As with the McCarthy controversy, he failed to provide moral leadership at a crucial moment.

In developing his foreign policy, Eisenhower tried to balance his desire for a reduced federal budget with the challenges posed by the cold war. Toward that end, he wanted to build a "new look" military that would get more bang for the buck by substituting nuclear weapons for mass conventional forces. Ike never specifically committed the United states to a nuclear assault on Moscow should the Soviets attack anywhere in the world, but he implied it. He also supported his secretary of state, John Foster Dulles, who frequently resorted to missile rattling. Dulles said the United States would meet aggression by "a great capacity to retaliate instantly by means and places of our own choosing."

In March 1954 Dulles said, "If the Russians attacked one of America's allies, there [is] no need for the President to go to Congress for a declaration of war." Critics ripped that comment for its threat to the Constitution, and they said Ike's reliance on nuclear weapons left America poorly prepared for regional or local conflicts that mandated a limited military response.

To continue Harry Truman's policy of containing the Soviet Union and its influence, Eisenhower used the Central Intelligence Agency (CIA) as a means to intervene in other countries. In 1953 the CIA staged a coup that overthrew Mohammed Mossadegh, the ruler of Iran, and returned Shah Mohammed Reza Pahlevi to power. Ike acted after Mossadegh seized the Anglo-Persian Oil Company and Britain, in retaliation, classified him as a communist. Soon after the coup, the shah concluded a deal beneficial to several American oil companies.

That same year Guatemalan president Jacobo Arbenz Guzmán nationalized 400,000 uncultivated acres held by the United Fruit Company in his country and distributed the land to peasants. The support Arbenz Guzmán received from left-wing radicals in Guatemala, including communists, along with the confiscation itself, unnerved the United States, especially since John Foster Dulles and his brother Allen Dulles, the head of the CIA, had business ties to United Fruit. When in May 1954 Arbenz Guzmán bought weapons from Soviet-bloc Czechoslovakia, Ike agreed to overthrow the Guatemalan president. A CIA coup succeeded, even though it violated the charter of the Organization of American States, which prohibited any member nation from interfering in the internal affairs of another. Guatemala's new leader quickly took the nationalized land from the peasants and gave it back to United Fruit.

These achievements through the use of stealth set the stage for a similar strategy in Vietnam. By 1954 France was fighting desperately to hold onto its colony of Vietnam against communist guerrillas led by Ho Chi Minh. As the French position deteriorated, Ike followed Harry Truman's lead and poured more money into the battle. By early 1954 the United States was paying 75 percent of the French war cost. Later that year, as France faced defeat at Dien Bien Phu, a remote village in North Vietnam, some of Eisenhower's advisers urged him to hit the communist rebels with nuclear weapons. Ike responded: "You boys must be crazy. We can't use those awful things against Asians for the second time in less than ten years. My God."

But Eisenhower decided that simply to walk away from Vietnam would expose Republicans to the same charges they had leveled against the Democrats: that they were weak on communism. As happened frequently in the cold war, domestic fears about the Red menace shaped foreign policy. In April 1954 the president spoke publicly about much-discussed domino analogy: Should Southeast Asia fall to the communist advance, so would Indochina, and then Burma, Thailand, Malaysia, and Indonesia, each collapsing in on the other like dominoes.

After France lost at Dien Bien Phu in 1954, the Geneva Accords prohibited military interference in Vietnam by any nation and provided for elections in 1956 to unify the entire country. Eisenhower refused to sign the accords, but he promised the United States would refrain from using force to "contradict" them.

Yet in August 1954 Ike sabotaged the agreement when he backed South Vietnam's dictator, Ngo Dinh Diem, by sending him military supplies. From then on, America replaced France in fighting the guerrillas. In September 1954 Eisenhower sponsored the Southeast Asia Treaty Organization (SEATO), a collective defense treaty with several Asian countries. He announced SEATO would protect South Vietnam, and in direct contradiction with the Geneva Accords, he placed South Vietnam on the same level as a sovereign country.

By the end of 1954, Ike was sending American military advisers to help the South Vietnamese army. Two years later, after a CIA report stated that the elections promised for all of Vietnam in 1956 would result in a victory for Ho Chi Minh, Eisenhower made sure they were cancelled. He refused, though, to send combat troops to the embattled region. In his diary he wrote: "The jungles of Indochina . . . would have swallowed up division after division of United States troops, who, unaccustomed to this kind of warfare, would have sustained heavy casualties." To later presidents confronted with the prospect of a communist victory, the jungle would appear not daunting but conquerable through the use of American military might.

Another Asian crisis erupted in 1954 when the People's Republic of China began shelling Quemoy and Matsu, islands under the control of the anticommunist Nationalist Chinese government on Formosa (present-day Taiwan). Republicans in particular cried out about protecting "free peoples," though Quemoy and Matsu, within sight of the Chinese mainland, were no more than specks in the sea. China shelled the islands because the Nationalists had stationed 75,000 troops on them and were using them as bases from which to attack the mainland. Eisenhower sent supplies to the beleaguered islands and obtained a resolution from Congress granting him the right to use force to protect Formosa and the nearby Pescadores, while leaving any commitment to Quemoy and Matsu ambiguous.

As the crisis continued, in March 1955 Secretary of State Dulles talked loosely about "new and powerful weapons of precision which can utterly destroy military targets without endangering unrelated civilian centers"—a veiled threat about using nuclear weapons. The president then scared the Chinese, and many Americans, when he responded to a question about whether he would employ small tactical nuclear devices by saying, "In any combat where these things can be used on strictly military targets and for strictly military purposes, I see no reason why they shouldn't be used just exactly as you would use a bullet or anything else." Amid such threatening words, China soon ended its shelling.

Eisenhower suffered a heart attack in 1955, and as the presidential election of 1956 approached, war erupted in the Mideast when Israel, Britain, and France invaded Egypt. They did so in response to that country's president, Gamal Abdel Nasser, nationalizing the Suez Canal. None of the invading countries informed Eisenhower they would attack, and he considered their act nothing less than heavy-handed imperialism. He sponsored a resolution in the United Nations calling for Israel to leave Egypt, and it passed with the support of both the United States and the Soviet Union. The Russians later threatened to use force in the Mideast. Ike reacted by placing America's forces on worldwide alert, but the crisis cooled after a cease-fire ended the fighting among the warring countries.

In order to contain communism, Ike asked for—and Congress passed— the Eisenhower Doctrine. This resolution authorized the president to give economic and military aid to any Middle Eastern country requesting it and declared the United States would send forces into the region should any country there ask for assistance "against armed aggression" from "international communism."

At about the same time, an uprising in Hungary against Soviet rule provided Eisenhower with the chance to make good on the Republican promise to liberate the oppressed people of Eastern Europe. But when Soviet tanks rumbled through Budapest to crush the rebellion (blanketed by the diversion of the Suez crisis), he did nothing, fully aware that to act with force might ignite a nuclear war.

In 1956 President Eisenhower again faced Adlai Stevenson in a run for the presidency, and once again the "I Like Ike" bandwagon rolled. This time Eisenhower won with 457 electoral votes to Stevenson's 73.

As Ike's second term began, he pushed a bill through Congress intended to guarantee African Americans the right to vote, but southern resistance and his own ineffective leadership weakened it. The final bill stipulated the attorney general could obtain an injunction against any person acting to prevent another from voting; yet the penalties for violating the law were so light and the obstacles to obtaining an injunction so great that the act carried little force.

In fall 1957 nine black students attempted to integrate Little Rock High School in Arkansas. To stop them, Governor Orval Faubus called out the national guard. Ike now faced a domestic crisis. Faubus had defied both the 1954 *Brown* case and a court order to let integration proceed, and a white mob had attacked some of the African-American students. At that point Eisenhower ordered the 101st Airborne Division into Little Rock, and in late September the black students entered the high school under the shadow of bayonets. In the end Ike acted not because he supported integration, but because he wanted to uphold the authority of the federal courts.

In November 1957, Eisenhower suffered a stroke. He later reported that he never completely recovered. "I reverse syllables in a long word and at times am compelled to speak slowly," he said.

Throughout his presidency, Eisenhower wanted to reach an arms agreement with the Soviet Union. Yet he continued to endorse disruptive CIA tactics and various forms of espionage, a dangerous strategy that soon blew up on him. While Ike arranged a disarmament conference with the Soviet Union, Britain, and France for 1960, he approved flights over Soviet airspace by America's secret high-altitude U2 spy plane. On May 1, two weeks before the scheduled summit, the Russians shot down a U2 piloted by Francis Gary Powers 1,200 miles within the Soviet Union.

The CIA told Ike he had nothing to worry about, that in any crash the aircraft would have been totally destroyed and Powers killed. With that in mind, he publicly denied Soviet charges that a spy plane had violated its borders. The Soviets then surprised him by exhibiting film retrieved from the plane and by parading Powers before the Russian public.

Caught in a lie, the mortified Eisenhower proceeded to the summit anyhow. Once there, Soviet Premier Nikita Khrushchev assailed him and the United States and then stormed out of the meeting. With the summit destroyed, any real chance to slow the arms race faded.

His second term over, Eisenhower retired to Gettysburg, Pennsylvania, where he wrote his memoirs. In the mid-1960s he conferred several times with President Lyndon Johnson's advisers and counseled them to seek victory in the Vietnam War. On March 24, 1969, Eisenhower's heart began failing him, and on March 28 he died.

When Dwight Eisenhower left the White House, he sounded a warning "In the councils of Government," he said, "we must guard against the acquisition of unwarranted influence, whether sought or unsought, by the military-industrial complex. We must never let the weight of this combination endanger our liberties or democratic processes. We should take nothing for granted." Essayist George W. S. Trow asserts that Dwight Eisenhower "flowed so easily within [the] events he dominated that he became indistinguishable from them." Trow adds that "I think Ike knew America had marinated on his watch." Eisenhower's warning, though, stands in stark contrast to unquestioned acceptance of the cold war, as if he were intent on awakening Trow's complacent country with his earlier promise: "I'm going to be as truthful as I can be"—the very words of trust that had won him the presidency eight years earlier.

Chronology

1890 Born October 14

1911 Enters U.S. Military Academy

1915 Commissioned second lieutenant

1916 Marries Mamie Doud

1917 Commands tank-training center

1922 Assigned to Panama

1925 Attends Command and General Staff School

1932 Serves on staff of General Douglas MacArthur

1935 Assigned to Philippines

1940 Named chief of staff of Third Army Division

1941 Wins mock battle in Louisiana

1942 Named assistant chief of staff to General Marshall

Assumes command of European Theater of Operations

Directs invasion of North Africa

1944 Directs Normandy invasion

1945 Accepts surrender of Germany

Becomes chief of staff, U.S. Army

1948 Named president of Columbia University

1952 Elected president

Visits Korea

1953 Names Earl Warren as chief justice

Directs CIA to overthrow Iranian government

Directs CIA to overthrow Guatemalan president

1954 Decides to provide military and economic aid to South Vietnam

1955 Suffers heart attack

1956 Condemns Israeli, British, French invasion of Egypt

Decides against providing military support to anticommunist rebellion in Hungary

Reelected president

1957 Announces Eisenhower Doctrine

Sends 101st Airborne Division to Little Rock, Arkansas

Suffers stroke

1959 Meets Soviet premier Nikita Khrushchev at Camp David

1960 Denies that he sent U-2 spy plane over the Soviet Union

Attends disarmament conference in Paris

1961 Retires to Gettysburg, Pennsylvania

1969 Dies March 28

Further Reading

Adams, Sherman. *Firsthand Report: The Story of the Eisenhower Administration.* New York: Harper & Bros., 1961.

Ambrose, Stephen E. *Eisenhower: Soldier and President.* New York: Simon & Schuster, 1990.

———. *The Supreme Commander: The War Years of General Dwight D. Eisenhower.* Garden City, N.Y.: Doubleday, 1970.

Cook, Blanche. *The Declassified Eisenhower.* Garden City, N.Y.: Doubleday, 1981.

D'Este, Carlo. *Eisenhower: A Soldier's Life.* New York: Henry Holt, 2002.

Divine, Robert A. *Eisenhower and the Cold War.* New York: Oxford University Press, 1981.

Eisenhower, Dwight D. *Crusade in Europe.* Garden City, N.Y.: Doubleday, 1967.

———. *Letters to Mamie*, ed. John S. D. Eisenhower. Garden City, N.Y.: Doubleday, 1978.

———. *Mandate for Change.* Garden City, N.Y.: Doubleday, 1963.

———. *Waging Peace.* Garden City, N.Y.: Doubleday, 1974.

Ewald, William Bragg, Jr. *Eisenhower the President: Crucial Days, 1951–1960.* Englewood Cliffs, N.J.: Prentice Hall, 1981.

Ferrell, Robert H., ed. *The Eisenhower Diaries.* N.Y.: W. W. Norton, 1981.

Greenstein, Fred I. The *Hidden-Hand Presidency: Eisenhower as Leader.* New York: Basic Books, 1982.

Wicker, Tom. *Dwight D. Eisenhower, 1953–1961.* New York: Times Books, 2002.

John Fitzgerald Kennedy (1917–1963)

Thirty-fifth President, 1961–1963

John Fitzgerald Kennedy
(John F. Kennedy Library)

"Let the word go forth from this time and place, to friend and foe alike, that the torch has been passed to a new generation of Americans—born in this century, tempered by war, disciplined by a hard and bitter peace, proud of our ancient heritage—and unwilling to witness or permit the slow undoing of those human rights to which this Nation has always been committed, and to which we are committed today at home and around the world."

—Inaugural words, January 20, 1961

After an assassin's bullets killed President John F. Kennedy in November 1963, Kennedy's family and those closely associated with his presidency promoted a Camelot-like legend: For one brief shining moment, there was an enlightened leader who ruled with compassion and a commitment to freedom, whose great deeds reshaped the country. The legend lives on, but revelations over the last 20 years have tarnished the knight's armor, casting Kennedy more as an opportunist than a moralist, and more as an egotist than a humanitarian.

—⁓—

John Fitzgerald Kennedy, called "Jack" by his family, was born on May 29, 1917, in Brookline, Massachusetts, in a modest clapboard house owned by his parents, Joseph Patrick Kennedy and Rose Fitzgerald Kennedy. Rose's father, John "Honey Fitz" Fitzgerald, once served as mayor of Boston, while Joseph's father was the son of a former state representative and Boston ward boss. At the time of Jack's birth, Joseph was the president of Columbia Trust, a bank in East Boston. Through stock investments, bootlegging, and an interest in a movie production company, he would soon become one of the wealthiest men in America.

At age three, Jack contracted scarlet fever and was sent to a sanitarium in Maine. Soon after he returned home three months later, his father bought a larger house and moved the Kennedy family into a two-story mansion. Although Joseph Kennedy cared for Jack's welfare and that of the youngster's brothers and sisters, business was his driving force. Hard-nosed, he saw life as a battle for survival where probity was excess baggage, and he had no qualms about engaging in insider trading on the stock market or other ethically wrong or illegal practices. Boston's elite shunned the elder Kennedy, partly because of his Irish background, but mainly because they considered him ruthless and brutish and found distasteful his sensational affair with actress Gloria Swanson in the 1920s.

In his later years Jack both respected and feared his father, from whom he learned that winning counted most. Given his father's priorities and his mother's distant character, Jack experienced a childhood devoid of parental warmth. Yet he was witty and outgoing, and Rose described him as a "funny little boy" who "said things in such an original, vivid way." For his postelementary education he enrolled in 1931 at Choate, an exclusive private school in Wallingford, Connecticut, where he formed The Muckers, a group dedicated to pranks; played football and hockey; struggled with Latin; and battled several illnesses.

Kennedy studied briefly at Princeton before entering Harvard in fall 1936. He majored in government, but in his first two years he earned a reputation as a playboy, one who preferred parties and racing his expensive boat at Cape Cod to academics. He played football until October 1937, when he suffered a severe back injury in a freak accident.

After President Franklin Roosevelt appointed Joseph Kennedy as ambassador to Britain in 1937, Jack visited London in the summer of 1938 and toured Europe. He returned to Harvard with a heightened interest in his studies, though he showed no signs of wanting to enter politics. A roommate later said of him: "Jack was a very stimulating person to live with. Very argumentative in a nice way. . . . I think the depth of his intellectual curiosity was shown in that he'd challenge anything you said. He had the best sense of humor of all the Kennedys."

Jack wrote an honors thesis in politics that analyzed Britain's appeasement of Nazi Germany, and with the help of one of his father's friends, it was published as *Why England Slept*. In his book Kennedy portrayed democracy as endangered, criticized the British for arming slowly while Hitler built his military machine, and called isolationism an unworthy response for any democratic country. As he graduated from Harvard in the summer of 1940, the book became a best-seller and served as a curious contrast to the elder Kennedy's own desire to appease Hitler.

After the Japanese attack at Pearl Harbor in December 1941, John Kennedy joined the U.S. Navy and served in the Pacific. In the early morning of August 2, 1943, Lieutenant Kennedy steered his boat, *PT 109*, from Rendova Harbor in the Solomon Islands into Blackett Strait, where he joined other PT boats on patrol. No enemy could be seen in the darkness until suddenly a crewman shouted, "Ship at two o'clock!" Seconds later, a Japanese warship slammed into *PT 109*, slicing its starboard side and causing an explosion. A fireball cut the sky. Radioman John Maguire recalled:

> We could see something out of the darkness. We're just cruising slow as we can. We're going six miles an hour. Kennedy says, "Sound general quarters!" Everybody was at their battle station anyway. . . . Kennedy got thrown against the wall of the cockpit. . . . The whole ocean was afire. I lift my helmet up. I hear voices. It was the Japanese running up and down the decks of their ship. They were on fire.

Two of the 12 men on board *PT 109* were killed as the stern of the boat sank instantly. Miraculously, Kennedy and the others survived as they clung to 15 feet of bow still jutting from the water. They waited to be rescued, not knowing that the navy had given them up for dead. After several hours the bow began sinking. Eight of the men held onto a log from a coconut tree while a ninth pushed it toward a nearby island. Pat McMahon, the boat's engineer, was so badly burned that Kennedy was forced to take the straps of the injured sailor's lifejacket, clench them in his teeth, and tow him to shore.

The survivors reached Plum Pudding Island, which they found deserted. They nicknamed it Bird Island because the only water they could find was the moisture they licked from the leaves of bushes spotted with bird droppings. After a while they swam to another island, where they found coconuts to eat. Kennedy and another sailor then searched a third island and retrieved a Japanese supply box that contained crackers and candy; they also found water, which they took back to their fellow survivors. After two South Pacific natives, working as scouts for the Allies, stumbled upon the desperate group, Kennedy scratched a message inside a coconut and asked them to take it and find help. The message read: "NAURO ISL NATIVE KNOWS POSIT HE CAN PILOT II ALIVE NEED SMALL BOAT KENNEDY." The British navy soon found the party.

Years later, after Kennedy won the presidency, he invited his two native rescuers to the White House. Before they could board their plane for Washington, they heard he had been assassinated. One said, "I . . . found [a] photo of him and I cried. I sat down with the picture and cried."

Kennedy, Sr., intended to direct Jack's older brother, Joseph, into the White House after World War II, but Joseph was killed while flying a mission over Europe. The elder Kennedy therefore pushed Jack to enter politics. Kennedy later recalled: "It was like being drafted. My father wanted [me] . . . in politics; 'wanted' isn't the right word. He demanded it."

In 1946 John F. Kennedy ran for Congress as a Democrat from a district that included portions of Boston and contained a heavily Italian and Irish population who found his Catholic background appealing. Many observers said Kennedy looked ill during the campaign. In fact, he suffered from his bad back and from Addison's disease, an ultimately fatal failure of the adrenal glands for which he took painful shots. The Kennedy family kept his illness a secret—as they would for the rest of his life—and portrayed him as a youthful, vigorous candidate.

Joseph Kennedy spent $300,000 on the race, a considerable sum at that time. He hired pollsters and handed out reprints of a magazine story depicting his son's heroism while captain of *PT 109*. Working with just four hours of sleep each day, JFK —as he came to be identified—campaigned hard and won. In Congress he compiled a forgettable record while he voted against the antilabor Taft-Hartley Act. He registered as a warrior in the cold war by supporting the Truman Doctrine and the Marshall Plan, as well as by sympathizing with the leader of the Red scare, Senator Joseph McCarthy.

Kennedy twice won reelection to the House. In 1952 he ran for the U.S. Senate against Henry Cabot Lodge, the incumbent and a scion of Boston's elite Brahmins. In a tough fight, the Irish-Catholic upstart charged Lodge with being soft on communism and used the slogan "Kennedy will do MORE for Massachusetts" to defeat him.

Liberals in the Senate embraced Kennedy, though to one friend he confided, "I'd be very happy to tell [letter writers] I'm not a liberal at all. . . . I'm not comfortable with those people." He gained national attention when he bucked sentiment in Massachusetts and supported the building of the St. Lawrence Seaway. He called for more defense spending to defeat communism, and he finally broke with Joseph McCarthy after the Army-McCarthy hearings of 1954 exposed the Republican senator's treachery.

Kennedy underwent major back surgery in 1954 that, with his Addison's disease, could easily have killed him. For the rest of his life he would be in considerable pain, often relying on crutches or a cane to relieve his back and taking amphetamines and pain-killing pills daily, sometimes hourly.

No amount of back pain kept Kennedy from womanizing. Despite having married wealthy Jacqueline Bouvier at a lavish ceremony in Newport, Rhode Island, on September 12, 1953, he had affairs with Hollywood actress Marilyn Monroe and with at least two Senate workers. (John and Jacqueline Kennedy had three children, one of whom died hours after birth.)

In 1955, while convalescing from a second back operation, JFK compiled *Profiles In Courage*, biographical sketches of senators who had put principles before politics. It was a best-seller in 1956 and the following year won him a Pulitzer Prize, though it was largely, if not completely, written by his legislative assistant, Theodore Sorenson. The *New York Times* said about *Profiles*, "It is refreshing and enlightening to have a first-rate politician write a thoughtful and persuasive book about political integrity."

Kennedy won reelection to the Senate in 1958 and then ran for the presidency in 1960 in a campaign managed by his younger brother Robert, while Joseph Kennedy continued to pour his money into the quest. JFK scored a crucial victory in the West Virginia primary when he defeated his leading challenger for the Democratic nomination, Senator Hubert H. Humphrey of Minnesota. His victory showed that a Catholic could win in a state 95 percent Protestant at a time when many voters questioned whether Kennedy would be more loyal to the pope than to his own country.

John Kennedy stunned the Democratic National Convention when he chose Texas senator Lyndon B. Johnson as his running mate. Both John and Robert Kennedy detested Johnson, the Senate majority leader and one of the country's most powerful politicians, for his politics and his character, which they considered crude. The traditional story says that JFK chose Johnson to balance the ticket, believing the Texan could carry his home state and much of the South. In *The Dark Side of Camelot*, Seymour Hersh offers the provocative view that Johnson and FBI Director J. Edgar Hoover "blackmailed" Kennedy into choosing Johnson by threatening to reveal secret files detailing the presidential nominee's sexual affairs.

Kennedy and his Republican opponent, Vice President Richard M. Nixon, differed little on the issues as each tried to prove himself the stronger cold warrior in fighting communism. Most notably, they engaged in the first debates ever televised during a presidential campaign. In terms of speaking points the two men dueled to a draw, but Kennedy won the contest for most attractive debater: Nixon looked drawn and poorly shaven, while his opponent looked rested and handsome. The debates made Kennedy a romantic idol, and screams from young women punctuated his campaign. Some analysts believe Kennedy's looks tipped the election to him, providing an affirmative answer to political commentator William F. Buckley's question, "Do we insist on a telegenic president?"

At least as equally decisive in the campaign, though, was the work of Chicago Mayor Richard Daley and Mafia don Sam Giancana, both of whom worked closely with the Kennedy campaign and secured enough votes in Chicago to put Illinois in his column. A shift of 4,500 ballots in that state to Nixon and 24,000 in Texas would have denied Kennedy the presidency. As it turned out, he won by a margin of about 115,000 votes out of a little more than 68 million cast. In his memoirs Richard Nixon claimed: "We were faced by an organization . . . that was led by the most ruthless group of political operators ever mobilized for a . . . campaign. Kennedy's organization approached . . . dirty tricks with a rougish relish." Nixon may have said what he did to make the point that he was not the only one to use reprehensible tactics in politics, but the statement nevertheless confirms Kennedy's Machiavellian talent.

John Fitzgerald Kennedy began his presidency in January 1961 with stirring words: "And so my fellow Americans: ask not what your country can do for you—ask what you can do for your country." Toward that end, in March he created the Peace Corps, which sent trained volunteers overseas to help people living in developing countries. Kennedy also created the Alliance for Progress to provide economic aid to Latin America, and later that year he committed the United States to landing a man on the moon by decade's end.

Campaign promises to the contrary, JFK showed little enthusiasm for civil rights during his first two years in office. He even rejected calls by the National Association for the Advancement of Colored People for legislation. He preferred instead to focus on his main interest, foreign policy. He had inherited from Dwight Eisenhower a clandestine plan to invade Cuba and overthrow communist dictator Fidel Castro. The CIA recruited Mafia leaders John Roselli, Sam Giancana, and Santo Trafficante to assassinate Castro, while it trained anti-Castro Cuban refugees for an amphibious assault on the island. The scheming was the CIA's worst-kept secret. In January 1961, days before Kennedy entered the presidency, the *New York Times* reported on the training underway in Guatemala.

While it remains unclear as to whether President Kennedy knew about specific CIA plans to assassinate Castro, many historians agree with the view stated by James T. Patterson in *Grand Expectations*: "It is doubtful that the CIA would have dared to kill a head of state on its own." Two assassination attempts were made before the invasion of Cuba, and killing Castro was an integral part of the Kennedy-approved plan.

In April 1961 the invasion began when refugee battalions numbering 1,450 soldiers landed at the Bay of Pigs on Cuba's southern coast. Castro quickly crushed the invaders, and the Cuban people rallied to support him rather than depose him—an outcome exactly opposite from what the CIA had predicted. During the battle Arleigh Burke, the navy chief of staff, requested that Kennedy send in air cover, but the president refused. According to Richard Reeves in *President Kennedy: Profile of Power*, an exchange between Burke and Kennedy went as follows:

> "No, I don't want the U.S. to get involved in this," Kennedy said.
>
> "Hell, Mr. President, we are involved," Burke answered.
>
> "Admiral, I don't want the United States involved in this," Kennedy snapped.

But Burke was right—the United States was involved, and the whole world knew it. When the Bay of Pigs invasion failed, it damaged Kennedy's credibility and made him appear deceitful and weak. Kennedy blamed the CIA and his advisers for the fiasco, but he could have abandoned the invasion plan at any time.

The Bay of Pigs incident hardened Kennedy's cold war resolve. He boosted defense spending, prompting Soviet premier Nikita Khrushchev to do the same, and launched Operation Mongoose, a $50-million secret program to disrupt Cuba by bombing factories, wrecking the sugar harvest, and killing Castro. With obsessive grandeur, the government developed at least 33 plans to assassinate the Cuban dictator, and President Kennedy again contacted Sam Giancana, though the record remains unclear as to whether he specifically ordered the Mafia don to have Castro killed. Aware of at least some of the plots, Castro warned through an American reporter that the attempts to kill him would lead to threats against leaders in the United States.

For reasons still unclear, but possibly because Castro and Khrushchev feared another invasion from the United States, the Soviet Union began arming Cuba with missiles in the summer of 1962. In fact, historian Michael Beschloss believes both the Cuban and Soviet leaders knew about Operation Mongoose and were convinced the United States would soon invade. By mid-October work was nearly complete on the launch pads for several short-range missiles carrying nuclear warheads, and it was proceeding rapidly on those for intermediate-range missiles that could reach several U.S. cities. JFK decided the weapons threatened American security and would boost Soviet prestige and must therefore be removed.

The president put together a special team of advisers, called ExComm, to discuss options. With a sense of urgency—for to allow the Soviets to complete the missiles would make it almost impossible to eliminate them—Kennedy and the advisers met nearly round the clock. Some of them wanted air strikes, accompanied by a land invasion to destroy the bases, an option fraught with danger, as evident in the following exchange involving President Kennedy, Secretary of Defense Robert McNamara, and General Maxwell Taylor, revealed on the tape recordings made at the White House:

> "We haven't any real report on what the state of the popular reaction would be to all this do we?" Kennedy asked. "We don't know whether . . ."
>
> "Great, great confusion and panic, don't you think? . . ." Taylor responded.
>
> "There's a real possibility you'd have to invade," McNamara said. "If you carried out an air strike, this might lead to an uprising, . . . to prevent the slaughter of the free Cubans, we would have to invade to reintroduce order into the country. And we would be prepared to do that."

On October 22, 1962, President Kennedy addressed the American people on national television and radio. He told them about the missiles in Cuba and warned the Soviets that if an attack was made on any nation in the Western Hemisphere, the United States would retaliate with a nuclear strike on Russia. Rather than strike Cuba by air, Kennedy announced a "quarantine," or blockade, of the island: Any Soviet ships approaching Cuba would be searched, and those carrying offensive weapons would be forced to stop.

With nuclear war in the balance, the world held its breath and waited to see how the Soviets would react. At that point Premier Khrushchev ordered Russian ships to turn around. Secretary of State Dean Rusk said, "We're eyeball to eyeball, and the other fellow just blinked." Actually, both sides blinked. Stepping back from the brink, Khrushchev and Kennedy reached an agreement stipulating that the Soviets would remove their missiles from Cuba and Kennedy would promise not to invade the island. In an addendum that Kennedy kept secret for fear it would show him to have compromised too much, he promised to remove American nuclear missiles stationed in Turkey.

The last point was important to the Soviets and to resolving the crisis. This was evident during the negotiations when Soviet ambassador Anatoly Dobrynin demanded of Robert Kennedy, "And what about Turkey?" to which Kennedy responded: "If that is the only obstacle . . . then the president doesn't see any unsurmountable difficulties in resolving this issue."

Many called John Kennedy's handling of the missile crisis his finest moment. He stood up to the Soviet Union but kept militarists in his own country at bay. Historian Michael R. Beschloss says that thanks to John and his brother Robert, ExComm "moved from an almost certain intention to bomb the missile sites and invade Cuba to what JFK finally did: throw a quarantine around the island and demand that

Nikita Khrushchev haul the missiles out. We now know that had Kennedy bombed, it might have easily escalated into a third world war." Others have criticized the president for brinkmanship and claim that the botched invasion at the Bay of Pigs had encouraged the Soviets to build the missile bases.

As a result of the crisis, the United States and the Soviet Union established a hot line between Washington and Moscow in 1963, and in June both countries, along with Britain, lessened tension by agreeing to a limited ban on nuclear atmospheric tests. Kennedy traveled to Germany that month and stood before the Berlin Wall, where he proclaimed the United States "will risk its cities to defend yours because we need your freedom to protect ours." He concluded with the words "*Ich bin ein Berliner*," meaning "I am a Berliner." To this day, many claim that what Kennedy actually said was "I am a doughnut" because *Berliner* was also a slang term for a pastry popular with Germans.

Despite the test ban treaty, America's cold war with the Soviet Union continued and heated up in Southeast Asia. JFK saw Vietnam as the place where the United States must show it could stop communist insurgencies anywhere in the world. While building America's nuclear arsenal at an accelerated pace, he strengthened conventional forces to respond to rebellions and formed a counterinsurgency unit called the Green Berets. Heading into 1963, he increased the number of American military advisers in South Vietnam to help the regime of Ngo Dinh Diem. As the war continued badly, and as Diem lost local support with his repressive policies, Kennedy considered him expendable. On November 1, 1963, after the CIA plotted with disaffected officers in the South Vietnamese army, Diem was overthrown and killed in a coup.

Whether Kennedy would have eventually reassessed his commitment to South Vietnam and withdrawn American advisers—numbering 15,000 by November 1963—remains debatable. Shortly before his death, he approved a plan to remove a small number of them, and at times he second-guessed his policy. But at other times his statements as a cold warrior indicated he would send more Americans to Vietnam.

The civil rights movement, meanwhile, was vexing Kennedy. In 1962, while Ross Barnett of Mississippi declared, "No school will be integrated in [this state] while I am your governor," a mob attacked black student James Meredith and the federal marshals escorting him as he tried to integrate the University of Mississippi at Oxford. The violence forced JFK to send in troops and shattered his hope for cooperation with southern governors.

Then in spring 1963 police in Birmingham, Alabama, used fire hoses and attack dogs against African Americans protesting segregation. As a result of the melee, civil rights leader Martin Luther King, Jr., was thrown in jail. Pictures of the violence appeared around the world and damaged America's standing as a land of freedom in the fight against communism. A few weeks later Alabama governor George C. Wallace tried to stop two black students from integrating the state university at Tuscaloosa.

Finally, in June 1963 Kennedy spoke out in a national address and called civil rights " a moral issue . . . as old as the scriptures and . . . as clear as the American Constitution." He proposed legislation that would end discrimination in jobs and in housing. In August 1963 he endorsed a massive march on Washington by more than 200,000 protesters demanding civil rights. He kept a close watch on it, though, by pressuring leaders to temper their speeches and by having members of his staff ready to pull the plug on the public address system should any of the speakers sound too radical. Despite the protest, Kennedy's civil rights bill stalled in Congress.

John Kennedy's extramarital affairs continued throughout his presidency, and they amounted to more than just inconsequential dalliances. An affair with Judith E. Campbell, the mistress of Sam Giancana, threatened to compromise a government investigation of the Mafia leader. Kennedy kept seeing Campbell until FBI director J. Edgar Hoover intervened with detailed information about her background. The president also had an affair with Ellen Rometsch, possibly a communist spy. According to Richard Reeves in *President Kennedy: Profile of Power*, "The logistics of Kennedy's liaisons with Judith Campbell and dozens of other women in the White House and in hotels, houses, and apartments around the country and around the world required secrecy and devotion rare even in the annals of the energetic service demanded by successful politicians." Beyond that, historian James M. Giglio observes that "the president's sexual indiscretions also created security difficulties regarding his physical protection since the Secret Service and FBI could not institute background checks on women discreetly smuggled into the White House."

In November 1963 President Kennedy embarked on a political trip to Texas, where he hoped to raise money for the Democrats and heal a rift within the state party. He received warm welcomes in Houston, San Antonio, and Fort Worth. On November 22 he arrived in Dallas. Shortly after noon, as his motorcade passed through Dealey Plaza, two rifle bullets, apparently fired from a window of the nearby Texas Book Depository, ripped through his head and throat. Another bullet wounded Governor John Connally, who was riding in the motorcade. The president was rushed to Parkland Hospital, where doctors pronounced him dead.

Some 90 minutes later, the police arrested Lee Harvey Oswald for killing Kennedy. On November 24, Jack Ruby, a Dallas nightclub operator with ties to organized crime, entered the city police station and shot and killed Oswald. Columnist William S. White reflected on Kennedy's assassination: "The plain fact is that I *was* crushed by grief and shock and all but physically knocked down by my horror that this unspeakable thing had occurred in my home state, where not long before a handful of harpies had spat upon [U.N. ambassador] Adlai Stevenson."

In 1964 a commission headed by Supreme Court Chief Justice Earl Warren concluded that Oswald had acted alone in assassinating the president, but controversy over the finding continues. Various conspiracy theories have emerged, some saying the Mafia arranged the killing, others linking it to Castro, and still others to agents within the U.S. government.

John F. Kennedy's murder made him a martyr, and many Americans embraced the image promoted by Jacqueline Kennedy of "gallant men" who "danced with beautiful women" and of artists and poets who gathered at the White House and "held back" the "barbarians beyond the walls." In an interview shortly after the assassination, she told how her husband liked to listen to the recording from the Broadway play *Camelot*, and she called the Kennedy presidency "a magic moment in American history." She added: "It will never be that way again. . . . There will never be another Camelot. . . ."

Chronology

1917 Born May 29

1935 Graduates from the Choate School
Studies at London School of Economics
Attends Princeton University briefly

1936 Enters Harvard University

1940 Graduates from Harvard University
Publishes *Why England Slept*

1941 Appointed ensign in naval reserve

1943 Sent to South Pacific
PT 109 sunk by Japanese destroyer
Returns to U.S. because of back injury and malaria

1945 Works as newspaper reporter

1946 Elected to U.S. House of Representatives

1947 Votes against Taft-Hartley Act

1948 Reelected to House of Representatives

1949 Criticizes Harry Truman's policy in China

1950 Reelected to House of Representatives

1952 Elected to U.S. Senate

1953 Marries Jacqueline Bouvier

1954 Undergoes spinal fusion operation

1956 Publishes *Profiles in Courage*

Campaigns for Democratic presidential nominee Adlai Stevenson

1957 Supports Civil Rights Act

Wins Pulitzer Prize for *Profiles in Courage*

1958 Reelected to Senate

1959 Launches campaign for presidency

1960 Elected president

1961 Inaugurated as president

Forms Peace Corps

Begins Alliance for Progress in Latin America

Orders invasion of Cuba at Bay of Pigs

1962 Sends federal troops to University of Mississippi

Orders Russian missiles out of Cuba during Cuban Missile Crisis

1963 Sends federal troops to Birmingham, to put down race riots

Increases numbers of U.S. advisers in Vietnam

Proposes new civil rights legislation

Assassinated in Dallas, Texas, on November 22

FURTHER READING

Bernstein, Irving. *Promises Kept: John F. Kennedy's New Frontier.* New York: Oxford University Press, 1991.

Beschloss, Michael. *The Crisis Years: Kennedy and Khrushchev, 1960–1963.* New York: Edward Burlingame, 1991.

Blight, James G., and David A. Welch. *On the Brink: Americans and Soviets Reexamine the Cuban Missile Crisis.* New York: Hill and Wang, 1988.

Brauer, Carl M. *John F. Kennedy and the Second Reconstruction.* New York: Columbia University Press, 1977.

Burner, David. *John F. Kennedy and a New Generation.* Glenview, Ill.: Scott, Foresman, 1988.

Clarke, Thurston. *Ask Not: The Inauguration of John F. Kennedy and the Speech That Changed America.* New York: Henry Holt, 2004.

Dallek, Robert. *An Unfinished Life: John F. Kennedy, 1917–1963.* New York: Little, Brown, 2003.

Frankel, Max. *High Noon in the Cold War: Kennedy, Khrushchev, and the Cuban Missile Crisis.* New York: Ballantine Books, 2004.

Giglio, James N. *The Presidency of John F. Kennedy.* Lawrence: University Press of Kansas, 1991.

Hamilton, Nigel. *JFK: Reckless Youth.* New York: Random House, 1992.

Hersh, Seymour M. *The Dark Side of Camelot.* New York: Little, Brown, 1997.

May, Ernest R., and Philip D. Zelikow. *The Kennedy Tapes: Inside the White House During the Cuban Missile Crisis.* Cambridge, Mass.: Harvard University Press, 1997.

Newman, John F. *JFK and Vietnam: Deception, Intrigue, and Struggle for Power.* New York: Warner Books, 1992.

Parmet, Herbert S. *Jack: The Struggles of John F. Kennedy.* New York: Dial Press, 1980.

———. *JFK: The Presidency of John F. Kennedy.* New York: Dial Press, 1983.

Reeves, Richard. *President Kennedy: Profile of Power.* New York: Simon & Schuster, 1993.

Reeves, Thomas C. *A Question of Character: The Life of John F. Kennedy.* New York: Free Press, 1991.

Rorabaugh, W. J. *Kennedy and the Promise of the Sixties.* New York: Cambridge University Press, 2002.

Smith, Sally Bedell. *Grace and Power: The Private World of the Kennedy White House.* New York: Random House, 2004.

Wills, Garry. *The Kennedy Imprisonment: A Meditation on Power.* Boston: Little, Brown, 1982.

Lyndon Baines Johnson (1908–1973)

Thirty-sixth President, 1963–1969

Lyndon Baines Johnson
(Lyndon B. Johnson Library)

"Let us now join reason to faith and action to experience, to transform our unity of interest into a unity of purpose. For the hour and the day and the time are here to achieve progress without strife, to achieve change without hatred. . . ."

—Inaugural words, second term, January 20, 1965

The differences between President Lyndon Johnson and his predecessor, John F. Kennedy, at least as they appeared on the surface, jarred many Americans. With Johnson in the White House, Kennedy's staunchest supporters thought they had descended into a demimonde, a barbaric hell where boorish behavior pricked sensibilities sharper than the cacti found in Johnson's Texas desert. Here was a president who talked crudely, swam in the White House pool naked, and met with his advisers while seated on the toilet; a president *Time* magazine described vividly in 1964 when he provided a self-guided automobile tour of his ranch:

At one point, Johnson pulled up near a small gathering of cattle, pushed a button under the dashboard—and a cow horn bawled from underneath the gleaming hood. . . Johnson talked about his cattle, [and] once plunged into what one startled newswoman called a "very graphic description of the sex life of a bull. . . ." Through all the fun, the President sipped beer from his paper cup. Eventually he ran dry. . . and took off at speeds up to 90 m.p.h. to get more. . . . Someone gasped at how fast Johnson was driving. Quickly Lyndon took one hand from the wheel, removed his five-gallon hat and flopped it on the dashboard to cover the speedometer.

Even worse to Johnson's critics was that his backcountry coarseness blended with a talent to tell tall stories and an unbridled ambition that overwhelmed any redeeming qualities. Yet Johnson's supporters pointed to his compassion born from his struggles growing up in the Texas hill country and his commitment to seek power not only for the sake of holding it but also for advancing the public good.

In 1968 African-American writer Ralph Ellison praised Johnson for a speech the president had given at Howard University three years earlier. According to Ellison, Johnson "spelled out the meaning of full integration for Negroes in a way that no one, no President, not Abraham Lincoln nor Franklin Roosevelt, no matter how much we loved and respected them, has ever done before. There was no hedging in it, no escape clauses."

Johnson's complexities and contradictions, his strengths and deficiencies, appeared in his policies: his War on Poverty that awoke Americans to shortcomings in their economic growth, his civil rights legislation that advanced black freedom, and his Vietnam War that cost hundreds of thousands of lives and bred deep distrust of government.

Lyndon Baines Johnson was born on August 27, 1908, near Stonewall, Texas, alongside the Pedernales River, to Samuel Ealy Johnson and Rebekah Baines Johnson. She was the daughter of Joseph Wilson Baines, a lawyer, educator, and lay preacher at the Baptist church in Blanco, Texas. Of her five children she favored Lyndon, imparting to him her fondness for books and learning. She also wrapped him in a possessive love that ensured if he did anything wrong or went against her wishes, she would turn cold and ignore him for days on end.

Sam Johnson farmed and invested in real estate, stocks, and cotton. He was moderately successful, but his fondness for the bottle often cost him. Lyndon Johnson later observed, "When he had too much to drink, he'd lose control of himself. He used bad language. He squandered the little money we had on the . . . markets. Sometimes he'd be lucky and make a lot of money. But more often he lost out."

When Lyndon was five, Sam moved his family to Johnson City. With a reputation for honesty, he won election to the state legislature six times, and Lyndon traveled with him on numerous campaigns. Sam liked to sit on his front porch and talk politics with his friends; the youngster would perch himself by the doorway and listen, enthralled by the stories. But he received a crushing blow at age 13 when his father's investments turned bad and dragged the entire family into poverty, making Sam rely on relatives to meet his mortgage payments. Lyndon hated the pain inflicted by being poor and determined he would live better.

As a teenager, Lyndon picked cotton, shined shoes, and distributed handbills. After graduating from high school, he continued to work at odd jobs, washing dishes, waiting on tables, and doing farmwork. After his mother convinced him to get a college degree, in 1927 he entered Southwest Texas State Teachers College in San Marcos.

Friendly and outgoing, the young man, now more than six feet tall, entered campus politics. He already had the habit of leaning his towering frame into people as he talked to them, grabbing them by the lapels, and placing his face next to theirs in order to make a point. He so often stretched the truth that his classmates nicknamed him "Bull" for throwing it around. Ambitious, he did whatever it took to win office. One friend recalled, "Everyone knew that if something wasn't straight, it was Lyndon Johnson who had done it."

While still in college he worked as the principal at an elementary school in Cotulla, Texas, that most Anglos wanted nothing to do with because of its Mexican students. He emphasized academic discipline and used some of his own money to buy bats and balls for the children so they could play games. They long remembered him as the Anglo who cared.

Johnson received his bachelor's degree from San Marcos in 1930 and taught high school in Houston, but his ambition made him want more. He later told historian Doris Kearns Goodwin, "I wouldn't want to be building great towers or big dams as an engineer, or big banks as a banker, or big insurance companies as a businessman. All those things are essential, but the thing that gives me the greatest satisfaction is dealing with human beings and watching the development of those human beings." For that he wanted the bigger stage politics could provide.

In 1932, Johnson left teaching for good when he joined the staff of Congressman Richard Kleberg in Washington, D.C. He was hired as Kleberg's legislative secretary, but with the congressman's devotion to golf, Johnson actually ran the office and honed his political skill. In September 1934 he met Claudia Alta Taylor, better known as Lady Bird, and in November they married. She bore him two daughters, Lynda Bird and Luci Baines.

The following year Johnson returned to Texas, where he served as the state director for President Franklin Roosevelt's National Youth Administration, a New Deal program to provide training and part-time jobs for young people during the Great Depression. Johnson gained a reputation for effective management and for compassion toward black and Mexican-American youths.

He gained politically as well when he expanded his contacts within the state and in 1937, at age 29, ran as a Democrat in a special election for a congressional seat in the Tenth District. Campaigning as an ardent New Dealer, he won. Once he returned to Washington, President Roosevelt adopted him as a protégé and made sure he gained appointment to the House Naval Affairs Committee.

Johnson worked Capitol Hill as effectively as any freshman congressman could by applying what he had learned as Richard Kleberg's secretary. In his first term and later, he obtained funding for local projects that brought electricity to rural homes in his district. He also developed a friendship with Sam Rayburn, a fellow Texan and the powerful Speaker of the House, even gaining entry into Rayburn's inner sanctum filled with power brokers. The two men eventually had a falling out when Johnson told Roosevelt that the Speaker opposed New Deal legislation when, in fact, he really favored it. Johnson spread the story as a way to loosen Rayburn's grip on patronage in Texas and gain more control over it for himself.

In 1941 Johnson ran for the U.S. Senate. He fully expected to defeat W. Lee "Pappy" O'Daniel, the Texas governor who campaigned with a hillbilly band. Instead he lost by about 1,300 votes after he made a big mistake: He allowed the political bosses under his control in the Mexican districts along the Rio Grande to report their largely fraudulent returns early, giving O'Daniel time to counter with his own rigged ballots.

Johnson returned to his seat in Congress while the United States entered World War II. During his Senate campaign, the Texan, who was a member of the naval reserve, had promised that should America go to war, he would "join the boys picked to defend our homes and our God and our liberties." Now he dragged his feet, trying to obtain from Roosevelt an appointment that would keep him out of combat. For several months he inspected bases on the West Coast, but pressure from political opponents convinced him it would look bad if the war ended without his ever having been in a combat zone.

In May 1942 Johnson finally went to the Pacific as an observer, appointed to report on conditions there. Soon after his arrival, he agreed to fly on a dangerous bombing run. While in the air, the plane in which he was riding developed engine problems, and as it returned to its base in New Guinea, Japanese fighters hit it. The plane managed to limp home. Johnson subsequently received a Silver Star from General Douglas MacArthur—a politically motivated bestowal, since no one else on that flight was given one—and returned to Washington. From the exaggerated stories Johnson told, no one would ever have guessed his harrowing flight experience was a one-time, 13-minute brush with combat. He even said that the men he flew with had nicknamed him "Raider" Johnson. To display his bravery, for the rest of his political career he nearly always wore on his lapel a small bar that indicated he had received the Silver Star.

Lyndon Johnson's wealth far exceeded his congressional salary after his wife, Lady Bird, bought KTBC, a radio station in Austin, Texas. Johnson always insisted he had nothing to do with the business, but in fact his influence turned the station into a valuable property. Lady Bird obtained unusually quick approval from the Federal Communications Commission to relocate KTBC to a more favorable spot on the AM dial and to broadcast 24 hours a day. In addition, the same supporters who funded Johnson's political campaigns bought commercial time; Johnson, in turn, helped them in Congress.

"Raider" Johnson soon obtained another nickname, this one related to his second try for the Senate. In 1948 he ran in the Democratic primary against former Texas governor Coke Stevenson. To align himself with his home state's increasing discontent with the New Deal, he turned conservative and in speeches emphasized his vote in Congress for the Taft-Hartley Act, which he called "anticommunist" but which was really antiunion. He also distributed campaign literature with the headline "Communists favor Coke."

As the initial vote returns showed a narrow victory for Stevenson, Johnson did what Texas political tradition and his own background called for: He stole ballots. Six days after the election, with Stevenson ahead by 157 votes, Johnson's political bosses reported a late tally from Precinct 13 along the Rio Grande that gave him 200 additional votes and made him the victor. Johnson finished with 494,191 ballots to Stevenson's 494,104—an 87-vote margin. Extensive research by Robert A. Caro, reported in his book *The Years of Lyndon Johnson: Means of Ascent*, proves that Johnson rigged the Precinct 13 results. Caro says, "In the context of the politics that was his life, Lyndon Johnson would do whatever was necessary to win." As a result of the way Johnson beat Stevenson, he arrived in the Senate with a new nickname, "Landslide Lyndon."

Johnson rose steadily, and with the support of Georgia's powerful Richard Russell, he was chosen minority leader in 1953. Two years later, after the Democrats regained control of the Senate, he became majority leader. Johnson used his knowledge of Congress and his considerable persuasive abilities to advance legislation. In 1957, after he recovered from a heart attack, he once more displayed his political talent when he attached amendments to President Eisenhower's civil rights bill to make it more acceptable to Southerners and move it through the Senate. Such efforts led some observers to call him the greatest majority leader ever and to talk about his potential for the White House.

Johnson wanted the presidency, and he went after it in 1960. *Time* magazine described his power and methods in the Senate and told about the candidate's character:

> He rolls out the welcome mat for every freshman Senator, works hard to maneuver the most promising men into the most advantageous committee assignments. No local bridge-building bill is too far from Texas or too petty for his full attention, if it will help a colleague's progress toward re-election. . . . Johnson is a back-slapper, a shoulder hugger, a knee squeezer. "I like to press the flesh," he says, "and look a man in the eye."

Johnson lost the Democratic nomination to Massachusetts senator John F. Kennedy, but for reasons still disputed, Kennedy offered him the vice-presidential spot, and he accepted. After the ticket's victory in November, Johnson found himself shunted from his powerful Senate seat to the nearly powerless vice presidency.

That changed with Kennedy's assassination at Dallas, Texas, on November 22, 1963. Lyndon Johnson was the one who had urged Kennedy to make the trip to Texas to help heal a rift within the state Democratic Party, and he was in the motorcade and heard the lethal gunshots that ripped through Dealey Plaza. He took the oath of office on *Air Force One* standing next to his wife and Jacqueline Kennedy, whose husband's blood still caked her suit.

Johnson intended to continue Kennedy's programs while developing his own distinct presidency, and a few days later said passage of a civil rights bill that had been stalled in Congress for months would honor the slain president. "We have talked long enough in this country about equal rights," he added. "We have talked for one hundred years or more. It is time now to write the next chapter, and to write it in the books of law."

In his State of the Union address, delivered in January 1964, President Johnson proclaimed: "This Administration today, here and now, declares unconditional war on poverty in America." To lead the fight, the president created an agency independent from his cabinet, much as Franklin Roosevelt had done with his New Deal programs. To maintain a connection to the Kennedys, he chose Sargent Shriver, the slain president's brother-in-law and successful head of the Peace Corps, to lead the War on Poverty, which was to be based on proposals originally developed under John Kennedy.

While Johnson let Shriver handle the details of the antipoverty legislation, he applied his political influence to get the measures approved. The programs reminded many of the New Deal in the way they rapidly poured forth from the Oval Office. Beginning in spring 1964 Congress debated his Economic Opportunity Act, which called for a Job Corps to provide training and work-study programs for poor youths. Volunteers in Service to America, or VISTA, created a domestic Peace Corps; the Community Action Program established antipoverty programs at the local level and most notably founded Head Start, an educational program for impoverished children. The Office of Economic Opportunity coordinated the entire War on Poverty, and Shriver was named its director.

In all, Congress authorized 10 separate antipoverty programs, costing nearly $1 billion. Johnson promoted the measures as helping more than the poor, stating that in the long run they would improve American society by reducing the crime that poverty bred. As Franklin Delano Roosevelt had done with the New Deal, Johnson avoided radicalism and emphasized broadening opportunities for poor people rather than redistributing wealth or income.

While Johnson's proposals moved through Congress, he unveiled a theme for his presidency. "We have the opportunity," he said, "to move not only toward the rich society and the powerful society, but upward to the Great Society. . . . It is a place where men are more concerned with the quality of their goals than the quantity of their goods." He called for rebuilding America's cities, constructing better housing, and improving transportation.

That July Congress finally passed the civil rights bill he and John Kennedy had requested. The bill made discrimination in public accommodations illegal; authorized the attorney general to file suits to desegregate schools; and prohibited most discriminatory employment practices based on race, color, religion, sex, or nationality.

Lyndon Johnson's domestic agenda came from a sincere desire to help the disadvantaged, fulfill the Kennedy legacy, enhance his own presidential reputation, and build support for his election in 1964. He much preferred domestic issues to foreign policy ones, but Vietnam soon overwhelmed him.

Johnson's entanglement in Indochina can be attributed in part to John Kennedy and the

White House advisers he had inherited from his predecessor. Shortly before Kennedy's death, the American military presence in South Vietnam was increased in an attempt to bolster the government in Saigon and prevent communists directed by North Vietnam from toppling it. Though JFK ultimately withdrew some of the military personnel, Johnson entered the White House to find Kennedy's advisers busy developing plans for a deeper commitment, with more money, more supplies, and more soldiers for South Vietnam.

For his part, Johnson feared that if he lost any territory in Southeast Asia to the communists, he would appear weak, and Republicans would attack him. Early on he expressed his belief in the domino theory, saying that if South Vietnam fell to communism, so too would Laos, Cambodia, Thailand, and the entire region. In a conversation with newspaper executive John S. Knight on February 3, 1964, Johnson said, "There's one of three things you can do. One is run and let the dominoes start falling over. And God Almighty, what they said about us [Democrats] leaving China [in 1949] would just be warming up, compared to what they'd say now."

One of Johnson's most telling actions in Vietnam occurred in February 1964 when he secretly ordered Plan 34A and launched commando raids by South Vietnamese PT boats against North Vietnam under the protection of American destroyers. It set the pattern for most of his strategy, as he would reveal little to the public about his directives and often lie about his motives and actions. As a result, he bred distrust in the government and failed to rally the support he needed for a prolonged war.

Like so many of Johnson's decisions, the commando raids drew America deeper into Vietnam. On August 2, 1964, three communist PT boats attacked the American destroyer *Maddox* in the Gulf of Tonkin some 16 miles from the North Vietnamese coast. Johnson said nothing publicly about the attack, though he ordered planes from an aircraft carrier to strike back, and they damaged one of the enemy boats.

On August 4 the *Maddox* and a nearby destroyer, the *Turner Joy*, reported another attack by the North Vietnamese. Even though the evidence for this second raid was flimsy—radar observations were likely misread—Johnson ordered air strikes against sites in North Vietnam and went on national television to claim that America had been assaulted on the high seas. He then asked Congress for support. With little debate Congress passed the Gulf of Tonkin Resolution, which gave him the authority "to take all necessary measures to repel any armed attack against forces of the United States and to prevent further aggression."

Johnson said nothing publicly about Plan 34A, nothing about American-sponsored raids on North Vietnam, and nothing about the *Maddox* having been involved in electronic surveillance to support the raids. He displayed anger when Vice President Hubert Humphrey indicated American culpability in the attack. To a friend, Johnson said "Yesterday morning he went on TV and . . . just blabbed everything that he had heard in a briefing. . . . Humphrey said, 'Well, we have been carrying on some operations in that area . . . where we have been going in and knocking out roads and petroleum things.' And that is exactly what we have been doing!" In a speech at Syracuse University, Johnson claimed: "The [North Vietnamese] attacks were deliberate. The attacks were unprovoked. The attacks have been answered. . . . Aggression—deliberate, willful, and systematic aggression—has unmasked its face to the entire world."

According to historian Robert Dallek in *Flawed Giant*, Lyndon Johnson doubted whether he should deepen American involvement in Vietnam and realized the danger of sending troops there. In his February 1964 conversation with James S. Knight, when Knight said "Long-range . . . the odds are certainly against us," Johnson replied: "Yes, there is no question about that. Any time you got that many people against you that far from your home base, it's bad." Dallek says that in 1964, at least, Johnson wanted the Gulf of Tonkin Resolution more to show resolve than to widen the war. Yet the president believed it gave him an added option, should at some later date he decide to expand the American combat role.

Whatever Johnson's doubts, he and his advisers believed the United States could defeat communism almost anywhere, particularly in what they considered "backward" Vietnam, or as Johnson called it, a "little piss-ant country." Such sense of strength mixed with hubris made it unlikely that Johnson would settle for anything less than complete victory. In fact, in 1964 he rejected overtures from Hanoi to discuss a settlement because it might result in communist participation in the South Vietnamese government.

As the 1964 presidential election neared, Johnson portrayed himself as standing firm against communism but using restraint so Americans would never have to fight in Vietnam. He successfully contrasted his policy with the Republican candidate, conservative Arizona senator Barry M. Goldwater, who advocated a strong military response. In what Robert Dallek calls the most famous TV campaign ad ever, the Democrats showed a little girl picking a daisy, her voice counting 10 before a mushroom cloud appeared and an announcer intoned that Americans must vote for Johnson, for the stakes were too high. That fall, crowds greeted Johnson with the chant "LBJ for the USA!" He defeated Goldwater in a landslide—among the most lopsided victories in presidential history.

With the election behind him, Johnson pushed his Great Society forward. In April 1965 Congress passed the Elementary and Secondary School Act, granting $1.3 billion to school districts based on the number of needy children they served. In July Medicare was passed to provide medical care for the elderly through a system financed by Social Security.

When in March 1965 sheriff's deputies and state troopers bludgeoned civil rights protesters at Selma, Alabama, Johnson told a national television audience that he was sending a Voting Rights Act to Congress. Passed in August, it suspended literacy and other voter tests and authorized federal agents to supervise voter registration in districts where discrimination prevailed.

When blacks rioted in the Watts district of Los Angeles later that month, Johnson reacted to a white backlash by retreating from additional civil rights proposals. An even worse riot in Detroit in 1965 forced LBJ to send troops into that city, and over the next several months more riots erupted elsewhere. Increasingly, whites feared blacks would turn from burning ghettoes to burning white neighborhoods, and Republicans criticized Johnson for allowing "anarchy" to spread.

Johnson never understood the anger among blacks and found it perplexing and discouraging given all he had done for civil rights. It was, to him, a slap in the face. As he saw it, every cry from African Americans for "black power" jeopardized his Great Society program and made Congress hostile to liberal reform.

Vietnam contributed to the national crisis and tore America apart. Johnson thought he could fight the war and advance his Great Society, but as the conflict expanded, it consumed more and more money—dwarfing spending on social programs—and more and more faith and trust.

In February 1965 Johnson reacted to a communist attack on U.S. soldiers at the South Vietnamese airbase of Pleiku by unleashing Operation Rolling Thunder, which sent wave after wave of B-52 bombers over North Vietnam. In time, the total number of bombs dropped in the American air war would exceed the number dropped on all nations in all previous wars. One of Johnson's advisers thought Operation Rolling Thunder would bring Hanoi to its knees within three months—a massive miscalculation.

On April 1, 1965, Johnson authorized American troops to take the offensive against communist forces in South Vietnam. Not only did he keep this crucial decision secret, but he also said at a press conference that he foresaw no change in America's combat role. Then on July 28 he made a critical decision to increase the number of troops in South Vietnam from 75,000 to 125,000, without calling up reserves or levying taxes to fight the war. As a result, he avoided an open debate with Congress that a declaration of emergency would have entailed and misled the public into thinking the sacrifice would be painless. When the pain from the loss of American lives became too great, antiwar protests intensified, as did the animosity between those who supported the war and those who condemned it. When these differences were added to divisions between whites and radical blacks and between young and older Americans—or what was called the generation gap—American society splintered.

As criticism of Johnson spread, the president demanded full loyalty from those around him. He also ranted about communists leading the dissenters, about communists taking over the nation. Some thought he had become completely unglued.

"We are [in Vietnam]," LBJ said, "because we have a promise to keep. . . . The central lesson of our time is that the appetite of aggression is never satisfied. To withdraw from one battlefield means only to prepare for the next." By October 1965 more than 200,000 American troops were in Vietnam, yet Johnson failed to discuss the escalation openly or reveal future prospects. Privately he saw a tough road ahead; publicly he said victory was just around the corner.

Although Johnson's social reforms contributed to a decline in poverty from 38 million poor people in 1959 to 25.9 million in 1967, internal disputes and funding problems imperiled his programs. When crime rates surged in 1966 and 1967, Americans opposed his leadership all the more. Johnson reacted by proposing a crime bill that included prohibitions on wiretapping and bugging, a surprising provision given that he had bugged opponents at the 1964 Democratic National Convention, bugged embassies and homes, and secretly recorded 10,000 conversations in the White House. Further, in 1967 Johnson and his National Security Council ordered the CIA to investigate possible links between foreign groups and student protesters in the United States. This mission, called Operation CHAOS, violated the National Security Act of 1947, which prohibited the CIA from engaging in "internal security functions."

Most Americans in 1967 backed their country's troop presence in Vietnam, but support was rapidly eroding, and in South Vietnam itself, military officers were saying the war could not be won. The greatest blow to Johnson's war came in January 1968 when the communists launched the Tet Offensive, a massive assault throughout South Vietnam. American troops beat back the enemy, but it showed that victory was distant and would require yet more soldiers above the 500,000 already stationed in the embattled country.

The Tet Offensive greatly damaged Johnson's approval rating and gave momentum to Minnesota senator Eugene McCarthy's campaign to wrest the Democratic presidential nomination from him. In March 1968 McCarthy, a sharp critic of the war, shocked the country when he won more delegates than LBJ in the New Hampshire primary. A few days later John Kennedy's brother, Robert Kennedy, entered the race.

In late March, Johnson presented his own surprise: He announced he would not seek reelection. Instead, he would try to open peace talks with Hanoi, and toward that end he declared a unilateral halt in air attacks over most of North Vietnam. For this action he received widespread praise. Preliminary peace negotiations began in May 1968 and more intensive ones in January 1969, but they would last several years.

When Johnson left the presidency, he retired to his ranch in the Texas hill country, along the Pedernales. There he died on January 22, 1973, following a heart attack.

The magnitude of the issues that confronted Lyndon Johnson, combined with the enormousness of his personality and the tragedy of his policies, encouraged some observers to present him as a Shakespearean figure. Barbara Garson did so viciously in 1966 when she staged the play

Macbird, a takeoff on *Macbeth*, that implied Lyndon Johnson had used palace intrigue and murdered John Kennedy. Others made Johnson into a King Lear, who realized his own faults but failed to rise above them and whose rages revealed an unstable mind. Johnson himself spoke in Learlike tones when in private he said, "People . . . think I want great power. And what I want is great solace—and a little love. That's all I want."

Any understanding of Lyndon Johnson's presidency should compare Ralph Ellison's words of 1968 with these from Shakespeare's *King Lear*:

O, sir, to wilful men
The injuries that they
Themselves procure
Must be their
Schoolmasters.

CHRONOLOGY

1908 Born August 27

1927 Graduates from Southwest Texas State Teachers College

1930 Begins teaching in Houston

1932 Hired as Congressman Richard Kleberg's legislative secretary

1934 Marries Claudia ("Lady Bird") Taylor

1935 Named director of National Youth Administration in Texas

1937 Elected to Congress as a Democrat

1938 Reelected to Congress

1940 Reelected to Congress for third term

1941 Loses bid for U.S. Senate seat

Goes on active duty in the navy

1942 Sent to Pacific by President Roosevelt to observe fighting conditions

1946 Reelected to fourth term in Congress

1947 Votes for Taft-Hartley Act

1948 Elected to U.S. Senate

1951 Elected Democratic Whip in the Senate

1953 Chosen Senate minority leader

1954 Reelected to Senate

Becomes Senate majority leader

1955 Suffers heart attack

1957 Directs passage of Civil Rights Act

1960 Loses Democratic presidential nomination to John F. Kennedy

Accepts vice-presidential nomination

Elected vice president

1963 Becomes president on assassination of John F. Kennedy

Urges passage of Civil Rights Act

1964 Announces War on Poverty

Signs Civil Rights Act

Orders retaliatory air strike on North Vietnam

Obtains passage of Gulf of Tonkin Resolution

Signs Economic Opportunity Act

Elected president

1965 Orders massive bombing of North Vietnam called Operation Rolling Thunder

Sends U.S. troops to end uprising in the Dominican Republic

Signs Medicare Act and Voting Rights Act

Orders American troops in South Vietnam to take the offensive and sends more troops without calling up the reserves or seeking higher taxes

1968 After Tet Offensive, announces pause in bombing of North Vietnam and that he will not seek reelection

1969 Retires to his ranch in the Texas hill country

1973 Dies January 22

Further Reading

Berman, Larry. *Planning A Tragedy: The Americanization of the War in Vietnam.* New York: W. W. Norton, 1982.

———. *Lyndon Johnson's War: The Road to Stalemate in Vietnam.* New York: Norton, 1989.

Beschloss, Michael R. *Reaching for Glory: Lyndon Johnson's Secret White House Tapes, 1964–1965.* New York: Simon & Schuster, 2001.

———. *Taking Charge: The Johnson White House Tapes, 1963–1964.* New York: Simon & Schuster, 1997.

Califano, Joseph A., Jr. *The Triumph & Tragedy of Lyndon Johnson.* New York: Simon & Schuster, 1991.

Caro, Robert A. *The Years of Lyndon Johnson: Master of the Senate.* New York: Alfred A. Knopf, 2002.

———. *The Years of Lyndon Johnson: Means of Ascent.* New York: Alfred A. Knopf, 1990.

———. *The Years of Lyndon Johnson: The Path to Power.* New York: Alfred A. Knopf, 1982.

Conklin, Paul. *Big Daddy from the Pedernales: Lyndon Baines Johnson.* Boston: Twayne, 1986.

Dallek, Robert. *Flawed Giant: Lyndon Johnson and His Times, 1961–1973.* New York: Oxford University Press, 1998.

———. *Lone Star Rising: Lyndon Johnson and His Times, 1908–1960.* New York: Oxford University Press, 1991.

———. *Lyndon B. Johnson: Portrait of a President.* New York: Oxford University Press, 2003.

Dugger, Ronnie. *The Politician: The Life and Times of Lyndon Johnson.* New York: W. W. Norton, 1982.

Gardner, Lloyd C. *Pay Any Price: Lyndon Johnson and the Wars for Vietnam.* Chicago: I. R. Dee, 1995.

Herring, George C. *LBJ and Vietnam: A Different Kind of War.* Austin: University of Texas Press, 1994.

Kaiser, David E. *American Tragedy: Kennedy, Johnson, and the Origin of the Vietnam War.* Cambridge, Mass.: Belknap Press, 2000.

Kearns, Doris. *Lyndon Johnson and the American Dream.* New York: St. Martin's Press, 1991.

Mann, Robert. *The Walls of Jericho: Lyndon Johnson, Hubert Humphrey, Richard Russell, and the Struggle for Civil Rights.* New York: Harcourt Brace, 1996.

McNamara, Robert S. *In Retrospect: The Tragedy and Lessons of Vietnam.* New York: Times Books, 1995.

RICHARD M. NIXON (1913–1994)

Thirty-seventh President, 1969–1974

RICHARD M. NIXON
(official White House photograph, Library of Congress)

"Let us pledge together to make these next four years the best four years in America's history, so that on its 200th birthday America will be as young and as vital as when it began, and as bright a beacon of hope for all the world."

—Inaugural words, second term,
January 20, 1973

When Richard Nixon accepted the Republican nomination for president in 1968, he recalled how as a child in Yorba Linda, California, the Santa Fe train passed through town and its whistle was "the sweetest music I ever heard." He would lay awake at night and listen as the train went by and think about faraway places where he would like to go.

He told his audience about the help he had received over the years from his parents, his teacher, his football coach, his wife, and his children and said, "You can see why I believe so deeply in the American dream." He indicated that just as glory once, and still, awaited him, so it awaited his country. "My fellow Americans," he concluded in referring to the crisis of war and protest in 1968, "the dark long night for America is about to end."

Yet Nixon's dreams foreshadowed a nightmare. His ruthless pursuit of power brought the United States to a constitutional crisis that shook its political system. Threatened with impeachment and forced to resign the presidency, he left with his country's faith in its government badly shaken, the White House shrouded in scorn, and Americans despairing of their future.

Richard Milhous Nixon was born in Yorba Linda, near Los Angeles, on January 9, 1913, the second of five sons of Frank Nixon and Hannah Milhous Nixon. Hannah was the daughter of Quaker parents in nearby Whittier; Frank converted to the Quaker faith after marrying her in June 1908. The two had contrasting personalities, with Frank argumentative and loud and Hannah compassionate and calm. In Yorba Linda, Frank owned a small lemon grove, but after it failed he was forced to work at odd jobs.

In 1922 Frank moved his family to Whittier, a bustling town. There he built a gas station and expanded it to include groceries, meats, and baked goods. Within a short time it provided a middle-class livelihood.

Richard worked in the store and learned from his father that determination meant winning, and winning meant everything. He also learned about politics as his father passionately condemned Democrats, and because Frank ruled his family through fear, Richard learned that power owed much to fear itself.

A serious child, Richard had a keen interest in current events and a remarkable ability to memorize almost anything. At age 16 he wrote the winning entry in his high school speech contest. His prescient theme—given his later pronouncements and actions as president—criticized journalists who used freedom of the press as a cover to slander others, foment riots, and attack patriotism. He said laws must be obeyed "for they have been passed for our own welfare."

In 1930 Richard graduated from Whittier High School and entered Whittier College. After getting up early each morning to prepare the fruits and vegetables at his father's store, he threw himself into campus activities. He was elected president of his freshman class, president of his fraternity, and president of the History Club. He joined the debate team and the glee club, acted in plays, and, despite his small size and lack of physical coordination, each fall he tried out for football. Even his coach winced at the beating the young man's body took as he failed to make the team.

For all his activities, Richard was awkward in personal relationships and made few friends. Nevertheless he excelled academically, graduated with a B.A. in history in 1934, and earned a scholarship to Duke Law School. For the next three years he lived a monastic existence, holding a job at the library and spending long hours at his studies. For a time he was too poor to afford a room and resided in an abandoned tool shack at the edge of the campus. He won election as president of the Duke Student Bar Association but socialized little. Many of his classmates thought him aloof and distant. One later said, "Nixon had a quality of intensity in him, worked hard, . . . he had a sense of privacy and [was] not terribly strong on humor."

Although Richard Nixon graduated third in his class in 1937, he was unable to connect with a New York firm. He therefore returned to Whittier, where he practiced law under Thomas Bewley. Soon after, he began dating Thelma Catherine "Pat" Ryan, whom he met during the rehearsal for a local play. They married on June 21, 1940, and later had two daughters, Julie and Tricia.

In late 1941 Nixon joined the Office of Price Administration in Washington, D.C. With World War II underway, in 1942 he obtained a commission in the navy. He served in the South Pacific and left the military in 1946 with the rank of lieutenant commander.

Nixon's political career began after he received a letter from a banker in Whittier who asked him to run for Congress. Whittier's Republicans wanted someone who could unseat incumbent Democrat Jerry Voorhis in the 12th District. Anxious to win office, in 1946 Nixon met with the banker and his Committee of 100, a group of small businessmen and farmers who disliked the New Deal and labor unions. Nixon's statements secured their support. He talked about two ideologies: "One advocated by the New Deal is government control in regulating our lives. The other calls for individual freedom and all that initiative can produce. I hold with the latter viewpoint."

Nixon used America's expanding Red scare to beat Voorhis. He accused his opponent of sympathizing with communism, a charge he knew to be untrue. According to Nixon's biographer, Stephen E. Ambrose, in *Nixon: The Education of a Politician*, the brash upstart engaged in a "dirty" campaign "characterized by a vicious, snarling approach." Yet Nixon was not acting alone with his smear tactics; in the late 1940s and 1950s, many Republicans won office by linking Democrats to communist causes.

In Congress Nixon served on the House Un-American Activities Committee (HUAC), then at the forefront of investigating communist influence in the United States. Nixon won reelection in 1948 and cosponsored a bill that would require members of the communist party to register with the government. Nixon said he wanted to expose Reds "for what they are." The bill passed the House but failed in the Senate.

As the Red scare intensified and the Soviet Union blockaded West Berlin and exploded its own atomic bomb, Whittaker Chambers, a senior editor of *Time* magazine, appeared before the HUAC and claimed that Alger Hiss, a former official in the State Department, was part of an "underground cell of government employees" who worked for the Communist Party. Chambers said he knew Hiss from years earlier when he himself had been a member of the party. Hiss testified before HUAC and denied the charges, saying he never knew Chambers. "The name means absolutely nothing to me," he insisted.

Nixon studied the testimony, met with Chambers, and came away convinced Alger Hiss was lying. He exposed Hiss by arranging what became a riveting confrontation between the alleged spy and Chambers in front of HUAC. Soon after, Chambers produced rolls of microfilm that contained copies of State Department documents from the mid-1930s, some written by Hiss. Chambers claimed Hiss had given him the documents in 1937 and 1938 as part of an espionage operation. In December 1948 a grand jury indicted Hiss for perjury, and in January 1950 he was convicted.

To Nixon the Hiss case confirmed his anticommunist views, and it made him a national figure. He ran for the U.S. Senate in 1950, and as in his race against Voorhis, he labeled his opponent, Helen Gahagan Douglas, a communist sympathizer. One of his staff members later said, "In almost every statement [Nixon] made, it was Helen Gahagan Douglas and Alger Hiss. . . . He got the two together somehow, ingeniously."

Once in the Senate, Nixon attacked President Harry Truman for failing to win the war in Korea. The Californian's rapid rise in politics continued in 1952 when Dwight Eisenhower chose him as his vice-presidential running mate. Eisenhower wanted a young candidate—Nixon was only 39—and one who could appeal to the conservative wing of the Republican Party.

As Eisenhower expected, Nixon attacked the Democratic presidential nominee, Adlai Stevenson, for being weak on communism, claiming that Stevenson held "a Ph.D. degree from [Secretary of State Dean] Acheson's College of Cowardly Communist Containment."

But Nixon's presence on the ticket nearly wrecked the campaign in September 1952 when a newspaper charged him with accepting about $18,000 from supporters as a slush fund to pay personal expenses. With Nixon having recently blamed the Democrats for corruption, the newspaper's accusation made him appear to be a hypocrite as well as a crook.

Eisenhower considered dumping him, but Nixon rescued himself when he appeared on national television and denied the charges. He admitted, however, that he had received a cocker spaniel named Checkers from a supporter and that he had given the dog to his children and would not give it back. Nixon's "Checkers speech" showed his effective use of television, and Republicans in the thousands convinced Eisenhower to retain him.

As vice president beginning in 1953, Richard Nixon achieved a higher profile than typical for the office. This partly stemmed from President Eisenhower's three major illnesses: a heart attack in 1955, a bout with ileitis in 1956, and a stroke in 1957 that nearly elevated the vice president into the White House. But it stemmed, too, from Nixon's work with congressional Republicans to rally them behind Eisenhower's requests for more foreign aid and from his several overseas trips.

One trip in particular boosted Nixon's standing. In 1959 he traveled to the Soviet Union, where he opened the United States Exhibition with Soviet premier Nikita Khrushchev. As the two men toured the show, they stopped in front of a model American house and engaged in a lively discussion about the relative values of communist and capitalist societies; this came to be known as the Kitchen Debate. Nixon performed well, and in the United States he earned praise for his rejoinders, such as: "The right to choose, the fact that we have a thousand different builders, that's the spice of life. We don't want to have a decision made at the top by one government official saying that we will have one type of house. That's the difference."

Nixon won the Republican presidential nomination in 1960 with little trouble. But the general election proved different as a close contest developed with the Democratic nominee, Senator John F. Kennedy. Nixon was no more extreme in his cold war views than Kennedy, and he refrained from attacking the senator on personal issues, such as his extramarital affairs and his Catholicism. A comment by Eisenhower, however, hurt Nixon. When asked by reporters to name one significant decision made by the vice president, Eisenhower said, "Give me a week." Subsequently, in the first of several televised debates with Kennedy, Nixon came across poorly when he looked uncomfortable. Still, Nixon nearly defeated Kennedy and may, in fact, have lost electoral votes due to corrupt balloting in Chicago, where the Democratic machine assured his opponent a victory in Illinois.

In 1962 most observers declared Nixon's political career at an end when he was defeated in a race for the California governorship. Nixon likely agreed with them. In parting remarks to reporters he said, "As I leave you I want you to know—just think how much you're going to be missing. You won't have Nixon to kick around anymore, because, gentlemen, this is my last press conference. . . ."

But Nixon made a stunning comeback. After helping Republicans win congressional seats in 1966, he captured his party's presidential nomination in 1968. He then surprised the delegates when he chose an obscure politician, Maryland governor Spiro Agnew, as his running mate. He liked Agnew for his tough stand against rioters in Baltimore and was convinced he would appeal to conservatives and take votes away from third-party presidential candidate George C. Wallace.

In confronting Wallace and Vice President Hubert Humphrey, the Democratic nominee, Nixon faced two challenges. First he had to convince voters who distrusted him that he could in fact be trusted, and second he had to convince them that he offered answers to the conflicts in American society generated by race, class, and age differences and by the Vietnam War.

In 1968 Nixon launched Operation Candor, a strategy where he talked openly and frankly with reporters. Regarding unity, Nixon said, "I want the Presidency to be a force for pulling our people back together once again, and for making our nation whole by making our people one."

Several gaffes by Agnew nearly cost Nixon the election. When reporters asked Agnew if he would visit any ghettoes, he replied, "When you've seen one slum, you've seen them all." At another point he commented on an Asian-American reporter sleeping in the back of the campaign plane: "What's wrong with the fat Jap?"

Richard Nixon crafted a widely popular appeal aimed primarily at white middle-class Americans and made little attempt to reach blacks, war protesters, or disenchanted youths. He claimed Humphrey would weaken the military, spend recklessly, and coddle lawbreakers, and he presented himself as best able to end the Vietnam War, though he never said exactly how he would do it.

In October 1968 Nixon appeared headed for a landslide victory as polls showed him 15 points ahead of Humphrey. But in the last days of the campaign, Humphrey closed the gap, and Nixon won by a margin of less than 1 percent in the popular vote. In his victory speech he told how on the road he had spotted a teenager carrying a sign that said, "Bring Us Together," and he announced: "That will be the great objective of this administration, . . . open to new ideas . . . open to the critics as well as those who support us. We want to bridge the generation gap. We want to bridge the gap between the races. We want to bring America together." At his inauguration, however, some 6,000 antiwar protesters chanted "Peace now!" and "Four more years of death!"

Nixon appealed to what he called America's "Silent Majority," or what *Time* magazine called "Middle Americans." *Time* defined this nebulous group as those who sported American-flag decals on their cars, wanted order in the streets, and opposed having their children bused to schools for desegregation. According to *Time*, "Middle Americans sing the national anthem at football games—and mean it." Although Nixon's strategy was aimed particularly at the South, it reached into all neighborhoods where Middle America reigned, primarily suburbs across the country.

To address Middle America's discontent with Vietnam, but also its opposition to losing any war, Nixon decided he would get out of the conflict on terms short of victory while making it appear America had won. Toward that end he embarked on a program that he called "Vietnamization," gradually turning over all the fighting to the South Vietnamese Army, even though he knew full well it had seldom fought credibly.

At the same time, he widened the air war, and in 1969 he ordered the secret bombing of Cambodia, taking the conflict into a neutral nation where the communists had established bases. For the most part, only Nixon and his national security adviser, Henry Kissinger, knew about the order. The State Department was bypassed, and to cover up the attack, pilot reports were altered. The bombing raids failed to destroy communist headquarters, but they did destroy Nixon's pledge of openness. They also revealed the continuing growth of an imperial presidency, one in which the chief executive's expanding powers went largely unchecked by Congress.

Nixon contemplated launching Operation Duck Hook, a plan to use nuclear weapons and bomb dikes to unleash flood waters on the North Vietnamese countryside, but massive antiwar demonstrations in the United States in October 1969 convinced him he lacked the support needed for such action. Yet in spring 1970 he sent American troops into Cambodia (while the aerial bombing continued) in another attempt to destroy the communist command.

Again the mission failed, but Nixon displayed a tough stand toward North Vietnam, his critics in Congress, and the antiwar movement. He knew the invasion would unleash a storm of protests, but he relished the opportunity to show his stamina. "We will not be humiliated, we will not be defeated," the president told a national television audience adding, "It is *not our power but our will* that is being tested." On May 4, 1970, at Kent State University in Ohio, national guardsmen shot and killed several student protestors; Spiro Agnew reacted by indicating they had deserved it.

In October 1969 Nixon advanced the cause for civil rights when he supported the Philadelphia Plan written by his secretary of labor, George Schultz. Under its terms, construction unions in Philadelphia working with federal contracts were required to establish "goals and timetables . . . for the hiring of black apprentices." This plan established the precedent for racial set-asides, popularly referred to as quotas. In addition, under Nixon the federal government desegregated more schools than ever before, and funding was increased for the enforcement of civil rights. In a move that would have greatly affected African Americans, Nixon proposed reforming the welfare system to provide a guaranteed minimum income to poor families, but Congress rejected it.

President Nixon appointed few women to important positions, but he supported the Equal Rights Amendment, named a White House adviser on women's issues, and instructed the Justice Department to pursue bias suits under the 1964 Civil Rights Act. When his first term neared its end, he signed Title IX, which banned sex discrimination in higher education.

When a massive oil spill at Santa Barbara, California, aroused public anger, Nixon supported a law that established the Environmental Protection Agency. He supported also the Clean Air Act that passed Congress in 1970 and the Endangered Species Act that followed three years later.

Despite Nixon's reforms, he angered liberals when he opposed busing and when he promoted conservative Supreme Court judge Warren Burger to chief justice. He stirred more controversy when he nominated Clement Haynsworth, an opponent of several desegregation rulings, to serve on the Supreme Court. After the Senate rejected Haynsworth, Nixon selected Harold Carswell, a poorly qualified judge who early in his career had expressed white supremacist views. The Senate rejected him, too, before approving Nixon's third choice, Minnesota jurist Harry Blackmun. The rancor from the Senate fight showed in the president's comments after Carswell's defeat: "I have reluctantly concluded that it is not possible to get confirmation for a judge on the Supreme Court of any man who believes in the strict construction of the Constitution."

Amid the furor over the court appointments, Vice President Spiro Agnew obeyed Nixon's orders and appealed to the nation's Silent Majority by vilifying antiwar protesters. Calling them "ideological eunuchs," he said, "It is time to question the credentials of their leaders. . . . If in challenging, we *polarize* the American people, I say it is time for a positive polarization. . . . It is time to rip away the rhetoric and to divide on authentic lines."

As the 1972 presidential election approached, Nixon's popularity grew. By removing American troops from Vietnam he subdued the antiwar protests. In 1972, while pursuing a Nixon Doctrine that said strategic interests should determine foreign commitments, he became the first president to visit communist China. His trip, broadcast on American television, paved the way for U.S. diplomatic recognition of that nation after he left office.

In May 1972 Nixon traveled to Moscow, where he met with Soviet leader Leonid Brezhnev. The two men signed SALT I, a treaty that limited the buildup of intercontinental ballistic missiles for five years, and another treaty that restricted the deployment of missile defense systems. By all appearances Nixon and Henry Kissinger were working in harmony to ease cold war tension. Behind the scenes, the two men distrusted each other. Kissinger called Nixon "basket case" and "meatball mind," while Nixon thought Kissinger treacherous. "There are times when Henry has to be kicked in the nuts," he told a friend. "Because Henry starts to think he's president."

After Richard Nixon won reelection in November 1972 with a landslide victory over

South Dakota Senator George McGovern, a liberal Democrat hampered by a divided party, he unleashed massive bombing attacks on North Vietnam. During the Christmas holiday season that year, B-52s devastated Hanoi and Haiphong, hitting factories, airports, train stations, houses, and hospitals. The *New York Times* called it "Stone Age barbarism." A peace agreement followed a week later, one many historians believe could have been reached much sooner. By its terms, Nixon conceded North Vietnam's most important demand: that it be allowed to keep its troops in South Vietnam. This assured an eventual communist victory.

Richard Nixon's personality and his style doomed his presidency. He isolated himself in the White House and allowed his two chief aides, H. R. "Bob" Haldeman and John Ehrlichman, to sequester him from almost everyone, including his cabinet. He later admitted, with a phrase remarkably echoing Kissinger's name-calling, "We were obsessed with secrecy. As a matter of fact, I was paranoiac or almost a basket case with regard to secrecy." He communicated mainly through memoranda, writings that, according to historian James T. Patterson, reveal "revengeful, aggressive, and violent feelings about people who seemed threatening."

On the surface Nixon's 1972 election victory appeared smooth and without problems, but in actuality a scandal festered, born from his deepening paranoia and covert activities. Even before the election, Nixon approved the Huston Plan, which would have placed the CIA and FBI intelligence operations under one supervisor, but opposition from FBI Director J. Edgar Hoover, who jealously guarded his turf, caused Nixon to cancel it. According to historian Joan Hoff, the plan "represented a segment of [the] Republican establishment whose fear of social and political chaos outweighed their normal respect for individual rights free from government interference." After Nixon ordered something be done about leaks of information to reporters, a special unit called the Plumbers engaged in break-ins, one of them at the office of a psychiatrist whose patient, Daniel Ellsberg, had given reporters the top secret government history of the Vietnam War, the Pentagon Papers.

In June 1972 operatives from the Committee to Re-Elect the President (CREEP) broke into the headquarters of the Democratic Party at the Watergate, an apartment complex in Washington. (Money for CREEP projects came from illegal fund-raising directed by Attorney General John Mitchell.) What they hoped to accomplish remains a mystery and may never be known, but they were arrested, and Richard Nixon subsequently began a cover-up. He feared that if the full extent of those implicated in the burglary became known, other illegal activities conducted by his administration would be exposed.

On June 23, 1972, Nixon met with Bob Haldeman, and they conspired to obstruct justice by telling the FBI that an investigation would jeopardize CIA operations. According to a transcribed version of their tape-recorded conversation, complete with the disjointed pattern often found in casual talk, Nixon instructed Haldeman to tell the CIA that "The President's belief is that this is going to open the whole Bay of Pigs [Cuban crisis] thing again. And because these people are plugging for, for keeps, and that they should call the FBI in and say that we wish for the country, don't go any further into this case, period. . . ."

Nixon later approved the payment of hush money to the operatives. On August 1, 1972, Nixon and Haldeman talked about the arrests:

> Haldeman: "They're all out of jail, they've all been take care of. We've done a lot of discreet checking to be sure there's no discontent in the ranks, and there isn't any. . . . It's very expensive, It's a costly—
>
> Nixon: "That's what the money is for."
>
> Haldeman: "—exercise, but that's better spent than—"
>
> Nixon: "Well, . . . they have to be paid. That's all there is to that."

At first the cover-up appeared to be working. The Watergate burglars maintained their silence, Nixon basked in his election victory, and few newspapers devoted space to the break-in. But two reporters, Carl Bernstein and Bob Woodward of the *Washington Post*, refused to accept Nixon's professions of ignorance. This was, after all, a president who had once said, "When I am the candidate, I run the campaign." They pursued leads, endured threats, and overcame stonewalling to produce articles raising doubts about the president's story.

Finally, one of the Watergate burglars began talking, first to the presiding judge in the break-in case, John Sirica, after he had threatened the defendants with tough sentences unless they revealed what had really happened, and then to a committee headed by North Carolina senator Sam Ervin. This led others involved in Watergate to talk, and in April 1973 Haldeman and Ehrlichman, along with John Dean, another top aide immersed in covering up the crime, resigned under pressure. The following month the Senate learned that Nixon had secretly taped conversations in the White House and that the tapes likely contained evidence crucial to the Watergate investigation.

Nixon reacted with his usual concern about disclosures and duplicity. In his memoirs he said, "It was as if a convulsion had seized Washington. Restraints that had governed professional and political conduct for decades were suddenly abandoned. The FBI and the Justice Department hemorrhaged with leaks of confidential testimony, grand jury materials, and prosecutorial speculation. And on Capitol Hill it seemed as if anything could be leaked and anything would be indulged, under the guise of righteous indignation over Watergate."

That October, Nixon tried to stymie the investigation by firing Watergate special prosecutor Archibald Cox. The president later said, "Strong conservatives in Congress and on my staff had long felt that he had to go, both because of the liberal enclave he had established and also because of the parasite he had become. . . . Firing him seemed the only way to rid the administration of the partisan viper . . . planted in our bosom." Nixon's attorney general and deputy attorney general resigned in protest of what was called the "Saturday Night Massacre."

At about the same time, Nixon publicly defended himself against charges that he had cheated on his income taxes. In an incredible statement he said, "I have never profited . . . from public service . . . I have never obstructed justice. . . . I am not a crook." As the country reeled from these events, Vice President Agnew was found to have been taking kickbacks and was forced to resign.

In February 1974 the House Judiciary Committee, chaired by New Jersey Democrat Peter W. Rodino, began an impeachment inquiry. While the committee met, Nixon fought orders to release his Watergate tapes to the investigation, but on July 24, 1974, the Supreme Court ruled in *United States v. Nixon* that he must turn them over. A few days later the judiciary committee recommended Nixon's impeachment for obstructing justice, committing perjury, and violating constitutional rights through the use of illegal wiretaps and the misuse of the FBI, the CIA, and the Internal Revenue Service (IRS). Nixon was accused of wielding the IRS as a weapon to cripple his political opponents by forcing them to endure costly audits. At one point, during the search for a new IRS commissioner, Nixon had said, "I want to be sure he is a ruthless son of a bitch, that he will do what he's told, that every income tax return I want to see I see, that he will go after our enemies." The judiciary committee, however, voted against charging Nixon with unconstitutional acts in the secret bombing of Cambodia—in effect refusing to condemn the imperial presidency over foreign policy.

When Nixon released several Watergate tapes on August 5, 1974, his remaining support in Congress and among the public dissolved. Even leading Republicans demanded he quit. The tapes included the one dealing with his attempt to get the CIA to prevent the FBI from investigating Watergate—the so-called smoking gun tape. Nixon soon realized the

House of Representatives would impeach him and the Senate would likely convict. Thus, on the night of August 8 he appeared on national television to announce his resignation, 22 years after the Checkers speech had kept his climb for higher office alive. "I no longer have a strong enough political base in the Congress to justify continuing," he told his audience.

Nixon's vice president, Gerald Ford, thought the statement lacking for its reference to political support rather than morality. "It would have had a better ring and a better response from the American people," he recalled, "if he had been more forthcoming, more contrite, and asked for forgiveness." Later that night, demonstrators gathered outside the White House and chanted, "Jail to the Chief." The following day Ford assumed the presidency.

In retirement Nixon, who was disbarred, fought hard to prevent the release of additional Watergate tapes (which were kept sealed until after his death) and wrote nine books on politics, mainly aimed at repairing his reputation. To a certain extent he succeeded in his effort, and many Americans viewed him as an elder statesman. Nixon died from a stroke on April 22, 1994, in New York City.

The Watergate tapes, along with observations by Nixon's former aides, present a damaging and in some ways frightening view of the presidency. Nixon swore effusively, lied profusely, and blurted out anti-Semitic remarks. He violated the Constitution and broke several laws.

Many observers wondered about his sanity, especially as the pressure from Watergate intensified. Some aides claimed that at crucial times Nixon was drunk, that during the Cambodian invasion he appeared incoherent at the Pentagon, and at that a crisis meeting in 1973 called to discuss the Arab-Israeli war he acted bizarrely. According to Anthony Summers in *The Arrogance of Power: The Secret World of Richard Nixon*, at this point the president began taking Dilantin, an anticonvulsant drug he thought would help him overcome anxiety and depression. He popped the pills without a doctor's prescription, probably unaware of the possible side effects that included mental confusion. During Nixon's final month in office, Defense Secretary James R. Schlesinger was so worried about Nixon's mental state that he instructed that no one obey military orders coming from the White House unless approved by him.

In 1968 Richard Nixon ran on a platform of bringing America together and always telling the truth. Yet 25 of his aides were indicted for criminal activities, and he was saved from criminal prosecution only by an unconditional pardon granted him by President Ford on September 8, 1974. Three years later, when asked in an interview whether the break-ins and bugging projects he had approved were wrong, Nixon said, "When the President does it, that means that it is not illegal."

Watergate often overshadows Nixon's presidential achievements: He improved relations with China and the Soviet Union, extricated the United States from Vietnam, and built a conservative coalition appealing to Middle America that the Republicans would use as a base of power in the late 1970s and 1980s. Yet Watergate, along with the credibility crisis that had surrounded the White House since the early 1960s, caused Americans to lose faith in their government and particularly in the presidency.

Although he was ultimately responsible for Watergate, Nixon's actions must be put in the context of his times. Joan Hoff asserts this point in her book *Nixon Reconsidered* when she says Watergate "was a disaster waiting to happen" because of the "decline in political ethics and practices during the cold war." She continues: "If we make [Nixon] an aberration rather than a normal product of the aprincipled . . . political system, we will have learned little from Watergate."

On August 9, 1974, Americans witnessed the remarkable sight of Richard Nixon climbing the stairs of an Air Force helicopter, turning to the crowd on the White House lawn, offering one last smile and wave of his hand, and then boarding for his departure. The president who as a boy listened to train whistles in the night and dreamed of faraway places filled with the promise of a better future departed to the sound of the chopper, leaving the scene of his greatest triumph and his greatest disgrace.

Chronology

1913 Born January 9

1930 Enters Whittier College

1934 Graduates from Whittier College
Enters Duke Law School

1937 Graduates from Duke Law School
Begins practicing law

1940 Marries Thelma "Pat" Ryan

1941 Begins working for Office of Price Administration

1942 Serves with the U.S. Navy in the South Pacific

1946 Elected to U.S. House of Representatives

1947 Serves on House Un-American Activities Committee

1948 Charges Alger Hiss with espionage

1950 Elected to U.S. Senate

1952 Nominated for vice presidency
Presents Checkers speech
Elected vice president

1959 Kitchen Debate with Nikita Khrushchev

1960 Loses presidential election

1962 Loses race for governor of California

1968 Elected president

1969 Orders secret bombing of Cambodia
Backs Philadelphia Plan for civil rights

1970 Sends U.S. troops into Cambodia
Supports formation of Environmental Protection Agency

1972 Visits Communist China
Signs SALT I Treaty with Soviet Union
Signs ABM Treaty with Soviet Union
Begins cover-up of Watergate break-in
Reelected president
Orders Christmas bombing of North Vietnam

1973 Fires special Watergate prosecutor Archibald Cox in Saturday Night Massacre

1974 Complies with Supreme Court ruling to turn over Watergate tapes
Releases "smoking-gun" tape
Resigns August 9
Receives full pardon from President Gerald Ford

1978 Publishes *Memoirs*

1994 Dies April 22

Further Reading

Abrahamsen, David. *Nixon Vs. Nixon: An Emotional Tragedy*. New York: Farrar, Straus and Giroux, 1977.

Aitken, Jonathan. *Nixon: A Life*. London: Weidenfeld and Nicolson, 1993.

Ambrose, Stephen E. *Nixon: The Education of a Politician, 1913–1962*. New York: Simon & Schuster, 1987.

———. *Nixon: The Triumph of a Politician, 1962–1972*. New York: Simon & Schuster, 1989.

Berman, Larry. *No Peace, No Honor: Nixon, Kissinger, and Betrayal in Vietnam*. New York: Free Press, 2001.

Brodie, Fawn M. *Richard Nixon: The Shaping of His Character*. New York: W. W. Norton, 1981.

Colodny, Len, and Robert Gettlin. *Silent Coup: The Removal of a President*. New York: St. Martin's Press, 1991.

Emery, Fred. *Watergate: The Corruption of American Politics and the Fall of Richard Nixon.* New York: Times Books, 1994.

Greenberg, David. *Nixon's Shadow: The History of an Image.* New York: W. W. Norton, 2003.

Hoff, Joan. *Nixon Reconsidered.* New York: Basic Books, 1994.

Kutler, Stanley I., ed. *Abuse of Power: The New Nixon Tapes.* New York: Free Press, 1997.

———. *The Wars of Watergate: The Last Crisis of Richard Nixon.* New York: W. W. Norton, 1992.

Morris, Roger. *Richard Milhous Nixon: The Rise of an American Politician.* New York: Holt, 1990.

Nixon, Richard. *RN: The Memoirs of Richard Nixon.* New York: Grosset and Dunlap, 1978.

———. *Six Crises.* Garden City, N.Y.: Doubleday, 1962.

Parmet, Herbert. *Richard Nixon and His America.* New York: Random House, 1990.

Reeves, Richard. *President Nixon: Alone in the White House.* New York: Simon & Schuster, 2001.

Schell, Jonathan. *The Time of Illusion.* New York: Vintage Books, 1975.

Wicker, Tom. *One of Us: Richard Nixon and the American Dream.* Boston: Little, Brown, 1991.

Woodward, Bob, and Carl Bernstein. *All the President's Men.* New York: Simon & Schuster, 1974.

———. *The Final Days.* New York: Simon & Schuster, 1976.

Gerald Ford (1913–)

Thirty-eighth President, 1974–1977

Gerald Ford
(official White House photograph, Library of Congress)

"As we bind up the internal wounds of Watergate, more painful and more poisonous than those of foreign wars, let us restore the golden rule to our political process, and let brotherly love purge our hearts of suspicion and of hate."

—Gerald Ford, speech in the East Room, August 9, 1974

In 1935 the University of Michigan yearbook said it was placing Gerald Ford in its Hall of Fame "because the football team chose him as their most valuable player; because he was a good student and got better grades than anyone else on the squad . . . because he never smokes, drinks, swears, or tells dirty stories . . . and because he's not a bit fraudulent and we can't find anything really nasty to say about him."

Nearly 40 years later, Americans turned to Ford's conservative midwestern values to lead them from President Richard Nixon's Watergate scandal and the crisis of confidence it had caused. While the country needed a strong dose of stability, decency, and honesty, Ford found himself struggling mightily against a collapsing economy, a citizenry demoralized by Vietnam, and his own limitations that kept Watergate and the questions surrounding presidential abuses very much alive.

Gerald Rudolph Ford, Jr., was born Leslie Lynch King, Jr., in Omaha, Nebraska, on July 14, 1913. He was the only child of Leslie Lynch King, a wool dealer, and Dorothy Ayer Gardner King. His parents divorced when he was two years old, and his mother took him to Grand Rapids, Michigan, where he grew up. In 1916 she married Gerald Rudolph Ford, and young Leslie took his stepfather's name.

The senior Ford instilled in Jerry, as his family and friends called him, the value of hard work and honesty. Jerry joined the Boy Scouts, worked in his stepfather's paint and varnish store on weekends and during the summers, and made solid grades at South High School, where he played football. After he earned all-city and all-state honors as a center in 1931, he accepted an offer from the head football coach at the University of Michigan in Ann Arbor to play there.

As in high school Ford's position was center, but he was not a starter until 1934, the year he earned national honors. He played in the 1935 Collegiate All-Star Game against the Chicago Bears and afterward received contract offers from the Green Bay Packers and the Detroit Lions. Since this was during the middle of the Great Depression and his stepfather was struggling to keep his paint business open, the offers tempted him. He had been an above-average student academically, though, and he longed to enter Yale Law School. Consequently, he decided against playing pro football and instead accepted a job at Yale University as assistant football coach, with the added duty of coaching boxers in the off-season. He believed that once he started working at Yale, he could convince the law school to accept him.

That, however, took time, and it was not until 1938 that he gained permission to enroll in law courses on a trial basis. He continued to coach while proving himself in the classroom. In 1940 politics attracted him, and during the summer he worked as a volunteer for the Wendell Wilkie presidential campaign. Although he earned no money, he learned much about politicking and attended the Republican National Convention in Philadelphia.

Ford graduated from Yale Law School in 1941 in the top third of his class and later that year returned to Grand Rapids to practice law. He said he belonged there, and having been bitten by the political bug, he believed Grand Rapids provided his best chance for winning public office. He formed a law partnership with another recent graduate, Philip Buchen, who later served on his staff in the White House.

Within a few months, Republican reformers approached Ford about helping them dump the local political boss. He agreed and formed the Home Front, which put up candidates to run against the machine in Kent County. Then World War II intervened, and in April 1942 he enlisted in the navy. Ford trained recruits at a flight school before receiving gunnery training at the naval station in Norfolk, Virginia. Assigned to the *U.S. Monterrey*, he saw duty in the South Pacific and was discharged in December 1945 as a lieutenant with 10 battle stars.

The war changed his view of the world. He later said, "I returned understanding we could never be isolated again. . . . It was clear to me, it was inevitable to me, that this country was obligated to lead in this new world. We had won the war. It was up to us to keep the peace." He had found his issue, and in 1948 he entered the Republican primary against Batel Jonkman, a congressman in the Grand Rapids Fifth Congressional District and a member of the House Foreign Affairs Committee who opposed aid to

Europe. Neither Jonkman nor almost anyone else took Ford seriously, but as the incumbent rested on his laurels, the challenger campaigned hard, stressing his war record and shaking hands at a feverish pitch. He shocked Jonkman, beating him by 9,300 votes, and in November outpolled his Democratic opponent by an even wider margin. Over the next two decades he won reelection handily every time.

On October 15, 1948, during the campaign, he married Elizabeth "Betty" Bloomer, who as a teenager had been a model at a store in Grand Rapids, Michigan, and after that a dancer with the Martha Graham group. The couple had four children. Later, as a first lady, Betty Ford endorsed the Equal Rights Amendment and won admiration for her brave fight against breast cancer and her openness in discussing her mastectomy.

Ford wanted to someday become Speaker of the House, and though Democratic majorities would deny him that position, he rose steadily in the congressional ranks through the 1950s and early 1960s. He earned a senior spot on the powerful Appropriations Committee and chaired the House Republican Conference. After Barry Goldwater and his right-wing supporters gained control of the Republican Party in 1963, Ford led a group of moderates who worked in Congress to point the party in a more mainstream direction. His leadership of the House Republican Conference attracted national attention, even more so after Goldwater went down to a devastating defeat in the 1964 presidential race.

In January 1965 Ford's fellow Republicans chose him to serve as minority leader, removing conservative Indianan Charles Halleck from that post. He continued to expand his influence by working Capitol Hill's inner rooms where the politicians made their deals.

Ford battled hard against President Lyndon Johnson's liberal Great Society social program and criticized the White House for its Vietnam policy. He thought Johnson weak in fighting the war and advocated using more military power. He gained so much prominence that in 1968 Richard Nixon offered him the vice-presidential spot on the Republican ticket. Thinking the Republicans might capture the House that year and he would therefore be elevated to Speaker, Ford declined. As it turned out, Nixon won the White House, but the Democrats maintained their majority in the House of Representatives.

Ford's relations with President Nixon were less than warm. Nixon wanted a Republican leadership he could control, and Ford thought the White House too overbearing. Nixon's domestic policy adviser, John Ehrlichman, said that Ford "wasn't excessively bright," and Ford complained that as far as presidential aides were concerned, Congress "existed . . . only to follow their instructions."

Still, Ford voted with the president's position on 83 percent of all roll calls, and he supported Nixon's many vetoes in 1973, a divisive year between Capitol Hill and the White House. In addition, at Nixon's behest he intervened with Wright Patman, chair of the House Banking Committee, to block an investigation into whether the Nixon presidential campaign had illegally laundered money.

On October 10, 1973, Vice President Spiro Agnew pleaded no contest to a charge of income tax evasion relating to kickbacks he had accepted. He was forced to resign, and Richard Nixon became the first president to act under the Twenty-fifth Amendment and appoint a new vice president, subject to congressional approval. He initially wanted to name former Texas governor John Connally, but he ultimately selected Gerald Ford, believing the congressman, with his 25 years of experience in the House, would be the easiest to get confirmed. Nixon's congressional liaison, his counselor, and Speaker of the House Carl Albert all told him that Ford was the only one among several potential candidates that Congress would approve. Ford accepted the appointment on October 11 and modestly told a gathering in the East Room of the White House: "I hope I have some assets that might be helpful in working with Congress."

With Nixon's Watergate problems mounting, most congressional representatives and senators realized that in confirming Ford they would likely be selecting the next president. As a result, they questioned him closely. He expressed support for Nixon's programs and stated he believed the president was "completely innocent" of any illegalities involving Watergate. After the House Judiciary Committee and the Senate Rules Committee voted overwhelmingly to approve him, the full House did likewise by a margin of 387 to 35 and the Senate by a margin of 92 to 3. Ford was sworn in by Chief Justice Warren E. Burger on December 6, 1973.

Over the next several months, Richard Nixon's position became untenable, and rather than face certain impeachment and conviction for his Watergate crimes, he resigned the presidency on August 9, 1974. At 12 noon that day, in the East Room of the White House, Gerald Ford placed his right hand on the Bible, its pages opened to the Book of Proverbs, and Chief Justice Warren Burger administered the oath of office. Ford told those crowded about him: "Our long national nightmare is over. Our Constitution works; our Great Republic is a government of laws and not of men. Here the people rule."

The new president immediately faced the problem of having to distance himself from the discredited Nixon. Yet he had to do so without any solid base of electoral support. As much as he believed "here the people rule," the people, and those only a small number, had never elected him to anything more than a seat in Congress from the Grand Rapids Fifth Congressional District. Making his ascension more difficult, Ford raised doubts as to whether he could cleanse the White House when he decided to keep Nixon's chief of staff, Alexander Haig, as his own.

Gerald Ford inherited an economic mess from Nixon. Inflation was surging and reached 3.7 percent for the month of August, boosted in part by oil price hikes in the aftermath of a boycott of the United States by the Organization of Petroleum Exporting Countries a year earlier. At the same time, unemployment was increasing. This unusual combination, dubbed "stagflation," presented the quandary of which economic weakness to tackle first. Ford placed the economy at the top of his agenda and showed he would concentrate on inflation when, during his initial hours in office, he told his cabinet he would control federal spending by wielding his veto power.

Conservatives disliked him for having opposed their ideological hero Barry Goldwater in the contest for the 1964 Republican presidential nomination and then, after Goldwater won the nomination, for refusing to endorse him. He angered them again in mid-August, when he announced a program to grant conditional amnesty to those who had evaded the draft or deserted the military during the Vietnam War and also when he nominated Nelson Rockefeller, the moderate former Republican governor of New York, as his vice president.

While most Americans trusted Ford and expressed guarded faith in his abilities, how he handled the continuing repercussions from Watergate would go a long way in determining whether he would maintain their trust and whether he would be able to develop lasting support. Many prominent leaders and groups called for Richard Nixon to stand trial for his crimes. The American Bar Association insisted justice must be equal for everyone involved in Watergate, and both Senate majority leader Mike Mansfield and House majority leader Tip O'Neill said they opposed Congress doing anything that would block an indictment of the former president.

Watergate Special Prosecutor Leon Jaworski was continuing his work, and it would be up to him and the grand jury over which he presided whether to indict Nixon. Every one of the senior lawyers on his staff argued for indictment. Soon after Ford entered the presidency, the House of Representatives voted 412-3 to accept its judiciary committee report on Nixon's impeachment. Although Nixon had resigned, the action was tantamount to impeaching him, and the House issued a statement saying it believed Nixon had indeed committed the offenses needed to place him on trial in the Senate.

On August 10 Ford was twice asked by reporters whether he would grant any kind of immunity to Nixon, and both times he said no. Alexander Haig had a different idea, and after Ford signaled his chief of staff's imminent demise by reducing his power in the White House, Haig committed himself to making sure that Nixon would receive a pardon. At the same time, Ford came under pressure from Nixon's family and perhaps even Nixon himself. Investigative reporter Seymour Hersh believes Nixon called Ford and threatened him, saying that unless a pardon were issued soon, he would tell the press that Ford had reneged on a deal the two had made before Nixon left the White House—namely the presidency for Ford in exchange for the pardon for Nixon. While many analysts dispute Hersh's account, most believe that Ford's decision on the pardon broke his presidency.

By September Ford was leaning toward pardoning Nixon for several reasons: To try the ex-president would expose him to undue embarrassment; the trials would last for years and divert attention from more important issues facing the country; and even if Nixon were found guilty, a later president might pardon him.

Finally, Ford thought that pardoning Nixon was the compassionate thing to do. He told Tip O'Neill, "I've made up my mind to pardon Nixon. I'm doing it because I think it's right for the country, and because it feels right in my heart. The man is so depressed, and I don't want to see a former president go to jail." O'Neill disagreed, telling Ford a pardon would damage him politically.

On September 8, 1974, Ford pardoned Richard Nixon for all "offenses" the former president "committed" or "may have committed." With that, Ford gained the dubious distinction of granting a pardon *before* the subject of the pardon had been indicted or tried. Americans expressed outrage. The president's public approval rating dropped 20 percent, and Sam Ervin, chair of the Senate Watergate Committee, stated: "President Ford ought to have allowed the legal processes to take their course, and not issued any pardon to former President Nixon until he had been indicted, tried, and convicted."

At the beginning of his presidency, Ford had said that "our Constitution works." With his pardon, millions of Americans concluded it worked to keep the full truth about Watergate hidden and to keep the main conspirator, Richard Nixon, from going to jail. Although many officials served time for Watergate crimes, Nixon served none, and he continued to receive the pension granted former presidents that provided him with material comfort. To make matters worse, Ford never insisted that Nixon admit guilt for what he had done as a condition for the pardon or even that he express complete contrition. The pardon thus kept Ford within the shadow of Watergate.

So intense was the controversy over Ford's action that he took the unusual step for a president of testifying before Congress. He admitted that prior to Nixon's resignation, Alexander Haig had raised the point with him that Nixon could quit and that Ford could then pardon him. Ford then said he had asked Haig whether a president could pardon a person even before an indictment had been issued, and Haig had said it could be done. But Ford insisted he later told Haig that Nixon must make a decision about whether to resign without the prospect of a pardon.

Most historians accept Ford's story, and quite possibly Haig realized he did not need a firm deal with Ford. He may have felt comfortable with Ford's sympathy for Nixon; he certainly realized that in their meeting Ford never denied the possibility of a pardon.

President Ford's economic policies fared little better than his Watergate measures. Still considering inflation to be the greatest problem, in October 1974 he proposed to Congress that it enact an income-tax surcharge and cut spending. On top of that, he began a program called Whip Inflation Now (WIN), under which the government printed coupons for people to fill out and pledge their efforts in the fight against higher prices. Hundreds of thousands of the coupons flooded the White House, which sent out WIN buttons for respondents to wear, but the program offered little more than hype.

Democrats, meanwhile, criticized Ford's tax proposal as the wrong prescription; they said a recession loomed, and they called instead for tax cuts. They turned out to be right, and after the November congressional elections in which the Republicans took a beating, Ford changed his course and proposed a $16 billion tax cut. After the Democratic Congress passed a much higher one than Ford wanted, the president was forced to accept it lest he appear to again be backtracking on the issue. Ford still disliked Capitol Hill's spending plans, and over the course of his presidency he used his veto 66 times. Congress overrode him only 12 times.

In 1975 New York City tottered on the edge of bankruptcy, and when its leaders asked Ford for help, he refused. The president insisted he would not arrange loans for a mismanaged government burdened with budget deficits. A banner headline in the *New York Daily News* shouted: "FORD TO CITY: DROP DEAD." The president changed his mind, though, after the New York state legislature devised a plan whereby the city would balance its budget, raise taxes, and freeze some wages. He now supported a bailout, and Congress passed a loan amounting to more than $2 billion. Ford's initial refusal likely pressured New York politicians to reform the city budget, but once again he had changed his mind, allowing his opponents to portray him as indecisive and weak.

A demoralized America struggling with Watergate and the economy encountered a ghost in late April 1975 when the Vietnam War reappeared on prime-time television. Newscasts showed workers at the American embassy in Saigon scrambling to board evacuation helicopters as communist troops approached the city. Jammed into the overcrowded choppers, the workers used clubs and fists to beat back panicked Vietnamese who were also trying to flee. The last American helicopter departed on April 29; the following day South Vietnam surrendered to the communists, and the victors triumphantly renamed Saigon, calling it Ho Chi Minh City. Keyes Beech, a reporter for the *Chicago Daily News*, said about his own escape: "My last view of Saigon was through the tail door of the helicopter. Tan Son Nhut was burning. So was Bien Hoa. Then the door closed—closed on the most humiliating chapter in American history."

Pushing lessons about Vietnam aside, that same year President Ford secretly involved the United States in a complex civil war in Angola, a former Portuguese colony in Africa scheduled to hold national elections soon. Ford sent money to back the rebel FNLA, or National Front, against the Soviet-backed MLPA, or Popular Movement. (These were but two of several rebel groups divided by ideology and tribal and ethnic loyalties.) Under Operation FEATURE, the president approved $25 million for weapons and supplies, and the Central Intelligence Agency hired mercenaries to fill the FNLA ranks. Ford's policy caused Cuba to help the MLPA by sending in troops, thus igniting a wider war.

When the *New York Times* leaked news about Ford's action, the Senate investigated. Congress then passed a law requiring Ford to end the intervention, and the president signed it. He subsequently issued an executive order that required intelligence agencies to report regularly to an oversight board and prohibited them from participating in any plans to kill foreign leaders—a back-door admission to what the United States had been doing for years. Despite these reforms, Operation FEATURE recalled the worst in presidential covert activities from the Vietnam era and, like the Nixon pardon, damaged Ford's credibility.

Presiding over a weakened presidency, Ford found an opportunity for toughness in May 1975, when communist Khmer Rouge forces in Cambodia captured an American merchant ship, the *Mayaguez*, in the Gulf of Siam. With the seizure coming just days after the American evacuation of South Vietnam, Ford heeded the words of his secretary of state, Henry Kissinger. "At some point, the United States must draw the line," Kissinger said. "This is not our idea of the best such situation. It is not our choice. But we must act upon it now, and act firmly."

President Ford could have opted for what the United States had done many previous times when foreign countries had confiscated American ships and negotiated to obtain their release. But he ruled out talks from the start. Instead, he called the capture piracy, sent aircraft carriers into the gulf, and ordered the landing of 100 marines on the tiny island of Koh Tang, where the Cambodians were holding the *Mayaguez* crew. While American planes hammered the Cambodian mainland, marines landed at Koh Tang and encountered an unexpected hail of bullets from the Cambodians. Within one hour, 15 marines were killed and eight American helicopters shot down. Yet soon after the assault began, the Cambodians released the crew.

Ford called the operation a victory, and Americans rejoiced over the freeing of the captives. One congressman said, "I am very proud of our country and our president today." Still, more marines had been killed than there were crew on the *Mayaguez*, and the release of the captives may have resulted less from the military attack than from pressure placed on Cambodia by China.

When former California governor Ronald Reagan announced early in 1976 that he would seek the Republican presidential nomination, most political observers believed the popular conservative would swamp Ford. Yet Ford beat Reagan in the New Hampshire primary—his first election victory outside his Michigan district—and went on to win the nomination, albeit by a razor-thin margin, with just 57 more delegate votes than the minimum of 1,130 that he needed.

Neither Ford's primary victories nor the *Mayaguez* incident saved him from defeat in November. Nixon's pardon burdened him, as did the worsening economy, his narrow electoral base, and voter disgust with the Republican Party. Democratic candidate Jimmy Carter, himself a virtual unknown, defeated Ford, though few Americans expressed any enthusiasm for him either. Carter pledged he would never lie, a comment that punctuated the low state of faith in the presidency. Of more than 81 million votes cast, Carter won with a plurality of 1.7 million.

Ford retired to Grand Rapids and in 1979 published his autobiography, *A Time to Heal.* Over the following years he distanced himself from politics and spent most of his time playing golf and vacationing in California and Colorado. In 1982 he presided over the opening of the Gerald R. Ford Library in Ann Arbor, Michigan. In the year 2000 Ford appeared at the Republican National Convention. Soon thereafter he suffered a stroke, from which he recovered. He attended the state funeral for Ronald Reagan in June 2004 but was too frail to attend the ceremony marking the opening of the Bill Clinton presidential library later that year.

Gerald Ford left the White House as a unique president, more accurately an oddity. Unlike any previous chief executive, he had never been elected as part of a national ticket. He was, in essence, a congressional appointee who failed to widen his base beyond Capitol Hill effectively. Had he built the trust he promised at the beginning of his term, he may well have won the popular mandate he so desperately desired.

Chronology

1913 Born July 14

1931 Wins all-city and all-state honors in high school football

Attends University of Michigan

1935 Plays in college football all-star game
Graduates from the University of Michigan
Begins work as assistant football coach at Yale University

1941 Graduates from Yale Law School
Begins practicing law

1942 Enlists in U.S. Navy

1945 Discharged from navy as a lieutenant

1948 Elected to U.S. House of Representatives
Marries Betty Bloomer

1965 Chosen minority leader

1968 Declines offer of vice presidential nomination

1973 Appointed vice president

1974 Becomes president
Selects Nelson Rockefeller to serve as vice president
Pardons Richard M. Nixon
Begins Whip Inflation Now program
Proposes tax cut

1975 Supports loan for New York City
Oversees evacuation of American embassy in Saigon
Approves Operation FEATURE in Angola
Orders rescue of the *Mayaguez* crew

1976 Wins Republican presidential nomination
Loses general election

1977 Retires to Grand Rapids, Michigan

1979 Publishes autobiography

1982 Presides over opening of the Gerald R. Ford Library

2000 Appears at Republican National Convention
Suffers stroke

2004 Attends state funeral for Ronald Reagan in Washington, D.C.

Further Reading

Cannon, James. *Time and Chance: Gerald Ford's Appointment with History.* New York: HarperCollins, 1994.

Ford, Gerald R. *A Time to Heal: The Autobiography of Gerald R. Ford.* New York: Harper and Row, 1979.

Greene, John Robert. *The Presidency of Gerald R. Ford.* Lawrence: University Press of Kansas, 1995.

Hartmann, Robert T. *Palace Politics: An Inside Account of the Ford Years.* New York: McGraw-Hill, 1980.

Hersey, John. *Aspects of the Presidency: Truman and Ford in Office.* New Haven, Conn.: Ticknor & Fields, 1980.

Mieczkowski, Yanek. *Gerald Ford and the Challenges of the 1970s.* Lexington: University Press of Kentucky, 2005.

Nessen, Ron. *It Sure Looks Different from the Inside.* New York: Simon & Schuster, 1978.

Osborne, John. *The White House Watch: The Ford Years.* Washington, D.C.: New Republic Books, 1977.

Reeves, Richard. *A Ford, Not a Lincoln.* New York: Harcourt, Brace, Jovanovich, 1975.

JAMES EARL CARTER, JR. (1924–)

Thirty-ninth President, 1977–1981

JAMES EARL CARTER, JR.
(official White House photograph, Library of Congress)

"Let our recent mistakes bring a resurgent commitment to the basic principles of our Nation, for we know that if we despise our own government we have no future."

—Inaugural words, January 20, 1977

For more than a decade, presidents deceived, lied, and even broke laws. Then in 1976 Jimmy Carter ran for the White House. During his paign he told the American people he would never lie to them inauguration he decided against riding in a limousine usually do, and instead walked down Penns honesty, morality, and warmth. Yet for al for all the longing Americans had f public support plummete presidency a discredite

James Earl "Jimmy" Carter, Jr., was born on October 1, 1924, in Plains, a small farming town, population 500, tucked away in southwestern Georgia amid dusty cotton and peanut fields. He grew up with two sisters—Gloria, born in 1926, and Ruth, born in 1929—and a much younger brother, Billy, born in 1937. When he ran for president, Jimmy Carter referred to his upbringing as the life of a poor boy, but he actually lived in comfort. His mother, Lillian Gordon Carter, worked as a registered nurse; she later bristled at her son's portrayal of their economic standing. The family had a nice house and a car, "Miss Lillian" said, and the first radio and the first television set in town. Jimmy's father, James Earl Carter, Sr., owned much farmland and operated a warehouse and brokerage business, mainly dealing in peanuts. As a child, Jimmy often awoke at four in the morning to work on his father's farm.

Carter graduated from the Plains public high school in 1941 and briefly studied at a nearby college before entering the Georgia Institute of Technology. Ever since he was a child, he had dreamed of attending Annapolis Naval Academy, and he won an appointment there in 1943. He graduated in 1946 ranked 60th in a class of 822 students.

That same year he married Rosalynn Smith, and over the next two decades they had four children: John William, born in 1947; James Earl III ("Chip"), in 1950; Donald Jeffrey, in 1952; and Amy, in 1967.

After graduating from Annapolis, Carter ...erving in the navy and obtained a choice ... help develop the first atomic sub- ... brilliant and egotistical Cap- ... Admiral) interviewed ... the young ... is.

Rickover assigned Carter to Schenectady, New York, where at Union College he took courses in reactor technology and nuclear physics. He then was appointed chief engineer of the *Seawolf*, a prototype for a nuclear sub. Carter expected to make the navy his career, but in 1953 his father, who months earlier had been elected to the state legislature, fell seriously ill.

The young Georgian returned home. He recalled: "I . . . spent a couple of weeks at Daddy's bedside while he was dying of cancer, talking to him quietly about our family, his business and his customers, and the general principles that guided his life." According to Carter, this tragedy caused him to reconsider his plans. He began to idolize his father's role as community leader and businessman—responsibilities that had made Daddy's life so admirable—and decided to quit the navy and run the family farm, warehouse, and brokerage. His decision, though, may have been based on an additional reason: He was convinced that promotions in the navy would be slow in coming.

Over the next eight years, Carter improved what had become a faltering business. As he did so, he developed a solid community reputation. He had all the right Plains credentials: a successful business, a prospering family, and, added to these, leadership in the Baptist church as lay reader, Sunday school teacher, and chairman of the board of deacons. He also served as chairman of the county school board. About the only serious problem Carter had with some townspeople involved race. The White Citizens Council wanted him to join their segregationist group to protect white power, but he refused. "That isn't the way I think we ought to go," he told them.

A hard worker, ambitious, and concerned about education issues likely to come before the Georgia legislature, Carter decided in 1962 to run for the state senate. He faced a tough fight in the Democratic primary against Homer ... a candidate supported by the county ... the election ended, Carter found ... found also that ballot boxes had been stuffed. "We had witnessed a case of dishonesty and election fraud worse than we had ever imagined." he said.

Carter forced a recount, was declared the victor, and went on to win the general election. "The events of the 1962 campaign opened my eyes not only to the ways in which democratic processes can be subverted," he said, "but also to the capacity of men and women of good will to engage the system and right such wrongs." The statement reflected his character well. He had mounted the white steed in 1962, the good knight on an errand to slay evil. He would stay on that steed for the rest of his political career, time and again seeing himself as defending what was right and just.

Jimmy Carter served two terms in the state senate and won high marks for promoting educational reform. With his reputation as one of Georgia's most powerful legislators, he entered the 1966 governor's race, advocated a progressive program . . . and lost, finishing third in the Democratic primary. The defeat shattered him and sent him into a deep depression, but he renewed his faith as a "born-again Christian" and committed himself to public service.

If religious faith were to be his guide, so too was the practical need to win votes. In his second run for the governorship in 1970, Carter dropped his progressive views and appealed to white racists by criticizing busing and by saying he would meet with Alabama governor George Wallace, a noted segregationist. His strategy worked, and he won the primary and general elections. One critic said of him: "He will do what it takes to win; he will change what views it takes for him to win." Carter may well have built his campaign on expediency, for as governor he returned to a progressive program. In January 1971 he said in his inaugural speech: "No poor, weak, or black person should ever again have to bear the additional burden of being deprived of the opportunity for an education, a job, or simple justice."

Carter's governorship displayed characteristics that would later define his presidency. He began his term by introducing a massive legislative package, one too large to work on effectively. He also ran into problems with his staff members: Young and inexperienced, they often rubbed legislative leaders the wrong way. Carter further antagonized legislators by considering himself morally superior to them and showing it. An example appeared in a story about the governor in the *Atlanta Constitution*:

> Carter badly needed votes in the Senate on a recent issue. One senator said he would vote with the governor if [Hamilton] Jordan [Carter's chief aide] would make one phone call assuring the senator's father (a state employee) of a slight promotion to an existing vacancy. The senator appeared at the time to hold the deciding vote. Jordan wanted to make the call. Carter said no. And the governor lost.

The self-righteous Carter hated to compromise, but when he did he often took the moral high ground and insisted he had given up little. That his insistence often conflicted with reality made him appear disingenuous and confused.

Yet Carter scored some impressive victories. The legislature approved a program to make the state government more efficient by condensing 300 state agencies into 22 and by implementing a new budget method. Carter authorized opening more than 100 community mental health centers, and he increased the number of minorities in government jobs. Several magazines hailed him as a "New South governor," a break with the region's reactionary and racist past. With such a reputation, in December 1974, as his administration neared its end (Georgia's constitution forbade a second consecutive term), he announced his candidacy for president.

The *Atlanta Constitution* said about Jimmy Carter early in his governorship: "Virtue is on [his] side, certainly, but how many votes has virtue?" As it turned out, among voters nationwide it had quite a few. In his race for president in 1976, Carter used virtue as his central issue so effectively that he seemed to come out of nowhere in winning the early Democratic primaries. After he captured the first primary in New Hampshire, *Time* and *Newsweek* magazines declared him the front-runner. Despite that boost, he lost several subsequent primaries and failed to win a northern industrial state until he finished first in Pennsylvania.

When the Georgian talked about virtue and making government work, he struck a sensitive chord with the public. At that time America had just gone through a tumultuous and discouraging period. In the late 1960s riots and rising crime shattered cities, protesters challenged traditional practices, and the Vietnam War tore society apart. In the early and mid-1970s the economy unraveled, the war ended in defeat, and the public learned about the lies and deceit used by presidents—from the early years of the Vietnam experience in the Eisenhower administration through the Watergate scandal of Nixon's presidency. Consequently, Carter's message was refreshing: "Why Not the Best?" To emphasize his crusade, when he accepted his nomination at the Democratic Convention in New York City in July 1976, whites and blacks held hands and sang, "We Shall Overcome."

Carter seemed assured of defeating the incumbent Republican president, Gerald Ford. Ford had the disadvantages of never having been elected to the office—he had assumed the presidency after Nixon resigned—of having taken the unpopular move of pardoning Nixon for his crimes, and of presiding over a faltering economy. To make matters worse, Ford committed a gaffe in a televised debate with Carter when he denied that the Soviet Union dominated Eastern Europe.

Carter blundered, though, when in an interview with *Playboy* magazine he used sexual slang and admitted to having "committed adultery in my heart many times." More important, as the campaign continued he avoided the issues and allowed Ford to effectively attack him for "fuzziness." By November, more and more voters thought that Carter had little substance. They didn't think much of Ford either. Polls gave Carter an 80 percent negative rating, and Ford a 76 percent negative rating.

On election day, voters cast their ballots for the least objectionable candidate. The Georgian squeaked out a victory with 50.1 percent of the popular vote to Ford's 48 percent. Carter would have lost had it not been for substantial support from African Americans.

In his inaugural address Jimmy Carter promised a "competent and compassionate" government and stressed pursuing a foreign policy in which the United States would be a "beacon of light" for human rights throughout the world. To underscore compassion, on his first day in office he unconditionally pardoned all Vietnam War draft resisters.

Also that same day, he ordered American nuclear weapons withdrawn from South Korea in a move he hoped would make the Soviet Union more receptive to arms negotiations. But his action revealed the same problems that had bedeviled him as governor: Inexperienced and still filled with self-righteous arrogance, he failed to consult adequately with Congress and the military and as a result opened himself to charges he had acted in haste and weakened America's defenses in Asia.

Carter sent mixed signals with his human rights policy. On the one hand, he appointed Cyrus Vance as secretary of state; as a moderate, Vance supported the president's goals. On the other hand, he appointed Zbigniew Brzezinski as his national security adviser; as a hard-liner, Brzezinski preferred protection of American security over human rights issues. Further, Carter pursued human rights selectively and unevenly. For example, he continued to send more and more weapons to the Shah in Iran despite that ruler's notorious use of his secret police, SAVAK, to imprison and torture political opponents. The president considered Iran's strategic value more important than its human rights record.

Mistakes and controversy enveloped Jimmy Carter's first year in the White House. Although, like the president, Congress was Democratic, Carter's aides, including his chief aide Hamilton Jordan, handled Capitol Hill ineptly. House Speaker Tip O'Neill complained that Jordan had never even introduced himself to him.

As he had with the Georgia legislature, Carter pursued an excessively ambitious program. Over a short time, he sent Congress proposals that dealt with everything from government reform to welfare reform. Anyone who balked at his ideas he regarded as selfish.

Carter inherited an economy reeling from foreign oil prices that had climbed from $6 a barrel to $12 since 1973. At the same time, America's dependence on foreign oil had increased from 35 to 50 percent. As a result, the price hikes caused inflation and dampened economic growth.

The president thought it imperative that Americans conserve energy, and in April 1977, at the time Congress enacted his proposal to form a cabinet-level department of energy, he revealed a plan that contained 113 provisions. He called America's energy problem the "moral equivalent of war," and many applauded him for acting boldly. But Carter once again stumbled when he failed to consult congressional leaders adequately, and the plan's complexity exposed it to criticism from many different quarters.

The president's moral reputation took a beating in a scandal involving Bert Lance, whom he had appointed as director of the Office of Management and Budget. Lance had been a bank executive before joining Carter's administration and owned considerable stock in the National Bank of Georgia. He was accused of having a conflict of interest in dealing with a policy affecting banking regulations and of using his influence to obtain a $3.4 million personal loan at deferred interest.

In August 1977 a report issued by the U.S. comptroller cleared Lance, and Carter praised him. But the report also said that when Lance was chairman of the small First National Bank of Calhoun in Georgia, he allowed large overdrafts on personal accounts held by the bank's officers and their relatives. As critics continued to attack Lance, Carter concluded that the controversy would overwhelm his presidency, and in September he asked for and received Lance's resignation. That Carter retained Lance so long, however, damaged the clean image he had projected for his presidency.

When inflation continued to rise in 1978—from August to September producer prices went up at a yearly rate of 11.4 percent—Carter announced that the government would monitor wages, benefits, and prices more closely to discourage any increases beyond a set level. The program, though, relied on voluntary compliance and ultimately failed.

In October Congress finally passed the president's energy legislation. Much of it had changed from what he originally wanted, stressing deregulation of the oil industry rather than conservation through taxation. Still, the president's intense lobbying had secured the bill's passage.

Carter scored a foreign policy coup involving Panama in 1978. For several years presidents had been negotiating to change the treaty that governed the Panama Canal. The United States maintained sovereignty over the 10-mile-wide canal zone and ran the canal itself under a perpetual lease. But discontent among Panamanians with American power in their country made change imperative. Carter promoted two treaties in the Senate that would quickly give operation of the canal to Panama and transfer sovereignty of the canal zone at the end of 1999. Opponents decried what they called a weakening of American power. Speaking in reference to how the United States originally got the canal, California senator S. I. Hayakawa, a Republican, said, "It's ours. We stole it fair and square."

In March 1978 the Senate narrowly ratified the treaties. Carter's effort had showed him at his best, skillfully dealing with Congress and guiding public opinion. *Time* magazine said, "Before the lobbying began last fall, polls showed that some 46 percent of the American public opposed the treaties. . . . A February Gallup Poll indicated that 45 percent of Americans favored the pact and 42 percent were opposed—a turnabout for which the administration can claim substantial credit."

Carter made progress in the Middle East as well. In September 1978 he brought together Anwar Sadat, president of Egypt, and Menachem Begin, prime minister of Israel, at Camp David, Maryland. There for 13 days he mediated discussions for a peace treaty between their countries. No treaty emerged, but a framework for future talks did, and after Carter visited Egypt and Israel several months later, an agreement resulted in which Egypt recognized Israel, and Israel withdrew its troops from the Sinai Peninsula.

As Carter basked in this achievement, a political storm blew in from Iran, where Islamic fundamentalists and other groups were fighting against Shah Mohammed Reza Pahlevi and his SAVAK regime. The uprising confused Carter. He reacted to it by sending the shah more weapons, yet hesitated at giving the Iranian leader his approval to crush the rebels at any cost. In short, he waffled—a word increasingly associated with his actions.

In January 1979 the shah fled Iran, and in early February the spiritual head of the Islamic fundamentalist rebels, Ayatollah Khomeini, took charge. The upheaval in Iran disrupted oil shipments from that country and caused higher prices and shortages in the United States. As consumers found their gas rationed, long lines formed at service stations and in a few instances fights broke out among motorists wielding knives and broken beer bottles. To encourage the domestic production of oil and discourage its consumption, Carter proposed ending all price controls on the fuel while levying windfall profits taxes on oil companies. His proposal promised higher consumer prices at a time when inflation hit 14 percent in May 1979.

The president traveled to Vienna in 1979 to meet with Soviet premier Leonid Brezhnev. They negotiated SALT II, a treaty to contain the spread of nuclear weapons. SALT II actually accomplished little; it ignored some dangerous new weapons technology, and rather than freeze the number of nuclear warheads, it allowed increases within specified limits. Even Carter seemed ambivalent about the treaty. He submitted it to the Senate, but when opponents attacked it for supposedly making too many concessions, and when the Soviets pursued what he thought was a belligerent foreign policy, he backed away. Once again, some said he waffled.

At home, inflation and high unemployment remained largely intractable as the energy crisis raged on. Disturbed by this, Carter went into retreat and talked privately to leaders from around the nation. When he reappeared in public, he presented his "crisis of spirit" speech in July 1979. "All the legislation in the world can't fix what's wrong with America . . . ," he said. "In a nation that was proud of hard work, strong families, close-knit communities, and our faith in God, too many of us now tend to worship self-indulgence and consumption. Human identity is no longer defined by what one does but by what one owns." Although many applauded his speech as accurate and forthright, it seemed to others too much like the jeremiads issued by Howard Beale, the fictional and embittered television newscaster in an acclaimed movie of the decade, *Network*—that is, it was depressing and something most people did not particularly want to hear. With this speech, therefore, the president opened himself up to charges that he was a defeatist.

As 1980 began and Carter looked toward his reelection campaign, problem after problem buffeted his administration, some beyond his control, some created or worsened by him. Because of this, the public mood turned increasingly sour. That spring, however, he achieved two big victories on the energy front. First, Congress, which had recently deregulated natural gas prices and provided for the gradual decontrol of domestic oil, passed his desired tax on windfall oil profits. Then it passed the Energy Security Act, which established the Synthetic Fuels Corporation to develop alternative energy sources.

Soon after this victory came embarrassment when Congress overrode his veto of a joint resolution that prevented him from placing a surcharge on imported oil. At about the same time, Congress authorized much more money for defense and much less for domestic programs than he wanted. And while inflation eased some, it remained high. "Across the nation," *Time* magazine reported, "inflation and the administration's inability to deal with it have caused widespread dismay." Ordinary Americans spoke to reporters about prices:

> "It has been six or eight months since I've taken my wife to a restaurant."
>
> "When I was 19, I could afford to buy a new car. Now I'm 26 and I can't afford to buy a used car."
>
> "I'm trying to find a house but it will take me ten years to earn the down payment."

Making matters worse, unemployment climbed to 7.8 percent during the summer of 1980 and was projected to reach 8.5 percent by year's end.

Although Carter had promised to improve relations with the Soviet Union, they instead deteriorated to a new low. This resulted in part from his criticism of the Russians for human rights violations but more so from the Soviet invasion of Afghanistan late in 1979 to support a Marxist regime against Islamic revolutionaries. Carter was convinced that the Russians would invade Iran from Afghanistan and thus threaten oil supplies in the Middle East. In retaliation, he quickened America's military buildup, placed an embargo on the sale of wheat and technology to the Soviet Union, and convinced the U.S. Olympic Committee to boycott the 1980 Olympics scheduled for Moscow. Critics said the president had overreacted, that the Russians had only invaded to defend their borders from the turmoil in a neighboring country. Most analysts later agreed with this view.

Iran proved more daunting to Carter, and much more damaging to his political future. In November 1979 Iranian militants, angered when Carter allowed the deposed shah into the United States for medical treatment, seized the U.S. embassy in Tehran and took a number of Americans hostage. When Ayatollah Khomeini ordered the militants to hold onto the hostages, Carter retaliated by suspending the purchase of oil from Iran and by freezing all Iranian assets held in American banks. Americans rallied behind the president, and in one poll his approval rating surpassed 60 percent.

Their feelings, though, changed to disenchantment as the hostage crisis dragged on into 1980. Day after day the media reminded Americans that the 53 hostages were still being held captive, and television aired humiliating and lasting pictures of the blindfolded prisoners. Carter intensified the crisis atmosphere by insisting that he thought about the captives every day and that he would stay at the White House instead of hitting the campaign trail in the presidential primaries so he could work on securing their release.

In April 1980 the president gave the go-ahead for a daring rescue mission, and American C-130 transport planes and RH-53 helicopters flew into Iran. The mission immediately fell apart. A desert sandstorm forced one helicopter back, mechanical problems plagued others, and Iranians in the usually desolate landing spot stumbled across the invaders. Finally, as the mission was aborted, a helicopter hit the fuselage of a C-130, causing a fire that burned eight soldiers to death. To add insult to the disaster, Iranians recovered the charred remains of the soldiers and displayed them on television. The mission's failure made the United States and Carter look inept.

The president faced a serious challenge in the 1980 Democratic primaries from Massachusetts senator Ted Kennedy. Just days before the Iranian rescue mission, Kennedy had scored stunning victories in the Connecticut and New York primaries. Carter still had a comfortable lead in delegates as a result of earlier primary victories, and Kennedy had little hope of winning in future primaries out west, but his continued sniping at Carter damaged the president for his run against the Republican nominee.

Carter secured his party's nomination in August and delivered an acceptance speech that *Time* magazine described as failing to communicate "a vision of his goals that would lead and inspire the nation." By that time his approval ratings in the polls had dropped below those for Richard Nixon during the lowest point of the Watergate scandal.

The Republican candidate, Ronald Reagan, held a large lead early in the presidential campaign, and he won a televised debate with Carter in late October by appearing relaxed and affable and by asking voters the cutting question: "Are you better off than you were four years ago?" Given the state of the economy, the answer was obvious, as Reagan intended.

Yet Carter fought back. The economy improved slightly before the election, and he effectively portrayed Reagan as a dangerous man who would drag the nation into a nuclear war. "Peace is my passion, peace is my pledge," Carter said. When the president accused Reagan of failing to understand foreign affairs, the Republican candidate satirically agreed by saying there were many things he did not understand; for example, "I don't understand why . . . Americans have been held hostage for a year now." With that dig he reminded voters of the Iranian hostage crisis and Carter's ineptitude. Two days before the election, the president announced progress in talks with Iran, but the statement made people suspect he was just trying to manipulate them.

Reagan soundly defeated the president; he won 51 percent of the popular vote compared to Carter's 41 percent (and 7 percent for John Anderson, a third-party candidate). The election, however, revealed more than Carter's personal loss; it revealed what historian William H. Chafe has called a "loss of faith" in the political system. An incredibly low 28 percent of those meeting voter qualifications actually registered and voted.

After the election, Carter reached an agreement with Iran. He unfroze $8 billion of Iranian assets in the United States in exchange for the hostages. But the Iranians kept their captives until Ronald Reagan's inauguration in January 1981, denying the defeated president their release under his administration. For Carter, the Iranian hostage crisis sealed his presidency's tragic end.

After his defeat, Carter worked on developing the Carter Center in Atlanta, Georgia, which promoted international democracy, worldwide health programs, and urban revitalization. He gained considerable attention for helping to resolve political disputes in several foreign countries. In addition, he earned praise for his work with Habitat for Humanity, repairing and building houses for the poor.

In 1994 Carter traveled to North Korea, where he helped that country negotiate a dispute with the United States over the production of nuclear weapons. North Korea announced it would freeze its nuclear program in exchange for Western aid to build nuclear reactors that produced less plutonium, an ingredient used in nuclear weapons, as a by-product. Later that year Carter participated in talks to return Jean-Bertrand Aristide to power as president of Haiti. Since leaving the White House, Carter has also written several books, among them *Turning Point* and *Talking Peace*, a children's book, both published in 1993 and *The Virtues of Aging*, published in 1998.

In the year 2000, Carter advocated that television stations dedicate five minutes of their airtime each night for one month prior to an election as periods in which candidates could discuss political issues. This, he said, would allow all candidates to present their views regardless of campaign funding. Two years later, Carter won the Nobel Peace Prize "for his decades of untiring effort to find peaceful solutions to international conflicts, to advance democracy and human rights, and to promote economic and social development." Despite his postpresidential accomplishments in humanitarian endeavors, Carter's record in the White House, marred by his myriad problems, made him for years persona non grata in the Democratic Party. No aspiring politician wanted to be associated with his reputation for weakness. In 1992, Bill Clinton insisted: "Jimmy Carter and I are as different as daylight and dark." Carter even told the *New York Times:* "Nobody wanted to be associated with me."

Gradually, however, his standing improved as more and more Americans forgot or chose to ignore his presidential problems in the wake of his more recent endeavors. Whereas Bill Clinton all but ignored Carter, in 2004 the Georgian was invited to speak at the Democratic National Convention. There he offered one of the most pointed criticisms of President George W. Bush. Carter said that in the months since 9/11, Americans had seen their relations with foreign allies deteriorate. He called it a squandering of goodwill "by a virtually unbroken series of mistakes and miscalculations." He added: "Unilateral acts and demands have isolated the United States from the very nations we need to join us in combating terrorism." In line with his humanitarian vision, he called on Americans to rededicate themselves to honest dealings among themselves and with other countries. He said:

> Today our dominant international challenge is to restore the greatness of America based on telling the truth, a commitment to peace and a respect for civil liberties at home and basic human rights abroad. . . . Without truth, without trust, America cannot flourish. Trust is at the very heart of our democracy, the sacred covenant between a president and the people. When that trust is violated, the bonds that hold our republic together begin to weaken.

Carter continued his work in 2004 to resolve international disputes. Later that summer, he and the Carter Center oversaw the recall election of President Hugo Chavez in Venezuela. He declared the Chavez victory a fair one.

Carter won recognition, too, as a writer. In 2003, he became the first sitting or former president to write a novel. *The Hornet's Nest,* as it was titled, told about families involved in the Revolutionary War in the South. One reviewer called the story "ambitious and deeply rewarding." Carter's *Sharing Good Times,* one of several memoirs he has written, appeared in 2004.

As president, Jimmy Carter fell victim to his own self-righteousness and inexperience. Despite his talk of virtue, he foundered by failing to provide a vision of where he wanted the country to go, while his inability to handle economic problems caused him to lose support even among loyal Democrats.

Carter came into office without a strong mandate and burdened by conflicts that pulled him in different directions. Domestically, he wanted liberal programs to help the disadvantaged and conservative economic policies to curb inflation. Overseas, he wanted to promote human rights and to protect American security in part by supporting authoritarian regimes.

Events beyond his control, such as foreign crises, hurt him, as did the political scene in Washington. In the perennial tug-of-war for power between Congress and president, Congress had taken the advantage after Watergate, while reforms limited the power of its committee chairs and made its members more independent and less manageable. Neither the president nor party leaders could do as much as in the past to whip Congress into line.

Yet other presidents have handled events beyond their control more skillfully than Carter. When the voters ousted him in 1980, many wanted to be released from his ineffectiveness, indecisiveness, and ineptitude. One political scientist called the election result a "landslide vote of no confidence in an incompetent administration." Despite government reform, energy legislation, and progress related to the Middle East talks at Camp David, Jimmy Carter's presidential legacy stands as one of noble purposes destroyed by poor leadership, and of great hopes turned into profound disappointment.

Chronology

1924 Born October 1

1941 Graduates from Plains, Georgia, high school
Enters Georgia Institute of Technology

1943 Enters Annapolis Naval Academy

1946 Graduates from Annapolis
Marries Rosalynn Smith

1953 Quits the navy to help ill father
Takes over peanut business

1962 Elected to Georgia state senate

1964 Reelected to state senate

1966 Defeated in bid for Georgia governorship

1970 Elected governor of Georgia

1971 Proposes reform package

1974 Announces candidacy for president

1975 Retires from governorship

1976 Elected president

1977 Orders nuclear weapons withdrawn from South Korea
Promote human rights as foreign policy
Convinces Congress to establish Department of Energy

1978 Signs bill to deregulate oil industry
Pushes Panama Canal treaty through Senate
Signs Camp David Accords

1979 Negotiates SALT II Treaty with Soviet Union
Backs away from SALT II Treaty
Presents "Crisis of Spirit" speech

1980 Imposes windfall profits tax on oil companies
Signs Energy Security Act
Boycotts Olympics in Moscow
Fails to rescue American hostages in Iran
Loses reelection

1981 Secures release of hostages in Iran
Retires to Georgia
Heads Carter Center in Atlanta

1983 Publishes *Keeping Faith: Memoirs of a President*

1993 Publishes *Turning Point* and *Talking Peace*

1994 Negotiates dispute between North Korea and the United States
Helps arrange for return to power of Haitian president Jean-Bertrand Aristide

2000 Advocates that television broadcasters provide free time for political candidates

2002 Wins Nobel Peace Prize

2004 Speaks at Democratic National Convention

FURTHER READING

Bill, James A. *The Eagle and the Lion: The Tragedy of American-Iranian Relations.* New Haven, Conn.: Yale University Press, 1983.

Biven, W. Carl. *Jimmy Carter's Economy: Policy in an Age of Limits.* Chapel Hill: University of North Carolina Press, 2002.

Brzezinski, Zbigniew. *Power and Principle: American Diplomacy in the Carter Years.* New York: Farrar, Straus, Giroux, 1986.

Carter, Jimmy. *An Hour before Daylight: Memories of My Rural Boyhood.* New York: Simon & Schuster, 2001.

———. *Keeping Faith: Memoirs of a President.* New York: Bantam Books, 1982.

———. *Sharing Good Times.* New York: Simon & Schuster, 2004.

———. *Talking Peace: A Vision for the Next Generation.* New York: Dutton Children's Books. 1993.

———. *Turning Point: A Candidate, a State, and a Nation Come of Age.* New York: Random House, 1992.

———. *Virtues of Aging.* New York: Ballantine Publishing, 1998.

Fink, Gary M. *Prelude to the Presidency: The Political Character and Legislative Leadership Style of Governor Jimmy Carter.* Westport, Conn.: Greenwood Press, 1980.

Harwood, Richard, ed. *The Pursuit of the Presidency, 1980.* New York: Berkley Books, 1980.

Jordan, Hamilton. *Crisis: The Last Year of the Carter Presidency.* New York: Putnam, 1982.

Kaufman, Burton I. *The Presidency of James Earl Carter, Jr.* Lawrence: University of Kansas, 1993.

Lasky, Victor. *Jimmy Carter: The Man and the Myth.* New York: Richard Marek, 1979.

Smith, Gaddis. *Morality, Reason, and Power: American Diplomacy in the Carter Years.* New York: Hill and Wang, 1986.

Thompson, Kenneth. *The Carter Presidency: Fourteen Intimate Perspectives of Jimmy Carter.* Lanham, Md.: University Press of America, 1990.

Ronald Reagan (1911–2004)

Fortieth President, 1981–1989

Ronald Reagan
(official White House photograph, Library of Congress)

"My fellow citizens, our Nation is poised for greatness. We must do what we know is right and do it with all our might. Let history say of us, 'These were golden years—when the American Revolution was reborn, when freedom gained new life, when America reached for her best.'"

—Inaugural words, second term,
January 21, 1985

In *Reagan's America*, Garry Wills presents a chapter titled "Hollywood on the Potomac" in which he discusses the merger between motion pictures and the presidency of Ronald Reagan. Reagan wanted to bring those around him into his "movie," to have them buy into his view and plans and see the world through his lens as actor and director, to play the roles he wanted them to play.

Reagan's chief of staff, Donald Regan, later said: "Every word was scripted, every place where Reagan was expected to stand was chalked with toe marks." Without a script, Reagan was prone to gaffes and unable to recall specifics. With it, he communicated forcefully, presenting his vision with so much fervor that he was able to rally wide support for his conservative agenda and reshape politics. So effectively did he project his friendly demeanor and so tightly did he coil American hopes around himself that he left office with widespread support, despite a scandal that involved impeachable offenses and nearly doomed his presidency.

Born on February 6, 1911, in Tampico, Illinois, a one-block dot of a town, Ronald Wilson Reagan had a happy childhood but one marred by his father's alcoholism. Jack Reagan, an inveterate storyteller (a gift Ron inherited), worked as a retailer and salesman, but his drinking imperiled his family's economic survival. Ron's mother, Nelle Wilson Reagan, a devout member of the Disciples of Christ Church and an amateur actress, took on odd jobs to help the family survive. Young Ron was friendly and outgoing, yet protective of his inner feelings, probably as a way to mask his embarrassment over his father. One biographer says, "Ronald Reagan rarely told you anything about himself."

The Reagans moved several times before settling in Dixon, Illinois, in 1920. Ron liked sports from an early age. As a teenager he worked as a lifeguard and once saved a swimmer from drowning. He graduated from Dixon High School in 1928, where he played football, and obtained a scholarship to Eureka College, a small school run by the Disciples of Christ, right in the middle of the Midwest and its heartland values. Reagan showed little interest in academics and earned only average grades. He joined the swim team and the football team and acted in several college plays. Reagan was elected student body president his senior year, but other than that, he showed no political drive. He graduated in 1932 with a bachelor's degree in economics and sociology.

A few months after his graduation, his baritone speaking voice and glib manner landed him a job as sports announcer at radio station WOC in Davenport, Iowa. From there he went to WHO in Des Moines as sports director. Known as Dutch Reagan—he used this childhood nickname because it sounded "sporty"—he became the most popular sportscaster in Iowa. He announced Chicago Cubs baseball games, but because the station lacked the money to send him to Wrigley Field, he was forced to present a running commentary based on reports from the wire services combined with details he fabricated.

On a trip to Hollywood in 1937, Reagan took a screen test at Warner Brothers Studios. When he was offered a seven-year contract for considerably more than his announcer's salary, he quit WHO and started making movies. Initially he landed lead roles only in B films and a few minor parts in better ones. His first substantial role came in 1939 when he starred in a comedy, *Brother Rat*. He met actress Jane Wyman on the set, and they married in 1940. The couple had two children, one of whom was adopted.

That same year Reagan received excellent reviews for his role as Notre Dame football player George Gipp in *Knute Rockne*, a movie he cherished for its sentimentalism and its theme of individual achievement. Better parts soon followed: the drama *Kings Row* in 1941—a box office hit that some reviewers have called his finest performance—and *Desperate Journey* in 1942, about American World War II pilots stranded in Germany.

When the United States first entered the war, Reagan obtained a draft deferment. He was later commissioned in the cavalry, but he never saw combat. Instead, he spent the entire war making films for the military and receiving leaves to make more movies—patriotic ones, including *This Is the Army*, for Warner Brothers.

In news releases the studio told about Reagan fighting overseas, and after the war he repeated these stories, all of them fictional.

As Jane Wyman's movie career advanced and Reagan's stagnated, friction developed within their marriage, and in 1948 they divorced. At about the same time Reagan was chosen president of the Screen Actors Guild (SAG), a union formed in the 1930s that was mild-mannered in its quest for labor rights. Reagan had his own mental picture about SAG and his work in it. He never saw it as a real union; to him it was altruism that bonded its members rather than common economic interests.

While Reagan led SAG, his preference for the Democratic Party and his pronounced, at times radical, New Deal outlook gradually changed. Jolted by waste in government contracts during World War II and by high taxes, he began gravitating toward the Republicans. A fear of communism also moved him, and despite reservations about intrusive government tactics, he supported the Red scare–era investigations by Congress and the FBI, as well as the blacklisting of actors by the major studios. He even told the FBI about Hollywood figures who he believed "invariably followed the Communist line." His marriage to Nancy Davis in 1952, the year he stepped down as SAG president, also encouraged his shift. She had been raised by her stepfather, Loyal Davis, a devout right-winger who had preached the conservative gospel to her, and she in turn preached it to Reagan.

In 1954 General Electric (GE) signed Ronald Reagan to act in and host its new television show, *General Electric Theater*. He immersed himself in the world of GE, the corporation that made "progress" its middle name. He made his house all-electric and acquiesced when GE censored the show to prevent anything from being telecast that reflected poorly on the company. Reagan's job included touring the country as GE's spokesman, and in addition to his hallelujah refrain about the company and corporate America, he spoke out against big government, criticized bureaucratic waste, and warned about the dangers of the welfare state. He claimed that programs such as farm subsidization meant creeping socialism and would open the gates of the republic to communism. His speeches often received standing ovations; according to one survey, by 1958 he ranked among the most recognized men in America.

Although still nominally a Democrat in 1960, Reagan campaigned for Richard Nixon, the Republican candidate in that year's presidential race. By 1961, as he increasingly spoke before right-wing groups, his speeches were more stridently anticommunist and critical of American foreign policy as defensive and weak in the fight against the Reds. An antitrust investigation in 1962 lapped at Reagan's door when the federal government suspected illegal collusion between the actor and MCA, a leading talent agency. When MCA settled with the government, the investigation of Reagan ended.

That same year, though, General Electric fired Reagan, thinking his antigovernment rhetoric had made him a liability. He went on to host *Death Valley Days*, a program sponsored by Borax. In 1964 he campaigned for conservative Republican presidential candidate Barry Goldwater. His nationally televised speech "A Time for Choosing" won widespread acclaim for its articulate, forceful character. After Goldwater was crushed by Lyndon Johnson in the November election, the party's right wing turned to Reagan as its best hope.

Two years later Ronald Reagan ran for governor of California as a Republican, backed by some of the state's wealthiest and most conservative businessmen. They had a blueprint laid out for him and wanted to make sure the road to Sacramento led to Washington. With all this planning for his future, Regan quipped, "If only I could think of it as a script that would run for four years."

In his campaign, Reagan condemned student radicals who were protesting against regulations at the University of California-Berkeley and against the Vietnam War. He said he would put them in their place, and he promised he would cut spending and make government more efficient. His identification with traditional American values in a time of great social and political upheaval, combined with his friendly demeanor, resulted in a landslide victory over the Democratic incumbent, Edmund G. Brown. Soon after his triumph, Reagan sent an explicit message to the Berkeley protesters: "No one is compelled to attend the university. Those who do attend should accept and obey the prescribed rules, or pack up and get out."

When Reagan was asked what kind of governor he would make, he said, "I don't know. I've never played a governor." As he promised in his campaign, he cut spending . . . until so many government agencies suffered he was forced to restore most of it. In another blow to conservative hopes, he convinced the legislature to pass the highest tax increase in state history. Yet his support within the Republican right, and among Californians in general, remained strong. He effectively blamed the tax increase on his predecessor, who he said had created a bureaucratic monster gobbling up revenues. He also continued to present himself as the true voice of American values opposed to the unwashed hippies, demonstrators, and other detritus intent on changing—and, in his mind, ruining—society. When in May 1969 police in Berkeley, California, fired tear gas and shotguns to disperse a crowd of countercultural youths who were trying to protect the communal People's Park from destruction, Reagan praised the authorities and sent in the National Guard, which quelled the outburst.

While critics complained about Reagan's detached governing style and about how he worked short hours and disliked details, he easily won reelection in 1970, though by a smaller margin than four years earlier. Having made a modest run for the Republican presidential nomination in 1968, he and his conservative backers set their sights on winning it in 1976, believing that when Richard Nixon's second term came to an end, Reagan would face a wide-open field. But Nixon's resignation in 1974 as a result of the Watergate scandal changed that scenario. Now Nixon's replacement, Gerald Ford, sought a full term in the White House. Reagan nevertheless decided to go ahead with his plan and run against Ford. Though he lost, he came close to denying the president his own party's nomination.

The Californian came away from the race with his credentials strengthened, for he had excited many a conservative with talk about Ford being too moderate. When Ford lost the general election to Democrat Jimmy Carter, Reagan's prospects for the White House brightened; he no longer had to worry about an incumbent Republican vice president grabbing the inside track for the nomination in 1980.

Conservative Republicans again rallied to Reagan's next presidential bid. Contributions poured in from wealthy Goldwater supporters, and evangelical Christians joined the campaign, convinced that Reagan would promote prayer in public schools and oppose abortion. When he expressed his doubts about the theory of evolution, they liked him even more.

Reagan's campaign received a boost from a tax revolt sweeping through California and several other states. When he promised he would cut federal taxes and still balance the budget, the tax rebels supported him. Reagan's main opponent for the Republican nomination, Congressman George Bush, called the Californian's plan "voodoo economics," but Reagan beat him and squared off against the incumbent, Jimmy Carter.

Almost everything worked against Carter. High unemployment and inflation bred widespread discontent; recent increases in oil prices angered car-dependent suburbanites; and radicals in Iran disgraced American honor by holding hostages at the U.S. embassy in Tehran. Where Carter talked about limitations and a crisis of spirit, Reagan talked about a better future and criticized the Democrats for their weakness overseas and economic incompetence at home. Over and over again Reagan asked Americans, "Are you better off today than you were four years ago?" He knew they would emphatically answer "no" and would remember the question and their answer when they voted.

Yet Americans thought about more than Carter's failures; they also thought back to the 1960s and early 1970s when America lost in Vietnam and experienced crime and domestic violence that liberals did nothing about. One anthropologist who studied a largely Jewish and Italian working-class district of New York City reported that in the mid-1970s its residents "embellished and modified the meaning of liberalism, associating it with profligacy, spinelessness, malevolence, masochism, elitism, fantasy, anarchy, idealism, softness, irresponsibility, and sanctimoniousness. The term *conservative* acquired connotations of pragmatism, character, reciprocity, truthfulness, stoicism, manliness, realism, hardness, vengeance, strictness, and responsibility."

Reagan tapped into these feelings and combined them with Carter's difficulties to perfect a formula for victory. He captured 489 electoral votes to Carter's 49 and finished with about 44 million popular votes to Carter's 35.5 million.

In his first inaugural address Reagan established the most important challenge facing him when he stated: "These United States are confronted with an economic affliction of great proportions. We suffer from the longest and one of the worst sustained inflations in our national history. It distorts our economic decisions, penalizes thrift and crushes the struggling young and the fixed-income elderly alike. It threatens to shatter the lives of millions of our people."

He addressed pessimists with: "We're not, as some would have us believe, doomed to an inevitable decline; I do not believe in a fate that will fall on us no matter what we do. I do believe in a fate that will fall on us if we do nothing." He also sowed in people's minds a tremendous distrust of federal action, while reinforcing his role as the Washington outsider, when he said, "In this present crisis, government is not the solution to our problem, government is the problem."

Soon after Ronald Reagan entered the White House, he launched what David Stockman, head of the Office of Management and the Budget, called a "blitzkrieg." Stockman had already told Reagan that movement toward a balanced budget would require "more sweeping and wrenching budget cuts than we had told the public . . . would be needed." On February 18, 1981, President Reagan appeared before a joint session of Congress and called for budget and tax cuts. Within weeks, Congress passed a bill to slash taxes by $750 billion over five years, and another to immediately cut welfare spending by $25 billion.

The president presented his plan as one that had been thoroughly analyzed and well calculated to enforce supply-side economics, a theory that said lower taxes, primarily for the wealthy, would boost the economy to the point where tax revenues would actually increase and the budget deficit would decline. According to Stockman, though, the plan was flawed from the beginning. He later confessed to using faulty and contrived figures to make it look as if the deficit would go down when it would not. Further, the plan suffered from two formidable limits. First, Reagan refused to reduce entitlement programs, mainly Social Security, Medicare, and veterans' benefits. As a result, the cuts in welfare made only a tiny dent in overall spending. Stockman said, "These three [programs] alone cost $250 billion per year. The programs we had cut saved $25 billion. The President and White House staff were seeing the tip of the budget iceberg. . . ."

Second, Reagan insisted on a massive boost in defense spending, more than $1 *trillion* over five years. On that point he was intractable. Stockman said, "The fundamentals of the Reagan fiscal program—the big tax cut, the defense buildup, an anti-inflation monetary policy, and a balanced budget—had been given *a priori*." They were not to be debated. By August 1981 Reagan "had driven through the Congress . . . the most sweeping and radical change in national economic policy since the New Deal."

Yet it was doomed. The tax cuts failed to generate the forecast revenue, and the military budget, by far the largest in the country's history, drained substantial sums from the treasury. As the deficit grew bigger—it would eventually exceed that of all previous deficits *combined*—Reagan stood by his statement: "Defense is not a budget issue. You spend what you need."

In keeping with supply-side economics, Reagan reduced business regulations. That meant easing environmental enforcement and practically giving away public oil and coal rights to companies. He also tempered safety and health enforcement, and in August 1981 he showed his firmness toward unions when he fired 13,000 air traffic controllers who had walked off their jobs.

Reagan supported Federal Reserve Board Chairman Paul Volcker in his policy to curb inflation through high interest rates. On that point, Stockman praised the president's perseverance: "When it counted, [he] gave Volcker the political latitude to do what had to be done. It was a genuine achievement."

President Reagan displayed personal fortitude when in March 1981 he survived an assassination attempt by John Hinckley, Jr., who shot him in the chest as he left a Washington hotel after giving a speech. Reagan reacted calmly as he was rushed to a nearby hospital, but it was a serious wound—he lost over 30 percent of his blood—that took months to heal. Oddly, Hinckley was infatuated with movies and planned his attack after having seen *Taxi Driver*—a film about a deranged man who tries to kill a presidential candidate, or apparently does so, depending on how the characters' actions are interpreted—at least 15 times. Hinckley stalked the scripted Reagan with his own script taken from the screen and applied to real life. According to one historian, Reagan's survival made him all the more formidable; it "elevated him . . . in people's affections. It made him almost a mythic figure." He was like a matinee idol.

In the short term, Paul Volcker's higher interest rates conflicted with the supply-side plan to expand the economy, and the bulging deficit drove interest rates higher yet. An economic recession followed—the worst since the Great Depression, although short-lived. In 1982 unemployment neared 11 percent, real income dropped, and exports declined.

While pursuing economic reform, President Reagan reshaped the Supreme Court with appointments that turned it to the right. He wanted judges who would side with victims rather than criminals, moderate civil rights measures, and weaken the right to abortion. For one vacancy on the court he chose Arizonan Sandra Day O'Connor; for another he appointed Antonin Scalia, a markedly conservative judge; and he elevated William H. Rehnquist, one of the court's most conservative members, to chief justice.

In 1983 the economy recovered as the auto industry revived, construction increased, and consumer spending improved. Unemployment decreased to 7.5 percent, though among African Americans it remained much higher. Reaganites pointed to the president's supply-side plan as the reason for the upturn. Few experts agreed with that assessment; they claimed the depression had simply bottomed out, and Reagan's plan had not created the mechanism for uninterrupted growth promised by its promoters.

In foreign policy, the president announced the Reagan Doctrine, the right of the United States to fight communist insurgency anywhere in the world. To Ronald Reagan, Latin America offered the most immediate danger. In El Salvador he backed a right-wing dictatorship that was fighting communist guerrillas and that, in protecting its power, used death squads to kill thousands of civilians, including the Catholic archbishop of San Salvador. In 1981 he froze military aid to Nicaragua to destabilize a leftist regime there. Then he provided money and supplies to Contras—he called them "freedom fighters"—who trained in Guatemala and attacked Nicaragua.

In 1982 Reagan involved the United States in a complex civil war in Lebanon when he landed 1,500 marines in Beirut on a mission to bring order to that city, then besieged by Israeli, Syrian, Palestinian, and Christian rebel forces. Reagan especially wanted to contain the Syrians, who were receiving aid from the Soviet Union, and create an environment conducive to peace talks. The mission, however, was poorly planned and the marines proved to be ineffectual.

With the communist threat still on Reagan's mind, in March 1983 he proposed the Strategic Defense Initiative (SDI), also called "Star Wars," a plan to use lasers and satellites to destroy incoming missiles and provide a shield for America against a Soviet nuclear attack. The "Evil Empire," as Reagan called the Soviets, would thus be rendered atomically impotent. Opponents, however, called SDI unworkable and claimed it would ignite a bigger arms race with the Soviet Union. Congress eventually approved money for it but only for a scaled-down planning program. Overall, the defense department received funds faster than it could use them, and it worked feverishly to spend the money, contributing to cost overruns, fraud, and waste on a scale far greater than any social program ever experienced from the New Deal onward.

In Lebanon the fighting among the various factions restricted the marines to Beirut's airport. There on October 23, 1983, Islamic terrorists, angered by the American presence, drove a truck filled with several tons of TNT into the marine compound and exploded it, killing 274 soldiers. Reagan said U.S. troops would stay, but their position was clearly untenable, and a few weeks later he withdrew them.

While the public might have been expected to condemn Reagan for the disaster in Lebanon, the same week of the Beirut explosion he launched an invasion of Grenada, a tiny Caribbean country shaken by a Marxist coup. Reagan acted ostensibly to rescue American medical students threatened by continued turmoil on the island, but he actually wanted to topple the government. American troops met little resistance from 110 Cuban soldiers sent by Fidel Castro to help build an airstrip on the island, and they brought the Marxist regime to a quick end. Reagan's public approval ratings soared, and Lebanon receded from memory as he talked about American pride and honor having been protected by brave soldiers.

In the 1984 presidential election Reagan reaped the benefits of a revived economy, the Grenada victory, and a campaign built around the slogan "Morning in America," the idea being that the country was once again on a glorious path. Americans looked at the Reagan advertising images on television of white picket fences, freckled kids, and puppy dogs and reacted like spectators of a Disney movie, their ideals packaged and wrapped in patriotic bunting, their worries soothed and doubts erased.

Ronald Reagan identified himself so firmly with the nationalist mood that to attack him was, in effect, to attack America. On television "He was like a canvas himself . . . ," says historian Haynes Johnson; "you could see the flag waving in the background, almost like he was old Uncle Sam." Reagan even co-opted Bruce Springsteen's rock song "Born in the USA," proclaiming it a modern celebratory anthem when its lyrics actually expressed deep reservations about society. Democratic presidential candidate Walter F. Mondale learned about Reagan's political punch in 1984 when the president won reelection in a landslide, capturing 49 of 50 states. Women, the young, the elderly, even union households supported him in droves.

For Reagan the fight against communism meant the Contras in Nicaragua had to be supported in their drive to topple that country's Marxist-infiltrated regime. His mission in Central America soon merged with an unrelated development in Lebanon, where a pro-Iranian terrorist group held several American hostages. In August 1985 he decided to work a deal with the terrorists and ordered the secret sale of 500 antitank missiles to Iran in exchange for the release of some of the hostages. Over the next several months Reagan sold the Iranians about 2,000 antitank missiles, along with other missiles and spare parts, but the terrorists refused to release another hostage. At one point national security adviser Robert McFarlane flew to Iran on a plane that carried military equipment, a Bible, and a cake, a strange combination of items meant to influence Iranians and convert them to Western ways.

In January 1986 the president's arms-for-hostages deal came together with his determination to help the Contras. That month, officials of the National Security Council (NSC) evaded a 1982 congressional law, the Boland Amendment, that prohibited the government from sending money to the Contras. They decided to overcharge Iran for the weapons sent them and transfer the inflated profits to the Contra cause.

In spring 1986, Congress lifted the Boland Amendment. But illegal acts had already been committed by the NSC, along with violation of the Constitution for having used government moneys unreported to the treasury. (Funds had been deposited in a secret account.)

Later that year a Beirut publication, *Al-Shiraa*, claimed the United States had sold arms in exchange for hostages. Reagan denied the report, and given his pronounced intransigence about dealing with terrorists, Americans believed him. Yet as more details surfaced, he changed his story and admitted the deed, inexplicably saying that it was done to encourage moderate factions in Iran and had no connection to the hostages.

Under intense pressure to uncover the complete story in the Iran-Contra scandal, President Reagan appointed an independent commission to investigate, headed by former Texas senator John Tower. The commission faulted Reagan's administrative procedure and claimed he was negligent but also said he had done nothing illegal. "The President did not seem to be aware of the way in which the operation was implemented and the full consequences of U.S. participation," said the commission's report. Soon after the findings, Reagan issued a national security directive barring the NSC staff (not the government as a whole) from engaging in covert operations.

Congress also investigated the affair and concluded that a runaway NSC, led by the president's national security adviser, Admiral John Poindexter and assisted by NSC staff member Colonel Oliver North, had circumvented the state department in order to run its own foreign policy, even to the point of a plan to create a rogue "Central Intelligence Agency" outside the existing CIA. (Officials in the state department had long complained about the White House intruding into even the smallest of foreign policy matters. Said one: "You've got a situation where very strong people are debating about the nickels and dimes of everyday decisions." The secretary of state, George P. Shultz, was a member of the NSC, but objected to the covert operation.) Yet when North testified before the Senate on national television, he presented himself as a patriot who had done nothing wrong in fighting communism, and most Americans cheered his commitment. To soothe Congress, Reagan promised in August 1987 to notify it in most instances should he decide to undertake covert activities.

Some observers believe that the congressional committee withheld material that would have been more damaging to the president. In any event, while Congress portrayed Reagan as detached and misled by his advisers, other evidence said differently. Robert McFarlane, who preceded Poindexter as national security adviser, testified to Congress that Reagan was briefed frequently about the Contras and that he asked detailed questions about them. In one instance he helped move an arms shipment through Honduras by contacting that country's president and speeding it along.

Special Prosecutor Lawrence E. Walsh issued a report after Reagan left the White House that also differed with the Senate findings. Walsh concluded that "President Reagan created the conditions which made possible the crimes committed by others by his secret deviations from announced national policy . . . and by his open determination to keep the contras together 'body and soul' despite a statutory ban on contra aid." Walsh admitted that "no direct evidence was developed that the President authorized . . . the diversion of proceeds to aid the contras." But he said it was unlikely Reagan was ignorant of the activity. Walsh pointed out that Poindexter's defense of the president and North's "wide destruction of records"—

the shredding machines operated day and night—made it impossible to uncover the complete story.

The special prosecutor criticized the Congressional investigation, saying:

> The disrespect for Congress by a popular and powerful President and his appointees was obscured when Congress accepted the tendered concept of a runaway conspiracy of subordinate officers. . . . Evidence obtained . . . established that the Iran/contra affair was not an aberrational scheme carried out by a "cabal of zealots" on the National Security Council staff. . . . Instead, it was the product of two foreign policy directives by President Reagan which skirted the law and which were executed by the NSC staff with the knowledge and support of high officials in the CIA, State and Defense departments. . . .

Walsh obtained indictments against 14 persons charged with criminal acts. Four of them were convicted of felonies, seven pleaded guilty either to felonies or misdemeanors, and one had his case dismissed. One of those who pled guilty was Robert McFarlane, who admitted he had unlawfully withheld information from Congress. During the scandal a despondent McFarlane had tried to commit suicide. Two other cases awaiting trial were closed when President Bush granted pardons to the accused.

Walsh claimed that "The lesson of Iran/contra is that if our system is to function properly, the branches of government must deal with one another honestly and cooperatively." He might have added what historian Arthur Schlesinger, Jr., found—that Reagan's actions in Iran-Contra resulted from the growth of a powerful presidency over the many years of the cold war. "The imperial temptation," Schlesinger said, "is the consequence of a global and messianic foreign policy."

He might have added that Iran-Contra resulted from President Reagan's immersion in his own mental image where every exertion in fighting communism was noble, every hesitation disloyal. This view made Reagan not so much detached, as the Tower Commission had concluded, as blinded. Indeed, Reagan never completely accepted the reality of what had happened. He later said, "I told the American people I did not trade arms for hostages. My heart and my best intentions still tell me that is true, but the facts and the evidence tell me it is not."

On Capitol Hill, congressmen and women talked of impeachment. But in the end Reagan was saved from such ignominy by his continued popularity and by the reluctance of Democrats, who had led the impeachment drive against Richard Nixon, of appearing to want to ruin all Republican presidents. They may have also disliked the thought of putting Vice President George Bush in the White House and giving him an advantage as an incumbent chief executive in the 1988 presidential race.

Reagan's wounded presidency received another blow in 1987 when economic reports revealed a widening gap between the wealthy and the poor and an increase in homelessness, while interest rates remained high. Then in October the stock market crashed, with the Dow Jones losing 13 percent of its value in one week.

Yet Reagan revived from the devastation, partly because the economy improved but mainly because of developments in the Soviet Union. Suddenly, Soviet president Mikhail Gorbachev, beset by his own economic problems, wanted to negotiate a momentous treaty on nuclear weapons. In December 1987 he and Reagan signed the Intermediate Nuclear Force Treaty, which committed their countries to dismantling and destroying all short- and medium-range missiles. A giant step had been taken: For the first time the United States and the Soviet Union advanced beyond arms control to arms elimination.

How much credit should Reagan be given for the treaty? Some historians say Gorbachev was ready to reach an agreement without any pressure from the United States. Others say that Reagan's arms buildup forced the issue. Most likely it was a bit of both. Historian Stephen E. Ambrose concludes that "Reagan's second term had seen more progress in ending the cold war . . . than had any other administration. Around the world, peace had broken out."

Reagan left the White House with a public approval rating of 50 percent, an unusually high number for an exiting president. As he departed by helicopter after George Bush's inauguration, cameras captured him and the new president saluting each other. The image felt heartwarming and looked spontaneous, but it was completely scripted.

Reagan retired to his home in Los Angeles, where in 1990 he wrote his autobiography, *An American Life*. In 1994, in a letter to the American people, Reagan disclosed he had been diagnosed with Alzheimer's disease, or degenerative cognitive dementia. Reagan said: "I now begin the journey that will lead me into the sunset of my life. . . ." Evidence indicates his mental faculties may actually have begun deteriorating late in his presidency.

Entering the 21st century, Reagan's health declined markedly. He died on June 5, 2004, at his home in Los Angeles, at age 93, making him the longest-lived former president. Reagan's career had been scripted as both an actor and a politician, down to the expressions he should make and the exact spot where he should stand when giving a speech. Under the watch of his wife Nancy Reagan, his funeral was also scripted. Indeed, preparations for it had begun years earlier, with the former first lady determined there should be a state funeral fitting her husband's accomplishments and promoting his place in history.

More than 100,000 mourners paid their respects to Reagan by making the pilgrimage to the Reagan presidential library in the Simi Valley, where his body lay in state. His casket was then placed aboard a plane at the Port Magu Naval Air Base and flown to Washington, D.C., for the first state funeral in the nation's capital since the death of Lyndon Johnson in 1973.

Amid an early heat wave that had descended on the city, there unfolded an elaborate ceremony, filled with drama and pathos. His body was carried to the Capitol Rotunda in a horse-drawn caisson and accompanied by a horse without rider, with the former president's boots affixed to the stirrups and, in accord with tradition, facing backward to commemorate a fallen hero. Jet fighters flew overhead, a 21-gun salute sounded, and a band played a muffled version of the "Battle Hymn of the Republic." His body was taken to the West Front of the Capitol rather than the usual entrance used for a state funeral, the East Front, which was blocked by construction, thus bringing him to the spot where he had sworn the oath of office for his first term.

A memorial service at the National Cathedral on June 11 attracted numerous prominent leaders, including all of the former U.S. presidents and Mikhail Gorbachev, who had headed the Soviet Union in its last throes. The current U.S. president, George W. Bush, presented a eulogy in which he said: "We lost Ronald Reagan only days ago but we have missed him a long time. We have missed his kindly presence, that reassuring voice and the happy ending we had wished for him. It has been 10 years since he said his own farewell, yet it is still very sad and hard to let him go. Ronald Reagan belongs to the ages now, but we preferred it when he belonged to us."

Reagan's body was then flown back across the country to California for a graveside service at sunset in the Simi Valley. In parting remarks, his son, Ronald Prescott Reagan, took a dig at President Bush while praising his own father. President Reagan, he said, was "a deeply unabashedly religious man, but he never made the fatal mistake of so many politicians—wearing his faith on his sleeve to gain political advantage."

During the funeral proceedings, CBS news reporter Bob Schieffer observed:

> I think it is very interesting . . . and also fitting that Ronald Reagan's funeral ceremonies began in California. He will then come to Washington and then they will end on Friday when he is buried at sunset in California. Because . . . unlike, say, Lyndon Johnson, who was a man of Washington, Ronald Reagan never really was. He was a man from the West. He came to Washington for a time and then he went back home to California. He

> never thought of himself as a part of this city. He loved being president. He enjoyed being here. But he never considered this his home.

Whatever Ronald Reagan's limitations, whatever scandals and economic reversals beset him, he reshaped the federal government and society with his conservative agenda. Some claimed he encouraged economic greed and a harsh partisanship. Yet he was a persuasive leader and a consummate actor whose "movie" played across the national landscape and left millions of Americans feeling more confident about their country's future.

CHRONOLOGY

1911 Born February 6

1920 Moves with family to Dixon, Illinois

1928 Graduates from Dixon High School
Enters Eureka College

1932 Graduates from Eureka College
Begins job as sports announcer at WOC

1937 Signs movie contract with Warner Brothers Studios

1939 Appears in *Brother Rat*

1940 Marries Jane Wyman
Appears in *Knute Rockne*

1947 Elected president of Screen Actors Guild

1948 Divorces Jane Wyman

1952 Marries Nancy Davis

1954 Hosts *General Electric Theater*

1960 Campaigns for Richard Nixon for president

1962 Hosts *Death Valley Days*

1964 Presents nationally televised speech supporting Barry Goldwater for president

1966 Elected governor of California

1970 Reelected governor

1976 Loses bid for Republican presidential nomination

1980 Elected president

1981 Announces supply-side economic program
Survives assassination attempt
Reduces taxes
Increases defense spending
Cuts spending for social programs
Crushes air traffic controllers' strike

1982 Sends U.S. Marines to Lebanon
Orders invasion of Grenada

1984 Reelected president

1985 Begins selling arms to Iran in exchange for release of American hostages

1987 Defends administration as Senate investigates Iran-Contra scandal
Signs Intermediate Nuclear Force Treaty with Soviet Union

1989 Retires from presidency

1990 Writes his autobiography

1994 Announces he suffers from Alzheimer's disease

2001 Sustains a broken right hip in a fall at his home

2004 Dies June 5

FURTHER READING

Bell, Coral. *The Reagan Paradox: American Foreign Policy in the 1980s*. New Brunswick, N.J.: Rutgers University Press, 1989.

Cannon, Lou. *President Reagan: The Role of a Lifetime*. New York: Public Affairs, 2000.

Johnson, Haynes. *Sleepwalking Through History: America in the Reagan Years*. New York: W. W. Norton, 1991.

Matlock, Jack. *Reagan and Gorbachev: How the Cold War Ended.* New York: Random House, 2004.

Mayer, Jane, and Doyle McManus. *Landslide: The Unmaking of the President, 1984–1988.* Boston: Houghton Mifflin, 1988.

Meese, Edwin, III. *With Reagan: The Inside Story.* Washington, D.C.: Regnery, 1992.

Skinner, Kiron K., Annelise Andersen, and Martin Anderson, eds., *Reagan: A Life in Letters.* New York: Free Press, 2003.

Stockman, David. *The Triumph of Politics: The Inside Story of the Reagan Revolution.* New York: Avon Books, 1986.

Vaughn, Stephen. *Ronald Reagan in Hollywood: Movies and Politics.* New York: Cambridge University Press, 1994.

Wills, Garry. *Reagan's America.* New York: Penguin Books, 1988.

George H. W. Bush (1924–)

Forty-first President, 1989–1993

George H. W. Bush
(official White House photograph, Library of Congress)

"For a new breeze is blowing, and a world refreshed by freedom seems reborn; for in man's heart, if not in fact, the day of the dictator is over. The totalitarian era is passing, its old ideas blown away like leaves from an ancient, lifeless tree."

—Inaugural words, January 20, 1989

When the Persian Gulf War ended in February 1991 after U.S. missiles and fighter planes shattered Iraq and ground forces defeated the enemy army within 100 hours, Americans rejoiced at the sureness of their weaponry, the swiftness of their victory, and the rightness of their cause. President George Bush reaped praise for his effective and strong leadership, and amid the hoopla surrounding the return home of U.S. soldiers, he proclaimed a new world order in which countries committed to moral leadership would contain aggressors and terrorists around the world.

Combined with the recent end to the cold war, the results of the Persian Gulf War indicated peace would reign and Bush would easily win reelection. His public approval rating, after all, had reached 90 percent, a level far higher than any previous president. Yet little more than 18 months later, the voters booted Bush from the White House. His term in office stands as one of the more remarkable examples of what can happen to a president who pursues foreign policy to the point of ignoring domestic issues.

Like several presidents before him, George Herbert Walker Bush came from a family known for its wealth and leadership in private and public service. He was born on June 12, 1924, in Milton, Massachusetts, but grew up in Greenwich, Connecticut, a well-to-do town near New York City. His father, Prescott Bush, was president of Brown Brothers, Harriman and Company investment bankers and served on the board of directors of Pan American Airways, the Columbia Broadcasting System, and Dresser Industries. He had close ties to Republican political leaders and had served in the U.S. Senate in the 1950s and early 1960s. George's mother, Dorothy Walker Bush, was from a prominent midwestern family. George spent summers at Walker's Point, his family's 10-bedroom home on 10 acres of land that jutted into the Atlantic Ocean at Kennebunkport, Maine.

George attended private school in Greenwich, and in 1936 he entered Phillips Academy, an exclusive all-boys prep school at Andover, Massachusetts. He was president of his senior class, president of the Greek fraternities, a member of the basketball team, and captain of both the baseball and soccer teams. While still a student, Bush met Barbara Pierce during a Christmas dance at the Greenwich Country Club. They soon fell in love and decided they would marry.

The day Japan attacked the United States at Pearl Harbor, Bush vowed he would fight to defend his country, and shortly after he graduated from Phillips Academy in June 1942, he joined the navy. For reasons that are unclear, officials waived the two years of college required for flight training, and Bush became America's youngest naval pilot.

On September 2, 1944, Bush's fighter plane was hit while he was on a mission to destroy a Japanese radio installation in the Pacific. As smoke filled the plane's cabin, he still managed to strike his target. He then struggled to keep the plane in the air. At 1,000 feet, one of the two men with him bailed out, but his parachute tangled and he was killed. Bush jumped next while a third crewman failed to escape. After plunging into the ocean, Bush grabbed a lifeboat that had been jettisoned from the plane, and he was rescued by a U.S. submarine. He was awarded the Distinguished Flying Cross and three air medals and returned home in December 1944.

On January 6, 1945, Bush married Barbara Pierce. The couple had six children. That fall he entered Yale University and majored in economics (a fascinating choice given that his presidency would founder over economic issues). As at Phillips Academy, he excelled academically and athletically. He played on the baseball team that reached the finals of the 1948 national championship, only to lose to the University of Southern California. Although he hit just .167 in the series, he was perfect in 32 fielding chances.

After Bush graduated from Yale, his father arranged a job for him at Dresser Industries, an oil company. In 1948 he began working for the firm in Odessa, Texas, as a trainee, cleaning and painting machinery. A few months later the company assigned him as a salesman to California, after which he was relocated to Midland, Texas.

George Bush left Dresser in 1951 to start his own business with a partner, creating the Bush-Overby Oil Development Company. He bought oil rights and then lined up financial backing for drilling the fields. Two years later, Bush-Overby merged with another company to form Zapata Petroleum; by 1954 they owned 71 oil wells. Bush established the headquarters for another business, Zapata Offshore, in Houston and in 1959 moved there from Midland.

George Bush cut his political teeth in 1960 when he ran for Harris County Republican Chairman in Houston. He won, and for two years under his leadership the party grew in size in a predominantly Democratic environment. In 1964 he ran for the U.S. Senate, but after easily winning the Republican primary he lost the general election to Ralph Yarborough, the incumbent. Many Texans considered Bush a presumptuous outsider, despite his having lived in Texas for 16 years. Hampered by his Eastern mannerisms, he adopted those of Texas, or at least tried to, when he wore cowboy boots and cowboy hats and affected a more down-to-earth attitude.

Bush ran for Congress in 1966 on a platform critical of President Lyndon Johnson's spending for social programs but supportive of the Vietnam War; he defeated his colorless Democratic opponent, Frank Briscoe. In Washington, Bush proposed no substantial legislation and took a moderately conservative stand on most issues. He backed cuts in government waste and wanted voluntary prayer in public schools. He pushed for a portion of federal funds to be returned to the states, opposed busing to achieve racial integration, and fought against the federal registration and licensing of guns. Bush changed his views about Vietnam and advocated American withdrawal from the war. Despite his vote on busing, he supported a civil rights bill, the Fair Housing Act of 1968. This angered some of his conservative backers, but he still won reelection that year.

Encouraged by Richard Nixon and other Republicans, Bush made another run for the Senate in 1970. He thought he would again be facing the liberal Ralph Yarborough in the contest, but Lloyd Bentsen defeated Yarborough in the Democratic primary. As a conservative, Bentsen cut into Bush's support and won the general election.

President Nixon then stepped in and appointed Bush as U.S. representative to the United Nations. In that post he defended the American preference for a "two-China policy," meaning representation for both Nationalist China and Communist China. His position was undercut in 1971, however, when the president shifted policy and agreed to a single seat for the communists.

Early in 1973 Nixon tapped Bush to serve as chairman of the Republican National Committee (RNC). Friction soon developed between the two men, though, when Nixon's advisers pressured Bush to defend the president in the rapidly worsening Watergate scandal. Bush refused, saying the RNC needed some independence. As the crisis deepened and Nixon's position became indefensible, Bush wrote the president on August 7, 1974: "It is my considered judgment that you should now resign. . . . I believe this view is held by most Republican leaders across the country."

When Nixon quit, Bush lobbied President Gerald Ford to appoint him as vice president, and he appeared on the chief executive's short list. In a memo written for Ford, White House aide Bryce Harlow listed Bush at the top with the words: "Strongest across the board; greatest weakness—regarded as intellectually 'light' by many top leaders in the country." But Ford chose New Yorker Nelson Rockefeller instead—"professionally the best qualified," according to Harlow—and allowed Bush to pick any other assignment he wanted. He chose to head the U.S. Liaison Office in Peking (Beijing), China.

Bush returned to Washington at the end of 1975 when President Ford appointed him director of the Central Intelligence Agency (CIA). He stepped in at a difficult time, as Senate investigations uncovered a wide range of illegal acts committed by the CIA since its founding in the 1940s. Bush worked to restore morale at the CIA and obtained $500 million from Congress to build two satellite reconnaissance systems and four ground stations for intercepting overseas communications.

But his tenure was short-lived; he resigned his post after Democrat Jimmy Carter won the presidency in November 1976. Bush then returned to Texas and his business interests, though he kept looking for an opportunity to reenter politics. As Carter's popularity plummeted, Bush considered running for the White House himself, and in 1979 he formally announced his bid for the Republican nomination.

He faced several formidable obstacles, among them his lack of name recognition, his weak record in winning elective office, and the candidacy of Ronald Reagan, the former governor of California, who was immensely popular with conservatives. Bush surprised many by finishing first in the Iowa caucuses, but Reagan solidly beat him in the New Hampshire primary. Although Bush's bid for the nomination failed, he gained notice for labeling Reagan's promise to both lower taxes and lower the budget deficit as "voodoo economics."

Despite the Texan's criticism, after Reagan won the nomination he picked Bush as his running mate, and together they easily defeated Jimmy Carter. In March 1981 Bush earned praise for calmly and competently handling the crisis when John Hinckley, Jr., shot President Reagan. Over the next several years, Bush headed one task force to stem the influx of illegal drugs into the United States and another to reduce government waste through deregulation.

As had all preceding vice presidents after World War II, Bush served on the National Security Council, but in his case the job ensnared him in a scandal. In 1986 and 1987 it was revealed that President Reagan had approved an NSC plan to sell weapons to Iran in exchange for that country's help in getting Islamic militants to release American hostages being held in Lebanon. In turn, Reagan's national security adviser, John Poindexter, used profits from the arms sales to illegally fund American-backed guerrilla forces fighting a leftist government in Nicaragua. These actions by the NSC not only broke the law, but they also violated Reagan's promise never to deal with terrorists.

As Congress investigated and some on Capitol Hill talked about impeaching the president, Bush denied any direct knowledge of the Iran-Contra scandal. He claimed the plan was carried out by lower-level members of the NSC staff. "I wish it hadn't happened," he said. "I think everybody, to the degree there were mistakes, should share in the blame."

Actually, Bush was being disingenuous, and when he said he was "out of the loop" on Iran-Contra, most Americans doubted him. Despite the scandal, he sought the presidency in 1988 and with Reagan's blessing won the Republican nomination.

To convince Republicans to choose him, Bush had abandoned his previous moderate positions and made promises conservatives wanted to hear. Foremost among them, he swore he would oppose any increase in taxes. If any congressmen should try to force him to do otherwise, he said, he would tell them: "Read my lips: no new taxes." Bush tied himself to Reagan's record, claiming he would continue to add jobs to the economy and lower inflation.

When Bush began his campaign against the Democratic nominee, Massachusetts governor Michael Dukakis, polls showed him nearly 20 points behind. Many voters still distrusted his answers about Iran-Contra, and others thought he lacked Ronald Reagan's guts and called him "a wimp." To counter that impression and play on fears that Dukakis was too liberal, he unleashed a harsh negative campaign. His manager, Lee Atwater, who considered anything fair and nothing sacred in politics, dragged him along the low road.

Bush claimed that Dukakis was unpatriotic for opposing the pledge of allegiance in schools —a barefaced exaggeration of the governor's stand on the issue. Bush's supporters portrayed Dukakis as soft on crime in advertisements that claimed that under the Massachusetts furlough system a black convict, Willie Horton, had committed rape while on a weekend release from prison. The Bush television ads displayed a prison with a revolving door letting out black inmates. Elizabeth Drew of the *New Yorker* said, "Never had the appeal to racism been so blatant and raw."

To many Americans, both candidates had little to offer, and the voters continued their tendency, evident since the late 1960s, to stay away from the polls. Conservative columnist George Will summed up the feelings of many when he called the first debate between Bush and Dukakis "a national embarrassment." He said, "Michael Dukakis was marginally less embarrassing than George Bush was, if only because his canned thoughts were ladled out in understandable syntax." Bush's negative attacks and his promise to continue the Reagan program brought him victory, but the Republicans failed to capture either the House or the Senate, and many Democrats never forgave Bush for his severe partisanship.

In his inaugural address President Bush tried to soften the acidic political atmosphere when he called for the United States "to make kinder the face of the nation and gentler the face of the world." He criticized the material greed of the Reagan years and praised those volunteers who gave their time for the good of society, the persons and organizations that made up what he called a "thousand points of light."

George Bush entered the White House as the decades-long cold war ended with the collapse of the Soviet empire and the communist system in Eastern Europe. Soon after Mikhail Gorbachev, president of the Soviet Union, withdrew his country's last troops from Afghanistan, he announced in June 1989 that Poland and Hungary were free to determine their own futures. In November the Berlin Wall fell, leading to the reunification of East and West Germany. By the end of 1989 the Russians had retreated to within their own borders, and the very survival of the Soviet Union itself was imperiled.

Many factors brought this change: the effects of America's containment policy in the cold war; discontent in Eastern Europe with Soviet domination; the Soviet military draining its country's budget; widespread corruption in the communist system; and Gorbachev's commitment to reform, particularly a new openness called *glasnost*. Bush reacted cautiously to the upheaval in Eastern Europe, neither exulting over the demise of Soviet power nor providing much aid to countries struggling to establish their independence.

Critics said Bush was still looking at Europe through the distorted scrim of the cold war and that he should have acted more firmly to support those governments emerging from Soviet rule. His supporters, however, said he moved at just the right pace, that massive intervention might cause reactionaries in the Soviet Union to undo Gorbachev's reforms. Bush's national security adviser, Brent Scowcroft, stated: "Our policy has to be based on our own national interest, and we have an interest in the stability of the Soviet Union. The instability of the USSR would be a great threat to us."

Where Eastern Europeans breathed freedom, the Chinese endured oppression. In June 1989 communist leader Deng Xiaoping ordered troops to fire into a huge crowd of pro-democracy demonstrators at Peking's Tiananmen Square. Hundreds, maybe thousands, died in the slaughter. Days later President Bush, acting in protest, suspended military sales to China and halted high-level diplomatic exchanges. At the same time, though, he sent an adviser to meet secretly with Chinese officials and assure them that relations would not worsen, and he soon agreed to sell satellites to China. Many Americans believed he pandered to the communist rulers, but he argued that the United States could best make China into a more open society through expanded trade.

Closer to home, President Bush sent American troops into Panama in December 1989 after that country's strongman, Manuel Noriega, rigged elections and declared that a "state of war" existed with the United States. Operation Just Cause, as Bush called it, resulted in the deaths of 24 American soldiers and numerous Panamanian civilians but also in the capture of Noriega, who was extradited to Miami, Florida and indicted for drug trafficking.

In June 1990 Bush met with Gorbachev, and they agreed to reduce long-range nuclear weapons by 30 percent and stockpiles of chemical weapons by 80 percent. Before the end of the year, the president formally announced that the cold war had ended.

Bush benefited from his improved relations with the Soviet Union when a crisis erupted in the Middle East. On August 1, 1990, Iraqi dictator Saddam Hussein invaded neighboring Kuwait and took over its oil fields. In a joint statement, Bush and Gorbachev labeled the invasion "brutal" and "illegal," and on August 2 the United Nations condemned Iraq and demanded it withdraw from Kuwait. Four days later the U.N. voted to impose sanctions, including an embargo on oil sales.

Still, Saddam refused to budge and instead declared Kuwait an Iraqi province. Bush worried that an emboldened Saddam would send his army's 5,000 tanks into Saudi Arabia and grab that country's oil fields, strategically crucial to the United States and Western Europe. In September he met with Gorbachev in Finland, and they reaffirmed their determination to pry Saddam out of Kuwait while rejecting the Iraqi leader's demand that any negotiations include talks to arrange a homeland for Palestinians. The summit showed how far the United States and the Soviet Union had come in their post–cold war relationship because previously the United States had sought to eliminate Soviet influence in the Middle East.

With Saddam standing firm, President Bush built a complex coalition to support the use of force against Iraq. He reached out to England, France, the Soviet Union, Arab states, and elsewhere—a diplomatic tour de force as he worked the phones and talked for hours with foreign leaders. And he built support at home by comparing Saddam Hussein to Adolf Hitler and warning that Iraq was developing nuclear weapons. Bush was determined to win any war quickly and forcefully. Consequently, he sent 550,000 troops to the Middle East, more than had fought in Vietnam, while obtaining some troops, air support, and considerable financial help from allied countries. (Japan ultimately contributed $14 billion, Germany $11 billion, and Saudi Arabia and Kuwait $16 billion each.)

On January 17, 1991, with the approval of Congress and the U.N. Security Council, Bush launched Operation Desert Storm. Planes struck Baghdad and B-52 bombers pounded Saddam's army, while naval ships hit targets with Tomahawk cruise missiles. The Iraqi army, already suffering from a recently ended 10-year war with Iran, unraveled, and on February 24, 1991, U.S. ground forces began their assault. They routed the Iraqis, who in their retreat from Kuwait set fire to oil fields. On February 27 Bush proclaimed an end to the war.

For two reasons, the resulting euphoria over the victory proved short-lived. First, in portraying Saddam as another Hitler, President Bush raised expectations that the Iraqi dictator would be driven from power. When this failed to occur, many Americans questioned Bush's fortitude and whether the United States and its coalition partners had really won. Second, congressional investigations revealed that decisions had been made under Bush that opened the door to Saddam's invasion. Until the Iraqi dictator attacked Kuwait, George Bush, as had previous presidents, supported him with military weapons and opposed efforts in Congress to place sanctions on him for having slaughtered Kurdish rebels. While Saddam threatened Kuwait, the American ambassador in Iraq indicated to him that the United States had no great concern over what might happen—in effect giving a diplomatic green light to the invasion.

In July 1991 Bush signed the Strategic Arms Reduction Treaty (START) with Gorbachev. START required the United States and the Soviet Union to reduce their strategic offensive arms by 30 percent over seven years. At the end of the year, though the Soviet Union collapsed, and Gorbachev resigned.

Despite President Bush's many foreign policy exploits, he still lost his bid for reelection. The conservative *National Review* called him "an other-directed man" in a pretentious 10-gallon hat, a leader who lacked vision, "a Connecticut

Yankee in the court of King Ronnie," the magazine said, and then asked: "Does he know what he really believes? Is there a there there?"

As Kuwait burned, Bush fiddled with America's economy, and as it worsened, he offered no plans to reverse its decline. In the 1992 campaign he dusted off his low-road tactics from four years earlier and tried to portray his Democratic opponent, Bill Clinton, as unpatriotic for supposedly making a trip to Moscow while he was a college student at Oxford; and as untrustworthy for having lied about avoiding the draft during the Vietnam War. But the attack failed to resonate, and every time Bush alluded to Clinton's character, he exposed himself to questions about Iran-Contra. By 1992 new evidence from former defense secretary Caspar Weinberger's notes, from Israeli intelligence reports, and from other sources showed that Bush had lied about the scandal, that he had approved the exchange of arms for hostages, and that he was clearly "in the loop" and involved in making important decisions about the deal.

At the same time, some Americans criticized Bush for refusing to use military force in the Balkans against Bosnian Serbs who had launched a war of "ethnic cleansing" on Bosnian Muslims. Bush, though, considered that battle a quagmire and unimportant to American security. In any event, the conflict had little influence on the presidential race. As Clinton's campaign manager said when asked to define the election's central issue: "It's the economy, stupid." With unemployment rising above 7 percent, Americans were unhappy, and on top of that, the man who had said "Read my lips: no new taxes," had approved a deal with Congress that raised them.

Several comments by Bush made him appear out of touch with ordinary Americans; for instance, in response to a reporter's question he was unable to state the price of a gallon of milk. In a three-way race that included independent candidate Ross Perot, Bush finished with the lowest percentage popular vote for an incumbent president since William Howard Taft. In addition, where Ronald Reagan had won 91 percent of the Republican vote in 1984, Bush won just 73 percent.

In December 1992 Bush sent 28,000 troops to Somalia to protect supplies shipped there for famine relief and to prevent armed groups from terrorizing humanitarian workers. On Christmas Eve he pardoned six officials indicted for their roles in Iran-Contra, most notably Caspar Weinberger. The president called his action compassionate and insisted, "Nobody is above the law. I believe when people break the law, that's a bad thing." Others saw his pardons as preventing trials that would reveal the truth—including the truth about him.

In January 1993 George Bush retired to Houston, Texas. Republicans subsequently ignored him for the most part, and in 1996 none of the party's contenders for president sought his endorsement. "I think Desert Storm lifted the morale of our country and healed some of the wounds of Vietnam. I'm sure of it," Bush said after the war. And he welcomed "an era in which the nations of the world, east and west, north and south, can prosper and live in harmony." But the era, if it were to materialize, would be minus his leadership.

Bush provided important advice to his son, George W. Bush, when he ran for the presidency in the year 2000. The elder Bush continued his role as an unofficial adviser to George W. after he entered the White House, although reports circulated that father and son disagreed over the invasion of Iraq, with the elder Bush more dubious about launching the attack. In January 2005, President George W. Bush recruited his father and former president Bill Clinton to raise money for the victims of a tsunami that devastated nations around the Indian Ocean.

CHRONOLOGY

1924 Born June 12

1942 Graduates from Phillips Academy
Joins U.S. Navy

1944 Survives crash of his fighter plane
Receives Distinguished Flying Cross

1945 Marries Barbara Pierce
Enters Yale University

1948 Plays in college baseball national championship series
Graduates from Yale
Begins working at Dresser Industries

1951 Forms Bush-Overby Oil Development Company

1953 Forms Zapata Petroleum

1959 Founds Zapata Offshore Headquarters in Houston, Texas

1960 Elected Harris County Republican chairman

1964 Loses U.S. Senate race

1966 Elected to U.S. House of Representatives

1968 Reelected to Congress

1970 Loses U.S. Senate race
Appointed U.S. representative to the United Nations

1973 Appointed chairman of Republican National Committee

1974 Recommends President Nixon resign
Arrives in Peking as chief of U.S. Liaison Office in China

1975 Appointed head of Central Intelligence Agency

1976 Resigns from CIA and returns to Texas

1980 Loses race for Republican presidential nomination
Chosen to run for vice president

1981 Begins vice presidency

1986 Denies participation in Iran-Contra scandal

1988 Elected president

1989 Imposes sanctions on China
Sends troops into Panama

1990 Promotes embargo of Iraq
Forms coalition against Iraq

1991 Launches Operation Desert Storm
Liberates Kuwait
Signs Strategic Arms Reduction Treaty with Soviet Union

1992 Loses reelection
Sends troops to Somalia
Pardons Iran-Contra figures

1993 Retires to Houston, Texas

2001 Attends presidential inauguration of his son George W. Bush

2001 Attends second presidential inauguration of his son George W. Bush

2005 Helps raise money for tsunami relief effort
Attends funeral of Pope John Paul II

Further Reading

Barilleaux, Ryan J. *Power and Prudence: The Presidency of George H. W. Bush.* College Station: Texas A&M University Press, 2004.

Beschloss, Michael R., and Strobe Talbott. *At the Highest Levels: The Inside Story of the End of the Cold War.* Boston: Little, Brown, 1993.

Feldman, Leslie D., and Rosanna Perotti, eds., *Honor and Loyalty: Inside the Politics of the George H. W. Bush White House.* Westport, Conn.: Greenwood Press, 2002.

Freedman, Lawrence, and Efraim Karsh. *The Gulf Conflict, 1990–1991: Diplomacy and War in the New World Order.* Princeton, N.J.: Princeton University Press, 1993.

Gordon, Michael R., and Bernard E. Trainor. *The General's War: The Inside Story of the Conflict in the Gulf.* Boston: Little, Brown, 1995.

Green, Fitzhugh. *George Bush: An Intimate Portrait.* New York: Hippocrene Books, 1989.

Jentleson, Bruce W. *With Friends Like These: Reagan, Bush, and Saddam, 1982–1990.* New York: W. W. Norton, 1994.

Kolb, Charles. *White House Daze: The Unmaking of Domestic Policy in the Bush Years.* New York: Free Press, 1994.

Phillips, Kevin P. *American Dynasty: Aristocracy, Fortune, and the Politics of Deceit in the House of Bush.* New York: Viking, 2004.

Tiefer, Charles. *The Semi-Sovereign Presidency: The Bush Administration's Strategy for Governing Without Congress.* Boulder, Colo.: Westview Press, 1994.

Unger, Craig. *House of Bush, House of Saud: The Secret Relationship Between the World's Two Most Powerful Dynasties.* New York: Scribner, 2004.

Wicker, Tom. *George Herbert Walker Bush.* New York: Lipper/Viking, 2004.

William Jefferson Clinton (1946–)

Forty-second President, 1993–2001

William Jefferson Clinton
(The White House)

"There is nothing wrong with America that cannot be cured by what is right about America. And so today we pledge an end to deadlock and drift, and a new season of American renewal has begun."
—Inaugural words, first term, January 20, 1993

When the Boys Nation buses arrived at the White House on July 24, 1963, the group on board, sponsored by the American Legion, included a 16-year-old Arkansan, Bill Clinton. Like the other boys, he had come to meet President John F. Kennedy. The president greeted his guests in the Rose Garden, and as he smiled and a gentle breeze tousled his hair, he told them about the hallowed ground on which they stood. "These trees which are just behind you were planted by Andrew Jackson when he was here in the White House," Kennedy said. "The tallest tree over there was planted by the first president who came to the White House, John Adams."

What feelings gripped Bill Clinton at that moment? Did patriotism overwhelm him when the president said, "I think all of us have a pride in our country"? Did ideals encourage him when Kennedy said the United States "stands guard all the way from Berlin to Saigon" in protecting freedom? Most likely they did, for Clinton believed in America's greatness.

Beyond that, he believed in himself and was convinced he would one day be president of the United States. After Kennedy finished his remarks, Clinton pushed to the front of the group as the boys angled to be near the president. He made sure the photographers standing nearby would capture him and Kennedy together. They did, and while the picture was later held up as a symbol of spontaneity and fate, it more accurately reflected the shrewd maneuvering, hard work, and determined planning that marked Clinton's political career.

Bill Clinton was born William Jefferson Blythe IV on August 19, 1946, in Hope, Arkansas, a small farming town near where the borders of Arkansas, Louisiana, and Texas converge. A few months before Bill's birth, his father, William Jefferson Blythe III, a traveling salesman, was killed in an automobile accident, leaving the boy to be raised by his mother, Virginia Dell Cassidy Blythe, then 23 years old, and by his maternal grandparents, Edith and Eldridge Cassidy.

When Bill was four years old, his mother married Roger Clinton, a car dealer. Three years later, in 1953, the family moved to Hot Springs, Arkansas. Years later, when he was running for president, Bill invoked images of Hope as his hometown, but he actually spent most of his youth and experienced his strongest childhood influences in Hot Springs, a wide-open city, at least for Arkansas, with its gambling and nightlife. The marriage of Virginia and Roger was tempestuous and stressful. Roger drank heavily and abused his wife verbally and physically. To escape this environment, at age eight Bill began attending the Park Place Baptist Church, arriving there every Sunday on his own, dressed in his best clothes.

His parents separated several times as their battles continued. The couple eventually divorced, but in 1962 they remarried. Roger Clinton then sat around the house drinking, while the family's life revolved around Bill, a bright youngster who Virginia believed was destined for greatness. Despite all of Bill's problems with his stepfather, in May 1962 he officially changed his last name from Blythe to Clinton for the sake, he later said, of "family solidarity."

Bill Clinton excelled at Hot Springs High, a school known for its demanding teachers and excellent facilities. He was a band major and junior class president, and he spoke frequently to community groups about his experiences with Boys Nation. His picture appeared more than 30 times in the high school yearbook, including the photo of him shaking hands with John Kennedy. He graduated in 1964 as a National Merit Scholarship semifinalist, ranked fourth in a senior class of 363 students.

Clinton applied to only one college: Georgetown University in Washington, D.C., which he wanted to attend so he could enroll in the School of Foreign Service and be at the country's political center. As an Arkansan at a college dominated by Easterners, he was an oddity; yet he quickly impressed his fellow students and professors with his intellect and friendliness. He entered Georgetown politicking from the start and won election as freshman class president.

Two years later Clinton began clerking for Arkansas senator J. William Fulbright and expressed his enthusiasm for the political world in a letter to his grandmother that provided a roll call of famous names: "It is of course exciting to be here around all the senators," he said, "and already this year I've seen the president, vice president, and senators Fulbright, Robert and Edward Kennedy, Javits, Long of Louisiana, Smathers of Florida, Yarborough of Texas, Anderson of New Mexico, McClellan, Thurmond of South Carolina, Church of

Idaho, Williams of New Jersey, Boggs of Delaware, McCarthy of Minnesota, Murphy of California, Stennis of Mississippi, and others."

At first a moderate supporter of the Vietnam War, Clinton began to change his views as he worked with Fulbright and his staff, who by 1966 were calling the American involvement a mistake. The following year he ran for student council president at Georgetown but lost when his opponent appealed to those discontent with the college's paternalistic administrators.

Clinton graduated from Georgetown in 1968 with a bachelor's degree in international studies and entered the graduate program at England's Oxford University as a Rhodes scholar. Like many other American college students during the Vietnam War, he was preoccupied with the draft, and his peculiar reaction to it has, over the years, provided fodder for his political opponents who continue to see duplicity and opportunism in his actions. Clinton received his draft notice in May 1969 and soon after joined an ROTC unit connected with the University of Arkansas Law School. He was to report there in the fall of 1969, a move that would allow him to study law while avoiding service in Vietnam, but when fall came, he returned to Oxford. He later said he had the permission of his ROTC commander to do so, but no record of an agreement exists, and letters written by Clinton to his friends at the time contradict his story.

In any event, in early October Clinton told his draft board to end his deferment. He later said he made the request because the deaths of friends in Vietnam made him uncomfortable about avoiding the war. Yet he could have requested the change earlier—in fact, he drafted a letter in mid-September to that effect but never sent it—or he could have enlisted.

Clinton's actions bespoke a person who wanted to avoid the draft but ultimately appear as if he had not avoided it—a coy move for someone looking to protect his reputation as he advanced his political prospects. Evidence indicates that he asked for an end to his deferment only after he realized that recent developments made it unlikely he would ever be drafted. The conscription law had just been changed to give graduate students a longer time to report to duty, and President Richard Nixon had stated that draft calls would be lowered as American troops gradually withdrew from Vietnam. In addition, Nixon announced the beginning of a draft lottery, and when the first one was held in December 1969, Bill Clinton received a high number that immunized him from induction.

According to Clinton biographer David Maraniss, by avoiding military service the Arkansan "did what 16 million other young American men did during that tumultuous era." In December 1969 Clinton wrote a lengthy letter to the colonel of the University of Arkansas ROTC explaining why he had chosen to remain at Oxford. At the time, military officials thought the letter exposed Clinton as a draft dodger, and later it came back to haunt him. Clinton said that in spite of his beliefs, he "decided to accept the draft" rather than become a resister, "for one reason: to maintain my political viability within the system."

It was a system that Clinton by and large supported. True, he opposed the war and in October 1969 briefly joined the activist cause when he helped organize an antiwar protest in London, but he stayed close to his moderate roots and rejected those who advocated radical change.

Anxious to develop his political career, Clinton left Oxford without a degree and in the fall of 1970 he enrolled at Yale Law School. He spent little time in class and instead politicked for Joseph D. Duffey, a Connecticut Democrat running for Congress on a peace and civil rights platform. Clinton gained a reputation for his boundless energy, his need for little sleep, and his incessant desire to talk. To several of his friends, Clinton lacked sincerity. One said, "You could never view his performance in a totally positive way. You wondered, is it real? There were moments that were so genuine that there was no doubt about it, and moments when you wondered—is this posture?"

In spring 1971 Clinton met Hillary Rodham, a second-year law student at Yale, and in 1972 both of them went to Texas, where they worked in Democrat George McGovern's presidential campaign. After graduating from Yale with his law degree in 1973, Clinton joined the faculty at the University of Arkansas School of Law at Fayetteville. The following year he sought public office for the first time when he ran for Congress as a Democrat from the Third Congressional District. Although he lost to the Republican incumbent, John Paul Hammerschmidt, he impressed fellow politicians by capturing 48 percent of the vote. In 1975 he married Hillary Rodham, who, in step with the feminist spirit then sweeping the country, kept her last name. In 1976 Clinton showed his statewide appeal when he won election as Arkansas attorney general.

Two years later Bill Clinton garnered 63 percent of the vote to become the youngest governor in the United States. But many voters soon regretted their choice after he and his staff mishandled several problems. His troubles began when he failed to keep two campaign promises: that he would submit a completed budget for the legislature on its opening day, and that he would have all of his bills drafted by then. When he finally presented his proposals, legislators scoffed at their complexity and large number.

Adding to his problems, Clinton mishandled a road improvement program. He hit on the project after an adviser, Dick Morris—a political hired gun who often worked for conservative Republicans—surveyed Arkansans and asked them what they considered to be the state's most important issue. They said "road improvements" and intimated they would be willing to pay higher car license fees to pay for them. Consequently, Clinton proposed increased rates on trucks and automobiles. Then when the trucking companies complained, he shifted the burden for the new fees to cars. At the same time he based the rates on vehicle weight—a move that upset Arkansans who drove older, heavier cars—and he hiked the tax on gasoline.

Angered by these tax increases, the voters turned against Clinton. His standing was further damaged when Cuban refugees at a resettlement camp at Fort Chaffee rioted. Clinton regained some of his support, however, by telling President Jimmy Carter, futilely as it turned out, that he would defy the federal government in refusing to accept additional refugees even if Washington brought "the whole United States Army down here."

In 1980 Bill Clinton's opponent for the governorship, Republican Frank White, attacked him for raising taxes and linked him to Carter's unpopular presidency. Voters responded to Clinton's travails and to his attempts to be all things to all people by electing White. A shattered and disheartened Clinton joined the law firm of Wright, Lindsey, and Jennings in Little Rock. But he had already begun planning his comeback, determined to regain the governor's mansion and with it the experience and background needed to eventually win the White House. Hillary Rodham directed his renewal, and she answered the unease Arkansans had with her feminist attitude by officially changing her last name to Clinton. With Dick Morris as his main adviser, Bill Clinton launched a negative campaign against White in 1982 and regained the governor's office.

This time around he recruited somewhat older and more experienced staff members and adopted education as his main issue. He appointed Hillary Clinton as chair of the Education Standards Committee, and the reforms it proposed, along with the taxes to support them, passed the legislature in the fall of 1983. In their wake, student test scores increased, as did the number of graduating seniors who enrolled in college. To appease conservatives, Clinton required that teachers take competency tests.

Along with the education reforms, Bill Clinton appealed to African Americans when he named the first black lawyer to the state supreme court and appointed more blacks to state boards and commissions than all previous

Arkansas governors combined. But he failed to push for a civil rights law, leaving his state as one of only two without such legislation. His reformist credentials also suffered in other ways: To appease business he loosened environmental enforcement and gave tax breaks to corporations, and to fund his education program he relied on the regressive sales tax. In fact, support for schools from the property tax remained so low that Arkansas still stood near the bottom among states in school funding.

Clinton won reelection as the "education governor" in 1984 when the gubernatorial term was increased from two to four years, and he won another term in 1988. While serving as governor he chaired the Education Commission of the States, the Democratic Governors' Association, the National Governors' Association and the Democratic Leadership Council, a group of moderates who wanted to make the Democratic Party more attractive to mainstream voters. He considered running for president in 1988 but instead gave the nominating speech for Governor Michael S. Dukakis of Massachusetts—a speech widely panned as long-winded.

He entered the Democratic presidential primaries in 1992, a year when dissatisfied voters criticized the incumbent, Republican George Bush, for ignoring domestic issues while the economy crumbled. Clinton finished second in the New Hampshire primary despite allegations he had carried on an affair with Gennifer Flowers, a nightclub singer. Although he denied the relationship, he went on the TV show *60 Minutes* with his wife and admitted he had caused "pain" in his marriage. This tactic worked, and he would use it again during his presidency. Clinton went on to win the Democratic nomination despite lingering doubts about his character.

During the general campaign, President Bush scored some points when he attacked Clinton for lying about how he had avoided military service in Vietnam. Clinton's tortured response, in which he denied ever having received a draft notice, encouraged use of the disparaging nickname "Slick Willie," given to him by his opponents. Writing in *On the Edge*, political analyst Elizabeth Drew says that "Slick Willie" derived from Clinton's abnormally strong desire to be liked and that this, in turn, "was a large factor behind his wanting to please everyone. 'Slick Willie' came from something deep inside him. When one of Clinton's closest advisers was asked why the Arkansan didn't talk about core principles more seriously, he replied, 'Because he wants to be all things to all people.'"

Clinton won the presidency, but with only 43 percent of the popular vote, compared to 38 percent for Bush and 19 percent for third-party candidate Ross Perot. Nonetheless, *Time* magazine said the election "places [Clinton] in a position to preside over one of the periodic reinventions of the country—those moments when Americans dig themselves out of their deepest problems by reimagining themselves." He came into the White House as one of the country's brightest presidents, supremely articulate and able to quickly grasp details and complexities, but also crafty and expedient—qualities that gave him the potential for great achievements and damaging self-destruction.

In one important way Clinton's presidency would differ from all others: The first lady would wield considerable power for an extended period. The evidence for this appeared early, when Hillary Clinton decided she would have an office in the West Wing, where the president and his top aides worked. And when Bill Clinton interviewed prospective cabinet members, she interviewed them too.

As with Bill Clinton's first entry into the governor's mansion, troubles at the White House beset him from the start. The first problem arose when he nominated Zoe Baird, counsel for Aetna Life and Casualty, as attorney general, even though she had violated the law in 1990 and hired illegal immigrants to work in her household. Forced to withdraw the nomination just two days into his presidency, Clinton looked inept. In April 1993, he nominated Lani Guinier to serve as assistant attorney general for civil rights. A lawyer for the

NAACP Legal Defense and Education Fund, Guinier had written academic articles in which she advocated that racial minorities should have veto power in legislatures. Conservatives damned her ideas as undemocratic and launched a withering attack against her. President Clinton failed to either end his support for her early or stand behind her, an indecisiveness that angered civil rights groups who rallied to Guinier's cause only to have Clinton eventually withdraw the nomination.

With the issue of the economy pressing down on him, Clinton allowed his presidency to be sidetracked by the controversy over whether to end the existing ban against gays in the military. The president let the matter fester for weeks before finally deciding in July 1993 on a "Don't ask, don't tell" policy, whereby gays would not be discriminated against provided they kept their homosexuality secret. It was a decision meant to please everyone that, in fact, pleased no one.

As medical costs mounted and 40 million Americans remained uncovered by any health care plan, and as opinion polls showed the public wanted something done about the problem, Clinton put together a task force to propose reforms. He realized that an effective plan would likely rally the middle class behind him and the Democratic Party. Republicans decided they could not let that happen, and they determined to oppose any "big government" health plan.

In putting together the task force, Bill Clinton made the first lady its leader. This proved to be a costly mistake as she and some 600 experts worked in secret, shutting out members of Congress and the cabinet in a move that raised suspicions about diabolical scheming. When the much-delayed proposal turned out to be over 1,300 pages long, its complexity stunned and confused both Congress and the public and lent itself to charges that it promised a more intrusive government. The country's four largest insurance companies, however, liked the plan, having helped the task force compile it.

Clinton's secretary of health and human services, Donna Shalala, admitted that the plan could raise rates for 40 percent of insured Americans. Those words and the other complications doomed the proposal and with it any hope for substantial health care reform. Clinton admitted his role in the defeat when he said, "We made the error of trying to do too much, took too long, and ended up achieving nothing."

While that failure unfolded, stories circulated about President Clinton's sexual promiscuity, along with charges that he and his wife had used state agencies in Arkansas and exerted their influence with a savings and loan bank to protect their investment in a land deal called Whitewater. More controversy ensued with the death in July 1993 of Clinton's consul, Vincent Foster. Although Foster killed himself, right-wing rumors asserted that he had been murdered as part of a Clintonian plot to cover-up Whitewater.

President Clinton managed to direct three important measures through the Democratic Congress, but in so doing he compromised considerably. First, in putting together an economic package, he dropped his campaign pledge of a middle-class tax cut. Added to that, Congress rejected his plan to boost spending on social programs, along with his proposal to raise money through an energy tax. Instead, the Senate passed an increase in the federal gasoline tax and set corporate taxes at less than half of what Clinton wanted. While the economic package cut social spending, it did increase taxes for the wealthy and gave the working poor the largest earned-income tax credit in history. Together, the tax hikes and program cuts reduced the deficit, and the economic growth that had begun before Clinton entered the White House accelerated, while inflation remained moderate and mortgage rates dropped.

In a second measure, Clinton won congressional approval for the North American Free Trade Agreement (NAFTA), which had been negotiated under President Bush. NAFTA liberalized trade among the United States, Mexico, and Canada, in line with Clinton's belief that lowered barriers would stimulate economic growth and bolster democratic government. NAFTA took effect on January 1, 1994.

Clinton's third measure, a crime bill, provided more than $30 billion for hiring police officers and building more prisons. The bill banned the sale of 19 types of assault weapons, required that sex offenders notify authorities of their whereabouts for at least 10 years after their release from jail, and extended the death penalty to more than 50 crimes.

President Clinton suffered a bitter defeat in the November 1994 elections when the Republicans gained 11 governorships, nine seats in the Senate, and 52 seats in the House, which shifted ideologically to the right. The GOP won votes by criticizing the president's approach toward health care and by promising a smaller government, lower taxes, and a balanced budget. At the same time, an investigation of Whitewater damaged Clinton by raising doubts about his credibility, especially after it was revealed that Webster L. Hubbell, third in command in the justice department and a close Clinton friend, had years earlier defrauded his clients at a law firm in Arkansas. (Hubbell was convicted and imprisoned for the crime in 1995.)

Nonetheless, after the 1994 elections Clinton launched one of his notable political comebacks. He hired Dick Morris as a consultant, and before long he was following Morris's advice that he appeal more strongly to the mainstream. Morris advocated what he called "triangulation," meaning Clinton should stand at the political center between the liberals of his own party and the escalating conservatism of the Republicans as a voice of moderation. He wanted Clinton to defuse the Republicans by advocating a middle-class tax cut and a balanced budget, along with other measures that would leave liberal Democrats little to claim except that they blocked the right-wing juggernaut.

Fortunately for Clinton, the Republicans, their heads swelled by their election triumph, alienated themselves from most Americans by pursuing a strident agenda under House Speaker Newt Gingrich that proposed too much too quickly (formerly Clinton's failing). When they attacked Medicare by calling for it to be reduced by $270 billion over five years, and when they sought a tax cut for the wealthy roughly equivalent to that amount, they allowed Clinton and the Democrats to portray them as taking from the elderly to fill the wallets of the rich. In November and again in December 1995, House Republicans shut down the federal government in an attempt to force the president to accept their budget, but this action only made them appear excessive and Clinton all the more reasonable.

As the 1996 presidential election neared, Clinton triangulated himself into accepting a welfare reform bill so at odds with the Democratic Party's past policies that several members of his own administration strenuously objected to it. Later, his secretary of labor, Robert Reich, described what had happened:

> The original idea had been to smooth the passage from welfare to work with guaranteed health care, child care, job training and a job paying enough to live on. The [August] 1996 legislation contained none of these supports—no health care or child care for people coming off welfare, no job training, no assurance of a job paying a living wage, not, for that matter, of a job at any wage. In effect, what was dubbed welfare "reform" merely ended the promise of help to the indigent and their children which Franklin D. Roosevelt had initiated. . . ."

Indeed, the bill terminated more than 60 years of guaranteed federal assistance to the needy and provided the states with block grants to develop their own welfare programs. Under no circumstances, however, could the states provide families with benefits for more than five years or provide block grant monies to persons convicted of drug-related felonies. Nonworking adults were required to find jobs within two years. By 1999 the number of people receiving welfare had dropped to 7.6 million, the lowest in 30 years, and by the year 2000 there was a drop in the number of children living in poverty, though it remained well above that for the 1970s. Much of the decline in the welfare rolls, though, resulted from economic growth, and how well the reform would work in times of decline remained to be seen.

Clinton was more interested in domestic than foreign policy, but as the first post–cold war president he linked the two together with his goal of "democratic enlargement." He believed that developing market economies overseas would lessen political oppression and make foreign countries pliable to American economic might (a vision parallel to President William Howard Taft's Dollar Diplomacy). President Clinton said to Congress in 1994, "We have put our economic competitiveness at the heart of our foreign policy." Toward that end, global free trade became imperative. In 1993 he convinced 15 Asian countries to promise they would develop a free-trade zone by the year 2010. The following year he signed a trade agreement that lowered tariffs worldwide by over $700 billion.

With the collapse of the Soviet Union, the dismantling of nuclear stockpiles assumed critical importance. In 1994 the United States–Russian–Ukraine Trilateral Statement and Annex resulted in the dismantling of all atomic weapons in Ukraine. That same year Clinton sent 20,000 American troops to Haiti as part of a multinational force to replace its military regime with a democratic government. The force withdrew in March 1995 after elections were held, and Clinton declared the mission a success. In Europe he helped craft the Dayton Accords, leading to an agreement among Serbs, Croatians, and Bosnians to end their fighting in the Balkans. Troops led by the North Atlantic Treaty Organization (NATO) enforced the agreement.

In the 1996 presidential election, Bill Clinton portrayed his Republican opponent, Kansas senator Robert Dole, as a tool of the unpopular House Speaker, Newt Gingrich. Clinton pointed to his own work in reducing the deficit, fighting crime, and reforming welfare as bringing significant results and appealing to the moderate course most voters preferred. He amassed a huge campaign war chest as money rolled in from influential Americans. But critics derided his sales plan of letting wealthy donors sleep in the Lincoln bedroom in exchange for their contributions, and they balked when he personally solicited money at 44 "coffee" meetings at the White House. In the end, Clinton convincingly beat Dole and third-party candidate Ross Perot, though again with less than 50 percent of the popular vote.

After Bill Clinton was inaugurated in January 1997, he testified in a sexual harassment lawsuit filed against him by Paula Corbin Jones, a former secretary in the Arkansas state government. As Jones's lawyers questioned him about his past behavior toward women (Clinton's own crime bill permitted a defendant in a sexual harassment lawsuit to be asked such questions), he denied he had ever had sexual relations with a White House intern, Monica Lewinsky. Clinton said he saw her on five occasions and might have been alone with her once. Then in January 1998 Linda Tripp, a Lewinsky confidant, turned over tape recordings to special prosecutor Kenneth Starr in which Lewinsky discussed her sexual affair with Clinton—one that had begun in November 1995. After the content of the Tripp tapes appeared in the press, scandal again rocked the Clinton White House.

President Clinton assured his cabinet he had never engaged in sexual relations with Lewinsky and that she was exaggerating and lying. When doubts about his story continued, he told the American people, "I want you to listen to me. I did not have sexual relations with that woman, Miss Lewinsky." Evidence gathered by Starr indicated otherwise, and in an unprecedented event, Clinton was forced to testify before a grand jury, where he insisted that he had answered the questions at the Jones deposition truthfully.

By late 1998 Starr had compiled considerable evidence to show that the president had lied when testifying in the Jones suit, a civil case, and again when testifying to the grand jury, a criminal proceeding. Other evidence indicated that Clinton had coached his secretary, Betty Currie, to answer questions in a way that would mislead prosecutors; that he may have encouraged Lewinsky to file a false affidavit in the Jones case (she denied this while admitting that Clinton suggested "if she were subpoenaed, she should file an affidavit to avoid being deposed"); and that he may have used his political influence to obtain a job for Lewinsky as a way to keep her quiet. Starr's written report contained so much lurid evidence about the sexual dalliances between Clinton and Lewinsky in the Oval Office area—details used to prove the president's lie—that it pulled the public's attention away from the crime of perjury to the question of whether Starr had invaded Clinton's privacy.

As the November 1998 congressional elections neared, most Americans condemned Clinton for his actions but objected to his removal from office. When Republicans lost seats in the House and saw their majority in it cut to six, Clinton felt confident he would avoid impeachment.

He seemed to be right as the election results forced Newt Gingrich from the Speakership and left the Republicans in disarray. But Clinton treated impeachment queries from the House so arrogantly that he even angered moderate congressmen. Then, as the House neared a vote on impeachment, he ordered an air attack on Iraq for having prevented arms inspectors from entering that country. While Clinton called the bombardment necessary to protect American security, others questioned the timing and suspected he had used it to divert attention from the Lewinsky scandal and rally Congress and the public behind him.

Whatever the case, in December 1998 the House impeached Clinton for lying under oath to the grand jury and for obstructing justice. The majority counsel for the House Judiciary Committee, David Schippers, said,

> The President . . . has lied under oath in a civil deposition, lied under oath in a criminal grand jury. He lied to the people, he lied to his Cabinet, he lied to his top aides, and now he's lied under oath to the Congress of the United States. *There's no one left to lie to.*"

On the eve of the impeachment vote, Clinton's counsel, Charles Ruff, stopped just short of saying the president had perjured himself. Ruff said Clinton had offered misleading testimony, but the president "believed that what he was doing was being evasive but truthful." Neither this statement nor Clinton's apology, in which he refused to admit he had broken the law, saved him from becoming only the second president ever to be impeached—"a big, permanent stain on his record," said one Clinton adviser.

Newsweek political analyst Jonathan Alter expressed the opinion of many Americans during the impeachment proceedings when he criticized both Clinton and Congress. "Clinton's squalid behavior helped strip his office of much of its grandeur," he said, and continued: "The House of Representatives has taken the solemn, even inspirational bipartisan process of 1974 [during the Richard Nixon impeachment hearings] and turned it into just another blunt political instrument."

According to the Constitution, an officeholder impeached by the House stands trial in the Senate. Conviction by two-thirds vote of all the senators results in removal from office. Consequently, Clinton's case was presented to the Senate, with Chief Justice William H. Rehnquist presiding. For 37 days the senators listened to testimony and read transcripts. "Is respondent William Jefferson Clinton guilty or not guilty?" By a vote of 55-45 they rejected a charge of perjury against the president. Then they split 50-50 on a second charge that accused Clinton of obstruction of justice. This tally was far short of the 67 votes needed to remove him from office.

A large number of Americans had opposed Clinton's impeachment. But after his acquittal, public opinion shifted, and a *USA Today*/CNN/Gallup Poll late in 1999 showed that fully half of all Americans believed that it was right that Clinton was impeached. Another poll by Gallup showed that most Americans—an overwhelming 71 percent—would best remember Clinton for the scandal, while an ABC/*Washington Post* poll revealed that they were "just plain tired of Bill Clinton."

Soon after his acquittal, Clinton displayed his resolve in a showdown with Serbian president Slobodan Milosevic. After Milosevic acted to crush an uprising in his country's province of Kosovo by using troops to kill some ethnic Albanians and force many more of them from their homes, Clinton and NATO demanded that Serbian troops withdraw. When Milosevic refused, NATO planes, led by the United States, bombed Serbian military and civilian targets for 78 days, beginning in March 1999. The attacks forced Milosevic to withdraw his army and accept NATO troops into the province along with NATO governance, though he convinced the United Nations Security Council to confirm Serbia's sovereignty over Kosovo.

In October 1999 the U.S. Senate handed Clinton a stinging political defeat when it refused to ratify the Comprehensive Test Ban Treaty which would forbid all underground nuclear weapons tests. Opponents called the treaty "unverifiable and unenforceable." The defeat marked the first time the Senate had rejected an international treaty since it voted down the Treaty of Versailles in 1920, following World War I. Around the same time, the president and Congress struggled over how to distribute a budget surplus, with Clinton wanting more money to fund programs for the elderly and Republicans on Capitol Hill wanting tax cuts.

Despite Clinton's victory in the Senate, his scandal woes continued. In spring 1999 Juanita Broaddrick offered credible, if ultimately unprovable, evidence that in the 1970s Clinton, while governor, had raped her. Then the judge in the Paula Corbin Jones case held the president in contempt of court and referred his perjury to a committee to decide whether he should be disbarred. In August 2000 independent counsel Robert Ray (who had succeeded Kenneth Starr) impaneled a grand jury to consider whether the events surrounding the Lewinsky scandal should necessitate indicting Clinton for criminal conduct after leaving the White House in January 2001.

As for Whitewater, the investigation finally ended in September 2000, with Ray concluding he did not have the evidence to indict either Bill Clinton or First Lady Hillary Rodham Clinton for criminal misconduct. Writing in the *New York Times*, James B. Stewart said that the Whitewater investigation was "preposterous" for the way it digressed from its original assignment, the way it took so long, and the way it cost so much money—nearly $60 million. He said, "From very early on, it should have been apparent that the criminal case could never be made against the Clintons. Who would testify against them?"

As Clinton prepared to leave the White House in January 2001, he seemed intent on restoring respectability to his presidency through accomplishments in foreign policy. He tried to broker a new Mideast peace accord between Palestinians and Israelis, but that effort failed. Instead he found himself scrambling to arrange a cease-fire after the violence on West Bank and in the Gaza Strip threatened to ignite a war between several Arab countries and Israel. In November 2000 Clinton became the first American president to travel to Vietnam since the U.S. war with that country ended in the mid-1970s. He was trying to help revive normal relations with Hanoi, and he promised to assist the Vietnamese in their effort to counter the effects of Agent Orange, a defoliant used in combat by the U.S. military. The chemical has harmed more than a million people and has caused many birth defects. Some commentators though it hypocritical for Clinton to travel to Vietnam and honor American war dead, as he did in the one ceremony at a rice paddy, when as a young man he had dodged the draft.

On the domestic scene, Clinton took bold steps to leave his mark as an environmental president. Among his final accomplishments, he banned road building and commercial logging on about 60 million acres of public forestland. In late 2000, the Wilderness Society declared Clinton "one of the top conservation presidents of all time."

President Clinton hoped that voters would express their approval of his presidency by electing Vice President Al Gore to the White House in November 2000 and by placing the Democrats in control of Congress. To Clinton's disappointment, although Gore finished ahead of Republican George W. Bush in the popular vote, he did so narrowly and lost the electoral count to his opponent; in Congress, the Democrats managed to win enough seats to reach a 50-50 tie in the Senate, but Republicans retained their razor-thin control of the House. Clinton publicly voiced his belief that Al Gore had really won the election and that political maneuvering in Florida by Gore's opponent, Republican George W. Bush, had caused the vice president to lose.

As much as controversy dogged Clinton during his presidency, it continued to do so in the days immediately after his departure. This time it stemmed from the 140 pardons that he granted during his final hours in the White House. Although presidents have an absolute constitutional right to grant pardons, several of those approved by Clinton raised suspicions that they came in exchange for contributions to his presidential library or to Hillary Clinton's campaign for the U.S. Senate.

At the center of attention was the pardon granted to Marc Rich, a fugitive billionaire who fled to Europe after his indictment on charges of tax evasion, fraud, and racketeering. Clinton defended this and his other pardons as "based on the merits," but critics pointed to the more than $400,000 donated by Rich's ex-wife, Denise Rich, to the Clinton library foundation. Added to this, newspapers revealed in late February 2001 that Hugh Rodham, the brother of Hillary Clinton, had received $400,000 in fees for successfully lobbying for a pardon and a prison commutation for two wealthy felons, one a businessman convicted of mail fraud and perjury, the other a cocaine trafficker. (After the controversy surfaced, Rodham returned the money.)

The opprobrium that descended on Clinton for his pardons was bipartisan and widespread. Former Democratic president Jimmy Carter called the Rich pardon "disgraceful," and Hamilton Jordan, Carter's chief aide in the White House, charged that Clinton "saw the pardon power as just another perk of the office." The *New York Times*, which had in the past largely supported Clinton, held nothing back in its editorial criticism. The last-minute pardon of Marc Rich, the paper said, "was a shocking abuse of presidential power and a reminder of why George W. Bush's vow to a restore integrity to the Oval Office resonates with millions of Americans. . . ." Reflecting back on Clinton's presidency, the paper said that he "constantly forced the nation to an unappetizing choice between investigations and the even more unsatisfactory route of ignoring outrageous and perhaps illegal conduct. . . . He throws our political and legal systems into arrest because he constantly comes up with ways of skirting the law or misrepresenting the facts that would never have occurred to anyone else in his position."

Both the House and the Senate began investigating the pardons (though without much enthusiasm, due in part to the fatigue over probing Clinton), and the U.S. attorney for New York launched a criminal investigation to determine if Denise Rich had used any of her former husband's money in backing the presidential library as a means to influence Clinton.

Yet in the broader context of the American presidency, other chief executives issued controversial pardons, none more so than Gerald Ford's pardon of Richard Nixon following the Watergate scandal and George Bush's pardon of Caspar Weinberger following the Iran-Contra scandal. Clinton's pardons, then, while reflecting a personal fault, may also have reflected a general trend by recent presidents to abuse the process.

In June 2004, Bill Clinton published his massive memoir, *My Life*, which traced his life from boyhood to his tumultuous years in the White House. "Early on the morning of August 19, 1946," he began, "I was born under a clear sky after a violent summer storm to a widowed mother in the Julia Chester Hospital in Hope, a town of about six thousand in southwest Arkansas, thirty-three miles east of the Texas border at Texarkana." Some reviewers found the book to be as windy as his political speeches; others called it "candid," "soul-searching," and "enlightening." Author Larry McMurtry called it "the richest American presidential autobiography." In a review he wrote: "No other book tells us as vividly or fully what it is like to be president of the United States for eight years." More than 3 million copies of the memoir were sold within the first eight days of its publication.

Clinton spoke at the Democratic National Convention in Boston in July to promote the presidential candidacy of John Kerry. For more than 30 minutes he held his audience spellbound. He criticized President George W. Bush for tax policies that favored the rich and for attacking Kerry as weak on terrorism. "Don't you believe it," he said in defense of Kerry. "Strength and wisdom are not opposing values." The Kerry campaign displayed no reluctance about gaining the controversial former president's backing; indeed, it was elated by Clinton's support, and that of Clinton's wife, Senator Hilary Clinton. "We welcome them in the race," said a Kerry spokesperson.

Bill Clinton's efforts for Kerry were hindered, however, by a serious illness. In late summer, he underwent quadruple bypass surgery. Gaunt and exhausted, he nevertheless hit the campaign trail in October.

In November, he attended the ceremony dedicating the Clinton Presidential Library in Little Rock, Arkansas. The following January, President George W. Bush asked him to join former President George H. W. Bush in leading a relief effort to raise money for the victims of a tsunami wave that brought massive destruction to several nations around the Indian Ocean.

Many political observers believe that Bill Clinton came into the White House with great promise but that he departed it with nothing better than modest accomplishments. His albatross turned out to be two developments of his own making: his desire to be well liked, which meant steering clear of risks that might have created a stellar record, and his refusal to admit responsibility for failure—a preference for deceit over forthrightness. On this last characteristic, his scandals thrived, leaving the imprint of impeachment that will forever detract from his legacy.

Chronology

1946 Born August 19

1953 Moves to Hot Springs, Arkansas

1962 Officially changes last name to Clinton

1964 Graduates from Hot Springs High School
Enters Georgetown University

1966 Clerks for Arkansas senator J. William Fulbright

1968 Graduates from Georgetown University
Enters Oxford University as a Rhodes scholar

1969 Maneuvers to avoid military draft

1970 Enters Yale University Law School

1972 Campaigns in Texas for Democratic presidential nominee George S. McGovern

1973 Receives law degree
Begins teaching at University of Arkansas Law School

1974 Loses election for U.S. House of Representatives

1975 Marries Hillary Rodham

1976 Elected Arkansas attorney general

1978 Elected governor of Arkansas

1980 Loses reelection campaign for governor

1982 Elected governor of Arkansas

1983 Gets education program passed by Arkansas legislature

1984 Reelected governor

1986 Chairs National Governors Association

1988 Presents presidential nominating speech at Democratic National Convention

Reelected governor

1992 Elected president

1993 Rescinds nomination for attorney general

Signs family leave bill

Establishes "Don't ask, don't tell" policy for gays in the military

Fails to get health care plan adopted

Embroiled in Whitewater investigation

Gets Congress to pass economic package

Convinces Congress to pass North Atlantic Free Trade Agreement

1994 Gets Congress to pass crime bill

Sends U.S. troops to Haiti

Suffers political setback when Republicans gain seats in Congress

1995 Helps arrange Dayton Accords

Engages in showdown with Congress over federal budget

1996 Signs welfare reform bill

Reelected president

1997 Testifies in sexual harassment lawsuit

1998 Sexual affair and false testimony revealed in tape recordings

Launches air attack on Iraq

Impeached by House of Representatives for perjury and obstruction of justice

1999 Acquitted by U.S. Senate

Directs air war against Serbia

Fails to get Congress to approve Comprehensive Test Ban Treaty

Found in contempt of court

2000 Undergoes investigation by independent counsel over whether he should be indicted for crimes relating to the Monica Lewinsky scandal

Arranges a cease-fire between Palestinians and Israelis in the Mideast

Visits Vietnam

2001 Doctors diagnose skin lesion on his back as cancerous

Retires from presidency

Issues 140 pardons

Moves to New York where Hillary Rodham Clinton has won a seat in the U.S. Senate

Arranges plea bargain with special counsel to avoid prosecution for perjury

2004 Publishes his memoir, *My Life*

Undergoes quadruple bypass surgery

2005 Heads relief effort for victims of a tsunami

Undergoes more surgery

Attends funderal of Pope John Paul II

Further Reading

Baker, Peter. *The Breach: Inside the Impeachment and Trial of William Jefferson Clinton.* New York: Scribner, 2000.

Campbell, Colin, and Bert A. Rockman, eds. *The Clinton Presidency: First Appraisals.* Chatham, N.J.: Chatham House, 1996.

Clinton, Bill. *My Life.* New York: Alfred A. Knopf, 2004.

Drew, Elizabeth. *On the Edge: The Clinton Presidency.* New York: Simon & Schuster, 1994.

———. *Showdown: The Struggle Between the Gingrich Congress and the Clinton White House.* New York: Simon & Schuster, 1996.

Hamilton, Nigel. *Bill Clinton: An American Journey.* New York: Random House, 2003.

Hitchens, Christopher. *No One Left to Lie To: The Triangulations of William Jefferson Clinton.* London: Verso, 1999.

Hyland, William G. *Clinton's World: Remaking American Foreign Policy.* Westport, Conn.: Praeger, 1999.

Johnson, Haynes. *The Best of Times: America in the Clinton Years.* New York: Harcourt, 2001.

Maraniss, David. *First in His Class: The Biography of Bill Clinton.* New York: Simon & Schuster, 1995.

Morris, Dick. *Behind the Oval Office: Winning the Presidency in the Nineties.* New York: Random House, 1997.

Reich, Robert. *Locked in the Cabinet.* New York: Alfred A. Knopf, 1997.

Renshon, Stanley A. *High Hopes: The Clinton Presidency and the Politics of Ambition.* New York: New York University Press, 1996.

Rozell, Mark J., and Clyde Wilcox, eds. *The Clinton Scandal and the Future of American Government.* Washington, D.C.: Georgetown University Press, 2000.

Stephanopolous, George. *All Too Human: A Political Education.* Boston: Little, Brown, 1999.

Walker, Martin. *The President We Deserve: Bill Clinton, His Rise, Falls, and Comebacks.* New York: Crown Publishers, 1996.

Woodward, Bob. *The Agenda: Inside the Clinton White House.* New York: Simon & Schuster, 1994.

George Walker Bush (1946–)

Forty-third president, 2001–

George W. Bush
(© AFP/CORBIS)

"Today we affirm a new commitment to live out our nation's promise through civility, courage, compassion, and character."
—Inaugural words, January 20, 2001

Not since 1876, when Rutherford B. Hayes defeated Samuel Tilden, had the United States seen a presidential election so confusing and controversial as that which occurred in the year 2000. As in the earlier balloting, the candidate who finished second in the popular vote, in this case George W. Bush, the Republican governor of Texas, won the presidency by amassing the most electoral votes. Also similar to the earlier election, the battle to determine a victor in this election extended well beyond election day, creating great uncertainty, with the state of Florida playing a crucial role in determining the winner.

When Bush began his presidential campaign in 1998, he held a big lead in public opinion surveys over Vice President Al Gore, the Democrat who eventually became his opponent. As late as Election Day in November 2000, the Bush campaign thought it would score a decisive victory over Gore. This assumption made Bush's second-place finish in the popular vote all the more stunning to him and his supporters.

George W. Bush was born on July 6, 1946, in New Haven, Connecticut, to George Herbert Walker Bush and Barbara Pierce Bush. He inherited wealth, prestige, and an impressive political lineage. His paternal grandfather, Prescott Bush, served as a U.S. senator from Connecticut for 10 years, from 1952 to 1962. His father, a student at Yale University at the time of his son's birth, won his first public office in 1966, when he was elected to the U.S. House of Representatives; he would go on to serve as vice president under Ronald Reagan and then succeed Reagan in the White House.

In the 1950s and 1960s, George W. lived in Midland, Texas, the town his father had moved to in the course of developing an oil business. But in 1961 the young man returned to the East when he enrolled at Phillips Academy (also known as Andover), the same prestigious prep school his father had graduated from in Andover, Massachusetts. George W. again followed in his father's footsteps when he entered Yale University in 1964. He showed far more attachment to fraternity life, parties, and pranks than he did to academics, but he graduated in 1968 with a bachelor's degree, after which he returned home and enlisted in the Texas Air National Guard's pilot-training program. With the Vietnam War under way in the 1960s, it was a controversial move, both at the time and even more so years later when he entered politics. Bush obtained one of the last two slots available in the National Guard despite scoring the minimum grade on a qualifying test.

An influential person helped him get his assignment, namely Ben Barnes, speaker of the Texas House of Representatives. After receiving a phone call from a family friend of the Bushes, Barnes contacted the general who was in charge of the Texas Air National Guard and recommended George W. for pilot training. Bush later said he had no knowledge of any such intervention and insisted that his assignment put him in line for service in Vietnam, but, in actuality, there was little chance his unit would be called into combat. The bottom line: Bush joined the National Guard so he could avoid having to fight in Vietnam, a tactic used by thousands of other young men. If, unlike President Bill Clinton, who was fiercely attacked by conservatives for dodging the draft, Bush eventually wore a uniform, he nevertheless used tactics equally self-serving and disingenuous.

While in the National Guard, Bush enjoyed preferential treatment. Most notably, in 1972, he obtained a transfer to Alabama so he could campaign for Republican Winton Blount, who was running for the U.S. Senate. Bush later claimed he performed his guard duty while helping Blount, but no records exist to prove the Texan ever reported to his new unit. General William Turnipseed, Bush's designated commander in Alabama, later said, "Had he reported in, I would have had some recall, and I do not. I had been in Texas, done my flight training there. If we had had a first lieutenant from Texas, I would have remembered."

In 1973, Bush enrolled in Harvard Business School, and though he disliked the faculty's liberalism, he earned his M.B.A. in 1975. At that point, he returned to Midland and founded an oil and gas exploration company. Bush later claimed he started his business on a shoestring, with limited money from his trust fund. In actuality, his family had many contacts with influential investors who, over the next few years, provided funds for George W.'s company at a time when the elder Bush was deeply involved in national politics as director of the Central Intelligence Agency, later as a presidential candidate, and as Ronald Reagan's vice president; clearly, the investors knew that to help George W. would curry favor with

Bush, Sr. In 1977, Bush married Laura Welch. They became the parents of twin girls, Barbara and Jenna, in 1982.

George W.'s involvement in the oil business again replicated the route followed by his father. One of the elder Bush's friends said of George W.: "He is always anxious to please his father, and he has done it by emulation. He went to Yale. He was a combat pilot. He went into the oil business in Midland. He ran for Congress. In his way, he tried to relive segments of his father's life."

The run for Congress occurred in 1978 when Bush campaigned as a Republican against Democrat Kent Hance for the open seat in the district that included Midland. Despite Bush's attraction to politics, his congressional race surprised some of his friends who remembered his apolitical years at Yale. Bush later said, "They were a little confused about why I was doing this, but at that time Jimmy Carter was president and he was trying to control natural gas prices, and I felt the United States was headed toward European-style socialism."

Hance attacked Bush by portraying him as an eastern elitist who had lost touch with Texas because he had spent time away from the state at schools in Massachusetts and Connecticut. The tactic worked; although Bush possessed the conservative credentials essential to west Texas politics, the equally conservative Hance outpolled him.

Bush returned to his oil business, by then called Arbusto Energy, seeded with money from George L. Ball, CEO of Prudential Bache Securities; William H. Draper III, a venture capitalist; Lewis Lehrman, a multimillionaire; and other investors. They soon encountered financial difficulty; when the price of oil suddenly dropped, Arbusto neared collapse. In 1982, businessman Philip Uzielli poured $1 million into Arbusto, but the company still faltered. Then, in 1984, two other prominent investors, Mercer Reynolds III and William O. Dewitt, bought Arbusto and merged it with another firm to form Spectrum 7—a move that made Bush the company's third-largest shareholder. After the Harken Energy Corporation acquired Spectrum 7, Bush was rewarded with a lucrative stock deal despite the company's continued difficulties. In June 1990 he sold two-thirds of his stock at a profit that exceeded $300,000.

The inflow of money came at a time Bush was working in his father's presidential campaign. In 1988, he went to Washington and, as a born-again Christian, he built close contacts with evangelicals, which helped the elder Bush receive 80 percent of their vote.

In 1989, just months before Bush sold most of his oil stock, he and 70 other investors bought the Texas Rangers, a professional baseball team in the American League, for $46 million. Bush expended $640,000 and became the owner most recognized by the public. He then obtained a lucrative deal with the city of Arlington, a Dallas suburb, after threatening to relocate the team if they did not get a new stadium. Arlington agreed to boost its sales tax to pay for the facility, while the Rangers agreed to pay $60 million in rent for its use. In return, they would get the title to the property in the year 2002. Since the stadium cost $191 million to build and its value would appreciate over the years, the Rangers stood to reap a handsome return.

In 1994, Bush decided to seek public office for the first time since his defeat in the 1978 congressional race. He set his sights on the Texas governorship and challenged the Democratic incumbent, Ann Richards. He benefited from America's conservative trend and its Republican mood—one that brought the GOP control of Congress—and from his own personable nature. Bush and his chief counselor, Karl Rove, himself a staunch conservative, crafted a right-of-center platform based on welfare reform, increased state financing of public education, and tougher juvenile justice laws. They also used the gun-control issue and attacked Richards for having vetoed legislation that would have allowed Texans to carry concealed weapons. Bush promised he would seek a new concealed-weapons bill.

As Bush suspected, Richards's veto had damaged her standing with conservatives, as had another of her positions, support of abortion rights for women. Rove, knowing that Bush had the tendency to become flustered and make contorted statements at unplanned events, kept him away from them. Bush defeated Richards by 350,000 votes out of 4.3 million cast.

George W. and his father made it seem as if the elder Bush took little part in the gubernatorial campaign, but behind the scenes, George, Sr., offered his son advice on issues and strategy and used his political contacts to the fullest (as he would in his son's presidential campaign). Having been recently defeated in his own reelection bid for president, George Bush saw his son's victory as something of a vindication for himself, as well as a rejuvenation of the Bush family political fortunes.

George W. entered an office that, constitutionally, was extremely limited; in Texas, most power resides not with the governor but with the legislature. The governor, however, could be instrumental in swaying public opinion and in bringing together competing groups, and Bush excelled in both endeavors. He won high marks for his ability to compromise and get along with the Democratic-controlled legislature. Bush said, "I worked hard to learn the legislative process and . . . to know individual legislators. I knew if I had strong relations with members, I would have stronger relations with their leaders."

Bush made refinancing of education the centerpiece of his term. The courts had already ordered that the disparity between rich and poor districts be lessened, and reforms were enacted under Ann Richards. In 1997, Bush asked the legislature to reduce property taxes substantially and make school funding more equitable by increasing the sales tax by one-half cent and by replacing the corporate franchise tax with a flat-rate business tax. The legislature took Bush's plan and reworked it, in part by lowering the property tax cut. According to Bush critics Molly Ivins and Lou Dubose in *Shrub: The Short but Happy Political Life of George W. Bush*, they made "the whole system much fairer." Bush later said that the reduction in property taxes was "significant for people on the outskirts of poverty, people with low incomes and senior citizens living on a fixed income."

At Bush's urging the legislature provided money for summer reading programs. He also obtained approval and funds to create more charter schools. Scandal, however, damaged the program when it was revealed that moneys had been mishandled; at one school in Waco, teachers' paychecks bounced despite the school's founder having received more than $750,000 in state funds.

Bush pushed for another education reform in late 1997 when he proposed that students pass a statewide reading test for promotion from the third to fourth grade; reading and math texts in the fifth grade; and reading, writing, and math tests in the eighth grade. Traditionally, school districts had set the standards for promotion, but the legislature approved his plan (though not until after his reelection). "I propose we begin the new century by putting an end to social promotion in Texas schools," Bush said.

In addition to educational reform, Bush pursued tort reform, and the legislature limited punitive damages that consumers, workers, and others could receive in suits against businesses. Bush claimed that the change would lead to lower insurance rates, but that failed to occur, even though profits for insurance companies increased.

Bush opposed a hate crimes bill that was debated in the legislature after James Byrd, Jr., a black man, was chained to a pickup truck and dragged to his death in the summer of 1998. When the bill passed the Texas House, he worked successfully to defeat it in the Senate because it provided protection for gays and lesbians.

Ever more desirous of winning the White House, Bush sought to solidify his political standing with a triumphant second term as governor. In 1998, he faced Democratic candidate Garry Mauro, the state land commissioner. After raising $20 million in campaign funds to Mauro's $3.5 million and promising more school reform and lower taxes, Bush won reelection in a landslide with nearly 69 percent of the vote. Bush claimed his victory showed "that a Leader who is compassionate and conservative can . . . open the doors of the Republican Party to new faces and new voices." That same year, he sold his interest in the Texas Rangers for about $15 million, a substantial return on his investment.

Throughout his governorship, Bush expressed strong support for property-rights legislation, a position that antagonized environmentalists. After stating "I understand full well the value of private property and its importance not only in our state but in capitalism in general," he signed legislation requiring that Texas, along with its local governments, compensate landowners whenever government policy impaired their property values.

An ardent supporter of the death penalty, Bush enforced it with enthusiasm and while insisting that the Texas legal system, rife with biased juries and incompetent lawyers, worked fairly. He opposed a bill to replace the death penalty with life sentences without parole for severely retarded criminals, and in 1999 he vetoed a bill that would have required each county to establish a system for appointing attorneys to represent indigent defendants.

With Karl Rove directing Bush's political advance, and with Bush anxious to win the White House, in 1999 the governor formally announced his candidacy for president. Many within and outside the Bush family had expected George W.'s younger brother, Jeb, recently elected governor of Florida, to be the Bush who would run for president. One observer said, "When it came to the family business, it was . . . Jeb who was supposed to take over and run the show."

As it turned out, the nation's Republican leaders quickly rallied around George W. Bush as the candidate best able to recapture the presidency for their party. Nevertheless, the Texas governor faced a surprisingly strong challenge from Arizona senator John McCain, who defeated him in the New Hampshire primary on February 1. Many voters in the primaries admired McCain for his forthrightness, while Bush showed little willingness to venture beyond his standard stump speeches. As the two candidates moved on to South Carolina, the campaign turned negative. In this acrimonious atmosphere, Bush invited criticism when he spoke at Bob Jones University, a conservative school known for its position against interracial dating and for its anti-Catholic bias. (Bush later apologized for his appearance there.) McCain, meanwhile, criticized the religious right when he called its leaders "agents of intolerance."

As Bush had done against Ann Richards in the Texas governor's race, he effectively positioned himself as the most conservative of the conservative candidates. His defeat of McCain, by a margin of 53 percent to 42 percent, followed by victories in Virginia and Washington state—while McCain won only in Michigan—rejuvenated his campaign. On March 7, Bush won nine of the 13 state primaries held that day, and on March 9, McCain suspended his own campaign, in effect assuring Bush the Republican nomination.

In the November general election, Bush faced Vice President Al Gore. Many potential voters cringed at the choice. They disliked Bush's shallow understanding of crucial issues; they disliked his limited experience, or what *Time* magazine called "one of the thinnest resumes in a century;" and they disliked his oral gaffes. At various points, Bush stated:

> "If you're sick and tired of the politics of cynicism and polls and principles, come and join this campaign."
>
> "The fact that he [Gore] relies on facts—says things that are not factual—are going to undermine his campaign."
>
> "We want [teachers] to know how to teach the science of reading. In order to make sure there's not this kind of federal—federal cufflink."

Other potential voters disliked Gore's exaggerations—he once claimed he had "invented" the Internet; they disliked his identification with the morally flawed outgoing president, Bill Clinton; and they disliked his stiff, wooden manner. In addition, the two men appealed so strongly to the political center, they took positions on issues only modestly different from each other. The *New York Times* offered two reasons for this: A less ideological electorate than in previous years, and a changed technology that made it more difficult for the candidates to appeal to one group without offending another, forcing them to take the safe ground to avoid upsetting anyone. But a third reason could be added to the list: that Bill Clinton and the Democratic Party had used the politics of blandness to achieve victories in the presidential elections of the 1990s and that Bush and Gore wanted to emulate that successful tactic.

In October 2000 they participated in three debates. In them, Bush reiterated his plans for a large tax cut, a revamping of Social Security to allow younger contributors to opt for placing their money in a fund that invested in stocks, and restraints on sending American troops overseas. Gore criticized Bush's tax-cut plan as so unbalanced it would, for the most part, benefit the wealthiest 1 percent of the population. On October 5, the vice presidential candidates, Republican Dick Cheney and Democrat Joseph Lieberman, also engaged in a debate.

Seeking an alternative to Bush and Gore, some voters turned to Ralph Nader, candidate of the Green Party, noted for his strong support of campaign finance reform, environmental protection, and programs that would address America's economic inequities. (Nader had been shut out of the presidential debates.) As the race between Bush and Gore tightened, Gore's campaign worried that Nader would attract liberals who would normally cast their ballots for Gore and would thus drain enough votes from the Democrat to deny him the presidency.

Their fears proved justified. With an electorate unexcited by the campaign—and voter turnout hovering around 51 percent, only a slight improvement from four years earlier—Nader took enough votes from Gore to cost him a victory in the crucial state of Florida (assuming that without Nader in the race nearly all of his supporters would have voted for Gore rather than Bush).

Despite public opinion polls indicating a tight race, on the eve of the November 7 election Karl Rove expressed what the *New York Times* called a "swaggering optimism" about Bush's prospects; he predicted that his candidate would get 320 electoral votes and would finish first in the popular vote. If that had happened, it would have meant a clear sweep for Bush and a significant mandate.

Unfortunately for the Bush campaign, in the final days of the election the momentum swung to Gore. The voters were listening to the vice president's statements that raised doubts about Bush's preparedness for the presidency, an assessment that Bush contributed to when he inaccurately indicated that social security was not a federal program. Concerns were also raised by news reports that Bush had been arrested in 1976 for drunk driving and had escaped punishment by falsely stating that he was only an occasional drinker. The reports revived suspicions that as a young man Bush had used cocaine and other drugs, and they called attention to his days of heavy drinking before he renounced alcohol in the 1980s.

Troubles with Rove's prediction and confusion over the election appeared even before the polls had closed across the country and Florida emerged as the most controversial battleground. During the afternoon of November 7, thousands of Democratic voters in Palm Beach County flooded local officials with complaints about the ballot layout. They claimed that the placement of punch holes for Gore and Reform Party candidate Patrick Buchanan had caused them to vote for Buchanan when they intended to vote for Gore. Indeed, Buchanan received 3,407 votes in the Democratic stronghold, three times higher than his totals in other South Florida counties.

At 8 P.M., the major television networks declared Gore the winner in Florida. Added to his victories in Pennsylvania and Michigan, it appeared he would be elected president. But at 10 P.M. the networks retracted their declaration, citing faulty data from exit polls in some precincts. As the returns continued, several other states, most notably New Mexico and Oregon, reported razor-thin margins between Bush and Gore that made it impossible to declare a winner.

Then, in the early morning of November 8, the networks declared Bush the victor in Florida and proclaimed him the president-elect. At 2:30 A.M. Gore conceded to Bush. But, in another odd turn, at 3:45 A.M., with Bush's lead in Florida dwindling to about 500 votes out of more than 5 million cast, Gore rescinded his concession, and a short time later the networks took back their declaration in Florida and classified that state's vote as too close to call.

In those Florida counties that had used punch-hole cards, a disproportionate number of ballots contained no votes whatsoever for president—more than 6,600 in Broward County alone. The Gore campaign suspected that the machine counts could have been wrong or that the mechanisms used in the voting booths could have been faulty and prevented voters from making a complete punch in their cards. Election officials began talking about "chads," small bits of cardboard that typically fall from computer cards anytime a hole has been punched through them. A chad that has not completely cleared the card and that might be hanging by a corner, or a card that might be only partially indented or dimpled would have failed to record a vote.

With that in mind, and his presidential campaign hanging in the balance, Gore began pressing for hand counts in Palm Beach County and in two other Democratic counties, Dade and Broward. Although manufacturers of the machines that used the punch-hole cards claimed that hand counts were more accurate and could resolve any discrepancies, and although several states, including Bush's home state of Texas, allowed the counting of dimpled cards, Bush went to court in order to stop Gore. (Florida law failed to specify how to handle chads or dimpled cards.) Bush feared that the counting of partially punched cards would give the state of Florida to his opponent. At the same time, voters in Palm Beach County demanded a new presidential vote there; in a legal suit, they claimed that the ballots had been "deceptive, confusing, and misleading."

Despite the uncertainty, Florida's secretary of state, Katherine Harris, a Republican and Bush supporter, certified Bush the winner, entitling him to the state's electoral votes. Her action sent Gore to the Florida Supreme Court, which overturned her decree and extended the deadline for counties to report their vote totals so that they could proceed with their recounts. The revised deadline, however, turned out to be too short (partly because Bush hampered the process). When the time for reporting the votes expired, Harris again certified Bush the winner, this time by 537 votes, after she refused to include hand recounts from Palm Beach County. Gore's running mate, Joseph Lieberman, reacted angrily, "How can we teach our children that every vote counts if we are not willing to make a good-faith effort to count every vote?"

At that point, the Florida Supreme Court ruled that "undervotes" in most of the states 67 counties, or about 170,000 ballots, should be recounted. With the deadline nearing for Florida's electors to meet and cast their votes for president, and with Bush claiming that votes had been counted and recounted ad nauseam, the Republican appealed to the U.S. Supreme Court. Bush, an avowed defender of states' rights, had decided that he wanted the federal government to overturn a state's decision in a presidential election: To the surprise of many legal scholars who knew that the Supreme Court seldom intervened in such elections and who realized that many of the justices themselves were conservatives who favored states' rights, the Supreme Court agreed to hear Bush's appeal.

A decidedly divided court, whose members had been primarily appointed by Republican presidents, ruled in Bush's favor. The majority in the decision said that the Florida Supreme Court had failed to specify guidelines needed to safeguard constitutional standards; as a result, there would be too many variations in how votes would be counted, with some county officials looking for mere indentations in the punch cards and others looking for hanging chads. That discrepancy, the court claimed, would violate the Fourteenth Amendment and its guarantee of equal protection to all citizens under the laws. (The decision begged the question, unasked in this case, of whether balloting had also to be uniform. In Florida, as well as several other states, various forms of ballots were used, such as punch cards and electronic ones.)

Many critics called the Court's decision political, based on a partisan and philosophical preference for conservative Republicans. Such criticism gained credence when *Newsweek* magazine reported that Justice Sandra Day O'Connor, who had sided with Bush, said on the night of November 7 when it looked like Gore might win the White House, that "this is terrible." (Of course, at the time O'Connor made the remark she had no idea she would be involved in the crucial election case.)

One of the dissenting justices, John Paul Stevens, believed so strongly that the Supreme Court had overstepped its bounds and damaged its credibility, that he stated: "Although we may never know with complete certainty the identity of the winner of this year's presidential election, the identity of the loser is perfectly clear. It is the nation's confidence in the judge as an impartial guardian of the rule of the law."

The Supreme Court's decision ended Gore's effort for a recount and left Bush the winner in Florida by less than one-half of 1 percent of the total state vote, giving him just enough electoral votes to win the presidency. Gore responded: "While I strongly disagree with the court's decision, I accept it. . . . And . . . for the sake of our unity . . . and the strength of our democracy, I offer my concession."

Many Americas reacted with dismay to the entire election ordeal. "I think the Constitution should be amended," said Ed Fine of Valley Village, California, "so the Supreme Court meets every four years to select the President, thereby sparing the country the expense and bother of an election." "This election opened my eyes, revealing truths I wish I did not know," said Nora Stoneman of Rockford, Illinois. "I'm appalled at the archaic voting systems that have been in place year after year that produce inaccurate voting results. . . . After seeing how this election has been handled, I may never choose to vote again." "After all the voting, it's as though a coin were flipped and landed on edge," said Stan Logue of San Diego, California. "The result is a selection, not an election, and the people in power have devised a rationale for pushing the coin over in one direction."

The election, or debacle as some called it, even caused former president Jimmy Carter, who had monitored dozens of elections overseas, to state, "I was really taken aback and embarrassed by what had happened in Florida. If we were invited to go into a foreign country to monitor the election, and they had similar election procedures, we would refuse to participate at all."

Some analysts blamed Al Gore's defeat on his failure to embrace Bill Clinton warmly and identify with the positive developments under Clinton's presidency. According to them, he should have, for example, more strongly identified with the economic prosperity of the Clinton years. Others claimed that Clinton was Gore's biggest liability. According to one survey, 44 percent of the voters thought the Clinton scandals very important or somewhat important, and of those voters the "vast majority" went for Bush. Pollster John Zogby claimed: "If we hadn't had the scandals, then Gore would probably have won clearly."

As Bush prepared to enter the White House, he declared that he would pursue his plans to boost defense spending and modernize the military, reform Social Security, make prescription-drug coverage affordable to Medicare patients, and convince Congress to cut taxes by $1.3 trillion. With the economy slowing in January 2001, he insisted that his tax cut would provide a needed stimulus. He said he would review several of President Bill Clinton's executive orders to protect the environment, with the implication that he would rescind some of them, and that he would ban federal funding to organizations operating overseas that supported or advocated abortions.

Bush appointed a diverse cabinet, in terms of race, ethnicity, and gender, as he did with his White House staff, which included Alberto R. Gonzales, a Hispanic, as his counsel, and Condoleezza Rice, an African-American woman, as his national security adviser.

Bush's prominent and high-powered choices for his cabinet indicated that he might well endow that group with substantial power, elevating it above the mere managerial role many recent presidents have allowed. "I'm not afraid to surround myself with strong and competent people," he told reporters. "I'm going to work with every cabinet member to set a series of goals for each cabinet, for each area of our government. And I'll work with the cabinet secretaries to help achieve those goals."

That possibility and the persons he selected brought mixed reactions from political analysts and politicians. Some saw in his appointments a strident conservatism that failed to recognize that he had lost the popular vote for the presidency to a moderate. Particularly galling to many Democrats were the nominations of Gale A. Norton as secretary of the interior and John Ashcroft as attorney general. Norton, a former Colorado attorney general, was a strong property-rights advocate. She had frequently expressed her preference for industries to police themselves in determining their compliance with environmental regulations.

Ashcroft, a former Missouri senator and governor, brought with him credentials as a born-again Christian who opposed women's abortion rights and had fought school desegregation plans in St. Louis. James C. Dobson, a leading religious conservative, stated, "If I were president-elect, John Ashcroft would be one of the people that I would be trying to find a spot for." Indeed, Bush received numerous phone calls from born-again Christians specifically urging him to appoint a religious and social conservative to the attorney general's office. Ashcroft certainly filled the bill. While serving in the U.S. Senate, he received a 100 percent rating from the Christian Coalition for his votes on issues such as abortion, education, the federal budget, and financing of the arts. The *New York Times* observed: "If confirmed by the Senate . . . Mr. Ashcroft would reach the highest office ever attained by a leading figure of the Christian right."

Thomas E. Mann, a scholar at the Brooking Institution, said, "Given the Florida recount, the Ashcroft nomination is just breathtaking. Democrats are going through the niceties of the transition period, but beneath the surface there is hostility and disbelief that Bush is proceeding in this fashion." Writing in *Time* magazine, political commentator Jack E. White asked, "What was president-elect George W. Bush thinking when he selected John Ashcroft as his nominee for Attorney General? That since he was designating three superbly qualified African Americans for high-level positions—Secretary of State Colin Powell, National Security Adviser Condoleezza Rice and Secretary of Education Rod Paige—blacks would somehow overlook Ashcroft's horrendous record on race?"

Although liberals and moderates complained about what they saw as the strident conservatism of Bush's cabinet nominees, other observers insisted that he had selected a pragmatic rather than an ideological group. His choice for secretary of state, former general Colin L. Powell, one of the most prominent and popular African Americans in the country, exuded this pragmatism because Powell attracted a diverse following with views difficult to label either conservative or liberal. And Bush reached out to the Democratic Party when he selected Norman Y. Mineta, President Clinton's secretary of commerce and a Japanese American, to serve as secretary of transportation. Yet for the most part, the moderates in his cabinet and on his White House staff tended to occupy foreign policy positions, while conservatives dominated the domestic agencies.

As Bush's cabinet choices faced confirmation by the Senate, troubles loomed. Women's and civil rights organizations prepared to fight Ashcroft's nomination; environmental groups vowed to rally against Norton; and Bush's candidate for secretary of labor, Linda Chavez, not only faced opposition from the president of the AFL-CIO, John Sweeny, who called her nomination "an insult to American working men and women," but also serious legal questions surrounding an illegal alien. Chavez had allowed the alien to stay at her house and perform odd jobs for which she received money, although Chavez said the woman was not an employee. Bush insisted, "I'm sure there's going to be some tough questioning for some of our nominees. But they're all fully prepared to handle tough questioning." In the end, though, the controversy surrounding Chavez and doubts within the FBI about her side of the illegal immigrant story forced her to withdraw from consideration.

During the presidential campaign, conservative columnist George Will said that Bush appeared to be a person imbued with "a lack of gravitas—a carelessness, even a recklessness, perhaps born of things having gone too easily so far." Clearly, Bush faced a challenge to prove such observations wrong.

He faced another challenge in building support after having been rejected for the presidency in the popular vote by more than 500,000 ballots cast. Al Gore, in fact, had won more popular votes than any other previous Democratic candidate, and his margin over Bush in that category exceeded that of John Kennedy over Richard Nixon in 1960 and Nixon over Hubert Humphrey in 1968. Bush also had to deal with a divided Congress, with the Senate evenly split between Republicans and Democrats.

It was an unusual scene when George Bush was inaugurated on January 20, 2001: He was sworn in by Chief Justice William Rehnquist, one of those on the court who had ruled in his favor. A few weeks later, Bush scored a major victory when Congress enacted his tax cut. But he also suffered several setbacks. His refusal to accept higher standards to fight arsenic contamination in water, his backing away from stricter regulation of carbon dioxide emissions at power plants, and his rejection of the Kyoto Treaty on global warming caused opponents to call him the "Toxic Texan." By September the economy had slowed, while in foreign policy his preference for unilateral action had alienated several countries, and his disengagement from the ongoing conflict between Palestinians and Israelis hampered efforts at reaching a peace agreement in the Middle East.

The direction of the Bush administration, and of America in general, changed on September 11, 2001, at 8:46 A.M., when a jet passenger airliner, commandeered by hijackers and loaded with almost-full fuel tanks, crashed into the north tower of the World Trade Center in New York City, striking the skyscraper near its top. Sixteen minutes later, as flames and dense smoke poured from the tower, a second airliner struck the south tower. Both buildings weakened as the fierce, fuel-fed fires raged. At 9:59 A.M., the south tower collapsed; at 10:28 A.M., the north tower followed. The disaster took the lives of more than 2,700 people.

In Washington, D.C., a third hijacked airliner plowed into the Pentagon at 9:37 A.M. A fourth plane, targeted for another site in the nation's capital, crashed into a field in Pennsylvania after its passengers overpowered the hijackers and forced the plane down.

The attacks were planned and staged by Al Qaeda, an Islamic terrorist group led by Osama bin Laden. He promoted a Holy War to establish an empire under Islamic law. Bin Laden and his followers viewed the United States as the primary obstacle toward their goal and as the great Satan, corrupting morals throughout the Islamic world. Al Qaeda particularly detested the U.S. military presence in Saudi Arabia (bin

Laden's birth country), the home of Mecca and Medina, the two holiest cities for Muslims.

President Bush was in Florida during the 9/11 attacks. On his return to Washington, he vowed the perpetrators would be punished. He soon boldly announced a War on Terror, and as Americans, stunned, saddened, and enormously angered by the attacks, rallied around him, his popularity soared. Support for Bush strengthened even further when the United States invaded Afghanistan on October 7, 2001, to topple its fundamentalist Islamic rulers, the Taliban. Afghanistan had given refuge to Al Qaeda and allowed bin Laden to set up terrorist training camps on its soil. The U.S. offensive caused the Taliban government to collapse in November, and a pro-American regime was established in the capital of Kabul. But bin Laden, a prime target of the assault, remained on the loose.

As part of the War on Terror, the United States disrupted the flow of money from various sources to Al Qaeda and shut down front organizations and charities that were funneling money to the terrorist group. By the end of 2002, a global hunt had resulted in the death or imprisonment of perhaps one-third of Al Qaeda's leaders, and in March 2003 Khalid Shaikh Muhammad, the alleged mastermind of 9/11, was captured.

At Bush's urging, Congress passed the Uniting and Strengthening America by Providing Appropriate Tools Required to Intercept and Obstruct Terrorism Act of 2001, more commonly called the PATRIOT Act. The House voted 98-1, and the Senate 356-66, for the legislation. The law allowed the United States to indefinitely imprison without trial any non-U.S. citizen determined by the attorney general to be a threat to national security. The government had neither to provide the detainees with a lawyer nor even make public the arrest.

In addition, among its other provisions, the PATRIOT Act allowed a wiretap to be issued against an individual instead of a specific telephone number; it allowed law enforcement agencies to obtain a warrant and search a residence without informing the occupants, as long as the attorney general had determined an issue of national security to be at stake; it allowed the FBI to order any person to turn over anything "tangible" for an authorized investigation "to protect against terrorism or clandestine intelligence activities"; it allowed law officers to obtain a warrant through an application that only had to show there existed an ongoing investigation, and to track which websites a person visits and any e-mail a person sends or receives; it allowed the government, under certain circumstances, to intercept the communications of a computer hacker without a court order; and it allowed the government to obtain library records that would show the books a person was reading.

Supporters of the PATRIOT Act insisted it was necessary to protect the country from terrorist intrigue that could kill thousands of people. Opponents said it was passed in a climate of fear and violated the Constitution and threatened civil liberties. Over subsequent months, four states (Hawaii, Alaska, Maine, and Vermont) and more than 330 cities passed resolutions condemning the PATRIOT Act as an assault on civil liberties. One city, Arcata, California, barred city workers, including the police and librarians, from cooperating with any federal investigations that, under the act, would violate a person's constitutional rights.

Most of the PATRIOT Act was due to expire at the end of 2005. President Bush, however, expressed his desire to continue it and perhaps expand its reach. The number of abuses under the act was difficult to determine because Attorney General John Ashcroft kept classified most of the information about the FBI's spy activities.

With the War on Terror, the president proclaimed a new foreign policy, subsequently called the Bush Doctrine. It contained two important elements: First, the United States would wage preventive war against any group or country that threatened American interests; and second, it would maintain military supremacy by preventing any other nation from emerging as its rival. The "strike first" strategy broke with the policy of deterrence that had been in effect for more than 50 years and had relied on primarily the prospect of a nuclear attack to deter an aggressor.

The Bush Doctrine was widely criticized as an arrogant flexing of U.S. military power and a threat to the role of international organizations, such as the United Nations. It opened the door to other countries also declaring they would determine when their interests were threatened and launch preventive war when they desired—policies that could degenerate into worldwide chaos.

The worst fears of the critics seemed to be coming true when Bush declared Iraq, Iran, and North Korea an "axis of evil." Through their weapons of mass destruction (WMD), Bush claimed, they threatened U.S. security and world peace. "Regime change" as a topic engulfed Washington—talk about how the United States should bring down the rulers of the three countries and in the process dismantle their chemical, biological, and nuclear weapons. The United States, it appeared, was going to use its military power to engage in wars against enemies on at least two continents.

Within the "axis of evil," Bush focused on the bugbear from his father's administration, Iraqi dictator Saddam Hussein. Even before 9/11, a powerful clique in the Bush administration, the neo-conservatives, or neocons, pushed for war against Iraq. They believed the United States should topple Hussein's regime and establish a democratic government in Iraq friendly to U.S. interests. Those interests included access to oil and policies supportive of Israel. Moreover, they believed once U.S. troops entered Iraq, the Americans would be universally greeted as liberators, and a democratic government would evolve quickly and painlessly. And once democracy took root in Iraq, they insisted, it would spread elsewhere in the Middle East, transforming Egypt, Syria, Saudi Arabia, and other countries. The neocons held secondary positions in the Bush administration, but one analyst later observed: "Absent the intellectual framework provided by the neocons, it is highly improbable that the result of this heightened attention [toward Iraq after 9/11] would have been a rapid lonely march into an essentially unprovoked war."

In October 2002 the House and Senate overwhelmingly voted the authorization Bush sought to attack Iraq, provided the evidence of a threat from Hussein proved solid. With each passing week, Bush insisted more strenuously that Hussein possessed WMD that posed an immediate threat to the United States. In his January 2003 State of the Union address, he claimed that evidence compiled by British intelligence showed Hussein had tried to acquire uranium from the country of Niger in Africa for use in making nuclear weapons. Yet the same charge had been removed from an earlier Bush speech because the CIA discovered it to be unfounded. Soon the White House itself came under investigation to determine whether administration officials had leaked the identity of an undercover CIA agent, Valerie Plame, whose husband, Joseph C. Wilson, had investigated the Niger story and, in a newspaper essay, declared it fake. The leak may have been a way to punish Wilson for his criticism and to send a message to anyone else who might dare to contradict the president.

Vice President Richard Cheney joined the neocons in pushing for war. He and Bush went so far as to imply that Hussein was connected to the 9/11 attacks. Yet administration officials were far from unanimous in their views. Many in the state department opposed attacking Iraq. Secretary of State Colin Powell thought the president should at least present his case to the United Nations, and he eventually persuaded him to do so. Bush chose Powell to appear before the UN, and the secretary obliged with descriptions and photographs apparently convincing enough to seal the case about Hussein's development and storage of WMD. As it turned out, however, most of the evidence was spurious at best.

As Bush moved closer to war, he tried to build an impressive coalition of nations who would join him. In this he failed. Except for Britain and Spain, only a few small countries supported Bush, and he was embarrassed by the refusal of Turkey to allow American troops on its soil to stage an attack on Iraq from the north. France and Germany especially denounced the movement toward war, with the French foreign minister, Dominque de Villepin, insisting that the UN weapons inspections imposed on Hussein were working. Moreover, he said the United States, Britain, and Spain were acting against the desire of the international community.

Indeed, the UN Weapons inspections program begun after the Persian Gulf War had been called by Cheney "the most intrusive system of arms control in history." In 1997, the inspectors reported that Hussein's nuclear weapons program had been dismantled and there existed no indications of weapon-usable nuclear material remaining in Iraq. The inspectors destroyed ballistic missiles, and in July 2002 Anthony Cordesman, of the Center for Strategic and International Studies, appeared before the Senate Foreign Relations Committee and said: "Iraq has not fired a Scud [missile] variant in nearly twelve years." As for chemical weapons, UN inspectors eliminated the main biological weapons facility at Al Hakam in 1996 and reported in 2002 that they found no renewed chemical or biological weapons programs.

The efforts of the neocons, Cheney, and of some older interventionists, such as Secretary of State Donald Rumsfeld, when combined with the power given to the executive branch over Congress after 9/11 (as Americans looked to strong leadership for guidance and to punish those they thought responsible for the terrorist attack), formed a potent movement toward war. Indeed, the combination propelled the United States into the conflict.

On March 18, 2003, President Bush presented his war message to the country. He said: "The Iraqi regime has used diplomacy as a ploy to gain time and advantage," and "it has uniformly defied Security Council resolutions demanding disarmament." Then he offered a series of accusations, none of which ultimately proved to be true:

> "Intelligence gathered by this and other governments leaves no doubt that the Iraq regime continues to possess and conceal some of the most lethal weapons ever devised."
>
> "The regime . . . has aided, trained, and harbored terrorists, including operatives of Al Qaeda."
>
> "The danger is clear: Using chemical, biological, or, one day, nuclear weapons obtained with the help of Iraq, the terrorists could fulfill their stated ambition and kill thousands or hundreds of thousands of innocent people in our country or any other."
>
> "Today, no nation can possibly claim that Iraq has disarmed. And it will not disarm as long as Saddam Hussein holds power."
>
> "Many nations . . . have the resolve and fortitude to act against this threat to peace, and a broad coalition is now gathering to enforce the just demands of the world."

To the Iraqi people, he added: "We will tear down the apparatus of terror, and we will help you to build a new Iraq that is prosperous and free. The tyrant will soon be gone. Your day of liberation is near."

Two days later, on March 20, American troops invaded Iraq. The assault followed an unsuccessful effort to kill Hussein through an air strike and came less than two hours after time had expired in an ultimatum Bush had given Hussein to abdicate and leave Iraq. White House spokesperson Ari Fleischer said the war was "a result of Saddam Hussein's failure to disarm and his possession of weapons of mass destruction."

Many Democrats who had voted against giving Bush the authority to attack Iraq reluctantly backed his decision. Senator Joseph Lieberman of Connecticut stated: "At a certain point—and we've reached it, I think—you've either got to go ahead and enforce the resolutions of the United Nations over 12 years to carry out the authority granted by Congress last fall with broad bipartisan support, or you make a mockery not just of the United Nations, but of the credibility of the United States."

Others, however, thought differently. Senator Edward Kennedy of Massachusetts said: "As long as the [United Nations weapons] inspectors are on the ground making progress, I continue to believe we should not be pulling the trigger of war. If inspectors do work, we avoid war; if they don't, we have a better chance of getting the world's support as we wage war and work to win the peace." Senator Tom Daschle of South Dakota said: "I'm saddened that the president failed so miserably at diplomacy that we are now forced to war. Saddened that we have to give up one life because this president couldn't create the kind of diplomatic effort that was so critical for our country." Fifteen House Democrats proclaimed they still opposed an "unnecessary and unjustified war." As U.S. troops entered Baghdad, Representative James Langevin of Rhode Island said: "Going into Iraq was a high-risk strategy. It's not so much that it was a military risk. Clearly, we're going to win, and I knew we would win decisively. It is a long-term risk in terms of how the world views the United States and its excessive power."

Bush and Rumsfeld decided to use a limited number of troops, as opposed to the massive assemblage of ground forces mobilized for the Persian Gulf War of 1991. The Americans moved through Iraq largely with ease, overwhelming Hussein's strategy of using paramilitary forces in the south to slow down the invaders. The Iraqis employed no chemical weapons against the Americans, who had prepared for the possibility of such an onslaught.

On May 1, Bush staged a landing on the aircraft carrier *Abraham Lincoln,* near the California coast, to proclaim that the combat phase of the war had ended. A huge sign placed aboard the ship declared "mission accomplished."

But the president and his advisers had gravely miscalculated the extent of the remaining opposition. There would be no unfettered adulation from Iraqis and no easy march to democracy. Trouble in the occupation of Iraq erupted immediately: Crowds looted everything from government buildings, from which they took office furniture and toilets, to weapons storage centers, from which they took armaments they would later use against U.S. troops. The looting was to a large degree organized, armed, and financed in a coordinated effort. Had the United States invaded with a larger force, the looting might have been prevented, or at least minimized. That, however, was not done. In fact, Bush ignored several preinvasion warnings from Secretary of State Powell concerning the difficulties likely to unfold following the toppling of Hussein.

By late summer 2003, the armed resistance in Iraq was making a mockery of "mission accomplished." Bush reacted to the first attacks by taunting the resistance fighters, telling them to "bring it on." They did, and the attacks intensified against the Americans, against workers from the United Nations and the Red Cross, and against fellow Iraqis, especially those who cooperated in any way with the United States. On August 19, a bomb exploded at the UN compound in Baghdad, killing 20 people, including the leading UN diplomat in Iraq, Sergio Vieira de Mello.

Terrorist groups combined with Hussein loyalists and Sunni religious radicals to spearhead the violence. Some fighters appeared to be coming in from Syria and Iran. Yet as the weeks passed, the Bush administration kept telling itself that victory was just around the corner. In the September/October issue of *Foreign Affairs,* Larry Diamond wrote: "As in Vietnam, a turning point always seemed imminent. And Washington refused to grasp the depth of popular disaffection." Moreover, he noted, too many Iraqis viewed the invasion not as an international effort, "but as an occupation by Western, Christian, and essentially Anglo-American powers, and this evoked powerful memories of previous subjugation and of the nationalist struggles against Iraq's former overlords."

In fall 2003, at about the same time the death toll of Americans from enemy fire following Bush's declaration had exceeded the total from before it, the president was forced to ask Congress for more money to fight in Iraq (and Afghanistan), a total of $87 billion. In October, a *New York Times*/CBS News poll showed that public faith in Bush's ability to handle an international crisis had declined from 66 percent to 45 percent.

On December 13, 2003, U.S. troops captured the elusive Hussein. American officials believed this would end or greatly reduce the violence in Iraq, but it abated only briefly.

Progress was made toward turning over the reigns of government in Iraq to the Iraqis, and on March 8, 2004, a governing council agreed to a democratic constitution and to elections being held by the end of January 2005. But throughout 2004 attacks escalated against U.S. and other foreign troops; foreign civilians; and Iraqi civilians, troops, and police. The rebels sought to show the Iraqis that Americans could not protect them, and they wanted to deepen the blame many Iraqis had placed on the Americans for the country's disorder and economic devastation. They may also have wanted to encourage sectarian strife between Sunnis and Shiites to plunge Iraq into a civil war and yet more chaos.

Suicide bombings, roadside bombings, and other assaults took their toll. On February 1, suicide bombers killed Kurds and their leaders; on March 2 they struck Shiites worshipping on holy day, killing at least 143. On March 31, four American contractors working for the U.S. military were killed, and their bodies were mutilated and hung from a bridge in Falluja. In April, several weeks of fighting began between the Americans and a militia attached to Shiite cleric Moktada al-Sadr. This fighting spread the violence beyond the Sunni communities of the north into the Shiite south. Hundreds of militiamen were killed before ceasefires halted the bloodshed in Karbala and Najaf.

On May 17, assassins murdered the president of the Iraqi governing council. A subsequent U.S. assault on Falluja disrupted the rebels but also gave rise to stories about Americans killing civilians, making the foreigners even more unpopular with many Iraqis. The U.S. troops pulled back from Falluja, until after the American presidential election in November, and then launched a new attack that turned the city into a virtual ghost town. The assault produced mixed results: Many rebels were killed or captured, but many others relocated to nearby towns.

The efforts of the United States to portray itself as a humane crusader in its pursuit of a democratic Middle East were dealt a severe blow in April, when photos appeared on the Internet and elsewhere revealing widespread abuse and torture at the Abu Ghraib prison near Baghdad. Military intelligence officers were extensively involved in the abuses that included one death, many beatings, and dogs terrorizing inmates. In an investigation, Major General George R. Fay documented the use of torture in some instances.

The responsibility for the abuses reached into the highest levels of the military and into the White House, as Secretary of Defense Rumsfeld had failed to provide clear guidance for interrogations. In September, the army acknowledged it had kept from prison rosters dozens of detainees at Abu Ghraib so their existence, and the treatment they received, could be concealed from the Red Cross. This procedure violated military policy and international law.

In December, the FBI, acting in response to a lawsuit against the U.S. government, released documents that told how witnesses had "described . . . such abuses [as] strangulation, beatings, placement of lit cigarettes into the detainees' ear openings and unauthorized interrogations." According to the *New York Times,* "The newly disclosed documents are the latest to show that such activities were known to a wide circle of government officials." In one memorandum an agent wrote:

> On a couple of occasions I entered interview rooms to find a detainee chained hand and foot in a fetal position to the floor, with no chair, food, or water. Most times they had urinated or defecated on themselves and had been left there for 18 to 24 hours or more.

The agent added:

> On another occasion the A/C had been turned off, making the temperature in the unventilated room probably well over 100 degrees. The detainee was almost unconscious on the floor, with a pile of hair next to him. He had apparently been literally pulling his own hair out throughout the night.

Other agents reported they saw detainees in Guantánamo Bay, Cuba, abused by their American captors. In fact, hundreds of foreign detainees were being kept at Guantánamo without the right to a trial or to know the charges against them. The United States insisted it could hold terrorist suspects indefinitely. The military officially claimed that the detainees possessed important information about terrorist groups. Numerous reports from within and outside the military, however, said that little, if any, important information had been gained from the captives.

In an annual report issued in January 2005, the group Human Rights Watch condemned American treatment of prisoners in Iraq, Afghanistan, and at Guantánamo. The group said:

> When the United States disregards human rights, it undermines . . . human rights culture and thus sabotages one of the most important tools for dissuading potential terrorists. Instead, U.S. abuses have provided a new rallying cry for terrorist recruiters and the pictures from Abu Ghraib have become the recruiting posters for Terrorism, Inc.

The group's executive director, Kenneth Roth, added: "The U.S. government is less and less able to push for justice abroad because it is unwilling to see justice done at home."

As scheduled elections neared for Iraq in late January 2005, Bush admitted that Iraqi troops were unprepared to take over from American forces the job of securing the country. The president said there had only been "mixed" success in training Iraqi troops. "They've got some generals in place and they've got foot soldiers in place," Bush said, "but the whole command structure necessary to have a viable military is not in place. And so they're going to have to spend a lot of time and effort on achieving that objective."

He might have added that the Iraqi army showed little desire to fight. Where it had engaged in combat alongside U.S. troops against the rebels, it had generally performed miserably and, in some instances, had even been infiltrated by the enemy. Senator John Warner, a Virginia Republican and chair of the Armed Services Committee, labeled Iraqi troops "bottom level."

Bush acknowledged, too, that without question "the bombers are having an effect" in terrorizing the Iraqi people and weakening American resolve in Iraq. Such words gave little comfort to those who thought the Iraqi elections could be held in an atmosphere of stability. In fact, as the elections approached, administration officials began scaling back their expectations, saying how many people voted would be of less importance than the country going through the process. Despite these problems, in January 2005 Bush said his reelection in 2004 was a ratification by the American people of his Iraq policy.

In mid-January, the United States officially admitted what had been the case from the start: No weapons of mass destruction existed in Iraq. The main reason for the United States attacking the country had proved to be smoke and mirrors. With that admittance, oil revenues from Iraq lagging far behind the cost of reconstruction, many Iraqis antagonized by the presence of U.S. troops, sectarian strife looming between Shiites and Sunnis, and the insurgency as vigorous as it ever had been, the picture in Iraq looked bleak.

In fact, in a chilling report, the National Intelligence Council (NIC), the CIA director's think tank, concluded that Bush's war in Iraq had accomplished the opposite from his professed intentions. Instead of dealing terrorism a crippling blow, it helped stimulate it. The instability produced by the U.S. invasion had made the country a thriving recruiting and training ground for terrorist groups. The analysis by 1,000 experts led NIC chairman Robert L. Hutchings to conclude that Iraq "is a magnate for international terrorist activity."

Bush battled terrorism, or in this case, an interpretation of the terrorist threat, on yet another front: a report released on July 22, 2004, from a bipartisan government commission that showed how the FBI, the CIA, and other government agencies, along with officials in the White House, had failed the country in the weeks leading up to 9/11. Bush had opposed the formation of the investigative commission and resisted cooperating with it until the political pressure to do so had become too great. He feared what it might conclude about any inadequacies on his part in the 9/11 tragedy. His fears proved on the mark.

The commission report concluded that the Bush administration had reacted inadequately to warnings of an attack, including having given short shrift to a report presented to Bush on August 6, 2001, titled "Bin Laden Determined to Strike in United States." Bush and his advisers were too focused on state actions rather than terrorist groups. (Bush had been critical of President Clinton for paying too much attention to such groups.) Moreover, the commission rejected the argument presented by Bush and Cheney when it found no connection between Osama bin Laden and Saddam Hussein. In the wake of the report, Bush reluctantly backed the commission recommendation to create a new national intelligence director.

In other matters, Bush pursued sharply conservative policies. Determined to help business and stimulate the economy, he convinced Congress to pass his $1.3 trillion tax cut in May 2001. Democrats largely opposed it, saying it would consume too much of the government surplus, the funds of which should be directed at correcting problems with social security and Medicare. Bush followed this with another tax cut in March 2002, and a third one early in 2003, totaling several hundred billion dollars more. It came after intense debate within the administration between those who worried about rising budget deficits and those who wanted to further stimulate the economy.

As it turned out, the cuts, coupled with an economic slowdown early in the Bush presidency, along with the costs from the war on terror, eliminated the existing budget surpluses and boosted the red ink. When Bush took office the government was forecasting a $5.6 trillion budget surplus by the year 2011. In 2004, it revised its forecast, replacing the surplus with a $3 trillion debt increase.

By 2004, the government was borrowing more than $1.1 billion a day to pay its bills. The annual amount it spent on interest payments to finance the debt exceeded its expenditures for education, homeland security, law enforcement, international aid, and space exploration combined.

Even the White House budget office attributed much of the debt to the tax cuts. The office concluded that about 50 percent of the debt resulted from a recession, declining stock prices, and the 9/11 attack. The other half, however, came from the president's policy choices, namely the tax cuts, along with the war in Afghanistan and the attack on Iraq. Indeed, in 2004 alone, Congress appropriated $174 billion for the Iraq war. One leading economist observed: "The Bush administration didn't just sit there and watch the deficit get wider. They actually exacerbated it."

Those who supported the tax cuts argued they would boost the economy with little increase in interest rates. The economy did pick up steam in the second half of 2004 on the crest of modest interest rate increases, though job creation lagged well behind the president's more optimistic predictions. An additional troubling development: The dollar was weakening, making foreign investors more reluctant to fund the deficit and forcing the government to pay higher interest rates.

Some economists predicted the end result would be steeper interest rates for borrowers and higher inflation. That, in turn, posed the danger of boosting prices, damaging consumer spending, and producing a recession. Other analysts worried that the bigger debt would mean such a heavy reliance on foreigners to fund it, the government would fall too heavily under their influence. Said one: "If China is financing the debt, how tough can we be the next time there is a Tiananmen Square?" Others insisted the U.S. economy was big enough to handle the debt, that it amounted to only 35 percent of the gross domestic product, much less than the debt ratio found in other countries.

Bush rejected the critics. In July 2004, he convinced Congress to extend for five years tax cuts set to expire. His economic policies, his advisers said, had been "an unqualified success."

Throughout 2004, Bush acted to firm up his conservative base to prepare him for reelection. In January, the administration filed a friend of the court brief with the Supreme Court, contending that the University of Michigan was using an unconstitutional quota system in its undergraduate and law school admissions. Ultimately, the court upheld the university's policies. His tax cut in May also appealed to conservatives. In July, he declared his support for a constitutional amendment that would prohibit gay marriages. And he made more emphatic his firm opposition to abortions.

Despite the problems with Iraq, Bush won reelection in 2004, defeating John Kerry, a Democratic senator from Massachusetts. The nation headed into the vote polarized, and it came out of it the same way. Little changed from the election of 2000, except the Republicans were able to motivate a greater number of their voters to get to the polls and offset a surge in Democratic voters, thus enabling Bush to capture about 51 percent of the popular count. Four years earlier he had to rely on victory in the electoral college to obtain the presidency. Most of the popular vote gains for the Republicans were in the South.

Some political analysts believed that the tactics by both parties, where they motivated their support base without reaching out substantially to independents, contributed to the prevailing polarization. Bush's slash-and-burn strategy, by which he pursued conservative policies without offering any significant compromises to his opponents, seemed especially to encourage political intolerance and a sense among both Republicans and Democrats that no quarter should be given. Even Republican strategists said it was time for the president to reach out to those who disagreed with him. Said one: "Bush needs to start thinking about his place in history as a uniter [sic], not a divider. It can't be a go it alone and we'll follow strategy anymore."

Analysts provided different reasons for the Bush victory. Some claimed that the president's attachment to mainstream values helped him to win, particularly his opposition to gay marriages. (Kerry opposed gay marriages too.) Others pointed to voters who felt more comfortable with Bush's ability to protect the country from terrorist attacks.

Another possible influence: A videotape released days before the election in which Al Qaeda leader Osama bin Laden derided Bush's actions overseas. One voter said the videotape left a deep impression: "When he made his presentation, looking all spiffed up, and condemned the president's foreign policy, I saw that as a clear sign I should vote for Bush." Writing in *Time* magazine, Charles Krauthammer said:

> With the election hanging in the balance, the campaign awaited some improbable development to tip the scale. Re-enter Osama bin Laden. The irony could not be richer, the circle more complete. By reminding us of 9/11 and the war on terrorism, bin Laden invoked the only thing that could trump Iraq—and save the president. His chilling appearance re-

> minded us of our peril, put Iraq in perspective, and played precisely to the President's success and strength—success and strength that he so squandered in Baghdad. Bin laden was never one to remotely understand the American mind—he spectacularly misjudged 9/11—and he pulled his nemesis over the finish line.

Other analysts noted that Americans were usually adverse to dismiss from office a president involved in a war. Still others blamed the loss on Kerry—that he failed to instill trust and came across as stiff and aloof.

Postelection surveys found several interesting trends in the election. Contrary to some widely held beliefs, churchgoers provided Bush with little more backing than they had four years earlier. Among those who attended church weekly, he received 58 percent of the vote, up only 1 percent from four years earlier. In fact, his greatest gains came from those who attended church infrequently, if at all. Moreover, though 22 percent of the voters cited moral values as the deciding issue in casting their vote, many more, some 34 percent, cited Iraq and terrorism. Additionally, while Democrats lamented the country's slide to the right, a slide assumed to be weakening their party, on many social issues the public remained moderate and thus closer to the Kerry than the Bush supporters. For example, by 69 percent to 22 percent people favored using discarded embryos for stem-cell research; only 9 percent supported a complete ban on abortions; and 60 percent approved recognition of gay unions, although they overwhelmingly opposed gay marriages.

In many ways the election was Bush's to lose, and he almost blew it. In the wake of 9/11, his popularity reached unprecedented heights; by November of 2004, it had diminished considerably, to the point he found himself in a dogfight to retain the White House. He was damaged by a sagging economy, but more so by Iraq. The failure to find WMD, the incessant violence, coupled with the rising toll the fighting took on the lives of Americans, and his inability to parry Kerry's criticism of Iraq in one of three presidential campaign debates, all took their toll.

In the election's closing days, victory depended on the state of Ohio. Whoever won there would take the White House. Kerry ran well upstate, primarily in and around Cleveland, but Bush carried the central and southern counties with enough votes to offset the Democrat's tally. In the end, Bush beat Kerry by nearly 140,000 votes, or 51 percent to 49 percent, and the state's 20 electoral votes went into the president's column.

Bush's reelection was accompanied by Republican gains in the House of Representatives and the Senate. In the Senate, the Republicans now held 55 seats—a mere five short of the number needed to overcome any Democratic filibuster—while in the House they held 229 seats to 200 for the Democrats (and one for an independent). A political analyst noted: "It may have been a narrow victory for Bush nationally, but everyone in these key Senate races benefited from his coattails." The 2004 results marked the first time since the 1920s that the Republican Party had won control of the White House, the Senate, and the House of Representatives in consecutive elections.

George W. Bush took the oath of office for his second term on a cold January 20, 2005. In his speech, he offered a strongly idealistic commitment to spreading democracy and liberty around the world. He said that the nation's "vital interests and our deepest beliefs are now one." Bush insisted: "We will encourage reform in other governments by making clear that success in our relations will require the decent treatment of their own people. America's belief in human dignity will guide our policies." He added: "We go forward with complete confidence in the eventual triumph of freedom. Not because history runs on the wheels of inevitability. It is human choices that move events. Not because we consider ourselves a chosen nation. God moves and chooses as he wills."

Bush obviously expected to turn around the bleak situation in Iraq and to defeat autocrats in Iran, North Korea, and elsewhere. Whether he would be able to do so, or whether he would be able to set the stage for a triumph many years down the road, of course remained to be seen. But whatever the case, Bush cast the worldwide pursuit of liberty and democracy as more than rhetoric; it had become a mission.

Protesters expressed their disapproval of Bush along the inaugural route, and overseas the reaction to his inaugural address was largely cool to hostile. The newspaper *La Republica* in Rome commented: " [Mr. Bush] is satisfied with himself and thus is even more disturbing. . . . There is the sense of a man who now considers the entire world as his own parish." *Frankfurter Rundschau* in Germany lamented events in Iraq and worried there could be more of the same. "He promised peace and democracy for Iraq," the paper said, "and turned the bloody dictatorship of Saddam into an anarchic stronghold of terror, paying with the lives of many thousands . . . ." And in Lebanon, the *Beirut Daily Star* stated: "The prevailing reaction in this region was that he has merely raised the level of American double standards in the world to a new level of incredulity, given the massive gap between America's rhetorical commitment to democracy and freedom and the reality of its often whimsical foreign policy priorities."

President Bush was adamant in his view about America's position in the world. He closed his inaugural speech with these words:

> When the Declaration of Independence was first read in public and the Liberty Bell was sounded in celebration, a witness said it rang as if it meant something. In our time it means something still. America, in this young century, proclaims liberty throughout all the world and to all the inhabitants thereof. Renewed in our strength, tested but not weary, we are ready for the greatest achievements in the history of freedom.

Chronology

1946 Born July 6

1961 Enrolls at Phillips Academy in Andover, Massachusetts

1964 Works in father's campaign for U.S. Senate

1968 Graduates from Yale University

Enlists in Texas Air National Guard

1973 Enrolls in Harvard Business School

1975 Graduates from Harvard Business School with an M.B.A.

Founds oil and gas exploration company

1977 Marries Laura Welch

1978 Loses congressional race

1984 Becomes third-largest shareholder in an oil company, Spectrum 7

1988 Helps father campaign for presidency

1989 Joins other investors to buy Texas Rangers baseball team

1994 Is elected governor of Texas

1997 Gets Texas legislature to pass property tax reform

Proposes statewide reading and math tests for public school students

1998 Is reelected governor

Sells his interest in the Texas Rangers

1999 Announces candidacy for Republican presidential nomination

2000 Wins Republican presidential nomination

Loses popular vote for president but certified as winner in Florida, which gives him a victory in the electoral college

Wins Supreme Court case that prevents recount of disputed votes in Florida

2001 Inaugurated as president

Gets Congress to pass tax cut

Declares war against terrorism

	Announces Bush Doctrine
	Declares Iraq, Iran, and North Korea to be an "axis of evil"
2002	Gets Congress to pass additional tax cuts
	Obtains authorization from Congress to attack Iraq
2003	Proclaims "mission accomplished" in Iraq only six weeks after attacking that country
	Gets Congress to pass an additional tax cut
	Asks Congress for $87 billion in additional funds to fight in Iraq
2004	Increases U.S. troop strength in Iraq
	Wins reelection by defeating Democrat John Kerry
	Admits Iraq troops unprepared to provide security for their country
2005	Is inaugurated to second term
	Announces bigger than expected federal budget deficit
	Attends funeral of Pope John Paul II

FURTHER READING

Begala, Paul. *Is Our Children Learning?: The Case Against George W. Bush.* New York: Simon & Schuster, 2000.

Bush, George W. *A Charge to Keep.* New York: William Morrow, 1999.

Clarke, Richard A. *Against All Enemies: Inside America's War on Terror.* New York: Free Press, 2004.

Dean, John. *Worse Than Watergate: The Secret Presidency of George W. Bush.* New York: Little, Brown, 2004.

Dionne, E. J., Jr., and William Kristol, eds. *Bush v. Gore: The Court Cases and the Commentary.* Washington, D.C.: Brookings Institute, 2001.

Frum, David. *The Right Man: The Surprise Presidency of George W. Bush.* New York: Random House, 2003.

Hatfield, J. H. *Fortunate Son: George W. Bush and the Making of an American President.* New York: Thomas Dunne Books, 1999.

Ivins, Molly, and Lou Dubose. *Shrub: The Short but Happy Political Life of George W. Bush.* New York: Random House, 2000.

Milbank, Dana. *Smashmouth: Two Years in the Gutter with Al Gore and George W. Bush.* New York: Basic Books, 2001.

Minutaglio, Bill. *First Son: George W. Bush and the Bush Family Dynasty.* New York: Times Books, 1999.

New York Times. *Thirty-six Days: The Complete Chronicle of the 2000 Presidential Election Crisis.* New York: Times Books, 2001.

Phillips, Kevin. *American Dynasty: Aristocracy, Fortune, and the Politics of Deceit in the House of Bush.* New York: Viking, 2004.

Unger, Craig. *House of Bush, House of Saud: The Secret Relationship Between the World's Two Most Powerful Dynasties.* New York: Scribner, 2004.

Woodward, Bob. *Bush at War.* New York: Simon & Schuster, 2002.

———. *Plan of Attack.* New York: Simon & Schuster, 2004.

APPENDIX

George Washington

Election of 1789

Candidate	Electoral Vote
George Washington	69
John Adams	34
John Jay	9
Nine others	26

Note: George Washington ran unopposed for president. According to rules then in effect, each elector cast two votes, with the person receiving the largest number becoming president and the second-largest becoming vice president. In this instance, Washington received the votes of all 69 electors from the first group of votes, while the electors split their second votes among 11 men. Since Adams had the most votes within this group, 34, he became vice president. The results made Washington the only presidential candidate ever to receive a unanimous vote from the electoral college.

Election of 1792

Candidate	Electoral Vote
George Washington	132
John Adams	77
George Clinton	50
Two others	5

Note: George Washington ran unopposed for president. According to rules then in effect, each elector cast two votes, with the person receiving the largest number becoming president and the second-largest becoming vice president. As in 1789, Washington was a unanimous choice, in this instance receiving the votes of all 132 electors from the first group of votes.

First Administration (March 4, 1789–March 3, 1793)

Vice President: John Adams
Secretary of State: Thomas Jefferson
Secretary of the Treasury: Alexander Hamilton
Secretary of War: Henry Knox
Attorney General: Edmund Randolph
Postmaster General: Samuel Osgood; Timothy Pickering (from August 1791)
Supreme Court Appointments: John Jay, Chief Justice (1789); John Rutledge (1789); William Cushing (1789); Robert H. Harrison (1789); James Wilson (1789); John Blair (1789); James Iredell (1790); Thomas Johnson (1791)
States Admitted: Vermont (1791); Kentucky (1792)

Second Administration (March 4, 1793–March 3, 1797)

Vice President: John Adams
Secretary of State: Thomas Jefferson; Edmund Randolph (from January 1794); Timothy Pickering (from August 1795)
Secretary of the Treasury: Alexander Hamilton; Oliver Wolcott, Jr. (from February 1795)
Secretary of War: Henry Knox; Timothy Pickering (from January 1795); James McHenry (from February 1796)
Attorney General: Edmund Randolph; William Bradford (from January 1794); Charles Lee (from December 1795)
Postmaster General: Timothy Pickering; Joseph Habersham (from February 1795)
Supreme Court Appointments: William Paterson (1793); John Rutledge, Chief Justice (1795; rejected by Senate); Samuel Chase (1796); Oliver Ellsworth, Chief Justice (1796)
State Admitted: Tennessee (1796)

Family Facts

Father: Augustine Washington (1694–1743)
Mother: Mary Ball Washington (1708–1789)

Wife: Martha Dandridge Custis (1731–1802)
Marriage: January 6, 1759
Children: John Parke Custis was adopted from wife's first marriage and died soon after the American Revolution.

Unusual Facts

George Washington owned 80,000 acres of land, and his Mount Vernon home included a village of several hundred slaves.

He chose the site for the new national capital along the Potomac River (it later became Washington, D.C.), commissioned Pierre l'Enfant to plan the city, and laid the cornerstone for the Capitol building.

He hired architect James Hoban to design the White House, and he drove the stakes that sited the building, though it was not finished until after his death.

Washington had one remaining tooth at the time of his inauguration. During his lifetime he wore dentures made of human, cow, or hippopotamus teeth, or invory or lead, but he never wore wooden teeth.

The six white horses in Washington's stables had their teeth brushed every morning on the president's orders.

When Washington was president, the national capital was located first in New York City, from 1789 to 1790 (it had been the capital under the Confederation government since 1785), and then in Philadelphia (where it remained until its relocation to Washington, D.C., in 1800).

Election of 1796

Candidate	Electoral Vote
John Adams Federalist	71
Thomas Jefferson Democratic-Republican	68
Thomas Pinckney Federalist	59
Aaron Burr Democratic-Republican	30
Samuel Adams Democratic-Republican	15
Oliver Ellsworth Federalist	11
Seven others	22

Note: According to rules then in effect, each elector cast two votes, with the person receiving the largest number becoming president and the second-largest becoming vice president.

Adams Administration (March 4, 1797–March 3, 1801)

Vice President: Thomas Jefferson
Secretary of State: Timothy Pickering; John Marshall (from June 1800)
Secretary of the Treasury: Oliver Wolcott, Jr.; Samuel Dexter (from January 1801)
Secretary of War: James McHenry; Samuel Dexter (from June 1800)
Attorney General: Charles Lee
Postmaster General: Joseph Habersham
Secretary of the Navy: (Department created by Congress in April 1798) Benjamin Stoddert
Supreme Court Appointments: Bushrod Washington (1798); Alfred Moore (1799); John Marshall, Chief Justice (1801)

Family Facts

Father: John Adams (1691–1761)
Mother: Susanna Boylston Adams (1699–1797)
Wife: Abigail Smith (1744–1818)
Marriage: October 25, 1764
Children: Abigail Amelia (1765–1813); John Quincy (1767–1848); Susanna (1768–1770); Charles (1770–1800); Thomas Boylston (1772–1832)

Unusual Facts

John Adams was the first president to live in the White House, then called the Executive Mansion or President's House.

When he moved into the President's House, the plaster walls were still wet and the flooring was unfinished.

He offered these words for future occupants of the mansion: "I pray Heaven to bestow the best blessings in this House and all that shall hereafter inhabit it. May none but honest and wise Men ever rule under this roof."

Thomas Jefferson

Election of 1800

Candidate	Electoral Vote
Thomas Jefferson Democratic-Republican	73
Aaron Burr Democratic-Republican	73
John Adams Federalist	65
Charles C. Pinckney Federalist	64
John Jay Federalist	1

Note: According to rules then in effect, each elector cast two votes, with the person receiving the largest number becoming president and the second-largest becoming vice president. A tie between Thomas Jefferson and Aaron Burr resulted, and after 36 ballots the House of Representatives elected Jefferson president.

Election of 1804

Candidate	Electoral Vote
Thomas Jefferson Democratic-Republican	162
Charles C. Pinckney Federalist	14

Note: The Twelfth Amendment, ratified in September 1804, required that separate votes be cast for president and vice president. This was intended to prevent a repetition of the Jefferson-Burr tie of 1800. As a result, from here on the candidate with the greatest number of votes on the presidential ballot became president, and the candidate with the greatest number of votes on the vice presidential ballot became vice president.

First Administration (March 4, 1801–March 3, 1805)

Vice President: Aaron Burr
Secretary of State: James Madison
Secretary of the Treasury: Samuel Dexter; Albert Gallatin (from May 1801)
Secretary of War: Henry Dearborn
Attorney General: Levi Lincoln
Postmaster General: Joseph Habersham; Gideon Granger (from November 1801)
Secretary of the Navy: Benjamin Stoddert; Robert Smith (from July 1801)
Supreme Court Appointment: William Johnson (1804)
State Admitted: Ohio (1803)

Second Administration (March 4, 1805–March 3, 1809)

Vice President: George Clinton
Secretary of State: James Madison
Secretary of the Treasury: Albert Gallatin
Secretary of War: Henry Dearborn
Attorney General: John Breckenridge; Caesar A. Rodney (from January 1807)
Postmaster General: Gideon Granger
Secretary of the Navy: Robert Smith
Supreme Court Appointments: Henry Brockholst Livingston (1806); Thomas Todd (1807)

Family Facts

Father: Peter Jefferson (1708–1757)
Mother: Jane Randolph Jefferson (1720–1776)
Wife: Martha Wayles Skelton (1748–1782)
Marriage: January 1, 1772
Children: Martha "Patsy" (1772–1836); Jane Randolph (1774–1775); Mary (1778–1804); Lucy (1780–1781); Lucy (1782–1785). A son died in infancy in 1777.
Jefferson likely fathered at least one child with his slave, Sally Hemings.

Unusual Facts

Thomas Jefferson was the first president elected by the House of Representatives.
When he became president, he had been a widower for 19 years. His daughter Martha or "Patsy" assumed the role of first lady.

Jefferson was the first president to be inaugurated in Washington, D.C. To lessen pomp, he eliminated the state carriage.

Bears brought back from Lewis and Clark's famous expedition were displayed in cages on the White House lawn. For years the White House was sometimes referred to as the "president's bear garden."

Jefferson once said, "I cannot live without books," and about 6,000 volumes from his private library were purchased for $23,950 to help start the Library of Congress.

Jefferson is credited with several inventions, including the swivel chair, a pedometer, a machine to make fiber from hemp, a letter-copying machine, a clock that kept track of the days of the week, and the lazy Susan.

Election of 1808

Candidate	Electoral Vote
James Madison Democratic-Republican	122
Charles C. Pinckney Federalist	47
George Clinton Independent-Republican	6

Election of 1812

Candidate	Electoral Vote
James Madison Democratic-Republican	128
DeWitt Clinton Federalist	89

First Administration (March 4, 1809–March 3, 1813)

Vice President: George Clinton (died 1812)
Secretary of State: Robert Smith; James Monroe (from April 1811)
Secretary of the Treasury: Albert Gallatin
Secretary of War: William Eustis; James Monroe (from January 1813); John Armstrong (from February 1813)
Attorney General: Caesar Augustus Rodney; William Pinkney (from January 1812)
Postmaster General: Gideon Granger
Secretary of the Navy: Robert Smith; Paul Hamilton (from May 1809); William Jones (from January 1813)
Supreme Court Appointments: Joseph Story (1811); Gabriel Duvall (1811)
State Admitted: Louisiana (1812)

Second Administration (March 4, 1813–March 3, 1817)

Vice President: Elbridge Gerry (died 1814)
Secretary of State: James Monroe
Secretary of the Treasury: Albert Gallatin; George W. Campbell (from February 1814); Alexander J. Dallas (from October 1814); William H. Crawford (from October 1816)
Secretary of War: John Armstrong; James Monroe (from October 1814); William H. Crawford (from August 1815)
Attorney General: William Pinkney; Richard Rush (from February 1814)
Postmaster General: Gideon Granger; Return J. Meigs, Jr. (from April 1814)
Secretary of the Navy: William Jones; Benjamin W. Crowninshield (from January 1815)
State Admitted: Indiana (1816)

Family Facts

Father: James Madison (1723–1801)
Mother: Eleanor Conway Madison (1731–1829)
Wife: Dorothea "Dolley" Payne Todd (1768–1849)
Marriage: September 15, 1794
Children: None

Unusual Facts

James Madison was the first president to have served in the U.S. House of Representatives.
He was the first president to wear long trousers. All previous presidents wore knee breeches (as did his successor, James Monroe, who continued to wear the traditional garb).
At 5'4" and less than 100 pounds, he was the shortest and lightest president.
Both of his vice presidents died in office.

Election of 1816

Candidate	Electoral Vote
James Monroe Democratic-Republican	183
Rufus King Federalist	34

Election of 1820

Candidate	Electoral Vote
James Monroe Democratic-Republican	231
John Quincy Adams Independent Republican	1

First Administration (March 4, 1817–March 3, 1821)

Vice President: Daniel D. Tompkins
Secretary of State: John Quincy Adams
Secretary of the Treasury: William Harris Crawford
Secretary of War: John C. Calhoun
Attorney General: Richard Rush; William Wirt (from November 1817)
Postmaster General: Return Jonathan Meigs, Jr.
Secretary of the Navy: Benjamin Crowninshield; Smith Thompson (from January 1819)
States Admitted: Mississippi (1817); Illinois (1818); Alabama (1819); Maine (1820)

Second Administration (March 4, 1821–March 3, 1825)

Vice President: Daniel D. Tompkins
Secretary of State: John Quincy Adams
Secretary of the Treasury: William Harris Crawford
Secretary of War: John C. Calhoun
Attorney General: William Wirt
Postmaster General: Return Jonathan Meigs, Jr.; John McLean (from July 1823)
Secretary of the Navy: Smith Thompson; Samuel L. Southard (from September 1823)
Supreme Court Appointment: Smith Thompson (1823)
State Admitted: Missouri (1821)

Family Facts

Father: Spence Monroe (?–1774)
Mother: Elizabeth Jones Monroe (n.d.)
Wife: Elizabeth Kortright (1768–1830)
Marriage: February 16, 1786
Children: Eliza Kortright (1786–1835); J. S. (most likely the initials stand for James Spence) (1799–1801); Maria Hester (1803–1850)

Unusual Facts

In the election of 1820, James Monroe received every electoral vote except one. A New Hampshire delegate cast his vote for John Quincy Adams to assure that George Washington remained the only president elected unanimously.

Monroe's inauguration in 1817 was the first to be held outdoors.

He was the first president to have been a U.S. senator.

He was the first president to ride on a steamboat.

Wanting to protect his privacy, in retirement he destroyed his personal papers.

John Quincy Adams

Election of 1828

Candidate	Electoral Vote	Popular Vote	Percent
John Quincy Adams Democratic-Republican	84	113,112	30.92
Andrew Jackson Democratic-Republican	99	151,271	41.34
William H. Crawford Democratic-Republican	41	40,876	11.17
Andrew Jackson Democratic-Republican	37	47,531	12.99
Other	. . .	13,053	3.57

Adams Administration (March 4, 1825–March 3, 1829)

Vice President: John C. Calhoun
Secretary of State: Henry Clay
Secretary of the Treasury: Richard Rush
Secretary of War: James Barbour; Peter Buell Porter (from June 1828)
Attorney General: William Wirt
Postmaster General: John McLean
Secretary of the Navy: Samuel L. Southard
Supreme Court Appointment: Robert Trimble (1826)

Family Facts

Father: John Adams (1735–1826)
Mother: Abigail Smith Adams (1744–1818)
Wife: Louisa Catherine Johnson (1775–1852)
Marriage: July 26, 1797
Children: George Washington (1801–1829); John (1803–1834); Charles Francis (1807–1886); Louisa Catherine (1811–1812)

Unusual Facts

When Anne Royall, the first American professional journalist, learned that President Adams regularly swam nude in the Potomac, she went to the river, gathered his clothes, and sat on them until he agreed to talk to her. This was the first time a woman reporter interviewed a president.

He was the first president to be photographed, this having been done after he left the White House.

Adams is the only former president to be elected to the House of Representatives. He served there for 17 years.

Andrew Jackson

Election of 1828

Candidate	Electoral Vote	Popular Vote	Percent
Andrew Jackson Democrat	178	642,553	55.97
John Quincy Adams National Republican	83	500,987	43.63
Other	. . .	4,568	0.40

Election of 1832

Candidate	Electoral Vote	Popular Vote	Percent
Andrew Jackson Democrat	219	701,780	54.23
Henry Clay National Republican	49	484,205	37.42
William Wirt Anti-Masonic	7	100,715	7.78
John Floyd Independent	11	. . .	. . .
Other	. . .	7,273	0.56

Note: John Floyd of Virginia received votes from electors chosen by several state legislatures, though he did not receive any popular votes.

First Administration (March 4, 1829–March 3, 1833)

Vice President: John C. Calhoun (resigned December 1832 to become senator from South Carolina)
Secretary of State: Martin Van Buren; Edward Livingston (from May 1831)
Secretary of the Treasury: Samuel D. Ingham; Louis McLane (from August 1831)
Secretary of War: John H. Eaton; Lewis Cass (from August 1831)
Attorney General: John M. Berrien; Roger B. Taney (from July 1831)
Postmaster General: John McLean; William T. Barry (from March 1829)
Secretary of the Navy: John Branch; Levi Woodbury (from May 1831)
Supreme Court Appointments: John McLean (1829); Henry Baldwin (1830)

Second Administration (March 4, 1833–March 3, 1837)

Vice President: Martin Van Buren
Secretary of State: Edward Livingston; Louis McLane (from May 1833); John Forsyth (from July 1834)
Secretary of the Treasury: Louis McLane; William J. Duane (from May 1833); Roger B. Taney (from September 1833); Levi Woodbury (from July 1834)
Secretary of War: Lewis Cass
Attorney General: Roger B. Taney; Benjamin F. Butler (from November 1833)

Postmaster General: John McLean; William T. Barry (from March 1829); Amos Kendall (from May 1835)
Secretary of the Navy: Levi Woodbury; Mahlon Dickerson (from June 1834)
Supreme Court Appointments: John McLean (1829); James M. Wayne (1835); Roger B. Taney, Chief Justice (1836); Philip P. Barbour (1836)
States Admitted: Arkansas (1836); Michigan (1837)

Family Facts

Father: Andrew Jackson (1730?–1767)
Mother: Elizabeth Hutchinson Jackson (1740?–1781)
Wife: Rachel Donelson Robards (1767–1828)
Marriage: August 1, 1791; second ceremony January 17, 1794
Child: Andrew Jackson, Jr. (adopted) (1810–1865)

Unusual Facts

Andrew Jackson was the first president born in a log cabin.

At Jackson's inauguration, celebrants poured into the White House, and in their enthusiasm they stood on the furniture, ripped curtains, broke glasses, and muddied carpets.

He was the first president to ride on a railroad train.

He survived the first attempt to assassinate a president.

During his presidency, running water was brought into the White House using a system of hollowed-out logs connected to a nearby reservoir.

In 1835 a 1,400-pound slab of cheddar cheese was delivered as a gift and placed in the entrance hall of the White House. The cheese, smell and all, stayed there for two years.

Martin Van Buren

Election of 1836

Candidate	Electoral Vote	Popular Vote	Percent
Martin Van Buren Democrat	170	764,716	50.83
William Henry Harrison Whig	73	550,816	36.63
Hugh L. White Whig	26	146,107	9.72
Daniel Webster Whig	14	41,201	2.74
Other	. . .	1,234	0.08

Van Buren Administration (March 4, 1837–March 3, 1841)

Vice President: Richard M. Johnson
Secretary of State: John Forsyth
Secretary of the Treasury: Levi Woodbury
Secretary of War: Joel R. Poinsett
Attorney General: Benjamin F. Butler; Felix Grundy (from September 1838); Henry D. Gilpin (from January 1840)
Postmaster General: Amos Kendall; John M. Niles (from May 1840)
Secretary of the Navy: Mahlon Dickerson; James K. Paulding (from July 1838)
Supreme Court Appointments: John Catron (1837); John McKinley (1837); Peter V. Daniel (1841)

Family Facts

Father: Abraham Van Buren (1737–1817)
Mother: Maria Hoes Van Alen Van Buren (1747–1817)
Wife: Hannah Hoes (1783–1819)
Marriage: February 21, 1807
Children: Abraham (1807–1873); John (1810–1866); Martin (1812–1855); Smith Thompson (1817–1876)

Unusual Facts

Martin Van Buren was the first president born in the United States (all previous ones having been born in the British colonies prior to American independence).

The term *O.K.* was popularized because of Van Buren. His hometown of Kinderhook, New York, was sometimes referred to as Old Kinderhook, and as a result organizations that formed to support his candidacy in 1840 were named O.K. Clubs. *O.K.* meaning "all correct," however, appeared as a slang term shortly before the Van Burenites adopted it.

A heating system was installed in the White House during Van Buren's presidency.

William Henry Harrison

Election of 1840

Candidate	Electoral Vote	Popular Vote	Percent
William Henry Harrison Whig	234	1,275,390	52.88
Martin Van Buren Democrat	60	1,128,854	46.81
James G. Birney Liberty	...	6,797	0.28
Other	...	767	0.03

Harrison Administration (March 4, 1841–April 4, 1841)

Vice President: John Tyler
Secretary of State: Daniel Webster
Secretary of the Treasury: Thomas Ewing
Secretary of War: John Bell
Attorney General: John J. Crittenden
Postmaster General: Francis Granger
Secretary of the Navy: George E. Badger

Family Facts

Father: Benjamin Harrison (1726–1791)
Mother: Elizabeth Bassett Harrison (1730–1792)
Wife: Anna Tuthill Symmes (1775–1864)
Marriage: November 22, 1795
Children: Elizabeth (1796–1846); John Cleves Symmes (1798–1832); Lucy Singleton (1800–1826); William Henry, Jr. (1802–1838); John Scott (1804–1878); Benjamin (1806–1840); Mary Symmes (1809–1842); Carter Bassett (1811–1839); Anna Tuthill (1813–1845); James Findlay (1814–1817)

Unusual Facts

William Henry Harrison's father was a signer of the Declaration of Independence.
Of Harrison's one month in office, he spent his final eight days in bed suffering from declining health.
He was the first president to die in office.

John Tyler

Note: John Tyler became president on April 6, 1841, after William Henry Harrison's death from illness.

Tyler Administration (April 6, 1841–March 3, 1845)

Vice President: None
Secretary of State: Daniel Webster; Abel P. Upshur (from July 1843); John C. Calhoun (from April 1844)
Secretary of the Treasury: Thomas Ewing; Walter Forward (from September 1841); John C. Spencer (from March 1843); George M. Bibb (from July 1844)
Secretary of War: John Bell; John C. Spencer (from October 1841); James M. Porter (from March 1843); William Wilkins (from February 1844)
Attorney General: John J. Crittenden; Hugh S. Legare (from September 1841); John Nelson (from July 1843)
Postmaster General: Francis Granger; Charles A. Wickliffe (from October 1841)
Secretary of the Navy: George E. Badger; Abel P. Upshur (from October 1841); David Henshaw (from July 1843); Thomas W. Gilmer (from February 1844); John Y. Mason (from March 1844)
Supreme Court Appointment: Samuel Nelson (1845)
State Admitted: Florida (1845)

Family Facts

Father: John Tyler (1747–1813)
Mother: Mary Marot Armistead Tyler (1761–1797)
First Wife: Letitia Christian (1790–1842)
First Marriage: March 29, 1813
Second Wife: Julia Gardiner (1820–1889)
Second Marriage: June 26, 1844
Children: (by his first wife) Mary (1815–1848); Robert (1816–1877); John, Jr. (1819–1896); Letitia (1821–1907); Elizabeth (1823–1850); Anne Contesse (1825); Alice (1827–1854); Tazewell (1830–1874); (by his second wife) David Gardiner (1846–1927); John Alexander (1848–1883); Julia (1849–1871); Lachlin (1851–1902); Lyon (1853–1935); Robert Fitzwalter (1856–1927); Pearl (1860–1947)

Unusual Facts

John Tyler's cabinet underwent more changes in personnel than that for any other president. There were 22 different cabinet secretaries for six positions.

He was elected in 1862 to the Confederate House of Representatives, making him the only president to have held office in the Confederacy.

James K. Polk

Election of 1844

Candidate	Electoral Vote	Popular Vote	Percent
James K. Polk Democrat	170	1,339,494	49.54
Henry Clay Whig	105	1,300,004	48.08
James G. Birney Liberty	. . .	62,103	2.30
Other	. . .	2,058	0.08

Polk Administration (March 4, 1845–March 3, 1849)

Vice President: George M. Dallas
Secretary of State: James Buchanan
Secretary of the Treasury: Robert J. Walker
Secretary of War: William L. Marcy
Attorney General: John Y. Mason; Nathan Clifford (from October 1846); Isaac Toucey (from June 1848)
Postmaster General: Cave Johnson
Secretary of the Navy: George Bancroft; John Y. Mason (from September 1846)
Supreme Court Appointments: Levi Woodbury (1845); Robert Cooper Grier (1846)
States Admitted: Texas (1845); Iowa (1846); Wisconsin (1848)

Family Facts

Father: Samuel Polk (1772–1827)
Mother: Jane Knox Polk (1776–1852)
Wife: Sara Childress (1803–1891)
Marriage: January 1, 1824
Children: None

Unusual Facts

News of James K. Polk's nomination was widely reported through a recent invention, the telegraph.

The president's wife, Sarah Polk, banned dancing, card-playing, and alcoholic beverages in the White House.

Polk added the most territory to the United States since the Louisiana Purchase of 1803.

He died just three and a half months after leaving the presidency.

Zachary Taylor

Election of 1848

Candidate	Electoral Vote	Popular Vote	Percent
Zachary Taylor Whig	163	1,361,393	47.28
Lewis Cass Democrat	127	1,223,460	42.49
Martin Van Buren Free-Soil	. . .	291,501	10.12
Other	. . .	2,830	0.10

Taylor Administration (March 4, 1849–July 9, 1850)

Vice President: Millard Fillmore
Secretary of State: John M. Clayton
Secretary of the Treasury: William M. Meredith
Secretary of War: George W. Crawford
Attorney General: Reverdy Johnson
Postmaster General: Jacob Collamer
Secretary of the Navy: William B. Preston
Secretary of the Interior: (Department created by Congress in March 1849) Thomas Ewing

Family Facts

Father: Richard Taylor (1744–1829)
Mother: Sarah Dabney Strother Taylor (1760–1822)
Wife: Margaret Mackall Smith (1788–1852)
Marriage: June 21, 1810
Children: Anne Margaret (1811–1875); Sarah Knox (1814–1835); Octavia (1816–1820); Margaret (1819–1820); Mary Elizabeth (1824–1909); Richard (1826–1879)

Unusual Facts

Zachary Taylor's defeat of the Mexicans at Buena Vista in February 1847 was one of the greatest victories in American military history.

He was the first president not previously elected to any other public office.

He neither smoked nor drank, but he chewed tobacco and in the White House had the reputation of never missing the sand-filled box that served as a spittoon in his office.

Visitors to the White House would take souvenir hairs from Whitey, his old Army horse, which he kept on the White House lawn.

He was the second president to die in office (like William Henry Harrison, from illness), and the second to die of the only two Whigs who ever won the White House.

Millard Fillmore

Note: Millard Fillmore became president on July 10, 1850, after Zachary Taylor's death from illness.

Fillmore Administration (July 10, 1850–March 3, 1853)

Vice President: None
Secretary of State: Daniel Webster; Edward Everett (from November 1852)
Secretary of the Treasury: William M. Meredith; Thomas Corwin (from July 1850)
Secretary of War: George Crawford; Charles M. Conrad (from July 1850)
Attorney General: Reverdy Johnson; John J. Crittenden (from July 1850)
Postmaster General: Nathan Hall; Samuel D. Hubbard (from September 1852)
Secretary of the Navy: William A. Graham; John P. Kennedy (from July 1852)
Secretary of the Interior: Thomas M. T. McKennan; Alexander H. H. Stuart (from September 1850)
Supreme Court Appointment: Benjamin R. Curtis (1851)
State Admitted: California (1850)

Family Facts

Father: Nathaniel Fillmore (1771–1863)
Mother: Phoebe Millard Fillmore (1780–1831)
First Wife: Abigail Powers (1798–1853)
First Marriage: February 5, 1826
Second Wife: Caroline Carmichael McIntosh (1813–1881)
Second Marriage: February 10, 1858
Children (by his first wife): Millard Powers (1828–1889); Mary Abigail (1832–1854)

Unusual Facts

Millard Fillmore and Andrew Jackson came from the most impoverished backgrounds of any of the presidents.

First Lady Abigail Powers Fillmore established a White House library.

His wife and his daughter, Mary Abigail, died within one year of each other.

Franklin Pierce

Election of 1852

Candidate	Electoral Vote	Popular Vote	Percent
Franklin Pierce Democrat	254	1,607,510	50.84
Winfield Scott Whig	42	1,386,942	43.87
John P. Hale Free-Soil	. . .	155,210	4.91
Other	. . .	12,168	0.38

Pierce Administration (March 4, 1853–March 3, 1857)

Vice President: William R. King (died April 1853)
Secretary of State: William L. Marcy
Secretary of the Treasury: James Guthrie
Secretary of War: Jefferson Davis
Attorney General: Caleb Cushing
Postmaster General: James Campbell
Secretary of the Navy: James C. Dobbin
Secretary of the Interior: Robert McClelland
Supreme Court Appointment: John A. Campbell (1853)

Family Facts

Father: Benjamin Pierce (1757–1839)
Mother: Anna Kendrick Pierce (1768–1838)
Wife: Jane Means Appleton (1806–1863)
Marriage: November 19, 1834
Children: Franklin (1836); Frank Robert (1839–1843); Benjamin "Benny" (1841–1853)

Unusual Facts

Franklin Pierce recited his inaugural address from memory.

Known for his good looks, he was called "Handsome Frank."

Pierce was kindly and charming and was described by one senator's wife as "courtly and polished."

He was responsible for the Gadsden Purchase, land bought from Mexico that consisted of southern New Mexico and southern Arizona.

Although popular in New Hampshire before the Civil War, during the war his pro-Southern views caused him to be labeled a traitor.

James Buchanan

Election of 1856

Candidate	Electoral Vote	Popular Vote	Percent
James Buchanan Democrat	174	1,836,072	45.28
John C. Fremont Republican	114	1,342,345	33.11
Millard Fillmore American (Know-Nothing)	8	873,053	21.53
Other	. . .	3,177	0.08

Buchanan Administration (March 4, 1857–March 3, 1861)

Vice President: John C. Breckenridge
Secretary of State: Lewis Cass; Jeremiah S. Black (from December 1860)
Secretary of the Treasury: Howell Cobb; Philip F. Thomas (from December 1860); John A. Dix (from January 1861)
Secretary of War: John B. Floyd; Joseph Holt (from January 1861)
Attorney General: Jeremiah S. Black; Edwin M. Stanton (from December 1860)
Postmaster General: Aaron V. Brown; Joseph Holt (from March 1859); Horatio King (from February 1861)
Secretary of the Navy: Isaac Toucey
Secretary of the Interior: Jacob Thompson
Supreme Court Appointment: Nathan Clifford (1858)
States Admitted: Minnesota (1858); Oregon (1859); Kansas (1861)

Family Facts

Father: James Buchanan (1761–1821)
Mother: Elizabeth Speer Buchanan (1767–1833)
Wife: None
Children: None

Unusual Facts

James Buchanan was the only bachelor president. His niece, Harriet Lane Johnston, served as White House hostess.

He had one eye that was nearsighted, causing him to tilt his head to his left.

He was often called a "dandy" for his meticulous dress and was famous for his almost total lack of humor.

Abraham Lincoln

Election of 1860

Candidate	Electoral Vote	Popular Vote	Percent
Abraham Lincoln Republican	180	1,865,908	39.82
Stephen A. Douglas Democrat	12	1,380,202	29.46
John C. Breckenridge Democrat	72	848,019	18.09
John Bell Constitutional Union	39	590,901	12.61
Other	. . .	531	0.01

Election of 1864

Candidate	Electoral Vote	Popular Vote	Percent
Abraham Lincoln Republican	212	2,218,388	55.02
George B. McClellan Democrat	21	1,812,807	44.96

Note: Because 11 southern states had seceded from the Union and were still in rebellion, they did not participate in the presidential election. As a result, their 81 electoral votes were not cast.

First Administration (March 4, 1861–March 3, 1865)

Vice President: Hannibal Hamlin
Secretary of State: William H. Seward
Secretary of the Treasury: Salmon P. Chase; William P. Fessenden (from July 1864)
Secretary of War: Simon Cameron; Edwin M. Stanton (from January 1862)
Attorney General: Edward Bates; James Speed (from December 1864)
Postmaster General: Montgomery Blair; William Dennison (from October 1864)
Secretary of the Navy: Gideon Welles
Secretary of the Interior: Caleb B. Smith; John P. Usher (from January 1863)
Supreme Court Appointments: Noah H. Swayne (1862); Samuel F. Miller (1862); David Davis (1862); Stephen J. Field (1863); Salmon P. Chase, Chief Justice (1864)
States Admitted: West Virginia (1863); Nevada (1864)

Second Administration (March 4, 1865–April 15, 1865)

Vice President: Andrew Johnson
Secretary of State: William H. Seward
Secretary of the Treasury: Hugh McCulloch
Secretary of War: Edwin M. Stanton
Attorney General: James Speed
Postmaster General: William Dennison
Secretary of the Navy: Gideon Welles
Secretary of the Interior: John P. Usher

Family Facts

Father: Thomas Lincoln (1778–1851)
Mother: Nancy Hanks Lincoln (1784–1818)
Stepmother: Sarah Bush Johnston
Wife: Mary Todd (1818–1882)

Marriage: November 4, 1842
Children: Robert Todd (1843–1926); Edward Baker (1846–1850); William Wallace (1850–1862); Thomas "Tad" (1853–1871)

Unusual Facts

Known as the "rail splitter," Abraham Lincoln hated manual labor.

He was the first president born outside of the original 13 colonies.

He liked being tall (6'4") and purposefully wore a stovepipe hat to add even more effect to his height.

In February 1860 Abraham Lincoln posed for a picture taken at Mathew Brady's photographic studio in New York City. Lincoln later credited the photo with being essential in winning him the Republican nomination, an early instance of photography assuming an important role in a presidential campaign.

First Lady Mary Todd Lincoln spent lavishly in refurbishing the White House, including $7,500 for draperies and furniture, $3,195 for a porcelain dining service, $1,500 for glassware, and additional sums for green velvet carpet and fancy matting. She exceeded her congressional budget of $26,000 by $6,000, causing Lincoln to complain about money spent on "flub dubs" while soldiers lacked blankets.

Lincoln invited more entertainers to the presidential residence than any previous chief executive. Among them were Larooqua, an American Indian singer known for her "mellifluous voice," the Hutchinson family, a singing troupe; and Meda Blanchard, the first opera singer to entertain at the White House.

Lincoln founded the United States Secret Service in 1865, but its original purpose was to investigate the counterfeiting of U.S. currency, not to guard the president.

He was the first president to be assassinated, an event that lent eerie credence to his words: "The death of . . . [a] president may not be without its use, in reminding us, that we, too, must die. . . . We are not so much roused . . . by the fall of many undistinguished, as that of one . . . well-known name. By the latter, we are forced to muse, and ponder."

Andrew Johnson

Note: Andrew Johnson became president on April 15, 1865, after Abraham Lincoln died from an assassin's bullet.

Johnson Administration (April 15, 1865–March 3, 1869)

Vice President: None
Secretary of State: William H. Seward
Secretary of the Treasury: Hugh McCulloch
Secretary of War: Edwin M. Stanton; John M. Schofield (from June 1868)
Attorney General: James Speed; Henry Stanbery (from 1866); William M. Evarts (from July 1868)
Postmaster General: William Dennison; Alexander W. Randall (from 1866)
Secretary of the Navy: Gideon Welles
Secretary of the Interior: John P. Usher; James Harlan (from May 1865); Orville H. Browning (from September 1866)
State Admitted: Nebraska (1867)

Family Facts

Father: Jacob Johnson (1778–1812)
Mother: Mary McDonough Johnson (1783–1856)
Wife: Eliza McCardle (1810–1876)
Marriage: May 17, 1827
Children: Martha (1828–1901); Charles (1830–1863); Mary (1832–1883); Robert (1834–1869); Andrew (1852–1879)

Unusual Facts

Andrew Johnson had no formal education.

Under Johnson's presidency, Alexander Gardner, Confederate commander of the prisoner-of-war camp at Andersonville, Georgia, was hanged. Johnson refused all requests for mercy.

He believed strongly that African Americans were inferior to whites and rhetorically asked, "Who believes for one instant that Mr. Jefferson, when he penned [the Declaration of Independence], had the negro population in his mind?"

He was the first president to be impeached; he was acquitted in the Senate by only one vote.

He was the only former president to be elected to the United States Senate.

Ulysses S. Grant

Election of 1868

Candidate	Electoral Vote	Popular Vote	Percent
Ulysses S. Grant Republican	214	3,013,650	52.66
Horatio S. Seymour Democrat	80	2,708,744	47.34
Other	. . .	46	. . .

Election of 1872

Candidate	Electoral Vote	Popular Vote	Percent
Ulysses S. Grant Republican	286	3,598,235	55.63
Horace Greeley Democrat/Liberal Republican	. . .	2,834,761	43.83
Charles O'Connor Straight Democrat	. . .	18,602	. . .
Other	. . .	16,081	. . .

Note: Horace Greeley carried six states, but because he died shortly after the general election, the 66 electoral votes from those states went to other individuals.

First Administration (March 4, 1869–March 3, 1873)

Vice President: Schuyler Colfax

Secretary of State: Elihu B. Washburne; Hamilton Fish (from March 17, 1869)

Secretary of the Treasury: George S. Boutwell

Secretary of War: John A. Rawlins; William T. Sherman (from September 1869); William W. Belknap (from November 1869)

Attorney General: Ebenezer Hoar; Amos T. Akerman (from July 1870); George H. Williams (from January 1871)

Postmaster General: John A. J. Creswell

Secretary of the Navy: Adolph E. Borie; George M. Robeson (from June 1869)

Secretary of the Interior: Jacob D. Cox; Columbus Delano (from November 1870)

Supreme Court Appointments: William Strong (1870); Joseph P. Bradley (1870); Ward Hunt (1872)

Second Administration (March 4, 1873–March 3, 1877)

Vice President: Henry Wilson

Secretary of State: Hamilton Fish

Secretary of the Treasury: William A. Richardson; Benjamin H. Bristow (from June 1874); Lot M. Morrill (from July 1876)

Secretary of War: William W. Belknap; Alphonso Taft (from March 1876); James D. Cameron (from June 1876)

Attorney General: George H. Williams; Edwards Pierrepont (from May 1875); Alphonso Taft (from June 1876)

Postmaster General: John A. J. Creswell; James W. Marshall (from July 1874); Marshall Jewell (from September 1874); James N. Tyner (from July 1876)
Secretary of the Navy: George M. Robeson
Secretary of the Interior: Columbus Delano; Zachariah Chandler (from October 1875)
Supreme Court Appointment: Morrison R. Waite, Chief Justice (1874)
State Admitted: Colorado (1876)

Family Facts

Father: Jesse Root Grant (1794–1873)
Mother: Hannah Simpson Grant (1798–1883)
Wife: Julia Boggs Dent (1826–1902)
Marriage: August 22, 1848
Children: Frederic Dent (1850–1912); Ulysses Simpson (1852–1929); Ellen Wrenshall (1855–1922); Jesse Root (1858–1934)

Unusual Facts

Ulysses S. Grant was once fined $20 for riding too fast on his horse.

By the end of his eight years as president, every one of his executive offices had come under congressional investigation for corruption.

Rutherford B. Hayes

Election of 1876

Candidate	Electoral Vote	Popular Vote	Percent
Rutherford B. Hayes Republican	185	4,034,311	47.95
Samuel J. Tilden Democrat	184	4,288,546	50.97
Peter Cooper Greenback	. . .	75,973	0.90
Other	. . .	14,271	0.17

Note: The disputed electoral votes of Florida, South Carolina, Louisiana, and Oregon were awarded to Hayes by a special commission appointed by Congress. Those votes were enough to make Hayes the winner by a margin of 185-184, even though he received fewer popular votes than Tilden.

Hayes Administration (March 4, 1877–March 3, 1881)

Vice President: William A. Wheeler
Secretary of State: William M. Evarts
Secretary of the Treasury: John Sherman
Secretary of War: George W. McCrary; Alexander Ramsey (from December 1879)
Attorney General: Charles Devens
Postmaster General: David M. Key; Horace Maynard (from August 1880)
Secretary of the Navy: Richard W. Thompson; Nathan Goff, Jr. (from January 1881)
Secretary of the Interior: Carl Schurz
Supreme Court Appointments: John Marshall Harlan (1877); William Burnham Woods (1880)

Family Facts

Father: Rutherford Hayes (1787–1822)
Mother: Sophia Birchard Hayes (1792–1866)
Wife: Lucy Ware Webb (1831–1889)
Marriage: December 30, 1852
Children: Sardis (1853–1926); James Webb Cook (1856–1934); Rutherford Platt (1858–1931); Joseph (1861–1863); George (1864–1866); Frances "Fanny" (1867–1950); Scott Russell (1871–1923); Manning Force (1873–1874)

Unusual Facts

When Rutherford Hayes was a child, he won elementary school contests in spelling.

His wife, Lucy Webb, was the first first lady to graduate from a college (Wesleyan). She began the annual Easter egg-rolling on the White House lawn.

Hayes installed the first telephone in the White House and placed his first call to Alexander Graham Bell.

He was the first president to travel to the West Coast while in office.

James A. Garfield

Election of 1880

Candidate	Electoral Vote	Popular Vote	Percent
James A. Garfield Republican	214	4,461,158	48.27
Winfield S. Hancock Democrat	155	4,444,260	48.25
James B. Weaver Greenback	...	305,997	3.32
Other	...	14,005	0.15

Garfield Administration (March 4, 1881–September 19, 1881)

Vice President: Chester A. Arthur
Secretary of State: James G. Blaine
Secretary of the Treasury: William Windom
Secretary of War: Robert T. Lincoln
Attorney General: Wayne MacVeagh
Postmaster General: Thomas L. James
Secretary of the Navy: William H. Hunt
Secretary of the Interior: Samuel J. Kirkwood
Supreme Court Appointment: Stanley Matthews (1881)

Family Facts

Father: Abram Garfield (1799–1833)
Mother: Eliza Ballou Garfield (1801–1888)
Wife: Lucretia Rudolph (1832–1918)
Marriage: November 11, 1858
Children: Eliza (1860–1863); Harry (1863–1942); James Rudolph (1865–1950); Mary (1867–1947); Irvin (1870–1951); Abram (1872–1958); Edward (1874–1876)

Unusual Facts

James A. Garfield was the youngest Union major general in the Civil War.

As a congressman he was known as the best speaker in the Republican Party.

He entertained friends by writing Latin with one hand and Greek with the other.

He was the last president born in a log cabin.

His mother, Elizabeth Ballou Garfield, was the first mother of a president to witness her son's inauguration.

Chester A. Arthur

Note: Chester A. Arthur became president on September 20, 1881, after James Garfield died from an assassin's bullet.

Arthur Administration (September 20, 1881–March 3, 1885)

Vice President: None
Secretary of State: James G. Blaine; Frederick T. Frelinghuysen (from December 1881)
Secretary of the Treasury: William Windom; Charles J. Folger (from November 1881); Walter Q. Gresham (from September 1884); Hugh McCulloch (from October 1884)
Secretary of War: Robert T. Lincoln
Attorney General: Wayne MacVeagh; Benjamin H. Brewster (from January 1882)
Postmaster General: Thomas L. James; Timothy O. Howe (from January 1882); Walter Q. Gresham (from April 1883); Frank Hatton (from October 1884)
Secretary of the Navy: William H. Hunt; William E. Chandler (from April 1882)
Secretary of the Interior: Samuel J. Kirkwood; Henry M. Teller (from April 1882)
Supreme Court Appointments: Horace Gary (1881); Samuel Blatchford (1882)

Family Facts

Father: William Arthur (1796–1875)
Mother: Malvina Stone Arthur (1802–1869)
Wife: Ellen Lewis Herndon (1837–1880)
Marriage: October 25, 1859
Children: William Lewis Herndon (1860–1863); Chester Alan, Jr. (1864–1937); Ellen (1871–1915)

Unusual Facts

Chester A. Arthur was an expert fisherman known for his success at catching trout, salmon, and striped bass.

His wife, Ellen, died just 10 months before he won the vice presidency.

In 1882 he hired Louis Tiffany to redecorate the interior of the White House.

Arthur was the first president to travel to Wyoming, which he did in 1883.

He liked to entertain and began weekly black-tie state dinners that sometimes included 14 courses of food and eight varieties of wine.

He dedicated the Washington Monument on February 21, 1885.

Grover Cleveland

Election of 1884

Candidate	Electoral Vote	Popular Vote	Percent
Grover Cleveland Democrat	219	4,874,621	48.50
James G. Blaine Republican	182	4,848,936	48.25
Benjamin F. Butler Greenback	. . .	175,096	1.74
John P. St. John Prohibition	. . .	147,482	1.47
Other	. . .	3,619	0.04

Election of 1892

Candidate	Electoral Vote	Popular Vote	Percent
Grover Cleveland Democrat	277	5,551,883	46.05
Benjamin Harrison Republican	145	5,179,244	42.96
James B. Weaver Populist	22	1,024,280	8.50
John Bidwell Prohibition	. . .	270,770	2.25
Other	. . .	29,920	0.25

First Administration (March 4, 1885–March 3, 1889)

Vice President: Thomas A. Hendricks
Secretary of State: Thomas F. Bayard
Secretary of the Treasury: Daniel Manning; Charles S. Fairchild (from April 1887)
Secretary of War: William C. Endicott
Attorney General: Augustus H. Garland
Postmaster General: William F. Vilas; Donald M. Dickinson (from January 1888)
Secretary of the Navy: William C. Whitney
Secretary of the Interior: Lucius Q. C. Lamar; William F. Vilas (from January 1888)
Secretary of Agriculture: (The Department of Agriculture was elevated by Congress to cabinet rank during the last days of the first Cleveland presidency, in February 1889) Norman J. Coleman
Supreme Court Appointments: Lucius Q. C. Lamar (1888); Melville W. Fuller, Chief Justice (1888)

Second Administration (March 4, 1893–March 3, 1897)

Vice President: Adlai E. Stevenson
Secretary of State: Walter Q. Gresham; Richard Olney (from June 1895)
Secretary of the Treasury: John G. Carlisle

Secretary of War: Daniel S. Lamont
Attorney General: Richard Olney; Judson Harmon (from June 1895)
Postmaster General: Wilson S. Bissell; William L. Wilson (from April 1895)
Secretary of the Navy: Hilary A. Herbert
Secretary of the Interior: Hoke Smith; David R. Francis (from September 1896)
Secretary of Agriculture: Julius Sterling Morton
Supreme Court Appointments: Edward D. White (1894); Rufus W. Peckham (1895)
State Admitted: Utah (1896)

Family Facts

Father: Richard Falley Cleveland (1804–1853)
Mother: Ann Neal Cleveland (1806–1882)
Wife: Frances Folsom (1864–1947)
Marriage: June 2, 1886
Children: Ruth (1891–1904); Esther (1893–1980); Marion (1895–1977); Richard Folsom (1897–1974); Francis Grover (1903–1995). Cleveland allegedly had an illegitimate son, Oscar (1874–?), with Maria Halpin.

Unusual Facts

Grover Cleveland is the only president to have been elected to two nonconsecutive terms.

During his first term, in 1886, the Statue of Liberty was unveiled in New York Harbor.

He was so fat in middle age that family members called him "Uncle Jumbo" after P. T. Barnum's famous elephant.

His wife, Frances Folsom, was 21 at the time of their marriage; he was 49. Their daughter Esther is the only president's child ever to be born in the White House.

As president, he often worked past midnight and into the early morning hours.

Benjamin Harrison

Election of 1888

Candidate	Electoral Vote	Popular Vote	Percent
Benjamin Harrison Republican	233	5,443,892	47.82
Grover Cleveland Democrat	168	5,534,488	48.62
Clinton B. Fisk Prohibition	. . .	249,813	2.19
Alson J. Streeter Union Labor	. . .	146,602	1.29
Other	. . .	8,519	0.07

Note: This was the second election in American history in which the candidate with the greatest number of popular votes finished second in electoral votes. The previous election was that of 1876.

Benjamin Harrison Administration (March 4, 1889–March 3, 1893)

Vice President: Levi P. Morton
Secretary of State: James G. Blaine; John W. Foster (from June 1892)
Secretary of the Treasury: William Windom; Charles Foster (from February 1891)
Secretary of War: Redfield Proctor; Stephen B. Elkins (from December 1891)
Attorney General: William H. H. Miller
Postmaster General: John Wanamaker
Secretary of the Navy: Benjamin F. Tracy
Secretary of the Interior: John W. Noble
Secretary of Agriculture: Jeremiah M. Rusk
Supreme Court Appointments: David J. Brewer (1889); Henry B. Brown (1890); George Shiras, Jr. (1892); Howell E. Jackson (1893)
States Admitted: North Dakota, South Dakota, Montana, Washington (all 1889); Idaho, Wyoming (both 1890)

Family Facts

Father: John Scott Harrison (1804–1878)
Mother: Elizabeth Irwin Harrison (1810–1850)
First Wife: Caroline "Carrie" Lavinia Scott (1832–1892)
First Marriage: October 20, 1853
Second Wife: Mary Scott Lord Dimmick (1858–1948)
Second Marriage: April 6, 1896
Children: (by his first wife) Russell Benjamin (1854–1936); Mary Scott (1858–1930); (by his second wife) Elizabeth (1897–1955)

Unusual Facts

Electric lights were installed in the White House during Benjamin Harrison's term, though his wife refused to turn them on because she was frightened of the switches.
He is the only president who is the grandson of another president, William Henry Harrison.
He is the only president ever to have been preceded and succeeded by the same president.
Quiet and withdrawn, Harrison was always formal in public and addressed even his close male friends as "Mister."

William McKinley

Election of 1896

Candidate	Electoral Vote	Popular Vote	Percent
William McKinley Republican	271	7,108,480	51.01
William J. Bryan Democrat/Populist	176	6,511,495	46.73
John A. Palmer National Democrat	. . .	133,435	0.96
Joshua Levering Prohibition	. . .	125,072	0.90
Other	. . .	57,256	0.41

Election of 1900

Candidate	Electoral Vote	Popular Vote	Percent
William McKinley Republican	292	7,218,039	51.67
William J. Bryan Democrat	155	6,358,345	45.51
John C. Wooley Prohibition	. . .	209,004	1.50
Eugene V. Debs Social Democrat	. . .	86,935	0.62
Other	. . .	98,147	0.70

First Administration (March 4, 1897–March 3, 1901)

Vice President: Garret A. Hobart
Secretary of State: John Sherman; William R. Day (April–September 1898); John Hay (from September 1898)
Secretary of the Treasury: Lyman J. Gage
Secretary of War: Russell A. Alger; Elihu Root (from August 1899)
Attorney General: Joseph McKenna; John W. Griggs (from February 1898)
Postmaster General: James A. Gary; Charles Emory Smith (from April 1898)
Secretary of the Navy: John D. Long
Secretary of the Interior: Cornelius N. Bliss; Ethan A. Hitchcock (from February 1899)
Secretary of Agriculture: James Wilson
Supreme Court Appointment: Joseph McKenna (1898)

Second Administration (March 4, 1901–September 14, 1901)

Vice President: Theodore Roosevelt
Secretary of State: John Hay
Secretary of the Treasury: Lyman J. Gage
Secretary of War: Elihu Root
Attorney General: John W. Griggs; Philander C. Knox (from April 1901)

Postmaster General: Charles Emory Smith
Secretary of the Navy: John D. Long
Secretary of the Interior: Ethan A. Hitchcock
Secretary of Agriculture: James Wilson

Family Facts

Father: William McKinley (1807–1892)
Mother: Nancy Allison McKinley (1809–1897)
Wife: Ida Saxton (1847–1907)
Marriage: January 25, 1871
Children: Katherine (1871–1875); Ida (1873)

Unusual Facts

William McKinley was the last president to have served in the Civil War.

During his front-porch presidential campaign of 1896, he answered only those questions submitted to him in advance.

He was the third president to be assassinated.

After he was struck by the assassin's bullets, his stomach wound was improperly drained in a poorly lighted operating room.

Theodore Roosevelt

Note: Theodore Roosevelt became president on September 14, 1901, after William McKinley died from an assassin's bullet.

Election of 1904

Candidate	Electoral Vote	Popular Vote	Percent
Theodore Roosevelt Republican	336	7,626,593	56.41
Alton B. Parker Democrat	140	5,082,898	37.60
Eugene V. Debs Socialist	. . .	402,489	2.98
Silas C. Swallow Prohibition	. . .	258,596	1.91
Other	. . .	148,388	1.10

First Administration (September 14, 1901–March 3, 1905)

Vice President: None
Secretary of State: John Hay
Secretary of the Treasury: Lyman J. Gage; Leslie M. Shaw (from February 1902)
Secretary of War: Elihu Root; William Howard Taft (from February 1904)
Attorney General: Philander C. Knox; William H. Moody (from July 1904)
Postmaster General: Charles Emory Smith; Henry C. Payne (from January 1902); Robert J. Wynne (from October 1904)
Secretary of the Navy: John D. Long; William H. Moody (from May 1902); Paul Morton (from July 1904)
Secretary of the Interior: Ethan A. Hitchcock
Secretary of Agriculture: James Wilson
Secretary of Commerce and Labor: (Department created by Congress in February 1903) George B. Cortelyou; Victor M. Metcalf (from July 1904)
Supreme Court Appointments: Oliver Wendell Holmes (1902); William R. Day (1903)

Second Administration (March 4, 1905–March 3, 1909)

Vice President: Charles Warren Fairbanks
Secretary of State: John Hay; Elihu Root (from July 1905); Robert Bacon (from January 1909)
Secretary of the Treasury: Leslie M. Shaw; George B. Cortelyou (from March 1907)
Secretary of War: William Howard Taft; Luke E. Wright (from July 1908)
Attorney General: William H. Moody; Charles J. Bonaparte (from December 1906)
Postmaster General: George B. Cortelyou; George von L. Meyer (from March 1907)
Secretary of the Navy: Paul Morton; Charles J. Bonaparte (from July 1905); Victor H. Metcalf (from December 1906); Truman H. Newberry (from December 1908)
Secretary of the Interior: Ethan A. Hitchcock; James R. Garfield (from March 1907)
Secretary of Agriculture: James Wilson
Secretary of Commerce and Labor: Victor H. Metcalf; Oscar S. Straus (from December 1906)

Supreme Court Appointment: William H. Moody (1906)
State Admitted: Oklahoma (1907)

Family Facts

Father: Theodore Roosevelt (1831–1878)
Mother: Martha Bulloch Roosevelt (1834–1884)
First Wife: Alice Hathaway Lee (1861–1884)
First Marriage: October 27, 1880
Second Wife: Edith Kermit Carow (1861–1948)
Second Marriage: December 2, 1886
Children: (by his first wife) Alice Lee (1884–1980); (by his second wife) Theodore, Jr. (1887–1944); Kermit (1889–1943); Ethel Carow (1891–1977); Archibald (1894–1981); Quentin (1897–1918)

Unusual Facts

Theodore Roosevelt was a sickly child who suffered from asthma, headaches, and bouts of vomiting.

While he was president, in 1902, the White House was extensively remodeled, including the addition of a West Wing, and most of the old furnishings were sold at auction.

Roosevelt was the first president to use the new medium of the wire services extensively to generate publicity for himself and his programs.

During Roosevelt's presidency in 1903, Orville and Wilbur Wright staged the first powered airplane flight in history at Kitty Hawk, North Carolina.

He was the first president to win the Nobel Peace Prize, which he was awarded for negotiating the Russo-Japanese Treaty.

After he was portrayed in a cartoon sparing the life of a bear cub, the phrase *Teddy bear* was given to stuffed toys representing the cuddly animal.

Guests at the Roosevelt White House included Rudyard Kipling, Bat Masterson, and John Burroughs.

On a safari to Africa in 1909, he bagged more than 500 assorted birds and animals, including 17 lions.

William Howard Taft

Election of 1908

Candidate	Electoral Vote	Popular Vote	Percent
William H. Taft Republican	321	7,662,258	51.58
William J. Bryan Democrat	162	6,406,801	43.05
Eugene V. Debs Socialist	. . .	420,380	2.82
Eugene W. Chafin Prohibition	. . .	252,821	1.70
Other	. . .	126,474	0.85

Taft Administration (March 4, 1909–March 3, 1913)

Vice President: James S. Sherman
Secretary of State: Philander C. Knox
Secretary of the Treasury: Franklin MacVeagh
Secretary of War: Jacob M. Dickinson; Henry L. Stimson (from May 1911)
Attorney General: George W. Wickersham
Postmaster General: Frank H. Hitchcock
Secretary of the Navy: George von L. Meyer
Secretary of the Interior: Richard A. Ballinger; Walter L. Fisher (from March 1911)
Secretary of Agriculture: James Wilson
Secretary of Commerce and Labor: Charles Nagel
Supreme Court Appointments: Horace H. Lurton (1909); Charles Evans Hughes (1910); Willis Van Devanter (1910); Edward D. White, Chief Justice (1910); Joseph R. Lamar (1911); Mahlon Pitney (1912)
States Admitted: New Mexico (1912); Arizona (1912)

Family Facts

Father: Alphonso Taft (1810–1891)
Mother: Louisa Maria Torrey Taft (1827–1907)
Wife: Helen Herron (1861–1943)
Marriage: June 19, 1886
Children: Robert Alphonso (1889–1953); Helen Herron (1891–1987); Charles Phelps (1897–1983)

Unusual Facts

William Howard Taft was the first and only president to finish third in a presidential election.

He was the first and thus far only president to serve on the Supreme Court.

He was the first president to have a presidential car.

Taft was so fat that a large bathtub was installed for him in the White House, reportedly after he got stuck in the old one.

Woodrow Wilson

Election of 1912

Candidate	Electoral Vote	Popular Vote	Percent
Woodrow Wilson Democrat	435	6,293,152	41.84
Theodore Roosevelt Progressive	88	4,119,207	27.39
William H. Taft Republican	8	3,486,333	23.18
Eugene V. Debs Socialist	. . .	900,369	5.99
Other	. . .	241,902	1.61

Election of 1916

Candidate	Electoral Vote	Popular Vote	Percent
Woodrow Wilson Democrat	277	9,126,300	49.24
Charles E. Hughes Republican	254	8,546,789	46.11
Allen L. Benson Socialist	. . .	589,924	3.18
James F. Hanly Prohibition	. . .	221,030	1.19
Other	. . .	50,979	0.28

First Administration (March 4, 1913–March 3, 1917)

Vice President: Thomas R. Marshall
Secretary of State: William Jennings Bryan; Robert Lansing (from June 1915)
Secretary of the Treasury: William G. McAdoo
Secretary of War: Lindley M. Garrison; Newton D. Baker (from March 1916)
Attorney General: James C. McReynolds; Thomas W. Gregory (from September 1914)
Postmaster General: Albert S. Burleson
Secretary of the Navy: Josephus Daniels
Secretary of the Interior: Franklin K. Lane
Secretary of Agriculture: David F. Houston
Secretary of Commerce: (Department created by Congress in March 1913 after it separated Commerce from the Labor Department) William C. Redfield
Secretary of Labor: (Department created by Congress in March 1913 after it separated Labor from the Commerce Department) William B. Wilson
Supreme Court Appointments: James C. McReynolds (1914); Louis D. Brandeis (1916); John H. Clarke (1916)

Second Administration (March 4, 1917–March 3, 1921)

Vice President: Thomas R. Marshall
Secretary of State: Robert Lansing; Bainbridge Colby (from March 1920)

Secretary of the Treasury: William G. McAdoo; Carter Glass (from December 1918); David F. Houston (from February 1920)
Secretary of War: Newton D. Baker
Attorney General: Thomas W. Gregory; A. Mitchell Palmer (from March 1919)
Postmaster General: Albert S. Burleson
Secretary of the Navy: Josephus Daniels
Secretary of the Interior: Franklin K. Lane; John B. Payne (from March 1920)
Secretary of Agriculture: David F. Houston; Edwin T. Meredith (from February 1920)
Secretary of Commerce: William C. Redfield; Joshua W. Alexander (from December 1919)
Secretary of Labor: William B. Wilson

Family Facts

Father: Joseph Ruggles Wilson (1822–1903)
Mother: Jessie Janet Woodrow Wilson (1826–1888)
First Wife: Ellen Louise Axson (1860–1914)
First Marriage: June 24, 1885
Second Wife: Edith Bolling Galt (1872–1961)
Second Marriage: December 18, 1915
Children: (by his first wife) Margaret Woodrow (1886–1944); Jessie Woodrow (1887–1933); Eleanor Randolph (1889–1967)

Unusual Facts

Woodrow Wilson was the only president to hold a doctorate.

He was one of only two presidents to win the Nobel Peace Prize.

He was the first president to travel to Europe while in office.

Warren G. Harding

Election of 1920

Candidate	Electoral Vote	Popular Vote	Percent
Warren G. Harding Republican	404	16,133,134	60.30
James M. Cox Democrat	127	9,140,884	34.17
Eugene V. Debs Socialist	. . .	913,664	3.42
Parley P. Christensen Farmer-Labor	. . .	264,540	0.99
Other	. . .	301,384	1.13

Harding Administration (March 4, 1921–August 2, 1923)

Vice President: Calvin Coolidge
Secretary of State: Charles Evans Hughes
Secretary of the Treasury: Andrew W. Mellon
Secretary of War: John W. Weeks
Attorney General: Harry M. Daugherty
Postmaster General: William H. Hays; Hubert Work; Harry S. New (from March 1923)
Secretary of the Navy: Edwin Denby
Secretary of the Interior: Albert B. Fall; Hubert Work (from March 1923)
Secretary of Agriculture: Henry C. Wallace
Secretary of Commerce: Herbert C. Hoover
Secretary of Labor: James J. Davis
Supreme Court Appointments: William Howard Taft, Chief Justice (1921); George Sutherland (1922); Pierce Butler (1922); Edward T. Sanford (1923)

Family Facts

Father: George Tyron Harding (1844–1928)
Mother: Phoebe Elizabeth Dickerson Harding (1843–1910)
Wife: Florence Kling De Wolfe (1860–1924)
Marriage: July 8, 1891
Children: Harding allegedly had a child born out of wedlock, Elizabeth Ann Christian (1919–?), with Nan Britton.

Unusual Facts

Warren Harding was the first politician to move directly from the U.S. Senate to the White House.

He was the first president to show motion pictures at the White House.

His image was transmitted as the first radio picture.

His secretary of the interior, Albert Fall, was the first cabinet officer convicted of a crime and sent to prison.

Calvin Coolidge

Note: Calvin Coolidge became president on August 3, 1923, after Warren G. Harding's death from an illness.

Election of 1924

Candidate	Electoral Vote	Popular Vote	Percent
Calvin Coolidge Republican	382	15,717,553	54.00
John W. Davis Democrat	136	8,386,169	28.84
Robert M. LaFollette Progressive/Socialist	13	4,814,050	16.56
Other	. . .	158,187	0.55

First Administration (August 3, 1923–March 3, 1925)

Vice President: None
Secretary of State: Charles Evans Hughes
Secretary of the Treasury: Andrew W. Mellon
Secretary of War: John W. Weeks
Attorney General: Harry M. Daugherty; Harlan F. Stone (from April 1924)
Postmaster General: Harry S. New
Secretary of the Navy: Edwin Denby; Curtis D. Wilbur (from March 1924)
Secretary of the Interior: Hubert Work
Secretary of Agriculture: Henry C. Wallace; Howard M. Gore (from November 1924)
Secretary of Commerce: Herbert C. Hoover
Secretary of Labor: James J. Davis

Second Administration (March 4, 1925–March 3, 1929)

Vice President: Charles G. Dawes
Secretary of State: Frank B. Kellogg
Secretary of the Treasury: Andrew W. Mellon
Secretary of War: John W. Weeks, Dwight F. Davis (from October 1925)
Attorney General: John G. Sargent
Postmaster General: Harry S. New
Secretary of the Navy: Curtis D. Wilbur
Secretary of the Interior: Hubert Work; Roy O. West (from July 1928)
Secretary of Agriculture: William M. Jardine
Secretary of Commerce: Herbert C. Hoover; William F. Whiting (from August 1928)
Secretary of Labor: James J. Davis
Supreme Court Appointment: Harlan Fiske Stone (1925)

Family Facts

Father: John Calvin Coolidge (1845–1926)
Mother: Victoria Josephine Moor Coolidge (1846–1885)
Wife: Grace Anna Goodhue (1879–1957)
Marriage: October 4, 1905
Children: John (1906–2000); Calvin, Jr. (1908–1924)

Unusual Facts

Parsimonious Calvin Coolidge found himself having to move out of the White House in March 1927 so that several hundred thousand dollars worth of repairs could be made to the residence.

During his presidency, audiences in movie theaters watched newsreels for the first time.

Herbert Hoover

Election of 1928

Candidate	Electoral Vote	Popular Vote	Percent
Herbert C. Hoover Republican	444	21,411,911	58.20
Alfred E. Smith Democrat	87	15,000,185	40.77
Norman Thomas Socialist	. . .	266,453	0.72
William Z. Foster Worker's	. . .	48,170	0.13
Other	. . .	63,565	0.17

Hoover Administration (March 4, 1929–March 3, 1933)

Vice President: Charles Curtis
Secretary of State: Henry L. Stimson
Secretary of the Treasury: Andrew Mellon; Ogden L. Mills (from February 1932)
Secretary of War: James W. Good; Patrick J. Hurley (from December 1929)
Attorney General: William DeWitt Mitchell
Postmaster General: Walter F. Brown
Secretary of the Navy: Charles F. Adams
Secretary of the Interior: Ray L. Wilbur
Secretary of Agriculture: Arthur M. Hyde
Secretary of Commerce: Robert P. Lamont; Roy D. Chapin (from August 1932)
Secretary of Labor: James J. Davis; William N. Doak (from December 1930)
Supreme Court Appointments: Charles Evans Hughes, Chief Justice (1930); Owen J. Roberts (1930); Benjamin N. Cardozo (1932)

Family Facts

Father: Jesse Clark Hoover (1847–1880)
Mother: Hulda Randall Minthorn Hoover (1848–1883)
Wife: Lou Henry (1875–1944)
Marriage: February 10, 1899
Children: Herbert Clark, Jr. (1903–1969); Allan Henry (1907–1993)

Unusual Facts

Herbert Hoover's death at age 90 made him second only to John Adams among presidents for longevity.

He was the first president born west of the Mississippi River.

He refused to accept a salary for serving as president.

Franklin Delano Roosevelt

Election of 1932

Candidate	Electoral Vote	Popular Vote	Percent
Franklin D. Roosevelt Democrat	472	22,825,016	57.42
Herbert C. Hoover Republican	59	15,758,397	39.64
Norman Thomas Socialist	...	883,990	2.22
William Z. Foster Communist	...	102,221	0.26
Other	...	179,758	0.45

Election of 1936

Candidate	Electoral Vote	Popular Vote	Percent
Franklin D. Roosevelt Democrat	523	27,747,636	60.79
Alfred M. Landon Republican	8	16,679,543	36.54
William Lemke Union	...	892,492	1.96
Norman Thomas Socialist	...	187,785	0.41
Other	...	134,847	0.30

Election of 1940

Candidate	Electoral Vote	Popular Vote	Percent
Franklin D. Roosevelt Democrat	449	27,263,448	54.70
Wendell Willkie Republican	82	22,336,260	44.82
Norman Thomas Socialist	...	116,827	0.23
Roger W. Babson Prohibition	...	58,685	0.12
Other	...	65,223	0.13

Election of 1944

Candidate	Electoral Vote	Popular Vote	Percent
Franklin D. Roosevelt Democrat	432	25,611,936	53.39
Thomas E. Dewey Republican	99	22,013,372	45.89
Norman Thomas Socialist	. . .	79,100	0.16
Claude A. Watson Prohibition	. . .	74,733	0.16
Other	. . .	195,778	0.41

First Administration (March 4, 1933–January 20, 1937)

Vice President: John N. Garner
Secretary of State: Cordell Hull
Secretary of the Treasury: William H. Woodin; Henry Morgenthau, Jr. (from January 1934)
Secretary of War: George H. Dern; Henry Woodring (from September 1936)
Attorney General: Homer S. Cummings
Postmaster General: James A. Farley
Secretary of the Navy: Claude A. Swanson
Secretary of the Interior: Harold L. Ickes
Secretary of Agriculture: Henry A. Wallace
Secretary of Commerce: Daniel C. Roper
Secretary of Labor: Frances Perkins

Second Administration (January 20, 1937–January 20, 1941)

Vice President: John N. Garner
Secretary of State: Cordell Hull
Secretary of the Treasury: Henry Morgenthau, Jr.
Secretary of War: Henry H. Woodring; Henry L. Stimson (from July 1940)
Attorney General: Homer S. Cummings; Frank Murphy (from January 1939); Robert H. Jackson (from January 1940)
Postmaster General: James A. Farley; Frank C. Walker (from September 1940)
Secretary of the Navy: Claude A. Swanson; Charles Edison (from January 1940); Frank Knox (from July 1940)
Secretary of the Interior: Harold L. Ickes
Secretary of Agriculture: Henry A. Wallace; Claude R. Wickard (from September 1940)
Secretary of Commerce: Daniel C. Roper; Harry L. Hopkins (from December 1938); Jesse H. Jones (from September 1940)
Secretary of Labor: Frances Perkins
Supreme Court Appointments: Hugo L. Black (1937); Stanley F. Reed (1938); Felix Frankfurter (1939); William O. Douglas (1939); Frank Murphy (1940)

Third Administration (January 20, 1941–January 20, 1945)

Vice President: Henry A. Wallace
Secretary of State: Cordell Hull; Edward R. Stettinius, Jr. (from December 1944)
Secretary of the Treasury: Henry Morgenthau, Jr.
Secretary of War: Henry L. Stimson
Attorney General: Robert H. Jackson; Francis Biddle (from September 1941)
Postmaster General: Frank C. Walker
Secretary of the Navy: Frank Knox; James V. Forrestal (from May 1944)
Secretary of the Interior: Harold L. Ickes
Secretary of Agriculture: Claude R. Wickard

Secretary of Commerce: Jesse H. Jones
Secretary of Labor: Frances Perkins
Supreme Court Appointments: Harlan Fiske Stone, Chief Justice (1941); James F. Byrnes (1941); Robert H. Jackson (1941); Wiley B. Rutledge (1943)

Fourth Administration (January 20, 1945–April 12, 1945)

Vice President: Harry S. Truman
Secretary of State: Edward R. Stettinius, Jr.
Secretary of the Treasury: Henry Morgenthau, Jr.
Secretary of War: Henry L. Stimson
Attorney General: Francis Biddle
Postmaster General: Frank C. Walker
Secretary of the Navy: James V. Forrestal
Secretary of the Interior: Harold L. Ickes
Secretary of Agriculture: Claude R. Wickard
Secretary of Commerce: Jesse H. Jones; Henry A. Wallace (from March 1945)
Secretary of Labor: Frances Perkins

Family Facts

Father: James Roosevelt (1828–1900)
Mother: Sara Delano Roosevelt (1854–1941)
Wife: Anna Eleanor Roosevelt (1884–1962)
Marriage: March 17, 1905
Children: Anna Eleanor (1906–1975); James (1907–1991); Franklin (1909); Elliott (1910–1990); Franklin Delano, Jr. (1914–1988); John Aspinwall (1916–1981)

Unusual Facts

Franklin Roosevelt appointed the first woman to a presidential cabinet: Frances Perkins, as secretary of labor.

Prohibition was repealed during his first term.

In accordance with the Twentieth Amendment, enacted in 1933, Roosevelt was the first president to begin a term in January rather than March, when he took the oath of office for his second term in 1937.

He died two weeks before Germany surrendered in World War II.

Harry S. Truman

Note: Harry S. Truman became president on April 12, 1945, after Franklin D. Roosevelt's death due to illness.

Election of 1948

Candidate	Electoral Vote	Popular Vote	Percent
Harry S. Truman Democrat	303	24,105,587	49.51
Thomas E. Dewey Republican	189	21,970,017	45.12
Strom Thurmond States' Rights	39	1,169,134	2.40
Henry A. Wallace Progressive	. . .	1,157,057	2.38
Other	. . .	290,647	0.60

First Administration (April 12, 1945–January 20, 1949)

Vice President: none
Secretary of State: Edward R. Stettinius, Jr.; James F. Byrnes (from July 1945); George C. Marshall (from January 1947)
Secretary of the Treasury: Henry Morgenthau, Jr.; Fred M. Vinson (from July 1945); John W. Snyder (from June 1946)
Secretary of War: Henry L. Stimson; Robert P. Patterson (from September 1945); Kenneth C. Royall (from July 1947); Department disbanded in September 1947 and replaced by Defense Department
Secretary of Defense: (Department created in September 1947 to replace War Department) James V. Forrestal
Attorney General: Francis Biddle; Thomas C. Clark (from July 1945)
Postmaster General: Frank C. Walker; Robert E. Hannegan (from July 1945); Jesse M. Donaldson (from December 1947)
Secretary of the Navy: James V. Forrestal (Department disbanded in September 1947)
Secretary of the Interior: Harold L. Ickes; Julius A. Krug (from March 1946)
Secretary of Agriculture: Claude R. Wickard; Clinton P. Anderson (from June 1945); Charles F. Brannan (from June 1948)
Secretary of Commerce: Henry A. Wallace; W. Averell Harriman (from October 1946); Charles Sawyer (from May 1948)
Secretary of Labor: Frances Perkins; Lewis B. Schwellenbach (from July 1945); Maurice J. Tobin (from August 1948)
Supreme Court Appointments: Harold H. Burton (1945); Fred M. Vinson, Chief Justice (1946)

Second Administration (January 20, 1949–January 20, 1953)

Vice President: Alben W. Barkley
Secretary of State: Dean Acheson
Secretary of the Treasury: John W. Snyder
Secretary of Defense: James V. Forrestal; Louis A. Johnson (from March 1949); George C. Marshall (from September 1950); Robert A. Lovett (from September 1951)
Attorney General: Thomas C. Clark; J. Howard McGrath (from August 1949); James P. McGranery (from May 1952)
Postmaster General: Jesse M. Donaldson

Secretary of the Interior: Julius A. Krug; Oscar L. Chapman (from January 1950)
Secretary of Agriculture: Charles F. Brannan
Secretary of Commerce: Charles Sawyer
Secretary of Labor: Maurice J. Tobin
Supreme Court Appointments: Thomas C. Clark (1949); Sherman Minton (1949)

Family Facts

Father: John Anderson Truman (1851–1914)
Mother: Martha Ellen Young Truman (1852–1947)
Wife: Elizabeth "Bess" Virginia Wallace (1885–1982)
Marriage: June 28, 1919
Child: Margaret (1924–)

Unusual Facts

Harry Truman was the first president to address the National Association for the Advancement of Colored People (NAACP).

His presidential address of October 5, 1947, was the first one ever telecast from the White House. He spoke about the world food crisis.

His presidential inauguration in 1949 was the first one broadcast on television. About 10 million viewers watched the ceremony.

Dwight David Eisenhower

Election of 1952

Candidate	Electoral Vote	Popular Vote	Percent
Dwight D. Eisenhower Republican	442	33,936,137	55.13
Adlai E. Stevenson Democrat	89	27,314,649	44.38
Vincent W. Hallinan Progressive	. . .	140,416	0.23
Stuart Hamblen Prohibition	. . .	73,413	0.12
Other	. . .	86,503	0.14

Election of 1956

Candidate	Electoral Vote	Popular Vote	Percent
Dwight D. Eisenhower Republican	457	35,585,247	57.37
Adlai E. Stevenson Democrat	73	26,030,172	41.97
T. Coleman Andrews States' Rights	. . .	108,055	0.17
Eric Hass Socialist-Labor	. . .	44,300	0.07
Other	. . .	257,600	0.42

First Administration (January 20, 1953–January 20, 1957)

Vice President: Richard M. Nixon
Secretary of State: John Foster Dulles
Secretary of the Treasury: George M. Humphrey
Secretary of Defense: Charles E. Wilson
Attorney General: Herbert Brownell, Jr.
Postmaster General: Arthur E. Summerfield
Secretary of the Interior: Douglas McKay; Frederick A. Seaton (from June 1956)
Secretary of Agriculture: Ezra Taft Benson
Secretary of Commerce: Sinclair Weeks
Secretary of Labor: Martin Durkin; James P. Mitchell (from January 1954)
Secretary of Health, Education, and Welfare (Department created April 1953): Oveta Culp Hobby; Marion B. Folsom (from August 1955)
Supreme Court Appointments: Earl Warren, Chief Justice (1953); John M. Harlan (1955); William J. Brennan, Jr. (1956)

Second Administration (January 20, 1957–January 20, 1961)

Vice President: Richard M. Nixon
Secretary of State: John Foster Dulles; Christian A. Herter (from April 1959)
Secretary of the Treasury: George M. Humphrey; Robert B. Anderson (from July 1957)

Secretary of Defense: Charles E. Wilson; Neil H. McElroy (from October 1957); Thomas S. Gates, Jr. (from December 1959)
Attorney General: Herbert Brownell, Jr.; William P. Rogers (from January 1958)
Postmaster General: Arthur E. Summerfield
Secretary of the Interior: Frederick A. Seaton
Secretary of Agriculture: Ezra Taft Benson
Secretary of Commerce: Sinclair Weeks; Lewis Strauss (from November 1958); Frederick H. Mueller (from August 1959)
Secretary of Labor: James P. Mitchell
Secretary of Health, Education, and Welfare: Marion B. Folsom; Arthur S. Flemming (from August 1958)
Supreme Court Appointments: Charles E. Whittaker (1957); Potter Stewart (1958)
States Admitted: Alaska (1959); Hawaii (1959)

Family Facts

Father: David Jacob Eisenhower (1863–1942)
Mother: Ida Elizabeth Stover Eisenhower (1862–1946)
Wife: Mary "Mamie" Geneva Doud (1896–1979)
Marriage: July 1, 1916
Children: Dwight (1917–1921); John Sheldon (1923–)

Unusual Facts

Dwight Eisenhower was the first president to fly aboard the jet aircraft *Air Force One.*
He was the first president to hold a televised press conference.
Eisenhower created the National Aeronautics and Space Administration (NASA).
He lived in 27 different homes during his 38 years in the army.

John Fitzgerald Kennedy

Election of 1960

Candidate	Electoral Vote	Popular Vote	Percent
John F. Kennedy Democrat	303	34,221,344	49.72
Richard M. Nixon Republican	219	34,106,671	49.55
Eric Hass Socialist-Labor	. . .	47,522	0.07
Other	15	337,175	0.48
Unpledged	. . .	116,248	0.17

Note: 15 electoral votes went to Democratic Senator Harry F. Byrd of West Virginia, distributed as eight from Mississippi, six from Alabama, and one from Oklahoma.

Kennedy Administration (January 20, 1961–November 22, 1963)

Vice President: Lyndon Baines Johnson
Secretary of State: Dean Rusk
Secretary of the Treasury: C. Douglas Dillon
Secretary of Defense: Robert S. McNamara
Attorney General: Robert F. Kennedy
Postmaster General: J. Edward Day; John A. Gronouski, Jr. (from September 1963)
Secretary of the Interior: Stewart L. Udall
Secretary of Agriculture: Orville L. Freeman
Secretary of Commerce: Luther H. Hodges
Secretary of Labor: Arthur J. Goldberg; W. Willard Wirtz (from September 1962)
Secretary of Health, Education, and Welfare: Abraham A. Ribicoff; Anthony J. Celebrezze (from July 1962)
Supreme Court Appointments: Byron R. White (1962); Arthur J. Goldberg (1962)

Family Facts

Father: Joseph Patrick Kennedy (1888–1969)
Mother: Rose Elizabeth Fitzgerald Kennedy (1891–1995)
Wife: Jacqueline Lee Bouvier (1929–1994)
Marriage: September 12, 1953
Children: Caroline Bouvier (1957–); John Fitzgerald Jr. (1960–1999); Patrick Bouvier (1963)

Unusual Facts

John Kennedy was the first president born in the 20th century and the youngest candidate ever elected to the office.

He was the first Roman Catholic president.

His reelection to the U.S. Senate in 1958 was by the largest plurality ever given a candidate in Massachusetts up to that time—875,000 more votes than his Republican opponent.

Lyndon Baines Johnson

Note: Lyndon B. Johnson became president on November 22, 1963, after the assassination of John F. Kennedy.

Election of 1964

Candidate	Electoral Vote	Popular Vote	Percent
Lyndon B. Johnson Democrat	486	43,126,584	61.05
Barry M. Goldwater Republican	52	27,177,838	38.47
Eric Hass Socialist-Labor	. . .	45,187	0.06
Clifton DeBerry Socialist Workers	. . .	32,701	0.05
Other	. . .	258,794	0.37

First Administration (November 22, 1963–January 20, 1965)

Vice President: None
Secretary of State: Dean Rusk
Secretary of the Treasury: C. Douglas Dillon
Secretary of Defense: Robert S. McNamara
Attorney General: Robert F. Kennedy
Postmaster General: John A. Gronouski
Secretary of the Interior: Stewart L. Udall
Secretary of Agriculture: Orville L. Freeman
Secretary of Commerce: Luther H. Hodges
Secretary of Labor: W. Willard Wirtz
Secretary of Health, Education and Welfare: Anthony J. Celebrezze

Second Administration (January 20, 1965–January 20, 1969)

Vice President: Hubert H. Humphrey
Secretary of State: Dean Rusk
Secretary of the Treasury: C. Douglas Dillon; Henry H. Fowler (from April 1965); Joseph W. Barr (from December 1968)
Secretary of Defense: Robert S. McNamara; Clark M. Clifford (from March 1968)
Attorney General: Nicholas Katzenbach; Ramsey Clark (from January 1967)
Postmaster General: John A. Gronouski; Lawrence F. O'Brien (from November 1965); Marvin Watson (from 1968)
Secretary of the Interior: Stewart L. Udall
Secretary of Agriculture: Orville L. Freeman
Secretary of Commerce: John T. Connor; Alexander B. Trowbridge (from June 1967); Cyrus R. Smith (from March 1968)
Secretary of Labor: W. Willard Wirtz
Secretary of Health, Education and Welfare: Anthony J. Celebrezze; John W. Gardner (from August 1965); Wilbur J. Cohen (from May 1968)
Secretary of Housing and Urban Development (Department created by Congress in September 1965): Robert C. Weaver; Robert C. Wood (January 1969)
Secretary of Transportation (Department created by Congress in October 1966): Alan S. Boyd (January 1967)
Supreme Court Appointments: Abe Fortas (1965); Thurgood Marshall (1967)

Family Facts

Father: Sam Ealy Johnson, Jr. (1877–1937)
Mother: Rebekah Baines Johnson (1881–1958)
Wife: Claudia "Lady Bird" Alta Taylor (1912–)
Marriage: November 17, 1934
Children: Lynda Bird (1944–); Luci Baines (1947–)

Unusual Facts

Lyndon Johnson's use of a helicopter during his race for the U.S. Senate in 1948 made him one of the first political candidates to campaign that way.

During Johnson's presidency both Martin Luther King, Jr., and Robert F. Kennedy were assassinated.

He nominated Thurgood Marshall to the Supreme Court, the first African American to serve on the bench.

Richard M. Nixon

Election of 1968

Candidate	Electoral Vote	Popular Vote	Percent
Richard M. Nixon Republican	301	31,785,148	43.42
Hubert H. Humphrey Democrat	191	31,274,503	42.72
George C. Wallace American Independent	46	901,151	13.53
Henning A. Blomen Socialist-Labor	. . .	52,591	0.07
Other	. . .	189,977	0.20

Election of 1972

Candidate	Electoral Vote	Popular Vote	Percent
Richard M. Nixon Republican	520	47,170,179	60.69
George S. McGovern Democrat	17	29,171,791	37.53
John G. Schmitz American Independent	. . .	1,090,673	1.40
Benjamin Spock People's	. . .	78,751	0.10
Other	1	216,196	0.28

Note: John Hospers of the Libertarian Party received one electoral vote from Virginia.

First Administration (January 20, 1969–January 20, 1973)

Vice President: Spiro T. Agnew
Secretary of State: William P. Rogers
Secretary of the Treasury: David M. Kennedy; John B. Connally (from February 1971); George P. Shultz (from June 1972)
Secretary of Defense: Melvin R. Laird
Attorney General: John N. Mitchell; Richard G. Kleindienst (from June 1972)
Postmaster General: Winton M. Blunt (until 1971, when position was removed from the cabinet)
Secretary of the Interior: Walter J. Hickel; Rogers Morton (from January 1971)
Secretary of Agriculture: Clifford M. Hardin; Earl L. Butz (from December 1971)
Secretary of Commerce: Maurice H. Stans; Peter G. Peterson (from February 1972)
Secretary of Labor: George P. Schultz; James D. Hodgson (from July 1970)
Secretary of Health, Education and Welfare: Robert H. Finch; Elliot L. Richardson (from June 1970)
Secretary of Housing and Urban Development: George Romney
Secretary of Transportation: John A. Volpe
Supreme Court Appointments: Warren E. Burger, Chief Justice (1969); Harry A. Blackmun (1970); Lewis F. Powell, Jr. (1972); William H. Rehnquist (1972)

Second Administration (January 20, 1973–August 9, 1974)

Vice President: Spiro T. Agnew; Gerald R. Ford (from December 1973)
Secretary of State: William P. Rogers; Henry A. Kissinger (from September 1973)
Secretary of the Treasury: George P. Schultz; William E. Simon (from May 1974)
Secretary of Defense: Elliot Richardson; James R. Schlesinger (from July 1973)
Attorney General: Richard G. Kleindienst; Elliot Richardson (for October 1973); William B. Saxbe (from January 1974)
Secretary of the Interior: Rogers Morton
Secretary of Agriculture: Earl L. Butz
Secretary of Commerce: Frederick B. Dent
Secretary of Labor: Peter J. Brennan
Secretary of Health, Education, and Welfare: Caspar W. Weinberger
Secretary of Housing and Urban Development: James T. Lynn
Secretary of Transportation: Claude S. Brinegar

Family Facts

Father: Francis Anthony Nixon (1878–1956)
Mother: Hannah Milhous Nixon (1885–1967)
Wife: Thelma "Pat" Catherine Ryan (1912–1993)
Marriage: June 21, 1940
Children: Patricia (1946–); Julie (1948–)

Unusual Facts

In 1960 Richard Nixon was the first presidential candidate to campaign in all 50 states.

He was the first president to appoint a vice president under the terms of the Twenty-fifth Amendment.

Nixon was the only president ever to resign his office.

He was the only president ever to receive a pardon for any crime he may have committed while in office.

Gerald Ford

Note: Gerald R. Ford was the first and, to date, only president never to have been elected to either the vice presidency or the presidency as a result of balloting by the electoral college. In October 1973 President Richard M. Nixon acted under the terms of the Twenty-fifth Amendment and nominated Ford, then a Republican congressman, to replace Vice President Spiro Agnew, who was forced to resign because of criminal misconduct. Ford was confirmed as vice president by both the House and the Senate and was sworn in on December 6, 1973. When, as a result of the Watergate scandal, Nixon resigned the presidency on August 9, 1974, Ford became president and was sworn in at 12:00 noon that day. He subsequently chose Nelson Rockefeller, former Republican governor of New York, to serve as his vice president, and Congress confirmed his choice.

Ford Administration (August 9, 1974–January 20, 1977)

Vice President: Nelson A. Rockefeller
Secretary of State: Henry A. Kissinger
Secretary of the Treasury: William E. Simon
Secretary of Defense: James R. Schlesinger; Donald Rumsfeld (from November 1975)
Attorney General: William B. Saxbe; Edward Levi (from February 1975)
Secretary of the Interior: Rogers Morton; Stanley K. Hathaway (from June 1975); Thomas S. Kleppe (from October 1975)
Secretary of Agriculture: Earl L. Butz; John A. Knebel (from November 1976)
Secretary of Commerce: Frederick B. Dent; Rogers Morton (from May 1975); Elliot L. Richardson (from February 1976)
Secretary of Labor: Peter J. Brennan; John T. Dunlop (from March 1975); W. J. Usery, Jr. (from February 1976)
Secretary of Health, Education, and Welfare: Caspar W. Weinberger; Forrest D. Mathews (from August 1975)
Secretary of Housing and Urban Development: James T. Lynn; Carla A. Hills (from March 1975)
Secretary of Transportation: Claude S. Brinegar; William T. Coleman, Jr. (from March 1975)
Supreme Court Appointment: John Paul Stevens (1975)

Family Facts

Father: Leslie Lynch King (1881–1941)
Stepfather: Gerald Rudolph Ford (1889–1962)
Mother: Dorothy Ayer Gardner King Ford (1892–1967)
Wife: Elizabeth "Betty" Bloomer Warren (1918—)
Marriage: October 15, 1948
Children: Michael Gerald (1950–); John "Jack" (1952–); Steven Meigs (1956–); Susan Elizabeth (1957–)

Unusual Facts

Gerald Ford did not learn that he was adopted until he was a teenager.

For the first few days while he was president, he commuted daily from his home in Alexandria, Virginia, while waiting for the White House to be readied for his occupancy.

Ford survived two assassination attempts within days of each other, one on September 5, 1975, the other on September 22, 1975.

James Earl Carter, Jr.

Election of 1976

Candidate	Electoral Vote	Popular Vote	Percent
James Earl Carter Democrat	297	40,830,763	50.06
Gerald R. Ford Republican	240	39,147,793	48.00
Eugene J. McCarthy Independent	. . .	756,691	0.93
Roger MacBride Libertarian	. . .	173,011	0.21
Other	1	647,631	0.79

Note: Former California governor Ronald Reagan received one electoral vote from an elector in Washington.

Carter Administration (January 20, 1977–January 20, 1981)

Vice President: Walter F. Mondale
Secretary of State: Cyrus R. Vance; Edmund S. Muskie (from May 1980)
Secretary of the Treasury: W. Michael Blumenthal; G. William Miller (from August 1979)
Secretary of Defense: Harold Brown
Attorney General: Griffin Bell; Benjamin R. Civiletti (from August 1979)
Secretary of the Interior: Cecil B. Andrus
Secretary of Agriculture: Robert Bergland
Secretary of Commerce: Juanita M. Kreps; Philip M. Klutznick (from January 1980)
Secretary of Labor: F. Ray Marshall
Secretary of Health, Education, and Welfare: (The Department of Health, Education, and Welfare was dissolved when it was split into the Department of Health and Human Services and the Department of Education by Congress in May 1980) Joseph A. Califano, Jr.; Patricia R. Harris (from August 1979)
Secretary of Health and Human Services: Patricia E. Harris (from May 1980)
Secretary of Housing and Urban Development: Patricia R. Harris, Moon Landrieu (from September 1979)
Secretary of Transportation: Brock Adams, Neil E. Goldschmidt (from September 1979)
Secretary of Energy: (Department created by Congress in August 1977) James R. Schlesinger; Charles W. Duncan, Jr. (from August 1979)
Secretary of Education: (Department created when the Department of Health, Education, and Welfare was split into the Department of Health and Human Services and the Department of Education by Congress in September 1979) Shirley Hufstedler

Family Facts

Father: James Earl Carter (1894–1953)
Mother: Lillian Gordy Carter (1898–1983)
Wife: Eleanor Rosalynn Smith (1928–)
Marriage: July 7, 1946
Children: John "Jack" (1947–); James Earl "Chip" III (1950–); Donnell Jeffrey (1952–); Amy Lynn (1967–)

Unusual Facts

Jimmy Carter was an avid reader as a child. In the third grade he won a prize for reading the most books in his class.

He was the first president elected from south of the Mason-Dixon Line and east of the Mississippi River in more than 100 years.

Carter was the first president since 1932 to lose reelection.

Ronald Reagan

Election of 1980

Candidate	Electoral Vote	Popular Vote	Percent
Ronald W. Reagan Republican	489	43,901,812	50.75
Jimmy Carter Democrat	49	35,483,820	41.02
John B. Anderson Independent	...	5,719,722	6.61
Edward E. Clark Libertarian	...	921,188	1.06
Other	...	486,754	0.56

Election of 1984

Candidate	Electoral Vote	Popular Vote	Percent
Ronald W. Reagan Republican	525	54,450,603	58.78
Walter F. Mondale Democrat	13	37,573,671	40.56
David Bergland Libertarian	...	227,949	0.25
Other	...	570,343	0.61

First Administration (January 20, 1981–January 20, 1985)

Vice President: George Bush
Secretary of State: Alexander Haig; George P. Shultz (from July 1982)
Secretary of the Treasury: Donald T. Regan
Secretary of Defense: Caspar W. Weinberger
Attorney General: William French Smith; Edwin Meese III (from February 1984)
Secretary of the Interior: James G. Watt; William P. Clark (from November 1983)
Secretary of Agriculture: John R. Block
Secretary of Commerce: Malcolm Baldridge
Secretary of Labor: Raymond J. Donovan
Secretary of Health and Human Services: Richard S. Schweiker; Margaret M. Heckler (from March 1983)
Secretary of Housing and Urban Development: Samuel R. Pierce, Jr.
Secretary of Transportation: Andrew L. "Drew" Lewis, Jr.; Elizabeth H. Dole (from February 1983)
Secretary of Energy: James B. Edwards; Donald Paul Hodel (from November 1982)
Secretary of Education: Terrel Bell
Supreme Court Appointment: Sandra Day O'Connor (1981)

Second Administration (January 20, 1985–January 20, 1989)

Vice President: George Bush
Secretary of State: George P. Shultz
Secretary of the Treasury: James A. Baker III; Nicholas F. Brady (from September 1988)

Secretary of Defense: Caspar W. Weinberger; Frank C. Carlucci (from November 1987)
Attorney General: Edwin Meese III; Richard Thornburgh (from January 1988)
Secretary of the Interior: Donald P. Hodel
Secretary of Agriculture: John R. Block; Richard Edmund Lyng (from March 1986)
Secretary of Commerce: Malcolm Baldridge; C. William Verity (from October 1987)
Secretary of Labor: Raymond J. Donovan; William E. Brock (from April 1985); Ann Dore McLaughlin (from December 1987)
Secretary of Health and Human Services: Margaret M. Heckler; Otis R. Bowen (from December 1985)
Secretary of Housing and Urban Development: Samuel R. Pierce, Jr.
Secretary of Transportation: Elizabeth H. Dole; James H. Burnley IV (from December 1987)
Secretary of Energy: John S. Herrington
Secretary of Education: William Bennett; Lauro F. Cavazos (from September 1988)
Supreme Court Appointments: William H. Rehnquist, Chief Justice (1986); Antonin Scalia (1986); Anthony M. Kennedy (1988)

Family Facts

Father: John Edward Reagan (1883–1941)
Mother: Nelle Wilson Reagan (1883–1962)
First Wife: Jane Wyman (1914–)
Marriage: January 26, 1940
Divorce: 1948
Second Wife: Nancy Davis (1923–)
Marriage: March 4, 1952
Children: (by his first wife) Maureen Elizabeth (1941–); Michael Edward (adopted, 1945–); (by his second wife) Patricia "Patti" (1952–); Ronald "Skip" (1958–)

Unusual Facts

Ronald Reagan was the oldest of all the presidents; he was 78 when he retired from the White House.
He acted in some 20 Hollywood movies.
He appointed the first woman to the Supreme Court, Justice Sandra Day O'Connor.
Reagan submitted the first trillion-dollar budget to Congress.

George H. W. Bush

Election of 1988

Candidate	Electoral Vote	Popular Vote	Percent
George H. W. Bush Republican	426	48,881,011	53.37
Michael S. Dukakis Democrat	111	41,828,350	45.67
Ron Paul Libertarian	. . .	431,499	0.47
Lenora Fulani Alliance	. . .	218,159	0.24
Other	1	226,852	0.25

Note: Lloyd Bentsen, the Democratic vice-presidential candidate, received one electoral vote for president.

Bush Administration (January 20, 1989–January 20, 1993)

Vice President: J. Danforth "Dan" Quayle
Secretary of State: James A. Baker III; Lawrence S. Eagleburger (from December 1992)
Secretary of the Treasury: Nicholas F. Brady
Secretary of Defense: Richard B. Cheney
Attorney General: Richard Thornburgh; William P. Barr (from November 1991)
Secretary of the Interior: Manuel Lujan, Jr.
Secretary of Agriculture: Clayton Yeutter; Edward R. Madigan (from March 1991)
Secretary of Commerce: Robert A. Mosbacher; Barbara H. Franklin (from February 1992)
Secretary of Labor: Elizabeth H. Dole; Lynn M. Martin (from February 1991)
Secretary of Health and Human Services: Louis W. Sullivan
Secretary of Housing and Urban Development: Jack F. Kemp
Secretary of Transportation: Samuel K. Skinner; Andrew H. Card, Jr. (from February 1992)
Secretary of Energy: James D. Watkins
Secretary of Education: Lauro Cavazos; Lamar Alexander (from March 1991)
Secretary of Veteran's Affairs: (Department created by Congress in October 1988, effective March 1989) Edward J. Derwinski
Supreme Court Appointments: David H. Souter (1990); Clarence Thomas (1991)

Family Facts

Father: Prescott Sheldon Bush (1895–1972)
Mother: Dorothy Walker Bush (1901–)
Wife: Barbara Pierce (1925–)
Marriage: January 6, 1945
Children: George W. (1946–); Pauline Robinson (1949–1953); John Ellis "Jeb" (1953–); Neil (1955–); Marvin (1956–); Dorothy Walker (1959–)

Unusual Facts

In college George Bush played as a starter on his school baseball team, which made it to the national championship series.

Bush was the first vice president elected president since Martin Van Buren.

He was the first vice president to lose reelection since Martin Van Buren.

He was the second president to have a son become president.

William Jefferson Clinton

Election of 1992

Candidate	Electoral Vote	Popular Vote	Percent
William Jefferson Clinton Democrat	370	44,908,233	42.95
George Bush Republican	168	39,102,282	37.40
Ross Perot Independent	. . .	19,721,433	18.86
Other	. . .	820,788	0.79

Election of 1996

Candidate	Electoral Vote	Popular Vote	Percent
William Jefferson Clinton Democrat	379	47,402,357	49.24
Bob Dole Republican	159	39,198,755	40.71
Ross Perot Reform	. . .	8,085,402	8.40
Ralph Nader Green	. . .	684,902	0.71
Harry Browne Libertarian	. . .	485,798	0.50
Other	. . .	420,009	0.44

First Administration (January 20, 1993–January 20, 1997)

Vice President: Al Gore, Jr.
Secretary of State: Warren M. Christopher
Secretary of the Treasury: Lloyd M. Bentsen; Robert E. Rubin (from January 1995)
Secretary of Defense: Les Aspin; William J. Perry (from February 1994)
Attorney General: Janet Reno
Secretary of the Interior: Bruce Babbitt
Secretary of Agriculture: Mike Espy; Daniel Robert Glickman (from March 1995)
Secretary of Commerce: Ronald H. Brown; Mickey Kantor (from April 1996)
Secretary of Labor: Robert B. Reich
Secretary of Health and Human Services: Donna E. Shalala
Secretary of Housing and Urban Development: Henry G. Cisneros
Secretary of Transportation: Federico Pena
Secretary of Energy: Hazel R. O'Leary
Secretary of Education: Richard Riley
Secretary of Veteran's Affairs: Jesse Brown
Supreme Court Appointments: Ruth Bader Ginsburg (1993); Stephen Breyer (1994)

Second Administration (January 20, 1997–January 20, 2001)

Vice President: Al Gore, Jr.
Secretary of State: Madeleine K. Albright

Secretary of the Treasury: Robert E. Rubin; Lawrence H. Summers (from July 1999)
Secretary of Defense: William J. Perry; William S. Cohen (from January 1997)
Attorney General: Janet Reno
Secretary of the Interior: Bruce Babbitt
Secretary of Agriculture: Daniel Robert Glickman
Secretary of Commerce: William M. Daley; Robert L. Mallett (from June 2000)
Secretary of Labor: Alexis Herman
Secretary of Health and Human Services: Donna E. Shalala
Secretary of Housing and Urban Development: Andrew M. Cuomo
Secretary of Transportation: Rodney E. Slater
Secretary of Energy: Federico N. Pena; Bill Richardson (from August 1998)
Secretary of Education: Richard Riley
Secretary of Veteran's Affairs: Jesse Brown; Togo D. West, Jr. (from May 1998)

Family Facts

Father: William Jefferson Blythe III (1918–1946)
Stepfather: Roger Clinton
Mother: Virginia Cassidy Blythe Clinton (1923–1994)
Wife: Hillary Rodham (1947–)
Marriage: October 11, 1975
Child: Chelsea Victoria (1980–)

Unusual Facts

As a senior at Georgetown University, Bill Clinton won a Rhodes Scholarship.

He was the only Democrat to be reelected president since Franklin Delano Roosevelt.

He was the second president to be impeached.

He was the 16th president to be elected without a majority of the popular vote, having received 43 percent of the vote in 1992 and 49 percent in 1996.

In the year 2000, his wife, Hillary Rodham Clinton, became the first first lady ever elected to the U.S. Senate.

George Walker Bush

Election of 2000

Candidate	Electoral Vote	Popular Vote	Percent
George Walker Bush Republican	271	50,456,169	47.9
Al Gore Democrat	266	50,996,116	48.4
Other	. . .	3,874,040	3.7

Note: The category "other" includes the votes recorded for Ralph Nader, presidential candidate of the Green Party, and Patrick Buchanan, presidential candidate of the Reform Party.

Election of 2004

Candidate	Electoral Vote	Popular Vote	Percent
George W. Bush Republican	274	59,245,671	51
John Kerry Democrat	252	55,709,805	48
Other	. . .	776,658	0.6

Note: The category "other" includes the votes cast for Ralph Nader, an independent presidential candidate, and Michael Badnarik, the presidential candidate of the Libertarian Party.

First Administration (January 20, 2001–January 20, 2005)

Vice President: Richard Cheney
Secretary of State: Colin L. Powell
Secretary of the Treasury: Paul O'Neill; John Snow (from February 2003)
Secretary of Defense: Donald Rumsfeld
Attorney General: John Ashcroft
Secretary of the Interior: Gale A. Norton
Secretary of Agriculture: Ann Veneman
Secretary of Commerce: Donald L. Evans
Secretary of Labor: Elaine L. Chao
Secretary of Health and Human Services: Tommy G. Thompson
Secretary of Housing and Urban Development: Melquiades R. Martinez; Alphonso Jackson (from April 2004)
Secretary of Transportation: Norman Y. Mineta
Secretary of Energy: Spencer Abraham
Secretary of Education: Rod Paige
Secretary of Veteran's Affairs: Anthony Principi
Secretary of Homeland Security: (cabinet post created 2003) Tom Ridge

Second Administration (January 20, 2005–)

Vice President: Richard Cheney
Secretary of State: Condoleeza Rice
Secretary of the Treasury: John Snow (from February 2003)
Secretary of Defense: Donald Rumsfeld
Attorney General: Alberto Gonzales
Secretary of the Interior: Gale A. Norton
Secretary of Agriculture: Mike Johanns
Secretary of Commerce: Carlos Gutierrez
Secretary of Labor: Elaine L. Chao

Secretary of Health and Human Services: Mike Leavitt
Secretary of Housing and Urban Development: Alphonso Jackson (from April 2004)
Secretary of Transportation: Norman Y. Mineta
Secretary of Energy: Sam Bodman
Secretary of Education: Margaret Spellings
Secretary of Veteran's Affairs: Jim Nicholson
Secretary of Homeland Security: Michael Chertoff

Family Facts

Father: George Herbert Walker Bush
Mother: Barbara Pierce Bush
Wife: Laura Welch (1947–)
Marriage: November 5, 1977
Children: Barbara (1982–); Jenna (1982–)

Unusual Facts

George W. Bush is the second son of a former president to be elected to the White House.

Like John Quincy Adams, the only other son of a former president to be elected to the White House, George W. Bush, in 2000, won the presidency while failing to garner a plurality of the popular vote.

The 2000 election made him the fourth candidate to be elected with a majority in the electoral college but with the second-highest number of popular votes.

BIBLIOGRAPHY

Overviews of the American Presidency

Barber, James David. *The Presidential Character: Predicting Performance in the White House.* 4th ed. Englewood Cliffs, N.J.: Prentice Hall, 1992.

Bennett, William J. *Presidential Leadership: Rating the Best and the Worst in the White House.* New York: Free Press, 2004.

Berman, Larry. *The New American Presidency.* Boston: Little, Brown, 1987.

Brinkley, Allan, and Davis Dyer, eds., *The American Presidency.* Boston: Houghton Mifflin, 2004.

Corwin, Edward S. *The President, Office and Powers, 1787–1957: History and Analysis of Practice and Opinion.* 4th ed. New York: New York University Press, 1957.

Cronin, Thomas E. *The State of the Presidency.* 2nd ed. Boston: Little, Brown, 1980.

Cronin, Thomas E., and Michael A. Genovese. *The Paradoxes of the American Presidency.* New York: Oxford University Press, 1998.

Dallek, Robert. *Hail to the Chief: The Making and Unmaking of American Presidents.* New York: Hyperion, 1996.

Edwards, George E., III, and Stephen J. Wayne, *Presidential Leadership: Politics and Policy Making.* 4th ed. New York: St. Martin's, 1997.

Gilbert, Robert E. *The Mortal Presidency: Illness and Anguish in the White House.* 2nd ed. New York: Fordham University Press, 1998.

Greenstein, Fred I. *Leadership in the Modern Presidency.* Cambridge, Mass.: Harvard University Press, 1988.

———. *The Presidential Difference: Leadership Style from FDR to Clinton.* New York: Free Press, 2000.

———. *The Presidential Difference: Leadership Style from FDR to George W. Bush.* Princeton, N.J.: Princeton University Press, 2004.

Hargrove, Erwin C. *The President as Leader: Appealing to the Better Angels of Our Nature.* Lawrence: University Press of Kansas, 1998.

Hart, John. *The Presidential Branch.* 2nd ed. Chatham, N.J.: Chatham House, 1995.

Herring, Pendleton. *Presidential Leadership: The Political Relations of Congress and the Chief Executive.* New York: Rinehart, 1940.

Jones, Charles O. *Passages to the Presidency: From Campaigning to Governing.* Washington, D.C.: Brookings Institution, 1998.

———. *The Presidency in a Separated System.* Washington, D.C.: Brookings Institution, 1994.

Koenig, Louis W. *The Chief Executive.* 4th ed. New York: Harcourt, Brace, Jovanovich, 1981.

Kunhardt, Philip B., Jr., Philip B. Kunhardt, III, and Peter W. Kunhardt. *The American President.* New York: Riverhead Books, 1999.

Laski, Harold Joseph. *The American Presidency: An Interpretation.* New York: Harper and Brothers, 1940.

Leuchtenburg, William E. *In the Shadow of FDR: From Harry Truman to Bill Clinton.* Rev. ed. Ithaca, N.Y.: Cornell University Press, 1993.

Lowi, Theodore. *The Personal President: Power Invested, Promise Unfulfilled.* Ithaca, N.Y.: Cornell University Press, 1985.

Murray, Robert K. *Greatness in the White House: Rating the Presidents from George Washington through Ronald Reagan.* University Park: Pennsylvania State University Press, 1994.

Neustadt, Richard E. *Presidential Power and the Modern Presidents: The Politics of Leadership from Roosevelt to Reagan.* New York: Free Press, 1990.

Pfiffner, James P. *The Modern Presidency.* 2nd ed. New York: St. Martin's, 1998.

———. *The Strategic Presidency.* 2nd ed. Lawrence: University Press of Kansas, 1996.

Riccards, Michael P. *The Ferocious Engine of Democracy: From Teddy Rossevelt through George W. Bush.* New York: Cooper Square Press, 2003.

Rossiter, Clinton. *The American Presidency.* 2nd ed. New York: Harcourt, Brace, 1960.

On the Organization of the Presidency

Burke, John P. *The Institutional Presidency.* Baltimore: Johns Hopkins University Press, 1992.

George, Alexander L. *Presidential Decision Making in Foreign Policy: The Effective Use of Advice and Information.* Boulder, Colo.: Westview Press,

1979.

Grover, William F. *The President as Prisoner: A Structural Critique of the Carter and Reagan Years.* Albany: State University of New York Press, 1989.

Hess, Stephen. *Organizing the Presidency.* New York: Harper & Row, 1974.

Hoxie, R. Gordon. *The White House: Organization and Operations.* New York: Center for the Study of the Presidency, 1971.

Schlesinger, Arthur M., Jr. *The Imperial Presidency.* New York: Houghton Mifflin, 1973.

Skowronek, Stephen. *The Politics Presidents Make: Leadership from John Adams to George Bush.* Cambridge, Mass.: Harvard University Press, 1993.

Walcott, Charles E., and Karen M. Hult. *Governing the White House: From Hoover through LBJ.* Lawrence: University Press of Kansas, 1995.

Warshaw, Shirley Anne. *The Domestic Presidency: Policy Making in the White House.* Boston: Allyn & Bacon, 1997.

Weko, Thomas J. *The Politicizing Presidency: The White House Personnel Office, 1948–1994.* Lawrence: University Press of Kansas, 1995.

On the Relationship Between Congress and the Presidency

Collier, Kenneth E. *Between the Branches: The White House Office of Legislative Affairs.* Pittsburgh, Pa.: University of Pittsburgh Press, 1997.

Edwards, George C., III. *At the Margins: Presidential Leadership and Congress.* New Haven, Conn.: Yale University Press, 1989.

Fisher, Louis. *The Politics of Shared Power: Congress and the Executive.* 4th ed. College Station: Texas A&M University Press, 1998.

Flynn, James J. *Winning the Presidency: The Difficulty of Election.* Brooklyn, N.Y.: Theo. Gauss, 1976.

Peterson, Mark A. *Legislating Together: The White House and Capitol Hill from Eisenhower to Reagan.* Cambridge, Mass.: Harvard University Press, 1990.

Watson, Richard A. *Presidential Vetoes and Public Policy.* Lawrence: University Press of Kansas, 1993.

On the Relationship Between the President and the Public

Brody, Richard A. *Assessing the President: The Media, Elite Opinion, and Public Support.* Stanford, Calif.: Stanford University Press, 1999.

Cohen, Jeffrey E. *Presidential Responsiveness and Public Policy-Making: The Public and the Politics that Presidents Choose.* Ann Arbor: University of Michigan Press, 1997.

Kernell, Samuel. *Going Public: New Strategies of Presidential Leadership.* 2nd ed. Washington, D.C.: CQ Press, 1993.

Mueller, John E. *War, Presidents, and Public Opinion.* New York: Wiley, 1973.

Detailed Compendium of Facts about the Presidents

Kane, Joseph Nathan. *Presidential Fact Book.* New York: Random House, 1999.

INDEX

Photos and illustrations are indicated by *italic* locators.
Locators for main entries are set in **boldface**.
Locators for material in the appendix are followed by *a*.

A

AAA (Agricultural Adjustment Act) 268
Abu Ghraib prison scandal 393
Ackerman, Amos T. 154
Adams, John *12,* **12–20,** 402*a*
 and John Quincy Adams 51
 birth and childhood 13
 chronology 19
 and the Constitution 16
 death of 19
 and Declaration of Independence 16
 early career 13–16
 election of 1796 16
 election of 1800 18
 election to presidency 16
 and Federalist Party 16–18
 and First Continental Congress 15–16
 foreign policy 16–18
 and France 16–18
 and Thomas Jefferson 16–17, 25
 post-presidential career 18–19
 and Republicans 17–18
 and Revolutionary War 14–16
 and Second Continental Congress 16
 as vice president 16
 and George Washington 4
Adams, John Quincy *49,* **49–57,** 407*a*
 birth and childhood 50
 cabinet of 54
 chronology 56–57
 death of 56
 and Democratic Party 55
 early career 50–53
 election of 1824 53
 election to presidency 53
 and Federalist Party 51–52
 in House of Representatives 55–56
 and Andrew Jackson 63
 as minister to Britain 52
 as minister to Netherlands 51
 and Monroe Doctrine 53
 and Native Americans 55
 post-presidential career 55–56
 and Republican Party 51–52, 54
 as secretary of state 53
 in Senate 51–52
 and slavery issue 56
 and Martin Van Buren 69, 70
 and War of 1812 52
Adams-Onís Treaty
 John Quincy Adams and 53
 James Monroe and 45
Afghanistan invasion (2001) 389
African Americans. *See also* civil rights; slavery; voting rights
 black codes 143
 black colonization 132
 Dred Scott decision 123, 124, 132
 Freedmen's Bureau 144
 in military service 135
Age of the Common Man 62
Agnew, Spiro
 and Gerald R. Ford 327
 and Richard M. Nixon 317–319, 321
Agricultural Adjustment Act (AAA) 268
agricultural policy. *See* farm policy
Alien and Sedition Acts
 John Adams and 17
 James Madison and 34
Al Qaeda 388–389
American Revolution. *See* Revolutionary War
Amistad case
 John Quincy Adams and 56
 Martin Van Buren and 73
Angola 330
antitrust action
 Theodore Roosevelt and 214
 William Howard Taft and 226
 Woodrow Wilson and 233–234
Aristide, Jean-Bertrand 340
arms negotiations/control. *See also* nuclear weapons
 Jimmy Carter and 336
 Richard M. Nixon and 319
 Ronald Reagan and 352–353
Arthur, Chester A. *175,* **175–182,** 425*a*
 assumption of presidency 175, 179
 birth and childhood 176
 chronology 181–182
 and civil rights 180–181
 as collector of customhouse, Port of New York 176–178
 death of 181
 early career 176–178
 election of 1880 178
 election of 1884 181
 and James A. Garfield 172
 and Rutherford B. Hayes 164, 165
 and Pendleton Act 180
 and Stalwarts 178–181
 and Star Routes fraud/trials 179–180
 as vice president 178–179
Ashcroft, John 387
 and George W. Bush 389
assassinations/assassination attempts
 James A. Garfield 167, 172–173
 John F. Kennedy 302
 Abraham Lincoln 136–137
 William McKinley 207–208
 Ronald Reagan 349
assistant secretary of the navy
 Franklin D. Roosevelt as 266
 Theodore Roosevelt as 213–214
assumption of presidency
 Chester A. Arthur and 175, 179
 Calvin Coolidge and 247–248, 251
 Millard Fillmore and 109
 Gerald R. Ford and 328
 Andrew Johnson and 143
 Lyndon B. Johnson and 308
 Theodore Roosevelt and 214–215
 Harry S. Truman and 280
 John Tyler and 85
atomic bomb 276, 280–281. *See also* nuclear weapons
Atwater, Lee 359

Austin, Harmon 168
"axis of evil" 390

B

Baird, Zoe 369
Balkans 362
Ballinger, Richard A. 224–225
Baltimore incident 197–198
banking. *See also* national bank
  Millard Fillmore and 106–107
  Franklin D. Roosevelt and 268
  John Tyler and 86
  Woodrow Wilson and 233
Battle of New Orleans 37, 61–62
Bay of Pigs 299
Belknap, William W. 154
Bentsen, Lloyd 358
Berlin Wall
  George H. W. Bush and 360
  John F. Kennedy and 301
bin Laden, Osama 388–389, 395
Birney, James G. 80
black codes 143
black colonization 132
Blaine, James G.
  and Grover Cleveland 185, 186
  and Benjamin Harrison 195–196
Bland-Allison Act 165
Blount, Winton 380
Bob Jones University 383
Boland Amendment 351
Bonaparte, Napoleon. *See* Napoleon Bonaparte
"Bonus Army" 260–261
"Born in the USA" (Bruce Springsteen) 350
Bosnia 362, 372, 374
Boston Massacre 14–15
Boston police strike 249–250
Boston Tea Party
  John Adams and 15
  Thomas Jefferson and 22
  James Madison and 32
  George Washington and 3
Boxer Rebellion 256
Brezhnev, Leonid
  and Jimmy Carter 338
  and Richard M. Nixon 319
Britain. *See* Great Britain
Broaddrick, Juanita 374
Brown v. Board of Education 290
Bryan, William Jennings 204
Buchanan, James *120*, **120–126**, 417*a*
  birth and childhood 121
  chronology 126
  death of 126
  and Democratic Party 122–125
  early career 121–123
  election of 1820 121
  election of 1828 122
  election of 1856 123
  election of 1858 125
  election of 1860 125
  election to presidency 123
  and Federalist Party 121
  in House of Representatives 121–122
  and Ostend Manifesto 123
  post-presidential career 126
  and Republican Party 124, 125
  in Senate 122–123
  and slavery issue 120, 123–126
Buchanan, Patrick 384
Bull Moose Party 218
Burke, Arleigh 299
Burleson, Albert S. 234
Burr, Aaron 27
Bush, George Herbert Walker *356*, **356–364**, 456*a*
  the Balkans 362
  and Lloyd Bentsen 358
  Berlin Wall, fall of 360
  birth and childhood 357
  Bosnia 362
  and George W. Bush 380–382
  as chairman of Republican National Committee 358
  China 360
  chronology 362–363
  and civil rights 358
  and Bill Clinton 362, 369, 376
  as director of CIA 358
  and Michael Dukakis 359–360
  early career 357–359
  election of 1966 358
  election of 1980 359
  election of 1992 362
  election of 2000 362
  election to presidency 359–360
  and Gerald R. Ford 358
  and Mikhail Gorbachev 360, 361
  in House of Representatives 358
  and Saddam Hussein 361
  and Iran-contra scandal 359
  Iraq 361
  and Richard M. Nixon 358
  Operation Desert Storm 361
  Panama invasion 360
  Persian Gulf War 361
  post-presidential career 362
  and Ronald Reagan 352, 353
  and Republican Party 358
  Strategic Arms Reduction Treaty 361
  Tiananmen Square 360
  as U.S. representative to United Nations 358
  as vice president 359
  and Watergate 358
Bush, George W. *379*, **379–399**, 459*a*–460*a*
  birth and childhood 380
  and George H. W. Bush 362, 381
  cabinet of 387–388
  and Jimmy Carter 341, 386
  chronology 398
  and Bill Clinton 375, 376
  early career 380–383
  education reform while governor 382
  election of 1978 381
  election of 1988 381
  election of 1994 381–382
  election of 1998 382–383
  election of 2000 379–380, 383–388
  election of 2004 395–396
  and Florida ballot 384–386
  and Al Gore 383–386, 388
  as governor 382–383
  and Katherine Harris 385
  and hate-crimes bill 382
  and Iraq War 390–396
  and Joseph Lieberman 385
  and John McCain 383
  and Ralph Nader 384
  and Sandra Day O'Connor 386
  and William H. Rehnquist 388
  and Republican Party 381
  and Ann Richards 381
  and September 11, 2001, terrorist attacks 388–389, 395
  and John Paul Stevens 386
  and terrorism 381–382
  Vietnam 380
Bush, Jeb 383
Bush, Prescott 357, 380
Bush Doctrine 389–390

C

Calhoun, John C.
  and Andrew Jackson 64
  and Franklin Pierce 114, 115
  and Zachary Taylor 103
  and John Tyler 87–88
  and Martin Van Buren 71
California
  Millard Fillmore and 108–109
  Zachary Taylor and 100, 102, 103
Callender, James 27–28
Cambodia
  Gerald R. Ford and 330–331
  Richard M. Nixon and 318–319

"Camelot" 295, 302
Camp David talks 338
Canada
Martin Van Buren and 73
John Tyler and 87
Carranza, Venustiano 234
Carter, James Earl, Jr. *333*, **333–338**, 452*a*–453*a*
and Jean-Bertrand Aristide 340
arms negotiations 336
and Bert Lance scandal 337
birth and childhood 334
and Leonid Brezhnev 338
and George W. Bush 386
cabinet of 336
Camp David talks 338
chronology 341–342
and Bill Clinton 368, 375
and Democratic Party 336
early career 334–336
economic policies 337
election of 1970 335
election of 1976 335–336
election of 1980 338–340
election to presidency 335–336
energy crisis 337
energy policy 337, 338
and Gerald R. Ford 331, 336
foreign policy 337–338
as governor 335
Haiti 340
human rights 336
inflation 339
Iranian hostage crisis 339, 340
and Ayatollah Khomeni 338, 339
Middle East peace talks 338
Moscow Olympics 339
and Nobel Peace Prize 340
North Korea 340
Panama Canal treaty 337
post-presidential career 340
and Ronald Reagan 340, 347–348
SALT II treaty 338
and September 11, 2001, terrorist attacks 341
Soviet Union 336, 338, 339
Castro, Fidel 299–300
CCC (Civilian Conservation Corps) 268
Central Intelligence Agency (CIA)
George H. W. Bush and 358
Dwight D. Eisenhower and 290–291, 293
Gerald R. Ford and 330
Lyndon B. Johnson and 311
John F. Kennedy and 299–300
Richard M. Nixon and 320
Chambers, Whittaker 316
Chase, Samuel 52
Chavez, Hugo 341
Chavez, Linda 388
"Checkers Speech" 317
Cheney, Richard 384, 390, 391
Chile 197–198
China
George H. W. Bush and 358, 360
Dwight D. Eisenhower and 291–292
Rutherford B. Hayes and 165
Herbert Hoover and 256
William Howard Taft and 226
Taiwan 291–292
John Tyler and 87
Chinese immigration
Chester A. Arthur and 181
James A. Garfield and 171
Rutherford B. Hayes and 165
Christian Coalition 387
chronologies
John Adams 19
John Quincy Adams 56–57
Chester A. Arthur 181–182
James Buchanan 126
George H. W. Bush 362–363
George W. Bush 398
Jimmy Carter 341–342
Grover Cleveland 191
Bill Clinton 376–377
Calvin Coolidge 254
Dwight D. Eisenhower 293–294
Millard Fillmore 111
Gerald R. Ford 331–332
James A. Garfield 173–174
Ulysses S. Grant 156
Warren G. Harding 244
Benjamin Harrison 199
William Henry Harrison 82
Rutherford B. Hayes 165–166
Herbert Hoover 262
Andrew Jackson 66–67
Thomas Jefferson 29–30
Andrew Johnson 146–147
Lyndon B. Johnson 312
John F. Kennedy 302–303
Abraham Lincoln 137–138
James Madison 38
William McKinley 208
James Monroe 47
Richard M. Nixon 323
Franklin Pierce 119
James K. Polk 96–97
Ronald Reagan 354
Franklin D. Roosevelt 274–275
Theodore Roosevelt 219
William Howard Taft 227–228
Zachary Taylor 104
Harry S. Truman 284
John Tyler 88
Martin Van Buren 74–75
George Washington 9–10
Woodrow Wilson 237–238
Churchill, Winston
and Franklin D. Roosevelt 272–273
and Harry S. Truman 280
CIA. *See* Central Intelligence Agency
Civilian Conservation Corps (CCC) 268
civil rights. *See also* voting rights
Chester A. Arthur and 180–181
George H. W. Bush and 358
Bill Clinton and 369
Dwight D. Eisenhower and 290, 292
James A. Garfield and 167, 169, 170
Warren G. Harding and 243
Benjamin Harrison and 197
Andrew Johnson and 144
Lyndon B. Johnson and 307, 308, 310
John F. Kennedy and 299, 301
William McKinley and 202
Richard M. Nixon and 319
Franklin D. Roosevelt and 270
Harry S. Truman and 278, 282–283
Woodrow Wilson and 234
civil service
Chester A. Arthur and 177, 180
James A. Garfield and 170, 172
Benjamin Harrison and 196
Rutherford B. Hayes and 163, 164
Thomas Jefferson and 26–27
Civil War. *See also* Reconstruction
James A. Garfield and 169
Ulysses S. Grant and 150–152
Benjamin Harrison and 194–195
Rutherford B. Hayes and 160
Andrew Johnson and 142–143
Abraham Lincoln and 134–136
William McKinley and 202–203
Clay, Henry
and John Quincy Adams 54
and Millard Fillmore 107
and William Henry Harrison 78, 79, 81
and Andrew Jackson 63, 64
and James K. Polk 92
and Zachary Taylor 103
and John Tyler 86–87
Clayton Antitrust Act 233–234
Clayton-Bulwar Treaty 103

Cleveland, Grover *183,* **183–191,** 426*a*–427*a*
birth and childhood 184
and Britain 191
chronology 191
death of 191
and Democratic Party 185–186
early career 184–185
election of 1884 185–186
election of 1888 188–189
election of 1892 189
election of 1896 191
election to presidency 185–186
foreign policy 190–191
as governor 185
and Hawaii 190–191
and Interstate Commerce Act 187
and labor 185, 189–191
monetary policy 183, 187, 189
and Mugwumps 185, 186
and Native Americans 188
post-presidential career 191
and Pullman Strike 183–184, 190, 191
tariffs 187–189
Clinton, Hillary Rodham 368–370, 374, 376
Clinton, William Jefferson *365,* **365–378,** 458*a*
birth and childhood 366
and George H. W. Bush 362
and George W. Bush 375, 384, 386
and Jimmy Carter 340
chronology 376–377
and Hillary Rodham Clinton 368–370, 374
Comprehensive Test Ban Treaty 374
and Democratic Party 368
and Robert Dole 372
and Michael S. Dukakis 369
early career 366–369
election of 1976 368
election of 1978 368
election of 1980 368
election of 1982 368
election of 1988 369
election of 1992 362, 369
election of 1994 371
election of 1996 372
election of 2000 375
election to presidency 369
environmental initiatives 375
extramarital affairs 369, 372–373
foreign policy 372, 374
and Vincent Foster 370
and J. William Fulbright 366–367
gays in the military 370
and Newt Gingrich 371, 373
and Al Gore 375
as governor 368–369
health-care reform 370
impeachment of 373–374
and John F. Kennedy 365–366
Kosovo 374
and Monica Lewinsky 372, 373
and Slobodan Milosevic 374
and Dick Morris 368, 371
and NAFTA 370–371
pardons 375
and Ross Perot 372
personal characteristics 376
and Robert Reich 371
and Marc Rich 375
Serbia 374
and Kenneth Starr 372
and Vietnam 367, 374
welfare reform 371
Whitewater 370, 371, 374
Clinton Presidential Library 376
Coercive Acts. *See* Intolerable Acts
cold war. *See also* Soviet Union
George H. W. Bush and 360
Dwight D. Eisenhower and 290–293
John F. Kennedy and 297, 299–301
Richard M. Nixon and 319
Harry S. Truman and 282–284
Colombia
William Henry Harrison and 78
Theodore Roosevelt and 216
Committee to Investigate the National Defense Program 279
communism
Dwight D. Eisenhower and 290, 292
Herbert Hoover and 257, 258
Lyndon B. Johnson and 310
Richard M. Nixon and 316
Ronald Reagan and 350
Harry S. Truman and 282, 283
Woodrow Wilson and 237
Comprehensive Test Ban Treaty 374
Compromise of 1850
Millard Fillmore and 108–110
Zachary Taylor and 103, 104
Confederation Congress 41
Conkling, Roscoe
and Chester A. Arthur 176, 178, 180
and James A. Garfield 170–172
and Rutherford B. Hayes 164–165
conservation
Bill Clinton and 375
Theodore Roosevelt and 215–218
William Howard Taft and 224–225
Constitution. *See also individual amendments*
John Adams and 16
Thomas Jefferson and 25
Andrew Johnson and 141
James Madison and 33
James Monroe and 42
William Howard Taft and 225
George Washington and 6
Constitutional Convention
John Adams and 15
Thomas Jefferson and 22–23
James Madison and 33
George Washington and 3, 6
Continental Congress, Second
John Adams and 16
Thomas Jefferson and 23–24
George Washington and 3–4
Contras 350
Conway, Thomas 5
Coolidge, Calvin *247,* **247–254,** 437*a*
assumption of presidency 247–248, 251
birth and childhood 248
and Boston police strike 249–250
cabinet of 252
chronology 254
death of 253
early career 248–251
and economics 251–252
election of 1920 250
election of 1924 252
and Federal Trade Commission 252
foreign policy 253
as governor 249–250
Great Depression, years leading up to 253
and labor relations 249–250
post-presidential career 253
and Republican Party 248, 250
and Teapot Dome scandal 252
as vice president 250–251
Cordesman, Anthony 391
Cornell, Alonzo
and Chester A. Arthur 178
and Rutherford B. Hayes 164, 165
Cornwallis, Lord 5
"court-packing bill" 270–271
Cox, Archibald 321
Coxey, Jacob 189
Credit Mobilier scandal 153
Creek 55

crime
George W. Bush and 382
Bill Clinton and 371
Lyndon B. Johnson and 311
Cuba
John F. Kennedy and 299–301
William McKinley and 204–207
Cuban missile crisis 300–301
Currie, Betty 373
Curtis, Edwin U. 249–250
customhouses 176–178
Czolgosz, Leon 208

D

Daniels, Josephus 266
Daschle, Tom 392
Daugherty, Harry M. 241–245
Dawes Act 188
Dayton Accords 372
death penalty 383
Declaration of Independence
John Adams and 16
Thomas Jefferson and 16, 23
defense spending
Ronald Reagan and 348–349
Harry S. Truman and 279
Democratic Party
John Quincy Adams and 55
James Buchanan and 122–125
George W. Bush and 391–392
Jimmy Carter and 336, 340
Grover Cleveland 185–186
Bill Clinton and 368
William Henry Harrison and 79
Rutherford B. Hayes and 162–163
Andrew Jackson and 63
Andrew Johnson and 140–143
Lyndon B. Johnson and 306, 308, 310
Abraham Lincoln and 136
Franklin Pierce and 115–116
James K. Polk and 91–92
Franklin D. Roosevelt and 265–267
Harry S. Truman and 279
John Tyler and 84–85, 88
Martin Van Buren and 70, 72
Woodrow Wilson and 232–233
Democratic Societies 8
Deng Xiaoping 360
Depression. *See* Great Depression
Dickinson, Charles 60–61
discrimination. *See* civil rights
Dobson, James C. 387
Dole, Robert 372
Dominican Republic
Ulysses S. Grant and 153
Theodore Roosevelt and 216
Dorr, Thomas W. 97
Dorsey, Stephen 179
Douglas, Stephen A.
and James Buchanan 124
and Abraham Lincoln 132–133
and Franklin Pierce 116–117
Douglass, Frederick
and Andrew Johnson 144
and Abraham Lincoln 135
draft dodgers, pardon of 336
Dred Scott decision
James Buchanan and 123, 124
Abraham Lincoln and 132
Duffey, Joseph D. 367
Dukakis, Michael S. 359–360, 369
Dulles, John Foster 290

E

Eastern Europe 360. *See also specific countries*
Eaton, John
and Martin Van Buren 71
and Andrew Jackson 63–64
economic policy. *See also* monetary policy
George H. W. Bush and 362
Jimmy Carter and 337
Grover Cleveland and 189
Bill Clinton and 370
Calvin Coolidge and 251–253
Millard Fillmore and 107
Gerald R. Ford and 329–330
Herbert Hoover and 259–261
Lyndon B. Johnson and 307
James Madison and 37–38
James K. Polk and 93
Ronald Reagan and 348–349
Franklin D. Roosevelt and 268, 271
education reform
George W. Bush and 382
Bill Clinton and 368, 369
Egypt
Jimmy Carter and 338
Dwight D. Eisenhower and 292
Ehrlichman, John 320, 321
Eisenhower, Dwight David *286,* **286–294,** 444*a*–445*a*
birth and childhood 287
and *Brown v. Board of Education* 290
Central Intelligence Agency 290–291, 293
chronology 293–294
civil rights 290, 292
and cold war 290–293
death of 293
early career 287–289
Egypt 292
and Eisenhower Doctrine 292
election of 1952 289–290
election of 1956 292
election to presidency 289–290
foreign policy 290–293
Guatemala 291
and Iran 290
and Korean conflict 290
and Little Rock High School Integration crisis 292
and Douglas MacArthur 288
and Joseph McCarthy 290
military career 287–289
and Richard M. Nixon 289–290, 316–317
and Normandy Beach invasion 288
nuclear weapons 290, 292
and Operation Overlord 288–289
and George Patton 288
post-presidential career 293
and Republican Party 289
Soviet Union 290, 292, 293
Taiwan 291–292
U2 spy plane crisis 293
Vietnam 291
and Earl Warren 290
World War II 288–289
Eisenhower Doctrine 292
election of 1789 6
election of 1792 7
election of 1796 16
election of 1798 33
election of 1800
John Adams and 18
Thomas Jefferson and 25–26
election of 1804 28
election of 1808 34
election of 1816 43–44
election of 1820
James Buchanan and 121
James Monroe and 46
election of 1824
John Quincy Adams and 53
Andrew Jackson and 63
election of 1825 78
election of 1827 84
election of 1828
James Buchanan and 122
William Henry Harrison and 79
Andrew Jackson and 63
Martin Van Buren and 70
election of 1832
Andrew Jackson and 65
Franklin Pierce and 114
Martin Van Buren and 71

election of 1836
  Franklin Pierce and 115
  Martin Van Buren and 71
election of 1840
  Millard Fillmore and 107
  William Henry Harrison and 76–77, 79–80, 82, 85
  James K. Polk and 92
  John Tyler and 85–88
  Martin Van Buren and 74
election of 1842 131
election of 1844
  James K. Polk and 88, 92
  John Tyler and 88
  Martin Van Buren and 74, 102
election of 1848
  Millard Fillmore and 108
  Franklin Pierce and 116
  Zachary Taylor and 102
election of 1852 110
election of 1856
  James Buchanan and 123
  Millard Fillmore and 111
  Franklin Pierce and 118
election of 1857 141
election of 1858 125
election of 1860
  James Buchanan and 125
  Abraham Lincoln and 133
election of 1862 169
election of 1864
  Millard Fillmore and 111
  Rutherford B. Hayes and 160
  Abraham Lincoln and 136
election of 1866
  Rutherford B. Hayes and 160
  Andrew Johnson and 144–145
election of 1868 152
election of 1872 161
election of 1874 155
election of 1876
  Ulysses S. Grant and 155
  Rutherford B. Hayes and 161–163
  William McKinley and 202
election of 1880
  Chester A. Arthur and 178
  James A. Garfield and 170–172
  Ulysses S. Grant and 155
  Benjamin Harrison and 195
election of 1884
  Chester A. Arthur and 181
  Grover Cleveland and 185–186
election of 1888
  Grover Cleveland and 188–189
  Benjamin Harrison and 195–196
election of 1892
  Grover Cleveland and 189
  Benjamin Harrison and 198–199
election of 1896
  Grover Cleveland and 191
  William McKinley and 203–204
election of 1898 214
election of 1900 214
election of 1904 216–217
election of 1908 223–224
election of 1912
  Theodore Roosevelt and 218
  William Howard Taft and 226
  Woodrow Wilson and 232–233
election of 1914 241
election of 1920
  Calvin Coolidge and 250
  Warren G. Harding and 242
  Franklin D. Roosevelt and 266
election of 1924 252
election of 1928
  Herbert Hoover and 258
  Franklin D. Roosevelt and 266
election of 1932
  Herbert Hoover and 261
  Franklin D. Roosevelt and 267
election of 1936 270
election of 1937 306
election of 1940 271
election of 1941 306
election of 1944
  Franklin D. Roosevelt and 273
  Harry S. Truman and 279
election of 1946
  John F. Kennedy and 297–298
  Richard M. Nixon and 316
election of 1948
  Gerald R. Ford and 326–327
  Lyndon B. Johnson and 307
  Harry S. Truman and 282
election of 1950 316
election of 1952
  Dwight D. Eisenhower and 289–290
  John F. Kennedy and 297
  Richard M. Nixon and 316–317
election of 1956 292
election of 1958 298
election of 1960
  Lyndon B. Johnson and 307–308
  John F. Kennedy and 298–299
  Richard M. Nixon and 317
  Ronald Reagan and 346
election of 1962 317
election of 1964
  Lyndon B. Johnson and 310
  Ronald Reagan and 346
election of 1966
  George H. W. Bush and 358
  Ronald Reagan and 346–347
election of 1968
  Gerald R. Ford and 327
  Richard M. Nixon and 317–318
election of 1970
  Jimmy Carter and 335
  Ronald Reagan and 347
election of 1972 319–320
election of 1976
  Jimmy Carter and 335–336
  Bill Clinton and 368
  Gerald R. Ford and 331
  Ronald Reagan and 347
election of 1978
  George W. Bush and 381
  Bill Clinton and 368
election of 1980
  George H. W. Bush and 359
  Jimmy Carter and 339–340
  Bill Clinton and 368
  Ronald Reagan and 347–348
election of 1982 368
election of 1984 350
election of 1988
  George H. W. Bush and 359–360
  George W. Bush and 381
  Bill Clinton and 369
election of 1992
  George H. W. Bush and 361–362
  Bill Clinton and 369
election of 1994
  George W. Bush and 381–382
  Bill Clinton and 371
election of 1996 372
election of 1998 382–383
election of 2000
  George H. W. Bush and 362
  George W. Bush and 379–380, 383–388
  Bill Clinton and 375
election of 2004
  George W. Bush and 396–397
  Bill Clinton and 376
election to presidency. *See also* assumption of presidency
  John Adams and 16
  John Quincy Adams and 53
  James Buchanan and 123
  George H. W. Bush and 359–360
  George W. Bush and 383–388, 396–397
  Jimmy Carter and 335–336
  Grover Cleveland and 185–186
  Bill Clinton and 369
  Dwight D. Eisenhower and 289–290
  James A. Garfield and 170–172
  Ulysses S. Grant and 152
  Warren G. Harding and 242

Benjamin Harrison and 195–196
William Henry Harrison and 79–80
Rutherford B. Hayes and 161–163
Herbert Hoover and 258
Andrew Jackson and 63
Thomas Jefferson and 25–26
John F. Kennedy and 298–299
Abraham Lincoln and 133
James Madison and 34
William McKinley and 203–204
James Monroe and 43–44
Richard M. Nixon and 317–318
Franklin Pierce and 116
Ronald Reagan and 347–348
Franklin D. Roosevelt and 267
William Howard Taft and 223–224
Zachary Taylor and 102
Martin Van Buren and 71
George Washington and 6
Woodrow Wilson and 232–233
Ellsberg, Daniel 320
El Salvador 349
Emancipation Proclamation 134–135
Embargo Act 27
energy crisis 337, 338
energy policy 337, 338
England. *See* Great Britain
environmentalism. *See also* conservation
Bill Clinton and 374–375
Benjamin Harrison and 197
Theodore Roosevelt and 215–218
William Howard Taft and 224–225
Environmental Protection Agency 319
Equal Rights Amendment 319
Era of Good Feelings 45
expansionism
William McKinley and 207
James K. Polk and 94
Theodore Roosevelt and 216
extramarital affairs
Bill Clinton and 369, 370, 372–373
John F. Kennedy and 301–302

F

Fair Deal 281
farm policy
Herbert Hoover and 258–259
Franklin D. Roosevelt and 268–270
Fay, George R. 393
FBI. *See* Federal Bureau of Investigation
Federal Bureau of Investigation (FBI)
Richard M. Nixon and 320, 321
Ronald Reagan and 346
The Federalist 33
Federalist Party
John Adams and 16–18
John Quincy Adams and 51–52
James Buchanan and 121
Hamiltonians and 9
Thomas Jefferson and 25–27
James Madison and 34–35
James Monroe and 42
partisan battles with Republican Party 25–27
Martin Van Buren and 70
George Washington and 9
Federalist Party (New England) 52
Federal Reserve Board 233
Federal Trade Commission 252
Fifteenth Amendment
James A. Garfield and 169–170
Ulysses S. Grant and 153
Fillmore, Millard *105*, **105–111**, 415*a*
assumption of presidency 109
birth and childhood 105–106
cabinet of 109
chronology 111
and Compromise of 1850 108–110
contributions of 105–106
death of 111
early career 106
election of 1840 107
election of 1848 108
election of 1852 110
election of 1856 111
election of 1864 111
and foreign policy 110
in House of Representatives 106–108
and Japan 110
and Know-Nothing Party 110, 111
personal characteristics 106
post-presidential career 110
and slavery issue 108–111
as vice president 108–109
and Whig Party 106–110
fireside chats 268
First Continental Congress
John Adams and 15–16
George Washington and 3
fiscal policy. *See* monetary policy
Fisk, James 153
Fleischer, Ari 391
Florida
George W. Bush and 384–386
James Monroe and 45
Flowers, Gennifer 369
Forbes, Charles 243, 245
Force Bill
Andrew Jackson and 64–65
John Tyler and 84
Ford, Gerald R. *325*, **325–332**, 451*a*
Angola 330
assumption of presidency 328
birth and childhood 326
and George H. W. Bush 358
cabinet of 328
and Jimmy Carter 331, 336
chronology 331–332
early career 326–328
economic policies 329–330
election of 1948 326–327
election of 1968 327
election of 1976 331
and Alexander Haig 328, 329
in House of Representatives 327
and Lyndon Johnson's programs 327
Mayaguez incident 330–331
as minority leader 327
New York City bailout 330
and Richard M. Nixon 322, 327–329
pardon of Nixon 328–329
personal characteristics 325
post-presidential career 331
and Ronald Reagan 347
and Republican Party 326, 327
and Spiro Agnew's resignation 327
as vice president 327–328
Vietnam 327, 330
Watergate 328
foreign policy
John Adams and 16–18
John Quincy Adams and 53
Martin Van Buren and 73
George H. W. Bush and 360–361
Jimmy Carter and 337–338
Grover Cleveland and 190–191
Bill Clinton and 372, 374
Calvin Coolidge and 253
Dwight D. Eisenhower and 290–293
Millard Fillmore and 110
Gerald R. Ford and 330–331
Ulysses S. Grant and 153
Warren G. Harding and 243
Benjamin Harrison and 197–198

Rutherford B. Hayes and 165
Thomas Jefferson and 26, 28
Andrew Johnson and 146
Lyndon B. Johnson and 308–311
John F. Kennedy and 299–301
James Madison and 35–38
William McKinley and 204–207
James Monroe and 45–47
Richard M. Nixon and 318–319
Franklin Pierce and 117
James K. Polk and 94–96
Ronald Reagan and 349–353
Theodore Roosevelt and 216–218
William Howard Taft and 226
Zachary Taylor and 103
Harry S. Truman and 281–283
John Tyler and 87–88
George Washington and 8–9
Woodrow Wilson and 234–237
Foster, Vincent 370
Fourteen Points 236–237
Fourteenth Amendment 144, 145
France
John Adams and 16–18
George W. Bush and 391
Thomas Jefferson and 25, 27
Andrew Johnson and 146
James Madison and 35–36
James Monroe and 42, 43
George Washington and 8, 9
Freedmen's Bureau 144
Free-Soil policy 131, 132
French and Indian War 3
French Revolution 8, 25
Fugitive Slave Law 117–118
Fulbright, J. William 366–367

G

Gallatin, Albert 35
Garfield, James A. *167,* **167–174,** 424*a*
birth and childhood 167
chronology 173–174
and civil rights 169, 170
on civil rights 167
and Civil War 169
death of 167, 172–173
early career 167–170
election of 1862 169
election of 1880 170–172
election to presidency 170–172
in House of Representatives 169
military career 169
and Reconstruction 169
and Republican Party 170
and slavery issue 169
and Stalwarts 170, 171, 173
and Star Routes fraud 172
gays in the military 370
Genet, Edward 9
Germany
George W. Bush and 391
Benjamin Harrison and 198
John F. Kennedy and 301
Franklin D. Roosevelt and 272–273
Woodrow Wilson and 235–236
gerrymandering 141
Gettysburg Address 135–136
Giles, William Branch 35
Gingrich, Newt 371–373
Glass-Steagall Act 260
Glavis, Louis 224, 225
Goldwater, Barry M.
and Lyndon B. Johnson 310
and Ronald Reagan 346
Gonzales, Alberto 387
Good Neighbor Policy 269
Gorbachev, Mikhail
and George H. W. Bush 360, 361
and Ronald Reagan 352–353
Gore, Al
and George W. Bush 379–380, 383–386, 388
and Bill Clinton 375
Gould, Jay
and Ulysses S.Grant 153
and Theodore Roosevelt 213
governor
George W. Bush as 382–383
Jimmy Carter as 335
Grover Cleveland as 185
Bill Clinton as 368–369
Calvin Coolidge as 249–250
Rutherford B. Hayes as 160–161
Thomas Jefferson as 24
Andrew Johnson as 141
William McKinley as 203
James Monroe as 42–43
James K. Polk as 92–93
Ronald Reagan as 347
Franklin D. Roosevelt as 267
Theodore Roosevelt as 214
John Tyler as 84
Martin Van Buren as 70
Woodrow Wilson as 232
Grant, Ulysses S. *148,* **148–156,** 421*a*–422*a*
birth and childhood 149
cabinet of 153, 154
chronology 156
and Civil War 150–152
death of 156
and Dominican Republic 153
early career 149–152
election of 1868 152
election of 1874 155
election of 1876 155
election of 1880 155
election to presidency 152
foreign policy 153
and James A. Garfield 170, 171
and Abraham Lincoln 135, 136
post-presidential career 155–156
and Republican Party 152, 155
Great Britain
John Quincy Adams and 52
Grover Cleveland 191
Ulysses S. Grant and 154
James Madison and 35–38
James Monroe and 46
James K. Polk and 94
Zachary Taylor and 103
John Tyler and 87–88
Martin Van Buren and 73
George Washington and 8–9
Woodrow Wilson and 235–236
Great Depression
Calvin Coolidge and 253
Herbert Hoover and 259–261
Franklin D. Roosevelt and 267–271
Great Society 308, 310
Greece 281, 282
Grenada 350
Grier, Robert C. 123
Guantánamo Bay, Cuba 394
Guatemala 291
Guinier, Lani 369–370
Guiteau, Charles 172–173
Gulf of Tonkin Resolution 309

H

Haig, Alexander 328, 329
Haiti
Jimmy Carter and 340
Bill Clinton and 372
Woodrow Wilson and 234
Haldeman, H. R. 320, 321
Halleck, Henry 151
Halpin, Maria 186
Hamilton, Alexander
and John Adams 17–18
and *The Federalist* 33
and Thomas Jefferson 25, 26
and monetary policy 6–8
and George Washington 5
Hamiltonians 7–9, 17–18
Hance, Kent 381
Hancock, Winfield S. 171
Hanna, Marcus Alonzo 203, 204
Hannegan, Robert 279

Harding, Warren G. *239,* **239–245,** 436*a*
birth and childhood 240
cabinet of 242–243
chronology 244
and civil rights 243
corruption in Harding administration 243–245
death of 244
early career 240–242
election of 1914 241
election of 1920 242
election to presidency 242
foreign policy 243
labor relations 243
as lieutenant governor 241
and national highway system 243
and Republican Party 241–242
in Senate 241
and Teapot Dome scandal 244–245
Harris, Katherine 385
Harrison, Benjamin *193,* **193–199,** 428*a*
and *Baltimore* incident 197–198
birth and childhood 194
and Chile 197–198
chronology 199
and civil rights 197
and Civil War 194–195
death 199
early career 194–195
election of 1880 195
election of 1888 195–196
election of 1892 198–199
election to presidency 195–196
and environmentalism 197
foreign policy 197–198
and Germany 198
and Hawaii 198
and Land Revision Act 197
military career 194–195
and monetary policy 197
personal characteristics 193–194
post-presidential career 199
and Republican Party 195
in Senate 195
and Sherman Antitrust Act 196–197
and tariffs 197
and voting rights 197
Harrison, William Henry *76,* **76–82,** 411*a*
birth and childhood 77
cabinet of 81, 85
death of 81
and Democratic Party 79
early career 77–79
election of 1825 78
election of 1828 79
election of 1840 76–77, 79–80, 82, 85
election to presidency 79–80
as governor of Indiana Territory 77
in House of Representatives 77
military career 77–78
as minister of Colombia 78
and Native Americans 77–78
as secretary of Northwest Territory 77
in Senate 78
and Martin Van Buren 74
and War of 1812 78
and Whig Party 79–81
Hartford Convention 37
hate-crimes bill 382
Hawaii
Grover Cleveland 190–191
Benjamin Harrison and 198
John Tyler and 87
Hayes, Rutherford B. *158,* **158–166,** 423*a*
birth and childhood 159
cabinet of 164
and China 165
chronology 165–166
and Civil War 160
death of 165
and Democratic Party 162–163
early career 159–161
election of 1864 160
election of 1866 160
election of 1872 161
election of 1876 161–163
election to presidency 161–163
foreign policy 165
and James A. Garfield 170
as governor 160–161
in House of Representatives 160
and Reconstruction 163–164
and Republican Party 160–165
health-care reform 370
Hemings, Sally 21, 25, 27–29
highway system, national 243
Hinckley, John, Jr. 349, 359
Hiroshima 276, 281
Hiss, Alger 316
Holocaust
Franklin D. Roosevelt and 273
Harry S. Truman and 279
homestead bill 141–142
Hoover, Herbert *255,* **255–262,** 438*a*
birth and childhood 256, 261
and "Bonus Army" 260–261
and Boxer Rebellion 256
chronology 262
and Calvin Coolidge 252
death of 261
early career 256–258
election of 1928 258
election of 1932 261
election to presidency 258
farm policy 258–259
as food administrator 257
and Glass-Steagall Act 260
and Great Depression 259–261
and Norris Dam project 259–260
post-presidential career 261
and Reconstruction Finance Corporation 260
and Republican Party 257–258
and Franklin D. Roosevelt 267
as secretary of commerce 258
and Smoot-Hawley Tariff 259, 260
stock market crash of 1929 259
and tariffs 259, 260
and taxation 260
and unions 257
and World War I 257
The Hornet's Nest (Jimmy Carter) 341
Horton, Willie 359–360
House of Representatives, U.S.
John Quincy Adams 55–56
James Buchanan 121–122
George H. W. Bush 358
Millard Fillmore 106–108
Gerald R. Ford 327
James A. Garfield 169
William Henry Harrison 77
Rutherford B. Hayes 160
Andrew Jackson 60
Andrew Johnson 141
Lyndon B. Johnson 306–307
John F. Kennedy 297
Abraham Lincoln 131–132
James Madison 33–34
William McKinley 202–203
Richard M. Nixon 316
Franklin Pierce 114
James K. Polk 91
John Tyler 84
House of Representatives (Confederate) 88
House Un-American Activities Committee 316
Hubbell, Webster L. 371
Hull, Gen. William 69
human rights 336
Humphrey, Hubert
and Lyndon B. Johnson 309
and Richard M. Nixon 317, 318
Hungary 292

Hussein, Saddam
and George H. W. Bush 361
and George W. Bush 390, 392, 393, 395
Huston Plan 320
Hutchings, Robert L. 395

I

immigration. *See also* Chinese immigration
James A. Garfield and 171
Rutherford B. Hayes and 165
impeachment
of Bill Clinton 373–374
of Andrew Johnson 145–146
Indiana Territory 77
Indian Ocean tsunami (2004)
George H. W. Bush and 362
Bill Clinton and 376
Indian Removal Act 65–66
INF (Intermediate Nuclear Force) treaty 352–353
inflation
Jimmy Carter and 339
Ronald Reagan and 349
Intermediate Nuclear Force (INF) treaty 352–353
Internal Revenue Service (IRS) 321
International Exposition and World's Fair (Philadelphia) 158–159, 162, 164
Interstate Commerce Act 187
Intolerable Acts
Thomas Jefferson and 22
James Madison and 32
Iran
Jimmy Carter and 338–340
Dwight D. Eisenhower and 290
Iran-Contra scandal
George H. W. Bush and 359
Ronald Reagan and 350–352
Iranian hostage crisis 339, 340
Iraq
George H. W. Bush and 361, 362
George W. Bush and 390
Bill Clinton and 373
Iraq War (2003)
George H. W. Bush and 362
George W. Bush and 390–396
IRS (Internal Revenue Service) 321
Israel 338. *See also* Middle East

J

Jackson, Andrew *58,* **58–67,** 408*a*–409*a*
and John Quincy Adams 53–55
and American Revolution 58
birth and childhood 59
and James Buchanan 121–122
cabinet of 63
chronology 66–67
death of 66
and Democratic Party 63
early career 59–63
election of 1824 63
election of 1828 63
election of 1832 65
election to presidency 63
and William Henry Harrison 79
in House of Representatives 60
military career 61–63
and James Monroe 45
and Native Americans 61, 62, 65–66
and James K. Polk 91, 92
post-presidential career 66
and Republican Party 60
and slavery issue 60
and John Tyler 84
and Martin Van Buren 70–72, 74
and War of 1812 61
James, Thomas L. 172
Japan
Millard Fillmore and 110
Franklin Pierce and 117
Franklin D. Roosevelt and 272
Theodore Roosevelt and 217, 218
Harry S. Truman and 280–281
Japanese-Americans, internment of 272
Jay, John
and *The Federalist* 33
and George Washington 9
Jay Treaty 8–9, 51
Jefferson, Thomas *21,* **21–30,** 403*a*–404*a*
and John Adams 16–17
birth and childhood 22
cabinet of 26
chronology 29–30
and Constitution 25
death of 29
and Declaration of Independence 16, 23
early career 22–25
election of 1800 25–26
election of 1804 28
election to presidency 25–26
and Federalist Party 25–27
and France 25, 27
as governor 24
and Andrew Jackson 60
and Louisiana Purchase 27
and James Madison 32–34
and monetary policy 6, 7
and James Monroe 41, 43
post-presidential career 28–29
and Republican Party 25–27
and Sally Hemings 21, 25, 27–29
and Second Continental Congress 23–24
and slavery issue 23, 29
Jeffersonians 7–9
Johnson, Andrew *139,* **139–147,** 420*a*
assumption of presidency 143
birth and childhood 140
chronology 146–147
and Civil War 142–143
death of 146
and Democratic Party 140–143
early career 140–142
election of 1857 141
election of 1866 144–145
foreign policy 146
and Fourteenth Amendment 144
and France 146
as governor 141
and Ulysses S. Grant 152
in House of Representatives 141
impeachment of 145–146
and Mexico 146
post-presidential career 146
and Reconstruction 143–145
and Russia 146
in Senate 141–142, 146
as vice president 142–143
Johnson, Lyndon Baines *304,* **304–312,** 447*a*–448*a*
assumption of presidency 308
birth and childhood 305
Central Intelligence Agency 311
chronology 312
and civil rights 307, 310
death of 311
Democratic Party 306, 308, 310
early career 305–308
election of 1937 306
election of 1941 306
election of 1948 307
election of 1960 307–308
election of 1964 310
and Gerald R. Ford 327
and Barry M. Goldwater 310
Great Society 308, 310
Gulf of Tonkin Resolution 309
in House of Representatives 306–307
and John F. Kennedy 298, 308
personal characteristics 304–305
in Senate 307
Tet Offensive 311

as vice president 308
Vietnam 308–311
Voting Rights Act 310
War on Poverty 308
World War II 306–307
Jones, Paula Corbin 372
Jordan, Hamilton 375

K

Kansas
James Buchanan and 124–125
Franklin Pierce and 117, 118
Kansas City political machine 278–279
Kansas-Nebraska Act
Abraham Lincoln and 131–132
Franklin Pierce and 117
Kennedy, Edward 339, 392
Kennedy, John Fitzgerald *295*, **295–303**, 446*a*
and Bay of Pigs 299
Berlin Wall 301
birth and childhood 296
and "Camelot" 295, 302
and Fidel Castro 299–300
Central Intelligence Agency 299–300
chronology 302–303
civil rights 299, 301
and Bill Clinton 365–366
and cold war 297, 299–301
Cuba 299–301
Cuban missile crisis 300–301
death of 295, 302
early career 296–298
election of 1946 297–298
election of 1952 297
election of 1958 298
election of 1960 298–299
election to presidency 298–299
extramarital affairs 301–302
foreign policy 299–301
Germany 301
in House of Representatives 297
and Lyndon B. Johnson 298, 308–309
and Nikita Khrushchev 299–301
and Joseph McCarthy 298
and Richard M. Nixon 298, 317
Peace Corps 299
PT 109 296–297
in Senate 297–298
Soviet Union 299–301
Vietnam 301
World War II 296–297
Kerry, John
and George W. Bush 395, 396
and Bill Clinton 376
Khalid Shaikh Muhammad 389
Khomeni, Ayatollah 338, 339
Khrushchev, Nikita
and John F. Kennedy 299–301
and Richard M. Nixon 317
Kissinger, Henry 318–320
Kitchen Debate 317
Know-Nothing Party 110, 111
Korean conflict
Dwight D. Eisenhower and 290
Harry S. Truman and 276, 283–284
Korea (North) 340, 390
Kosovo 374
KTBC radio 307
Ku Klux Klan 154
Kuwait 361
Kyoto Treaty 388

L

labor policy
Grover Cleveland and 185
Calvin Coolidge and 249–250
Warren G. Harding and 243
Herbert Hoover and 257
Franklin D. Roosevelt and 269
Theodore Roosevelt and 215
William Howard Taft and 225–226
Harry S. Truman and 281
labor strikes
Calvin Coolidge and 249
Rutherford B. Hayes and 164
Harry S. Truman and 281
labor unions
Grover Cleveland and 187
Calvin Coolidge and 249–250
William Howard Taft and 223
Lance, Bert 337
Land Revision Act 197
Langevin, James 392
Latin America
James Monroe and 46
Ronald Reagan and 349
William Howard Taft and 226
League of Nations 237
Lebanon 349–350
Lecompton constitution (Kansas) 124–125
Lee, Charles (general) 5
lend-lease agreement 271
Lewinsky, Monica 372, 373
Lewis and Clark expedition 27
Lieberman, Joseph 384, 385, 391–392
lieutenant governor, Warren G. Harding as 241
Lincoln, Abraham *128*, **128–138**, 418*a*–419*a*
assassination of 136–137
birth and childhood 129
and James Buchanan 124–126
chronology 137–138
and Civil War 134–136
death of 137
and Democratic Party 136
early career 130–133
early views on slavery 129, 130
election of 1842 131
election of 1860 133
election of 1864 136
election to presidency 133
and Emancipation Proclamation 134–135
and Gettysburg Address 135–136
in House of Representatives 131–132
and Andrew Johnson 142
and Lincoln-Douglas debates 132–133
personal characteristics 129
and Republican Party 132–134
and slavery issue 131–134
and Martin Van Buren 74
Lincoln-Douglas debates 132–133
Little Rock High School Integration crisis 292
Louisiana Purchase
John Quincy Adams and 51–52
Thomas Jefferson and 27
James Monroe and 43

M

MacArthur, Douglas
and Dwight D. Eisenhower 288
and Herbert Hoover 261
and Harry S. Truman 283–284
Macon's Bill No. 2 35
Madison, James *31*, **31–39**, 405*a*
and John Quincy Adams 52
and American Revolution 32
birth and childhood 32
and Britain 35–38
chronology 38
and Constitution 33
and Constitutional Convention 33
and Continental Congress 33
death of 38
early career 32–34
election of 1798 33
election of 1808 34
election to presidency 34
and *The Federalist* 33

and Federalist Party 34
foreign policy 35–38
in House of Representatives 33–34
and Andrew Jackson 62
and monetary policy 6, 7
and James Monroe 43
post-presidential career 38
and Republican Party 34
and Revolutionary War 32
and slavery issue 33
and Martin Van Buren 69
and War of 1812 35–38
Maine (battleship) 201–202, 205
Manhattan Project 279
Manifest Destiny 93, 94, 96
Manning, Daniel 185
Marshall, George C.
and Dwight D. Eisenhower 288
and Harry S. Truman 282
Marshall Plan 282
materialism 251
Mauro, Garry 382
Mayaguez incident 330–331
McCain, John 383
McCarthy, Joseph
and Dwight D. Eisenhower 290
and John F. Kennedy 298
and Harry S. Truman 282
McClellan, George B. 134, 135
McDonald, John 154–155
McFarlane, Robert 350–352
McGovern, George 320, 368
McKinley, William *201,* **201–208,** 429*a*–430*a*
birth and childhood 202
chronology 208
and civil rights 202
and Civil War 202–203
and Cuba 204–207
death of 207–208
early career 202–203
election of 1876 202
election of 1896 203–204
election to presidency 203–204
foreign policy 204–207
as governor 203
in House of Representatives 202–203
and monetary policy 204, 207
and Philippines 206–207
and Republican Party 202–203
and Spain 201–202, 204–207
and Spanish-American War 201–202, 204–207
and tariff 202–203
and voting rights 202
McNary-Haugen Farm Relief Bill 253
Mellon, Andrew 251
Mexico
Andrew Johnson and 146
James K. Polk and 94–96
John Tyler and 87
Woodrow Wilson and 234–235
Middle East
George H. W. Bush and 361
Jimmy Carter and 338
Bill Clinton and 374
Ronald Reagan and 349–350
military career
of Dwight D. Eisenhower 287–289
of James A. Garfield 169
of Benjamin Harrison 194–195
of William Henry Harrison 77–78
of Andrew Jackson 61–62
of Zachary Taylor 99–102
of George Washington 3–6
military service, African Americans in 135
military spending. *See* defense spending
Milosevic, Slobodan 374
Mineta, Norman Y. 387–388
minority leader, Gerald R. Ford as 327
Missouri Compromise
James Buchanan and 123
James Monroe and 45–46
Franklin Pierce and 117
John Tyler and 84
Molotov, Vyacheslav 280
Mondale, Walter F. 350
monetary policy. *See also* banking; economic policy
Grover Cleveland and 183, 187, 189
Alexander Hamilton and 6–8
Benjamin Harrison and 197
Rutherford B. Hayes and 165
Andrew Jackson and 65
Thomas Jefferson and 6, 7
James Madison and 6, 7
William McKinley and 204, 207
William Howard Taft and 225
Martin Van Buren and 72
Woodrow Wilson and 233
Monroe, James *40,* **40–48,** 406*a*
and John Quincy Adams 53
birth and childhood 41
and Britain 46
cabinet of 45
chronology 47
and Confederation Congress 41
and Constitution 42
death of 47
early career 41–43
election of 1816 43–44
election of 1820 46
election to presidency 43–44
and Era of Good Feelings 45
foreign policy 45–47
and France 42, 43
as governor 42–43
and Andrew Jackson 62
and Latin America 46
and Louisiana Purchase 27
and Missouri Compromise 46
and Monroe Doctrine 46–47
and Native Americans 45
personal characteristics 41
post-presidential career 47
and Republican Party 42–43
and Revolutionary War 41
as secretary of state 43
in Senate 42
and slavery issue 45–46
and Spain 45, 46
Monroe Doctrine
John Quincy Adams and 53
James Monroe and 46–47
Theodore Roosevelt and 216
John Tyler and 87
Morris, Dick 368, 371
Moscow Olympics (1980) 339
Mugwumps 185, 186
Mulligan, James 186
Murphy, Thomas 154
My Life (Bill Clinton) 375–376

N

Nader, Ralph 384
NAFTA (North American Free Trade Agreement) 370–371
Nagasaki 276, 281
Napoleon Bonaparte
and Thomas Jefferson 27
Thomas Jefferson and 27
and James Madison 35–36
James Madison and 35–36
national bank
Millard Fillmore and 106–107
Franklin Pierce and 114
John Tyler and 86
Woodrow Wilson and 233
national debt
Thomas Jefferson and 26
James Madison and 35, 38
national highway system 243
National Industrial Recovery Act (NIRA) 268
National Intelligence Council (NIC) 395
Nationalist China. *See* Taiwan

National Labor Relations Board (NLRB) 269
National Security Council (NSC)
  George H. W. Bush and 359
  Ronald Reagan and 351
Native Americans
  John Quincy Adams and 55
  Grover Cleveland and 188
  William Henry Harrison and 77–78
  Andrew Jackson and 61, 62, 65–66
  James Madison and 35
  James Monroe and 45
NATO. *See* North Atlantic Treaty Organization
Navy, U.S.
  Benjamin Harrison and 198
  William McKinley and 206
Nebraska 116–117
Netherlands 51
Neutrality Acts 271
New Deal
  Lyndon B. Johnson and 306
  Richard M. Nixon and 316
  Franklin D. Roosevelt and 268–271
  Harry S. Truman and 278
New Mexico
  Millard Fillmore and 108–109
  Zachary Taylor and 102, 103
New Nationalism 226
New York City
  Gerald R. Ford and 330
  Theodore Roosevelt and 213, 214
Nicaragua
  Ronald Reagan and 350–351
  Woodrow Wilson and 234
NIC (National Intelligence Council) 395
Niger 390
NIRA (National Industrial Recovery Act) 268
Nixon, Richard M. *314,* **314–323,** 449*a*–450*a*
  and Spiro Agnew 317–319, 321
  arms control 319
  birth and childhood 315
  and Leonid Brezhnev 319
  and George H. W. Bush 358
  Cambodia 318–319
  Central Intelligence Agency 320
  "Checkers Speech" 317
  chronology 323
  and civil rights 319
  Clean Air Act 319
  and Archibald Cox 321
  death of 322
  early career 315–317
  and John Ehrlichman 320
  and Dwight D. Eisenhower 289–290, 316–317
  election of 1946 316
  election of 1950 316
  election of 1952 316–317
  election of 1960 317
  election of 1962 317
  election of 1968 317–318
  election of 1972 319–320
  election to presidency 317–318
  and Daniel Ellsberg 320
  Endangered Species Act 319
  Environmental Protection Agency 319
  Equal Rights Amendment 319
  and Gerald R. Ford 322, 327–329
  and H. R. Haldeman 320
  and Alger Hiss 316
  in House of Representatives 316
  and House Un-American Activities Committee 316
  and John F. Kennedy 298, 299, 317
  and Nikita Khrushchev 317
  and Henry Kissinger 318, 319
  and Kitchen Debate 317
  pardon of 322
  Pentagon Papers 320
  post-presidential career 322
  and Ronald Reagan 346
  and Republican Party 316, 317
  resignation of presidency 322–323
  SALT I treaty 319
  "Saturday Night Massacre" 321
  in Senate 316
  Supreme Court 319
  as vice president 317
  Vietnam 318–320
  Watergate 320–322
  World War II 316
NLRB (National Labor Relations Board) 269
Nobel Peace Prize (James Earl Carter, Jr.) 340
Noriega, Manuel 360
Normandy Beach invasion 288
Norris Dam project 259–260
North, Oliver 350, 351
North American Free Trade Agreement (NAFTA) 370–371
North Atlantic Treaty Organization (NATO)
  Bill Clinton and 374
  Harry S. Truman and 283
Northern Securities 214
Northwest Territory 77
Norton, Gale A. 387, 388
NSC. *See* National Security Council
NSC-68 283
nuclear weapons. *See also* arms negotiations/control
  Bill Clinton and 372, 374
  Dwight D. Eisenhower and 290, 292
  Ronald Reagan and 352
  Harry S. Truman and 276, 279–281

O

O'Connor, Sandra Day
  and George W. Bush 386
  and Ronald Reagan 349
Olney, Richard 190
Open Door Policy 226
Operation Desert Storm 361
Operation FEATURE 330
Operation Just Cause 360
Operation Mongoose 299, 300
Operation Overlord 288–289
Oregon 92–95
Ostend Manifesto
  James Buchanan and 123
  Franklin Pierce and 117
Otis, James 12, 14
Owen-Glass Act 233

P

Paine, Thomas 51
Panama
  George H. W. Bush and 360
  Jimmy Carter and 337
  Theodore Roosevelt and 216
Pan-American Conference 55
pardons, presidential
  Jimmy Carter and 336
  Bill Clinton and 375
  Gerald R. Ford and 328–329
  Richard M. Nixon and 322
Patton, George 288
Peace Corps 299
Pearl Harbor 272
Pendergast, Tom 278–279
Pendleton Act 180
Pentagon Papers 320
Pentagon terrorist attack. *See* September 11, 2001, terrorist attacks
Perot, Ross 362, 372
Perry, Matthew 110
Persian Gulf War (1990–1991) 356, 361
Philadelphia Plan 319

Philippines
William McKinley and 206–207
William Howard Taft and 223
Pierce, Franklin *113*, **113–119**, 416*a*
birth and childhood 114
and James Buchanan 122, 123
cabinet of 116
chronology 119
death of 119
and Democratic Party 115–116
early career 114–115
election of 1832 114
election of 1836 115
election of 1848 116
election of 1856 118
election to presidency 116
and foreign policy 117
in House of Representatives 114
and Japan 117
and Kansas-Nebraska Act 117
and nullification of Missouri Compromise 117
and Ostend Manifesto 117
post-presidential career 118
in Senate 115
and slavery issue 114–118
and Spain 117
Pinchot, Gifford 225
Plame, Valerie 390
Platt, Thomas C.
and James A. Garfield 172
and Theodore Roosevelt 214
Platt Amendment 207
Poindexter, John 351–352, 359
Poland 280
Polk, James K. *90*, **90–97**, 413*a*
birth and childhood 91
and Britain 94
and James Buchanan 122
chronology 96–97
death of 96
and Democratic Party 91–92
early career 91–92
election of 1840 92
election of 1844 88, 92
foreign policy 94–96
as governor 92–93
in House of Representatives 91
and Mexico 94–96
and Oregon 92–95
and slavery issue 95–96
as Speaker of the House 92
and Zachary Taylor 101
and U.S.-Mexican War 96
and Martin Van Buren 74
Populists 204
Potsdam conference 280
Powell, Colin L. 387, 390
presidential powers 233
Princeton University 231–232
Progressives
Theodore Roosevelt and 215, 216, 218
William Howard Taft and 223–225
Woodrow Wilson and 233
PT 109 296–297
public works projects
Herbert Hoover and 258
Franklin D. Roosevelt and 268, 269
Pullman Strike
Grover Cleveland and 183–184
Theodore Roosevelt and 214
William Howard Taft and 223
Pure Food and Drug Act 217

R

Radical Party
Rutherford B. Hayes and 160
Andrew Johnson and 145
railroads
Grover Cleveland and 187
Rutherford B. Hayes and 164
Randolph, Edmund 9
Ray, Robert 374
Reagan, Nancy 353
Reagan, Ronald Prescott (Ron Reagan, Jr.) 353
Reagan, Ronald Wilson *344*, **344–355**, 454*a*–455*a*
assassination attempt 349
birth and childhood 345
and George H. W. Bush 359
and Jimmy Carter 340, 348
chronology 354
death of 353
early career 345–347
economic policies 348–349
election of 1960 346
election of 1964 346
election of 1966 346–347
election of 1970 347
election of 1976 347
election of 1980 347–348
election of 1984 350
election to presidency 347–348
El Salvador 349
and Gerald R. Ford 347
foreign policy 349–353
and Barry Goldwater 346
and Mikhail Gorbachev 352–353
as governor 347
Grenada 350
and John Hinckley, Jr. 349
INF treaty 352–353
Iran-Contra scandal 350–352
Latin America 349
Lebanon 349–350
and Walter F. Mondale 350
Nicaragua 350–351
and Richard M. Nixon 346
and Sandra Day O'Connor 349
post-presidential career 353–354
Reagan Doctrine 349
and William H. Rehnquist 349
and Republican Party 347
shift from Democrat to Republican 346
Soviet Union 352–353
"Star Wars" 350
and David Stockman 348
Strategic Defense Initiative 350
supply-side economics 348, 349
Supreme Court 349
tax cuts 348
Reagan Doctrine 349
Reconstruction
James A. Garfield and 169
Rutherford B. Hayes and 163–164
Andrew Johnson and 143–145
Reconstruction Finance Corporation 260
Red Scare
Richard M. Nixon and 316
Ronald Reagan and 346
Harry S. Truman and 282
Rehnquist, William H. 349, 373, 388
Reich, Robert 371
religious freedom 24
relocation centers (WWII) 272
Republican National Committee 358
Republican Party
John Adams and 17–18
John Quincy Adams and 51–52, 54
James Buchanan and 124, 125
George H. W. Bush and 358
George W. Bush and 381
Calvin Coolidge and 248, 250
Dwight D. Eisenhower and 289
Gerald R. Ford and 326, 327
James A. Garfield and 170
Ulysses S. Grant and 152, 155
Warren G. Harding and 241–242
Benjamin Harrison and 195
Rutherford B. Hayes and 160–165
Herbert Hoover and 257–258
Andrew Jackson and 60
Thomas Jefferson and 25–27
Jeffersonians and 9

Abraham Lincoln and 132–134
James Madison and 34
William McKinley and 202–203
James Monroe and 42–45
Richard M. Nixon and 316, 317
partisan battles with Federalist Party 25–27
Ronald Reagan and 347
Theodore Roosevelt and 214
William Howard Taft and 223–224, 226
Martin Van Buren and 69
George Washington and 9
resignation of presidency, Richard M. Nixon and 322–323
Revenue Act of 1935 270
Revolutionary War
John Adams and 14–16
Andrew Jackson and 59
James Madison and 32
James Monroe and 41
George Washington and 3–6
Rhode Island 97
Rice, Condoleezza 387
Rich, Marc 375
Richards, Ann 381–382
Rickover, Hyman 334
The Rights of Man (Thomas Paine) 51
Rodham, Hugh 375
Roosevelt, Franklin Delano *263*, **263–275**, 440*a*–441*a*
Agricultural Adjustment Act 268
as assistant secretary of the navy 266
birth and childhood 264–265
cabinet of 267
chronology 274–275
and Winston Churchill 272–273
Civilian Conservation Corps 268
civil rights 270
"court-packing bill" 270–271
death of 273–274
and Democratic Party 265–267
early career 265–267
election of 1920 266
election of 1928 266
election of 1932 267
election of 1936 270
election of 1940 271
election of 1944 273
election to presidency 267
farm policy 268–270
fireside chats 268
Good Neighbor Policy 269
as governor 267
and Great Depression 267–271
and the Holocaust 273
Japanese-Americans, internment of 272
labor policy 269
lend-lease agreement 271
National Industrial Recovery Act 268
National Labor Relations Board 269
New Deal 268–271
Pearl Harbor 272
personal characteristics 264
polio 264, 266
Revenue Act of 1935 270
Second New Deal 269
and Joseph Stalin 272–273
stock market crash of 1929 267
Tennessee Valley Authority 268
and United Nations 273
Works Progress Administration 269
and World War I 266
World War II 271–274
Yalta Conference 273
Roosevelt, Theodore *210*, **210–220**, 431*a*–432*a*
as assistant secretary of the Navy 213–214
assumption of presidency 214–215
birth and childhood 211
and Bull Moose Party 218
chronology 219
and conservation 215–218
death of 219
and Dominican Republic 216
early career 212–214
election of 1898 214
election of 1900 214
election of 1904 216–217
election of 1912 218
and environmentalism 215–218
foreign policy 216–218
as governor 214
and labor/management relations 215
and Panama 216
post-presidential career 218–219
and Progressives 215, 216, 218
and Republican Party 214
and Spanish-American War 214
and William Howard Taft 223–224, 226
as vice president 214
Roth, Kenneth 394
Rove, Karl 381–384
Ruff, Charles 373
Rumsfeld, Donald 391–393
Russia. *See also* Soviet Union
James Buchanan and 122
Herbert Hoover and 258
Andrew Johnson and 146
Theodore Roosevelt and 217, 218
Woodrow Wilson and 237

S

al-Sadr, Moktada 393
SALT I treaty 319
SALT II treaty 338
Santa Anna, Antonio Lopéz de 95
Santo Domingo. *See also* Dominican Republic
Ulysses S. Grant and 153
Woodrow Wilson and 234
"Saturday Night Massacre" 321
Saudi Arabia 361
Schippers, David 373
Schultz, George P. 351
Scott, Dred. *See Dred Scott* decision
Scott, Winfield 116
Scowcroft, Brent 360
SDI (Strategic Defense Initiative) 350
Second New Deal 269
secretary of commerce, Herbert Hoover as 258
secretary of state
John Quincy Adams as 53
James Monroe as 43
Martin Van Buren as 70–71
secretary of war
James Monroe as 43
William Howard Taft as 223
sectionalism
Millard Fillmore and 111
Zachary Taylor and 103
Sedition Act 17, 18
segregation. *See* civil rights
Senate (members of)
John Quincy Adams 51–52
James Buchanan 122–123
Warren G. Harding 241
Benjamin Harrison 195
William Henry Harrison 78
Andrew Johnson 141–142, 146
Lyndon B. Johnson 307
John F. Kennedy 297–298
James Monroe 42
Richard M. Nixon 316
Franklin Pierce 115
Harry S. Truman 278–279
John Tyler 84–85
Martin Van Buren 69–70
September 11, 2001, terrorist attacks
George W. Bush and 388–389, 395
Jimmy Carter and 341
Serbia 374
Seventeenth Amendment 225

Shalala, Donna 370
Sharing Good Times (Jimmy Carter) 341
Sherman, John 170
Sherman Antitrust Act 196–197
Silver Purchase Act
Grover Cleveland and 189
Benjamin Harrison and 197
Sixteenth Amendment 225
slavery
John Quincy Adams and 56
James Buchanan and 120, 123–126
Millard Fillmore and 108–111
James A. Garfield and 169
Andrew Jackson and 60
James G. Birney and 80
Thomas Jefferson and 23, 29
Andrew Johnson and 141
Abraham Lincoln and 131–134
James Madison and 33
James Monroe and 45–46
Franklin Pierce and 114–118
James K. Polk and 95–96
Zachary Taylor and 102–103
John Tyler and 84, 87–88
Martin Van Buren and 70–73
George Washington and 6
Smith, Jesse 244
Smoot-Hawley Tariff 259, 260
Social Security reform 384, 395
Somalia 362
Soviet Union. *See also* cold war; Russia
George H. W. Bush and 360, 361
Jimmy Carter and 336, 338, 339
Dwight D. Eisenhower and 290, 292, 293
John F. Kennedy and 299–301
Richard M. Nixon and 319
Ronald Reagan and 350, 352–353
Franklin D. Roosevelt and 272–273
Harry S. Truman and 281–284
Spain
William McKinley and 201–202, 204–207
James Monroe and 45, 46
Franklin Pierce and 117
Theodore Roosevelt and 214
Speaker of the House, James K. Polk as 92
Specie Circular 72
spoils system
Chester A. Arthur and 177
Rutherford B. Hayes and 161–162, 164
Springsteen, Bruce 350
Stalin, Joseph
and Franklin D. Roosevelt 272–273
and Harry S. Truman 280–282
Stalwarts
Chester A. Arthur and 178–181
James A. Garfield and 170, 171, 173
Stamp Act 14
Starr, Kenneth 372, 373
Star Routes fraud/trials
Chester A. Arthur and 179–180
James A. Garfield and 172
START Treaty 361
"Star Wars." *See* Strategic Defense Initiative
states' rights
Franklin Pierce and 116
James K. Polk and 93
Stevens, John Paul 386
Stevenson, Coke 307
Stockman, David 348
stock market crash of 1929
Herbert Hoover and 259
Franklin D. Roosevelt and 267
Strategic Arms Reduction Treaty (START) 361
Strategic Defense Initiative (SDI; "Star Wars") 350
student protests 346–347
suffrage. *See* voting rights
supply-side economics 348, 349
Supreme Court
George W. Bush and 384–385
Dred Scott decision 123, 124, 132
Richard M. Nixon and 319
Ronald Reagan and 349
Franklin D. Roosevelt and 270–271
William Howard Taft and 227
Sussex Pledge 235–236
Sweeny, John 388

T

Taft, William Howard *221*, **221–228,** 433*a*
and antitrust action 226
birth and childhood 222
cabinet of 224
as Chief Justice 227
and China 226
chronology 227–228
as civil governor of Philippines 223
and conservation 224–225
death of 227
early career 222–223
election of 1908 223–224
election of 1912 226
election to presidency 223–224
and environmentalism 224–225
foreign policy 226
and labor 225–226
and Open Door Policy 226
post-presidential career 227
and Republican Party 223–224, 226
as secretary of war 223
and tariff 224
Taft-Hartley Act 281
Taiwan 291–292
Taliban 389
Tariff of Abominations 55
tariffs
Chester A. Arthur and 181
Grover Cleveland and 187–189
Millard Fillmore and 107
Benjamin Harrison and 197
Herbert Hoover and 259, 260
William McKinley and 202–203
James K. Polk and 93
William Howard Taft and 224
John Tyler and 84
Woodrow Wilson and 233
taxation
George H. W. Bush and 359
George W. Bush and 382, 395
Bill Clinton and 370
Calvin Coolidge and 252
Gerald R. Ford and 330
Herbert Hoover and 260
James Madison and 35
Ronald Reagan and 348
Taylor, John W. 54, 55
Taylor, Zachary *98*, **98–104,** 414*a*
birth and childhood 99
and Britain 103
chronology 104
death of 104
early career 99–102
election of 1848 102
election to presidency 102
and Millard Fillmore 108
foreign policy 103
military career 99–102
and slavery issue 102–103
and U.S.-Mexican War 99–101
and Martin Van Buren 74
and War of 1812 99
and Whig Party 101–102
Teapot Dome scandal
Calvin Coolidge and 252
Warren G. Harding and 244–245
Tennessee Valley Authority (TVA) 268

Tenure of Office Act
Grover Cleveland and 188
Andrew Johnson and 145–146
terrorism 388–390, 395
Tet Offensive 311
Texas
Millard Fillmore and 109
James K. Polk and 94
Zachary Taylor and 102, 103
John Tyler and 87–88
Tiananmen Square 360
Tower, John 351
Tower Commission 351–352
Townshend Acts 14, 15
"Trail of Tears" 66
Treasury, U.S.
Millard Fillmore and 106–107
James K. Polk and 93
Treaty of Fort Wayne 78
Treaty of Ghent
Andrew Jackson and 62
James Madison and 37
Treaty of Guadalupe Hidalgo 96
Treaty of Morfontaine 18
Treaty of Paris
John Adams and 16
William McKinley and 207
Tripp, Linda 372
Truman, Harry S. *276,* **276–284,** 442*a*–443*a*
assumption of presidency 280
and atomic bomb 276, 280–281
birth and childhood 277
chronology 284
and Winston Churchill 280
civil rights 278
and cold war 282–284
death of 284
and Democratic Party 279
early career 277–279
election of 1944 279
election of 1948 282
Fair Deal 281
Hiroshima 276, 281
on Holocaust 279
and Kansas City political machine 278–279
Korean conflict 276, 283–284
labor policy 281
and Douglas MacArthur 283–284
Marshall Plan 282
and Joseph McCarthy 282
Nagasaki 276, 281
and New Deal 278
North Atlantic Treaty Organization 283
and Tom Pendergast 278–279
post-presidential career 284
Potsdam conference 280
in Senate 278–279
and Soviet Union 281–284
and Joseph Stalin 280
Taft-Hartley Act 281
Truman Doctrine 281
as vice president 279–280
World War I 277–278
World War II 279–281
Truman Committee 279
Truman Doctrine 281
Turkey 391
Turnipseed, William 380
TVA (Tennessee Valley Authority) 268
Tyler, John *83,* **83–89,** 412*a*
and annexation of Texas 87–88
assumption of presidency 85
birth and childhood 84
and Britain 87–88
and Canada 87
and China 87
chronology 88
in Confederate House of Representatives 88
death of 88
and Democratic Party 84–85, 88
early career 84–85
election of 1827 84
election of 1840 85–88
election of 1844 88
foreign policy 87–88
as governor 84
and William Henry Harrison 80, 81
in House of Representatives 84
and Mexico 87
and national bank bill 86, 87
personal characteristics 83
and political struggles with Henry Clay 86–87
post-presidential career 88–89
in Senate 84–85
and slavery issue 84, 87–88
and Martin Van Buren 74
and Whig Party 85–88
Tyler Doctrine 87

U

U2 spy plane crisis 293
underconsumption 253
unions. *See* labor unions
United Fruit Company 291
United Nations 273, 358, 390, 391
U.S.-Mexican War
Ulysses S. Grant and 149–150
Abraham Lincoln and 131
Franklin Pierce and 115
James K. Polk and 95, 96
Zachary Taylor and 99–101
USA PATRIOT Act 389

V

Van Buren, Martin *68,* **68–75,** 410*a*
birth and childhood 69
and Britain 73
and Canada 73
chronology 74–75
death of 74
and Democratic Party 70, 72
early career 69–70
election of 1828 70
election of 1832 71
election of 1836 71
election of 1840 74
election of 1844 74, 102
election to presidency 71
foreign policy 73
as governor 70
and William Henry Harrison 79, 80
and Andrew Jackson 63, 64, 66
personal characteristics 68–69, 71–72
post-presidential career 74
and Republican Party 69
as secretary of state 70–71
in Senate 69–70
and slavery issue 70, 71–73
as vice president 71
and Whig Party 72–74
veto power 81
vice president
John Adams as 16
Chester A. Arthur as 178–179
George H. W. Bush as 359
Calvin Coolidge as 250–251
and death of president 85
Millard Fillmore as 108–109
Gerald R. Ford as 327–328
Lyndon B. Johnson as 308
Richard M. Nixon as 317
Theodore Roosevelt as 214
Harry S. Truman as 279–280
John Tyler as 85
Martin Van Buren as 71
Vieira de Mello, Sergio 392
Vietnam
George W. Bush and 380
Bill Clinton and 367, 374
Dwight D. Eisenhower and 291
Gerald R. Ford and 327, 330
Lyndon B. Johnson and 308–311
John F. Kennedy and 301
Richard M. Nixon and 318–320

Villepin, Dominique de 391
Virginia Plan 33
Virginia Ratifying Convention 42
voting rights
  Dwight D. Eisenhower and 292
  Benjamin Harrison and 197
  Andrew Johnson and 144, 145
  Lyndon B. Johnson and 310
  William McKinley and 202
  Woodrow Wilson and 234
Voting Rights Act 310

W

Walsh, Lawrence E. 351–352
Warner, John 394
War of 1812
  John Quincy Adams and 52
  William Henry Harrison and 78
  Andrew Jackson and 61
  James Madison and 35–38
  James Monroe and 43
  Zachary Taylor and 99
War on Poverty 308
War on Terror 389–390
Warren, Earl 290
Washington, George 1, **1–11**, 400*a*–401*a*
  and John Adams 16
  and John Quincy Adams 51
  birth and childhood 2
  and Britain 8–9
  chronology 9–10
  and Constitution 6
  and Constitutional Convention 6
  death of 9
  early career 2–6
  election of 1789 6
  election of 1792 7
  election to presidency 6
  and Federalist Party 9
  and First Continental Congress 3
  foreign policy 8–9
  and France 8, 9
  and French and Indian War 3
  and Andrew Jackson 60
  and Thomas Jefferson 25
  military career 3–6
  personal characteristics 1, 2
  post-presidential career 9
  and Republican Party 9
  and Revolutionary War 3–6
  and Second Continental Congress 3–4
  and slavery issue 6
Watergate
  George H. W. Bush and 358
  Gerald R. Ford and 328, 329
  Richard M. Nixon and 320–322
Webster-Ashburton Treaty
  Martin Van Buren and 72
  John Tyler and 87
Weed, Thurlow 106–108
Weinberger, Caspar 362
welfare
  Bill Clinton and 371–372
  Ronald Reagan and 348
  Franklin D. Roosevelt and 270
Westbrook, Theodore 213
Whig Party
  Millard Fillmore and 106–110
  William Henry Harrison and 79–81
  Zachary Taylor and 101–102
  John Tyler and 85–88
  Martin Van Buren and 72–74
Whip Inflation Now (WIN) 330
Whiskey Rebellion 7–8
Whiskey Ring 154–155
White, Frank 368
Whitewater 370, 371, 374
Wilkinson, James (general) 35
Will, George 388
Wilson, Joseph C. 390
Wilson, Woodrow *229*, **229–238**, 434*a*–435*a*
  birth and childhood 230
  and Britain 235–236
  chronology 237–238
  and civil rights 234
  and Clayton Antitrust Act 233–234
  death of 237
  and Democratic Party 232–233
  early career 230–232
  election of 1912 232–233
  election to presidency 232–233
  foreign policy 234–237
  and Fourteen Points 236–237
  and Germany 235–236
  as governor 232
  and Haiti 234
  and League of Nations 237
  and Mexico 234–235
  and monetary policy 233
  and Nicaragua 234
  and Progressives 233
  and Russia 237
  and Santo Domingo 234
  and tariff 233
  and voting rights 234
  World War I 235–237
WIN (Whip Inflation Now) 330
Works Progress Administration (WPA) 269
World Trade Center terrorist attack. *See* September 11, 2001, terrorist attacks
World War I
  Herbert Hoover and 257
  Franklin D. Roosevelt and 266
  Harry S. Truman and 277–278
  Woodrow Wilson and 235–237
World War II
  George H. W. Bush and 357
  Dwight D. Eisenhower and 288–289
  Gerald R. Ford and 326
  Lyndon B. Johnson and 306–307
  John F. Kennedy and 296–297
  Richard M. Nixon and 316
  Franklin D. Roosevelt and 271–274
  Harry S. Truman and 279–281
WPA (Works Progress Administration) 269

Y

Yalta agreement 280
Yalta Conference 273
Yarborough, Ralph 358

Z

Zogby, John 386